FREQUENTLY USED SYMBOLS AND ABBREVIATIONS

AAI	Average Age of Inventory	EOQ	Economic Order Quantity
ACH	Automated Clearinghouse	EPS	Earnings Per Share
ACP	Average Collection Period	FC	Fixed Operating Cost
AF_j	Amount of Funds Available from Financing Source j at a Given Cost	FCF	Free Cash Flow
A/P	Accounts Payable	FDI	Foreign Direct Investment
APP	Average Payment Period	FLM	Financial Leverage Multiplier
APR	Annual Percentage Rate	FV	Future Value
APY	Annual Percentage Yield	FVA_n	Future Value of an n-Year Annuity
A/R	Accounts Receivable	$FVIF_{i,n}$	Future Value Interest Factor for a Single Amount Compounded at i Percent for n Periods
b_j	Beta Coefficient or Index of Nondiversifiable Risk for Asset j	$FVIFA_{i,n}$	Future Value Interest Factor for an Annuity When Interest Is Compounded Annually at i Percent for n Periods
b_p	Portfolio Beta		
B_0	Value of a Bond	GAAP	Generally accepted accounting principles
BP_j	Break Point for Financing Source j	g	Growth Rate
C	Carrying Cost per Unit per Period	i	Annual Rate of Interest
CAPM	Capital Asset Pricing Model	I	Interest Payment
CCC	Cash Conversion Cycle	IOS	Investment Opportunities Schedule
CD	Stated Cash Discount in Percentage Terms	IPO	Initial Public Offering
CF_0	Initial Investment	IRR	Internal Rate of Return
CF_t	Cash Inflow in Period t	JIT	Just-In-Time System
CV	Coefficient of Variation	m	Number of times per year interest is compounded
D_p	Preferred Stock Dividend		
D_t	• Per-Share Dividend Expected at the End of Year t • Depreciation Expense in Year t	M	Bond's Par Value
		M/B	Market/Book Ratio
DFL	Degree of Financial Leverage	MACRS	Modified Accelerated Cost Recovery System
DOL	Degree of Operating Leverage	MNC	Multinational Company
DPS	Dividends per Share	MRP	Materials Requirement Planning
DTC	Depository Transfer Check	n	• Number of Outcomes Considered
DTL	Degree of Total Leverage		• Number of Periods—Typically, Years
e	Exponential Function = 2.7183		• Years to Maturity
EAR	Effective Annual Rate	N	Number of Days Payment Can Be Delayed by Giving up the Cash Discount
EBIT	Earnings Before Interest and Taxes		
EOM	End of the Month	N_d	Net Proceeds from the Sale of Debt (Bond)

N_n	Net Proceeds from the Sale of New Common Stock
N_p	Net Proceeds from the Sale of the Preferred Stock
NCAI	Net Current Asset Investment
NFAI	Net Fixed Asset Investment
NOPAT	Net operating profits after taxes
NPV	Net Present Value
O	Order Cost Per Order
OC	Operating Cycle
OCF	Operating Cash Flow
P	Price (value) of asset
P_0	Value of Common Stock
$PBDT_t$	Profits Before Depreciation and Taxes in year t
PD	Preferred Stock Dividend
P/E	Price/Earnings Ratio
PMT	Amount of Payment
Pr	Probability
PV	Present Value
PVA_n	Present Value of an n-Year Annuity
$PVIF_{i,n}$	Present Value Interest Factor for a Single Amount Discounted at i Percent for n Periods
$PVIFA_{i,n}$	Present Value Interest Factor for an Annuity When Interest is Discounted Annually at i Percent for n Periods
Q	• Order Quantity in Units
	• Sales Quantity in Units
r	• Actual, Expected ($\bar{r}$), or Required Rate of Return
	• Cost of Capital
r_a	Weighted Average Cost of Capital
r_d	Required Return on Bond
r_i	After-Tax Cost of Debt

r_j	Required Return on Asset j
r_m	Market Return; Return on the Market Portfolio of Assets
r_p	• Cost of Preferred Stock
	• Portfolio Return
r_r	Cost of Retained Earnings
r_s	Required Return on Common Stock
R_F	Risk-Free Rate of Interest
RADR	Risk-Adjusted Discount Rate
ROA	Return on Total Assets
ROE	Return on Common Equity
S	Usage in Units per Period
SML	Security Market Line
t	Time
T	Firm's Marginal Tax Rate
V	Value of an Asset or Firm
V_C	Value of Entire Company
V_D	Value of All Debt
V_P	Value of Preferred Stock
V_S	Value of Common Stock
VC	Variable Operating Cost per Unit
w_j	• Proportion of the Portfolio's Total Dollar Value Represented by Asset j
	• Proportion of a Specific Source of Financing j in the Firm's Capital Structure
WACC	Weighted Average Cost of Capital
WMCC	Weighted Marginal Cost of Captial
YTM	Yield to Maturity
ZBA	Zero Balance Account
σ	Standard Deviation
Σ	Summation Sign

PRINCIPLES OF
MANAGERIAL
FINANCE

BRIEF

The Prentice Hall Series in Finance

Alexander/Sharpe/Bailey
Fundamentals of Investments

Andersen
Global Derivatives: A Strategic Risk Management Perspective

Bear/Moldonado-Bear
Free Markets, Finance, Ethics, and Law

Berk/DeMarzo
Corporate Finance*
Corporate Finance: The Core*

Bierman/Smidt
The Capital Budgeting Decision: Economic Analysis of Investment Projects

Bodie/Merton/Cleeton
Financial Economics

Click/Coval
The Theory and Practice of International Financial Management

Copeland/Weston/Shastri
Financial Theory and Corporate Policy

Cornwall/Vang/Hartman
Entrepreneurial Financial Management

Cox/Rubinstein
Options Markets

Dorfman
Introduction to Risk Management and Insurance

Dietrich
Financial Services and Financial Institutions: Value Creation in Theory and Practice

Dufey/Giddy
Cases in International Finance

Eakins
Finance in .learn

Eiteman/Stonehill/Moffett
Multinational Business Finance

Emery/Finnerty/Stowe
Corporate Financial Management

Fabozzi
Bond Markets: Analysis and Strategies

Fabozzi/Modigliani
Capital Markets: Institutions and Instruments

Fabozzi/Modigliani/Jones/Ferri
Foundations of Financial Markets and Institutions

Finkler
Financial Management for Public, Health, and Not-for-Profit Organizations

Francis/Ibbotson
Investments: A Global Perspective

Fraser/Ormiston
Understanding Financial Statements

Geisst
Investment Banking in the Financial System

Gitman
Principles of Managerial Finance*
Principles of Managerial Finance—Brief Edition*

Gitman/Joehnk
Fundamentals of Investing*

Gitman/Madura
Introduction to Finance

Guthrie/Lemon
Mathematics of Interest Rates and Finance

Haugen
The Inefficient Stock Market: What Pays Off and Why
Modern Investment Theory
The New Finance: Overreaction, Complexity, and Uniqueness

Holden
Excel Modeling and Estimation in the Fundamentals of Corporate Finance
Excel Modeling and Estimation in the Fundamentals of Investments
Excel Modeling and Estimation in Investments
Excel Modeling and Estimation in Corporate Finance

Hughes/MacDonald
International Banking: Text and Cases

Hull
Fundamentals of Futures and Options Markets
Options, Futures, and Other Derivatives
Risk Management and Financial Institutions

Keown
Personal Finance: Turning Money into Wealth

Keown/Martin/Petty/Scott
Financial Management: Principles and Applications
Foundations of Finance: The Logic and Practice of Financial Management

Kim/Nofsinger
Corporate Governance

Levy/Post
Investments

May/May/Andrew
Effective Writing: A Handbook for Finance People

Madura
Personal Finance

Marthinsen
Risk Takers: Uses and Abuses of Financial Derivatives

McDonald
Derivatives Markets
Fundamentals of Derivatives Markets

Megginson
Corporate Finance Theory

Melvin
International Money and Finance

Mishkin/Eakins
Financial Markets and Institutions

Moffett
Cases in International Finance

Moffett/Stonehill/Eiteman
Fundamentals of Multinational Finance

Nofsinger
Psychology of Investing

Ogden/Jen/O'Connor
Advanced Corporate Finance

Pennacchi
Theory of Asset Pricing

Rejda
Principles of Risk Management and Insurance

Schoenebeck
Interpreting and Analyzing Financial Statements

Scott/ Martin/ Petty/Keown/Thatcher
Cases in Finance

Seiler
Performing Financial Studies: A Methodological Cookbook

Shapiro
Capital Budgeting and Investment Analysis

Sharpe/Alexander/Bailey
Investments

Solnik/McLeavey
Global Investments

Stretcher/Michael
Cases in Financial Management

Titman/Martin
Valuation: The Art and Science of Corporate Investment Decisions

Trivoli
Personal Portfolio Management: Fundamentals and Strategies

Van Horne
Financial Management and Policy
Financial Market Rates and Flows

Van Horne/Wachowicz
Fundamentals of Financial Management

Vaughn
Financial Planning for the Entrepreneur

Weston/Mitchel/Mulherin
Takeovers, Restructuring, and Corporate Governance

Winger/Frasca
Personal Finance

* denotes titles   Log onto www.myfinancelab.com to learn more

PRINCIPLES OF
MANAGERIAL FINANCE

BRIEF FIFTH EDITION

LAWRENCE J. GITMAN
SAN DIEGO STATE UNIVERSITY

Boston San Francisco New York
London Toronto Sydney Tokyo Singapore Madrid
Mexico City Munich Paris Cape Town Hong Kong Montreal

Editor-in-Chief: Denise Clinton
Executive Editor: Donna Battista
Development Editor: Ann Torbert
Project Manager/EA: Mina Kim
Editorial Assistant: Kerri McQueen
Managing Editor: Nancy Fenton
Senior Marketing Manager: Andrew Watts
Senior Media Producer: Bethany Tidd
Associate Media Producer: Miguel Leonarte
Supplements Editor: Heather McNally
Permissions Editor: Dana Weightman
Project Coordination, Text Design, Art Studio,
    and Electronic Page Makeup: Thompson Steele, Inc.
Design Manager: Joyce Wells
Cover Photograph: George Hammerstein/Solus Photography/Veer
Senior Manufacturing Buyer: Carol Melville

Credits: 51: Data from Dun & Bradstreet, "Industry Norms and Ratios, 2006"; 294: From *The Wall Street Journal*, 3/28/07; 292: © 2007 MetroPCS Wireless, Inc. All Rights Reserved; 466: © 2006 by Risk Management Association.

For information on obtaining permission for the use of material from this work, please submit a written request to Pearson Education, Inc., Rights and Contracts Department, 75 Arlington Street, Suite 300, Boston, MA 02116 or fax your request to (617) 848-7047. Printed in the United States.

ISBN 0-321-56655-6

1 2 3 4 5 6 7 8 9 10

Dedicated to the memory
of my mother, Dr. Edith Gitman,
who instilled in me the importance
of education and hard work

The Key to Your Success in Three Easy Steps!

❶ Take a Sample Test to assess your knowledge.

❷ Review your personalized Study Plan to see where you need more work.

❸ Use the Study Plan exercises and step-by-step tutorials to get practice—and individualized feedback—where you need it.

If your Instructor assigns homework and tests using MyFinanceLab…

The MyFinanceLab Course Home page makes it easy for you to stay on track by displaying class announcements and automatic reminders of upcoming assignments.

Did your textbook come bundled with a MyFinanceLab access code? If so, simply go to www.myfinancelab.com to register using the code. If not, you can purchase access to MyFinanceLab online at www.myfinancelab.com.

Gitman's
Proven Teaching/Learning System

Users of *Principles of Managerial Finance, Brief* have praised the effectiveness of the book's teaching/learning system, which they hail as one of its hallmarks. The system, driven by a set of carefully developed learning goals, has been retained and polished in the Fifth Edition. The "walkthrough" on the pages that follow illustrates and describes the key elements of the teaching/learning system. We encourage both students and instructors to acquaint themselves at the start of the semester with the many useful features the book offers.

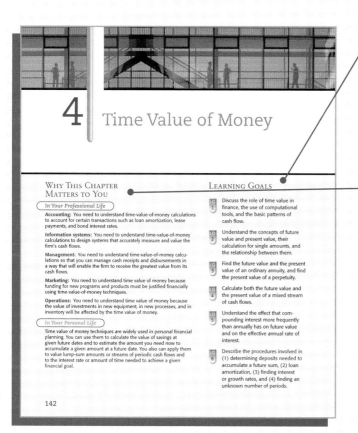

Six **Learning Goals** at the start of the chapter anchor the most important concepts and techniques in the chapter. The learning goal icons reappear next to related text sections and again in the chapter-end summary, end-of-chapter homework materials, and supplements such as the Study Guide, Test Bank, and MyFinanceLab.

Every chapter opens with a feature, titled **Why This Chapter Matters to You**, that helps motivate student interest.

Its first part, **In Your Professional Life**, discusses the intersection of the finance topics covered in the chapter with the concerns of other major business disciplines. It encourages students majoring in accounting, information systems, management, marketing, and operations to appreciate the numerous cross-disciplinary interactions that routinely occur in business.

The second part, **In Your Personal Life**, identifies topics in the chapter that will have particular application to personal finance.

Learning goal icons, which appear next to first-level text headings, tie chapter content to the learning goals.

LG 5 LG 6 **6.4 Bond Valuation**

The basic valuation equation can be customized for use in valuing specific securities: bonds, common stock, and preferred stock. We describe bond valuation in this chapter, and valuation of common stock and preferred stock in Chapter 7.

For help in study and review, **key terms** are printed in boldface type, and their definitions appear in the margin where they are first introduced. These terms are also boldfaced in the book's index and appear in the end-of-book glossary.

annual percentage yield (APY)
The *effective annual rate* of interest that must be disclosed to consumers by banks on their savings products as a result of "truth-in-savings laws."

"Truth-in-savings laws," on the other hand, require banks to quote the **annual percentage yield (APY)** on their savings products. The APY is the *effective annual rate* a savings product pays. For example, a savings account that pays 0.5 percent per month would have an APY of 6.17 percent $[(1.005)^{12} - 1]$.

Quoting loan interest rates at their lower nominal annual rate (the APR) and savings interest rates at the higher effective annual rate (the APY) offers two advantages: It tends to standardize disclosure to consumers, and it enables financial institutions to quote the most attractive interest rates: low loan rates and high savings rates.

Examples are an important component of the book's learning system. Clearly set off from the text, they provide an immediate and concrete demonstration of how to apply financial concepts, tools, and techniques.

Examples in certain chapters demonstrate time value of money techniques. These examples show the use of time lines, financial calculators, spreadsheets (with cell formulas), and factor tables.

New! **Personal Finance Examples** demonstrate how students can apply managerial finance concepts, tools, and techniques to their personal financial decisions.

Example

Braden Company, as we have noted, wants to find the present value of a 5-year ordinary annuity of $700, assuming an 8% opportunity cost.

Calculator Use Using the calculator's inputs shown at the left, you will find the present value of the ordinary annuity to be $2,794.90. The value obtained with the calculator is more accurate than those found using the equation or the table (shown below).

Spreadsheet Use The present value of the ordinary annuity also can be calculated as shown on the following Excel spreadsheet.

	A	B
1	PRESENT VALUE OF AN ORDINARY ANNUITY	
2	Annual payment	$700
3	Annual rate of interest, compounded annually	8%
4	Number of years	5
5	Present value of an ordinary annuity	$2,794.90

Entry in Cell B5 is =PV(B3,B4,–B2)
The minus sign appears before B2 because
the annual payment is a cash outflow.

Personal Finance Example Marilyn Carbo has $10 that she can spend on candy costing $0.25 per piece. She could buy 40 pieces of candy ($10.00/$0.25) today. The nominal rate of interest on a 1-year deposit is currently 7%, and the expected rate of inflation over the coming year is 4%. Instead of buying the 40 pieces of candy today, Marilyn could invest the $10 in a 1-year deposit account now. At the end of 1 year she would have $10.70 because she would have earned 7% interest—an additional $0.70 (0.07 × $10.00)—on her $10 deposit. The 4% inflation rate would over the 1-year period increase the cost of the candy by 4%—an additional $0.01 (0.04 × $0.25)—to $0.26 per piece. As a result, at the end of the 1-year period Marilyn would be able to buy about 41.2 pieces of candy ($10.70/$0.26), or roughly 3% more (41.2/40.0 = 1.03). The increase in the amount of money available to Marilyn at the end of 1 year is merely her nominal rate of return (7%), which must be reduced by the rate of inflation (4%) during the period to determine her real rate of return of 3%. Marilyn's increased buying power therefore equals her 3% real rate of return.

Key equations are printed in blue throughout the text to help readers identify the most important mathematical relationships. The variables used in these equations are, for convenience, printed on the *front endpapers* of the book.

Appendix Table A–2 presents present value interest factors for $1. By letting $PVIF_{i,n}$ represent the appropriate factor, we can rewrite the general equation for present value (Equation 4.9) as follows:

$$PV = FV_n \times (PVIF_{i,n}) \tag{4.12}$$

This expression indicates that to find the present value of an amount to be received in a future period, n, we have merely to multiply the future amount, FV_n, by the appropriate present value interest factor.

Marginal hints add useful ideas, comments, and pieces of information to enrich the text discussion and boost student learning.

Hint Anyone familiar with an electronic spreadsheet, such as Excel, realizes that most of the time-value-of-money calculations can be performed expeditiously by using the special functions contained in the spreadsheet.

Electronic Spreadsheets

Like financial calculators, electronic spreadsheets have built-in routines that simplify time value calculations. We provide in the text a number of spreadsheet solutions that identify the cell entries for calculating time values. The value for each variable is entered in a cell in the spreadsheet, and the calculation is programmed using an equation that links the individual cells. If values of the variables are changed, the solution automatically changes as a result of the equation linking the cells. In the spreadsheet solutions in this book, the equation that determines the calculation is shown at the bottom of the spreadsheet.

Review Questions appear at the end of each major text section. These questions challenge readers to stop and test their understanding of key concepts, tools, techniques, and practices before moving on to the next section.

(Focus on Ethics) Loan Fraud

IN PRACTICE

In June 2007, the creator of the Backstreet Boys and 'N Sync was indicted by a federal grand jury on charges that he defrauded a bank out of $20 million. He was accused of fraudulently securing millions in bank loans with documents from a fake accounting firm.

What constitutes *loan fraud?* A loan fraud is a scheme or

"S&L Kingpin" statute. This law provides for fines of up to $20 million for organizational defendants and up to $10 million and life imprisonment for individuals.

Common types of loan fraud include making false application, loans to nonexistent borrowers, nominee loans, double pledging of collateral, and misapplication of loan funds. *False applications*

and without telling the lenders. *Misapplication of loan funds* involves using the money for a purpose other than that stated in the loan.

How does a bank or lending institution protect itself from loan fraud? Deterioration in a borrower's finances can be a red flag. Lenders can calculate horizontal analyses by comparing

In Practice boxes offer insights into important topics in managerial finance through the experiences of real companies, both large and small. There are two categories of In Practice boxes:

(Focus on Practice) Free Cash Flow at eBay

IN PRACTICE

Free cash flow is the lifeblood of any company and is the only true way to measure how much cash a company is generating. Free cash flow is, broadly, operating cash flow minus investments in net fixed assets and net current assets. It represents the net amount of cash flow available to creditors and owners. Free cash flow is an ideal way to measure a company's health and cash-generating growth.

Take **eBay**, for example. The company which brings together millions of people every day in its online marketplace produced $1.73 billion in free cash flow for the year ending December 31, 2006. Net cash provided by operating activities was $2.24 billion, and the company invested $0.51 billion in property, equipment, and net current assets during 2006, leaving $1.73 billion in free cash flow, a 10.09 percent increase over the previous year.

However, despite the increase in free cash flow, eBay faces some challenges. Users

of eBay generated a total of 610 million listings in the fourth quarter of 2006, a 12 percent increase over the fourth quarter of 2005. But the company is spending more and more, mostly paying Google, a chief competitor, to draw traffic to the site. When expenses start to increase more than free cash flow, it suggests that a company's competitive edge is under attack.

Having free cash flows is one thing; what a company does with it is quite another. According to the Motley Fool (www.fool.com), as an investor you are much better served by companies that use free cash flow to buy back their stock (if the stock is undervalued) or, better yet, use it toward a regular cash dividend. The investor then has the option to reinvest the dividend back into the company or use the dividend to pursue a different opportunity.

In 2006, eBay chose to use its excess cash to buy back stock. Since announcing a share buyback program in July 2006, the

company repurchased approximately 50 million shares of its common stock at a total cost of nearly $1.7 billion. In addition, the company has the capacity to buy back an additional $300 million of stock under the initial plan, and the company's board of directors has authorized an expansion of the stock repurchase program to provide for the repurchase of up to an additional $2 billion of the company's common stock within the next 2 years. For the time being, stockholders expecting the start of a dividend stream can put those expectations on hold. The company's intentions are clearly not to begin paying dividends for the foreseeable future.

■ *Free cash flow is often considered a more reliable measure of a company's income than reported earnings. What are some possible ways that corporate accountants might be able to change their earnings to portray a more favorable earnings statement?*

Focus on Ethics boxes help readers understand and appreciate important ethical issues and problems related to managerial finance.

Focus on Practice boxes take a corporate focus that relates a business event or situation to a specific financial concept or technique.

Both types of In Practice boxes end with a *critical thinking question* to help readers broaden the lesson from the content of the box. Guideline answers to these questions can be found at the book's Companion Website.

Summary

Focus on Value

Financial managers review and analyze the firm's financial statements periodically, both to uncover developing problems and to assess the firm's progress toward achieving its goals. These actions are aimed at **preserving and creating value for the firm's owners.** Financial ratios enable financial managers to monitor the pulse of the firm and its progress toward its strategic goals. Although financial statements and financial ratios rely on accrual concepts, they can provide useful insights into important aspects of risk and return (cash flow) that affect share price.

Review of Learning Goals

LG 1 Understand tax depreciation procedures and the effect of depreciation on the firm's cash flows. Depreciation is an important factor affecting a firm's cash flow. An asset's depreciable value and depreciable life are determined by using the MACRS standards in the federal tax code. MACRS groups assets (excluding real estate) into six property classes based on length of recovery period.

The end-of-chapter **Summary** consists of two sections. The first section, **Focus on Value,** explains how the chapter's content relates to the firm's goal of maximizing owner wealth. The feature helps reinforce understanding of the link between the financial manager's actions and share value.

The second part of the Summary, the **Review of Learning Goals,** restates each learning goal and summarizes the key material that was presented to support mastery of that goal.

Self-Test Problems, keyed to the learning goals, give readers an opportunity to strengthen their understanding of topics by doing a sample problem. For reinforcement, solutions to the Self-Test Problems appear in Appendix B at the back of the book.

Warm-Up Exercises follow the Self-Test Problems. These short, numerical exercises give students practice in applying tools and techniques presented in the chapter.

A blue box indicates the **Exercises** and **Problems** available in **MyFinanceLab**.

Comprehensive **Problems**, keyed to the learning goals, are longer and more complex than the Warm-Up Exercises. In this section, instructors will find multiple problems that address the important concepts, tools, and techniques in the chapter.

New! **Personal Finance Problems** specifically relate to personal finance situations and examples in each chapter. These new problems will help students see how they can apply the tools and techniques of managerial finance in managing their own finances.

A short descriptor identifies the essential concept or technique of the problem. Problems labeled as **Integrative** tie together related topics. Guideline answers to selected end-of-chapter problems appear in Appendix C.

The last item in the chapter Problems is an **Ethics Problem**. The ethics problem gives students another opportunity to think about and apply ethics principles to managerial financial situations.

Chapter 2 Case

Assessing Martin Manufacturing's Current Financial Position

Terri Spiro, an experienced budget analyst at Martin Manufacturing Company, has been charged with assessing the firm's financial performance during 2009 and its financial position at year-end 2009. To complete this assignment, she gathered the firm's 2009 financial statements (below and on page 99). In addition, Terri obtained the firm's ratio values for 2007 and 2008, along with the 2009 industry average ratios (also applicable to 2007 and 2008). These are presented in the table on page 100.

Chapter Cases call for application of concepts and techniques to a more complex, realistic situation than in the regular Problems. These cases help strengthen practical application of financial tools and techniques.

Spreadsheet Exercise

The income statement and balance sheet are the basic reports that a firm constructs for use by management and for distribution to stockholders, regulatory bodies, and the general public. They are the primary sources of historical financial information about the firm. Dayton Products, Inc., is a moderate-sized manufacturer. The company's management has asked you to perform a detailed financial statement analysis of the firm.

The income statement data for the years ending December 31, 2009 and 2008, respectively, is presented in the table at the top of page 101. (*Note:* Purchases of inventory during 2009 amounted to $109,865.)

Every chapter includes a **Spreadsheet Exercise**. This exercise gives students an opportunity to use Excel® software to create one or more spreadsheets with which to analyze a financial problem. The spreadsheet to be created often is modeled on a table in the chapter or a spreadsheet template that can be viewed at the book's Companion Website.

Web Exercise

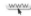

Go to the book's companion website at www.prenhall.com/gitman to find the Web Exercise for this chapter.

> Remember to check the book's website at www.prenhall.com/gitman to find additional resources, including Web Exercises and a Web Case.

Now available online at the book's Companion Website, a **Web Exercise** for every chapter links the chapter topic to a related site on the Internet and asks students to use information found there to answer questions. These exercises capture student interest while showing sources of finance information online.

Brief Contents

Contents

Part Two | Important Financial Concepts   141

Chapter 7
Stock Valuation   281

Part Three | Long-Term Investment Decisions   321

Part Four | Long-Term Financial Decisions   411

Part Five | Short-Term Financial Decisions 523

Preface

The desire to write *Principles of Managerial Finance* came out of my experience teaching the introductory managerial finance course early in my career. I was not very far removed from my own undergraduate studies and therefore could appreciate the difficulties some of my students were having with the textbook we used. They wanted a book that spoke to them in plain English. They wanted a book that tied concepts to reality. And they wanted not just description, but demonstration of concepts, tools, and techniques. Recognizing that, I decided to write an introductory finance text that would effectively resolve these concerns.

Courses and students have changed since that initial book, but the goals of the text have not changed. The conversational tone and wide use of examples set off in the text still characterize *Principles of Managerial Finance, Brief*. Building on those strengths, over numerous editions and translations and well over half a million U.S. users, I've continued to listen carefully to feedback from both instructors and students, from adopters, nonadopters, and practitioners.

The Fifth Edition

Like the first edition, *Principles of Managerial Finance, Brief*, Fifth Edition, still uses plain English, ties concepts to reality, and demonstrates concepts, tools, and techniques. It incorporates a proven learning system, which integrates pedagogy with concepts and practical applications. It concentrates on the knowledge that is needed to make keen financial decisions in an increasingly competitive business environment. The strong pedagogy and generous use of examples—including, new in this edition, personal finance examples—make the text an easily accessible resource for long-distance learning, online courses, and self-study programs.

The Fifth Edition of *Principles of Managerial Finance, Brief*, has been specifically designed to fit the one-term financial management course. It is intended for those professors who want to provide students with a thorough introduction to corporate finance that focuses on the fundamental concepts, tools, techniques, and practices of financial management. I've "right-sized" the book for the one-term course by eliminating from my longer *Principles* book topics that will be covered in subsequent courses. Specifically, I've eliminated the chapter on corporate mergers and the separate chapter on international managerial finance, although discussions and examples of international finance appear in appropriate chapter discussions throughout. In addition, the chapter from the longer book that contains discussion of hybrid and derivative securities is not included in this Brief Edition. Also, coverage of capital budgeting in the Brief Edition is presented in two chapters, compared to three chapters in the longer book. Finally, presentation of many topics has been streamlined throughout. The resulting presentation thoroughly covers all basic topics, yet is four chapters and about 250 pages shorter than *Principles of Managerial Finance*, Twlefth Edition, upon which it is based.

Organization

The text's organization, described in detail in the following pages, conceptually links the firm's actions and its value as determined in the securities market. Each major decision area is presented in terms of both risk and return factors and their potential impact on owners' wealth. A *Focus on Value* element at the end of each chapter helps reinforce the student's understanding of the link between the financial manager's actions and the firm's share value.

In organizing each chapter, I have adhered to a managerial decision-making perspective, relating decisions to the firm's overall goal of wealth maximization. Once a particular concept has been developed, its application is illustrated by an example—a hallmark feature of this book. These examples demonstrate, and solidify in the student's thought, financial decision-making considerations and their consequences. As described next, this edition expands this feature with the addition of examples related to *personal finance*.

International Considerations

We live in a world where international considerations cannot be divorced from the study of business in general and finance in particular. As in prior editions, discussions of international dimensions of chapter topics are integrated throughout the book. A marginal icon of a globe highlights these discussions, and international material is integrated into learning goals and end-of-chapter materials. In addition, for those who want to spend more time addressing the topic, a separate chapter on international managerial finance is available at the book's Web site, www.prenhall.com/gitman.

Personal Finance Linkages

The Fifth Edition has responded to reviewers' requests for more personal finance linkages and to calls for educators to help improve the financial literacy of young people. At the start of each chapter, the feature titled *Why This Chapter Matters to You* helps motivate student interest by discussing how the topic of the chapter relates to the concerns of other major business disciplines and to personal finance. Within the chapter, *Personal Finance Examples* explicitly link the concepts, tools, and techniques of each chapter to personal finance applications. In the homework material, the book also has more than 75 personal finance problems. The purpose of these personal finance materials is to demonstrate to students the usefulness of managerial finance knowledge in both business and personal financial dealings.

Ethical Issues

The need for ethics in business remains as important as ever. Students need to understand the ethical issues that financial managers face as they attempt to maximize shareholder value and to solve business problems. Thus, half the chapters include an In Practice box that focuses on ethical issues. Most of these ethics boxes are new in this edition, and those that are not new have been updated.

Homework Opportunities

Of course, practice is essential for students' learning of managerial finance concepts, tools, and techniques. To meet that need, the book offers a rich and varied menu of homework assignments: short, numerical Warm-Up Exercises; a comprehensive set of Problems, including more than one problem for each important concept or technique and now also including personal finance problems; an Ethics Problem in almost every chapter; a Chapter Case; a Spreadsheet Exercise; and an online Web Exercise. In addition, most of the end-of-chapter problems are available in algorithmic form in myfinancelab. These materials (see pages vi through xi for detailed descriptions) offer students solid learning opportunities, and they offer instructors opportunities to expand and enrich the classroom environment.

From classroom to boardroom, the Fifth Edition of *Principles of Managerial Finance, Brief* can help users get to where they want to be. I believe that it is the best edition yet—more relevant, more accurate, and more effective than ever. I hope you agree that *Principles of Managerial Finance, Brief*, Fifth Edition, is the most effective introductory managerial finance text for your students.

Lawrence J. Gitman
La Jolla, California

Revised Content

As we made plans to publish *Principles of Managerial Finance, Brief*, Fifth Edition, we carefully assessed market feedback about content changes that would better meet the needs of instructors teaching the course.

The chapter sequence remains the same as in the prior edition. Although the text content is sequential, instructors can assign almost any chapter as a self-contained unit, enabling instructors to customize the text to various teaching strategies and course lengths. For those instructors who want to assign an entire chapter on financial institutions and markets as a foundational chapter in the managerial finance course, a complete chapter on institutions and markets is available online at the book's Companion Website, www.prenhall.com/gitman. A chapter on international managerial finance is also available at the Web site.

A number of new topics have been added at appropriate places, and existing discussions have been updated and/or smoothed. In Chapter 5 and beyond, we have changed the notation for returns from "k" to "r" to improve familiarity with notational use in other courses.

The following list details the chapter-by-chapter content changes in the Fifth Edition.

Chapter 1   The Role and Environment of Managerial Finance
- Revised discussion of the role of business ethics
- Significantly revised and restructured presentation of "Securities Exchanges," now labeled "Broker Markets and Dealer Markets"
- Added one new Personal Finance Example
- Revised Focus on Practice box (Warren Buffett's leadership at Berkshire Hathaway)
- Added one new Personal Finance Problem

Chapter 2   Financial Statements and Analysis
- Added three new Personal Finance Examples
- New Focus on Practice box evaluating the effects of the Sarbanes-Oxley Act
- Added three new Personal Finance Problems

Chapter 3   Cash Flow and Financial Planning
- Added two new Personal Finance Examples
- New Focus on Practice box (free cash flow at eBay)
- Added one new Personal Finance Problem
- Revised Spreadsheet Exercise and Group Exercise
- Added to Companion Website detailed discussion of developing the statement of cash flows

Chapter 4   Time Value of Money
- Shifted computational emphasis to calculator and spreadsheet use, de-emphasizing the use of financial tables
- Re-labeled 22 existing Examples as Personal Finance Examples
- Revised Focus on Practice box (subprime mortgages)
- Re-labeled 32 existing Problems as Personal Finance Problems

Chapter 5   Risk and Return
- Changed notation for returns from "k" to "r" beginning in this chapter and throughout entire text to improve familiarity
- Switched emphasis from "Sensitivity Analysis" to "Scenario Analysis"
- Updated discussion of country risk in Venezuela
- Added one new Personal Finance Example
- Revised Focus on Ethics box (moral risk)
- Added one new Personal Finance Problem

Chapter 6   Interest Rates and Bond Valuation
- Revised discussion of bond yields and bond prices
- Added footnotes on bond duration and bond yield to call
- Re-labeled five existing Examples as Personal Finance Examples
- Revised Focus on Ethics box (new legislation affecting the credit-rating agencies)
- Re-labeled four Problems as Personal Finance Problems

Chapter 7   Stock Valuation
- Revised discussion of American depositary receipts and American depositary shares
- Revised discussion of interpreting stock quotations consistent with latest format of stock quotations
- Re-labeled three existing Examples as Personal Finance Examples
- New Focus on Ethics box (additional costs of pre-earnings guidance)
- Re-labeled six Problems as Personal Finance Problems

Chapter 8   Capital Budgeting Cash Flows
- Added two new Personal Finance Examples
- New Focus on Practice box (foreign direct investment in China)
- Added three new Personal Finance Problems

Chapter 9   Capital Budgeting Techniques: Certainty and Risk
- Clarified tabular explanation of project preferences with extreme discount rates and dissimilar cash inflow patterns
- Added four new Personal Finance Examples
- Changed terminology and clarified discussion relating to scenario analysis
- New Focus on Ethics box (environmental compliance costs)
- Added six new Personal Finance Problems
- Added new Ethics Problem

Chapter 10 The Cost of Capital

- Moved text coverage of EVA® to Companion Website
- Added two new Personal Finance Examples
- Revised Focus on Practice box (EVA®)
- Added three new Personal Finance Problems
- Added new Ethics Problem

Chapter 11 Leverage and Capital Structure

- Added three new Personal Finance Examples
- Revised Focus on Practice box (Adobe's operating leverage)
- Added three new Personal Finance Problems

Chapter 12 Dividend Policy

- Added two new Personal Finance Examples
- New Focus on Ethics box (motives for stock buybacks)
- Added one new Personal Finance Problem and re-labeled three existing Problems as Personal Finance Problems
- Added new Ethics Problem

Chapter 13 Working Capital and Current Assets Management

- Added two new Personal Finance Examples
- New Focus on Ethics box (stretching accounts payable)
- Added two new Personal Finance Problems
- Added new Ethics Problem

Chapter 14 Current Liabilities Management

- Added two new Personal Finance Examples
- New Focus on Ethics box (loan fraud)
- Added two new Personal Finance Problems

Supplements to the Fifth Edition

The *PMF* Teaching/Learning System includes a variety of useful supplements for teachers and for students.

Teaching Tools for Instructors

The key teaching tools available to instructors are the *Instructor's Manual*, testing materials, and *PowerPoint® Lecture Presentations*.

Instructor's Manual   Revised by Thomas Krueger, University of Wisconsin at La Crosse. This comprehensive resource pulls together the teaching tools so that instructors can use the textbook easily and effectively in the classroom. Each chapter provides an overview of key topics and detailed answers and solutions to all review questions, Warm-Up Exercises, end-of-chapter problems, and chapter cases, plus suggested answers to all critical thinking questions in chapter openers and boxes, Ethics Problems, Group Exercises, and Web Exercises. At the end of the manual are practice quizzes and solutions. The complete Instructor's Manual, including Spreadsheet Exercises, is available online at the Instructor's Resource Center (http://www.prenhall.com/irc) and on the Instructor's Resource CD-ROM.

Test Bank   Created by Daniel J. Borgia, Florida Gulf Coast University. Thoroughly revised to accommodate changes in the text, the Test Bank consists of a mix of true/false, multiple-choice, and essay questions. Each test question includes identifiers for type of question, skill tested by learning goal, and key topic tested plus, where appropriate, the formula(s) or equation(s) used in deriving the answer. The Test Bank is available in both printed and electronic formats, including Windows or Macintosh *TestGen* files and Microsoft Word files. The Test Bank and TestGen are available online at the Instructor's Resource Center (http://www.prenhall.com/irc) and on the Instructor's Resource CD-ROM.

Instructors can download the *TestGen* version of the Test Bank into *QuizMaster,* an online testing program for Windows and Macintosh that enables users to conduct timed or untimed exams at computer workstations. After completing tests, students can see their scores and view or print a diagnostic report of those topics or objectives requiring more attention. When installed on a local area network, *QuizMaster* allows instructors to save the scores on disk, print study diagnoses, and monitor progress of students individually or by class section and by all sections of the course.

PowerPoint Lecture Presentation   Created by Daniel J. Borgia, Florida Gulf Coast University. This presentation combines lecture notes with all of the art from the textbook. The PowerPoint Lecture Presentation is available online at the

Instructor's Resource Center (http://www.prenhall.com/irc) and on the Instructor's Resource CD-ROM.

Instructor's Resource CD-ROM Electronic files of the *Instructor's Manual, Test Bank, Computerized Test Bank*, and *PowerPoint Lecture Presentations* are available on one convenient CD-ROM, compatible with both Windows and Macintosh computers. The electronic versions allow instructors to customize the support materials to their individual classroom needs. All the resources on the Instructor's Resource CD-ROM are also available online at the Instructor's Resource Center (http://www.prenhall.com/irc).

Learning Tools for Students

Beyond the book itself, students have access to several resources for success in this course: MyFinanceLab, *Study Guide*, and the *Principles of Managerial Finance, Brief*, Fifth Edition Companion Website.

MyFinanceLab The Student Access Kit for MyFinanceLab opens the door to a powerful Web-based diagnostic testing and tutorial system designed specifically for the Gitman, *Principles of Managerial Finance* textbooks. With MyFinanceLab, instructors can create, edit, and assign online homework, and test and track all student work in the online gradebook. MyFinanceLab allows students to take practice tests correlated to the textbook and receive a customized study plan based on the test results. Most end-of-chapter problems are available in MyFinanceLab, and because the problems have algorithmically generated values, no student will have the same homework as another, and there is an unlimited opportunity for practice and testing. Students get the help they need, when they need it, from the robust tutorial options, including "View an Example" and "Help Me Solve This," which breaks the problem into its steps and links to the relevant textbook page.

Students can use MyFinanceLab with no instructor intervention. However, to take advantage of the full capabilities of MyFinanceLab, including assigning homework and tracking student progress in the automated gradebook, instructors will want to set up their class. To view a demo of MyFinanceLab or to request instructor access go to www.myfinancelab.com.

Study Guide *Updated by Thomas Kreuger, University of Wisconsin at La Crosse.* The *Study Guide* is an integral component of the *PMF* Learning System. It offers many tools for studying finance. Each chapter contains the following features: chapter summary enumerated by learning goals; topical chapter outline, also broken down by learning goals for quick review; sample problem solutions; study tips and a full sample exam with the answers at the end of the chapter. A financial dictionary of key terms is located at the end of the Study Guide, along with an appendix with tips on using financial calculators.

Principles of Managerial Finance, Brief, Fifth Edition Companion Website The website to accompany this textbook, located at www.prenhall.com/gitman, contains many additional resources. For each chapter on the website you will find

- Web Cases, which ask students to use the Web to find information and solve finance problems
- Web Exercises

- Self-Assessment Quizzes
- Case Studies in Finance, *updated by Michael Seiler of Hawaii Pacific University*

In addition to the chapter resources, you will find

- Two Web chapters: (1) "Financial Markets and Institutions," from the text *Introduction to Finance* by Lawrence J. Gitman and Jeff Madura, and (2) "International Managerial Finance," from *Principles of Managerial Finance*, Twelfth Edition, by Lawrence J. Gitman
- An online glossary, both as review flashcards and as a quick-reference document
- Spreadsheet examples from the textbook
- A Financial Calculator Guide
- Our Online Career Center

In addition to the Companion Website, the course content is available in Blackboard® and WebCT. Please contact your local sales representative for more information on obtaining course content in these various formats.

Acknowledgments

To My Colleagues, Friends, and Family

No textbook can consistently meet market needs without continual feedback from colleagues, students, practitioners, and members of the publishing team. Once again, I invite colleagues to relate their classroom experiences using this book and its package to me in care of the Acquisitions Editor in Finance, Prentice Hall Publishing Company, 75 Arlington Street, Suite 300, Boston, Massachusetts 02116. Your constructive criticism will help me to continue to improve the textbook and its Teaching/Learning System still further.

Prentice Hall and former publisher HarperCollins sought the advice of a great many excellent reviewers, all of whom strongly influenced various aspects of this book. The following individuals provided extremely thoughtful and useful comments for the preparation of the Fifth Edition:

Omar Benkato, *Ball State University*
Boyd D. Collier, *Tarleton State University*
Michael Giuliano, *University of Maryland–Asia Division*
John E. Harper, *Texas A&M at Commerce*
Raj K. Kohli, *Indiana University–South Bend*
Inayat Mangla, *Western Michigan University*
Bala Maniam, *Sam Houston State University*
Brian Maris, *Northern Arizona University*
Lee McClain, *Western Washington University*
Mukunthan Santhanakrishnan, *Idaho State University*
Tom Schmidt, *Simpson College*
Sandeep Singh, *SUNY Brockport*
Gordon M. Stringer, *University of Colorado–Colorado Springs*
Faye (Hefei) Wang, *University of Illinois–Chicago*

My special thanks go to the following individuals who analyzed the manuscript in previous editions:

Saul W. Adelman	Scott Besley	Omer Carey
M. Fall Ainina	Douglas S. Bible	Patrick A. Casabona
Gary A. Anderson	Charles W. Blackwell	Robert Chatfield
Ronald F. Anderson	Russell L. Block	K. C. Chen
James M. Andre	Calvin M. Boardman	Roger G. Clarke
Gene L. Andrusco	Paul Bolster	Terrence M. Clauretie
Antonio Apap	Robert J. Bondi	Ronnie J. Clayton
David A. Arbeit	Jeffrey A. Born	Mark Cockalingam
Allen Arkins	Jerry D. Boswell	Thomas Cook
Saul H. Auslander	Denis O. Boudreaux	Maurice P. Corrigan
Peter W. Bacon	Kenneth J. Boudreaux	Mike Cudd
Richard E. Ball	Wayne Boyet	Donnie L. Daniel
Thomas Bankston	Ron Braswell	Prabir Datta
Alexander Barges	Christopher Brown	Joel J. Dauten
Charles Barngrover	William Brunsen	Lee E. Davis
Michael Becker	Samuel B. Bulmash	Irv DeGraw
Omar Benkato	Francis E. Canda	Richard F. DeMong

Peter A. DeVito
James P. D'Mello
Mario A. Dipp
R. Gordon Dippel
Carleton Donchess
Thomas W. Donohue
Shannon Donovan
Vincent R. Driscoll
Betty A. Driver
Lorna Dotts
David R. Durst
Dwayne O. Eberhardt
Ronald L. Ehresman
Ted Ellis
F. Barney English
Greg Filbeck
Ross A. Flaherty
Rich Fortin
Timothy J. Gallagher
George W. Gallinger
Sharon Garrison
Gerald D. Gay
Deborah Giarusso
R. H. Gilmer
Anthony J. Giovino
Philip W. Glasgo
Jeffrey W. Glazer
Joel Gold
Ron B. Goldfarb
Dennis W. Goodwin
David A. Gordon
J. Charles Granicz
C. Ramon Griffin
Reynolds Griffith
Arthur Guarino
Lewell F. Gunter
Linda U. Hadley
Melvin W. Harju
Phil Harrington
George F. Harris
George T. Harris
John D. Harris
Mary Hartman
Richard Harvey
R. Stevenson Hawkey
Roger G. Hehman
Harvey Heinowitz
Glenn Henderson
Russell H. Hereth
Kathleen T. Hevert
J. Lawrence Hexter
Douglas A. Hibbert
Roger P. Hill
Linda C. Hittle

James Hoban
Hugh A. Hobson
Keith Howe
Kenneth M. Huggins
Jerry G. Hunt
Zahid Iqbal
Mahmood Islam
James F. Jackson
Stanley Jacobs
Dale W. Janowsky
Jeannette R. Jesinger
Nalina Jeypalan
Timothy E. Johnson
Roger Juchau
Ashok K. Kapoor
Daniel J. Kaufman, Jr.
Jim Keys
Joseph K. Kiely
Terrance E. Kingston
Thomas M. Krueger
Lawrence Kryzanowski
Harry R. Kuniansky
Richard E. La Near
William R. Lane
James Larsen
Rick LeCompte
B. E. Lee
Scott Lee
Michael A. Lenarcic
A. Joseph Lerro
Thomas J. Liesz
Alan Lines
Christopher K. Ma
James C. Ma
Dilip B. Madan
Judy Maese
James Mallet
Timothy A. Manuel
Brian Maris
Daniel S. Marrone
William H. Marsh
John F. Marshall
Linda J. Martin
Stanley A. Martin
Charles E. Maxwell
Timothy Hoyt McCaughey
Jay Meiselman
Vincent A. Mercurio
Joseph Messina
John B. Mitchell
Daniel F. Mohan
Charles Mohundro
Gene P. Morris
Edward A. Moses

Tarun K. Mukherjee
William T. Murphy
Randy Myers
Lance Nail
Kiseok Nam
Donald A. Nast
Vivian F. Nazar
G. Newbould
Charles Ngassam
Gary Noreiko
Dennis T. Officer
Kathleen J. Oldfather
Kathleen F. Oppenheimer
Richard M. Osborne
Jerome S. Osteryoung
Prasad Padmanabahn
Roger R. Palmer
Don B. Panton
John Park
Ronda S. Paul
Bruce C. Payne
Gerald W. Perritt
Gladys E. Perry
Stanley Piascik
Gregory Pierce
Mary L. Piotrowski
D. Anthony Plath
Jerry B. Poe
Gerald A. Pogue
Suzanne Polley
Ronald S. Pretekin
Fran Quinn
Rich Ravichandran
David Rayone
Walter J. Reinhart
Jack H. Reubens
Benedicte Reyes
William B. Riley, Jr.
Ron Rizzuto
Gayle A. Russell
Patricia A. Ryan
Murray Sabrin
Kanwal S. Sachedeva
R. Daniel Sadlier
Hadi Salavitabar
Gary Sanger
William L. Sartoris
Michael Schinski
Carl J. Schwendiman
Carl Schweser
Jim Scott
John W. Settle
Richard A. Shick
A. M. Sibley

Surendra S. Singhvi
Stacy Sirmans
Barry D. Smith
Gerald Smolen
Ira Smolowitz
Jean Snavely
Joseph V. Stanford
John A. Stocker
Lester B. Strickler
Elizabeth Strock
Donald H. Stuhlman
Sankar Sundarrajan
Philip R. Swensen
S. Tabriztchi
John C. Talbott
Gary Tallman
Harry Tamule
Richard W. Taylor

Rolf K. Tedefalk
Richard Teweles
Kenneth J. Thygerson
Robert D. Tollen
Emery A. Trahan
Pieter A. Vandenberg
Nikhil P. Varaiya
Oscar Varela
Kenneth J. Venuto
James A. Verbrugge
Ronald P. Volpe
John M. Wachowicz, Jr.
William H. Weber III
Herbert Weinraub
Jonathan B. Welch
Grant J. Wells
Larry R. White
Peter Wichert

C. Don Wiggins
Howard A. Williams
Richard E. Williams
Glenn A. Wilt, Jr.
Bernard J. Winger
Tony R. Wingler
Alan Wong
I. R. Woods
John C. Woods
Robert J. Wright
Richard H. Yanow
Seung J. Yoon
Charles W. Young
Philip J. Young
Joe W. Zeman
J. Kenton Zumwalt
John T. Zeitlow
Tom Zwirlein

My special thanks go to all members of my book team whose vision, creativity, and ongoing support helped me to engineer all elements of the Teaching/Learning System: to Michael J. Woodworth of Purdue University for the chapter-opening vignettes and the *In Practice:* Focus on Practice, Ethics, and Global Focus boxes; to Mehdi Salehizadeh of San Diego State University for help in revising the chapter on International Finance; to Steven Lifland of High Point University for the new personal finance problems, and for updating the in-chapter spreadsheet examples, Spreadsheet Exercises, Warm-Up Exercises, Group Exercises, and Web Exercises; to Daniel J. Borgia of Florida Gulf Coast University for revising the Test Banks and the PowerPoint Lecture Presentations; to Thomas Kreuger of the University of Wisconsin at La Crosse for updating the *Instructor's Manual* and *Study Guide;* to Michael Seiler of Hawaii Pacific University for updating the Case Studies in Finance on the book's website; and to Nikhil Varaiya of San Diego State University for assistance in obtaining data. I'm pleased by and proud of all their efforts.

A hearty round of applause also goes to the publishing team assembled by Prentice Hall—including Donna Battista, Mina Kim, Nancy Fenton, Bethany Tidd, Dana Weightman, Heather McNally, Andrew Watts, and others who worked on the book—for the inspiration and the perspiration that define teamwork. Nancy Freihofer and all the people at Thompson Steele, Inc. deserve an equally resounding ovation. A standing ovation is due Ann Torbert, whose development expertise and hard work have contributed to the book's standard of excellence. Also, special thanks to the formidable Prentice Hall sales force in finance, whose ongoing efforts keep the business fun!

Finally, and most important, many thanks to my wife, Robin, and to our children, Zachary and Jessica, for patiently providing support, understanding, and good humor throughout the revision process. To them, I will be forever grateful.

Lawrence J. Gitman
La Jolla, California

To the Student

Because you have a good many options for getting your assigned reading materials, I appreciate your choosing this textbook as the best means for learning in your managerial finance course. You should not be disappointed. I was not far removed from my own undergraduate studies when I wrote the first edition of this book, and so I set out to write a book that would meet the needs of students. In every edition, I have been mindful of students and careful to maintain a student focus.

The learning system in this book has been used by many of your predecessors in the course and proven effective. It integrates various learning tools with the concepts, tools, techniques, and practical applications you will need to learn about managerial finance. I have worked hard to present in a clear and interesting way the information you will need. This book is loaded with features designed to motivate your study of finance and to help you learn the course material. Go to pages vii-xii ("Gitman's Proven Learning/Teaching System") for an overview and walkthrough of those features. Notice that the book includes Personal Finance Examples (and related end-of-chapter problems) that show how to apply managerial finance concepts and tools to your personal financial life.

About some of the specific features: First, pay attention to the Learning Goals, which will help you focus on what material you need to learn, where you can find it in the chapter, and whether you've mastered it by the end of the chapter.

Second, avoid the temptation to rush past the Review Questions at the end of each major text section. Pausing briefly to test your understanding of the section content will help you cement your understanding of it. Give yourself an honest assessment. If some details are fuzzy, go back (even briefly) and review anything that still seems unclear.

Third, look for (or make) opportunities to talk with classmates or friends about what you are reading and learning in the course. Talking about the concepts and techniques of finance demonstrates how much you've learned, uncovers things you haven't yet understood fully, and gives you valuable practice for class and (eventually) the business world. While you're talking, don't neglect to discuss the issues raised in the *Focus on Ethics* boxes, which look at some of the opportunities to do right (or not) that business people face.

The Student Access Kit for MyFinanceLab opens the door to a powerful Web-based diagnostic testing and tutorial system designed for this text. MyFinanceLab allows you to take practice tests correlated to the textbook and receive a customized study plan based on your results. The assignment Problems in MyFinanceLab, based on selected end-of-chapter Problems in the book, have algorithmically generated values. Thus, the numbers in your homework will differ from those of your classmates, and there is an unlimited opportunity for practice and testing. You can get the help you need, when you need it, from the robust tutorial options, including "View an Example" and "Help Me Solve This," which breaks the problem into steps and links to the relevant textbook page.

Given today's rapidly changing technology, who knows what might be available next? Prentice Hall and I are striving to keep pace with your needs and interests, and would like to hear your ideas for improving the teaching and learning of finance. Please feel free to share your ideas with us by e-mailing finance@prenhall.com.

I wish you all the best in this course, and in your academic and professional careers.

Lawrence J. Gitman
La Jolla, California

Part One
Introduction to Managerial Finance

Chapters in This Part

1 **The Role and Environment of Managerial Finance**

2 **Financial Statements and Analysis**

3 **Cash Flow and Financial Planning**

1

The Role and Environment of Managerial Finance

WHY THIS CHAPTER MATTERS TO YOU

In Your Professional Life

Accounting: You need to understand the relationships between the firm's accounting and finance functions; how the financial statements you prepare will be used; business ethics; agency costs and why the firm must bear them; and how to calculate the tax effects of proposed transactions.

Information systems: You need to understand the organization of the firm; why finance personnel require both historical and projected data; and what data are necessary for determining the firm's tax liability.

Management: You need to understand the legal forms of business organization; the tasks that will be performed by finance personnel; the goal of the firm; management compensation; ethics in the firm; the agency problem; and the role of financial institutions and markets.

Marketing: You need to understand how the activities you pursue will be affected by the finance function, such as the firm's cash and credit management policies; ethical behaviors; and the role of financial markets in raising capital.

Operations: You need to understand the organization of the firm and of the finance function in particular; why maximizing profit is not the main goal of the firm; the role of financial institutions and markets in financing; and ethics and the agency problem.

In Your Personal Life

Many of the principles of managerial finance apply to your personal life: to making purchase and sale transactions, borrowing money, and saving and investing to achieve financial goals. These actions require you to interact with financial institutions and markets. You also need to consider the impact of taxes on your financial plans. Learning the basics of managerial finance can help you manage your personal finances effectively.

LEARNING GOALS

LG 1 Define *finance,* its major areas and opportunities, and the legal forms of business organization.

LG 2 Describe the managerial finance function and its relationship to economics and accounting.

LG 3 Identify the primary activities of the financial manager.

LG 4 Explain the goal of the firm, corporate governance, the role of ethics, and the agency issue.

LG 5 Understand financial institutions and markets, and the role they play in managerial finance.

LG 6 Discuss business taxes and their importance in financial decisions.

The field of finance directly affects the lives of every person and every organization. Many areas for study and a large number of career opportunities are available in finance. The purpose of this chapter is to acquaint you with the study of finance, the managerial finance function, and the goal of the firm, including corporate governance issues. The chapter also describes financial institutions and markets, and business taxation. Finance will affect your working life in whatever area of study you choose to concentrate.

1.1 | Finance and Business

The field of finance is broad and dynamic. Basic principles of finance, such as those you will learn in this textbook, can be universally applied in business organizations of different types. In addition, many of these principles are applicable to your personal financial life.

What Is Finance?

finance
The art and science of managing money.

Finance can be defined as the art and science of managing money. Virtually all individuals and organizations earn or raise money and spend or invest money. Finance is concerned with the process, institutions, markets, and instruments involved in the transfer of money among individuals, businesses, and governments. Most adults will benefit from an understanding of finance, which will enable them to make better personal financial decisions.

Major Areas and Opportunities in Finance

The major areas of finance can be summarized by reviewing the career opportunities in finance. These opportunities can, for convenience, be divided into two broad areas: financial services and managerial finance.

Financial Services

financial services
The area of finance concerned with the design and delivery of advice and financial products to individuals, business, and government.

Financial services is the area of finance concerned with the design and delivery of advice and financial products to individuals, business, and government. It involves a variety of interesting career opportunities within the areas of banking and related institutions, personal financial planning, investments, real estate, and insurance. Career opportunities available in each of these areas are described at this textbook's website.

Managerial Finance

managerial finance
Concerns the duties of the *financial manager* in the business firm.

financial manager
Actively manages the financial affairs of any type of business, whether financial or nonfinancial, private or public, large or small, profit-seeking or not-for-profit.

Managerial finance is concerned with the duties of the *financial manager* in the business firm. **Financial managers** actively manage the financial affairs of any type of businesses—financial and nonfinancial, private and public, large and small, profit-seeking and not-for-profit. They perform such varied financial tasks as planning, extending credit to customers, evaluating proposed large expenditures, and raising money to fund the firm's operations. In recent years, changing economic, competitive, and regulatory environments have increased the importance and complexity of the financial manager's duties. Today's financial manager is more actively involved in developing and implementing corporate strategies aimed at "growing the firm" and improving its competitive position. As a result, many top executives have come from the finance area.

Another ongoing trend has been the globalization of business activity. U.S. corporations have dramatically increased their sales, purchases, investments, and fund raising in other countries, and foreign corporations have likewise increased their corresponding activities in the United States. These changes have increased the need for financial managers who can manage cash flows in different currencies and protect against the risks that naturally arise from international transactions. Although these changes make the managerial finance function more complex, they can lead to a more rewarding and fulfilling career.

Legal Forms of Business Organization

The three most common legal forms of business organization are the *sole proprietorship*, the *partnership*, and the *corporation*. Other specialized forms of business organization also exist. Sole proprietorships are the most numerous. However, corporations are overwhelmingly dominant with respect to business receipts and net profits. Corporations are given primary emphasis in this textbook.

Sole Proprietorships

sole proprietorship
A business owned by one person and operated for his or her own profit.

A **sole proprietorship** is a business owned by one person who operates it for his or her own profit. About 75 percent of all business firms are sole proprietorships. The typical sole proprietorship is a small business, such as a bike shop, personal trainer, or plumber. The majority of sole proprietorships are found in the wholesale, retail, service, and construction industries.

unlimited liability
The condition of a sole proprietorship (or general partnership) allowing the owner's total wealth to be taken to satisfy creditors.

Typically, the proprietor, along with a few employees, operates the proprietorship. He or she normally raises capital from personal resources or by borrowing and is responsible for all business decisions. The sole proprietor has **unlimited liability;** his or her total wealth—not merely the amount originally invested—can be taken to satisfy creditors. The key strengths and weaknesses of sole proprietorships are summarized in Table 1.1.

Partnerships

partnership
A business owned by two or more people and operated for profit.

A **partnership** consists of two or more owners doing business together for profit. Partnerships account for about 10 percent of all businesses, and they are typically larger than sole proprietorships. Finance, insurance, and real estate firms are the most common types of partnership. Public accounting and stock brokerage partnerships often have large numbers of partners.

articles of partnership
The written contract used to formally establish a business partnership.

Most partnerships are established by a written contract known as **articles of partnership.** In a *general* (or *regular*) *partnership*, all partners have unlimited liability, and each partner is legally liable for *all* of the debts of the partnership. Strengths and weaknesses of partnerships are summarized in Table 1.1.

corporation
An artificial being created by law (often called a "legal entity").

Corporations

Hint Many small corporations, as well as small proprietorships and partnerships, have no access to financial markets. In addition, whenever the owners take out a loan, they usually must personally cosign the loan.

A **corporation** is an artificial being created by law. Often called a "legal entity," a corporation has the powers of an individual in that it can sue and be sued, make and be party to contracts, and acquire property in its own name. Although only

TABLE 1.1	Strengths and Weaknesses of the Common Legal Forms of Business Organization		
	Sole proprietorship	Partnership	Corporation
Strengths	• Owner receives all profits (and sustains all losses) • Low organizational costs • Income included and taxed on proprietor's personal tax return • Independence • Secrecy • Ease of dissolution	• Can raise more funds than sole proprietorships • Borrowing power enhanced by more owners • More available brain power and managerial skill • Income included and taxed on partner's personal tax return	• Owners have *limited liability,* which guarantees that they cannot lose more than they invested • Can achieve large size via sale of ownership (stock) • Ownership (stock) is readily transferable • Long life of firm • Can hire professional managers • Has better access to financing • Can offer attractive retirement plans
Weaknesses	• Owner has *unlimited liability*—total wealth can be taken to satisfy debts • Limited fund-raising power tends to inhibit growth • Proprietor must be jack-of-all-trades • Difficult to give employees long-run career opportunities • Lacks continuity when proprietor dies	• Owners have *unlimited liability* and may have to cover debts of other partners • Partnership is dissolved when a partner dies • Difficult to liquidate or transfer partnership	• Taxes generally higher, because corporate income is taxed, and dividends paid to owners are also taxed at a maximum 15% rate • More expensive to organize than other business forms • Subject to greater government regulation • Lacks secrecy, because stockholders must receive financial reports

stockholders
The owners of a corporation, whose ownership, or *equity,* is evidenced by either common stock or preferred stock.

common stock
The purest and most basic form of corporate ownership.

dividends
Periodic distributions of earnings to the stockholders of a firm.

board of directors
Group elected by the firm's stockholders and typically responsible for developing strategic goals and plans, setting general policy, guiding corporate affairs, approving major expenditures, and hiring/firing, compensating, and monitoring key officers and executives.

about 15 percent of all businesses are incorporated, the corporation is the dominant form of business organization in terms of receipts and profits. It accounts for nearly 90 percent of business receipts and 80 percent of net profits. Although corporations are involved in all types of businesses, manufacturing corporations account for the largest portion of corporate business receipts and net profits. The key strengths and weaknesses of large corporations are summarized in Table 1.1.

The owners of a corporation are its **stockholders,** whose ownership, or *equity,* is evidenced by either common stock or preferred stock.[1] These forms of ownership are discussed in detail in Chapter 7; at this point it is enough to say that **common stock** is the purest and most basic form of corporate ownership. Stockholders expect to earn a return by receiving **dividends**—periodic distributions of earnings—or by realizing gains through increases in share price.

As noted in the upper portion of Figure 1.1 (see page 6), control of the corporation is structured as a democracy. The stockholders (owners) vote periodically to elect members of the *board of directors* and to decide other issues such as amending the corporate charter. The **board of directors** is typically responsible for developing strategic goals and plans, setting general policy, guiding corporate affairs, approving major expenditures, and hiring/firing, compensating,

---

1. Some corporations do not have stockholders but rather have "members" who often have rights similar to those of stockholders—that is, they are entitled to vote and receive dividends. Examples include mutual savings banks, credit unions, mutual insurance companies, and a whole host of charitable organizations.

FIGURE 1.1

Corporate Organization
The general organization of a corporation and the finance function (which is shown in yellow)

Stockholders

elect

Board of Directors · · · · · · · **Owners**

hires

President (CEO) · · · · · · · **Managers**

Vice President Human Resources · Vice President Manufacturing · Vice President Finance (CFO) · Vice President Marketing · Vice President Information Resources

Treasurer · Controller

Capital Expenditure Manager · Credit Manager · Foreign Exchange Manager · Tax Manager · Cost Accounting Manager

Financial Planning and Fund-Raising Manager · Cash Manager · Pension Fund Manager · Corporate Accounting Manager · Financial Accounting Manager

and monitoring key officers and executives. The directors typically include both "inside directors," such as key corporate executives, and "outside directors," such as executives from other companies, major shareholders, and national or community leaders. Outside directors for major corporations are generally paid an annual fee of $15,000 to $25,000 or more. Also, they are frequently granted options to buy a specified number of shares of the firm's stock at a stated—and often attractive—price.

president or chief executive officer (CEO)
Corporate official responsible for managing the firm's day-to-day operations and carrying out the policies established by the board of directors.

limited partnership (LP)
S corporation (S corp)
limited liability corporation (LLC)
limited liability partnership (LLP)
See Table 1.2.

The **president or chief executive officer (CEO)** is responsible for managing day-to-day operations and carrying out the policies established by the board of directors. The CEO is required to report periodically to the firm's directors.

It is important to note the division between owners and managers in a large corporation, as shown by the dashed horizontal line in Figure 1.1. This separation and some of the issues surrounding it will be addressed in the discussion of *the agency issue* later in this chapter.

Other Limited Liability Organizations

A number of other organizational forms provide owners with limited liability. The most popular are **limited partnerships (LPs)**, **S corporations (S corps)**, **limited liability corporations (LLCs)**, and **limited liability partnerships (LLPs)**. Each rep-

TABLE 1.2	Other Limited Liability Organizations
Organization	Description
Limited partnership (LP)	A partnership in which one or more partners have limited liability as long as at least *one* partner (the general partner) has unlimited liability. The *limited partners* cannot take an active role in the firm's management; they are passive investors.
S corporation (S corp)	A tax-reporting entity that (under Subchapter S of the Internal Revenue Code) allows certain corporations with 100 or fewer stockholders to choose to be taxed as partnerships. Its stockholders receive the organizational benefits of a corporation and the tax advantages of a partnership. But S corps lose certain tax advantages related to pension plans.
Limited liability corporation (LLC)	Permitted in most states, the LLC gives its owners, like those of S corps, limited liability and taxation as a partnership. But unlike an S corp, the LLC can own more than 80% of another corporation, and corporations, partnerships, or non-U.S. residents can own LLC shares. LLCs work well for corporate joint ventures or projects developed through a subsidiary.
Limited liability partnership (LLP)	A partnership permitted in many states; governing statutes vary by state. All LLP partners have limited liability. They are liable for their own acts of malpractice, but not for those of other partners. The LLP is taxed as a partnership. LLPs are frequently used by legal and accounting professionals.

resents a specialized form or blending of the characteristics of the organizational forms described previously. What they have in common is that their owners enjoy limited liability, and they typically have fewer than 100 owners. Each of these limited liability organizations is briefly described in Table 1.2.

Why Study Managerial Finance?

An understanding of the concepts, techniques, and practices presented throughout this text will fully acquaint you with the financial manager's activities and decisions. Because most business decisions are measured in financial terms, the financial manager plays a key role in the operation of the firm. People in all areas of responsibility—accounting, information systems, management, marketing, operations, and so forth—need a basic understanding of the managerial finance function.

Okay, so you're not planning to major in finance! You still will need to understand the activities of the financial manager to improve your chance of success in your chosen business career. All managers in the firm, regardless of their job descriptions, work with financial personnel to justify labor requirements, negotiate operating budgets, deal with financial performance appraisals, and sell proposals at least partly on the basis of their financial merits. Clearly, those managers who understand the financial decision-making process will be better able to address financial concerns and will therefore more often get the resources they need to attain their own goals. The "Why This Chapter Matters to You" section that appears on each chapter-opening page should help you understand the importance of each chapter in both your professional and personal life.

As you study this text, you will learn about the career opportunities in managerial finance, which are briefly described in Table 1.3 (see page 8). Although this

TABLE 1.3	Career Opportunities in Managerial Finance
Position	**Description**
Financial analyst	Primarily prepares the firm's financial plans and budgets. Other duties include financial forecasting, performing financial comparisons, and working closely with accounting.
Capital expenditures manager	Evaluates and recommends proposed long-term investments. May be involved in the financial aspects of implementing approved investments.
Project finance manager	In large firms, arranges financing for approved long-term investments. Coordinates consultants, investment bankers, and legal counsel.
Cash manager	Maintains and controls the firm's daily cash balances. Frequently manages the firm's cash collection and disbursement activities and short-term investments; coordinates short-term borrowing and banking relationships.
Credit analyst/manager	Administers the firm's credit policy by evaluating credit applications, extending credit, and monitoring and collecting accounts receivable.
Pension fund manager	In large companies, oversees or manages the assets and liabilities of the employees' pension fund.
Foreign exchange manager	Manages specific foreign operations and the firm's exposure to fluctuations in exchange rates.

text focuses on publicly held profit-seeking firms, the principles presented here are equally applicable to private and not-for-profit organizations. The decision-making principles developed in this text can also be applied to personal financial decisions. I hope that this first exposure to the exciting field of finance will provide the foundation and initiative for further study and possibly even a future career.

REVIEW QUESTIONS

1–1   What is *finance?* Explain how this field affects the life of everyone and of every organization.

1–2   What is the *financial services* area of finance? Describe the field of *managerial finance.*

1–3   Which legal form of business organization is most common? Which form is dominant in terms of business receipts and net profits?

1–4   Describe the roles and the basic relationship among the major parties in a corporation—stockholders, board of directors, and president. How are corporate owners compensated?

1–5   Briefly name and describe some organizational forms other than corporations that provide owners with limited liability.

1–6   Why is the study of managerial finance important to your professional life regardless of the specific area of responsibility you may have within the business firm? Why is it important to your personal life?

1.2 | The Managerial Finance Function

People in all areas of responsibility within the firm must interact with finance personnel and procedures to get their jobs done. For financial personnel to make useful forecasts and decisions, they must be willing and able to talk to individuals in other areas of the firm. For example, when considering a new product, the financial manager needs to obtain sales forecasts, pricing guidelines, and advertising and promotion budget estimates from marketing personnel. The managerial finance function can be broadly described by considering its role within the organization, its relationship to economics and accounting, and the primary activities of the financial manager.

Organization of the Finance Function

treasurer
The firm's chief financial manager, who is responsible for the firm's financial activities, such as financial planning and fund raising, making capital expenditure decisions, and managing cash, credit, the pension fund, and foreign exchange.

controller
The firm's chief accountant, who is responsible for the firm's accounting activities, such as corporate accounting, tax management, financial accounting, and cost accounting.

Hint A *controller* is sometimes referred to as a *comptroller.* Not-for-profit and governmental organizations frequently use the title of comptroller.

The size and importance of the managerial finance function depend on the size of the firm. In small firms, the finance function is generally performed by the accounting department. As a firm grows, the finance function typically evolves into a separate department linked directly to the company president or CEO through the chief financial officer (CFO). The lower portion of the organizational chart in Figure 1.1 (on page 6) shows the structure of the finance function in a typical medium-to-large-size firm.

Reporting to the CFO are the treasurer and the controller. The **treasurer** (the chief financial manager) is commonly responsible for handling financial activities, such as financial planning and fund raising, making capital expenditure decisions, managing cash, managing credit activities, managing the pension fund, and managing foreign exchange. The **controller** (the chief accountant) typically handles the accounting activities, such as corporate accounting, tax management, financial accounting, and cost accounting. The treasurer's focus tends to be more external, the controller's focus more internal. *The activities of the treasurer, or financial manager, are the primary concern of this text.*

If international sales or purchases are important to a firm, it may well employ one or more finance professionals whose job is to monitor and manage the firm's exposure to loss from currency fluctuations. A trained financial manager can "hedge," or protect against such a loss, at reasonable cost by using a variety of financial instruments. These **foreign exchange managers** typically report to the firm's treasurer.

Relationship to Economics

foreign exchange manager
The manager responsible for monitoring and managing the firm's exposure to loss from currency fluctuations.

marginal cost–benefit analysis
Economic principle that states that financial decisions should be made and actions taken only when the added benefits exceed the added costs.

The field of finance is closely related to economics. Financial managers must understand the economic framework and be alert to the consequences of varying levels of economic activity and changes in economic policy. They must also be able to use economic theories as guidelines for efficient business operation. Examples include supply-and-demand analysis, profit-maximizing strategies, and price theory. The primary economic principle used in managerial finance is **marginal cost–benefit analysis,** the principle that financial decisions should be made and actions taken only when the added benefits exceed the added costs. Nearly all financial decisions ultimately come down to an assessment of their marginal benefits and marginal costs.

Example

Jamie Teng is a financial manager for Nord Department Stores, a large chain of upscale department stores operating primarily in the western United States. She is currently trying to decide whether to replace one of the firm's online computers with a new, more sophisticated one that would both speed processing and handle a larger volume of transactions. The new computer would require a cash outlay of $80,000, and the old computer could be sold to net $28,000. The total benefits from the new computer (measured in today's dollars) would be $100,000. The benefits over a similar time period from the old computer (measured in today's dollars) would be $35,000. Applying marginal cost–benefit analysis, Jamie organizes the data as follows:

Benefits with new computer	$100,000	
Less: Benefits with old computer	35,000	
(1) Marginal (added) benefits		$65,000
Cost of new computer	$ 80,000	
Less: Proceeds from sale of old computer	28,000	
(2) Marginal (added) costs		52,000
Net benefit [(1) − (2)]		$13,000

Because the marginal (added) benefits of $65,000 exceed the marginal (added) costs of $52,000, Jamie recommends that the firm purchase the new computer to replace the old one. The firm will experience a net benefit of $13,000 as a result of this action.

Relationship to Accounting

The firm's finance (treasurer) and accounting (controller) activities are closely related and generally overlap. Indeed, managerial finance and accounting are often not easily distinguishable. In small firms the controller often carries out the finance function, and in large firms many accountants are closely involved in various finance activities. However, there are two basic differences between finance and accounting; one is related to the emphasis on cash flows and the other to decision making.

Emphasis on Cash Flows

accrual basis
In preparation of financial statements, recognizes revenue at the time of sale and recognizes expenses when they are incurred.

cash basis
Recognizes revenues and expenses only with respect to actual inflows and outflows of cash.

The accountant's primary function is to develop and report data for measuring the performance of the firm, assess its financial position, comply with and file reports required by securities regulators, and file and pay taxes. Using certain standardized and generally accepted principles, the accountant prepares financial statements that recognize revenue at the time of sale (whether payment has been received or not) and recognize expenses when they are incurred. This approach is referred to as the **accrual basis.**

The financial manager, on the other hand, places primary emphasis on *cash flows*, the intake and outgo of cash. He or she maintains the firm's solvency by planning the cash flows necessary to satisfy its obligations and to acquire assets needed to achieve the firm's goals. The financial manager uses this **cash basis** to recognize the revenues and expenses only with respect to actual inflows and outflows of cash. Regardless of its profit or loss, *a firm must have a sufficient flow of cash to meet its obligations as they come due.*

Example

Nassau Corporation, a small yacht dealer, sold one yacht for $100,000 in the calendar year just ended. The yacht was purchased during the year at a total cost of $80,000. Although the firm paid in full for the yacht during the year, at year-end it has yet to collect the $100,000 from the customer. The accounting view and the financial view of the firm's performance during the year are given by the following income and cash flow statements, respectively.

Accounting view (accrual basis)		Financial view (cash basis)	
Nassau Corporation income statement for the year ended 12/31		**Nassau Corporation** cash flow statement for the year ended 12/31	
Sales revenue	$100,000	Cash inflow	$ 0
Less: Costs	80,000	Less: Cash outflow	80,000
Net profit	$ 20,000	Net cash flow	($80,000)

In an accounting sense Nassau Corporation is profitable, but in terms of actual cash flow it is a financial failure. Its lack of cash flow resulted from the uncollected account receivable of $100,000. Without adequate cash inflows to meet its obligations, the firm will not survive, regardless of its level of profits.

Hint The primary emphasis of accounting is on accrual methods; the primary emphasis of financial management is on cash flow methods.

As the example shows, accrual accounting data do not fully describe the circumstances of a firm. Thus the financial manager must look beyond financial statements to obtain insight into existing or developing problems. Of course, accountants are well aware of the importance of cash flows, and financial managers use and understand accrual-based financial statements. Nevertheless, the financial manager, by concentrating on cash flows, should be able to avoid insolvency and achieve the firm's financial goals.

Personal Finance Example

Individuals do not use accrual concepts. Rather, they rely solely on cash flows to measure their financial outcomes. Generally, individuals plan, monitor, and assess their financial activities using cash flows over a given period, typically a month or a year. Ann Bach projects her cash flows during October 2009 as follows:

Item	Amount Inflow	Outflow
Net pay received	$4,400	
Rent		$1,200
Car payment		450
Utilities		300
Groceries		800
Clothes		750
Dining out		650
Gasoline		260
Interest received	220	
Misc. expense		425
Totals	$4,620	$4,835

Ann subtracts her total outflows of $4,835 from her total inflows of $4,620, and finds that her *net cash flow* for October will be −$215. To cover the $215 shortfall, Ann would have to either borrow $215 (putting it on a credit card is a form of borrowing), or withdraw $215 from her savings. Or she could decide to reduce her outflows in areas of discretionary spending—e.g., clothing purchases, dining out, or areas that make up the $425 of miscellaneous expense.

Decision Making

The second major difference between finance and accounting has to do with decision making. Accountants devote most of their attention to the *collection and presentation of financial data*. Financial managers evaluate the accounting statements, develop additional data, and *make decisions* on the basis of their assessment of the associated returns and risks. Of course, this does not mean that accountants never make decisions or that financial managers never gather data. Rather, the primary focuses of accounting and finance are distinctly different.

Primary Activities of the Financial Manager

Hint Technically, financial managers make recommendations with regard to decisions that are ultimately made by the CEO and/or corporate board of directors.

In addition to ongoing involvement in financial analysis and planning, the financial manager's primary activities are making investment decisions and making financing decisions. Investment decisions determine both the mix and the type of assets held by the firm. Financing decisions determine both the mix and the type of financing used by the firm. These sorts of decisions can be conveniently viewed in terms of the firm's balance sheet, as shown in Figure 1.2. However, the decisions are actually made on the basis of their cash flow effects on the overall value of the firm.

REVIEW QUESTIONS

1–7 What financial activities is the treasurer, or financial manager, responsible for handling in the mature firm?

1–8 What is the primary economic principle used in managerial finance?

1–9 What are the major differences between accounting and finance with respect to emphasis on cash flows and decision making?

1–10 What are the two primary activities of the financial manager that are related to the firm's balance sheet?

FIGURE 1.2

Financial Activities
Primary activities of the financial manager

1.3 | Goal of the Firm

As noted earlier, the owners of a corporation are normally distinct from its managers. Actions of the financial manager should be taken to achieve the objectives of the firm's owners, its stockholders. In most cases, if financial managers are successful in this endeavor, they will also achieve their own financial and professional objectives. Thus financial managers need to know what the objectives of the firm's owners are.

Maximize Profit?

earnings per share (EPS)
The amount earned during the period on behalf of each outstanding share of common stock, calculated by dividing the period's total earnings available for the firm's common stockholders by the number of shares of common stock outstanding.

Some people believe that the firm's objective is always to maximize profit. To achieve this goal, the financial manager would take only those actions that were expected to make a major contribution to the firm's overall profits. For each alternative being considered, the financial manager would select the one that is expected to result in the highest monetary return.

Corporations commonly measure profits in terms of **earnings per share (EPS),** which represent the amount earned during the period on behalf of each outstanding share of common stock. EPS are calculated by dividing the period's total earnings available for the firm's common stockholders by the number of shares of common stock outstanding.

Example

Nick Dukakis, the financial manager of Neptune Manufacturing, a producer of marine engine components, is choosing between two investments, Rotor and Valve. The following table shows the EPS that each investment is expected to have over its 3-year life.

| | Earnings per share (EPS) | | | |
Investment	Year 1	Year 2	Year 3	Total for years 1, 2, and 3
Rotor	$1.40	$1.00	$0.40	$2.80
Valve	0.60	1.00	1.40	3.00

In terms of the profit maximization goal, Valve would be preferred over Rotor, because it results in higher total earnings per share over the 3-year period ($3.00 EPS compared with $2.80 EPS).

But is profit maximization a reasonable goal? No. It fails for a number of reasons: It ignores (1) the timing of returns, (2) cash flows available to stockholders, and (3) risk.

Timing

Because the firm can earn a return on funds it receives, *the receipt of funds sooner rather than later is preferred.* In our example, in spite of the fact that the total earnings from Rotor are smaller than those from Valve, Rotor provides much greater earnings per share in the first year. The larger returns in year 1 could be reinvested to provide greater future earnings.

Cash Flows

Profits do *not* necessarily result in cash flows available to the stockholders. Owners receive cash flow in the form of either cash dividends paid them or the proceeds from selling their shares for a higher price than initially paid. Greater EPS do not necessarily mean that a firm's board of directors will vote to increase dividend payments.

Furthermore, higher EPS do not necessarily translate into a higher stock price. Firms sometimes experience earnings increases without any correspondingly favorable change in stock price. Only when earnings increases are accompanied by increased future cash flows would a higher stock price be expected.

Risk

risk
The chance that actual outcomes may differ from those expected.

Profit maximization also disregards **risk**—the chance that actual outcomes may differ from those expected. A basic premise in managerial finance is that a tradeoff exists between return (cash flow) and risk. *Return and risk are, in fact, the key determinants of share price, which represents the wealth of the owners in the firm.*

Hint The relationship between risk and return is one of the most important concepts in the book. Investors who seek to avoid risk will *always* require a bigger return for taking bigger risks.

Cash flow and risk affect share price differently: Higher cash flow is generally associated with a higher share price. Higher risk tends to result in a lower share price because the stockholder must be compensated for the greater risk. In general, stockholders are **risk-averse**—that is, they want to avoid risk. When risk is involved, stockholders expect to earn higher rates of return on investments of higher risk and lower rates on lower-risk investments. The key point, which will be fully developed in Chapter 5, is that differences in risk can significantly affect the value of an investment.

risk-averse
Seeking to avoid risk.

Because profit maximization does not achieve the objectives of the firm's owners, it should *not* be the primary goal of the financial manager.

Maximize Shareholder Wealth

The goal of the firm, and therefore of all managers and employees, is *to maximize the wealth of the owners for whom it is being operated.* The wealth of corporate owners is measured by the share price of the stock, which in turn is based on the timing of returns (cash flows), their magnitude, and their risk.

When considering each financial decision alternative or possible action in terms of its effect on the share price of the firm's stock, *financial managers should accept only those actions that are expected to increase share price.* Figure 1.3 depicts this process. Because share price represents the owners' wealth in the firm, maximizing share price will maximize owner wealth. Note that *return (cash flows) and risk are the key decision variables in maximizing owner wealth.* It is important to recognize that earnings per share, because they are viewed as an indicator of the firm's future returns (cash flows), often appear to affect share price.

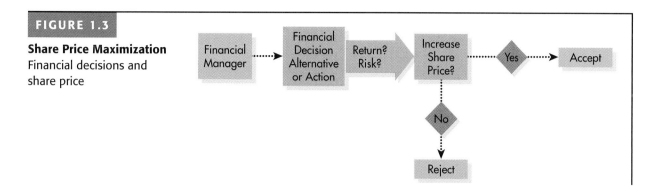

FIGURE 1.3

Share Price Maximization
Financial decisions and
share price

What About Stakeholders?

Although maximization of shareholder wealth is the primary goal, many firms broaden their focus to include the interests of *stakeholders* as well as shareholders. **Stakeholders** are groups such as employees, customers, suppliers, creditors, owners, and others who have a direct economic link to the firm. A firm with a *stakeholder focus* consciously avoids actions that would prove detrimental to stakeholders. The goal is not to maximize stakeholder well-being but to preserve it.

The stakeholder view does not alter the goal of maximizing shareholder wealth. Such a view is often considered part of the firm's "social responsibility." It is expected to provide long-run benefit to shareholders by maintaining positive stakeholder relationships. Such relationships should minimize stakeholder turnover, conflicts, and litigation. Clearly, the firm can better achieve its goal of shareholder wealth maximization by fostering cooperation with its other stakeholders, rather than conflict with them.

stakeholders
Groups such as employees,
customers, suppliers,
creditors, owners, and
others who have a direct
economic link to the firm.

Corporate Governance

The system used to direct and control a corporation is referred to as **corporate governance.** It defines the rights and responsibilities of the key corporate participants such as the shareholders, board of directors, officers and managers, and other stakeholders, and the rules and procedures for making corporate decisions. It also typically specifies the structure through which the company sets objectives, develops plans for achieving them, and establishes procedures for monitoring performance.

Figure 1.1 on page 6 depicts the typical corporate governance structure, in which the stockholders (owners) elect a board of directors (their representatives), who in turn hire officers and managers (professional managers) to operate the firm in a manner consistent with the goals, plans, and policies established and monitored by the board on behalf of the shareholders. Typically, the board's policies specify ethical practices and provide for the protection of stakeholder interests.

corporate governance
The system used to direct and
control a corporation. Defines
the rights and responsibilities
of key corporate participants,
decision-making procedures,
and the way in which the firm
will set, achieve, and monitor
its objectives.

Individual versus Institutional Investors

Clearly, the corporate board's first responsibility is to the shareholders. To better understand this responsibility it is helpful to differentiate between the two broad classes of owners—individuals and institutions. **Individual investors** are investors who buy relatively small quantities of shares so as to earn a return on idle funds, build a source of retirement income, or provide financial security. **Institutional investors** are investment professionals that are paid to manage other people's money. They hold and trade large quantities of securities for individuals, businesses, and governments. Institutional investors include banks, insurance companies, mutual funds, and pension funds, which invest large sums of money to earn competitive returns for their clients/plan participants.

Because they hold and trade large blocks of stock, institutional investors tend to have a much greater influence on corporate governance than do individual investors. Simply stated, because they own large amounts of common stock and have the resources to buy and sell large blocks of shares, institutional investors are able to maintain management's attention. If a large institutional investor sells or buys a sizable block of shares, the share price will likely be driven down or up, respectively. Clearly, these large investors speak in a much louder voice than does the individual investor.

The Sarbanes-Oxley Act of 2002

Beginning in 2000, numerous corporate misdeeds were uncovered and disclosed by various regulatory bodies. The misdeeds derived from two main types of issues: (1) false disclosures in financial reporting and other information releases, and (2) undisclosed conflicts of interest between corporations and their analysts, auditors, and attorneys and between corporate directors, officers, and shareholders. In response to these fraudulent disclosures and conflicts of interest, in July 2002 Congress passed the **Sarbanes-Oxley Act of 2002** (commonly called **SOX**).

Sarbanes-Oxley focused on eliminating the many disclosure and conflict of interest problems that had surfaced. It did the following: established an oversight board to monitor the accounting industry; tightened audit regulations and controls; toughened penalties against executives who commit corporate fraud; strengthened accounting disclosure requirements and ethical guidelines for corporate officers; established corporate board structure and membership guidelines; established guidelines with regard to analyst conflicts of interest; mandated instant disclosure of stock sales by corporate executives; and increased securities regulation authority and budgets for auditors and investigators.

Although most commentators believe SOX is effective in reducing fraudulent disclosures and conflicts of interest in corporations, its implementation has placed a huge financial burden on the corporations that must comply with its requirements. Regulators and corporations continue to discuss how to simplify compliance with SOX. As a result, future modifications aimed at simplifying SOX are widely anticipated.

The Role of Business Ethics

Business ethics are the standards of conduct or moral judgment that apply to persons engaged in commerce. Violations of these standards in finance involve a variety of actions: "creative accounting," earnings management, misleading finan-

individual investors
Investors who buy relatively small quantities of shares so as to meet personal investment goals.

institutional investors
Investment professionals, such as banks, insurance companies, mutual funds, and pension funds, that are paid to manage other people's money and that hold and trade large quantities of securities.

Sarbanes-Oxley Act of 2002 (SOX)
An act aimed at eliminating corporate disclosure and conflict of interest problems. Contains provisions about corporate financial disclosures and the relationships among corporations, analysts, auditors, attorneys, directors, officers, and shareholders.

business ethics
Standards of conduct or moral judgment that apply to persons engaged in commerce.

cial forecasts, insider trading, fraud, excessive executive compensation, options backdating, bribery, and kickbacks. The financial press has reported many such violations in recent years, involving such well-known companies as **Apple, Boeing, Enron,** and **Tyco.** As a result, the business community in general and the financial community in particular are developing and enforcing ethical standards. The goal of these ethical standards is to motivate business and market participants to adhere to both the letter and the spirit of laws and regulations concerned with business and professional practice. Most business leaders believe businesses actually strengthen their competitive positions by maintaining high ethical standards.

Considering Ethics

Robert A. Cooke, a noted ethicist, suggests that the following questions be used to assess the ethical viability of a proposed action.[2]

1. Is the action arbitrary or capricious? Does it unfairly single out an individual or group?
2. Does the action violate the moral or legal rights of any individual or group?
3. Does the action conform to accepted moral standards?
4. Are there alternative courses of action that are less likely to cause actual or potential harm?

Clearly, considering such questions before taking an action can help to ensure its ethical viability.

Today, an increasing number of firms are directly addressing the issue of ethics by establishing corporate ethics policies and requiring employee compliance with them. A major impetus toward the development of corporate ethics policies has been the *Sarbanes-Oxley Act of 2002* described earlier. Frequently, employees are required to sign a formal pledge to uphold the firm's ethics policies. Such policies typically apply to employee actions in dealing with all corporate stakeholders, including the public. Many companies also require employees to participate in ethics seminars and training programs.

To provide further insight into the ethical dilemmas and issues sometimes facing the financial manager, in many chapters, the *In Practice* box focuses on ethics.

Ethics and Share Price

An effective ethics program is believed to enhance corporate value. An ethics program can produce a number of positive benefits. It can reduce potential litigation and judgment costs; maintain a positive corporate image; build shareholder confidence; and gain the loyalty, commitment, and respect of the firm's stakeholders. Such actions, by maintaining and enhancing cash flow and reducing perceived risk, can positively affect the firm's share price. *Ethical behavior is therefore viewed as necessary for achieving the firm's goal of owner wealth maximization.*[3]

The Agency Issue

We have seen that the goal of the financial manager should be to maximize the wealth of the firm's owners. Thus managers can be viewed as *agents* of the owners who have hired them and given them decision-making authority to

---

2. Robert A. Cooke, "Business Ethics: A Perspective," in *Arthur Andersen Cases on Business Ethics* (Chicago: Arthur Andersen, September 1991), pp. 2 and 5.

3. For an excellent discussion of this and related issues by a number of finance academics and practitioners who have given a lot of thought to financial ethics, see James S. Ang, "On Financial Ethics," *Financial Management* (Autumn 1993), pp. 32–59.

manage the firm. Technically, any manager who owns less than 100 percent of the firm is to some degree an agent of the other owners. This separation of owners and managers is shown by the dashed horizontal line in Figure 1.1 on page 6.

In theory, most financial managers would agree with the goal of owner wealth maximization. In practice, however, managers are also concerned with their personal wealth, job security, and fringe benefits. Such concerns may make managers reluctant or unwilling to take more than moderate risk if they perceive that taking too much risk might jeopardize their jobs or reduce their personal wealth. The result is a less-than-maximum return and a potential loss of wealth for the owners.

Hint A stockbroker confronts the same issue. If she gets you to buy and sell more stock, it's good for *her*, but it may *not* be good for you.

The Agency Problem

agency problem
The likelihood that managers may place personal goals ahead of corporate goals.

From this conflict of owner and personal goals arises what has been called the **agency problem,** the likelihood that managers may place personal goals ahead of corporate goals. Two factors—market forces and *agency costs*—serve to prevent or minimize agency problems.

Market Forces   One market force is major shareholders, particularly large *institutional investors* such as life insurance companies, mutual funds, and pension funds. These holders of large blocks of a firm's stock exert pressure on management to perform, by communicating their concerns to the firm's board. They often threaten to exercise their voting rights or liquidate their holdings if the board does not respond positively to their concerns.

Another market force is the *threat of takeover* by another firm that believes it can enhance the target firm's value by restructuring its management, operations, and financing. The constant threat of a takeover tends to motivate management to act in the best interests of the firm's owners.

agency costs
The costs borne by stockholders to maintain a *corporate governance structure* that minimizes agency problems and contributes to the maximization of owner wealth.

Agency Costs   To minimize agency problems and contribute to the maximization of owners' wealth, stockholders incur **agency costs.** These are the costs of maintaining a *corporate governance structure* that monitors management behavior, ensures against dishonest acts of management, and gives managers the financial incentive to maximize share price.

The most popular, powerful, and expensive approach is to *structure management compensation* to correspond with share price maximization. The objective is to give managers incentives to act in the best interests of the owners. In addition, the resulting compensation packages allow firms to compete for and hire the best managers available. The two key types of compensation plans are incentive plans and performance plans.

incentive plans
Management compensation plans that tend to tie management compensation to share price; the most popular incentive plan involves the grant of *stock options.*

stock options
An incentive allowing managers to purchase stock at the market price set at the time of the grant.

Incentive plans tend to tie management compensation to share price. The most popular incentive plan is the granting of **stock options** to management. These options allow managers to purchase stock at the market price set at the time of the grant. If the market price rises, managers will be rewarded by being able to resell the shares at the higher market price.

performance plans
Plans that tie management compensation to measures such as EPS, growth in EPS, and other ratios of return. *Performance shares* and/or *cash bonuses* are used as compensation under these plans.

performance shares
Shares of stock given to management for meeting stated performance goals.

Many firms also offer **performance plans,** which tie management compensation to measures such as earnings per share (EPS), growth in EPS, and other ratios of return. **Performance shares,** shares of stock given to management as a result of meeting the stated performance goals, are often used in these plans.

cash bonuses
Cash paid to management for achieving certain performance goals.

Another form of performance-based compensation is **cash bonuses,** cash payments tied to the achievement of certain performance goals.

The Current View of Management Compensation

The execution of many compensation plans has been closely scrutinized in recent years. Both individuals and institutional stockholders, as well as the Securities and Exchange Commission (SEC), continue to publicly question the appropriateness of the multimillion-dollar compensation packages that many corporate executives receive. For example, the three highest-paid CEOs in 2006 were (1) Steven P. Jobs of Apple Inc., who earned $646.60 million; (2) Ray R. Irani of Occidental Petroleum, who earned $321.64 million; and (3) Barry Diller of IAC/InterActive-Corp, who earned $295.14 million. Tenth on the same list was Henry C. Duques of First Data, who earned $98.21 million. During 2006, the average compensation of the CEOs of America's 500 biggest companies surveyed by *Forbes*.com using data from a variety of sources was $15.20 million, up 38 percent from 2005. The average compensation of the top 20 highest-paid CEOs was $144.66 million.

Recent studies have failed to find a strong relationship between CEO compensation and share price. During the past few years, publicity surrounding these large compensation packages (without corresponding share price performance) has driven down executive compensation. Contributing to this publicity is the SEC requirement that publicly traded companies disclose to shareholders and others the amount of compensation to their CEO, CFO, three other highest-paid executives, and directors, the method used to determine it and a narrative discussion regarding the underlying compensation policies. At the same time, new compensation plans that better link managers' performance with regard to shareholder wealth to their compensation are being developed and implemented.

Unconstrained, managers may have other goals in addition to share price maximization, but much of the evidence suggests that share price maximization—the focus of this book—is the primary goal of most firms.

REVIEW QUESTIONS

1–11 For what three basic reasons is profit maximization inconsistent with wealth maximization?

1–12 What is *risk?* Why must risk as well as return be considered by the financial manager who is evaluating a decision alternative or action?

1–13 What is the goal of the firm and, therefore, of all managers and employees? Discuss how one measures achievement of this goal.

1–14 What is *corporate governance?* How has the Sarbanes-Oxley Act of 2002 affected it? Explain.

1–15 Describe the role of corporate ethics policies and guidelines, and discuss the relationship that is believed to exist between ethics and share price.

1–16 How do market forces—both shareholder activism and the threat of takeover—act to prevent or minimize the *agency problem?* What role do *institutional investors* play in shareholder activism?

1–17 Define *agency costs,* and explain their relationship to a firm's *corporate governance structure.* How can the firm *structure management compensation* to minimize agency problems? What is the current view with regard to the execution of many compensation plans?

1.4 | Financial Institutions and Markets

Most successful firms have ongoing needs for funds. They can obtain funds from external sources in three ways. The first source is through a *financial institution* that accepts savings and transfers them to those that need funds. A second source is through *financial markets,* organized forums in which the suppliers and demanders of various types of funds can make transactions. A third source is through *private placement.* Because of the unstructured nature of private placements, here we focus primarily on the role of financial institutions and financial markets in facilitating business financing.

For an in-depth, chapter-length discussion of financial institutions and financial markets, see the online chapter at the book's website.

Financial Institutions

financial institution
An intermediary that channels the savings of individuals, businesses, and governments into loans or investments.

Financial institutions serve as intermediaries by channeling the savings of individuals, businesses, and governments into loans or investments. Many financial institutions directly or indirectly pay savers interest on deposited funds; others provide services for a fee (for example, checking accounts for which customers pay service charges). Some financial institutions accept customers' savings deposits and lend this money to other customers or to firms; others invest customers' savings in earning assets such as real estate or stocks and bonds; and some do both. Financial institutions are required by the government to operate within established regulatory guidelines.

Hint Think about how inefficient it would be if each individual saver had to negotiate with each potential user of savings. Institutions make the process very efficient by becoming intermediaries between savers and users.

Key Customers of Financial Institutions

For financial institutions, the key suppliers of funds and the key demanders of funds are individuals, businesses, and governments. The savings that individual consumers place in financial institutions provide these institutions with a large portion of their funds. Individuals not only supply funds to financial institutions but also demand funds from them in the form of loans. However, individuals as a group are the *net suppliers* for financial institutions: They save more money than they borrow.

Business firms also deposit some of their funds in financial institutions, primarily in checking accounts with various commercial banks. Like individuals, firms borrow funds from these institutions, but firms are *net demanders* of funds: They borrow more money than they save.

Governments maintain deposits of temporarily idle funds, certain tax payments, and Social Security payments in commercial banks. They do not borrow funds *directly* from financial institutions, although by selling their debt securities to various institutions, governments indirectly borrow from them. The government, like business firms, is typically a *net demander* of funds: It typically borrows more than it saves. We've all heard about the federal budget deficit.

Major Financial Institutions

The major financial institutions in the U.S. economy are commercial banks, savings and loans, credit unions, savings banks, insurance companies, mutual funds, and pension funds. These institutions attract funds from individuals, businesses, and governments, combine them, and make loans available to individuals and businesses. Descriptions of the major financial institutions are found at the textbook's website.

Financial Markets

financial markets
Forums in which suppliers of funds and demanders of funds can transact business directly.

private placement
The sale of a new security issue, typically bonds or preferred stock, directly to an investor or group of investors.

public offering
The nonexclusive sale of either bonds or stocks to the general public.

primary market
Financial market in which securities are initially issued; the only market in which the issuer is directly involved in the transaction.

secondary market
Financial market in which preowned securities (those that are not new issues) are traded.

Financial markets are forums in which suppliers of funds and demanders of funds can transact business directly. Whereas the loans and investments of institutions are made without the direct knowledge of the suppliers of funds (savers), suppliers in the financial markets know where their funds are being lent or invested. The two key financial markets are the money market and the capital market. Transactions in short-term debt instruments, or marketable securities, take place in the *money market*. Long-term securities—bonds and stocks—are traded in the *capital market*.

To raise money, firms can use either private placements or public offerings. **Private placement** involves the sale of a new security issue, typically bonds or preferred stock, directly to an investor or group of investors, such as an insurance company or pension fund. Most firms, however, raise money through a **public offering** of securities, which is the nonexclusive sale of either bonds or stocks to the general public.

All securities are initially issued in the **primary market.** This is the only market in which the corporate or government issuer is directly involved in the transaction and receives direct benefit from the issue. That is, the company actually receives the proceeds from the sale of securities. Once the securities begin to trade between savers and investors, they become part of the **secondary market.** The primary market is the one in which "new" securities are sold. The secondary market can be viewed as a "preowned" securities market.

The Relationship between Institutions and Markets

Financial institutions actively participate in the financial markets as both suppliers and demanders of funds. Figure 1.4 (see page 22) depicts the general flow of funds through and between financial institutions and financial markets; private placement transactions are also shown. The individuals, businesses, and governments that supply and demand funds may be domestic or foreign. We next briefly discuss the money market, including its international equivalent—the *Eurocurrency market*. We then end this section with a discussion of the capital market, which is of key importance to the firm.

The Money Market

money market
A financial relationship created between suppliers and demanders of *short-term funds.*

The **money market** is created by a financial relationship between suppliers and demanders of *short-term funds* (funds with maturities of one year or less). The money market exists because some individuals, businesses, governments, and financial institutions have temporarily idle funds that they wish to put to some interest earning use. At the same time, other individuals, businesses, governments, and financial institutions find themselves in need of seasonal or temporary

FIGURE 1.4

Flow of Funds
Flow of funds for financial
institutions and markets

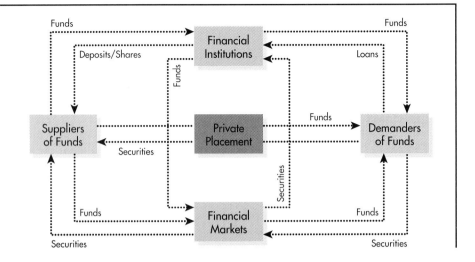

financing. The money market brings together these suppliers and demanders of short-term funds.

Most money market transactions are made in **marketable securities**—short-term debt instruments, such as U.S. Treasury bills, commercial paper, and negotiable certificates of deposit issued by government, business, and financial institutions, respectively. (Marketable securities are described in Chapter 13.)

The Eurocurrency Market

The international equivalent of the domestic money market is called the **Eurocurrency market**. This is a market for short-term bank deposits denominated in U.S. dollars or other easily convertible currencies. Eurocurrency deposits arise when a corporation or individual makes a bank deposit in a currency other than the local currency of the country where the bank is located. If, for example, a multinational corporation were to deposit U.S. dollars in a London bank, this would create a Eurodollar deposit (a dollar deposit at a bank in Europe). Nearly all Eurodollar deposits are *time deposits*. This means that the bank would promise to repay the deposit, with interest, at a fixed date in the future—say, in 6 months. During the interim, the bank is free to lend this dollar deposit to creditworthy corporate or government borrowers. If the bank cannot find a borrower on its own, it may lend the deposit to another international bank.

The Capital Market

The **capital market** is a market that enables suppliers and demanders of *long-term funds* to make transactions. Included are securities issues of business and government. The backbone of the capital market is formed by the broker and dealer markets that provide a forum for bond and stock transactions. International capital markets also exist.

Key Securities Traded: Bonds and Stocks

The key capital market securities are *bonds* (long-term debt) and both *common stock* and *preferred stock* (equity, or ownership).

bond
Long-term debt instrument used by business and government to raise large sums of money, generally from a diverse group of lenders.

Bonds are long-term debt instruments used by business and government to raise large sums of money, generally from a diverse group of lenders. *Corporate bonds* typically pay interest *semiannually* (every 6 months) at a stated *coupon interest rate*. They have an initial *maturity* of from 10 to 30 years, and a *par, or face, value* of $l,000 that must be repaid at maturity. Bonds are described in detail in Chapter 6.

Example	Lakeview Industries, a major microprocessor manufacturer, has issued a 9 percent coupon interest rate, 20-year bond with a $1,000 par value that pays interest semiannually. Investors who buy this bond receive the contractual right to $90 annual interest (9% coupon interest rate × $1,000 par value) distributed as $45 at the end of each 6 months (1/2 × $90) for 20 years, plus the $1,000 par value at the end of year 20.

preferred stock
A special form of ownership having a fixed periodic dividend that must be paid prior to payment of any dividends to common stockholders.

As noted earlier, shares of *common stock* are units of ownership, or equity, in a corporation. Common stockholders earn a return by receiving dividends—periodic distributions of earnings—or by realizing increases in share price. **Preferred stock** is a special form of ownership that has features of both a bond and common stock. Preferred stockholders are promised a fixed periodic dividend that must be paid prior to payment of any dividends to common stockholders. In other words, preferred stock has "preference" over common stock. Preferred and common stock are described in detail in Chapter 7.

broker market
The securities exchanges on which the two sides of a transaction, the buyer and seller, are brought together to trade securities.

Broker Markets and Dealer Markets

By far, the vast majority of trades made by individual investors take place in the secondary market. When you look at the secondary market *on the basis of how securities are traded,* you will find you can essentially divide the market into two segments: broker markets and dealer markets.

The key difference between broker and dealer markets is a technical point dealing with the way trades are executed. That is, when a trade occurs in a **broker market,** the two sides to the transaction, the buyer and the seller, are brought together and the trade takes place at that point: Party A sells his or her securities directly to the buyer, Party B. In a sense, with the help of a *broker,* the securities effectively change hands on the floor of the exchange. The broker market consists of national and regional **securities exchanges,** which are organizations that provide a marketplace in which firms can raise funds through the sale of new securities and purchasers can resell securities.

securities exchanges
Organizations that provide the marketplace in which firms can raise funds through the sale of new securities and purchasers can resell securities.

dealer market
The market in which the buyer and seller are not brought together directly but instead have their orders executed by securities dealers that "make markets" in the given security.

In contrast, when trades are made in a **dealer market,** the buyer and the seller are never brought together directly. Instead, **market makers** execute the buy/sell orders. Market makers are *securities dealers* who "make markets" by offering to buy or sell certain securities at stated prices. Essentially, two separate trades are made: Party A sells his or her securities (in, say, Dell) to a dealer, and Party B buys his or her securities (in Dell) from another, or possibly even the same, dealer. Thus, there is always a dealer (*market maker*) on one side of a dealer-market transaction. The dealer market is made up of both the **Nasdaq market,** an all-electronic trading platform used to execute securities trades, and the **over-the-counter (OTC) market,** where smaller, unlisted securities are traded.

market makers
Securities dealers who "make markets" by offering to buy or sell certain securities at stated prices.

Nasdaq market
An all-electronic trading platform used to execute securities trades.

over-the-counter (OTC) market
Market where smaller, unlisted securities are traded.

Broker Markets   If you are like most individual investors, when you think of the "stock market" the first name to come to mind is the New York Stock

Exchange (NYSE). In point of fact, the NYSE is the dominant broker market. Also included in this market are the American Stock Exchange (AMEX), which is another *national exchange,* and several so-called *regional exchanges.* These exchanges account for about 60 percent of *the total dollar volume* of all shares traded in the U.S. stock market. In broker markets all the trading takes place on centralized trading floors.

Most exchanges are modeled after the New York Stock Exchange. For a firm's securities to be listed for trading on a stock exchange, a firm must file an application for listing and meet a number of requirements. For example, to be eligible for listing on the NYSE, a firm must have at least 2,200 stockholders owning 100 or more shares; a minimum of 1.1 million shares of publicly held stock outstanding; pretax earnings of at least $10 million over the previous 3 years, with no loss in the previous 2 years; and a minimum market value of public shares of $100 million. Clearly, only large, widely held firms are candidates for NYSE listing.

Once placed, an order to buy or sell on the NYSE can be executed in minutes, thanks to sophisticated telecommunication devices. New Internet-based brokerage systems enable investors to place their buy and sell orders electronically. Information on publicly traded securities is reported in various media, both print, such as the *Wall Street Journal,* and electronic, such as MSN Money (**www.moneycentral.msn.com**).

Dealer Markets   One of the key features of the *dealer market* is that it has no centralized trading floors. Instead, it is made up of a large number of *market makers* who are linked together via a mass-telecommunications network.

Each market maker is actually a securities dealer who makes a market in one or more securities by offering to buy or sell them at stated bid/ask prices. The **bid price** and **ask price** represent, respectively, the highest price offered to purchase a given security and the lowest price at which the security is offered for sale. In effect, an investor pays the ask price when buying securities and receives the bid price when selling them.

As described earlier, the dealer market is made up of both the *Nasdaq market* and the *over-the-counter (OTC) market,* which together account for about 40 percent of all shares traded in the U.S. market—with the Nasdaq accounting for the overwhelming majority of those trades. (As an aside, the *primary market* is also a dealer market, because all new issues are sold to the investing public by securities dealers, acting on behalf of the investment banker.)

The largest dealer market consists of a select group of stocks that are listed and traded on the *National Association of Securities Dealers Automated Quotation System,* typically referred to as *Nasdaq.* Founded in 1971, Nasdaq had its origins in the OTC market, but is today considered *a totally separate entity that's no longer a part of the OTC market.* In fact, in 2006 the Nasdaq was formally recognized by the SEC as a "listed exchange," essentially giving it the same stature and prestige as the NYSE.

bid price
The highest price offered to purchase a security.

ask price
The lowest price at which a security is offered for sale.

Eurobond market
The market in which corporations and governments typically issue bonds denominated in dollars and sell them to investors located outside the United States.

International Capital Markets

Although U.S. capital markets are by far the world's largest, there are important debt and equity markets outside the United States. In the **Eurobond market,** corporations and governments typically issue bonds denominated in dollars and sell them to investors located outside the United States. A U.S. corporation might, for example, issue dollar-denominated bonds that would be purchased by investors in Belgium, Germany, or Switzerland. Through the Eurobond market, issuing firms and governments can tap a much larger pool of investors than would be generally available in the local market.

The *foreign bond market* is another international market for long-term debt securities. A **foreign bond** is a bond issued by a foreign corporation or government that is denominated in the investor's home currency and sold in the investor's home market. A bond issued by a U.S. company that is denominated in Swiss francs and sold in Switzerland is an example of a foreign bond. Although the foreign bond market is much smaller than the Eurobond market, many issuers have found it to be an attractive way of tapping debt markets in Germany, Japan, Switzerland, and the United States.

Finally, the **international equity market** allows corporations to sell blocks of shares to investors in a number of different countries simultaneously. This market enables corporations to raise far larger amounts of capital than they could raise in any single national market. International equity sales have also proven to be indispensable to governments that have sold state-owned companies to private investors during recent years.

foreign bond
Bond that is issued by a foreign corporation or government and is denominated in the investor's home currency and sold in the investor's home market.

international equity market
A market that allows corporations to sell blocks of shares to investors in a number of different countries simultaneously.

The Role of Capital Markets

The capital market creates continuous liquid markets in which firms can obtain needed financing. It also creates **efficient markets** that allocate funds to their most productive uses. This is especially true for securities that are actively traded in broker or dealer markets, where the competition among wealth-maximizing investors determines and publicizes prices that are believed to be close to their true value. See *Focus on Practice* box on page 26 for the story of one legendary stock price, and the equally legendary man who brought it about.

The price of an individual security is determined by the demand for and supply of the security. Figure 1.5 depicts the interaction of the forces of demand (represented by line D_0) and supply (represented by line S) for a given security currently selling at an equilibrium price P_0. At that price, Q_0 shares of the stock are traded.

efficient market
A market that allocates funds to their most productive uses as a result of competition among wealth-maximizing investors that determines and publicizes prices that are believed to be close to their true value.

FIGURE 1.5

Supply and Demand
Supply and demand for a security

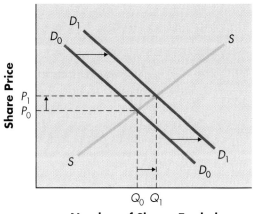

Number of Shares Traded

Focus on Practice   Berkshire Hathaway—Can Buffett Be Replaced?

In early 1980, investors could buy one share of **Berkshire Hathaway** Class A common stock (stock symbol: BRKA) for $285. That may have seemed expensive at the time, but by mid-2007 the price of just one share had climbed to $111,000. The wizard behind such phenomenal growth in shareholder value is the chairman of Berkshire Hathaway, Warren Buffett, nicknamed the Oracle of Omaha.

With his partner, Vice-Chairman Charlie Munger, Buffett runs a large conglomerate of 73 businesses with 217,000 employees and nearly $100 billion in annual revenues. He makes it look easy. In his words, "I've taken the easy route, just sitting back and working through great managers who run their own shows. My only tasks are to cheer them on, sculpt and harden our corporate culture, and make major capital-allocation decisions. Our managers have returned this trust by working hard and effectively."

Buffett's style of corporate leadership seems rather laid back, but behind that "aw-shucks" manner lies one of the best analytical minds in business. He believes in aligning managerial incentives with performance. Berkshire employs many different incentive arrangements, with their terms depending on such elements as the economic potential or capital intensity of a CEO's business. Whatever the compensation arrangement, Buffett tries to keep it both simple and fair. Buffett himself receives an annual salary of $100,000—not much in this age of super-sized CEO compensation packages. However, with nearly 31 percent ownership in Berkshire Hathaway, valued at nearly $44 billion, Buffett is doing fine financially, even after announcing recently his plans to donate $40 billion to philanthropic causes.

Berkshire's annual report is a must-read for many investors due to the popularity of Buffett's annual letter to shareholders with his homespun take on such topics as investing, corporate governance, and corporate leadership. Shareholder meetings in Omaha, Nebraska, have turned into cult-like gatherings, with thousands traveling to listen to Buffett answer questions from shareholders. One question that has been firmly answered is the question of Mr. Buffett's ability to create shareholder value.

The next question that needs to be answered is whether Berkshire Hathaway can successfully replace Buffett (age 77), Munger (age 83), and the board of directors (average age of 70). Time will tell. Given its track record, the company is likely to be successful in finding a new generation of leadership that takes action based on the best interests of employees, customers, and shareholders, as long as Warren Buffett is able to impart his special wisdom to the process.

■ *The share price of BRKA has never been split. Why might the company refuse to split its shares to make them more affordable to average investors?*

Changing evaluations of a firm's prospects cause changes in the demand for and supply of its securities and ultimately result in a new price for the securities. Suppose, for example, that the firm shown in Figure 1.5 announces a favorable discovery. Investors expect rewarding results from the discovery, so they increase their valuations of the firm's shares. The changing evaluation results in a shift in demand from D_0 to D_1. At that new level of demand, Q_1 shares will be traded, and a new, higher equilibrium price of P_1 will result. The competitive market created by the major securities exchanges provides a forum in which share prices are continuously adjusted to changing demand and supply.

REVIEW QUESTIONS

1–18 Who are the key participants in the transactions of financial institutions? Who are *net suppliers* and who are *net demanders?*

1–19 What role do *financial markets* play in our economy? What are *primary* and *secondary* markets? What relationship exists between financial institutions and financial markets?

1–20 What is the *money market?* What is the *Eurocurrency market?*

1–21 What is the *capital market?* What are the primary securities traded in it?

1–22 What are *broker markets?* What are *dealer markets?* How do they differ?

1–23 Briefly describe the international capital markets, particularly the *Eurobond market* and the *international equity market.*

1–24 What are *efficient markets?* What determines the price of an individual security in such a market?

1.5 | Business Taxes

Taxes are a fact of life, and businesses, like individuals, must pay taxes on income. The income of sole proprietorships and partnerships is taxed as the income of the individual owners; corporate income is subject to corporate taxes.

Regardless of their legal form, all businesses can earn two types of income: ordinary and capital gains. Under current law, these two types of income are treated differently in the taxation of individuals; they are not treated differently for entities subject to corporate taxes. Frequent amendments are made to the tax code.

Ordinary Income

ordinary income
Income earned through the sale of a firm's goods or services.

The **ordinary income** of a corporation is income earned through the sale of goods or services. Ordinary income in 2007 was taxed subject to the rates depicted in the corporate tax rate schedule in Table 1.4.

TABLE 1.4   Corporate Tax Rate Schedule

Range of taxable income	Base tax	+	(Marginal rate × amount over base bracket)
$ 0 to $ 50,000	$ 0	+	(15% × amount over $ 0)
50,000 to 75,000	7,500	+	(25 × amount over 50,000)
75,000 to 100,000	13,750	+	(34 × amount over 75,000)
100,000 to 335,000	22,250	+	(39 × amount over 100,000)
335,000 to 10,000,000	113,900	+	(34 × amount over 335,000)
10,000,000 to 15,000,000	3,400,000	+	(35 × amount over 10,000,000)
15,000,000 to 18,333,333	5,150,000	+	(38 × amount over 15,000,000)
Over 18,333,333	6,416,667	+	(35 × amount over 18,333,333)

Example

Webster Manufacturing, Inc., a small manufacturer of kitchen knives, has before-tax earnings of $250,000. The tax on these earnings can be found by using the tax rate schedule in Table 1.4:

$$\text{Total taxes due} = \$22,250 + [0.39 \times (\$250,000 - \$100,000)]$$
$$= \$22,250 + (0.39 \times \$150,000)$$
$$= \$22,250 + \$58,500 = \underline{\$80,750}$$

From a financial point of view, it is important to understand the difference between average and marginal tax rates, the treatment of interest and dividend income, and the effects of tax deductibility.

Average versus Marginal Tax Rates

average tax rate
A firm's taxes divided by its taxable income.

The **average tax rate** paid on the firm's ordinary income can be calculated by dividing its taxes by its taxable income. For firms with taxable income of $10 million or less, the average tax rate ranges from 15 to 34 percent, reaching 34 percent when taxable income equals or exceeds $335,000. For firms with taxable income in excess of $10 million, the average tax rate ranges between 34 and 35 percent. The average tax rate paid by Webster Manufacturing, Inc., in the preceding example was 32.3 percent ($80,750 ÷ $250,000). As a corporation's taxable income increases, its average tax rate approaches and finally reaches 34 percent. It remains at that level up to $10 million of taxable income, beyond which it rises toward and reaches 35 percent at $18,333,333.

marginal tax rate
The rate at which *additional income* is taxed.

The **marginal tax rate** represents the rate at which *additional income* is taxed. In the current corporate tax structure, the marginal tax rate on income up to $50,000 is 15 percent; from $50,000 to $75,000 it is 25 percent; and so on, as shown in Table 1.4. Webster Manufacturing's marginal tax rate is currently 39 percent because its next dollar of taxable income (bringing its before-tax earnings to $250,001) would be taxed at that rate.

Example

If Webster Manufacturing's earnings go up to $300,000, the marginal tax rate on the additional $50,000 of income will be 39 percent. The company will therefore have to pay additional taxes of $19,500 (0.39 × $50,000). Total taxes on the $300,000, then, will be $100,250 ($80,750 + $19,500). To check this figure using the tax rate schedule in Table 1.4, we would get a total tax liability of $22,500 + [0.39 × ($300,000 + $100,000)] = $22,250 + $78,000 = $100,250—the same value obtained by applying the marginal tax rate to the added income and adjusting the known tax liability.

To simplify calculations in the text, we assume *a fixed 40 percent tax rate to be applicable to ordinary corporate income*. Given our focus on financial decision making, this rate is assumed to represent the firm's *marginal tax rate*.

Interest and Dividend Income

double taxation
Occurs when the already once-taxed earnings of a corporation are distributed as cash dividends to stockholders, who must pay taxes of up to a maximum rate of 15 percent on them.

In the process of determining taxable income, any *interest received* by the corporation is included as ordinary income. Dividends, on the other hand, are treated differently. This different treatment moderates the effect of **double taxation,** which occurs when the already once-taxed earnings of a corporation are distributed as cash dividends to stockholders, who must pay taxes of up to a maximum rate of 15 percent on them. Therefore, dividends that the firm receives on common and preferred stock held in other corporations, and representing less than 20 percent ownership in them, are subject to a 70 percent exclusion for tax purposes.[4] The dividend exclusion in effect eliminates most of the potential tax liability from the dividends received by the second and any subsequent corporations.

Tax-Deductible Expenses

In calculating their taxes, corporations are allowed to deduct operating expenses, as well as interest expense. The tax deductibility of these expenses reduces their after-tax cost. The following example illustrates the benefit of tax deductibility.

Example

Two companies, Debt Co. and No-Debt Co., both expect in the coming year to have earnings before interest and taxes of $200,000. Debt Co. during the year will have to pay $30,000 in interest. No-Debt Co. has no debt and therefore will have no interest expense. Calculation of the earnings after taxes for these two firms is as follows:

	Debt Co.	No-Debt Co.
Earnings before interest and taxes	$200,000	$200,000
Less: Interest expense	30,000	0
Earnings before taxes	$170,000	$200,000
Less: Taxes (40%)	68,000	80,000
Earnings after taxes	$102,000	$120,000
Difference in earnings after taxes	$18,000	

Debt Co. had $30,000 more interest expense than No-Debt Co., but Debt Co.'s earnings after taxes are only $18,000 less than those of No-Debt Co. This difference is attributable to the fact that Debt Co.'s $30,000 interest expense deduction provided a tax savings of $12,000 ($68,000 for Debt Co. versus $80,000 for No-Debt Co.). This amount can be calculated directly by multiplying the tax rate by the amount of interest expense $(0.40 \times \$30,000 = \$12,000)$. Similarly, the $18,000 *after-tax cost* of the interest expense can be calculated directly by multiplying one minus the tax rate by the amount of interest expense $[(1 - 0.40) \times \$30,000 = \$18,000]$.

For discussion of another corporate tax provision—a tax loss carryback— see the book's website. WWW

The tax deductibility of certain expenses reduces their actual (after-tax) cost to the profitable firm. Note that both for accounting and tax purposes *interest is a tax-deductible expense, whereas dividends are not.* Because dividends are not tax deductible, their after-tax cost is equal to the amount of the dividend. Thus a $30,000 cash dividend has an after-tax cost of $30,000.

---

4. The exclusion is 80% if the corporation owns between 20% and 80% of the stock in the corporation paying it dividends; 100% of the dividends received are excluded if it owns more than 80% of the corporation paying it dividends. For convenience, we are assuming here that the ownership interest in the dividend-paying corporation is less than 20%.

Capital Gains

capital gain
The amount by which the sale price of an asset exceeds the asset's initial purchase price.

If a firm sells a capital asset (such as stock held as an investment) for more than its initial purchase price, the difference between the sale price and the purchase price is called a **capital gain.** For corporations, capital gains are added to ordinary corporate income and taxed at the regular corporate rates, with a maximum marginal tax rate of 39 percent. To simplify the computations presented in the text, as for ordinary income, *a fixed 40 percent tax rate is assumed to be applicable to corporate capital gains.*

Example

Ross Company, a manufacturer of pharmaceuticals, has pretax operating earnings of $500,000 and has just sold for $150,000 an asset that was purchased 2 years ago for $125,000. Because the asset was sold for more than its initial purchase price, there is a capital gain of $25,000 ($150,000 sale price − $125,000 initial purchase price). The corporation's taxable income will total $525,000 ($500,000 ordinary income plus $25,000 capital gain). Because this total exceeds $335,000, the capital gain will be taxed at the 34% rate (see Table 1.4), resulting in a tax of $8,500 (0.34 × $25,000).

REVIEW QUESTIONS

Hint If you have not done so already, look at the "To the Student" letter on p. xxxvii. It describes organization of this book and how you can make best use of its various features.

1–25 Describe the tax treatment of *ordinary income* and that of *capital gains.* What is the difference between the *average tax rate* and the *marginal tax rate?*

1–26 How does the tax treatment of dividend income by the corporation moderate the effects of *double taxation?*

1–27 What benefit results from the tax deductibility of certain corporate expenses?

Summary

Focus on Value

Chapter 1 established the primary goal of the firm—to maximize the wealth of the owners for whom the firm is being operated. For public companies, value at any time is reflected in the stock price. Therefore, management should act only on those opportunities that are expected to create value for owners by increasing the stock price. Doing this requires management to consider the returns (magnitude and timing of cash flows), the risk of each proposed action, and their combined effect on value.

Review of Learning Goals

LG 1 Define *finance,* its major areas and opportunities, and the legal forms of business organization. Finance is the art and science of managing money. It affects the life of every person and of every organization. Major opportunities in financial services exist within banking and related institutions, personal financial planning, investments, real estate, and insurance. Managerial finance is concerned with the duties of the financial manager in the business firm. The recent trend toward globalization of business activity has created new demands and opportunities in managerial finance.

The legal forms of business organization are the sole proprietorship, the partnership, and the corporation. The corporation is dominant in terms of business receipts and profits, and its owners are its common and preferred stockholders. Stockholders expect to earn a return by receiving dividends or by realizing gains through increases in share price.

LG 2 **Describe the managerial finance function and its relationship to economics and accounting.** All areas of responsibility within a firm interact with finance personnel and procedures. The financial manager must understand the economic environment and relies heavily on the economic principle of marginal cost–benefit analysis to make financial decisions. Financial managers use accounting but concentrate on cash flows and decision making.

LG 3 **Identify the primary activities of the financial manager.** The primary activities of the financial manager, in addition to ongoing involvement in financial analysis and planning, are making investment decisions and making financing decisions.

LG 4 **Explain the goal of the firm, corporate governance, the role of ethics, and the agency issue.** The goal of the financial manager is to maximize the owners' wealth, as evidenced by stock price. The financial manager who is evaluating decision alternatives must assess both return and risk. The wealth-maximizing actions of financial managers should also reflect the interests of stakeholders.

The corporate governance structure is used to direct and control the corporation by defining the rights and responsibilities of the key corporate participants. Both individual and institutional investors hold the stock of most companies, but institutional investors tend to have much greater influence on corporate governance. The Sarbanes-Oxley Act of 2002 (SOX) was passed to eliminate fraudulent financial disclosure and conflict of interest problems. Positive ethical practices help a firm and its managers to achieve the firm's goal of owner wealth maximization. SOX has provided impetus toward such practices.

An agency problem results when managers, as agents for owners, place personal goals ahead of corporate goals. Market forces, in the form of shareholder activism and the threat of takeover, tend to prevent or minimize agency problems. Firms incur agency costs to maintain a corporate governance structure that monitors managers' actions and provides incentives for them to act in the best interests of owners. Stock options and performance plans are examples of such agency costs.

LG 5 **Understand financial institutions and markets, and the role they play in managerial finance.** Financial institutions serve as intermediaries by channeling into loans or investments the savings of individuals, businesses, and governments. The financial markets are forums in which suppliers and demanders of funds can transact business directly. Financial institutions actively participate in the financial markets as both suppliers and demanders of funds.

In the money market, suppliers and demanders of short-term funds trade marketable securities (short-term debt instruments). The Eurocurrency market is the international equivalent of the domestic money market.

In the capital market, investors make transactions in long-term debt (bonds) and equity (common and preferred stock). Broker markets and dealer markets provide secondary markets for securities. The broker market consists of national and regional securities exchanges, which bring together buyers and sellers. Dealer markets, which include the Nasdaq and over-the-counter (OTC) markets, have orders executed by dealers who "make markets" in given securities. The primary market is a dealer market. Important international debt and equity markets are the Eurobond market and the international equity market. The capital market creates continuous liquid markets for needed financing and allocates funds to their most productive uses.

Discuss business taxes and their importance in financial decisions. Corporate income is subject to corporate taxes. Corporate tax rates apply to both ordinary income (after deduction of allowable expenses) and capital gains. The average tax rate paid by a corporation ranges from 15 to 35 percent. Corporate taxpayers can reduce their taxes through certain provisions in the tax code: dividend income exclusions and tax-deductible expenses. A capital gain occurs when an asset is sold for more than its initial purchase price; they are added to ordinary corporate income and taxed at regular corporate tax rates. (For convenience, we assume a 40 percent marginal tax rate in this book.)

Self-Test Problem (Solution in Appendix B)

ST1–1 **Corporate taxes** Montgomery Enterprises, Inc., had operating earnings of $280,000 for the year just ended. During the year the firm sold stock that it held in another company for $180,000, which was $30,000 above its original purchase price of $150,000, paid 1 year earlier.
a. What is the amount, if any, of capital gains realized during the year?
b. How much total taxable income did the firm earn during the year?
c. Use the corporate tax rate schedule given in Table 1.4 to calculate the firm's total taxes due.
d. Calculate both the *average tax rate* and the *marginal tax rate* on the basis of your findings.

Warm-Up Exercises   A blue box (■) indicates exercises available in 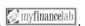.

E1–1 Ann and Jack have been partners for several years. Their firm, A & J Tax Preparation, has been very successful, as the pair agree on most business-related questions. One disagreement, however, concerns the legal form of their business.

Ann has tried for the past 2 years to get Jack to agree to incorporate. She believes that there is no downside to incorporating and sees only benefits. Jack strongly disagrees; he thinks that the business should remain a partnership forever.

First, take Ann's side and explain the positive side to incorporating the business. Next, take Jack's side and state the advantages to remaining a partnership. Lastly, what information would you want if you were asked to make the decision for Ann and Jack?

E1–2   You have been made treasurer for a day at AIMCO, Inc. AIMCO develops technology for video conferencing. A manager of the satellite division has asked you to authorize a capital expenditure in the amount of $10,000. The manager states that this expenditure is necessary to continue a long-running project designed to use satellites to allow video conferencing anywhere on the planet. The manager admits that the satellite concept has been surpassed by recent technological advances in telephony, but he feels that AIMCO should continue the project. His reasoning is based on the fact that $2.5 million has already been spent over the past 15 years on this project. Although the project has little chance to be viable, the manager believes it would be a shame to waste the money and time already spent.

Use *marginal cost–benefit analysis* to make your decision regarding whether you should authorize the $10,000 expenditure to continue the project.

E1–3   The end-of-year parties at Yearling, Inc., are known for their extravagance. Management provides the best food and entertainment to thank the employees for their hard work. During the planning for this year's bash, a disagreement broke out between the treasurer's staff and the controller's staff. The treasurer's staff contended that the firm was running low on cash and might have trouble paying its bills over the coming months; they requested that cuts be made to the budget for the party. The controller's staff felt that any cuts were unwarranted as the firm continued to be very profitable.

Can both sides be right? Explain your answer.

E1–4   Recently, some branches of Donut Shop, Inc., have dropped the practice of allowing employees to accept tips. Customers who once said, "Keep the change," now have to get used to waiting for their nickels. Management even instituted a policy of requiring that the change be thrown out if a customer drives off without it. As a frequent customer who gets coffee and doughnuts for the office, you notice that the lines are longer and that more mistakes are being made in your order.

Explain why tips could be viewed as similar to stock options and why the delays and incorrect orders could represent a case of *agency costs*. If tips are gone forever, how could Donut Shop reduce these agency costs?

E1–5   Reston, Inc., has asked your corporation, Pruro, Inc., for financial assistance. As a long-time customer of Reston, your firm has decided to give that assistance. The question you are debating is whether Pruro should take Reston stock with a 5% annual dividend or a promissory note paying 5% annual interest.

Assuming payment is guaranteed and the dollar amounts for annual interest and dividend income are identical, which option will result in greater after-tax income for the first year?

Problems

A blue box (■) indicates problems available in .

P1–1   Liability comparisons   Merideth Harper has invested $25,000 in Southwest Development Company. The firm has recently declared bankruptcy and has $60,000 in unpaid debts. Explain the nature of payments, if any, by Ms. Harper in each of the following situations.

a. Southwest Development Company is a *sole proprietorship* owned by Ms. Harper.

b. Southwest Development Company is a 50–50 *partnership* of Ms. Harper and Christopher Black.

c. Southwest Development Company is a *corporation*.

P1–2   Marginal cost–benefit analysis and the goal of the firm   Ken Allen, capital budgeting analyst for Bally Gears, Inc., has been asked to evaluate a proposal. The manager of the automotive division believes that replacing the robotics used on the heavy truck gear line will produce total benefits of $560,000 (in today's dollars) over the next 5 years. The existing robotics would produce benefits of $400,000 (also in today's dollars) over that same time period. An initial cash investment of $220,000 would be required to install the new equipment. The manager estimates that the existing robotics can be sold for $70,000. Show how Ken will apply *marginal cost–benefit analysis* techniques to determine the following:

a. The marginal (added) benefits of the proposed new robotics.

b. The marginal (added) cost of the proposed new robotics.

c. The net benefit of the proposed new robotics.

d. What should Ken Allen recommend that the company do? Why?

e. What factors besides the costs and benefits should be considered before the final decision is made?

P1–3   Accrual income versus cash flow for a period   Thomas Book Sales, Inc., supplies textbooks to college and university bookstores. The books are shipped with a proviso that they must be paid for within 30 days but can be returned for a full refund credit within 90 days. In 2009, Thomas shipped and billed book titles totaling $760,000. Collections, net of return credits, during the year totaled $690,000. The company spent $300,000 acquiring the books that it shipped.

a. Using accrual accounting and the preceding values, show the firm's net profit for the past year.

b. Using cash accounting and the preceding values, show the firm's net cash flow for the past year.

c. Which of these statements is more useful to the financial manager? Why?

P1–4   Cash flows   It is typical for Jane to plan, monitor, and assess her financial position using cash flows over a given period, typically a month. Jane has a savings account, and her bank loans money at 6% per year while it offers short-term investment rates of 5%. Jane's cash flows during August were as follows:

Item	Cash inflow	Cash outflow
Clothes		$1,000
Interest received	$ 450	
Dining out		500
Groceries		800
Salary	4,500	
Auto payment		355
Utilities		280
Mortgage		1,200
Gas		222

a. Determine Jane's total cash inflows and cash outflows.
b. Determine the *net cash flow* for the month of August.
c. If there is a shortage, what are a few options open to Jane?
d. If there is a surplus, what would be a prudent strategy for her to follow?

P1–5 **Identifying agency problems, costs, and resolutions**   Explain why each of the following situations is an agency problem and what costs to the firm might result from it.
Suggest how the problem might be dealt with short of firing the individual(s) involved.
a. The front desk receptionist routinely takes an extra 20 minutes of lunch to run
personal errands.
b. Division managers are padding cost estimates so as to show short-term efficiency
gains when the costs come in lower than the estimates.
c. The firm's chief executive officer has secret talks with a competitor about the possibility of a merger in which (s)he would become the CEO of the combined firms.
d. A branch manager lays off experienced full-time employees and staffs customer
service positions with part-time or temporary workers to lower employment
costs and raise this year's branch profit. The manager's bonus is based on profitability.

P1–6 **Corporate taxes**   Tantor Supply, Inc., is a small corporation acting as the exclusive
distributor of a major line of sporting goods. During 2009 the firm earned $92,500
before taxes.
a. Calculate the firm's tax liability using the corporate tax rate schedule given in
Table 1.4.
b. How much are Tantor Supply's 2009 after-tax earnings?
c. What was the firm's *average tax rate*, based on your findings in part **a**?
d. What is the firm's *marginal tax rate*, based on your findings in part **a**?

P1–7 **Average corporate tax rates**   Using the corporate tax rate schedule given in
Table 1.4, perform the following:
a. Calculate the tax liability, after-tax earnings, and average tax rates for the following levels of corporate earnings before taxes: $10,000; $80,000; $300,000;
$500,000; $1.5 million; $10 million; and $20 million.
b. Plot the *average tax rates* (measured on the *y* axis) against the pretax income
levels (measured on the *x* axis). What generalization can be made concerning the
relationship between these variables?

P1–8 **Marginal corporate tax rates**   Using the corporate tax rate schedule given in Table 1.4, perform the following:

a. Find the marginal tax rate for the following levels of corporate earnings before taxes: $15,000; $60,000; $90,000; $200,000; $400,000; $1 million; and $20 million.

b. Plot the *marginal tax rates* (measured on the *y* axis) against the pretax income levels (measured on the *x* axis). Explain the relationship between these variables.

P1–9 **Interest versus dividend income**   During the year just ended, Shering Distributors, Inc., had pretax earnings from operations of $490,000. In addition, during the year it received $20,000 in income from interest on bonds it held in Zig Manufacturing and received $20,000 in income from dividends on its 5% common stock holding in Tank Industries, Inc. Shering is in the 40% tax bracket and is eligible for a 70% dividend exclusion on its Tank Industries stock.

a. Calculate the firm's tax on its operating earnings only.

b. Find the tax and the after-tax amount attributable to the interest income from Zig Manufacturing bonds.

c. Find the tax and the after-tax amount attributable to the dividend income from the Tank Industries, Inc., common stock.

d. Compare, contrast, and discuss the after-tax amounts resulting from the interest income and dividend income calculated in parts **b** and **c**.

e. What is the firm's total tax liability for the year?

P1–10 **Interest versus dividend expense**   Michaels Corporation expects earnings before interest and taxes to be $40,000 for this period. Assuming an ordinary tax rate of 40%, compute the firm's earnings after taxes and earnings available for common stockholders (earnings after taxes and preferred stock dividends, if any) under the following conditions:

a. The firm pays $10,000 in interest.

b. The firm pays $10,000 in preferred stock dividends.

P1–11 **Capital gains taxes**   Perkins Manufacturing is considering the sale of two nondepreciable assets, X and Y. Asset X was purchased for $2,000 and will be sold today for $2,250. Asset Y was purchased for $30,000 and will be sold today for $35,000. The firm is subject to a 40% tax rate on capital gains.

a. Calculate the amount of capital gain, if any, realized on each of the assets.

b. Calculate the tax on the sale of each asset.

P1–12 **Capital gains taxes**   The following table contains purchase and sale prices for the nondepreciable capital assets of a major corporation. The firm paid taxes of 40% on capital gains.

Asset	Purchase price	Sale price
A	$ 3,000	$ 3,400
B	12,000	12,000
C	62,000	80,000
D	41,000	45,000
E	16,500	18,000

a. Determine the amount of capital gain realized on each of the five assets.
b. Calculate the amount of tax paid on each of the assets.

 P1–13 ETHICS PROBLEM   What does it mean to say that managers should maximize shareholder wealth "subject to ethical constraints"? What ethical considerations might enter into decisions that result in cash flow and stock price effects that are less than they might otherwise have been?

Chapter 1 Case

Assessing the Goal of Sports Products, Inc.

Loren Seguara and Dale Johnson both work for Sports Products, Inc., a major producer of boating equipment and accessories. Loren works as a clerical assistant in the Accounting Department, and Dale works as a packager in the Shipping Department. During their lunch break one day, they began talking about the company. Dale complained that he had always worked hard trying not to waste packing materials and efficiently and cost-effectively performing his job. In spite of his efforts and those of his co-workers in the department, the firm's stock price had declined nearly $2 per share over the past 9 months. Loren indicated that she shared Dale's frustration, particularly because the firm's profits had been rising. Neither could understand why the firm's stock price was falling as profits rose.

Loren indicated that she had seen documents describing the firm's profit-sharing plan under which all managers were partially compensated on the basis of the firm's profits. She suggested that maybe it was profit that was important to management, because it directly affected their pay. Dale said, "That doesn't make sense, because the stockholders own the firm. Shouldn't management do what's best for stockholders? Something's wrong!" Loren responded, "Well, maybe that explains why the company hasn't concerned itself with the stock price. Look, the only profits that stockholders receive are in the form of cash dividends, and this firm has never paid dividends during its 20-year history. We as stockholders therefore don't directly benefit from profits. The only way we benefit is for the stock price to rise." Dale chimed in, "That probably explains why the firm is being sued by state and federal environmental officials for dumping pollutants in the adjacent stream. Why spend money for pollution control? It increases costs, lowers profits, and therefore lowers management's earnings!"

Loren and Dale realized that the lunch break had ended and they must quickly return to work. Before leaving, they decided to meet the next day to continue their discussion.

To Do

a. What should the management of Sports Products, Inc., pursue as its overriding goal? Why?
b. Does the firm appear to have an *agency problem?* Explain.

    c. Evaluate the firm's approach to pollution control. Does it seem to be *ethical?* Why might incurring the expense to control pollution be in the best interests of the firm's owners despite its negative effect on profits?

    d. Does the firm appear to have an effective *corporate governance structure?* Explain any shortcomings.

    e. On the basis of the information provided, what specific recommendations would you offer the firm?

Spreadsheet Exercise

Assume that Monsanto Corporation is considering the renovation and/or replacement of some of its older and outdated carpet-manufacturing equipment. Its objective is to improve the efficiency of operations in terms of both speed and reduction in the number of defects. The company's finance department has compiled pertinent data that will allow it to conduct a *marginal cost–benefit analysis* for the proposed equipment replacement.

The cash outlay for new equipment would be approximately $600,000. The net book value of the old equipment and its potential net selling price is $250,000. The total benefits from the new equipment (measured in today's dollars) would be $900,000. The benefits of the old equipment over a similar period of time (measured in today's dollars) would be $300,000.

To Do

Create a spreadsheet to conduct a *marginal cost–benefit analysis* for Monsanto Corporation and determine the following:

a. The marginal (added) benefits of the proposed new equipment.
b. The marginal (added) cost of the proposed new equipment.
c. The net benefit of the proposed new equipment.
d. What would you recommend that the firm do? Why?

Web Exercise

The World Wide Web (a part of the larger Internet) has become such a powerful force in every aspect of our society that to ignore its potential would lessen your learning experience. As a source of timely information, the Web is unrivaled. Anyone in the world now has the ability to do in-depth research into almost any topic with just a few mouse clicks. The Web exercise in each chapter of this book will continue the work done within the chapter, applying real-world and real-time data to the subjects taught therein. A relatively brief "deliverable" is attached with the assigned searches. These documents are meant to serve as verification of your time spent online. Often the exercises will build on past exercises and match closely the work done in the group exercises; this correspondence is created purposefully. The chapter, its examples and problems, and the group and Web exercises should all be seen as continuous tools whereby overlap reinforces the key elements of the material.

Go to the book's companion website at www.prenhall.com/gitman to find the Web Exercise for this chapter.

Remember to check the book's website at www.prenhall.com/gitman to find additional resources, including Web Exercises and a Web Case.

2

Financial Statements and Analysis

WHY THIS CHAPTER MATTERS TO YOU

In Your Professional Life

Accounting: You need to understand the stockholders' report and preparation of the four key financial statements; how firms consolidate international financial statements; and how to calculate and interpret financial ratios for decision making.

Information systems: You need to understand what data are included in the firm's financial statements to design systems that will supply such data to those who prepare the statements and to those in the firm who use the data for ratio calculations.

Management: You need to understand what parties are interested in the stockholders' report and why; how the financial statements will be analyzed by those both inside and outside the firm to assess various aspects of performance; the caution that should be exercised in using financial ratio analysis; and how the financial statements affect the value of the firm.

Marketing: You need to understand the effects your decisions will have on the financial statements, particularly the income statement and the statement of cash flows, and how analysis of ratios, especially those involving sales figures, will affect the firm's decisions about levels of inventory, credit policies, and pricing decisions.

Operations: You need to understand how the costs of operations are reflected in the firm's financial statements and how analysis of ratios, particularly those involving assets, cost of goods sold, or inventory, may affect requests for new equipment or facilities.

In Your Personal Life

A routine step in personal financial planning is to prepare and analyze personal financial statements, so that you can monitor progress toward your financial goals. Also, you need to understand and analyze corporate financial statements to build and monitor your investment portfolio.

LEARNING GOALS

LG 1 Review the contents of the stockholders' report and the procedures for consolidating international financial statements.

LG 2 Understand who uses financial ratios, and how.

LG 3 Use ratios to analyze a firm's liquidity and activity.

LG 4 Discuss the relationship between debt and financial leverage and the ratios used to analyze a firm's debt.

LG 5 Use ratios to analyze a firm's profitability and its market value.

LG 6 Use a summary of financial ratios and the DuPont system of analysis to perform a complete ratio analysis.

Å ll companies gather financial data about their operations and report this information in financial statements for interested parties. These statements are widely standardized, and so we can use the data in them to make comparisons between firms and over time. Analysis of certain items of financial data can identify areas where the firm excels and, also, areas of opportunity for improvement. This chapter reviews the content of financial statements and explains categories of financial ratios and their use.

2.1 | The Stockholders' Report

generally accepted accounting principles (GAAP)
The practice and procedure guidelines used to prepare and maintain financial records and reports; authorized by the *Financial Accounting Standards Board (FASB).*

Financial Accounting Standards Board (FASB)
The accounting profession's rule-setting body, which authorizes *generally accepted accounting principles (GAAP).*

Public Company Accounting Oversight Board (PCAOB)
A not-for-profit corporation established by the *Sarbanes-Oxley Act of 2002* to protect the interests of investors and further the public interest in the preparation of informative, fair, and independent audit reports.

Securities and Exchange Commission (SEC)
The federal regulatory body that governs the sale and listing of securities.

stockholders' report
Annual report that publicly owned corporations must provide to stockholders; it summarizes and documents the firm's financial activities during the past year.

letter to stockholders
Typically, the first element of the annual stockholders' report and the primary communication from management.

Every corporation has many and varied uses for the standardized records and reports of its financial activities. Periodically, reports must be prepared for regulators, creditors (lenders), owners, and management. The guidelines used to prepare and maintain financial records and reports are known as **generally accepted accounting principles (GAAP).** These accounting practices and procedures are authorized by the accounting profession's rule-setting body, the **Financial Accounting Standards Board (FASB).**

In addition, the *Sarbanes-Oxley Act of 2002*, enacted in an effort to eliminate the many disclosure and conflict of interest problems of corporations, established the **Public Company Accounting Oversight Board (PCAOB),** a not-for-profit corporation that oversees auditors of public corporations. The PCAOB is charged with protecting the interes ts of investors and furthering the public interest in the preparation of informative, fair, and independent audit reports. The expectation is that it will instill confidence in investors with regard to the accuracy of the audited financial statements of public companies.

Publicly owned corporations with more than $5 million in assets and 500 or more stockholders[1] are required by the **Securities and Exchange Commission (SEC)**—the federal regulatory body that governs the sale and listing of securities—to provide their stockholders with an annual **stockholders' report.** The stockholders' report summarizes and documents the firm's financial activities during the past year. It begins with a letter to the stockholders from the firm's president and/or chairman of the board.

The Letter to Stockholders

The **letter to stockholders** is the primary communication from management. It describes the events that are considered to have had the greatest effect on the firm during the year. It also generally discusses management philosophy, corporate governance issues, strategies, and actions, as well as plans for the coming year. Links at this book's website (www.prenhall.com/gitman) will take you to some representative letters to stockholders.

---

1. Although the Securities and Exchange Commission (SEC) does not have an official definition of *publicly owned*, these financial measures mark the cutoff point it uses to require informational reporting, regardless of whether the firm publicly sells its securities. Firms that do not meet these requirements are commonly called "closely owned" firms.

The Four Key Financial Statements

The four key financial statements required by the SEC for reporting to share-holders are (1) the income statement, (2) the balance sheet, (3) the statement of stockholders' equity, and (4) the statement of cash flows.[2] The financial statements from the 2009 stockholders' report of Bartlett Company, a manufacturer of metal fasteners, are presented and briefly discussed. Most likely, you have studied these four financial statements in an accounting course, so the purpose of looking at them here is to refresh your memory of the basics, rather than provide an exhaustive review.

Income Statement

income statement
Provides a financial summary of the firm's operating results during a specified period.

The **income statement** provides a financial summary of the firm's operating results during a specified period. Most common are income statements covering a 1-year period ending at a specified date, ordinarily December 31 of the calendar year. Many large firms, however, operate on a 12-month financial cycle, or *fiscal year,* that ends at a time other than December 31. In addition, monthly income statements are typically prepared for use by management, and quarterly statements must be made available to the stockholders of publicly owned corporations.

Table 2.1 presents Bartlett Company's income statements for the years ended December 31, 2009 and 2008. The 2009 statement begins with *sales revenue*—the total dollar amount of sales during the period—from which the *cost of goods sold* is deducted. The resulting *gross profits* of $986,000 represent the amount remaining to satisfy operating, financial, and tax costs. Next, *operating expenses,* which include selling expense, general and administrative expense, lease expense, and depreciation expense, are deducted from gross profits.[3] The resulting *operating profits* of $418,000 represent the profits earned from producing and selling products; this amount does not consider financial and tax costs. (Operating profit is often called *earnings before interest and taxes,* or *EBIT.*) Next, the financial cost—*interest expense*—is subtracted from operating profits to find *net profits* (or *earnings*) *before taxes.* After subtracting $93,000 in 2009 interest, Bartlett Company had $325,000 of net profits before taxes.

Next, taxes are calculated at the appropriate tax rates and deducted to determine *net profits* (or *earnings*) *after taxes.* Bartlett Company's net profits after taxes for 2009 were $231,000. Any preferred stock dividends must be subtracted from net profits after taxes to arrive at *earnings available for common stockholders.* This is the amount earned by the firm on behalf of the common stockholders during the period.

Dividing earnings available for common stockholders by the number of shares of common stock outstanding results in *earnings per share (EPS).* EPS represent the number of dollars earned during the period on behalf of each outstanding

Hint Some firms, such as retailers and agricultural firms, end their fiscal year at the end of their operating cycle rather than at the end of the calendar year—for example, retailers at the end of January and agricultural firms at the end of September.

---

2. Whereas these statement titles are consistently used throughout this text, it is important to recognize that in practice, companies frequently use different titles. For example, General Electric uses "Statement of Earnings" rather than "Income Statement" and "Statement of Financial Position" rather than "Balance Sheet." Both Sprint Nextel and Qualcomm use "Statement of Operations" rather than "Income Statement."

3. Depreciation expense can be, and frequently is, included in manufacturing costs—cost of goods sold—to calculate gross profits. Depreciation is shown as an expense in this text to isolate its effect on cash flows.

TABLE 2.1	Bartlett Company Income Statements ($000)		
		For the years ended December 31	
		2009	2008
Sales revenue		$3,074	$2,567
Less: Cost of goods sold		2,088	1,711
Gross profits		$ 986	$ 856
Less: Operating expenses			
Selling expense		$ 100	$ 108
General and administrative expenses		194	187
Lease expense[a]		35	35
Depreciation expense		239	223
Total operating expense		$ 568	$ 553
Operating profits		$ 418	$ 303
Less: Interest expense		93	91
Net profits before taxes		$ 325	$ 212
Less: Taxes (rate = 29%)[b]		94	64
Net profits after taxes		$ 231	$ 148
Less: Preferred stock dividends		10	10
Earnings available for common stockholders		$ 221	$ 138
Earnings per share (EPS)[c]		$2.90	$1.81
Dividend per share (DPS)[d]		$1.29	$0.75

[a]Lease expense is shown here as a separate item rather than being included as part of interest expense, as specified by the FASB for financial reporting purposes. The approach used here is consistent with tax reporting rather than financial reporting procedures.

[b]The 29% tax rate for 2009 results because the firm has certain special tax write-offs that do not show up directly on its income statement.

[c]Calculated by dividing the earnings available for common stockholders by the number of shares of common stock outstanding—76,262 in 2009 and 76,244 in 2008. Earnings per share in 2009: $221,000 ÷ 76,262 = $2.90; in 2008: $138,000 ÷ 76,244 = $1.81.

[d]Calculated by dividing the dollar amount of dividends paid to common stockholders by the number of shares of common stock outstanding. Dividends per share in 2009: $98,000 ÷ 76,262 = $1.29; in 2008: $57,183 ÷ 76,244 = $0.75.

dividend per share (DPS)
The dollar amount of cash distributed during the period on behalf of each outstanding share of common stock.

share of common stock. In 2009, Bartlett Company earned $221,000 for its common stockholders, which represents $2.90 for each outstanding share. The actual cash **dividend per share** (DPS), which is the dollar amount of cash distributed during the period on behalf of each outstanding share of common stock, paid in 2009 was $1.29.

Personal Finance Example

Jan and Jon Smith, a mid-30s married couple with no children, prepared a personal income and expense statement, which is similar to a corporate income statement. A condensed version of their income and expense statement appears on the next page. A more detailed version appears at the book's website.

Jan and Jon Smith
Income and Expense Statement
for the year ended December 31, 2009

Income

Salaries (incl. sales commissions)	$72,725
Interest received	195
Dividends received	120
(1) Total income	$73,040

Expenses

Mortgage payments	$16,864
Auto loan payments	2,520
Utilities (incl. cable)	2,470
Home repairs & maintenance	1,050
Food (incl. dining out)	5,825
Car expense	2,265
Health care and insurance	1,505
Clothes, shoes, accessories	1,700
Insurance (homeowners, auto, & life)	1,380
Taxes (income, Soc. Security, prop.)	16,430
Appliance and furniture payments	1,250
Recreation and entertainment	4,630
Tuition and books for Jan	1,400
Personal care & other items	2,415
(2) Total expenses	$61,704
(3) Cash surplus (or deficit)	
[(1) − (2)]	$11,336

During the year, the Smiths had total income of $73,040 and total expenses of $61,704, which left them with a cash surplus of $11,336. They can use the surplus to increase their savings and investments.

Balance Sheet

balance sheet
Summary statement of the firm's financial position at a given point in time.

The **balance sheet** presents a summary statement of the firm's financial position at a given point in time. The statement balances the firm's *assets* (what it owns) against its financing, which can be either *debt* (what it owes) or *equity* (what was provided by owners). Bartlett Company's balance sheets as of December 31 of 2009 and 2008 are presented in Table 2.2. They show a variety of asset, liability (debt), and equity accounts.

current assets
Short-term assets, expected to be converted into cash within 1 year or less.

An important distinction is made between short-term and long-term assets and liabilities. The **current assets** and **current liabilities** are *short-term* assets and liabilities. This means that they are expected to be converted into cash (current assets) or paid (current liabilities) within 1 year or less. All other assets and liabilities, along with stockholders' equity, which is assumed to have an infinite life, are considered *long-term*, or *fixed*, because they are expected to remain on the firm's books for more than 1 year.

current liabilities
Short-term liabilities, expected to be paid within 1 year or less.

As is customary, the assets are listed from the most liquid—*cash*—down to the least liquid. *Marketable securities* are very liquid short-term investments, such

Hint The key components
of the balance sheet can be
shown as:

Current assets	Current liabilities
	Long-term debt
Fixed assets	Stockholders' equity

or

Total assets =	Total liabilities and stockholders' equity

TABLE 2.2   Bartlett Company Balance Sheets ($000)

	December 31	
Assets	2009	2008
Current assets		
Cash	$ 363	$ 288
Marketable securities	68	51
Accounts receivable	503	365
Inventories	289	300
Total current assets	$1,223	$1,004
Gross fixed assets (at cost)[a]		
Land and buildings	$2,072	$1,903
Machinery and equipment	1,866	1,693
Furniture and fixtures	358	316
Vehicles	275	314
Other (includes financial leases)	98	96
Total gross fixed assets (at cost)	$4,669	$4,322
Less: Accumulated depreciation	2,295	2,056
Net fixed assets	$2,374	$2,266
Total assets	$3,597	$3,270

Liabilities and Stockholders' Equity		
Current liabilities		
Accounts payable	$ 382	$ 270
Notes payable	79	99
Accruals	159	114
Total current liabilities	$ 620	$ 483
Long-term debt (includes financial leases)[b]	$1,023	$ 967
Total liabilities	$1,643	$1,450
Stockholders' equity		
Preferred stock—cumulative 5%, $100 par, 2,000 shares authorized and issued[c]	$ 200	$ 200
Common stock—$2.50 par, 100,000 shares authorized, shares issued and outstanding in 2009: 76,262; in 2008: 76,244	191	190
Paid-in capital in excess of par on common stock	428	418
Retained earnings	1,135	1,012
Total stockholders' equity	$1,954	$1,820
Total liabilities and stockholders' equity	$3,597	$3,270

[a]In 2009, the firm has a 6-year financial lease requiring annual beginning-of-year payments of $35,000. Four years of the lease have yet to run.

[b]Annual principal repayments on a portion of the firm's total outstanding debt amount to $71,000.

[c]The annual preferred stock dividend would be $5 per share (5% × $100 par), or a total of $10,000 annually ($5 per share × 2,000 shares).

Hint Another interpretation of the balance sheet is that on one side are the assets that have been purchased to be used to increase the profit of the firm. The other side indicates how these assets were acquired, either by borrowing or by investing the owners' money.

long-term debt
Debts for which payment is not due in the current year.

paid-in capital in excess of par
The amount of proceeds in excess of the par value received from the original sale of common stock.

retained earnings
The cumulative total of all earnings, net of dividends, that have been retained and reinvested in the firm since its inception.

as U.S. Treasury bills or certificates of deposit, held by the firm. Because they are highly liquid, marketable securities are viewed as a form of cash ("near cash"). *Accounts receivable* represent the total monies owed the firm by its customers on credit sales made to them. *Inventories* include raw materials, work in process (partially finished goods), and finished goods held by the firm. The entry for *gross fixed assets* is the original cost of all fixed (long-term) assets owned by the firm.[4] *Net fixed assets* represent the difference between gross fixed assets and *accumulated depreciation*—the total expense recorded for the depreciation of fixed assets. (The net value of fixed assets is called their *book value*.)

Like assets, the liabilities and equity accounts are listed from short-term to long-term. Current liabilities include *accounts payable*, amounts owed for credit purchases by the firm; *notes payable*, outstanding short-term loans, typically from commercial banks; and *accruals*, amounts owed for services for which a bill may not or will not be received. (Examples of accruals include taxes due the government and wages due employees.) **Long-term debt** represents debt for which payment is not due in the current year. *Stockholders' equity* represents the owners' claims on the firm. The *preferred stock* entry shows the historical proceeds from the sale of preferred stock ($200,000 for Bartlett Company).

Next, the amount paid by the original purchasers of common stock is shown by two entries: common stock and paid-in capital in excess of par on common stock. The *common stock* entry is the *par value* of common stock. **Paid-in capital in excess of par** represents the amount of proceeds in excess of the par value received from the original sale of common stock. The sum of the common stock and paid-in capital accounts divided by the number of shares outstanding represents the original price per share received by the firm on a single issue of common stock. Bartlett Company therefore received about $8.12 per share [($191,000 par + $428,000 paid-in capital in excess of par) ÷ 76,262 shares] from the sale of its common stock.

Finally, **retained earnings** represent the cumulative total of all earnings, net of dividends, that have been retained and reinvested in the firm since its inception. It is important to recognize that retained earnings *are not cash* but rather have been utilized to finance the firm's assets.

Bartlett Company's balance sheets in Table 2.2 show that the firm's total assets increased from $3,270,000 in 2008 to $3,597,000 in 2009. The $327,000 increase was due primarily to the $219,000 increase in current assets. The asset increase, in turn, appears to have been financed primarily by an increase of $193,000 in total liabilities. Better insight into these changes can be derived from the statement of cash flows, which we will discuss shortly.

Personal Finance Example   The following personal balance sheet for Jan and Jon Smith—the couple introduced earlier, who are married, in their mid-30s, and have no children—is similar to a corporate balance sheet. Again, a more detailed version appears at the book's website.

---

4. For convenience the term *fixed assets* is used throughout this text to refer to what, in a strict accounting sense, is captioned "property, plant, and equipment." This simplification of terminology permits certain financial concepts to be more easily developed.

Jan and Jon Smith
Balance Sheet
December 31, 2009

Assets		Liabilities and Net Worth	
Cash on hand	$ 90	Credit card balances	$ 665
Checking accounts	575	Utility bills	120
Savings accounts	760	Medical bills	75
Money market funds	800	Other current liab.	45
Total liquid assets	$ 2,225	Total cur. liab.	$ 905
Stocks & bonds	$ 2,250	Real estate mortg.	$ 92,000
Mutual funds	1,500	Auto loans	4,250
Retirement funds, IRA	2,000	Education loan	3,800
Total investments	$ 5,750	Personal loan	4,000
Real estate	$120,000	Furniture loan	800
Cars	14,000	Tot. L-T liab.	$104,850
Household furnishings	3,700	Tot. liab.	$105,755
Jewelry & artwork	1,500	Net worth (N/W)	$ 41,420
Total personal prop.	$139,200	Tot. liab. & N/W	$147,175
Total assets	$147,175		

statement of stockholders' equity
Shows all equity account transactions that occurred during a given year.

statement of retained earnings
Reconciles the net income earned during a given year, and any cash dividends paid, with the change in retained earnings between the start and the end of that year. An abbreviated form of the *statement of stockholders' equity.*

The Smiths have total assets of $147,175 and total liabilities of $105,755. Personal net worth (N/W) is a "plug figure"—the difference between total assets and total liabilities—which in the case of Jan and Jon Smith is $41,420.

Statement of Retained Earnings

The *statement of retained earnings* is an abbreviated form of the statement of stockholders' equity. Unlike the **statement of stockholders' equity,** which shows all equity account transactions that occurred during a given year, the **statement of retained earnings** reconciles the net income earned during a given year, and any cash dividends paid, with the change in retained earnings between the start and the end of that year. Table 2.3 presents this statement for Bartlett Company for the year ended December 31, 2009. The statement shows that the company began the year with $1,012,000 in retained earnings and had net profits after taxes of $231,000,

TABLE 2.3   Bartlett Company Statement of Retained Earnings ($000) for the Year Ended December 31, 2009

Retained earnings balance (January 1, 2009)		$1,012
Plus: Net profits after taxes (for 2009)		231
Less: Cash dividends (paid during 2009)		
Preferred stock	$10	
Common stock	98	
Total dividends paid		108
Retained earnings balance (December 31, 2009)		$1,135

from which it paid a total of $108,000 in dividends, resulting in year-end retained earnings of $1,135,000. Thus the net increase for Bartlett Company was $123,000 ($231,000 net profits after taxes minus $108,000 in dividends) during 2009.

Statement of Cash Flows

statement of cash flows
Provides a summary of the firm's operating, investment, and financing cash flows and reconciles them with changes in its cash and marketable securities during the period.

The **statement of cash flows** is a summary of the cash flows over the period of concern. The statement provides insight into the firm's operating, investment, and financing cash flows and reconciles them with changes in its cash and marketable securities during the period. Bartlett Company's statement of cash flows for the year ended December 31, 2009, is presented in Table 2.4. Further insight into this statement is included in the discussion of cash flow in Chapter 3.

Notes to the Financial Statements

notes to the financial statements
Explanatory notes keyed to relevant accounts in the statements; they provide detailed information on the accounting policies, procedures, calculations, and transactions underlying entries in the financial statements.

Included with published financial statements are explanatory notes keyed to the relevant accounts in the statements. These **notes to the financial statements** provide detailed information on the accounting policies, procedures, calculations, and transactions underlying entries in the financial statements. Common issues

TABLE 2.4	Bartlett Company Statement of Cash Flows ($000) for the Year Ended December 31, 2009		
Cash Flow from Operating Activities			
Net profits after taxes		$231	
Depreciation		239	
Increase in accounts receivable		(138)[a]	
Decrease in inventories		11	
Increase in accounts payable		112	
Increase in accruals		45	
Cash provided by operating activities			$500
Cash Flow from Investment Activities			
Increase in gross fixed assets		($347)	
Change in equity investments in other firms		0	
Cash provided by investment activities			(347)
Cash Flow from Financing Activities			
Decrease in notes payable		($ 20)	
Increase in long-term debts		56	
Changes in stockholders' equity[b]		11	
Dividends paid		(108)	
Cash provided by financing activities			(61)
Net increase in cash and marketable securities			$ 92

[a]As is customary, parentheses are used to denote a negative number, which in this case is a cash outflow.

[b]Retained earnings are excluded here, because their change is actually reflected in the combination of the "net profits after taxes" and "dividends paid" entries.

Focus on Practice

Is It Time to Change SOX?

IN PRACTICE

In 2000 and 2001, accounting irregularities at a number of large corporations forced Congress to take action, passing the Sarbanes-Oxley Act of 2002 (SOX). However, not everyone is pleased with the law. Many companies complain that compliance with the Sarbanes-Oxley corporate reporting regulations require them to spend much time and money. Large corporations, for example, spent an average of $3.8 million in 2005 to comply with the law. The most onerous aspect of SOX appears to be Section 404, which requires companies to first review their own systems for ensuring accurate financial reports and then have them tested by outside auditors.

Several high-ranking government officials have weighed in on the debate. In a speech to the Economic Club in November 2006, U.S. Treasury Secretary Henry Paulson acknowledged the impact of the accounting provi-

sions, especially on small businesses. Rather than passing a new law to amend the act, he said, Section 404 should be implemented in a more efficient and cost-effective manner. Also, Securities and Exchange Commission (SEC) Chairman Christopher Cox wrote a letter to the Public Company Accounting Oversight Board (the auditing industry's overseer) urging that the rule be adapted to companies based on company size.

Supporters of SOX claim that the law and related reforms have produced more reliable corporate financial statements, which investors rely on when deciding whether to buy or sell shares. According to Duncan W. Richardson, chief equity investment officer at Eaton Vance Management and overseer of $80 billion in stock holdings, even the act's much-disparaged requirements for testing internal financial controls could drive gains in corporate productivity

and profits. Thompson Financial's Earnings Purity Index, which tracks earnings adjusted for unusual charges and write-offs—techniques used to make earnings look better—reports that improvements have been shown in each of the past 4 years.

The jury is still out on whether Sarbanes-Oxley will be changed to alleviate the burden on U.S. corporations. However, consider this: On the day SOX was signed into law, the market value of the Wilshire 5000, a proxy for all public companies in the United States, stood at $10.5 trillion. By April 2007, the value of the Wilshire 5000 was $14.5 trillion. While the markets factor in many events, the passage of SOX has not had a significantly negative impact, as some might argue.

■ *In addition to investors, who else might be benefiting directly from the implementation of the Sarbanes-Oxley Act?*

addressed by these notes include revenue recognition, income taxes, breakdowns of fixed asset accounts, debt and lease terms, and contingencies. Since passage of Sarbanes-Oxley, notes to the financial statements have also included some details about compliance with that law. The *Focus on Practice* box above discusses issues relating to SOX compliance. Professional securities analysts use the data in the statements and notes to develop estimates of the value of securities that the firm issues, and these estimates influence the actions of investors and therefore the firm's share value.

Financial Accounting Standards Board (FASB) Standard No. 52
Mandates that U.S.-based companies translate their foreign-currency-denominated assets and liabilities into dollars, for consolidation with the parent company's financial statements. This is done by using the *current rate (translation) method.*

Consolidating International Financial Statements

So far, we've discussed financial statements involving only one currency, the U.S. dollar. The issue of how to consolidate a company's foreign and domestic financial statements has bedeviled the accounting profession for many years. The current policy is described in **Financial Accounting Standards Board (FASB) Standard No. 52,** which mandates that U.S.-based companies translate their

current rate (translation) method
Technique used by U.S.-based companies to translate their foreign-currency-denominated assets and liabilities into dollars, for consolidation with the parent company's financial statements, using the year-end (current) exchange rate.

foreign-currency-denominated assets and liabilities into dollars, for consolidation with the parent company's financial statements. This is done by using a technique called the **current rate (translation) method,** under which all of a U.S. parent company's foreign-currency-denominated assets and liabilities are converted into dollar values using the exchange rate prevailing at the fiscal year ending date (the current rate). Income statement items are treated similarly. Equity accounts, on the other hand, are translated into dollars by using the exchange rate that prevailed when the parent's equity investment was made (the historical rate). Retained earnings are adjusted to reflect each year's operating profits or losses. For an example that demonstrates consolidation of international financial statements, go to the book's website.

REVIEW QUESTIONS

2–1   What roles do GAAP, the FASB, and the PCAOB play in the financial reporting activities of public companies?
2–2   Describe the purpose of each of the four major financial statements.
2–3   Why are the notes to the financial statements important to professional securities analysts?
2–4   How is the *current rate (translation) method* used to consolidate a firm's foreign and domestic financial statements?

2.2 | Using Financial Ratios

ratio analysis
Involves methods of calculating and interpreting financial ratios to analyze and monitor the firm's performance.

The information contained in the four basic financial statements is of major significance to a variety of interested parties who regularly need to have relative measures of the company's performance. *Relative* is the key word here, because the analysis of financial statements is based on the use of *ratios* or *relative values*. **Ratio analysis** involves methods of calculating and interpreting financial ratios to analyze and monitor the firm's performance. The basic inputs to ratio analysis are the firm's income statement and balance sheet.

Interested Parties

Hint Management should be the most interested party of this group. Managers not only have to worry about the financial situation of the firm, but they are also critically interested in what the other parties think about the firm.

Ratio analysis of a firm's financial statements is of interest to shareholders, creditors, and the firm's own management. Both current and prospective shareholders are interested in the firm's current and future level of risk and return, which directly affect share price. The firm's creditors are interested primarily in the short-term liquidity of the company and its ability to make interest and principal payments. A secondary concern of creditors is the firm's profitability; they want assurance that the business is healthy. Management, like stockholders, is concerned with all aspects of the firm's financial situation, and it attempts to produce financial ratios that will be considered favorable by both owners and creditors. In addition, management uses ratios to monitor the firm's performance from period to period.

Types of Ratio Comparisons

Ratio analysis is not merely the calculation of a given ratio. More important is the *interpretation* of the ratio value. A meaningful basis for comparison is needed to answer such questions as "Is it too high or too low?" and "Is it good or bad?" Two types of ratio comparisons can be made: cross-sectional and time-series.

cross-sectional analysis
Comparison of different firms' financial ratios at the same point in time; involves comparing the firm's ratios to those of other firms in its industry or to industry averages.

benchmarking
A type of *cross-sectional analysis* in which the firm's ratio values are compared to those of a key competitor or group of competitors that it wishes to emulate.

Cross-Sectional Analysis

Cross-sectional analysis involves the comparison of different firms' financial ratios at the same point in time. Analysts are often interested in how well a firm has performed in relation to other firms in its industry. Frequently, a firm will compare its ratio values to those of a key competitor or group of competitors that it wishes to emulate. This type of cross-sectional analysis, called **benchmarking**, has become very popular.

Comparison to industry averages is also popular. These figures can be found in the *Almanac of Business and Industrial Financial Ratios, Dun & Bradstreet's Industry Norms and Key Business Ratios, RMA Annual Statement Studies, Value Line,* and industry sources.[5] A sample from one available source of industry averages is given in Table 2.5.

TABLE 2.5   Industry Average Ratios for Selected Lines of Business[a]

Line of business (number of concerns reporting)[b]	Current ratio (X)	Quick ratio (X)	Sales to inventory (X)	Collection period (days)	Total assets to sales (%)	Total liabilities to net worth (%)	Return on sales (%)	Return on total assets (%)	Return on net worth (%)
Department	4.9	1.4	6.6	1.8	32.0	25.1	2.8	6.8	16.2
stores	2.6	0.6	4.6	6.1	43.8	76.6	1.0	2.3	4.5
(143)	1.6	0.2	3.5	21.2	64.9	176.9	0.1	0.1	0.2
Electronic	2.3	1.5	31.6	27.4	24.6	54.3	3.4	7.3	20.6
computers	1.6	0.9	11.3	40.9	58.9	114.3	0.5	1.3	4.6
(76)	1.2	0.7	6.8	68.5	104.1	238.3	(9.7)	(10.4)	(20.6)
Grocery	2.6	1.0	29.6	1.1	15.3	48.5	2.2	9.4	24.8
stores	1.6	0.5	19.6	2.9	21.3	105.2	1.0	4.4	10.0
(455)	1.1	0.2	13.9	6.9	31.2	277.3	0.3	1.4	3.5
Motor	2.9	1.1	11.4	16.1	27.8	56.4	4.2	10.3	26.9
vehicles	1.7	0.7	8.3	24.1	37.4	150.8	1.5	4.1	9.6
(42)	1.2	0.5	5.5	40.5	47.3	357.2	0.2	0.8	1.2

[a]These values are given for each ratio for each line of business. The center value is the median, and the values immediately above and below it are the upper and lower quartiles, respectively.
[b]Standard Industrial Classification (SIC) codes for the lines of business shown are, respectively: SIC #5311, SIC #3571, SIC #5411, SIC #3711.
Source: "Industry Norms and Key Business Ratios," Dun & Bradstreet, Inc. Reprinted with permission.

5. Cross-sectional comparisons of firms operating in several lines of business are difficult to perform. Weighted-average industry average ratios based on the firm's product-line mix can be used or, if data are available, analysis of the firm on a product-line basis can be performed to evaluate a multiproduct firm.

Hint Industry averages
are not particularly useful
for analyzing firms with
multiproduct lines. In the
case of multiproduct firms,
it is difficult to select the
appropriate benchmark
industry.

Many people mistakenly believe that as long as the firm being analyzed has a
value "better than" the industry average, it can be viewed favorably. However,
this "better than average" viewpoint can be misleading. Quite often a ratio value
that is far better than the norm can indicate problems that, on more careful
analysis, may be more severe than had the ratio been worse than the industry
average. It is therefore important to investigate significant deviations *to either
side* of the industry standard.

Example

In early 2010, Mary Boyle, the chief financial analyst at Caldwell Manufacturing,
a producer of heat exchangers, gathered data on the firm's financial performance
during 2009, the year just ended. She calculated a variety of ratios and obtained
industry averages. She was especially interested in inventory turnover, which
reflects the speed with which the firm moves its inventory from raw materials
through production into finished goods and to the customer as a completed sale.
Generally, higher values of this ratio are preferred, because they indicate a
quicker turnover of inventory. Caldwell Manufacturing's calculated inventory
turnover for 2009 and the industry average inventory turnover were as follows:

	Inventory turnover, 2009
Caldwell Manufacturing	14.8
Industry average	9.7

Mary's initial reaction to these data was that the firm had managed its inventory significantly *better than* the average firm in the industry. The turnover was
nearly 53% faster than the industry average. Upon reflection, however, she realized that a very high inventory turnover could also mean very low levels of inventory. The consequence of low inventory could be excessive stockouts (insufficient
inventory). Discussions with people in the manufacturing and marketing departments did, in fact, uncover such a problem: Inventories during the year were
extremely low, the result of numerous production delays that hindered the firm's
ability to meet demand and resulted in lost sales. A ratio that initially appeared to
reflect extremely efficient inventory management was actually the symptom of a
major problem.

Time-Series Analysis

time-series analysis
Evaluation of the firm's
financial performance over
time using financial ratio
analysis.

Time-series analysis evaluates performance over time. Comparison of current to
past performance, using ratios, enables analysts to assess the firm's progress.
Developing trends can be seen by using multiyear comparisons. Any significant
year-to-year changes may be symptomatic of a major problem.

Combined Analysis

The most informative approach to ratio analysis combines cross-sectional and
time-series analyses. A combined view makes it possible to assess the trend in the
behavior of the ratio in relation to the trend for the industry. Figure 2.1 depicts
this type of approach using the average collection period ratio of Bartlett
Company, over the years 2006–2009. This ratio reflects the average amount of
time (in days) it takes the firm to collect bills, and lower values of this ratio generally are preferred. The figure quickly discloses that (1) Bartlett's effectiveness in

FIGURE 2.1

Combined Analysis
Combined cross-sectional and time-series view of Bartlett Company's average collection period, 2006–2009

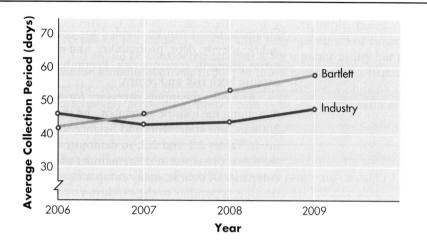

collecting its receivables is poor in comparison to the industry, and (2) Bartlett's trend is toward longer collection periods. Clearly, Bartlett needs to shorten its collection period.

Cautions about Using Ratio Analysis

Before discussing specific ratios, we should consider the following cautions about their use:

1. Ratios that reveal large deviations from the norm merely indicate *symptoms* of a problem. Additional analysis is typically needed to isolate the *causes* of the problem.
2. A single ratio does not generally provide sufficient information from which to judge the *overall* performance of the firm. However, if an analysis is concerned only with certain *specific* aspects of a firm's financial position, one or two ratios may suffice.
3. The ratios being compared should be calculated using financial statements dated at the same point in time during the year. If they are not, the effects of *seasonality* may produce erroneous conclusions and decisions.
4. It is preferable to use *audited financial statements* for ratio analysis. If they have not been audited, the data in them may not reflect the firm's true financial condition.
5. The financial data being compared should have been developed in the same way. The use of differing accounting treatments—especially relative to inventory and depreciation—can distort the results of ratio comparisons, regardless of whether cross-sectional or time-series analysis is used.
6. Results can be distorted by *inflation*, which can cause the book values of inventory and depreciable assets to differ greatly from their replacement values. Additionally, inventory costs and depreciation write-offs can differ from their true values, thereby distorting profits. Without adjustment, inflation tends to cause older firms (older assets) to appear more efficient and profitable than newer firms (newer assets). Clearly, in using ratios, you must be careful when comparing older to newer firms or a firm to itself over a long period of time.

Average Payment Period

The **average payment period**, or average age of accounts payable, is calculated in the same manner as the average collection period:

$$\text{Average payment period} = \frac{\text{Accounts payable}}{\text{Average purchases per day}}$$

$$= \frac{\text{Accounts payable}}{\dfrac{\text{Annual purchases}}{365}}$$

The difficulty in calculating this ratio stems from the need to find annual purchases,[11] a value not available in published financial statements. Ordinarily, purchases are estimated as a given percentage of cost of goods sold. If we assume that Bartlett Company's purchases equaled 70 percent of its cost of goods sold in 2009, its average payment period is

$$\frac{\$382,000}{\dfrac{0.70 \times \$2,088,000}{365}} = \frac{\$382,000}{\$4,004} = 95.4 \text{ days}$$

This figure is meaningful only in relation to the average credit terms extended to the firm. If Bartlett Company's suppliers have extended, on average, 30-day credit terms, an analyst would give Bartlett a low credit rating. Prospective lenders and suppliers of trade credit are most interested in the average payment period because it provides insight into the firm's bill-paying patterns.

Total Asset Turnover

The **total asset turnover** indicates the efficiency with which the firm uses its assets to generate sales. Total asset turnover is calculated as follows:

$$\text{Total asset turnover} = \frac{\text{Sales}}{\text{Total assets}}$$

The value of Bartlett Company's total asset turnover in 2009 is

$$\frac{\$3,074,000}{\$3,597,000} = 0.85$$

This means the company turns over its assets 0.85 times per year.

Generally, the higher a firm's total asset turnover, the more efficiently its assets have been used. This measure is probably of greatest interest to management, because it indicates whether the firm's operations have been financially efficient.

---

11. Technically, annual *credit* purchases—rather than annual purchases—should be used in calculating this ratio. For simplicity, this refinement is ignored here.

REVIEW QUESTION

2–10 To assess the firm's average collection period and average payment period ratios, what additional information is needed, and why?

2.5 | Debt Ratios

The *debt position* of a firm indicates the amount of other people's money being used to generate profits. In general, the financial analyst is most concerned with long-term debts, because these commit the firm to a stream of contractual payments over the long run. The more debt a firm has, the greater its risk of being unable to meet its contractual debt payments. Because creditors' claims must be satisfied before the earnings can be distributed to shareholders, current and prospective shareholders pay close attention to the firm's ability to repay debts. Lenders are also concerned about the firm's indebtedness.

financial leverage
The magnification of risk and return through the use of fixed-cost financing, such as debt and preferred stock.

In general, the more debt a firm uses in relation to its total assets, the greater its *financial leverage*. **Financial leverage** is the magnification of risk and return through the use of fixed-cost financing, such as debt and preferred stock. The more fixed-cost debt a firm uses, the greater will be its expected risk and return.

Example

Patty Akers is in the process of incorporating her new business. After much analysis she determined that an initial investment of $50,000—$20,000 in current assets and $30,000 in fixed assets—is necessary. These funds can be obtained in either of two ways. The first is the *no-debt plan*, under which she would invest the full $50,000 without borrowing. The other alternative, the *debt plan*, involves investing $25,000 and borrowing the balance of $25,000 at 12% annual interest.

Regardless of which alternative she chooses, Patty expects sales to average $30,000, costs and operating expenses to average $18,000, and earnings to be taxed at a 40% rate. Projected balance sheets and income statements associated with the two plans are summarized in Table 2.6 (see page 60). The no-debt plan results in after-tax profits of $7,200, which represent a 14.4% rate of return on Patty's $50,000 investment. The debt plan results in $5,400 of after-tax profits, which represent a 21.6% rate of return on Patty's investment of $25,000. The debt plan provides Patty with a higher rate of return, but the risk of this plan is also greater, because the annual $3,000 of interest must be paid before receipt of earnings.

The example demonstrates that *with increased debt comes greater risk as well as higher potential return.* Therefore, the greater the financial leverage, the greater the potential risk and return. A detailed discussion of the impact of debt on the firm's risk, return, and value is included in Chapter 11. Here, we emphasize the use of financial debt ratios to assess externally a firm's debt position.

degree of indebtedness
Measures the amount of debt relative to other significant balance sheet amounts.

There are two general types of debt measures: measures of the degree of indebtedness and measures of the ability to service debts. The **degree of indebtedness** measures the amount of debt relative to other significant balance sheet amounts. A popular measure of the degree of indebtedness is the debt ratio.

TABLE 2.6	**Financial Statements Associated with Patty's Alternatives**	
	No-debt plan	Debt plan
Balance Sheets		
Current assets	$20,000	$20,000
Fixed assets	30,000	30,000
Total assets	$50,000	$50,000
Debt (12% interest)	$ 0	$25,000
(1) Equity	50,000	25,000
Total liabilities and equity	$50,000	$50,000
Income Statements		
Sales	$30,000	$30,000
Less: Costs and operating expenses	18,000	18,000
Operating profits	$12,000	$12,000
Less: Interest expense	0	$0.12 \times \$25,000 =$ 3,000
Net profits before taxes	$12,000	$ 9,000
Less: Taxes (rate = 40%)	4,800	3,600
(2) Net profits after taxes	$ 7,200	$ 5,400
Return on equity [(2) ÷ (1)]	$\dfrac{\$7,200}{\$50,000} = 14.4\%$	$\dfrac{\$5,400}{\$25,000} = 21.6\%$

ability to service debts
The ability of a firm to make the payments required on a scheduled basis over the life of a debt.

coverage ratios
Ratios that measure the firm's ability to pay certain fixed charges.

   The second type of debt measure, the **ability to service debts,** reflects a firm's ability to make the payments required on a scheduled basis over the life of a debt.[12] The firm's ability to pay certain fixed charges is measured using **coverage ratios.** Typically, higher coverage ratios are preferred, but too high a ratio (above industry norms) may result in unnecessarily low risk and return. In general, the lower the firm's coverage ratios, the less certain it is to be able to pay fixed obligations. If a firm is unable to pay these obligations, its creditors may seek immediate repayment, which in most instances would force a firm into bankruptcy. Two popular coverage ratios are the times interest earned ratio and the fixed-payment coverage ratio.

Debt Ratio

debt ratio
Measures the proportion of total assets financed by the firm's creditors.

The **debt ratio** measures the proportion of total assets financed by the firm's creditors. The higher this ratio, the greater the amount of other people's money being used to generate profits. The ratio is calculated as follows:

$$\text{Debt ratio} = \frac{\text{Total liabilities}}{\text{Total assets}}$$

---

12. The term *service* refers to the payment of interest and repayment of principal associated with a firm's debt obligations. When a firm services its debts, it pays—or fulfills—these obligations.

The debt ratio for Bartlett Company in 2009 is

$$\frac{\$1,643,000}{\$3,597,000} = 0.457 = 45.7\%$$

This value indicates that the company has financed close to half of its assets with debt. The higher this ratio, the greater the firm's degree of indebtedness and the more financial leverage it has.

Times Interest Earned Ratio

times interest earned ratio
Measures the firm's ability to make contractual interest payments; sometimes called the *interest coverage ratio.*

The **times interest earned ratio,** sometimes called the *interest coverage ratio,* measures the firm's ability to make contractual interest payments. The higher its value, the better able the firm is to fulfill its interest obligations. The times interest earned ratio is calculated as follows:

$$\text{Times interest earned ratio} = \frac{\text{Earnings before interest and taxes}}{\text{Interest}}$$

The figure for *earnings before interest and taxes* is the same as that for *operating profits* shown in the income statement. Applying this ratio to Bartlett Company yields the following 2009 value:

$$\text{Times interest earned ratio} = \frac{\$418,000}{\$93,000} = 4.5$$

The times interest earned ratio for Bartlett Company seems acceptable. A value of at least 3.0—and preferably closer to 5.0—is often suggested. The firm's earnings before interest and taxes could shrink by as much as 78 percent $[(4.5 - 1.0) \div 4.5]$, and the firm would still be able to pay the $93,000 in interest it owes. Thus it has a good margin of safety.

Fixed-Payment Coverage Ratio

fixed-payment coverage ratio
Measures the firm's ability to meet all fixed-payment obligations.

The **fixed-payment coverage ratio** measures the firm's ability to meet all fixed-payment obligations, such as loan interest and principal, lease payments, and preferred stock dividends.[13] As is true of the times interest earned ratio, the higher this value, the better. The formula for the fixed-payment coverage ratio is

$$\frac{\text{Fixed-payment coverage ratio}}{} = \frac{\text{Earnings before interest and taxes} + \text{Lease payments}}{\text{Interest} + \text{Lease payments} + \{(\text{Principal payments} + \text{Preferred stock dividends}) \times [1/(1 - T)]\}}$$

where T is the corporate tax rate applicable to the firm's income. The term $1/(1 - T)$ is included to adjust the after-tax principal and preferred stock dividend payments

13. Although preferred stock dividends, which are stated at the time of issue, can be "passed" (not paid) at the option of the firm's directors, it is generally believed that the payment of such dividends is necessary. *This text therefore treats the preferred stock dividend as a contractual obligation, to be paid as a fixed amount, as scheduled.*

back to a before-tax equivalent that is consistent with the before-tax values of all other terms. Applying the formula to Bartlett Company's 2009 data yields

$$\frac{\text{Fixed-payment}}{\text{coverage ratio}} = \frac{\$418,000 + \$35,000}{\$93,000 + \$35,000 + \{(\$71,000 + \$10,000) \times [1/(1 - 0.29)]\}}$$

$$= \frac{\$453,000}{\$242,000} = 1.9$$

Because the earnings available are nearly twice as large as its fixed-payment obligations, the firm appears safely able to meet the latter.

Like the times interest earned ratio, the fixed-payment coverage ratio measures risk. The lower the ratio, the greater the risk to both lenders and owners; the greater the ratio, the lower the risk. This ratio allows interested parties to assess the firm's ability to meet additional fixed-payment obligations without being driven into bankruptcy.

REVIEW QUESTIONS

2–11 What is *financial leverage?*

2–12 What ratio measures the firm's *degree of indebtedness?* What ratios assess the firm's *ability to service debts?*

2.6 | Profitability Ratios

There are many measures of profitability. As a group, these measures enable analysts to evaluate the firm's profits with respect to a given level of sales, a certain level of assets, or the owners' investment. Without profits, a firm could not attract outside capital. Owners, creditors, and management pay close attention to boosting profits because of the great importance the market places on earnings.

Common-Size Income Statements

common-size income statement
An income statement in which each item is expressed as a percentage of sales.

A popular tool for evaluating profitability in relation to sales is the **common-size income statement.** Each item on this statement is expressed as a percentage of sales. Common-size income statements are especially useful in comparing performance across years. Three frequently cited ratios of profitability that can be read directly from the common-size income statement are (1) the gross profit margin, (2) the operating profit margin, and (3) the net profit margin.

Common-size income statements for 2009 and 2008 for Bartlett Company are presented and evaluated in Table 2.7. These statements reveal that the firm's cost of goods sold increased from 66.7 percent of sales in 2008 to 67.9 percent in 2009, resulting in a worsening gross profit margin. However, thanks to a decrease in total operating expenses, the firm's net profit margin rose from 5.4 percent of sales in 2008 to 7.2 percent in 2009. The decrease in expenses more than compensated for the increase in the cost of goods sold. A decrease in the firm's 2009 interest expense (3.0 percent of sales versus 3.5 percent in 2008) added to the increase in 2009 profits.

TABLE 2.7   Bartlett Company Common-Size Income Statements

	For the years ended December 31 2009	2008	Evaluation[a] 2008–2009
Sales revenue	100.0%	100.0%	same
Less: Cost of goods sold	67.9	66.7	worse
(1) Gross profit margin	32.1%	33.3%	worse
Less: Operating expenses			
Selling expense	3.3%	4.2%	better
General and administrative expenses	6.8	6.7	better
Lease expense	1.1	1.3	better
Depreciation expense	7.3	9.3	better
Total operating expense	18.5%	21.5%	better
(2) Operating profit margin	13.6%	11.8%	better
Less: Interest expense	3.0	3.5	better
Net profits before taxes	10.6%	8.3%	better
Less: Taxes	3.1	2.5	worse[b]
Net profits after taxes	7.5%	5.8%	better
Less: Preferred stock dividends	0.3	0.4	better
(3) Net profit margin	7.2%	5.4%	better

[a]Subjective assessments based on data provided.

[b]Taxes as a percentage of sales increased noticeably between 2008 and 2009 because of differing costs and expenses, whereas the average tax rates (taxes ÷ net profits before taxes) for 2008 and 2009 remained about the same—30% and 29%, respectively.

Gross Profit Margin

gross profit margin
Measures the percentage of each sales dollar remaining after the firm has paid for its goods.

The **gross profit margin** measures the percentage of each sales dollar remaining after the firm has paid for its goods. The higher the gross profit margin, the better (that is, the lower the relative cost of merchandise sold). The gross profit margin is calculated as follows:

Hint This is a very significant ratio for small retailers, especially during times of inflationary prices. If the owner of the firm does not raise prices when the cost of sales is rising, the gross profit margin will erode.

$$\text{Gross profit margin} = \frac{\text{Sales} - \text{Cost of goods sold}}{\text{Sales}} = \frac{\text{Gross profits}}{\text{Sales}}$$

Bartlett Company's gross profit margin for 2009 is

$$\frac{\$3,074,000 - \$2,088,000}{\$3,074,000} = \frac{\$986,000}{\$3,074,000} = 32.1\%$$

This value is labeled (1) on the common-size income statement in Table 2.7.

Operating Profit Margin

operating profit margin
Measures the percentage of each sales dollar remaining after all costs and expenses *other than* interest, taxes, and preferred stock dividends are deducted; the "pure profits" earned on each sales dollar.

The **operating profit margin** measures the percentage of each sales dollar remaining after all costs and expenses *other than* interest, taxes, and preferred stock dividends are deducted. It represents the "pure profits" earned on each sales dollar.

Operating profits are "pure" because they measure only the profits earned on operations and ignore interest, taxes, and preferred stock dividends. A high operating profit margin is preferred. The operating profit margin is calculated as follows:

$$\text{Operating profit margin} = \frac{\text{Operating profits}}{\text{Sales}}$$

Bartlett Company's operating profit margin for 2009 is

$$\frac{\$418,000}{\$3,074,000} = 13.6\%$$

This value is labeled (2) on the common-size income statement in Table 2.7.

Net Profit Margin

net profit margin
Measures the percentage of each sales dollar remaining after all costs and expenses, *including* interest, taxes, and preferred stock dividends, have been deducted.

The **net profit margin** measures the percentage of each sales dollar remaining after all costs and expenses, *including* interest, taxes, and preferred stock dividends, have been deducted. The higher the firm's net profit margin, the better. The net profit margin is calculated as follows:

$$\text{Net profit margin} = \frac{\text{Earnings available for common stockholders}}{\text{Sales}}$$

Bartlett Company's net profit margin for 2009 is

$$\frac{\$221,000}{\$3,074,000} = 7.2\%$$

This value is labeled (3) on the common-size income statement in Table 2.7.

Hint The net profit margin is sometimes defined as net profits after taxes divided by sales. The formula used here places greater emphasis on the common stockholders.

The net profit margin is a commonly cited measure of the firm's success with respect to earnings on sales. "Good" net profit margins differ considerably across industries. A net profit margin of 1 percent or less would not be unusual for a grocery store, whereas a net profit margin of 10 percent would be low for a retail jewelry store.

Earnings per Share (EPS)

Hint EPS represents the dollar amount earned *on behalf of* each outstanding share of common stock—not the amount of earnings *actually distributed* to shareholders.

The firm's *earnings per share (EPS)* is generally of interest to present or prospective stockholders and management. As we noted earlier, EPS represents the number of dollars earned during the period on behalf of each outstanding share of common stock. Earnings per share is calculated as follows:

$$\text{Earnings per share} = \frac{\text{Earnings available for common stockholders}}{\text{Number of shares of common stock outstanding}}$$

Bartlett Company's earnings per share in 2009 is

$$\frac{\$221,000}{76,262} = \$2.90$$

This figure represents the dollar amount earned *on behalf of* each outstanding share of common stock. The dollar amount of cash *actually distributed* to each shareholder is the *dividend per share (DPS)*, which, as noted in Bartlett Company's income statement (Table 2.1), rose to $1.29 in 2009 from $0.75 in 2008. EPS is closely watched by the investing public and is considered an important indicator of corporate success.

Return on Total Assets (ROA)

return on total assets (ROA)
Measures the overall effectiveness of management in generating profits with its available assets; also called the *return on investment (ROI)*.

The **return on total assets (ROA),** often called the *return on investment (ROI)*, measures the overall effectiveness of management in generating profits with its available assets. The higher the firm's return on total assets, the better. The return on total assets is calculated as follows:

$$\text{Return on total assets} = \frac{\text{Earnings available for common stockholders}}{\text{Total assets}}$$

Hint Some firms use this measure as a simple decision technique for evaluating proposed fixed-asset investments.

Bartlett Company's return on total assets in 2009 is

$$\frac{\$221{,}000}{\$3{,}597{,}000} = 6.1\%$$

This value indicates that the company earned 6.1 cents on each dollar of asset investment.

Return on Common Equity (ROE)

return on common equity (ROE)
Measures the return earned on the common stockholders' investment in the firm.

The **return on common equity (ROE)** measures the return earned on the common stockholders' investment in the firm. Generally, the higher this return, the better off are the owners. Return on common equity is calculated as follows:

$$\text{Return on common equity} = \frac{\text{Earnings available for common stockholders}}{\text{Common stock equity}}$$

This ratio for Bartlett Company in 2009 is

$$\frac{\$221{,}000}{\$1{,}754{,}000} = 12.6\%$$

Note that the value for common stock equity ($1,754,000) was found by subtracting the $200,000 of preferred stock equity from the total stockholders' equity of $1,954,000 (see Bartlett Company's 2009 balance sheet in Table 2.2). The calculated ROE of 12.6 percent indicates that during 2009 Bartlett earned 12.6 cents on each dollar of common stock equity.

REVIEW QUESTIONS

2–13 What three ratios of profitability are found on a *common-size income statement?*

2–14 What would explain a firm's having a high gross profit margin and a low net profit margin?

2–15 Which measure of profitability is probably of greatest interest to the investing public? Why?

2.7 | Market Ratios

market ratios
Relate a firm's market value, as measured by its current share price, to certain accounting values.

Market ratios relate the firm's market value, as measured by its current share price, to certain accounting values. These ratios give insight into how well investors in the marketplace feel the firm is doing in terms of risk and return. They tend to reflect, on a relative basis, the common stockholders' assessment of all aspects of the firm's past and expected future performance. Here we consider two popular market ratios, one that focuses on earnings and another that considers book value.

Price/Earnings (P/E) Ratio

price/earnings (P/E) ratio
Measures the amount that investors are willing to pay for each dollar of a firm's earnings; the higher the P/E ratio, the greater the investor confidence.

The **price/earnings (P/E) ratio** is commonly used to assess the owners' appraisal of share value. The P/E ratio measures the amount that investors are willing to pay for each dollar of a firm's earnings. The level of this ratio indicates the degree of confidence that investors have in the firm's future performance. The higher the P/E ratio, the greater the investor confidence. The P/E ratio is calculated as follows:

$$\text{Price/earnings (P/E) ratio} = \frac{\text{Market price per share of common stock}}{\text{Earnings per share}}$$

If Bartlett Company's common stock at the end of 2009 was selling at $32.25, using the EPS of $2.90, the P/E ratio at year-end 2009 is

$$\frac{\$32.25}{\$2.90} = 11.1$$

This figure indicates that investors were paying $11.10 for each $1.00 of earnings. The P/E ratio is most informative when applied in cross-sectional analysis using an industry average P/E ratio or the P/E ratio of a benchmark firm.

Market/Book (M/B) Ratio

market/book (M/B) ratio
Provides an assessment of how investors view the firm's performance. Firms expected to earn high returns relative to their risk typically sell at higher M/B multiples.

The **market/book (M/B) ratio** provides an assessment of how investors view the firm's performance. It relates the market value of the firm's shares to their book—strict accounting—value. To calculate the firm's M/B ratio, we first need to find the *book value per share of common stock:*

$$\frac{\text{Book value per share}}{\text{of common stock}} = \frac{\text{Common stock equity}}{\text{Number of shares of common stock outstanding}}$$

Substituting the appropriate values for Bartlett Company from its 2009 balance sheet, we get

$$\frac{\text{Book value per share}}{\text{of common stock}} = \frac{\$1,754,000}{76,262} = \$23.00$$

The formula for the market/book ratio is

$$\text{Market/book (M/B) ratio} = \frac{\text{Market price per share of common stock}}{\text{Book value per share of common stock}}$$

Substituting Bartlett Company's end of 2009 common stock price of $32.25 and its $23.00 book value per share of common stock (calculated above) into the M/B ratio formula, we get

$$\text{Market/book (M/B) ratio} = \frac{\$32.25}{\$23.00} = 1.40$$

This M/B ratio means that investors are currently paying $1.40 for each $1.00 of book value of Bartlett Company's stock.

The stocks of firms that are expected to perform well—improve profits, increase their market share, or launch successful products—typically sell at higher M/B ratios than the stocks of firms with less attractive outlooks. Simply stated, firms expected to earn high returns relative to their risk typically sell at higher M/B multiples. Clearly, Bartlett's future prospects are being viewed favorably by investors, who are willing to pay more than its book value for the firm's shares. Like P/E ratios, M/B ratios are typically assessed cross-sectionally, to get a feel for the firm's return and risk compared to peer firms.

REVIEW QUESTION

2–16 How do the *price/earnings (P/E) ratio* and the *market/book (M/B) ratio* provide a feel for the firm's return and risk?

2.8 | A Complete Ratio Analysis

Analysts frequently wish to take an overall look at the firm's financial performance and status. Here we consider two popular approaches to a complete ratio analysis: (1) summarizing all ratios and (2) the DuPont system of analysis. The summary analysis approach tends to view *all aspects* of the firm's financial activities to isolate key areas of responsibility. The DuPont system acts as a search technique aimed at finding the *key areas* responsible for the firm's financial condition.

Summarizing All Ratios

We can use Bartlett Company's ratios to perform a complete ratio analysis using both cross-sectional and time-series analysis approaches. The 2009 ratio values calculated earlier and the ratio values calculated for 2007 and 2008 for Bartlett Company, along with the industry average ratios for 2009, are summarized in Table 2.8 (see pages 68 and 69), which also shows the formula used to calculate each ratio. Using these data, we can discuss the five key aspects of Bartlett's performance—liquidity, activity, debt, profitability, and market.

Liquidity

The overall liquidity of the firm seems to exhibit a reasonably stable trend, having been maintained at a level that is relatively consistent with the industry average in 2009. The firm's liquidity seems to be good.

TABLE 2.8 Summary of Bartlett Company Ratios (2007–2009, Including 2009 Industry Averages)

Ratio	Formula	Year			Industry average 2009[c]	Evaluation[d]		
		2007[a]	2008[b]	2009[b]		Cross-sectional 2009	Time-series 2007–2009	Overall
Liquidity								
Current ratio	$\dfrac{\text{Current assets}}{\text{Current liabilities}}$	2.04	2.08	1.97	2.05	OK	OK	OK
Quick (acid-test) ratio	$\dfrac{\text{Current assets} - \text{Inventory}}{\text{Current liabilities}}$	1.32	1.46	1.51	1.43	OK	good	good
Activity								
Inventory turnover	$\dfrac{\text{Cost of goods sold}}{\text{Inventory}}$	5.1	5.7	7.2	6.6	good	good	good
Average collection period	$\dfrac{\text{Accounts receivable}}{\text{Average sales per day}}$	43.9 days	51.2 days	59.7 days	44.3 days	poor	poor	poor
Average payment period	$\dfrac{\text{Accounts payable}}{\text{Average purchases per day}}$	75.8 days	81.2 days	95.4 days	66.5 days	poor	poor	poor
Total asset turnover	$\dfrac{\text{Sales}}{\text{Total assets}}$	0.94	0.79	0.85	0.75	OK	OK	OK
Debt								
Debt ratio	$\dfrac{\text{Total liabilities}}{\text{Total assets}}$	36.8%	44.3%	45.7%	40.0%	OK	OK	OK
Times interest earned ratio	$\dfrac{\text{Earnings before interest and taxes}}{\text{Interest}}$	5.6	3.3	4.5	4.3	good	OK	OK
Fixed-payment coverage ratio	$\dfrac{\text{Earnings before interest and taxes} + \text{Lease payments}}{\text{Int.} + \text{Lease pay.} + \{(\text{Prin.} + \text{Pref. div.}) \times [1/(1 - T)]\}}$	2.4	1.4	1.9	1.5	good	OK	good

Ratio	Formula	Year			Industry average 2009[c]	Evaluation[d]		
		2007[a]	2008[b]	2009[b]		Cross-sectional 2009	Time-series 2007–2009	Overall
Profitability								
Gross profit margin	$\dfrac{\text{Gross profits}}{\text{Sales}}$	31.4%	33.3%	32.1%	30.0%	OK	OK	OK
Operating profit margin	$\dfrac{\text{Operating profits}}{\text{Sales}}$	14.6%	11.8%	13.6%	11.0%	good	OK	good
Net profit margin	$\dfrac{\text{Earnings available for common stockholders}}{\text{Sales}}$	8.2%	5.4%	7.2%	6.2%	good	OK	good
Earnings per share (EPS)	$\dfrac{\text{Earnings available for common stockholders}}{\text{Number of shares of common stock outstanding}}$	$3.26	$1.81	$2.90	$2.26	good	OK	good
Return on total assets (ROA)	$\dfrac{\text{Earnings available for common stockholders}}{\text{Total assets}}$	7.8%	4.2%	6.1%	4.6%	good	OK	good
Return on common equity (ROE)	$\dfrac{\text{Earnings available for common stockholders}}{\text{Common stock equity}}$	13.7%	8.5%	12.6%	8.5%	good	OK	good
Market								
Price/earnings (P/E) ratio	$\dfrac{\text{Market price per share of common stock}}{\text{Earnings per share}}$	10.5	10.0[e]	11.1	12.5	OK	OK	OK
Market/book (M/B) ratio	$\dfrac{\text{Market price per share of common stock}}{\text{Book value per share of common stock}}$	1.25	0.85[e]	1.40	1.30	OK	OK	OK

[a]Calculated from data not included in the chapter.
[b]Calculated by using the financial statements presented in Tables 2.1 and 2.2.
[c]Obtained from sources not included in this chapter.
[d]Subjective assessments based on data provided.
[e]The market price per share at the end of 2008 was $18.06.

Activity

Bartlett Company's inventory appears to be in good shape. Its inventory management seems to have improved, and in 2009 it performed at a level above that of the industry. The firm may be experiencing some problems with accounts receivable. The average collection period seems to have crept up above that of the industry. Bartlett also appears to be slow in paying its bills; it pays nearly 30 days slower than the industry average. This could adversely affect the firm's credit standing. Although overall liquidity appears to be good, the management of receivables and payables should be examined. Bartlett's total asset turnover reflects a decline in the efficiency of total asset utilization between 2007 and 2008. Although in 2009 it rose to a level considerably above the industry average, it appears that the pre-2008 level of efficiency has not yet been achieved.

Debt

Bartlett Company's indebtedness increased over the 2007–2009 period and is currently above the industry average. Although this increase in the debt ratio could be cause for alarm, the firm's ability to meet interest and fixed-payment obligations improved, from 2008 to 2009, to a level that outperforms the industry. The firm's increased indebtedness in 2008 apparently caused a deterioration in its ability to pay debt adequately. However, Bartlett has evidently improved its income in 2009 so that it is able to meet its interest and fixed-payment obligations at a level consistent with the average in the industry. In summary, it appears that although 2008 was an off year, the company's improved ability to pay debts in 2009 compensates for its increased degree of indebtedness.

Profitability

Bartlett's profitability relative to sales in 2009 was better than the average company in the industry, although it did not match the firm's 2007 performance. Although the *gross* profit margin was better in 2008 and 2009 than in 2007, higher levels of operating and interest expenses in 2008 and 2009 appear to have caused the 2009 *net* profit margin to fall below that of 2007. However, Bartlett Company's 2009 net profit margin is quite favorable when compared to the industry average.

The firm's earnings per share, return on total assets, and return on common equity behaved much as its net profit margin did over the 2007–2009 period. Bartlett appears to have experienced either a sizable drop in sales between 2007 and 2008 or a rapid expansion in assets during that period. The exceptionally high 2009 level of return on common equity suggests that the firm is performing quite well. The firm's above-average returns—net profit margin, EPS, ROA, and ROE—may be attributable to the fact that it is more risky than average. A look at market ratios is helpful in assessing risk.

Market

Investors have greater confidence in the firm in 2009 than in the prior two years, as reflected in the price/earnings (P/E) ratio of 11.1. However, this ratio is below the industry average. The P/E ratio suggests that the firm's risk has declined but remains above that of the average firm in its industry. The firm's market/book

(M/B) ratio has increased over the 2007–2009 period, and in 2009 it exceeds the industry average. This implies that investors are optimistic about the firm's future performance. The P/E and M/B ratios reflect the firm's increased profitability over the 2007–2009 period: Investors expect to earn high future returns as compensation for the firm's above-average risk.

In summary, the firm appears to be growing and has recently undergone an expansion in assets, financed primarily through the use of debt. The 2008–2009 period seems to reflect a phase of adjustment and recovery from the rapid growth in assets. Bartlett's sales, profits, and other performance factors seem to be growing with the increase in the size of the operation. In addition, the market response to these accomplishments appears to have been positive. In short, the firm seems to have done well in 2009.

DuPont System of Analysis

DuPont system of analysis
System used to dissect the firm's financial statements and to assess its financial condition.

The **DuPont system of analysis** is used to dissect the firm's financial statements and to assess its financial condition. It merges the income statement and balance sheet into two summary measures of profitability: return on total assets (ROA) and return on common equity (ROE). Figure 2.2 (see page 72) depicts the basic DuPont system with Bartlett Company's 2009 monetary and ratio values. The upper portion of the chart summarizes the income statement activities; the lower portion summarizes the balance sheet activities.

DuPont Formula

The DuPont system first brings together the *net profit margin*, which measures the firm's profitability on sales, with its *total asset turnover*, which indicates how efficiently the firm has used its assets to generate sales. In the **DuPont formula**, the product of these two ratios results in the *return on total assets (ROA)*:

DuPont formula
Multiplies the firm's *net profit margin* by its *total asset turnover* to calculate the firm's *return on total assets (ROA)*.

$$ROA = \text{Net profit margin} \times \text{Total asset turnover}$$

Substituting the appropriate formulas into the equation and simplifying results in the formula given earlier,

$$ROA = \frac{\text{Earnings available for common stockholders}}{\text{Sales}} \times \frac{\text{Sales}}{\text{Total assets}} = \frac{\text{Earnings available for common stockholders}}{\text{Total assets}}$$

When the 2009 values of the net profit margin and total asset turnover for Bartlett Company, calculated earlier, are substituted into the DuPont formula, the result is

$$ROA = 7.2\% \times 0.85 = 6.1\%$$

This value is the same as that calculated directly in an earlier section (page 65). The DuPont formula enables the firm to break down its return into profit-on-sales and efficiency-of-asset-use components. Typically, a firm with a low net profit margin has a high total asset turnover, which results in a reasonably good return on total assets. Often, the opposite situation exists.

FIGURE 2.2   **DuPont System of Analysis**

The DuPont system of analysis with application to Bartlett Company (2009)

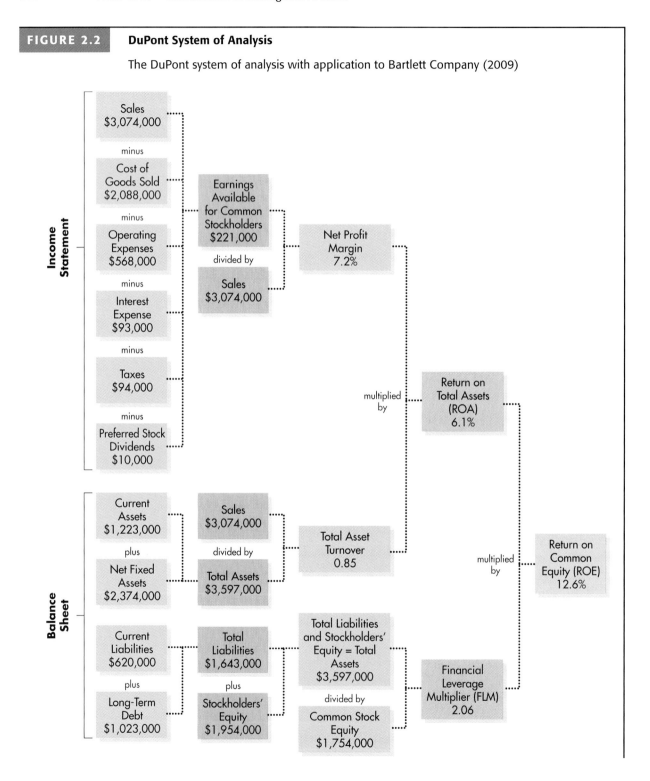

Modified DuPont Formula

modified DuPont formula
Relates the firm's *return on total assets (ROA)* to its *return on common equity (ROE)* using the *financial leverage multiplier (FLM)*.

financial leverage multiplier (FLM)
The ratio of the firm's total assets to its common stock equity.

The second step in the DuPont system employs the **modified DuPont formula.** This formula relates the firm's *return on total assets (ROA)* to its *return on common equity (ROE)*. The latter is calculated by multiplying the return on total assets (ROA) by the **financial leverage multiplier (FLM)**, which is the ratio of total assets to common stock equity:

$$ROE = ROA \times FLM$$

Substituting the appropriate formulas into the equation and simplifying results in the formula given earlier,

$$ROE = \frac{\text{Earnings available for common stockholders}}{\text{Total assets}} \times \frac{\text{Total assets}}{\text{Common stock equity}} = \frac{\text{Earnings available for common stockholders}}{\text{Common stock equity}}$$

Use of the financial leverage multiplier (FLM) to convert the ROA into the ROE reflects the impact of financial leverage on owners' return. Substituting the values for Bartlett Company's ROA of 6.1 percent, calculated earlier, and Bartlett's FLM of 2.06 ($3,597,000 total assets ÷ $1,754,000 common stock equity) into the modified DuPont formula yields

$$ROE = 6.1\% \times 2.06 = 12.6\%$$

The 12.6 percent ROE calculated by using the modified DuPont formula is the same as that calculated directly (page 65).

Applying the DuPont System

The advantage of the DuPont system is that it allows the firm to break its return on equity into a profit-on-sales component (net profit margin), an efficiency-of-asset-use component (total asset turnover), and a use-of-financial-leverage component (financial leverage multiplier). The total return to owners therefore can be analyzed in these important dimensions.

The use of the DuPont system of analysis as a diagnostic tool is best explained using Figure 2.2. Beginning with the rightmost value—the ROE—the financial analyst moves to the left, dissecting and analyzing the inputs to the formula to isolate the probable cause of the resulting above-average (or below-average) value.

Example

For the sake of demonstration, let's ignore all industry average data in Table 2.8 and assume that Bartlett's ROE of 12.6 % is actually below the industry average. Moving to the left in Figure 2.2, we would examine the inputs to the ROE—the ROA and the FLM—relative to the industry averages. Let's assume that the FLM is in line with the industry average, but the ROA is below the industry average. Moving farther to the left, we examine the two inputs to the ROA—the net profit margin and total asset turnover. Assume that the net profit margin is in line with the industry average, but the total asset turnover is below the industry average. Moving still farther to the left, we find that whereas the firm's sales are consistent with the industry value, Bartlett's total assets have grown significantly during the past year. Looking farther to the left, we would review the firm's activity ratios for current assets. Let's say that whereas the firm's inventory turnover is in line with the industry average, its average collection period is well above the industry average.

We can readily trace the possible problem back to its cause: Bartlett's low ROE is primarily the consequence of slow collections of accounts receivable, which resulted in high levels of receivables and therefore high levels of total assets. The high total assets slowed Bartlett's total asset turnover, driving down its ROA, which then drove down its ROE. By using the DuPont system of analysis to dissect Bartlett's overall returns as measured by its ROE, we found that slow collections of receivables caused the below-industry-average ROE. Clearly, the firm needs to better manage its credit operations.

REVIEW QUESTIONS

2–17 Financial ratio analysis is often divided into five areas: *liquidity, activity, debt, profitability,* and *market* ratios. Differentiate each of these areas of analysis from the others. Which is of the greatest concern to creditors?

2–18 Describe how you would use a large number of ratios to perform a complete ratio analysis of the firm.

2–19 What three areas of analysis are combined in the *modified DuPont formula?* Explain how the *DuPont system of analysis* is used to dissect the firm's results and isolate their causes.

Summary

Focus on Value

Financial managers review and analyze the firm's financial statements periodically, both to uncover developing problems and to assess the firm's progress toward achieving its goals. These actions are aimed at **preserving and creating value for the firm's owners.** Financial ratios enable financial managers to monitor the pulse of the firm and its progress toward its strategic goals. Although financial statements and financial ratios rely on accrual concepts, they can provide useful insights into important aspects of risk and return (cash flow) that affect share price.

Review of Learning Goals

LG 1 **Review the contents of the stockholders' report and the procedures for consolidating international financial statements.** The annual stockholders' report, which publicly owned corporations must provide to stockholders, documents the firm's financial activities of the past year. It includes the letter to stockholders and various subjective and factual information. It also contains four key financial statements: the income statement, the balance sheet, the statement of stockholders' equity (or its abbreviated form, the statement of retained earnings), and the statement of cash flows. Notes describing the technical aspects of the financial statements follow. Financial statements of companies that have operations whose cash flows are denominated in one or more foreign currencies must be translated into dollars in accordance with *FASB Standard No. 52.*

Understand who uses financial ratios, and how. Ratio analysis enables stockholders, lenders, and the firm's managers to evaluate the firm's financial performance. It can be performed on a cross-sectional or a time-series basis. Benchmarking is a popular type of cross-sectional analysis. Users of ratios should understand the cautions that apply to their use.

Use ratios to analyze a firm's liquidity and activity. Liquidity, or the ability of the firm to pay its bills as they come due, can be measured by the current ratio and the quick (acid-test) ratio. Activity ratios measure the speed with which accounts are converted into sales or cash—inflows or outflows. The activity of inventory can be measured by its turnover; that of accounts receivable by the average collection period; and that of accounts payable by the average payment period. Total asset turnover measures the efficiency with which the firm uses its assets to generate sales.

Discuss the relationship between debt and financial leverage and the ratios used to analyze a firm's debt. The more debt a firm uses, the greater its financial leverage, which magnifies both risk and return. Financial debt ratios measure both the degree of indebtedness and the ability to service debts. A common measure of indebtedness is the debt ratio. The ability to pay fixed charges can be measured by times interest earned and fixed-payment coverage ratios.

Use ratios to analyze a firm's profitability and its market value. The common-size income statement, which shows all items as a percentage of sales, can be used to determine gross profit margin, operating profit margin, and net profit margin. Other measures of profitability include earnings per share, return on total assets, and return on common equity. Market ratios include the price/earnings ratio and the market/book ratio.

Use a summary of financial ratios and the DuPont system of analysis to perform a complete ratio analysis. A summary of all ratios can be used to perform a complete ratio analysis using cross-sectional and time-series analysis. The DuPont system of analysis is a diagnostic tool used to find the key areas responsible for the firm's financial performance. It enables the firm to break the return on common equity into three components: profit on sales, efficiency of asset use, and use of financial leverage.

Self-Test Problems (Solutions in Appendix B)

ST2–1   Ratio formulas and interpretations   Without referring to the text, indicate for each of the following ratios the formula for calculating it and the kinds of problems, if any, the firm is likely to have if that ratio is too high relative to the industry average. What if the ratio is too low relative to the industry average? Create a table similar to the one on the next page and fill in the empty blocks.

Ratio	Too high	Too low
Current ratio =		
Inventory turnover =		
Times interest earned =	✕	
Gross profit margin =		
Return on total assets =	✕	
Price/earnings (P/E) ratio =		

   ST2–2 **Balance sheet completion using ratios**   Complete the 2009 balance sheet for O'Keefe Industries using the information that follows it.

O'Keefe Industries
Balance Sheet
December 31, 2009

Assets		Liabilities and Stockholders' Equity	
Cash	$32,720	Accounts payable	$120,000
Marketable securities	25,000	Notes payable	_____
Accounts receivable	_____	Accruals	20,000
Inventories	_____	Total current liabilities	_____
Total current assets	_____	Long-term debt	_____
Net fixed assets	_____	Stockholders' equity	$600,000
Total assets	$_____	Total liabilities and stockholders' equity	$_____

The following financial data for 2009 are also available:
(1) Sales totaled $1,800,000.
(2) The gross profit margin was 25%.
(3) Inventory turnover was 6.0.
(4) There are 365 days in the year.
(5) The average collection period was 40 days.
(6) The current ratio was 1.60.
(7) The total asset turnover ratio was 1.20.
(8) The debt ratio was 60%.

Warm-Up Exercises

A blue box (■) indicates exercises available in .

  You are a summer intern at the office of a local tax-preparer. To test your basic knowledge of financial statements, your manager, who graduated from your alma mater 2 years ago, gives you the following list of accounts and asks you to prepare a simple income statement using those accounts.

Accounts	($000,000)
Depreciation	25
General and administrative expenses	22
Sales	345
Sales expenses	18
Cost of goods sold	255
Lease expense	4
Interest expense	3

a. Arrange the accounts into a well-labeled income statement. Make sure you label and solve for gross profit, operating profit, and net profit before taxes.
b. Using a 35% tax rate, calculate taxes paid and net profit after taxes.
c. Assuming a dividend of $1.10 per share with 4.25 million shares outstanding, calculate EPS and additions to retained earnings.

E2–2 Explain why the income statement can also be called a "profit and loss statement." What exactly does the word "balance" mean in the title of the balance sheet? Why do we balance the two halves?

E2–3 Cooper Industries, Inc., began 2009 with retained earnings of $25.32 million. During the year it paid four quarterly dividends of $0.35 per share to 2.75 million common stockholders. Preferred stockholders, holding 500,000 shares, were paid two semiannual dividends of $0.75 per share. The firm had a net profit after taxes of $5.15 million. Prepare the statement of retained earnings for the year ended December 31, 2009.

E2–4 Bluestone Metals, Inc., is a metal fabrication firm which manufactures prefabricated metal parts for customers in a variety of industries. The firm's motto is "If you need it, we can make it." The CEO of Bluestone recently held a board meeting during which he extolled the virtues of the corporation. The company, he stated confidently, had the capability to build any product and could do so using a lean manufacturing model. The firm would soon be profitable, claimed the CEO, because the company used state-of-the-art technology to build a variety of products while keeping inventory levels low. As a business press reporter, you have calculated some ratios to analyze the financial health of the firm. Bluestone's current ratios and quick ratios for the past 6 years are shown in the table below:

	2004	2005	2006	2007	2008	2009
Current ratio	1.2	1.4	1.3	1.6	1.8	2.2
Quick ratio	1.1	1.3	1.2	0.8	0.6	0.4

What do you think of the CEO's claim that the firm is lean and soon to be profitable? (*Hint*: Is there a possible warning sign in the relationship between the two ratios?)

E2–5 If we know that a firm has a net profit margin of 4.5%, total asset turnover of 0.72, and a financial leverage multiplier of 1.43, what is its ROE? What is the advantage to using the DuPont system to calculate ROE over the direct calculation of earnings available for common stockholders divided by common stock equity?

Problems

A blue box (■) indicates problems available in myfinancelab.

P2–1 **Reviewing basic financial statements** The income statement for the year ended December 31, 2009, the balance sheets for December 31, 2009 and 2008, and the statement of retained earnings for the year ended December 31, 2009, for Technica, Inc., are given below and on page 79. Briefly discuss the form and informational content of each of these statements.

Technica, Inc. Income Statement for the Year Ended December 31, 2009		
Sales revenue		$600,000
Less: Cost of goods sold		460,000
Gross profits		$140,000
Less: Operating expenses		
General and administrative expenses	$30,000	
Depreciation expense	30,000	
Total operating expense		60,000
Operating profits		$ 80,000
Less: Interest expense		10,000
Net profits before taxes		$ 70,000
Less: Taxes		27,100
Earnings available for common stockholders		$ 42,900
Earnings per share (EPS)		$2.15

Technica, Inc. Balance Sheets					
	December 31			December 31	
Assets	2009	2008	Liabilities and Stockholders' Equity	2009	2008
Cash	$ 15,000	$ 16,000	Accounts payable	$ 57,000	$ 49,000
Marketable securities	7,200	8,000	Notes payable	13,000	16,000
Accounts receivable	34,100	42,200	Accruals	5,000	6,000
Inventories	82,000	50,000	Total current liabilities	$ 75,000	$ 71,000
Total current assets	$138,300	$116,200	Long-term debt	$150,000	$160,000
Land and buildings	$150,000	$150,000	Stockholders' equity		
Machinery and equipment	200,000	190,000	Common stock equity (shares outstanding: 19,500 in 2009 and 20,000 in 2008)	$110,200	$120,000
Furniture and fixtures	54,000	50,000			
Other	11,000	10,000			
Total gross fixed assets	$415,000	$400,000	Retained earnings	73,100	50,200
Less: Accumulated depreciation	145,000	115,000	Total stockholders' equity	$183,300	$170,200
Net fixed assets	$270,000	$285,000	Total liabilities and stockholders' equity	$408,300	$401,200
Total assets	$408,300	$401,200			

Technica, Inc. Statement of Retained Earnings for the Year Ended December 31, 2009	
Retained earnings balance (January 1, 2009)	$50,200
Plus: Net profits after taxes (for 2009)	42,900
Less: Cash dividends (paid during 2009)	20,000
Retained earnings balance (December 31, 2009)	$73,100

P2–2 **Financial statement account identification**   Mark each of the accounts listed in the following table as follows:

a. In column (1), indicate in which statement—income statement (IS) or balance sheet (BS)—the account belongs.

b. In column (2), indicate whether the account is a current asset (CA), current liability (CL), expense (E), fixed asset (FA), long-term debt (LTD), revenue (R), or stockholders' equity (SE).

Account name	(1) Statement	(2) Type of account
Accounts payable	_____	_____
Accounts receivable	_____	_____
Accruals	_____	_____
Accumulated depreciation	_____	_____
Administrative expense	_____	_____
Buildings	_____	_____
Cash	_____	_____
Common stock (at par)	_____	_____
Cost of goods sold	_____	_____
Depreciation	_____	_____
Equipment	_____	_____
General expense	_____	_____
Interest expense	_____	_____
Inventories	_____	_____
Land	_____	_____
Long-term debts	_____	_____
Machinery	_____	_____
Marketable securities	_____	_____
Notes payable	_____	_____
Operating expense	_____	_____
Paid-in capital in excess of par	_____	_____
Preferred stock	_____	_____
Preferred stock dividends	_____	_____
Retained earnings	_____	_____
Sales revenue	_____	_____
Selling expense	_____	_____
Taxes	_____	_____
Vehicles	_____	_____

Conrad Air, Inc. Balance Sheet as of December 31, 2009			
Assets		**Liabilities and Stockholders' Equity**	
Cash	$ 120,000	Accounts payable	$ 70,000
Marketable securities	35,000	Short-term notes	55,000
Accounts receivable	45,000	Current liabilities	$ 125,000
Inventories	130,000	Long-term debt	$2,700,000
Current assets	$ 330,000	Total liabilities	$2,825,000
Equipment	$2,970,000	Common stock	$ 500,000
Buildings	1,600,000	Retained earnings	1,575,000
Fixed assets	$4,570,000	Stockholders' equity	$2,075,000
Total assets	$4,900,000	Total liabilities and equity	$4,900,000

a. Conrad paid no dividends during the year and invested the funds in marketable securities.
b. Conrad paid dividends totaling $500,000 and used the balance of the net income to retire (pay off) long-term debt.
c. Conrad paid dividends totaling $500,000 and invested the balance of the net income in building a new hangar.
d. Conrad paid out all $1,365,000 as dividends to its stockholders.

P2–9 Initial sale price of common stock Beck Corporation has one issue of preferred stock and one issue of common stock outstanding. Given Beck's stockholders' equity account that follows, determine the original price per share at which the firm sold its single issue of common stock.

Stockholders' equity ($000)	
Preferred stock	$ 125
Common stock ($0.75 par, 300,000 shares outstanding)	225
Paid-in capital in excess of par on common stock	2,625
Retained earnings	900
Total stockholders' equity	$3,875

P2–10 Statement of retained earnings Hayes Enterprises began 2009 with a retained earnings balance of $928,000. During 2009, the firm earned $377,000 after taxes. From this amount, preferred stockholders were paid $47,000 in dividends. At year-end 2009, the firm's retained earnings totaled $1,048,000. The firm had 140,000 shares of common stock outstanding during 2009.
a. Prepare a statement of retained earnings for the year ended December 31, 2009, for Hayes Enterprises. (*Note:* Be sure to calculate and include the amount of cash dividends paid in 2009.)
b. Calculate the firm's 2009 earnings per share (EPS).
c. How large a per-share cash dividend did the firm pay on common stock during 2009?

P2–11 **Ratio comparisons**   Robert Arias recently inherited a stock portfolio from his uncle. Wishing to learn more about the companies in which he is now invested, Robert performs a ratio analysis on each one and decides to compare them to each other. Some of his ratios are listed below.

Ratio	Island Electric Utility	Burger Heaven	Fink Software	Roland Motors
Current ratio	1.10	1.3	6.8	4.5
Quick ratio	0.90	0.82	5.2	3.7
Debt ratio	0.68	0.46	0	0.35
Net profit margin	6.2%	14.3%	28.5%	8.4%

Assuming that his uncle was a wise investor who assembled the portfolio with care, Robert finds the wide differences in these ratios confusing. Help him out.
a. What problems might Robert encounter in comparing these companies to one another on the basis of their ratios?
b. Why might the current and quick ratios for the electric utility and the fast-food stock be so much lower than the same ratios for the other companies?
c. Why might it be all right for the electric utility to carry a large amount of debt, but not the software company?
d. Why wouldn't investors invest all of their money in software companies instead of in less profitable companies? (Focus on risk and return.)

  Liquidity management   Bauman Company's total current assets, total current liabilities, and inventory for each of the past 4 years follow:

Item	2006	2007	2008	2009
Total current assets	$16,950	$21,900	$22,500	$27,000
Total current liabilities	9,000	12,600	12,600	17,400
Inventory	6,000	6,900	6,900	7,200

a. Calculate the firm's current and quick ratios for each year. Compare the resulting time series for these measures of liquidity.
b. Comment on the firm's liquidity over the 2006–2009 period.
c. If you were told that Bauman Company's inventory turnover for each year in the 2006–2009 period and the industry averages were as follows, would this information support or conflict with your evaluation in part **b**? Why?

Inventory turnover	2006	2007	2008	2009
Bauman Company	6.3	6.8	7.0	6.4
Industry average	10.6	11.2	10.8	11.0

PERSONAL FINANCE PROBLEM

 P2–13 **Liquidity ratio** Josh Smith has compiled some of his personal financial data in order to determine his liquidity position. The data are as follows.

Account	Amount
Cash	$3,200
Marketable securities	1,000
Checking account	800
Credit card payables	1,200
Short-term notes payable	900

a. Calculate Josh's *liquidity ratio*.
b. Several of Josh's friends have told him that they have liquidity ratios of about 1.8. How would you analyze Josh's liquidity relative to his friends?

 P2–14 **Inventory management** Wilkins Manufacturing has annual sales of $4 million and a gross profit margin of 40%. Its *end-of-quarter inventories* are

Quarter	Inventory
1	$ 400,000
2	800,000
3	1,200,000
4	200,000

a. Find the average quarterly inventory and use it to calculate the firm's inventory turnover and the average age of inventory.
b. Assuming that the company is in an industry with an average inventory turnover of 2.0, how would you evaluate the activity of Wilkins' inventory?

 P2–15 **Accounts receivable management** An evaluation of the books of Blair Supply, which follows, gives the end-of-year accounts receivable balance, which is believed to consist of amounts originating in the months indicated. The company had annual sales of $2.4 million. The firm extends 30-day credit terms.

Month of origin	Amounts receivable
July	$ 3,875
August	2,000
September	34,025
October	15,100
November	52,000
December	193,000
Year-end accounts receivable	$300,000

a. Use the year-end total to evaluate the firm's collection system.
b. If 70% of the firm's sales occur between July and December, would this affect the validity of your conclusion in part **a**? Explain.

P2–16 Debt analysis Springfield Bank is evaluating Creek Enterprises, which has requested a $4,000,000 loan, to assess the firm's financial leverage and financial risk. On the basis of the debt ratios for Creek, along with the industry averages (see top of page 86) and Creek's recent financial statements (below), evaluate and recommend appropriate action on the loan request.

Creek Enterprises
Income Statement
for the Year Ended December 31, 2009

Sales revenue		$30,000,000
Less: Cost of goods sold		21,000,000
Gross profits		$ 9,000,000
Less: Operating expenses		
Selling expense	$3,000,000	
General and administrative expenses	1,800,000	
Lease expense	200,000	
Depreciation expense	1,000,000	
Total operating expense		6,000,000
Operating profits		$ 3,000,000
Less: Interest expense		1,000,000
Net profits before taxes		$ 2,000,000
Less: Taxes (rate = 40%)		800,000
Net profits after taxes		$ 1,200,000
Less: Preferred stock dividends		100,000
Earnings available for common stockholders		$ 1,100,000

Creek Enterprises
Balance Sheet
December 31, 2009

Assets		Liabilities and Stockholders' Equity	
Current assets		Current liabilities	
Cash	$ 1,000,000	Accounts payable	$ 8,000,000
Marketable securities	3,000,000	Notes payable	8,000,000
Accounts receivable	12,000,000	Accruals	500,000
Inventories	7,500,000	Total current liabilities	$16,500,000
Total current assets	$23,500,000	Long-term debt (includes financial leases)[b]	$20,000,000
Gross fixed assets (at cost)[a]		Stockholders' equity	
Land and buildings	$11,000,000	Preferred stock (25,000 shares,	
Machinery and equipment	20,500,000	$4 dividend)	$ 2,500,000
Furniture and fixtures	8,000,000	Common stock (1 million shares at $5 par)	5,000,000
Gross fixed assets	$39,500,000	Paid-in capital in excess of par value	4,000,000
Less: Accumulated depreciation	13,000,000	Retained earnings	2,000,000
Net fixed assets	$26,500,000	Total stockholders' equity	$13,500,000
Total assets	$50,000,000	Total liabilities and stockholders' equity	$50,000,000

[a]The firm has a 4-year financial lease requiring annual beginning-of-year payments of $200,000. Three years of the lease have yet to run.
[b]Required annual principal payments are $800,000.

Industry averages	
Debt ratio	0.51
Times interest earned ratio	7.30
Fixed-payment coverage ratio	1.85

P2–17 **Common-size statement analysis**   A common-size income statement for Creek Enterprises' 2008 operations follows. Using the firm's 2009 income statement presented in Problem 2–16, develop the 2009 common-size income statement and compare it to the 2008 statement. Which areas require further analysis and investigation?

Creek Enterprises Common-Size Income Statement for the Year Ended December 31, 2008		
Sales revenue ($35,000,000)		100.0%
Less: Cost of goods sold		65.9
Gross profits		34.1%
Less: Operating expenses		
Selling expense	12.7%	
General and administrative expenses	6.3	
Lease expense	0.6	
Depreciation expense	3.6	
Total operating expense		23.2
Operating profits		10.9%
Less: Interest expense		1.5
Net profits before taxes		9.4%
Less: Taxes (rate = 40%)		3.8
Net profits after taxes		5.6%
Less: Preferred stock dividends		0.1
Earnings available for common stockholders		5.5%

P2–18 **Ratio proficiency**   McDougal Printing, Inc., had sales totaling $40,000,000 in fiscal year 2009. Some ratios for the company are listed below. Use this information to determine the dollar values of various income statement and balance sheet accounts as requested.

McDougal Printing, Inc. Year Ended December 31, 2009	
Sales	$40,000,000
Gross profit margin	80%
Operating profit margin	35%
Net profit margin	8%
Return on total assets	16%
Return on common equity	20%
Total asset turnover	2
Average collection period	62.2 days

Calculate values for the following:

a. Gross profits
b. Cost of goods sold
c. Operating profits
d. Operating expenses

e. Earnings available for common stockholders
f. Total assets
g. Total common stock equity
h. Accounts receivable

 P2–19 **Cross-sectional ratio analysis**   Use the financial statements below for Fox Manufacturing Company for the year ended December 31, 2009, along with the industry average ratios at the top of page 88, to:

a. Prepare and interpret a complete ratio analysis of the firm's 2009 operations.
b. Summarize your findings and make recommendations.

Fox Manufacturing Company
Income Statement
for the Year Ended December 31, 2009

Sales revenue		$600,000
Less: Cost of goods sold		460,000
Gross profits		$140,000
Less: Operating expenses		
General and administrative expenses	$30,000	
Depreciation expense	30,000	
Total operating expense		60,000
Operating profits		$ 80,000
Less: Interest expense		10,000
Net profits before taxes		$ 70,000
Less: Taxes		27,100
Net profits after taxes (earnings available for common stockholders)		$ 42,900
Earnings per share (EPS)		$2.15

Fox Manufacturing Company
Balance Sheet
December 31, 2009

Assets		Liabilities and Stockholders' Equity	
Cash	$ 15,000	Accounts payable	$ 57,000
Marketable securities	7,200	Notes payable	13,000
Accounts receivable	34,100	Accruals	5,000
Inventories	82,000	Total current liabilities	$ 75,000
Total current assets	$138,300	Long-term debt	$150,000
Net fixed assets	$270,000	Stockholders' equity	
Total assets	$408,300	Common stock equity	
		(20,000 shares outstanding)	$110,200
		Retained earnings	73,100
		Total stockholders' equity	$183,300
		Total liabilities and stockholders' equity	$408,300

Ratio	Industry average, 2009
Current ratio	2.35
Quick ratio	0.87
Inventory turnover[a]	4.55
Average collection period[a]	35.8 days
Total asset turnover	1.09
Debt ratio	0.300
Times interest earned ratio	12.3
Gross profit margin	0.202
Operating profit margin	0.135
Net profit margin	0.091
Return on total assets (ROA)	0.099
Return on common equity (ROE)	0.167
Earnings per share (EPS)	$3.10

[a]Based on a 365-day year and on end-of-year figures.

P2–20   Financial statement analysis   The financial statements of Zach Industries for the year ended December 31, 2009, follow.

Zach Industries Income Statement for the Year Ended December 31, 2009	
Sales revenue	$160,000
Less: Cost of goods sold	106,000
Gross profits	$ 54,000
Less: Operating expenses	
Selling expense	$ 16,000
General and administrative expenses	10,000
Lease expense	1,000
Depreciation expense	10,000
Total operating expense	$ 37,000
Operating profits	$ 17,000
Less: Interest expense	6,100
Net profits before taxes	$ 10,900
Less: Taxes	4,360
Net profits after taxes	$ 6,540

Zach Industries Balance Sheet December 31, 2009	
Assets	
Cash	$ 500
Marketable securities	1,000
Accounts receivable	25,000
Inventories	45,500
Total current assets	$ 72,000
Land	$ 26,000
Buildings and equipment	90,000
Less: Accumulated depreciation	38,000
Net fixed assets	$ 78,000
Total assets	$150,000
Liabilities and Stockholders' Equity	
Accounts payable	$ 22,000
Notes payable	47,000
Total current liabilities	$ 69,000
Long-term debt	$ 22,950
Common stock[a]	$ 31,500
Retained earnings	$ 26,550
Total liabilities and stockholders' equity	$150,000

[a]The firm's 3,000 outstanding shares of common stock closed 2009 at a price of $25 per share.

a. Use the preceding financial statements to complete the following table. Assume the industry averages given in the table are applicable for both 2008 and 2009.

Ratio	Industry average	Actual 2008	Actual 2009
Current ratio	1.80	1.84	_____
Quick ratio	0.70	0.78	_____
Inventory turnover[a]	2.50	2.59	_____
Average collection period[a]	37.5 days	36.5 days	_____
Debt ratio	65%	67%	_____
Times interest earned ratio	3.8	4.0	_____
Gross profit margin	38%	40%	_____
Net profit margin	3.5%	3.6%	_____
Return on total assets	4.0%	4.0%	_____
Return on common equity	9.5%	8.0%	_____
Market/book ratio	1.1	1.2	_____

[a]Based on a 365-day year and on end-of-year figures.

b. Analyze Zach Industries' financial condition as it is related to (1) liquidity, (2) activity, (3) debt, (4) profitability, and (5) market. Summarize the company's overall financial condition.

P2–21 DuPont system of analysis   Use the following ratio information for Johnson International and the industry averages for Johnson's line of business to:
a. Construct the DuPont system of analysis for both Johnson and the industry.
b. Evaluate Johnson (and the industry) over the 3-year period.
c. Indicate in which areas Johnson requires further analysis. Why?

Johnson	2007	2008	2009
Financial leverage multiplier	1.75	1.75	1.85
Net profit margin	0.059	0.058	0.049
Total asset turnover	2.11	2.18	2.34

Industry Averages			
Financial leverage multiplier	1.67	1.69	1.64
Net profit margin	0.054	0.047	0.041
Total asset turnover	2.05	2.13	2.15

P2–22 ETHICS PROBLEM   Do some reading in periodicals and/or on the Internet to find out more about the Sarbanes-Oxley Act's provisions for companies. Select one of those provisions, and indicate why you think financial statements will be more trustworthy if company financial executives implement this provision of SOX.

Chapter 2 Case

Assessing Martin Manufacturing's Current Financial Position

Terri Spiro, an experienced budget analyst at Martin Manufacturing Company, has been charged with assessing the firm's financial performance during 2009 and its financial position at year-end 2009. To complete this assignment, she gathered the firm's 2009 financial statements (below and on page 91). In addition, Terri obtained the firm's ratio values for 2007 and 2008, along with the 2009 industry average ratios (also applicable to 2007 and 2008). These are presented in the table on page 92.

Martin Manufacturing Company Income Statement for the Year Ended December 31, 2009		
Sales revenue		$5,075,000
Less: Cost of goods sold		3,704,000
Gross profits		$1,371,000
Less: Operating expenses		
Selling expense	$650,000	
General and administrative expenses	416,000	
Depreciation expense	152,000	
Total operating expense		1,218,000
Operating profits		$ 153,000
Less: Interest expense		93,000
Net profits before taxes		$ 60,000
Less: Taxes (rate = 40%)		24,000
Net profits after taxes		$ 36,000
Less: Preferred stock dividends		3,000
Earnings available for common stockholders		$ 33,000
Earnings per share (EPS)		$0.33

Martin Manufacturing Company
Balance Sheets

Assets	December 31	
	2009	2008
Current assets		
Cash	$ 25,000	$ 24,100
Accounts receivable	805,556	763,900
Inventories	700,625	763,445
Total current assets	$1,531,181	$1,551,445
Gross fixed assets (at cost)	$2,093,819	$1,691,707
Less: Accumulated depreciation	500,000	348,000
Net fixed assets	$1,593,819	$1,343,707
Total assets	$3,125,000	$2,895,152

Liabilities and Stockholders' Equity		
Current liabilities		
Accounts payable	$ 230,000	$ 400,500
Notes payable	311,000	370,000
Accruals	75,000	100,902
Total current liabilities	$ 616,000	$ 871,402
Long-term debt	$1,165,250	$ 700,000
Total liabilities	$1,781,250	$1,571,402
Stockholders' equity		
Preferred stock (2,500 shares, $1.20 dividend)	$ 50,000	$ 50,000
Common stock (100,000 shares at $4 par)[a]	400,000	400,000
Paid-in capital in excess of par value	593,750	593,750
Retained earnings	300,000	280,000
Total stockholders' equity	$1,343,750	$1,323,750
Total liabilities and stockholders' equity	$3,125,000	$2,895,152

[a]The firm's 100,000 outstanding shares of common stock closed 2009 at a price of $11.38 per share.

| | | Martin Manufacturing Company Historical and Industry Average Ratios | | |
Ratio	Actual 2007	Actual 2008	Actual 2009	Industry average 2009
Current ratio	1.7	1.8	_____	1.5
Quick ratio	1.0	0.9	_____	1.2
Inventory turnover (times)	5.2	5.0	_____	10.2
Average collection period	50.7 days	55.8 days	_____	46 days
Total asset turnover (times)	1.5	1.5	_____	2.0
Debt ratio	45.8%	54.3%	_____	24.5%
Times interest earned ratio	2.2	1.9	_____	2.5
Gross profit margin	27.5%	28.0%	_____	26.0%
Net profit margin	1.1%	1.0%	_____	1.2%
Return on total assets (ROA)	1.7%	1.5%	_____	2.4%
Return on common equity (ROE)	3.1%	3.3%	_____	3.2%
Price/earnings (P/E) ratio	33.5	38.7	_____	43.4
Market/book (M/B) ratio	1.0	1.1	_____	1.2

To Do

a. Calculate the firm's 2009 financial ratios, and then fill in the preceding table. (Assume a 365-day year.)
b. Analyze the firm's current financial position from both a cross-sectional and a time-series viewpoint. Break your analysis into evaluations of the firm's liquidity, activity, debt, profitability, and market.
c. Summarize the firm's overall financial position on the basis of your findings in part b.

Spreadsheet Exercise

The income statement and balance sheet are the basic reports that a firm constructs for use by management and for distribution to stockholders, regulatory bodies, and the general public. They are the primary sources of historical financial information about the firm. Dayton Products, Inc., is a moderate-sized manufacturer. The company's management has asked you to perform a detailed financial statement analysis of the firm.

The income statement data for the years ending December 31, 2009 and 2008, respectively, is presented in the table at the top of page 93. (*Note:* Purchases of inventory during 2009 amounted to $109,865.)

Annual Income Statement (Values in millions)	For the year ended	
	December 31, 2009	December 31, 2008
Sales	$178,909.00	$187,510.00
Cost of goods sold	?	111,631.00
Selling, general, and administrative expenses	12,356.00	12,900.00
Other tax expense	33,572.00	33,377.00
Depreciation and amortization	12,103.00	7,944.00
Other income (add to EBIT to arrive at EBT)	3,147.00	3,323.00
Interest expense	398	293
Income tax rate (average)	35.324%	37.945%
Dividends paid per share	$1.47	$0.91
Basic EPS from total operations	$1.71	$2.25

You also have the following balance sheet information as of December 31, 2009 and 2008, respectively.

Annual Balance Sheet (Values in millions)	December 31, 2009	December, 31, 2008
Cash and equivalents	$ 7,229.00	$ 6,547.00
Receivables	21,163.00	19,549.00
Inventories	8,068.00	7,904.00
Other current assets	1,831.00	1,681.00
Property, plant, and equipment, gross	204,960.00	187,519.00
Accumulated depreciation and depletion	110,020.00	97,917.00
Other noncurrent assets	19,413.00	17,891.00
Accounts payable	$ 13,792.00	$ 22,862.00
Short-term debt payable	4,093.00	3,703.00
Other current liabilities	15,290.00	3,549.00
Long-term debt payable	6,655.00	7,099.00
Deferred income taxes	16,484.00	16,359.00
Other noncurrent liabilities	21,733.00	16,441.00
Retained earnings	$ 74,597.00	$ 73,161.00
Total common shares outstanding	6.7 billion	6.8 billion

To Do

a. Create a spreadsheet similar to the spreadsheet in Table 2.1 (which can be viewed at **www.prenhall.com/gitman**) to model the following:

    (1) A multiple-step comparative income statement for Dayton, Inc., for the periods ending December 31, 2009 and 2008. You must calculate the cost of goods sold for the year 2009.

    (2) A common-size income statement for Dayton, Inc., covering the years 2009 and 2008.

b. Create a spreadsheet similar to the spreadsheet in Table 2.2 (which can be viewed at **www.prenhall.com/gitman**) to model the following:

    (1) A detailed, comparative balance sheet for Dayton, Inc., for the years ended December 31, 2009 and 2008.

    (2) A common-size balance sheet for Dayton, Inc., covering the years 2009 and 2008.

c. Create a spreadsheet similar to the spreadsheet in Table 2.8 (which can be viewed at **www.prenhall.com/gitman**) to perform the following analysis:

    (1) Create a table that reflects both 2009 and 2008 operating ratios for Dayton, Inc., segmented into (a) liquidity, (b) activity, (c) debt, (d) profitability, and (e) market. Assume that the current market price for the stock is $90.

    (2) Compare the 2009 ratios to the 2008 ratios. Indicate whether the results "outperformed the prior year" or "underperformed relative to the prior year."

Web Exercise

Go to the book's companion website at **www.prenhall.com/gitman** to find the Web Exercise for this chapter.

> Remember to check the book's website at **www.prenhall.com/gitman** to find additional resources, including Web Exercises and a Web Case.

3 Cash Flow and Financial Planning

WHY THIS CHAPTER MATTERS TO YOU

In Your Professional Life

Accounting: You need to understand how depreciation is used for both tax and financial reporting purposes; how to develop the statement of cash flows; the primary focus on cash flows, rather than accruals, in financial decision making; and how pro forma financial statements are used within the firm.

Information systems: You need to understand the data that must be kept to record depreciation for tax and financial reporting; the information needs for strategic and operating plans; and what data are needed as inputs for preparing cash plans and profit plans.

Management: You need to understand the difference between strategic and operating plans, and the role of each; the importance of focusing on the firm's cash flows; and how use of pro forma statements can head off trouble for the firm.

Marketing: You need to understand the central role that marketing plays in formulating the firm's long-term, strategic plans, and the importance of the sales forecast as the key input for both cash planning and profit planning.

Operations: You need to understand how depreciation affects the value of the firm's plant assets; how the results of operations are captured in the statement of cash flows; that operations provide key inputs into the firm's short-term financial plans; and the distinction between fixed and variable operating costs.

In Your Personal Life

Individuals, like corporations, should focus on cash flow when planning and monitoring finances. You should establish short- and long-term financial goals (destinations) and develop personal financial plans (road maps) that will guide their achievement. Cash flows and financial plans are as important for individuals as for corporations.

LEARNING GOALS

LG 1 Understand tax depreciation procedures and the effect of depreciation on the firm's cash flows.

LG 2 Discuss the firm's statement of cash flows, operating cash flow, and free cash flow.

LG 3 Understand the financial planning process, including long-term (strategic) financial plans and short-term (operating) financial plans.

LG 4 Discuss the cash-planning process and the preparation, evaluation, and use of the cash budget.

LG 5 Explain the simplified procedures used to prepare and evaluate the pro forma income statement and the pro forma balance sheet.

LG 6 Evaluate the simplified approaches to pro forma financial statement preparation and the common uses of pro forma statements.

Cash flow is the primary focus of financial management. The goal is twofold: to meet the firm's financial obligations and to generate positive cash flow for its owners. Financial planning focuses on the firm's cash and profits—both of which are key elements of continued financial success, and even survival. This chapter outlines how the firm analyzes its cash flows, including the effects of depreciation and the roles of operating and free cash flows, and how it uses cash budgets and pro forma statements in the financial planning process.

3.1 | Analyzing the Firm's Cash Flow

Cash flow, the lifeblood of the firm, is the primary focus of the financial manager both in managing day-to-day finances and in planning and making strategic decisions focused on creating shareholder value. We therefore place major emphasis on estimating and analyzing the cash flows associated with the major financial decisions discussed and demonstrated throughout this book.

An important factor affecting a firm's cash flow is depreciation (and any other noncash charges). From an accounting perspective, a firm's cash flows can be summarized in the statement of cash flows, which was described in Chapter 2. From a strict financial perspective, firms often focus on both *operating cash flow*, which is used in managerial decision making, and *free cash flow*, which is closely watched by participants in the capital market. We begin our analysis of cash flow by considering the key aspects of depreciation, which is closely related to the firm's cash flow.

Depreciation

depreciation
The systematic charging of a portion of the costs of fixed assets against annual revenues over time.

Business firms are permitted for tax and financial reporting purposes to charge a portion of the costs of fixed assets systematically against annual revenues. This allocation of historical cost over time is called **depreciation.** For tax purposes, the depreciation of business assets is regulated by the Internal Revenue Code. Because the objectives of financial reporting sometimes differ from those of tax legislation, firms often use different depreciation methods for financial reporting than those required for tax purposes. Keeping two different sets of records for these two different purposes is legal.

modified accelerated cost recovery system (MACRS)
System used to determine the depreciation of assets for tax purposes.

Depreciation for tax purposes is determined by using the **modified accelerated cost recovery system (MACRS);** a variety of depreciation methods are available for financial reporting purposes. Before we discuss the methods of depreciating an asset, you must understand the depreciable value of an asset and the depreciable life of an asset.

Depreciable Value of an Asset

Under the basic MACRS procedures, the depreciable value of an asset (the amount to be depreciated) is its *full* cost, including outlays for installation.[1] No adjustment is required for expected salvage value.

---

1. Land values are *not* depreciable. Therefore, to determine the depreciable value of real estate, the value of the land is subtracted from the cost of real estate. In other words, only buildings and other improvements are depreciable.

TABLE 3.1	First Four Property Classes under MACRS

Property class (recovery period)	Definition
3 years	Research equipment and certain special tools
5 years	Computers, typewriters, copiers, duplicating equipment, cars, light-duty trucks, qualified technological equipment, and similar assets
7 years	Office furniture, fixtures, most manufacturing equipment, railroad track, and single-purpose agricultural and horticultural structures
10 years	Equipment used in petroleum refining or in the manufacture of tobacco products and certain food products

Example

Baker Corporation acquired a new machine at a cost of $38,000, with installation costs of $2,000. Regardless of its expected salvage value, the depreciable value of the machine is $40,000: $38,000 cost + $2,000 installation cost.

Depreciable Life of an Asset

depreciable life
Time period over which an asset is depreciated.

The time period over which an asset is depreciated—its **depreciable life**—can significantly affect the pattern of cash flows. The shorter the depreciable life, the more quickly the cash flow created by the depreciation write-off will be received. Given the financial manager's preference for faster receipt of cash flows, a shorter depreciable life is preferred to a longer one. However, the firm must abide by certain Internal Revenue Service (IRS) requirements for determining depreciable life. These MACRS standards, which apply to both new and used assets, require the taxpayer to use as an asset's depreciable life the appropriate MACRS **recovery period**.[2] There are six MACRS recovery periods—3, 5, 7, 10, 15, and 20 years—excluding real estate. It is customary to refer to the property classes as 3-, 5-, 7-, 10-, 15-, and 20-year property. The first four property classes—those routinely used by business—are defined in Table 3.1.

recovery period
The appropriate depreciable life of a particular asset as determined by MACRS.

Depreciation Methods

For *financial reporting purposes*, companies can use a variety of depreciation methods (straight-line, double-declining balance, and sum-of-the-years'-digits[3]). For *tax purposes*, assets in the first four MACRS property classes are depreciated by the double-declining balance (200%) method, using the half-year convention and switching to straight-line when advantageous. The *approximate percentages* (rounded to the nearest whole percent) written off each year for the first four property classes are shown in Table 3.2 (see page 98). Rather than using the percentages in the table, the firm can either use straight-line depreciation over the asset's recovery period with the half-year convention or use the alternative depreciation system. For purposes of this text, we will use the MACRS depreciation percentages, because they generally provide for the fastest write-off and therefore the best cash flow effects for the profitable firm.

---

2. An exception occurs in the case of assets depreciated under the *alternative depreciation system*. For convenience, in this text we ignore the depreciation of assets under this system.

3. For a review of these depreciation methods as well as other aspects of financial reporting, see any recently published financial accounting text.

TABLE 3.2	Rounded Depreciation Percentages by Recovery Year Using MACRS for First Four Property Classes

| | Percentage by recovery year[a] | | | |
Recovery year	3 years	5 years	7 years	10 years
1	33%	20%	14%	10%
2	45	32	25	18
3	15	19	18	14
4	7	12	12	12
5		12	9	9
6		5	9	8
7			9	7
8			4	6
9				6
10				6
11				4
Totals	100%	100%	100%	100%

[a]These percentages have been rounded to the nearest whole percent to simplify calculations while retaining realism. To calculate the *actual* depreciation for tax purposes, be sure to apply the actual unrounded percentages or directly apply double-declining balance (200%) depreciation using the half-year convention.

Because MACRS requires use of the half-year convention, assets are assumed to be acquired in the middle of the year; therefore only one-half of the first year's depreciation is recovered in the first year. As a result, the final half-year of depreciation is recovered in the year immediately following the asset's stated recovery period. In Table 3.2, the depreciation percentages for an n-year class asset are given for $n + 1$ years. For example, a 5-year asset is depreciated over 6 recovery years. The application of the tax depreciation percentages given in Table 3.2 can be demonstrated by a simple example.

Example

Baker Corporation acquired, for an installed cost of $40,000, a machine having a recovery period of 5 years. Using the applicable percentages from Table 3.2, Baker calculates the depreciation in each year as follows:

Year	Cost (1)	Percentages (from Table 3.2) (2)	Depreciation [(1) × (2)] (3)
1	$40,000	20%	$ 8,000
2	40,000	32	12,800
3	40,000	19	7,600
4	40,000	12	4,800
5	40,000	12	4,800
6	40,000	5	2,000
Totals		100%	$40,000

Column 3 shows that the full cost of the asset is written off over 6 recovery years.

Because financial managers focus primarily on cash flows, *only tax depreciation methods will be utilized throughout this textbook.*

Developing the Statement of Cash Flows

The *statement of cash flows,* introduced in Chapter 2, summarizes the firm's cash flow over a given period of time. Before discussing the statement and its interpretation, we will review the cash flow through the firm and the classification of inflows and outflows of cash.

The Firm's Cash Flows

Hint In finance, cash is king. Income statement profits are good, but they don't pay the bills, nor do asset owners accept them in place of cash.

Figure 3.1 (see page 100) illustrates the firm's cash flows. Note that marketable securities are considered the same as cash because of their highly liquid nature. Both cash and marketable securities represent a reservoir of liquidity that is *increased by cash inflows* and *decreased by cash outflows.*

operating flows
Cash flows directly related to sale and production of the firm's products and services.

investment flows
Cash flows associated with purchase and sale of both fixed assets and equity investments in other firms.

financing flows
Cash flows that result from debt and equity financing transactions; include incurrence and repayment of debt, cash inflow from the sale of stock, and cash outflows to repurchase stock or pay cash dividends.

Also note that the firm's cash flows can be divided into (1) operating flows, (2) investment flows, and (3) financing flows. The **operating flows** are cash inflows and outflows directly related to the sale and production of the firm's products and services. **Investment flows** are cash flows associated with the purchase and sale of both fixed assets and equity investments in other firms. Clearly, purchase transactions would result in cash outflows, whereas sales transactions would generate cash inflows. The **financing flows** result from debt and equity financing transactions. Incurring either short-term or long-term debt would result in a corresponding cash inflow; repaying debt would result in an outflow. Similarly, the sale of the company's stock would result in a cash inflow; the repurchase of stock or payment of cash dividends would result in an outflow.

Classifying Inflows and Outflows of Cash

The statement of cash flows, in effect, summarizes the inflows and outflows of cash during a given period. Table 3.3 (see page 100) classifies the basic inflows (sources) and outflows (uses) of cash. For example, if a firm's accounts payable balance increased by $1,000 during the year, the change would be an *inflow of cash.* If the firm's inventory increased by $2,500, the change would be an *outflow of cash.*

A few additional points can be made with respect to the classification scheme in Table 3.3:

1. A *decrease* in an asset, such as the firm's cash balance, is an *inflow of cash.* Why? Because cash that has been tied up in the asset is released and can be used for some other purpose, such as repaying a loan. On the other hand, an *increase* in the firm's cash balance is an *outflow of cash,* because additional cash is being tied up in the firm's cash balance.

noncash charge
An expense that is deducted on the income statement but does not involve the actual outlay of cash during the period; includes depreciation, amortization, and depletion.

2. Depreciation (like amortization and depletion) is a **noncash charge**—an expense that is deducted on the income statement but does not involve the

FIGURE 3.1   **Cash Flows**

The firm's cash flows

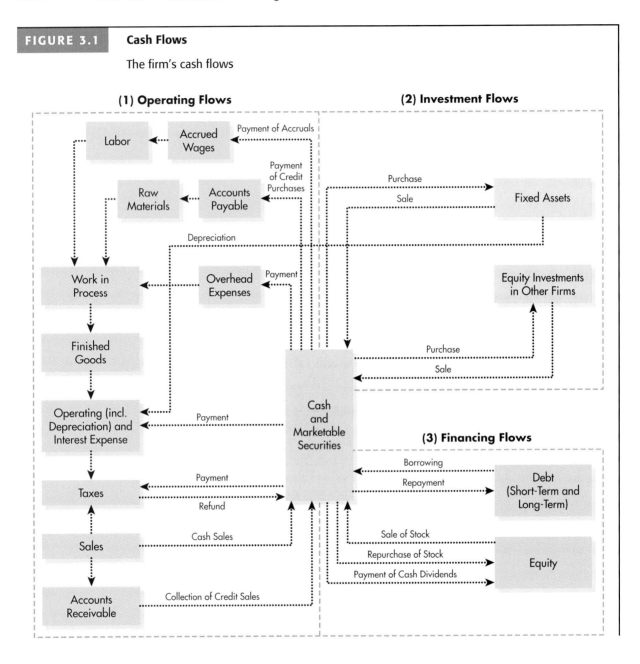

TABLE 3.3   **Inflows and Outflows of Cash**

Inflows (sources)	Outflows (uses)
Decrease in any asset	Increase in any asset
Increase in any liability	Decrease in any liability
Net profits after taxes	Net loss
Depreciation and other noncash charges	Dividends paid
Sale of stock	Repurchase or retirement of stock

actual outlay of cash during the period. Because it shields the firm from taxes by lowering taxable income, the noncash charge is considered a cash inflow. From a strict accounting perspective, adding depreciation back to the firm's net profits after taxes provides an estimate of cash flow from operations:[4]

$$\text{Cash flow from operations} = \\ \text{Net profits after taxes} + \text{Depreciation and other noncash charges} \quad \text{(3.1)}$$

Note that a firm can have a *net loss* (negative net profits after taxes) and still have positive cash flow from operations when depreciation (and other non-cash charges) during the period is greater than the net loss. In the statement of cash flows, net profits after taxes (or net losses) and depreciation (and other noncash charges) are therefore treated as separate entries.

3. We will refine Equation 3.1 in the next section and apply the revised equation (Equation 3.4) in Chapter 8 to estimate the relevant operating cash inflows associated with a firm's present and proposed fixed-asset investments.

4. Because depreciation is treated as a separate cash inflow, only *gross* rather than *net* changes in fixed assets appear on the statement of cash flows. This treatment avoids the potential double counting of depreciation.

5. Direct entries of changes in retained earnings are not included on the statement of cash flows. Instead, entries for items that affect retained earnings appear as net profits or losses after taxes and dividends paid.

Preparing the Statement of Cash Flows

The statement of cash flows for a given period is developed using the income statement for the period, along with the beginning- and end-of-period balance sheets. The income statement for the year ended December 31, 2009, and the December 31 balance sheets for 2008 and 2009 for Baker Corporation are given in Tables 3.4 (see page 102) and 3.5 (see page 103), respectively. The statement of cash flows for the year ended December 31, 2009, for Baker Corporation is presented in Table 3.6 (see page 104). Note that all cash inflows as well as net profits after taxes and depreciation are treated as positive values. All cash outflows, any losses, and dividends paid are treated as negative values. The items in each category—operating, investment, and financing—are totaled, and the three totals are added to get the "Net increase (decrease) in cash and marketable securities" for the period. As a check, this value should reconcile with the actual change in cash and marketable securities for the year, which is obtained from the beginning- and end-of-period balance sheets. A detailed description of the procedures used to prepare Baker Corporation's statement of cash flows is posted on this book's website.

Interpreting the Statement

The statement of cash flows allows the financial manager and other interested parties to analyze the firm's cash flow. The manager should pay special attention both to the major categories of cash flow and to the individual items of cash

---

4. This equation is merely an estimate because it is based on the assumption that the firm's accounts receivable, inventory, accounts payable, and accruals remain unchanged during the period. Generally, these account balances will change over the period.

TABLE 3.4	Baker Corporation Income Statement ($000) for the Year Ended December 31, 2009	
Sales revenue		$1,700
Less: Cost of goods sold		1,000
Gross profits		$ 700
Less: Operating expenses		
Selling expense	$ 70	
General and administrative expenses	120	
Lease expense[a]	40	
Depreciation expense	100	
Total operating expense		$ 330
Earnings before interest and taxes (EBIT)		$ 370
Less: Interest expense		70
Net profits before taxes		$ 300
Less: Taxes (rate = 40%)		120
Net profits after taxes		$ 180
Less: Preferred stock dividends		10
Earnings available for common stockholders		$ 170
Earnings per share (EPS)[b]		$1.70

[a]Lease expense is shown here as a separate item rather than included as interest expense as specified by the FASB for financial reporting purposes. The approach used here is consistent with tax reporting rather than financial reporting procedures.

[b]Calculated by dividing the earnings available for common stockholders by the number of shares of common stock outstanding ($170,000 ÷ 100,000 shares = $1.70 per share).

inflow and outflow, to assess whether any developments have occurred that are contrary to the company's financial policies. In addition, the statement can be used to evaluate progress toward projected goals or to isolate inefficiencies. The financial manager also can prepare a statement of cash flows developed from projected financial statements to determine whether planned actions are desirable in view of the resulting cash flows.

Operating Cash Flow

operating cash flow (OCF)
The cash flow a firm generates from its normal operations; calculated as *net operating profits after taxes (NOPAT)* plus depreciation.

A firm's **operating cash flow (OCF)** is the cash flow it generates from its normal operations—producing and selling its output of goods or services. A variety of definitions of OCF can be found in the financial literature. Equation 3.1 introduced the simple accounting definition of cash flow from operations. Here we refine this definition to estimate cash flows more accurately. Unlike the earlier definition, this one excludes interest and taxes to enable us to focus on the true cash flow resulting from operations without regard to interest expense and taxes.

TABLE 3.5	Baker Corporation Balance Sheets ($000)		
		December 31	
Assets		2009	2008
Current assets			
Cash		$ 400	$ 300
Marketable securities		600	200
Accounts receivable		400	500
Inventories		600	900
Total current assets		$2,000	$1,900
Gross fixed assets (at cost)			
Land and buildings		$1,200	$1,050
Machinery and equipment		850	800
Furniture and fixtures		300	220
Vehicles		100	80
Other (includes certain leases)		50	50
Total gross fixed assets (at cost)		$2,500	$2,200
Less: Accumulated depreciation		1,300	1,200
Net fixed assets		$1,200	$1,000
Total assets		$3,200	$2,900
Liabilities and Stockholders' Equity			
Current liabilities			
Accounts payable		$ 700	$ 500
Notes payable		600	700
Accruals		100	200
Total current liabilities		$1,400	$1,400
Long-term debt		$ 600	$ 400
Total liabilities		$2,000	$1,800
Stockholders' equity			
Preferred stock		$ 100	$ 100
Common stock—$1.20 par, 100,000 shares outstanding in 2009 and 2008		120	120
Paid-in capital in excess of par on common stock		380	380
Retained earnings		600	500
Total stockholders' equity		$1,200	$1,100
Total liabilities and stockholders' equity		$3,200	$2,900

net operating profits after taxes (NOPAT)
A firm's earnings before interest and after taxes, $EBIT \times (1 - T)$.

The first step is to calculate **net operating profits after taxes (NOPAT)**, which represent the firm's earnings before interest and after taxes. Letting T equal the applicable corporate tax rate, NOPAT is calculated as follows:

$$NOPAT = EBIT \times (1 - T) \tag{3.2}$$

To convert NOPAT to operating cash flow (OCF), we merely add back depreciation:

$$OCF = NOPAT + Depreciation \tag{3.3}$$

TABLE 3.6	Baker Corporation Statement of Cash Flows ($000) for the Year Ended December 31, 2009		
Cash Flow from Operating Activities			
Net profits after taxes		$180	
Depreciation		100	
Decrease in accounts receivable		100	
Decrease in inventories		300	
Increase in accounts payable		200	
Decrease in accruals		(100)^a	
Cash provided by operating activities			$780
Cash Flow from Investment Activities			
Increase in gross fixed assets		($300)	
Changes in equity investments in other firms		0	
Cash provided by investment activities			(300)
Cash Flow from Financing Activities			
Decrease in notes payable		($100)	
Increase in long-term debts		200	
Changes in stockholders' equity^b		0	
Dividends paid		(80)	
Cash provided by financing activities			20
Net increase in cash and marketable securities			$500

^{a}As is customary, parentheses are used to denote a negative number, which in this case is a cash outflow.

^{b}Retained earnings are excluded here, because their change is actually reflected in the combination of the "Net profits after taxes" and "Dividends paid" entries.

We can substitute the expression for NOPAT from Equation 3.2 into Equation 3.3 to get a single equation for OCF:

$$OCF = [EBIT \times (1 - T)] + Depreciation \qquad (3.4)$$

Example

Substituting the values for Baker Corporation from its income statement (Table 3.4) into Equation 3.4, we get

$$OCF = [\$370 \times (1.00 - 0.40)] + \$100 = \$222 + \$100 = \$322$$

During 2009, Baker Corporation generated $322,000 of cash flow from producing and selling its output. Therefore, we can conclude that Baker's operations are generating positive cash flows.

Comparing Equations 3.1 and 3.4 reveals the key difference between the accounting and finance definitions of operating cash flow: The finance definition excludes interest—a financing cost—as an operating cash flow, whereas the accounting definition includes it as an operating flow. In the unlikely case that a firm has no interest expense, the accounting definition (Equation 3.1) and the finance definition (Equation 3.4) of operating cash flow would be the same.

Free Cash Flow

free cash flow (FCF)
The amount of cash flow available to investors (creditors and owners) after the firm has met all operating needs and paid for investments in net fixed assets and net current assets.

The firm's **free cash flow** (**FCF**) represents the amount of cash flow available to investors—the providers of debt (creditors) and equity (owners)—after the firm has met all operating needs and paid for investments in net fixed assets and net current assets. It represents the summation of the net amount of cash flow available to creditors and owners during the period. Free cash flow can be defined as follows:

$$\text{FCF} = \text{OCF} - \text{Net fixed asset investment (NFAI)} - \text{Net current asset investment (NCAI)} \quad (3.5)$$

The *net fixed asset investment (NFAI)* can be calculated as shown here:

$$\text{NFAI} = \text{Change in net fixed assets} + \text{Depreciation} \quad (3.6)$$

Example

Using the Baker Corporation's balance sheets in Table 3.5, we see that its change in net fixed assets between 2008 and 2009 was +$200 ($1,200 in 2009 − $1,000 in 2008). Substituting this value and the $100 of depreciation for 2009 into Equation 3.6, we get Baker's net fixed asset investment (NFAI) for 2009:

$$\text{NFAI} = \$200 + \$100 = \$300$$

Baker Corporation therefore invested a net $300,000 in fixed assets during 2009. This amount would, of course, represent a net cash outflow to acquire fixed assets during 2009.

Looking at Equation 3.6, we can see that if the depreciation during a year is less than the *decrease* during that year in net fixed assets, the NFAI would be negative. A negative NFAI represents a net cash *inflow* attributable to the fact that the firm sold more assets than it acquired during the year.

The *net current asset investment (NCAI)* represents the net investment made by the firm in its current (operating) assets. "Net" refers to the difference between current assets and the sum of accounts payable and accruals. Notes payable are not included in the NCAI calculation because they represent a negotiated creditor claim on the firm's free cash flow. Equation 3.7 shows the NCAI calculation.

$$\text{NCAI} = \text{Change in current assets} - \text{Change in (accounts payable + accruals)} \quad (3.7)$$

Example

Looking at the Baker Corporation's balance sheets for 2008 and 2009 in Table 3.5, we see that the change in current assets between 2008 and 2009 is +$100 ($2,000 in 2009 − $1,900 in 2008). The difference between Baker's accounts payable plus accruals of $800 in 2009 ($700 in accounts payable + $100 in accruals) and of $700 in 2008 ($500 in accounts payable + $200 in accruals) is +$100 ($800 in 2009 − $700 in 2008). Substituting into Equation 3.7 the change in current assets and the change in the sum of accounts payable plus accruals for Baker Corporation, we get its 2009 NCAI:

$$\text{NCAI} = \$100 - \$100 = \$0$$

Focus on Practice

Free Cash Flow at eBay

IN PRACTICE

Free cash flow is the lifeblood of any company and is the only true way to measure how much cash a company is generating. Free cash flow is, broadly, operating cash flow minus investments in net fixed assets and net current assets. It represents the net amount of cash flow available to creditors and owners. Free cash flow is an ideal way to measure a company's health and cash-generating growth.

Take **eBay,** for example. The company which brings together millions of people every day in its online marketplace produced $1.73 billion in free cash flow for the year ending December 31, 2006. Net cash provided by operating activities was $2.24 billion, and the company invested $0.51 billion in property, equipment, and net current assets during 2006, leaving $1.73 billion in free cash flow, a 10.09 percent increase over the previous year.

However, despite the increase in free cash flow, eBay faces some challenges. Users

of eBay generated a total of 610 million listings in the fourth quarter of 2006, a 12 percent increase over the fourth quarter of 2005. But the company is spending more and more, mostly paying Google, a chief competitor, to draw traffic to the site. When expenses start to increase more than free cash flow, it suggests that a company's competitive edge is under attack.

Having free cash flows is one thing; what a company does with it is quite another. According to the Motley Fool (www.fool.com), as an investor you are much better served by companies that use free cash flow to buy back their stock (if the stock is undervalued) or, better yet, use it toward a regular cash dividend. The investor then has the option to reinvest the dividend back into the company or use the dividend to pursue a different opportunity.

In 2006, eBay chose to use its excess cash to buy back stock. Since announcing a share buyback program in July 2006, the

company repurchased approximately 50 million shares of its common stock at a total cost of nearly $1.7 billion. In addition, the company has the capacity to buy back an additional $300 million of stock under the initial plan, and the company's board of directors has authorized an expansion of the stock repurchase program to provide for the repurchase of up to an additional $2 billion of the company's common stock within the next 2 years. For the time being, stockholders expecting the start of a dividend stream can put those expectations on hold. The company's intentions are clearly not to begin paying dividends for the foreseeable future.

■ *Free cash flow is often considered a more reliable measure of a company's income than reported earnings. What are some possible ways that corporate accountants might be able to change their earnings to portray a more favorable earnings statement?*

This means that during 2009 Baker Corporation made no investment ($0) in its current assets net of accounts payable and accruals.

Now we can substitute Baker Corporation's 2009 operating cash flow (OCF) of $322, its net fixed asset investment (NFAI) of $300, and its net current asset investment (NCAI) of $0 into Equation 3.5 to find its free cash flow (FCF):

$$FCF = \$322 - \$300 - \$0 = \$22$$

We can see that during 2009 Baker generated $22,000 of free cash flow, which it can use to pay its investors—creditors (payment of interest) and owners (payment of dividends). Thus, the firm generated adequate cash flow to cover all of its operating costs and investments and had free cash flow available to pay investors.

Clearly, cash flow is the lifeblood of the firm. The *Focus on Practice* box at the top of this page discusses eBay's free cash flow.

In the next section, we consider various aspects of financial planning for cash flow and profit.

REVIEW QUESTIONS

3–1 Briefly describe the first four *modified accelerated cost recovery system (MACRS)* property classes and recovery periods. Explain how the depreciation percentages are determined by using the MACRS recovery periods.

3–2 Describe the overall cash flow through the firm in terms of operating flows, investments flows, and financing flows.

3–3 Explain why a decrease in cash is classified as a *cash inflow (source)* and why an increase in cash is classified as a *cash outflow (use)* in preparing the statement of cash flows.

3–4 Why is depreciation (as well as amortization and depletion) considered a *noncash charge?* How do accountants estimate *cash flow from operations?*

3–5 Describe the general format of the statement of cash flows. How are cash inflows differentiated from cash outflows on this statement?

3–6 What is the difference between the accounting and finance definitions of *operating cash flow?* Under what circumstances are they the same?

3–7 From a strict financial perspective, define and differentiate between a firm's *operating cash flow (OCF)* and its *free cash flow (FCF).*

3.2 | The Financial Planning Process

Financial planning is an important aspect of the firm's operations because it provides road maps for guiding, coordinating, and controlling the firm's actions to achieve its objectives. Two key aspects of the financial planning process are *cash planning* and *profit planning*. Cash planning involves preparation of the firm's cash budget. Profit planning involves preparation of pro forma statements. Both the cash budget and the pro forma statements are useful for internal financial planning; they also are routinely required by existing and prospective lenders.

The **financial planning process** begins with long-term, or *strategic*, financial plans. These, in turn, guide the formulation of short-term, or *operating*, plans and budgets. Generally, the short-term plans and budgets implement the firm's long-term strategic objectives. Although the remainder of this chapter places primary emphasis on short-term financial plans and budgets, a few preliminary comments on long-term financial plans are in order.

financial planning process
Planning that begins with long-term, or *strategic*, financial plans that in turn guide the formulation of short-term, or *operating*, plans and budgets.

Long-Term (Strategic) Financial Plans

Long-term (strategic) financial plans lay out a company's planned financial actions and the anticipated impact of those actions over periods ranging from 2 to 10 years. Five-year strategic plans, which are revised as significant new information becomes available, are common. Generally, firms that are subject to high degrees of operating uncertainty, relatively short production cycles, or both, tend to use shorter planning horizons.

long-term (strategic) financial plans
Lay out a company's planned financial actions and the anticipated impact of those actions over periods ranging from 2 to 10 years.

Long-term financial plans are part of an integrated strategy that, along with production and marketing plans, guides the firm toward strategic goals. Those long-term plans consider proposed outlays for fixed assets, research and development activities, marketing and product development actions, capital structure, and major sources of financing. Also included would be termination of existing projects, product lines, or lines of business; repayment or retirement of outstanding debts; and any planned acquisitions. Such plans tend to be supported by a series of annual budgets.

Hint Preparation of the annual budget is an important part of the firm's planning process that involves all managers. It represents a tedious but important management activity.

Short-Term (Operating) Financial Plans

short-term (operating) financial plans
Specify short-term financial actions and the anticipated impact of those actions.

Short-term (operating) financial plans specify short-term financial actions and the anticipated impact of those actions. These plans most often cover a 1- to 2-year period. Key inputs include the sales forecast and various forms of operating and financial data. Key outputs include a number of operating budgets, the cash budget, and pro forma financial statements. The entire short-term financial planning process is outlined in Figure 3.2. Here we focus solely on cash and profit planning from the financial manager's perspective.

Short-term financial planning begins with the sales forecast. From it, companies develop production plans that take into account lead (preparation) times and include estimates of the required raw materials. Using the production plans, the firm can estimate direct labor requirements, factory overhead outlays, and operating expenses. Once these estimates have been made, the firm can prepare a pro forma income statement and cash budget. With these basic inputs, the firm can finally develop a pro forma balance sheet.

Hint Excel spreadsheets are widely used to streamline the process of preparing and evaluating these short-term financial planning statements.

Personal Finance Example   The first step in personal financial planning requires you to define your goals. Whereas in a corporation, the goal is to maximize owner wealth (i.e., share price), individuals typically have a number of major goals.

Generally personal goals can be short-term (1 year), intermediate-term (2–5 years), or long-term (6+ years). The short- and intermediate-term goals support the long-term goals. Clearly, types of long-term personal goals depend on the individual's or family's age, and goals will continue to change with one's life situation.

You should set your personal financial goals carefully and realistically. Each goal should be clearly defined and have a priority, time frame, and cost estimate. For example, a college senior's intermediate-term goal in 2009 might include earning a master's degree at a cost of $40,000 by 2012, and his or her long-term goal might be to buy a condominium at a cost of $125,000 by 2016.

Throughout the remainder of this chapter, we will concentrate on the key outputs of the short-term financial planning process: the cash budget, the pro forma income statement, and the pro forma balance sheet.

REVIEW QUESTIONS

3–8   What is the *financial planning process?* Contrast *long-term (strategic) financial plans* and *short-term (operating) financial plans.*

3–9   Which three statements result as part of the short-term (operating) financial planning process?

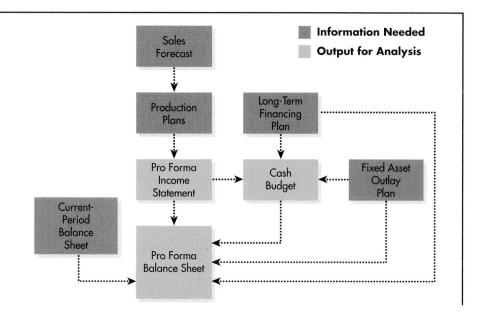

FIGURE 3.2

Short-Term Financial Planning
The short-term (operating) financial planning process

3.3 | Cash Planning: Cash Budgets

cash budget (cash forecast)
A statement of the firm's planned inflows and outflows of cash that is used to estimate its short-term cash requirements.

The **cash budget,** or **cash forecast,** is a statement of the firm's planned inflows and outflows of cash. It is used by the firm to estimate its short-term cash requirements, with particular attention being paid to planning for surplus cash and for cash shortages.

Typically, the cash budget is designed to cover a 1-year period, divided into smaller time intervals. The number and type of intervals depend on the nature of the business. The more seasonal and uncertain a firm's cash flows, the greater the number of intervals. Because many firms are confronted with a seasonal cash flow pattern, the cash budget is quite often presented on a *monthly basis.* Firms with stable patterns of cash flow may use quarterly or annual time intervals.

The Sales Forecast

sales forecast
The prediction of the firm's sales over a given period, based on external and/or internal data; used as the key input to the short-term financial planning process.

The key input to the short-term financial planning process is the firm's **sales forecast.** This prediction of the firm's sales over a given period is ordinarily prepared by the marketing department. On the basis of the sales forecast, the financial manager estimates the monthly cash flows that will result from projected sales and from outlays related to production, inventory, and sales. The manager also determines the level of fixed assets required and the amount of financing, if any, needed to support the forecast level of sales and production. In practice, obtaining good data is the most difficult aspect of forecasting. The sales forecast may be based on an analysis of external data, internal data, or a combination of the two.

external forecast
A sales forecast based on the relationships observed between the firm's sales and certain key external economic indicators.

An **external forecast** is based on the relationships observed between the firm's sales and certain key external economic indicators such as the gross domestic product (GDP), new housing starts, consumer confidence, and disposable personal income. Forecasts containing these indicators are readily available.

Internal forecasts are based on a consensus of sales forecasts through the firm's own sales channels. Typically, the firm's salespeople in the field are asked to estimate how many units of each type of product they expect to sell in the coming year. These forecasts are collected and totaled by the sales manager, who may adjust the figures using knowledge of specific markets or of the salesperson's forecasting ability. Finally, adjustments may be made for additional internal factors, such as production capabilities.

Firms generally use a combination of external and internal forecast data to make the final sales forecast. The internal data provide insight into sales expectations, and the external data provide a means of adjusting these expectations to take into account general economic factors. The nature of the firm's product also often affects the mix and types of forecasting methods used.

Preparing the Cash Budget

The general format of the cash budget is presented in Table 3.7. We will discuss each of its components individually.

Cash Receipts

Cash receipts include all of a firm's inflows of cash during a given financial period. The most common components of cash receipts are cash sales, collections of accounts receivable, and other cash receipts.

internal forecast
A sales forecast based on a buildup, or consensus, of sales forecasts through the firm's own sales channels.

Hint The firm needs to spend a great deal of time and effort to make the sales forecast as precise as possible. An "after-the-fact" analysis of the prior year's forecast can help the firm determine which approach or combination of approaches will give it the most accurate forecasts.

cash receipts
All of a firm's inflows of cash during a given financial period.

Example ▸ Coulson Industries, a defense contractor, is developing a cash budget for October, November, and December. Coulson's sales in August and September were $100,000 and $200,000, respectively. Sales of $400,000, $300,000, and $200,000 have been forecast for October, November, and December, respectively. Historically, 20% of the firm's sales have been for cash, 50% have generated accounts receivable collected after 1 month, and the remaining 30% have generated accounts receivable collected after 2 months. Bad-debt expenses (uncol-

TABLE 3.7   The General Format of the Cash Budget

	Jan.	Feb.	...	Nov.	Dec.
Cash receipts	$XXX	$XXG		$XXM	$XXT
Less: Cash disbursements	XXA	XXH	...	XXN	XXU
Net cash flow	$XXB	$XXI		$XXO	$XXV
Add: Beginning cash	XXC	XXD	XXJ	XXP	XXQ
Ending cash	$XXD	$XXJ		$XXQ	$XXW
Less: Minimum cash balance	XXE	XXK	...	XXR	XXY
Required total financing		$XXL		$XXS	
Excess cash balance	$XXF				$XXZ

TABLE 3.8	**A Schedule of Projected Cash Receipts for Coulson Industries ($000)**					

	Aug. $100	Sept. $200	Oct. $400	Nov. $300	Dec. $200
Forecast sales					
Cash sales (0.20)	$20	$40	$ 80	$ 60	$ 40
Collections of A/R:					
Lagged 1 month (0.50)		50	100	200	150
Lagged 2 months (0.30)			30	60	120
Other cash receipts					30
Total cash receipts			$210	$320	$340

lectible accounts) have been negligible.[5] In December, the firm will receive a $30,000 dividend from stock in a subsidiary. The schedule of expected cash receipts for the company is presented in Table 3.8. It contains the following items:

Forecast sales   This initial entry is *merely informational.* It is provided as an aid in calculating other sales-related items.

Cash sales   The cash sales shown for each month represent 20% of the total sales forecast for that month.

Collections of A/R   These entries represent the collection of accounts receivable (A/R) resulting from sales in earlier months.

   Lagged 1 month   These figures represent sales made in the preceding month that generated accounts receivable collected in the current month. Because 50% of the current month's sales are collected 1 month later, the collections of A/R with a 1-month lag shown for September represent 50% of the sales in August, collections for October represent 50% of September sales, and so on.

   Lagged 2 months   These figures represent sales made 2 months earlier that generated accounts receivable collected in the current month. Because 30% of sales are collected 2 months later, the collections with a 2-month lag shown for October represent 30% of the sales in August, and so on.

Other cash receipts   These are cash receipts expected from sources other than sales. Interest received, dividends received, proceeds from the sale of equipment, stock and bond sale proceeds, and lease receipts may show up here. For Coulson Industries, the only other cash receipt is the $30,000 dividend due in December.

Total cash receipts   This figure represents the total of all the cash receipts listed for each month. For Coulson Industries, we are concerned only with October, November, and December, as shown in Table 3.8.

---

5. Normally, it would be expected that the collection percentages would total slightly less than 100%, because some of the accounts receivable would be uncollectible. In this example, the sum of the collection percentages is 100% (20% + 50% + 30%), which reflects the fact that all sales are assumed to be collected.

Cash Disbursements

cash disbursements
All outlays of cash by the
firm during a given financial
period.

Cash disbursements include all outlays of cash by the firm during a given financial period. The most common cash disbursements are

Cash purchases	Fixed-asset outlays
Payments of accounts payable	Interest payments
Rent (and lease) payments	Cash dividend payments
Wages and salaries	Principal payments (loans)
Tax payments	Repurchases or retirements of stock

It is important to recognize that *depreciation and other noncash charges are NOT included in the cash budget*, because they merely represent a scheduled write-off of an earlier cash outflow. The impact of depreciation, as we noted earlier, is reflected in the reduced cash outflow for tax payments.

Example

Coulson Industries has gathered the following data needed for the preparation of a cash disbursements schedule for October, November, and December.

Purchases   The firm's purchases represent 70% of sales. Of this amount, 10% is paid in cash, 70% is paid in the month immediately following the month of purchase, and the remaining 20% is paid 2 months following the month of purchase.[6]

Rent payments   Rent of $5,000 will be paid each month.

Wages and salaries   Fixed salary cost for the year is $96,000, or $8,000 per month. In addition, wages are estimated as 10% of monthly sales.

Tax payments   Taxes of $25,000 must be paid in December.

Fixed-asset outlays   New machinery costing $130,000 will be purchased and paid for in November.

Interest payments   An interest payment of $10,000 is due in December.

Cash dividend payments   Cash dividends of $20,000 will be paid in October.

Principal payments (loans)   A $20,000 principal payment is due in December.

Repurchases or retirements of stock   No repurchase or retirement of stock is expected between October and December.

The firm's cash disbursements schedule, using the preceding data, is shown in Table 3.9. Some items in the table are explained in greater detail below.

Purchases   This entry is *merely informational*. The figures represent 70% of the forecast sales for each month. They have been included to facilitate calculation of the cash purchases and related payments.

Cash purchases   The cash purchases for each month represent 10% of the month's purchases.

Payments of A/P   These entries represent the payment of accounts payable (A/P) resulting from purchases in earlier months.

---

6. Unlike the collection percentages for sales, the total of the payment percentages should equal 100%, because it is expected that the firm will pay off all of its accounts payable.

TABLE 3.9   A Schedule of Projected Cash Disbursements for Coulson Industries ($000)

	Aug.	Sept.	Oct.	Nov.	Dec.
Purchases (0.70 × sales)	$70	$140	$280	$210	$140
Cash purchases (0.10)	$7	$14	$ 28	$ 21	$ 14
Payments of A/P:					
Lagged 1 month (0.70)		49	98	196	147
Lagged 2 months (0.20)			14	28	56
Rent payments			5	5	5
Wages and salaries			48	38	28
Tax payments					25
Fixed-asset outlays				130	
Interest payments					10
Cash dividend payments			20		
Principal payments					20
Total cash disbursements			$213	$418	$305

Lagged 1 month   These figures represent purchases made in the preceding month that are paid for in the current month. Because 70% of the firm's purchases are paid for 1 month later, the payments with a 1-month lag shown for September represent 70% of the August purchases, payments for October represent 70% of September purchases, and so on.

Lagged 2 months   These figures represent purchases made 2 months earlier that are paid for in the current month. Because 20% of the firm's purchases are paid for 2 months later, the payments with a 2-month lag for October represent 20% of the August purchases, and so on.

Wages and salaries   These amounts were obtained by adding $8,000 to 10% of the *sales* in each month. The $8,000 represents the salary component; the rest represents wages.

The remaining items on the cash disbursements schedule are self-explanatory.

net cash flow
The mathematical difference between the firm's cash receipts and its cash disbursements in each period.

ending cash
The sum of the firm's beginning cash and its net cash flow for the period.

required total financing
Amount of funds needed by the firm if the ending cash for the period is less than the desired minimum cash balance; typically represented by notes payable.

excess cash balance
The (excess) amount available for investment by the firm if the period's ending cash is greater than the desired minimum cash balance; assumed to be invested in marketable securities.

Net Cash Flow, Ending Cash, Financing, and Excess Cash

Look back at the general-format cash budget in Table 3.7. We have inputs for the first two entries, and we now continue calculating the firm's cash needs. The firm's **net cash flow** is found by subtracting the cash disbursements from cash receipts in each period. Then we add beginning cash to the firm's net cash flow to determine the **ending cash** for each period.

Finally, we subtract the desired minimum cash balance from ending cash to find the **required total financing** or the **excess cash balance.** If the ending cash is less than the minimum cash balance, *financing* is required. Such financing is typically viewed as short-term and is therefore represented by notes payable. If the ending cash is greater than the minimum cash balance, *excess cash* exists. Any excess cash is assumed to be invested in a liquid, short-term, interest-paying vehicle—that is, in marketable securities.

Example

Table 3.10 presents Coulson Industries' cash budget, based on the data already developed. At the end of September, Coulson's cash balance was $50,000, and its notes payable and marketable securities equaled $0. The company wishes to maintain, as a reserve for unexpected needs, a minimum cash balance of $25,000.

For Coulson Industries to maintain its required $25,000 ending cash balance, it will need total borrowing of $76,000 in November and $41,000 in December. In October the firm will have an excess cash balance of $22,000, which can be held in an interest-earning marketable security. The required total financing figures in the cash budget refer to *how much will be owed at the end of the month;* they do *not* represent the monthly changes in borrowing.

The monthly changes in borrowing and in excess cash can be found by further analyzing the cash budget. In October the $50,000 beginning cash, which becomes $47,000 after the $3,000 net cash outflow, results in a $22,000 excess cash balance once the $25,000 minimum cash is deducted. In November the $76,000 of required total financing resulted from the $98,000 net cash outflow less the $22,000 of excess cash from October. The $41,000 of required total financing in December resulted from reducing November's $76,000 of required total financing by the $35,000 of net cash inflow during December. Summarizing, the *financial activities for each month* would be as follows:

October: **Invest the $22,000** excess cash balance in marketable securities.

November: Liquidate the $22,000 of marketable securities and **borrow $76,000** (notes payable).

December: **Repay $35,000** of notes payable to leave $41,000 of outstanding required total financing.

TABLE 3.10   A Cash Budget for Coulson Industries ($000)

	Oct.	Nov.	Dec.
Total cash receipts[a]	$210	$320	$340
Less: Total cash disbursements[b]	213	418	305
Net cash flow	($ 3)	($ 98)	$ 35
Add: Beginning cash	50	47	(51)
Ending cash	$ 47	($ 51)	($ 16)
Less: Minimum cash balance	25	25	25
Required total financing (notes payable)[c]	—	$ 76	$ 41
Excess cash balance (marketable securities)[d]	$ 22	—	—

[a]From Table 3.8.
[b]From Table 3.9.
[c]Values are placed in this line when the ending cash is less than the desired minimum cash balance. These amounts are typically financed short-term and therefore are represented by notes payable.
[d]Values are placed in this line when the ending cash is greater than the desired minimum cash balance. These amounts are typically assumed to be invested short-term and therefore are represented by marketable securities.

Evaluating the Cash Budget

Hint Not only is the cash budget a great tool to let management know when it has cash shortages or excesses, but it may be a document required by potential creditors. It communicates to them what the money will be used for, and how and when their loans will be repaid.

The cash budget indicates whether a cash shortage or surplus is expected in each of the months covered by the forecast. Each month's figure is based on the internally imposed requirement of a minimum cash balance and *represents the total balance at the end of the month.*

At the end of each of the 3 months, Coulson expects the following balances in cash, marketable securities, and notes payable:

| Account | End-of-month balance ($000) | | |
	Oct.	Nov.	Dec.
Cash	$25	$25	$25
Marketable securities	22	0	0
Notes payable	0	76	41

Hint Because of the uncertainty of the ending cash values, the financial manager will usually seek to borrow more than the maximum financing indicated in the cash budget.

Note that the firm is assumed first to liquidate its marketable securities to meet deficits and then to borrow with notes payable if additional financing is needed. As a result, it will not have marketable securities and notes payable on its books at the same time. Because it may be necessary to borrow up to $76,000 for the 3-month period, the financial manager should be certain that some arrangement is made to ensure the availability of these funds.

Personal Finance Example   Because individuals receive only a finite amount of income (cash inflow) during a given period, they need to prepare budgets in order to make sure they can cover their expenses (cash outflows) during the period. The *personal budget* is a short-term financial planning report that helps an individual or family achieve its short-term financial goals. Personal budgets typically cover a 1-year period, broken into months.

A condensed version of a personal budget for the first quarter (3 months) is shown below. You can see a more detailed version (with breakouts of expenses) at the book's companion website.

	Jan.	Feb.	Mar.
Income			
Take-home pay	$4,775	$4,775	$4,775
Investment income			90
(1) Total income	$4,775	$4,775	$4,865
Expenses			
(2) Total expenses	$4,026	$5,291	7,396
Cash surplus or deficit [(1) − (2)]	$ 749	($ 516)	($2,531)
Cumulative cash surplus or deficit	$ 749	$ 233	($2,298)

Preceding Year's Financial Statements

The income statement for the firm's 2009 operations is given in Table 3.12. It indicates that Vectra had sales of $100,000, total cost of goods sold of $80,000, net profits before taxes of $9,000, and net profits after taxes of $7,650. The firm paid $4,000 in cash dividends, leaving $3,650 to be transferred to retained earnings. The firm's balance sheet for 2009 is given in Table 3.13.

TABLE 3.12	Vectra Manufacturing's Income Statement for the Year Ended December 31, 2009		
Sales revenue			
Model X (1,000 units at $20/unit)		$20,000	
Model Y (2,000 units at $40/unit)		80,000	
Total sales			$100,000
Less: Cost of goods sold			
Labor		$28,500	
Material A		8,000	
Material B		5,500	
Overhead		38,000	
Total cost of goods sold			80,000
Gross profits			$ 20,000
Less: Operating expenses			10,000
Operating profits			$ 10,000
Less: Interest expense			1,000
Net profits before taxes			$ 9,000
Less: Taxes ($0.15 \times \$9,000$)			1,350
Net profits after taxes			$ 7,650
Less: Common stock dividends			4,000
To retained earnings			$ 3,650

TABLE 3.13	Vectra Manufacturing's Balance Sheet, December 31, 2009		
Assets		**Liabilities and Stockholders' Equity**	
Cash	$ 6,000	Accounts payable	$ 7,000
Marketable securities	4,000	Taxes payable	300
Accounts receivable	13,000	Notes payable	8,300
Inventories	16,000	Other current liabilities	3,400
Total current assets	$39,000	Total current liabilities	$19,000
Net fixed assets	$51,000	Long-term debt	$18,000
Total assets	$90,000	Stockholders' equity	
		Common stock	$30,000
		Retained earnings	$23,000
		Total liabilities and stockholders' equity	$90,000

TABLE 3.14	2010 Sales Forecast for Vectra Manufacturing
Unit sales	
Model X	1,500
Model Y	1,950
Dollar sales	
Model X ($25/unit)	$ 37,500
Model Y ($50/unit)	97,500
Total	$135,000

Sales Forecast

Just as for the cash budget, the key input for pro forma statements is the sales forecast. Vectra Manufacturing's sales forecast for the coming year (2010), based on both external and internal data, is presented in Table 3.14. The unit sale prices of the products reflect an increase from $20 to $25 for model X and from $40 to $50 for model Y. These increases are necessary to cover anticipated increases in costs.

REVIEW QUESTION

3–14 What is the purpose of *pro forma statements?* What inputs are required for preparing them using the simplified approaches?

3.5 | Preparing the Pro Forma Income Statement

percent-of-sales method
A simple method for developing the pro forma income statement; it forecasts sales and then expresses the various income statement items as percentages of projected sales.

A simple method for developing a pro forma income statement is the **percent-of-sales method.** It forecasts sales and then expresses the various income statement items as percentages of projected sales. The percentages used are likely to be the percentages of sales for those items in the previous year. By using dollar values taken from Vectra's 2009 income statement (Table 3.12), we find that these percentages are

$$\frac{\text{Cost of goods sold}}{\text{Sales}} = \frac{\$80,000}{\$100,000} = 80.0\%$$

$$\frac{\text{Operating expenses}}{\text{Sales}} = \frac{\$10,000}{\$100,000} = 10.0\%$$

$$\frac{\text{Interest expense}}{\text{Sales}} = \frac{\$1,000}{\$100,000} = 1.0\%$$

Applying these percentages to the firm's forecast sales of $135,000 (developed in Table 3.14), we get the 2010 pro forma income statement shown in Table 3.15.

120

Part Two
Important Financial Concepts

Chapters in This Part

4 Time Value of Money

WHY THIS CHAPTER MATTERS TO YOU

In Your Professional Life

Accounting: You need to understand time-value-of-money calculations to account for certain transactions such as loan amortization, lease payments, and bond interest rates.

Information systems: You need to understand time-value-of-money calculations to design systems that accurately measure and value the firm's cash flows.

Management: You need to understand time-value-of-money calculations so that you can manage cash receipts and disbursements in a way that will enable the firm to receive the greatest value from its cash flows.

Marketing: You need to understand time value of money because funding for new programs and products must be justified financially using time-value-of-money techniques.

Operations: You need to understand time value of money because the value of investments in new equipment, in new processes, and in inventory will be affected by the time value of money.

In Your Personal Life

Time value of money techniques are widely used in personal financial planning. You can use them to calculate the value of savings at given future dates and to estimate the amount you need now to accumulate a given amount at a future date. You also can apply them to value lump-sum amounts or streams of periodic cash flows and to the interest rate or amount of time needed to achieve a given financial goal.

LEARNING GOALS

LG 1 Discuss the role of time value in finance, the use of computational tools, and the basic patterns of cash flow.

LG 2 Understand the concepts of future value and present value, their calculation for single amounts, and the relationship between them.

LG 3 Find the future value and the present value of an ordinary annuity, and find the present value of a perpetuity.

LG 4 Calculate both the future value and the present value of a mixed stream of cash flows.

LG 5 Understand the effect that compounding interest more frequently than annually has on future value and on the effective annual rate of interest.

LG 6 Describe the procedures involved in (1) determining deposits needed to accumulate a future sum, (2) loan amortization, (3) finding interest or growth rates, and (4) finding an unknown number of periods.

B ecause we view the firm as a going concern, we assess the decisions of its financial managers, and ultimately the value of the firm itself, in light of its cash flows. The opportunity to earn interest on the firm's funds makes the timing of its cash flows important, because a dollar received in the future is not the same as a dollar received today. Thus, money has a time value, which affects everyone—individuals, businesses, and government. In this chapter we explore the concepts related to the time value of money.

LG 1   4.1 | The Role of Time Value in Finance

Hint The time value of money is one of the most important concepts in finance. Money that the firm has in its possession today is more valuable than money in the future because the money it now has can be invested and earn positive returns.

Financial managers and investors are always confronted with opportunities to earn positive rates of return on their funds, whether through investment in attractive projects or in interest-bearing securities or deposits. Therefore, the timing of cash outflows and inflows has important economic consequences, which financial managers explicitly recognize as the *time value of money*. Time value is based on the belief that a dollar today is worth more than a dollar that will be received at some future date. We begin our study of time value in finance by considering the two views of time value—future value and present value, the computational tools used to streamline time value calculations, and the basic patterns of cash flow.

Future Value versus Present Value

Financial values and decisions can be assessed by using either future value or present value techniques. Although these techniques will result in the same decisions, they view the decision differently. Future value techniques typically measure cash flows at the *end* of a project's life. Present value techniques measure cash flows at the *start* of a project's life (time zero). *Future value* is cash you will receive at a given future date, and *present value* is just like cash in hand today.

time line
A horizontal line on which time zero appears at the leftmost end and future periods are marked from left to right; can be used to depict investment cash flows.

A **time line** can be used to depict the cash flows associated with a given investment. It is a horizontal line on which time zero appears at the leftmost end and future periods are marked from left to right. A time line covering five periods (in this case, years) is given in Figure 4.1. The cash flows occurring at time zero and at the end of each year are shown above the line; the negative values represent *cash outflows* ($10,000 at time zero) and the positive values represent *cash inflows* ($3,000 inflow at the end of year 1, $5,000 inflow at the end of year 2, and so on).

Because money has a time value, all of the cash flows associated with an investment, such as those in Figure 4.1, must be measured at the same point in time. Typically, that point is either the end or the beginning of the investment's

Time Line
Time line depicting an investment's cash flows

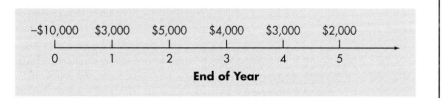

Compounding and Discounting
Time line showing compounding to find future value and discounting to find present value

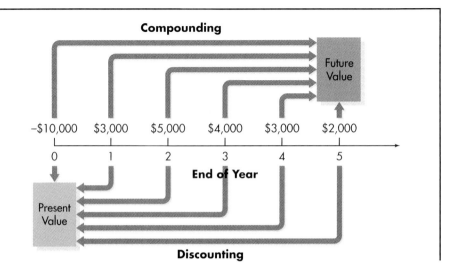

life. The future value technique uses *compounding* to find the *future value* of each cash flow at the end of the investment's life and then sums these values to find the investment's future value. This approach is depicted above the time line in Figure 4.2. The figure shows that the future value of each cash flow is measured at the end of the investment's 5-year life. Alternatively, the present value technique uses *discounting* to find the *present value* of each cash flow at time zero and then sums these values to find the investment's value today. Application of this approach is depicted below the time line in Figure 4.2.

The meaning and mechanics of compounding to find future value and of discounting to find present value are covered in this chapter. Although future value and present value result in the same decisions, *financial managers—because they make decisions at time zero—tend to rely primarily on present value techniques.*

Computational Tools

Time-consuming calculations are often involved in finding future and present values. Although you should understand the concepts and mathematics underlying these calculations, the application of time value techniques can be streamlined. We focus on the use of hand-held financial calculators, electronic spreadsheets, and financial tables as aids in computation.

Financial Calculators

Financial calculators can be used to simplify time value computations. Generally, *financial calculators* include numerous preprogrammed financial routines. This chapter and those that follow show the keystrokes for calculating interest factors and making other financial computations. For convenience, we use the important financial keys, labeled in a fashion consistent with most major financial calculators.

We focus primarily on the keys pictured and defined in Figure 4.3. We typically use four of the first five keys shown in the left column, along with the compute (**CPT**) key. One of the four keys represents the unknown value being

Calculator Keys
Important financial keys on the typical calculator

N — Number of periods

I — Interest rate per period

PV — Present value

PMT — Amount of payment (used only for annuities)

FV — Future value

CPT — Compute key used to initiate financial calculation once all values are input

calculated. (Occasionally, all five of the keys are used, with one representing the unknown value.) The keystrokes on some of the more sophisticated calculators are menu-driven: After you select the appropriate routine, the calculator prompts you to input each value; on these calculators, a compute key is not needed to obtain a solution. Regardless, any calculator with the basic future and present value functions can be used to simplify time value calculations. See Appendix A for keystrokes for some of the more popular calculators. The keystrokes for other financial calculators are explained in the reference guides that accompany them.

Once you understand the basic underlying concepts, you probably will want to use a calculator to streamline routine financial calculations. With a little practice, you can increase both the speed and the accuracy of your financial computations. Remember that *conceptual understanding of the material is the objective.* An ability to solve problems with the aid of a calculator does not necessarily reflect such an understanding, so don't just settle for answers. Work with the material until you are sure you also understand the concepts.

Electronic Spreadsheets

Hint Anyone familiar with an electronic spreadsheet, such as Excel, realizes that most of the time-value-of-money calculations can be performed expeditiously by using the special functions contained in the spreadsheet.

Like financial calculators, electronic spreadsheets have built-in routines that simplify time value calculations. We provide in the text a number of spreadsheet solutions that identify the cell entries for calculating time values. The value for each variable is entered in a cell in the spreadsheet, and the calculation is programmed using an equation that links the individual cells. If values of the variables are changed, the solution automatically changes as a result of the equation linking the cells. In the spreadsheet solutions in this book, the equation that determines the calculation is shown at the bottom of the spreadsheet.

The ability to use electronic spreadsheets has become a prime skill for today's managers. As the saying goes, "Get aboard the bandwagon, or get run over." The spreadsheet solutions we present in this book will help you climb up onto that bandwagon!

Financial Tables

Financial tables include various future and present value interest factors that simplify time value calculations. The values shown in these tables are easily developed from formulas, with various degrees of rounding. As a result, slight differences are likely to exist between table-based calculations and the more precise values obtained using a financial calculator or spreadsheet.

FIGURE 4.4

Financial Tables
Layout and use of
a financial table

				Interest Rate		↓		
Period	1%	2%	...	10%	...	**20%**	...	50%
1			...		...	:	...	
2			...		...	:	...	
3			...		...	:	...	
:	:	:	...	:	...	:	...	:
→ 10	...	...	...	...	...	**X.XXX**	...	...
:	:	:	...	:	...	:	...	:
20			...		...		...	
:	:	:	...	:	...	:	...	:
50			...		...		...	

The financial tables are typically indexed by the interest rate (in columns) and the number of periods (in rows). Figure 4.4 shows this general layout. The interest factor at a 20 percent interest rate for 10 years would be found at the intersection of the 20% column and the 10-period row, as shown by the dark blue box. A full set of the four basic financial tables is included in Appendix A at the end of the book. These tables are described more fully later in the chapter.

Basic Patterns of Cash Flow

The cash flow—both inflows and outflows—of a firm can be described by its general pattern. It can be defined as a single amount, an annuity, or a mixed stream.

Single amount: A lump-sum amount either currently held or expected at some future date. Examples include $1,000 today and $650 to be received at the end of 10 years.

Annuity: A level periodic stream of cash flow. For our purposes, we'll work primarily with *annual* cash flows. Examples include either paying out or receiving $800 at the end of each of the next 7 years.

Mixed stream: A stream of cash flow that is *not* an annuity; a stream of unequal periodic cash flows that reflect no particular pattern. Examples include the following two cash flow streams A and B.

	Mixed cash flow stream	
End of year	A	B
1	$ 100	−$ 50
2	800	100
3	1,200	80
4	1,200	− 60
5	1,400	
6	300	

Note that neither cash flow stream has equal, periodic cash flows and that A is a 6-year mixed stream and B is a 4-year mixed stream.

In the next three sections of this chapter, we develop the concepts and techniques for finding future and present values of single amounts, annuities, and mixed streams, respectively. Detailed demonstrations of these cash flow patterns are included.

REVIEW QUESTIONS

4–1   What is the difference between *future value* and *present value?* Which approach is generally preferred by financial managers? Why?

4–2   Define and differentiate among the three basic patterns of cash flow: (1) a single amount, (2) an annuity, and (3) a mixed stream.

4.2 | Single Amounts

Imagine that at age 25 you began making annual purchases of $2,000 of an investment that earns a guaranteed 5 percent annually. At the end of 40 years, at age 65, you would have invested a total of $80,000 (40 years × $2,000 per year). Assuming that all funds remain invested, how much would you have accumulated at the end of the fortieth year? $100,000? $150,000? $200,000? No, your $80,000 would have grown to $242,000! Why? Because the time value of money allowed your investments to generate returns that built on each other over the 40 years.

Future Value of a Single Amount

The most basic future value and present value concepts and computations concern single amounts, either present or future amounts. We begin by considering the future value of present amounts. Then we will use the underlying concepts to determine the present value of future amounts. You will see that although future value is more intuitively appealing, present value is more useful in financial decision making.

We often need to find the value at some future date of a given amount of money placed on deposit today. For example, if you deposit $500 today into an account that pays 5 percent annual interest, how much would you have in the account at the end of exactly 10 years? **Future value** is the value at a given future date of a present amount placed on deposit today and earning interest at a specified rate. It depends on the rate of interest earned and the length of time a given amount is left on deposit. Here we explore the future value of a single amount.

future value
The value at a given future date of a present amount placed on deposit today and earning interest at a specified rate. Found by applying *compound interest* over a specified period of time.

The Concept of Future Value

We speak of **compound interest** to indicate that the amount of interest earned on a given deposit has become part of the *principal* at the end of a specified period. The term **principal** refers to the amount of money on which the interest is paid. Annual compounding is the most common type.

compound interest
Interest that is earned on a given deposit and has become part of the *principal* at the end of a specified period.

principal
The amount of money on which interest is paid.

The *future value* of a present amount is found by applying *compound interest* over a specified period of time. Savings institutions advertise compound interest returns at a rate of *x* percent, or *x* percent interest, compounded annually, semiannually, quarterly, monthly, weekly, daily, or even continuously. The concept of future value with annual compounding can be illustrated by a simple example.

Personal Finance Example If Fred Moreno places $100 in a savings account paying 8% interest compounded annually, at the end of 1 year he will have $108 in the account—the initial principal of $100 plus 8% ($8) in interest. The future value at the end of the first year is calculated by using Equation 4.1:

$$\text{Future value at end of year 1} = \$100 \times (1 + 0.08) = \$108 \qquad \textbf{(4.1)}$$

If Fred were to leave this money in the account for another year, he would be paid interest at the rate of 8% on the new principal of $108. At the end of this second year there would be $116.64 in the account. This amount would represent the principal at the beginning of year 2 ($108) plus 8% of the $108 ($8.64) in interest. The future value at the end of the second year is calculated by using Equation 4.2:

$$\text{Future value at end of year 2} = \$108 \times (1 + 0.08) \qquad \textbf{(4.2)}$$
$$= \$116.64$$

Substituting the expression between the equals signs in Equation 4.1 for the $108 figure in Equation 4.2 gives us Equation 4.3:

$$\text{Future value at end of year 2} = \$100 \times (1 + 0.08) \times (1 + 0.08) \qquad \textbf{(4.3)}$$
$$= \$100 \times (1 + 0.08)^2$$
$$= \$116.64$$

The equations in the preceding example lead to a more general formula for calculating future value.

The Equation for Future Value

The basic relationship in Equation 4.3 can be generalized to find the future value after any number of periods. We use the following notation for the various inputs:

FV_n = future value at the end of period n

PV = initial principal, or present value

i = annual rate of interest paid. (*Note:* On financial calculators, **I** is typically used to represent this rate.)

n = number of periods (typically years) that the money is left on deposit

The general equation for the future value at the end of period n is

$$FV_n = PV \times (1 + i)^n \qquad \textbf{(4.4)}$$

A simple example will illustrate how to apply Equation 4.4.

Personal Finance Example Jane Farber places $800 in a savings account paying 6% interest compounded annually. She wants to know how much money will be in the account at the end of 5 years. Substituting $PV = \$800$, $i = 0.06$, and $n = 5$ into Equation 4.4 gives the amount at the end of year 5.

$$FV_5 = \$800 \times (1 + 0.06)^5 = \$800 \times (1.338) = \$1,070.40$$

This analysis can be depicted on a time line as follows:

Time line for future value of a single amount ($800 initial principal, earning 6%, at the end of 5 years)

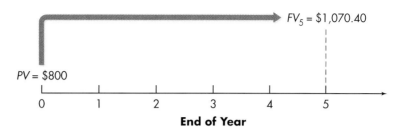

Using Computational Tools to Find Future Value

Solving the equation in the preceding example involves raising 1.06 to the fifth power. Using a financial calculator, an electronic spreadsheet, or a future value interest table greatly simplifies the calculation. A table that provides values for $(1 + i)^n$ in Equation 4.4 is included near the back of the book in Appendix Table A–1. The value in each cell of the table is called the **future value interest factor**. This factor is the multiplier used to calculate, at a specified interest rate, the future value of a present amount as of a given time. The future value interest factor for an initial principal of $1 compounded at i percent for n periods is referred to as $FVIF_{i,n}$.

future value interest factor
The multiplier used to calculate, at a specified interest rate, the future value of a present amount as of a given time.

$$\text{Future value interest factor} = FVIF_{i,n} = (1 + i)^n \qquad (4.5)$$

By finding the intersection of the annual interest rate, i, and the appropriate periods, n, you will find the future value interest factor that is relevant to a particular problem.[1] Using $FVIF_{i,n}$ as the appropriate factor, we can rewrite the general equation for future value (Equation 4.4) as follows:

$$FV_n = PV \times (FVIF_{i,n}) \qquad (4.6)$$

This expression indicates that to find the future value at the end of period n of an initial deposit, we have merely to multiply the initial deposit, PV, by the appropriate future value interest factor.[2]

Personal Finance Example   In the preceding example, Jane Farber placed $800 in her savings account at 6% interest compounded annually and wishes to find out how much will be in the account at the end of 5 years.

Calculator Use[3]   The financial calculator can be used to calculate the future value directly.[4] First punch in $800 and depress **PV**; next punch in 5 and depress

---

1. Although we commonly deal with years rather than periods, financial tables are frequently presented in terms of periods to provide maximum flexibility.

2. Occasionally, you may want to estimate roughly how long a given sum must earn at a given annual rate to double the amount. The *Rule of 72* is used to make this estimate; dividing the annual rate of interest into 72 results in the approximate number of periods it will take to double one's money at the given rate. For example, to double one's money at a 10% annual rate of interest will take about 7.2 years (72 ÷ 10 = 7.2). Looking at Table A–1, we can see that the future value interest factor for 10% and 7 years is slightly less than 2 (1.949); this approximation therefore appears to be reasonably accurate.

3. Many calculators allow the user to set the number of payments per year. Most of these calculators are preset for monthly payments—12 payments per year. Because we work primarily with annual payments—one payment per year—it is important to *be sure that your calculator is set for one payment per year*. And although most calculators are preset to recognize that all payments occur at the end of the period, it is important to *make sure that your calculator is correctly set on the END mode*. Consult the reference guide that accompanies your calculator for instructions for setting these values.

4. To avoid including previous data in current calculations, *always clear all registers of your calculator before inputting values and making each computation*.

Input | Function
800 | PV
5 | N
6 | I
| CPT
| FV

Solution
1,070.58

N; then punch in 6 and depress **I** (which is equivalent to "*i*" in our notation)[5]; finally, to calculate the future value, depress **CPT** and then **FV.** The future value of $1,070.58 should appear on the calculator display as shown at the left. On many calculators, this value will be preceded by a minus sign (−1,070.58). *If a minus sign appears on your calculator, ignore it here as well as in all other "Calculator Use" illustrations in this text.*[6] (*Note:* In future examples of calculator use, we will use only a display similar to that shown on this page. If you need a reminder of the procedures involved, go back and review this paragraph.)

Spreadsheet Use   The future value of the single amount also can be calculated as shown on the following Excel spreadsheet.

	A	B
1	FUTURE VALUE OF A SINGLE AMOUNT	
2	Present value	$800
3	Interest rate, pct per year compounded annually	6%
4	Number of years	5
5	Future value	$1,070.58
	Entry in Cell B5 is =FV(B3,B4,0,−B2,0) The minus sign appears before B2 because the present value is an outflow (i.e., a deposit made by Jane Farber).	

Table Use   The future value interest factor for an initial principal of $1 on deposit for 5 years at 6% interest compounded annually, $FVIF_{6\%, \, 5yrs}$, found in Table A–1, is 1.338. Using Equation 4.6, $800 \times 1.338 = \$1,070.40$. Therefore, the future value of Jane's deposit at the end of year 5 will be $1,070.40.

Because both the calculator and the spreadsheet are more accurate than the future value factors, which have been rounded to the nearest 0.001, a slight difference—in this case, $0.18—will frequently exist between the values found by these alternative methods. Clearly, the improved accuracy and ease of calculation tend to favor the use of the calculator.

A Graphical View of Future Value

Remember that we measure future value at the *end* of the given period. Figure 4.5 illustrates the relationship among various interest rates, the number of periods interest is earned, and the future value of one dollar. The figure shows that (1) the higher the interest rate, the higher the future value, and (2) the longer the period of time, the higher the future value. Note that for an interest rate of 0 percent, the future value always equals the present value ($1.00). But for any interest rate greater than zero, the future value is greater than the present value of $1.00.

---

5. The known values *can be punched into the calculator in any order;* the order specified in this as well as other demonstrations of calculator use included in this text merely reflects convenience and personal preference.

6. The calculator differentiates inflows from outflows by preceding the outflows with a negative sign. For example, in the problem just demonstrated, the $800 present value (PV), because it was keyed as a positive number (800), is considered an inflow or deposit. Therefore, the calculated future value (FV) of −1,070.58 is preceded by a minus sign to show that it is the resulting outflow or withdrawal. Had the $800 present value been keyed in as a negative number (−800), the future value of $1,070.58 would have been displayed as a positive number (1,070.58). Simply stated, *the cash flows—present value (PV) and future value (FV)—will have opposite signs.*

FIGURE 4.5

Future Value Relationship
Interest rates, time periods, and future value of one dollar

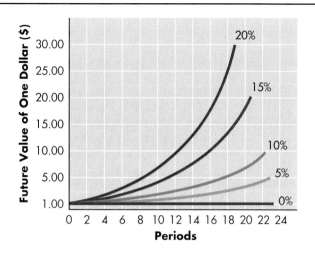

Present Value of a Single Amount

present value
The current dollar value of a future amount—the amount of money that would have to be invested today at a given interest rate over a specified period to equal the future amount.

It is often useful to determine the value today of a future amount of money. For example, how much would I have to deposit today into an account paying 7 percent annual interest to accumulate $3,000 at the end of 5 years? **Present value** is the current dollar value of a future amount—the amount of money that would have to be invested today at a given interest rate over a specified period to equal the future amount. Present value depends largely on the investment opportunities and the point in time at which the amount is to be received. This section explores the present value of a single amount.

The Concept of Present Value

discounting cash flows
The process of finding present values; the inverse of compounding interest.

The process of finding present values is often referred to as **discounting cash flows**. It is concerned with answering the following question: If I can earn i percent on my money, what is the most I would be willing to pay now for an opportunity to receive FV_n dollars n periods from today?

This process is actually the inverse of compounding interest. Instead of finding the future value of present dollars invested at a given rate, discounting determines the present value of a future amount, assuming an opportunity to earn a certain return on the money. This annual rate of return is variously referred to as the *discount rate, required return, cost of capital,* and *opportunity cost.* These terms will be used interchangeably in this text.

Personal Finance Example   Paul Shorter has an opportunity to receive $300 one year from now. If he can earn 6% on his investments in the normal course of events, what is the most he should pay now for this opportunity? To answer this question, Paul must determine how many dollars he would have to invest at 6% today to have $300 one year from now. Letting PV equal this unknown amount and using the same notation as in the future value discussion, we have

$$PV \times (1 + 0.06) = \$300 \qquad \textbf{(4.7)}$$

Solving Equation 4.7 for *PV* gives us Equation 4.8:

$$PV = \frac{\$300}{(1 + 0.06)} \qquad (4.8)$$
$$= \$283.02$$

The value today ("present value") of $300 received one year from today, given an opportunity cost of 6%, is $283.02. That is, investing $283.02 today at the 6% opportunity cost would result in $300 at the end of one year.

The Equation for Present Value

The present value of a future amount can be found mathematically by solving Equation 4.4 for *PV*. In other words, the present value, *PV*, of some future amount, FV^n, to be received *n* periods from now, assuming an opportunity cost of *i*, is calculated as follows:

$$PV = \frac{FV_n}{(1 + i)^n} = FV_n \times \left[\frac{1}{(1 + i)^n} \right] \qquad (4.9)$$

Note the similarity between this general equation for present value and the equation in the preceding example (Equation 4.8). Let's use this equation in an example.

Personal Finance Example   Pam Valenti wishes to find the present value of $1,700 that will be received 8 years from now. Pam's opportunity cost is 8%. Substituting $FV_8 = \$1,700$, $n = 8$, and $i = 0.08$ into Equation 4.9 yields Equation 4.10:

$$PV = \frac{\$1,700}{(1 + 0.08)^8} = \frac{\$1,700}{1.851} = \$918.42 \qquad (4.10)$$

The following time line shows this analysis.

Time line for present value of a single amount ($1,700 future amount, discounted at 8%, from the end of 8 years)

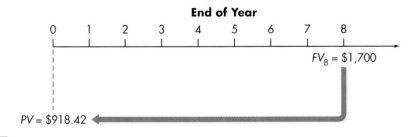

Using Computational Tools to Find Present Value

present value interest factor
The multiplier used to calculate, at a specified discount rate, the present value of an amount to be received in a future period.

The present value calculation can be simplified by using a **present value interest factor**. This factor is the multiplier used to calculate, at a specified discount rate, the present value of an amount to be received in a future period. The present value interest factor for the present value of $1 discounted at *i* percent for *n* periods is referred to as $PVIF_{i,n}$.

$$\text{Present value interest factor} = PVIF_{i,n} = \frac{1}{(1 + i)^n} \qquad (4.11)$$

Appendix Table A–2 presents present value interest factors for $1. By letting $PVIF_{i,n}$ represent the appropriate factor, we can rewrite the general equation for present value (Equation 4.9) as follows:

$$PV = FV_n \times (PVIF_{i,n}) \qquad \text{(4.12)}$$

This expression indicates that to find the present value of an amount to be received in a future period, n, we have merely to multiply the future amount, FV_n, by the appropriate present value interest factor.

Personal Finance Example   As noted, Pam Valenti wishes to find the present value of $1,700 to be received 8 years from now, assuming an 8% opportunity cost.

Input	Function
1700	FV
8	N
8	I
	CPT
	PV

Solution
918.46

Calculator Use   Using the calculator's financial functions and the inputs shown at the left, you should find the present value to be $918.46. The value obtained with the calculator is more accurate than the values found using the equation or the table (shown below), although for the purposes of this text, these differences are insignificant.

Spreadsheet Use   The present value of the single future amount also can be calculated as shown on the following Excel spreadsheet.

	A	B
1	PRESENT VALUE OF A SINGLE AMOUNT	
2	Future value	$1,700
3	Interest rate, pct per year compounded annually	8%
4	Number of years	8
5	Present value	$918.46

Entry in Cell B5 is =−PV(B3,B4,0,B2)
The minus sign appears before PV to change
the present value to a positive amount.

Table Use   The present value interest factor for 8% and 8 years, $PVIF_{8\%,8 \text{ yrs}}$, found in Table A–2, is 0.540. Using Equation 4.12, $1,700 \times 0.540 = $918. The present value of the $1,700 Pam expects to receive in 8 years is $918.

A Graphical View of Present Value

Remember that present value calculations assume that the future values are measured at the *end* of the given period. The relationships among the factors in a present value calculation are illustrated in Figure 4.6 (see page 154). The figure clearly shows that, everything else being equal, (1) the higher the discount rate, the lower the present value, and (2) the longer the period of time, the lower the present value. Also note that given a discount rate of 0 percent, the present value always equals the future value ($1.00). But for any discount rate greater than zero, the present value is less than the future value of $1.00.

Comparing Present Value and Future Value

We will close this section with some important observations about present values. One is that the expression for the present value interest factor for i percent and n periods, $1/(1 + i)^n$, is the *inverse* of the future value interest factor for i percent and

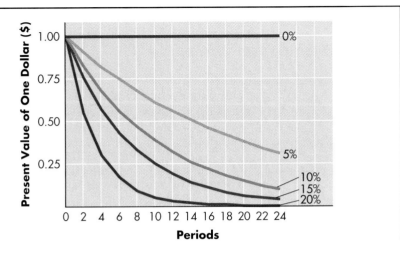

FIGURE 4.6

Present Value Relationship
Discount rates, time periods, and present value of one dollar

n periods, $(1 + i)^n$. You can confirm this very simply: Divide a present value interest factor for i percent and n periods, $PVIF_{i,n}$, given in Table A–2, into 1.0, and compare the resulting value to the future value interest factor given in Table A–1 for i percent and n periods, $FVIF_{i,n}$. The two values should be equivalent.

Second, because of the relationship between present value interest factors and future value interest factors, we can find the present value interest factors given a table of future value interest factors, and vice versa. For example, the future value interest factor (from Table A–1) for 10 percent and 5 periods is 1.611. Dividing this value into 1.0 yields 0.621, which is the present value interest factor (given in Table A–2) for 10 percent and 5 periods.

REVIEW QUESTIONS

4–3 How is the *compounding process* related to the payment of interest on savings? What is the general equation for future value?

4–4 What effect would a *decrease* in the interest rate have on the future value of a deposit? What effect would an *increase* in the holding period have on future value?

4–5 What is meant by "the present value of a future amount"? What is the general equation for present value?

4–6 What effect does *increasing* the required return have on the present value of a future amount? Why?

4–7 How are present value and future value calculations related?

4.3 | Annuities

How much would you pay today, given that you can earn 7 percent on low-risk investments, to receive a guaranteed $3,000 at the end of *each* of the next 20 years? How much will you have at the end of 5 years if your employer withholds and invests $1,000 of your year-end bonus at the end of *each* of the next 5 years,

annuity
A stream of equal periodic cash flows, over a specified time period. These cash flows can be *inflows* of returns earned on investments or *outflows* of funds invested to earn future returns.

ordinary annuity
An annuity for which the cash flow occurs at the *end* of each period.

annuity due
An annuity for which the cash flow occurs at the *beginning* of each period.

guaranteeing you a 9 percent annual rate of return? To answer these questions, you need to understand the application of the time value of money to *annuities*.

An **annuity** is a stream of equal periodic cash flows, over a specified time period. These cash flows are usually annual but can occur at other intervals, such as monthly (rent, car payments). The cash flows in an annuity can be *inflows* (the $3,000 received at the end of each of the next 20 years) or *outflows* (the $1,000 invested at the end of each of the next 5 years).

Types of Annuities

There are two basic types of annuities. For an **ordinary annuity,** the cash flow occurs at the *end* of each period. For an **annuity due,** the cash flow occurs at the *beginning* of each period.

Personal Finance Example   Fran Abrams is choosing which of two annuities to receive. Both are 5-year, $1,000 annuities; annuity A is an ordinary annuity, and annuity B is an annuity due. To better understand the difference between these annuities, she has listed their cash flows in Table 4.1. Note that the amount of each annuity totals $5,000. The two annuities differ in the timing of their cash flows: The cash flows are received sooner with the annuity due than with the ordinary annuity.

Although the cash flows of both annuities in Table 4.1 total $5,000, the annuity due would have a higher future value than the ordinary annuity, because each of its five annual cash flows can earn interest for one year more than each of the ordinary annuity's cash flows. In general, as will be demonstrated later in this chapter, *both the future value and the present value of an annuity due are always greater than the future value and the present value, respectively, of an otherwise identical ordinary annuity.*

Because ordinary annuities are more frequently used in finance, *unless otherwise specified, the term* annuity *is intended throughout this book to refer to ordinary annuities.* Discussions of annuities in this book concentrate on ordinary annuities. For discussion and computation of annuities due, see the book's website.

	Annual cash flows	
End of year[a]	**Annuity A (***ordinary***)**	**Annuity B (***annuity due***)**
0	$ 0	$1,000
1	1,000	1,000
2	1,000	1,000
3	1,000	1,000
4	1,000	1,000
5	1,000	0
Totals	$5,000	$5,000

TABLE 4.1   Comparison of Ordinary Annuity and Annuity Due Cash Flows ($1,000, 5 Years)

[a]The ends of years 0, 1, 2, 3, and 4 are equivalent to the beginnings of years 1, 2, 3, 4, and 5, respectively.

Finding the Future Value of an Ordinary Annuity

The calculations required to find the future value of an ordinary annuity are illustrated in the following example.

Personal Finance Example   Fran Abrams wishes to determine how much money she will have at the end of 5 years if she chooses annuity A, the ordinary annuity. It represents deposits of $1,000 annually, at the *end of each* of the next 5 years, into a savings account paying 7% annual interest. This situation is depicted on the following time line:

Time line for future value of an ordinary annuity ($1,000 end-of-year deposit, earning 7%, at the end of 5 years)

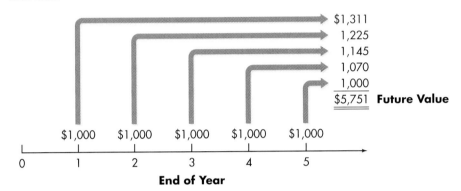

As the figure shows, at the end of year 5, Fran will have $5,751 in her account. Note that because the deposits are made at the end of the year, the first deposit will earn interest for 4 years, the second for 3 years, and so on.

Using Computational Tools to Find the Future Value of an Ordinary Annuity

Annuity calculations can be simplified by using a financial calculator, an electronic spreadsheet, or an interest table. A table for the future value of a $1 *ordinary annuity* is given in Appendix Table A–3. The factors in the table are derived by summing the future value interest factors for the appropriate number of years. For example, the factor for the annuity in the preceding example is the sum of the factors for the five years (years 4 through 0): $1.311 + 1.225 + 1.145 + 1.070 + 1.000 = 5.751$. Because the deposits occur at the end of each year, they will earn interest from the end of the year in which each occurs to the end of year 5. Therefore, the first deposit earns interest for 4 years (end of year 1 through end of year 5), and the last deposit earns interest for zero years. The future value interest factor for zero years at any interest rate i, $FVIF_{i,0}$, is 1.000, as we have noted. The formula for the **future value interest factor for an ordinary annuity** when interest is compounded annually at i percent for n periods, $FVIFA_{i,n}$, is[7]

future value interest factor for an ordinary annuity The multiplier used to calculate the future value of an *ordinary annuity* at a specified interest rate over a given period of time.

$$FVIFA_{i,n} = \sum_{t=1}^{n}(1+i)^{t-1}$$ (4.13)

---

7. A mathematical expression that can be applied to calculate the future value interest factor for an ordinary annuity more efficiently is

$$FVIFA_{i,n} = \frac{1}{i} \times [(1+i)^n - 1]$$ (4.13a)

The use of this expression is especially attractive in the absence of any financial calculator, electronic spreadsheet, or the appropriate financial tables.

This factor is the multiplier used to calculate the future value of an *ordinary annuity* at a specified interest rate over a given period of time.

Using FVA_n for the future value of an *n*-year annuity, *PMT* for the amount to be deposited annually at the *end* of each year, and $FVIFA_{i,n}$ for the appropriate *future value interest factor for a one-dollar ordinary annuity compounded at i percent for* n *years*, we can express the relationship among these variables as

$$FVA_n = PMT \times (FVIFA_{i,n}) \tag{4.14}$$

The following example illustrates this calculation using a calculator, a spreadsheet, and a table.

Input   Function
1000   PMT
5   N
7   I
      CPT
      FV

Solution
5,750.74

Personal Finance Example   As noted earlier, Fran Abrams wishes to find the future value (FVA_n) at the end of 5 years (*n*) of an annual *end-of-year deposit* of $1,000 (*PMT*) into an account paying 7% annual interest (*i*) during the next 5 years.

Calculator Use   Using the calculator inputs shown at the left, you will find the future value of the ordinary annuity to be $5,750.74, a slightly more precise answer than that found using the table (shown below).

Spreadsheet Use   The future value of the ordinary annuity also can be calculated as shown on the following Excel spreadsheet.

	A	B
1	FUTURE VALUE OF AN ORDINARY ANNUITY	
2	Annual payment	$1,000
3	Annual rate of interest, compounded annually	7%
4	Number of years	5
5	Future value of an ordinary annuity	$5,750.74

Entry in Cell B5 is =FV(B3,B4,−B2)
The minus sign appears before B2 because
the annual payment is a cash outflow.

Table Use   The future value interest factor for an ordinary 5-year annuity at 7% ($FVIFA_{7\%,5yrs}$), found in Table A–3, is 5.751. Using Equation 4.14, the $1,000 deposit $\times$ 5.751 results in a future value for the annuity of $5,751.

Finding the Present Value of an Ordinary Annuity

Quite often in finance, there is a need to find the present value of a *stream* of cash flows to be received in future periods. An annuity is, of course, a stream of equal periodic cash flows. (We'll explore the case of mixed streams of cash flows in a later section.) The method for finding the present value of an ordinary annuity is similar to the method just discussed. There are long and short methods for making this calculation.

Example   Braden Company, a small producer of plastic toys, wants to determine the most it should pay to purchase a particular ordinary annuity. The annuity consists of cash flows of $700 at the end of each year for 5 years. The firm requires the

As the equation shows, the appropriate factor, $PVIFA_{i,\infty}$, is found simply by dividing the discount rate, i (stated as a decimal), into 1. The validity of this method can be seen by looking at the factors in Table A–4 for 8, 10, 20, and 40 percent: As the number of periods (typically years) approaches 50, these factors approach the values calculated using Equation 4.17: $1 \div 0.08 = 12.50$; $1 \div 0.10 = 10.00$; $1 \div 0.20 = 5.00$; and $1 \div 0.40 = 2.50$.

Personal Finance Example   Ross Clark wishes to endow a chair in finance at his alma mater. The university indicated that it requires $200,000 per year to support the chair, and the endowment would earn 10% per year. To determine the amount Ross must give the university to fund the chair, we must determine the present value of a $200,000 perpetuity discounted at 10%. The appropriate present value interest factor can be found by dividing 1 by 0.10, as noted in Equation 4.17. Substituting the resulting factor, $PVIFA_{10\%,\infty} = 10$, and the amount of the perpetuity, $PMT = \$200,000$, into Equation 4.16 results in a present value of $2,000,000 for the perpetuity. In other words, to generate $200,000 every year for an indefinite period requires $2,000,000 today if Ross Clark's alma mater can earn 10% on its investments. If the university earns 10% interest annually on the $2,000,000, it can withdraw $200,000 per year indefinitely without touching the initial $2,000,000, which would never be drawn upon.

REVIEW QUESTIONS

4–8   What is the difference between an *ordinary annuity* and an *annuity due?* Which always has greater future value and present value for identical annuities and interest rates? Why?

4–9   What are the most efficient ways to calculate the present value of an ordinary annuity? What is the relationship between the *PVIF* and *PVIFA* interest factors given in Tables A–2 and A–4, respectively?

4–10   What is a *perpetuity?* How can the present value interest factor for such a stream of cash flows be determined?

4.4 | Mixed Streams

mixed stream
A stream of unequal periodic cash flows that reflect no particular pattern.

Two basic types of cash flow streams are possible: the annuity and the mixed stream. Whereas an *annuity* is a pattern of equal periodic cash flows, a **mixed stream** is a stream of unequal periodic cash flows that reflect no particular pattern. Financial managers frequently need to evaluate opportunities that are expected to provide mixed streams of cash flows. Here we consider both the future value and the present value of mixed streams.

Future Value of a Mixed Stream

Determining the future value of a mixed stream of cash flows is straightforward. We determine the future value of each cash flow at the specified future date and then add all the individual future values to find the total future value.

Example   Shrell Industries, a cabinet manufacturer, expects to receive the following mixed stream of cash flows over the next 5 years from one of its small customers.

End of year	Cash flow
1	$11,500
2	14,000
3	12,900
4	16,000
5	18,000

If Shrell expects to earn 8% on its investments, how much will it accumulate by the end of year 5 if it immediately invests these cash flows when they are received? This situation is depicted on the following time line:

Time line for future value of a mixed stream (end-of-year cash flows, compounded at 8% to the end of year 5)

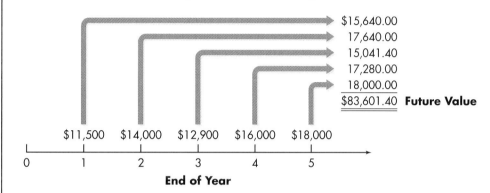

Calculator Use   You can use your calculator to find the future value of each individual cash flow, as demonstrated earlier (pages 149 and 150), and then sum the future values, to get the future value of the stream. Unfortunately, unless you can program your calculator, most calculators lack a function that would allow you to input *all of the cash flows*, specify the interest rate, and directly calculate the future value of the entire cash flow stream. Had you used your calculator to find the individual cash flow future values and then summed them, the future value of Shrell Industries' cash flow stream at the end of year 5 would have been $83,608.15.

Spreadsheet Use   The future value of the mixed stream also can be calculated as shown on the following Excel spreadsheet.

	A	B
1	FUTURE VALUE OF A MIXED STREAM	
2	Interest rate, pct/year	8%
3	Year	Year-End Cash Flow
4	1	$11,500
5	2	$14,000
6	3	$12,900
7	4	$16,000
8	5	$18,000
9	Future value	$83,608.15

Entry in Cell B9 is
=−FV(B2,A8,0,NPV(B2,B4:B8)).
The minus sign appears before FV to convert
the future value to a positive amount.

| | | | TABLE 4.3 | Future Value of a Mixed Stream of Cash Flows |

TABLE 4.3   **Future Value of a Mixed Stream of Cash Flows**

Year	Cash flow (1)	Number of years earning interest (n) (2)	$FVIF_{8\%,n}{}^a$ (3)	Future value [(1) × (3)] (4)
1	$11,500	5 − 1 = 4	1.360	$15,640.00
2	14,000	5 − 2 = 3	1.260	17,640.00
3	12,900	5 − 3 = 2	1.166	15,041.40
4	16,000	5 − 4 = 1	1.080	17,280.00
5	18,000	5 − 5 = 0	1.000^b	18,000.00
			Future value of mixed stream	$83,601.40

[a]Future value interest factors at 8% are from Table A–1.

[b]The future value of the end-of-year-5 deposit at the end of year 5 is its present value because it earns interest for zero years and $(1 + 0.08)^0 = 1.000$.

Table Use   To solve this problem, we determine the future value of each cash flow compounded at 8% for the appropriate number of years. Note that the first cash flow of $11,500, received at the end of year 1, will earn interest for 4 years (end of year 1 through end of year 5); the second cash flow of $14,000, received at the end of year 2, will earn interest for 3 years (end of year 2 through end of year 5); and so on. The sum of the individual end-of-year-5 future values is the future value of the mixed cash flow stream. The future value interest factors required are those shown in Table A–1. Table 4.3 presents the calculations needed to find the future value of the cash flow stream, which turns out to be $83,601.40. This value is less precise than the value obtained using a calculator or spreadsheet.

If Shrell Industries invests at 8% interest the cash flows received from its customer over the next 5 years, the company will accumulate about $83,600 by the end of year 5.

Present Value of a Mixed Stream

Finding the present value of a mixed stream of cash flows is similar to finding the future value of a mixed stream. We determine the present value of each future amount and then add all the individual present values together to find the total present value.

Example   Frey Company, a shoe manufacturer, has been offered an opportunity to receive the following mixed stream of cash flows over the next 5 years:

End of year	Cash flow
1	$400
2	800
3	500
4	400
5	300

If the firm must earn at least 9% on its investments, what is the most it should pay for this opportunity? This situation is depicted on the following time line:

Time line for present value of a mixed stream (end-of-year cash flows, discounted at 9% over the corresponding number of years)

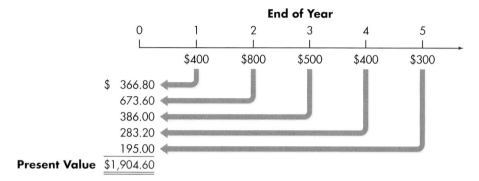

Calculator Use   You can use a calculator to find the present value of each individual cash flow, as demonstrated earlier (page 153), and then sum the present values, to get the present value of the stream. However, most financial calculators have a function that allows you to punch in *all cash flows*, specify the discount rate, and then directly calculate the present value of the entire cash flow stream. Because calculators provide solutions more precise than those based on rounded table factors, the present value of Frey Company's cash flow stream found using a calculator is $1,904.76.

Spreadsheet Use   The present value of the mixed stream of future cash flows also can be calculated as shown on the following Excel spreadsheet.

	A	B
1	PRESENT VALUE OF A MIXED STREAM OF CASH FLOWS	
2	Interest rate, pct/year	9%
3	Year	Year-End Cash Flow
4	1	$400
5	2	$800
6	3	$500
7	4	$400
8	5	$300
9	Present value	$1,904.76
	Entry in Cell B9 is =NPV(B2,B4:B8).	

Table Use   To solve this problem, determine the present value of each cash flow discounted at 9% for the appropriate number of years. The sum of these individual values is the present value of the total stream. The present value interest factors required are those shown in Table A–2. Table 4.4 (see page 164) presents the calculations needed to find the present value of the cash flow stream, which turns out to be $1,904.60. This value is close to the more precise value of $1,904.76 found by using a calculator or spreadsheet.

Paying about $1,905 would provide exactly a 9% return. Frey should pay no more than that amount for the opportunity to receive these cash flows.

			Present value
	Cash flow	$PVIF_{9\%,n}{}^a$	[(1) × (2)]
Year (n)	(1)	(2)	(3)
1	$400	0.917	$ 366.80
2	800	0.842	673.60
3	500	0.772	386.00
4	400	0.708	283.20
5	300	0.650	195.00
		Present value of mixed stream	$1,904.60

TABLE 4.4   Present Value of a Mixed Stream of Cash Flows

[a]Present value interest factors at 9% are from Table A–2.

REVIEW QUESTION

4–11 How is the future value of a mixed stream of cash flows calculated? How is the present value of a mixed stream of cash flows calculated?

4.5 | Compounding Interest More Frequently Than Annually

Interest is often compounded more frequently than once a year. Savings institutions compound interest semiannually, quarterly, monthly, weekly, daily, or even continuously. This section discusses various issues and techniques related to these more frequent compounding intervals.

Semiannual Compounding

semiannual compounding
Compounding of interest over two periods within the year.

Semiannual compounding of interest involves two compounding periods within the year. Instead of the stated interest rate being paid once a year, one-half of the stated interest rate is paid twice a year.

Personal Finance Example   Fred Moreno has decided to invest $100 in a savings account paying 8% interest *compounded semiannually*. If he leaves his money in the account for 24 months (2 years), he will be paid 4% interest compounded over four periods, each of which is 6 months long. Table 4.5 uses interest factors to show that at the end of 12 months (1 year) with 8% semiannual compounding, Fred will have $108.16; at the end of 24 months (2 years), he will have $116.99.

Quarterly Compounding

quarterly compounding
Compounding of interest over four periods within the year.

Quarterly compounding of interest involves four compounding periods within the year. One-fourth of the stated interest rate is paid four times a year.

TABLE 4.5   **Future Value from Investing $100 at 8% Interest Compounded Semiannually over 24 Months (2 Years)**

Period	Beginning principal (1)	Future value interest factor (2)	Future value at end of period [(1) × (2)] (3)
6 months	$100.00	1.04	$104.00
12 months	104.00	1.04	108.16
18 months	108.16	1.04	112.49
24 months	112.49	1.04	116.99

Personal Finance Example   Fred Moreno has found an institution that will pay him 8% interest *compounded quarterly*. If he leaves his money in this account for 24 months (2 years), he will be paid 2% interest compounded over eight periods, each of which is 3 months long. Table 4.6 uses interest factors to show the amount Fred will have at the end of each period. At the end of 12 months (1 year), with 8% quarterly compounding, Fred will have $108.24; at the end of 24 months (2 years), he will have $117.17.

Table 4.7 (see page 166) compares values for Fred Moreno's $100 at the end of years 1 and 2 given annual, semiannual, and quarterly compounding periods at the 8 percent rate. As shown, *the more frequently interest is compounded, the greater the amount of money accumulated*. This is true for *any interest rate* for *any period of time*.

A General Equation for Compounding More Frequently Than Annually

The interest-factor formula for annual compounding (Equation 4.5) can be rewritten for use when compounding takes place more frequently. If *m* equals the

TABLE 4.6   **Future Value from Investing $100 at 8% Interest Compounded Quarterly over 24 Months (2 Years)**

Period	Beginning principal (1)	Future value interest factor (2)	Future value at end of period [(1) × (2)] (3)
3 months	$100.00	1.02	$102.00
6 months	102.00	1.02	104.04
9 months	104.04	1.02	106.12
12 months	106.12	1.02	108.24
15 months	108.24	1.02	110.41
18 months	110.40	1.02	112.62
21 months	112.61	1.02	114.87
24 months	114.86	1.02	117.17

| TABLE 4.7 | Future Value at the End of Years 1 and 2 from Investing $100 at 8% Interest, Given Various Compounding Periods |

	Compounding period		
End of year	Annual	Semiannual	Quarterly
1	$108.00	$108.16	$108.24
2	116.64	116.99	117.17

number of times per year interest is compounded, the interest-factor formula for annual compounding can be rewritten as

$$FVIF_{i,n} = \left(1 + \frac{i}{m}\right)^{m \times n} \tag{4.18}$$

The basic equation for future value (Equation 4.4) can now be rewritten as

$$FV_n = PV \times \left(1 + \frac{i}{m}\right)^{m \times n} \tag{4.19}$$

If $m = 1$, Equation 4.19 reduces to Equation 4.4. Thus, if interest is compounded annually (once a year), Equation 4.19 will provide the same result as Equation 4.4. The general use of Equation 4.19 can be illustrated with a simple example.

Personal Finance Example   The preceding examples calculated the amount that Fred Moreno would have at the end of 2 years if he deposited $100 at 8% interest compounded semiannually and compounded quarterly. For semiannual compounding, m would equal 2 in Equation 4.19; for quarterly compounding, m would equal 4. Substituting the appropriate values for semiannual and quarterly compounding into Equation 4.19, we find that

1. *For semiannual compounding:*

$$FV_2 = \$100 \times \left(1 + \frac{0.08}{2}\right)^{2 \times 2} = \$100 \times (1 + 0.04)^4 = \$116.99$$

2. *For quarterly compounding:*

$$FV_2 = \$100 \times \left(1 + \frac{0.08}{4}\right)^{4 \times 2} = \$100 \times (1 + 0.02)^8 = \$117.17$$

These results agree with the values for FV_2 in Tables 4.5 and 4.6.

If the interest were compounded monthly, weekly, or daily, m would equal 12, 52, or 365, respectively.

Using Computational Tools for Compounding More Frequently Than Annually

We can use the future value interest factors for one dollar, given in Table A–1, when interest is compounded m times each year. Instead of indexing the table for i percent and n years, as we do when interest is compounded annually, we index it for $(i \div m)$ percent and $(m \times n)$ periods. However, the table is less useful, because it includes only selected rates for a limited number of periods. Instead, a financial calculator or an electronic spreadsheet is typically required.

Personal Finance Example   Fred Moreno wished to find the future value of $100 invested at 8% interest compounded both semiannually and quarterly for 2 years. The number of compounding periods m, the interest rate $(i \div m)$, and the number of periods $(m \times n)$ used, along with the future value interest factor, are as follows:

Compounding period	m	Interest rate $(i \div m)$	Periods $(m \times n)$	Future value interest factor from Table A–1
Semiannual	2	8% ÷ 2 = 4%	2 × 2 = 4	1.170
Quarterly	4	8% ÷ 4 = 2%	4 × 2 = 8	1.172

Calculator Use   If the calculator were used for the semiannual compounding calculation, the number of periods would be 4 and the interest rate would be 4%. The future value of $116.99 will appear on the calculator display as shown at the top left.

For the quarterly compounding case, the number of periods would be 8 and the interest rate would be 2%. The future value of $117.17 will appear on the calculator display as shown in the second display at the left.

Spreadsheet Use   The future value of the single amount with semiannual and quarterly compounding also can be calculated as shown on the following Excel spreadsheet.

	A	B
1	FUTURE VALUE OF A SINGLE AMOUNT WITH SEMIANNUAL AND QUARTERLY COMPOUNDING	
2	Present value	$100
3	Interest rate, pct per year compounded semiannually	8%
4	Number of years	2
5	Future value with semiannual compounding	$116.99
6	Present value	$100
7	Interest rate, pct per year compounded quarterly	8%
8	Number of years	2
9	Future value with quarterly compounding	$117.17

Entry in Cell B5 is =FV(B3/2,B4*2,0,–B2,0).
Entry in Cell B9 is =FV(B7/4,B8*4,0,–B2,0).
The minus sign appears before B2 because the present value is a cash outflow (i.e., a deposit made by Fred Moreno).

Table Use   Multiplying each of the future value interest factors by the initial $100 deposit results in a value of $117.00 (1.170 × $100) for semiannual compounding and a value of $117.20 (1.172 × $100) for quarterly compounding.

Comparing the calculator, spreadsheet, and table values, we can see that the calculator and spreadsheet values agree with the values in Table 4.7 but are more precise because the table factors have been rounded.

Continuous Compounding

continuous compounding
Compounding of interest an infinite number of times per year at intervals of microseconds.

In the extreme case, interest can be compounded continuously. **Continuous compounding** involves compounding over every microsecond—the smallest time period imaginable. In this case, m in Equation 4.18 would approach infinity. Through the use of calculus, we know that as m approaches infinity, the interest-factor equation becomes

$$FVIF_{i,n} \text{ (continuous compounding)} = e^{i \times n} \qquad (4.20)$$

where e is the exponential function,[9] which has a value of 2.7183. The future value for continuous compounding is therefore

$$FV_n \text{ (continuous compounding)} = PV \times (e^{i \times n}) \qquad (4.21)$$

Personal Finance Example   To find the value at the end of 2 years ($n = 2$) of Fred Moreno's $100 deposit ($PV = \$100$) in an account paying 8% annual interest ($i = 0.08$) compounded continuously, we can substitute into Equation 4.21:

$$\begin{aligned} FV_2 \text{ (continuous compounding)} &= \$100 \times e^{0.08 \times 2} \\ &= \$100 \times 2.7183^{0.16} \\ &= \$100 \times 1.1735 = \$117.35 \end{aligned}$$

Calculator Use   To find this value using the calculator, you need first to find the value of $e^{0.16}$ by punching in 0.16 and then pressing **2nd** and then e^x to get 1.1735. Next multiply this value by $100 to get the future value of $117.35 as shown at the left. (*Note:* On some calculators, you may not have to press **2nd** before pressing e^x.)

Spreadsheet Use   The future value of the single amount with continuous compounding of Fred's deposit also can be calculated as shown on the following Excel spreadsheet.

	A	B
1	FUTURE VALUE OF A SINGLE AMOUNT WITH CONTINUOUS COMPOUNDING	
2	Present value	$100
3	Annual rate of interest, compounded continuously	8%
4	Number of years	2
5	Future value with continuous compounding	$117.35
	Entry in Cell B5 is =B2*EXP(B3*B4).	

The future value with continuous compounding therefore equals $117.35. As expected, the continuously compounded value is larger than the future value of interest compounded semiannually ($116.99) or quarterly ($117.17). Contin-

---

9. Most calculators have the exponential function, typically noted by e^x, built into them. The use of this key is especially helpful in calculating future value when interest is compounded continuously.

uous compounding results in the largest future value that would result from compounding interest more frequently than annually at a given rate over a stated period of time.

Nominal and Effective Annual Rates of Interest

nominal (stated) annual rate
Contractual annual rate of interest charged by a lender or promised by a borrower.

effective (true) annual rate (EAR)
The annual rate of interest actually paid or earned.

Both businesses and investors need to make objective comparisons of loan costs or investment returns over different compounding periods. To put interest rates on a common basis, so as to allow comparison, we distinguish between nominal and effective annual rates. The **nominal, or stated, annual rate** is the contractual annual rate of interest charged by a lender or promised by a borrower. The **effective, or true, annual rate (EAR)** is the annual rate of interest actually paid or earned. The effective annual rate reflects the effects of compounding frequency, whereas the nominal annual rate does not.

Using the notation introduced earlier, we can calculate the effective annual rate, EAR, by substituting values for the nominal annual rate, i, and the compounding frequency, m, into Equation 4.22:

$$EAR = \left(1 + \frac{i}{m}\right)^m - 1 \tag{4.22}$$

We can apply this equation using data from preceding examples.

Personal Finance Example   Fred Moreno wishes to find the effective annual rate associated with an 8% nominal annual rate ($i = 0.08$) when interest is compounded (1) annually ($m = 1$); (2) semiannually ($m = 2$); and (3) quarterly ($m = 4$). Substituting these values into Equation 4.22, we get

1. *For annual compounding:*

$$EAR = \left(1 + \frac{0.08}{1}\right)^1 - 1 = (1 + 0.08)^1 - 1 = 1 + 0.08 - 1 = 0.08 = 8\%$$

2. *For semiannual compounding:*

$$EAR = \left(1 + \frac{0.08}{2}\right)^2 - 1 = (1 + 0.04)^2 - 1 = 1.0816 - 1 = 0.0816 = 8.16\%$$

3. *For quarterly compounding:*

$$EAR = \left(1 + \frac{0.08}{4}\right)^4 - 1 = (1 + 0.02)^4 - 1 = 1.0824 - 1 = 0.0824 = 8.24\%$$

These values demonstrate two important points: The first is that nominal and effective annual rates are equivalent for annual compounding. The second is that the effective annual rate increases with increasing compounding frequency, up to a limit that occurs with *continuous compounding.*[10]

---

10. The effective annual rate for this extreme case can be found by using the following equation:

$$EAR \text{ (continuous compounding)} = e^i - 1 \tag{4.22a}$$

For the 8% nominal annual rate ($i = 0.08$), substitution into Equation 4.24a results in an effective annual rate of

$$e^{0.08} - 1 = 1.0833 - 1 = 0.0833 = 8.33\%$$

in the case of continuous compounding. This is the highest effective annual rate attainable with an 8% nominal rate.

At the consumer level, "truth-in-lending laws" require disclosure on credit card and loan agreements of the **annual percentage rate (APR).** The APR is the *nominal annual rate* found by multiplying the periodic rate by the number of periods in one year. For example, a bank credit card that charges $1^1/_2$ percent per month (the periodic rate) would have an APR of 18 percent (1.5% per month $\times$ 12 months per year).

"Truth-in-savings laws," on the other hand, require banks to quote the **annual percentage yield (APY)** on their savings products. The APY is the *effective annual rate* a savings product pays. For example, a savings account that pays 0.5 percent per month would have an APY of 6.17 percent $[(1.005)^{12} - 1]$.

Quoting loan interest rates at their lower nominal annual rate (the APR) and savings interest rates at the higher effective annual rate (the APY) offers two advantages: It tends to standardize disclosure to consumers, and it enables financial institutions to quote the most attractive interest rates: low loan rates and high savings rates.

REVIEW QUESTIONS

4–12 What effect does compounding interest more frequently than annually have on (**a**) future value and (**b**) the *effective annual rate (EAR)?* Why?

4–13 How does the future value of a deposit subject to continuous compounding compare to the value obtained by annual compounding?

4–14 Differentiate between a *nominal annual rate* and an *effective annual rate (EAR)*. Define *annual percentage rate (APR)* and *annual percentage yield (APY)*.

4.6 | Special Applications of Time Value

Future value and present value techniques have a number of important applications in finance. We'll study four of them in this section: (1) determining deposits needed to accumulate a future sum, (2) loan amortization, (3) finding interest or growth rates, and (4) finding an unknown number of periods.

Determining Deposits Needed to Accumulate a Future Sum

Suppose you want to buy a house 5 years from now, and you estimate that an initial down payment of $30,000 will be required at that time. To accumulate the $30,000, you will wish to make equal annual end-of-year deposits into an account paying annual interest of 6 percent. The solution to this problem is closely related to the process of finding the future value of an annuity. You must determine what size annuity will result in a single amount equal to $30,000 at the end of year 5.

Earlier in the chapter we found the future value of an *n*-year ordinary annuity, FVA_n, by multiplying the annual deposit, PMT, by the appropriate interest factor, $FVIFA_{i,n}$. The relationship of the three variables was defined by Equation 4.14, which is repeated here as Equation 4.23:

$$FVA_n = PMT \times (FVIFA_{i,n}) \qquad \text{(4.23)}$$

We can find the annual deposit required to accumulate FVA_n dollars by solving Equation 4.23 for PMT. Isolating PMT on the left side of the equation gives us

$$PMT = \frac{FVA_n}{FVIFA_{i,n}}$$

(4.24)

Once this is done, we have only to substitute the known values of FVA_n and $FVIFA_{i,n}$ into the right side of the equation to find the annual deposit required.

Personal Finance Example   As just stated, you want to determine the equal annual end-of-year deposits required to accumulate $30,000 at the end of 5 years, given an interest rate of 6%.

Input	Function
30000	FV
5	N
6	I
	CPT
	PMT

Solution
5,321.89

Calculator Use   Using the calculator inputs shown at the left, you will find the annual deposit amount to be $5,321.89. Thus, if $5,321.89 is deposited at the end of each year for 5 years at 6% interest, there will be $30,000 in the account at the end of 5 years.

Spreadsheet Use   The annual deposit needed to accumulate the future sum also can be calculated as shown on the following Excel spreadsheet.

	A	B
1	ANNUAL DEPOSITS NEEDED TO ACCUMULATE A FUTURE SUM	
2	Future value	$30,000
3	Number of years	5
4	Annual rate of interest	6%
5	Annual deposit	$5,321.89
	Entry in Cell B5 is =−PMT(B4,B3,0,B2). The minus sign appears before PMT because the annual deposits are cash outflows.	

Table Use   Table A–3 indicates that the future value interest factor for an ordinary annuity at 6% for 5 years ($FVIFA_{6\%,5yrs}$) is 5.637. Substituting $FVA_5 = $30,000$ and $FVIFA_{6\%,5yrs} = 5.637$ into Equation 4.26 yields an annual required deposit, PMT, of $5,321.98. Note that this value, except for a slight rounding difference, agrees with the value found using a calculator and spreadsheet.

loan amortization
The determination of the equal periodic loan payments necessary to provide a lender with a specified interest return and to repay the loan principal over a specified period.

loan amortization schedule
A schedule of equal payments to repay a loan. It shows the allocation of each loan payment to interest and principal.

Loan Amortization

The term **loan amortization** refers to the determination of equal periodic loan payments. These payments provide a lender with a specified interest return and repay the loan principal over a specified period. The loan amortization process involves finding the future payments, over the term of the loan, whose present value at the loan interest rate equals the amount of initial principal borrowed. Lenders use a **loan amortization schedule** to determine these payment amounts and the allocation of each payment to interest and principal. In the case of home mortgages, these tables are used to find the equal *monthly* payments necessary to *amortize*, or pay off, the mortgage at a specified interest rate over a 15- to 30-year period.

Amortizing a loan actually involves creating an annuity out of a present amount. For example, say you borrow $6,000 at 10 percent and agree to make equal annual end-of-year payments over 4 years. To find the size of the payments, the lender determines the amount of a 4-year annuity discounted at 10 percent that has a present value of $6,000. This process is actually the inverse of finding the present value of an annuity.

Earlier in the chapter, we found the present value, PVA_n, of an n-year ordinary annuity by multiplying the annual amount, PMT, by the present value interest factor for an annuity, $PVIFA_{i,n}$. This relationship, which was originally expressed as Equation 4.16, is repeated here as Equation 4.25:

$$PVA_n = PMT \times (PVIFA_{i,n}) \tag{4.25}$$

To find the equal annual payment required to pay off, or amortize, the loan, PVA_n, over a certain number of years at a specified interest rate, we need to solve Equation 4.25 for PMT. Isolating PMT on the left side of the equation gives us

$$PMT = \frac{PVA_n}{PVIFA_{i,n}} \tag{4.26}$$

Once this is done, we have only to substitute the known values into the righthand side of the equation to find the annual payment required.

Personal Finance Example   As just stated, you want to determine the equal annual end-of-year payments necessary to amortize fully a $6,000, 10% loan over 4 years.

Input	Function
6000	PV
4	N
10	I
	CPT
	PMT

Solution
1,892.82

Calculator Use   Using the calculator inputs shown at the left, you will find the annual payment amount to be $1,892.82. Thus, to repay the interest and principal on a $6,000, 10%, 4-year loan, equal annual end-of-year payments of $1,892.82 are necessary.

The allocation of each loan payment (based on table use, a payment of $1,892.74) to interest and principal can be seen in columns 3 and 4 of the *loan amortization schedule* in Table 4.8. The portion of each payment that represents interest (column 3) declines over the repayment period, and the portion going to

TABLE 4.8   **Loan Amortization Schedule**
($6,000 Principal, 10% Interest, 4-Year Repayment Period)

End of year	Beginning-of-year principal (1)	Loan payment[a] (2)	Payments		End-of-year principal [(1) − (4)] (5)
			Interest [0.10 × (1)] (3)	Principal [(2) − (3)] (4)	
1	$6,000.00	$1,892.74	$600.00	$1,292.74	$4,707.26
2	4,707.26	1,892.74	470.73	1,422.01	3,285.25
3	3,285.25	1,892.74	328.53	1,564.21	1,721.04
4	1,721.04	1,892.74	172.10	1,720.64	—[b]

[a]Based on the use of tables.

[b]Because of rounding, a slight difference ($0.40) exists between the beginning-of-year-4 principal (in column 1) and the year-4 principal payment (in column 4).

principal repayment (column 4) increases. This pattern is typical of amortized loans; as the principal is reduced, the interest component declines, leaving a larger portion of each subsequent loan payment to repay principal.

Spreadsheet Use   The annual payment to repay the loan also can be calculated as shown on the first Excel spreadsheet below. The amortization schedule allocating each loan payment to interest and principal can be calculated precisely as shown on the second spreadsheet.

	A	B
1	ANNUAL PAYMENT TO REPAY A LOAN	
2	Loan principal (present value)	$6,000
3	Annual rate of interest	10%
4	Number of years	4
5	Annual payment	$1,892.82

Entry in Cell B5 is =–PMT(B3,B4,B2).
The minus sign appears before PMT because
the annual payments are cash outflows.

	A	B	C	D	E
1		LOAN AMORTIZATION SCHEDULE			
2		Data: Loan principal		$6,000	
3		Annual rate of interest		10%	
4		Number of years		4	
5		Annual Payments			
6	Year	Total	To Interest	To Principal	Year-End Principal
7	0				$6,000.00
8	1	$1,892.82	$600.00	$1,292.82	4,707.18
9	2	$1,892.82	$470.72	$1,422.11	3,285.07
10	3	$1,892.82	$328.51	$1,564.32	1,720.75
11	4	$1,892.82	$172.07	$1,720.75	0.00

Key Cell Entries
Cell B8: =–PMT(D3,D4,D2), copy to B9:B11
Cell C8: =–CUMIPMT(D3,D4,D2,A8,A8,0), copy to C9:C11
Cell D8: =–CUMPRINC(D3,D4,D2,A8,A8,0), copy to D9:D11
Cell E8: =E7–D8, copy to E9:E11
The minus signs appear before the entries in Cells B8, C8, and D8
because these are cash outflows.

Table Use   Table A–4 indicates that the present value interest factor for an ordinary annuity corresponding to 10% and 4 years ($PVIFA_{10\%,4yrs}$) is 3.170. Substituting $PVA_4 = \$6,000$ and $PVIFA_{10\%,4yrs} = 3.170$ into Equation 4.28 and solving for PMT yield an annual loan payment of $1,892.74. Except for a slight rounding difference, this agrees with the calculator and spreadsheet value.

To attract buyers who could not immediately afford 15- to 30-year mortgages of equal annual payments, lenders offered mortgages whose interest rates adjusted at certain points. The *Focus on Practice* box on page 174 discusses how such mortgages have worked out for some "subprime" borrowers.

Focus on Practice   New Century Brings Trouble for Subprime Mortgages

IN PRACTICE

As the housing market began to boom at the end of the twentieth century and into the early twenty-first, the market share of subprime mortgages climbed from near 0 percent in 1997 to about 20 percent of mortgage originations in 2006. Several factors combined to fuel the rapid growth of lending to borrowers with tarnished credit, including a low interest rate environment, loose underwriting standards, and innovations in mortgage financing such as "affordability programs" to increase rates of homeownership among lower-income borrowers.

Particularly attractive to new homebuyers was the hybrid adjustable rate mortgage (ARM), which featured a low introductory interest rate that reset upward after a preset period of time. Interest rates began a steady upward trend beginning in late 2004. In 2006, some $300 billion worth of adjustable ARMs were reset to higher rates. In 2007, that figure will triple. The rise in interest rates will push monthly payments beyond what some homeowners can afford. For those who cannot make their payments, foreclosure and repossession by the lender may be the only way out.

Foreclosure on a nonproductive mortgage is particularly unwelcome and unrewarding for subprime mortgages. With very small equity margins in the original purchase, any drop in housing prices, as is currently happening in some overheated housing markets, exposes the lender to losses. They simply cannot sell the repossessed home for more than the outstanding loan. Typical of such lenders is **New Century Financial Corp.** The company, based in Irvine, California, entered Chapter 11 bankruptcy in April 2007, cutting 3,200 of its 7,200 employees as part of its reorganization. One of the largest providers of subprime mortgages, New Century made $51.6 billion in subprime loans in 2006.

Problems with subprime loans were not limited to New Century. The Mortgage Bankers Association estimates that subprime loans were used to finance about 17 percent of home purchases in 2006. The mortgage bankers group reported in March 2007 that 13 percent of all subprime loans were in delinquency, more than five times the delinquency rate for home loans to borrowers with the best credit ratings. Like most bubbles, excesses will lead to corrections and the financial fallout from the subprime delinquencies will eventually run its course.

■ *As a reaction to problems in the subprime area, lenders are already tightening lending standards. What effect will this have on the housing market?*

Finding Interest or Growth Rates

It is often necessary to calculate the compound annual interest or *growth rate* (that is, the annual rate of change in values) of a series of cash flows. Examples include finding the interest rate on a loan, the rate of growth in sales, and the rate of growth in earnings. In doing this, we can use either future value or present value interest factors. The use of present value interest factors is described in this section. The simplest situation is one in which a person wishes to find the rate of interest or growth in a *series of cash flows*.[11]

Personal Finance Example   Ray Noble wishes to find the rate of interest or growth reflected in the stream of cash flows he received from a real estate investment over the period 2005 through 2009. The following table lists those cash flows:

---

11. Because the calculations required for finding interest rates and growth rates, given the series of cash flows, are the same, this section refers to the calculations as those required to find interest *or* growth rates.

Year	Cash flow
2009	$1,520 ⌉4
2008	1,440 ⌉3
2007	1,370 ⌉2
2006	1,300 ⌉1
2005	1,250

By using the first year (2005) as a base year, we see that interest has been earned (or growth experienced) for 4 years.

Calculator Use   Using the calculator to find the interest or growth rate, we treat the earliest value as a present value, PV, and the latest value as a future value, FV_n. (*Note:* Most calculators require *either* the PV or the FV value to be input as a negative number to calculate an unknown interest or growth rate. That approach is used here.) Using the inputs shown at the left, you will find the interest or growth rate to be 5.01%.

Input | Function
1250 | PV
−1520 | FV
4 | N
| CPT
| I
Solution
5.01

Spreadsheet Use   The interest or growth rate for the series of cash flows also can be calculated as shown on the following Excel spreadsheet.

	A	B
1	INTEREST OR GROWTH RATE–	SERIES OF CASH FLOWS
2	Year	Cash Flow
3	2009	$1,520
4	2008	$1,440
5	2007	$1,370
6	2006	$1,300
7	2005	$1,250
8	Annual growth rate	5.01%

Entry in Cell B8 is =RATE((A3–A7),0,B7,–B3,0). The expression A3–A7 in the entry calculates the number of years of growth. The minus sign appears before B3 because the investment in 2009 is treated as a cash outflow.

Table Use   The first step is to divide the amount received in the earliest year (PV) by the amount received in the latest year (FV_n). Looking back at Equation 4.12, we see that this results in the present value interest factor for a *single amount* for 4 years, $PVIF_{i,4yrs}$, which is 0.822 ($1,250 ÷ $1,520). The interest rate in Table A–2 associated with the factor closest to 0.822 for 4 years is the interest or growth rate of Ray's cash flows. In the row for year 4 in Table A–2, the factor for 5 percent is 0.823—almost exactly the 0.822 value. Therefore, the interest or growth rate of the given cash flows is approximately (to the nearest whole percent) 5%, which is consistent with the value found using a calculator or spreadsheet.[12]

Another type of interest-rate problem involves finding the interest rate associated with an *annuity*, or equal-payment loan.

12. To obtain more precise estimates of interest or growth rates, *interpolation*—a mathematical technique for estimating unknown intermediate values—can be applied. For information on how to interpolate a more precise answer in this example, see the book's home page at www.prenhall.com/gitman.

Personal Finance Example Jan Jacobs can borrow $2,000 to be repaid in equal annual end-of-year amounts of $514.14 for the next 5 years. She wants to find the interest rate on this loan.

Calculator Use (*Note:* Most calculators require *either* the *PMT* or the *PV* value to be input as a negative number to calculate an unknown interest rate on an equal-payment loan. That approach is used here.) Using the inputs shown at the left, you will find the interest rate to be 9.00%.

Spreadsheet Use The interest or growth rate for the annuity also can be calculated as shown on the following Excel spreadsheet.

	A	B
1	INTEREST OR GROWTH RATE–ANNUITY	
2	Present value (loan principal)	$2,000
3	Number of years	5
4	Annual payments	$514.14
5	Annual interest rate	9.00%

Entry in Cell B5 is =RATE(B3,B4,–B2).
The minus sign appears before B2 because
the loan principal is treated as a cash outflow.

Table Use Substituting $PVA_5 = \$2,000$ and $PMT = \$514.14$ into Equation 4.25 and rearranging the equation to solve for $PVIFA_{i,5yrs}$, we get

$$PVIFA_{i,5yrs} = \frac{PVA_5}{PMT} = \frac{\$2,000}{\$514.14} = 3.890 \qquad \text{(4.27)}$$

The interest rate for 5 years associated with the annuity factor closest to 3.890 in Table A–4 is 9%. Therefore, the interest rate on the loan is approximately (to the nearest whole percent) 9%, which is consistent with the value found using a calculator or spreadsheet.

Finding an Unknown Number of Periods

Sometimes it is necessary to calculate the number of time periods needed to generate a given amount of cash flow from an initial amount. Here we briefly consider this calculation for both single amounts and annuities. This simplest case is when a person wishes to determine the number of periods, n, it will take for an initial deposit, PV, to grow to a specified future amount, FV_n, given a stated interest rate, i.

Personal Finance Example Ann Bates wishes to determine the number of years it will take for her initial $1,000 deposit, earning 8% annual interest, to grow to equal $2,500. Simply stated, at an 8% annual rate of interest, how many years, n, will it take for Ann's $1,000, PV, to grow to $2,500, FV_n?

Input / Function: 514.14 PMT; −2000 PV; 5 N; CPT; I; Solution 9.00

Input | Function
1000 | PV
−2500 | FV
8 | I
| CPT
| N

Solution
11.91

Calculator Use Using the calculator, we treat the initial value as the present value, *PV*, and the latest value as the future value, FV_n. (*Note:* Most calculators require *either* the *PV* or the *FV* value to be input as a negative number to calculate an unknown number of periods. That approach is used here.) Using the inputs shown at the left, we find the number of periods to be 11.91 years.

Spreadsheet Use The number of years for the present value to grow to a specified future value also can be calculated as shown on the following Excel spreadsheet.

	A	B
1	YEARS FOR A PRESENT VALUE TO GROW TO A SPECIFIED FUTURE VALUE	
2	Present value (deposit)	$1,000
3	Annual rate of interest, compounded annually	8%
4	Future value	$2,500
5	Number of years	11.91
Entry in Cell B5 is =NPER(B3,0,B2,−B4). The minus sign appears before B4 because the future value is treated as a cash outflow.		

Table Use In a manner similar to our approach for finding an unknown interest or growth rate in a series of cash flows, we begin by dividing the amount deposited in the earliest year by the amount received in the latest year. This results in the present value interest factor for 8% and *n* years, $PVIF_{8\%,n}$, which is 0.400 ($1,000 ÷ $2,500). The number of years (periods) in Table A–2 associated with the factor closest to 0.400 for an 8% interest rate is the number of years required for $1,000 to grow to $2,500 at 8%. In the 8% column of Table A–2, the factor for 12 years is 0.397—almost exactly the 0.400 value. Therefore, the number of years necessary for the $1,000 to grow to a future value of $2,500 at 8% is approximately (to the nearest year) 12. This number is consistent with, but not as precise as, the value found using a calculator or spreadsheet.

Another type of number-of-periods problem involves finding the number of periods associated with an *annuity*. Occasionally we wish to find the unknown life, *n*, of an annuity, *PMT*, that is intended to achieve a specific objective, such as repaying a loan of a given amount, PVA_n, with a stated interest rate, *i*.

Personal Finance Example Bill Smart can borrow $25,000 at an 11% annual interest rate; equal, annual, end-of-year payments of $4,800 are required. He wishes to determine how long it will take to fully repay the loan. In other words, he wishes to determine how many years, *n*, it will take to repay the $25,000, 11% loan, PVA_n, if the payments of $4,800, *PMT*, are made at the end of each year.

Input | Function
−4800 | PMT
25000 | PV
11 | I
| CPT
| N

Solution
8.15

Calculator Use (*Note:* Most calculators require *either* the *PV* or the *PMT* value to be input as a negative number to calculate an unknown number of periods. That approach is used here.) Using the inputs shown at the left, you will find the number of periods to be 8.15 years.

Spreadsheet Use The number of years to pay off the loan also can be calculated as shown on the Excel spreadsheet on page 178.

	A	B
1	YEARS TO PAY OFF A LOAN	
2	Annual payment	$4,800
3	Annual rate of interest, compounded annually	11%
4	Present value (loan principal)	$25,000
5	Number of years to pay off the loan	8.15

Entry in Cell B5 is =NPER(B3,–B2,B4).
The minus sign appears before B2 because
the payments are treated as cash outflows.

Table Use   Substituting $PVA_n = \$25,000$ and $PMT = \$4,800$ into Equation 4.25 and rearranging the equation to solve $PVIFA_{11\%,n}$, we get

$$PVIFA_{11\%,n} = \frac{PVA_n}{PMT} = \frac{\$25,000}{\$4,800} = 5.208 \qquad (4.28)$$

The number of periods for an 11% interest rate associated with the annuity factor closest to 5.208 in Table A–4 is 8 years. Therefore, the number of periods necessary to repay the loan fully is approximately (to the nearest year) 8 years. This value is consistent with the number of periods found using a calculator or spreadsheet.

REVIEW QUESTIONS

4–15 How can you determine the size of the equal, annual, end-of-period deposits necessary to accumulate a certain future sum at the end of a specified future period at a given annual interest rate?

4–16 Describe the procedure used to amortize a loan into a series of equal periodic payments.

4–17 Which present value interest factors would be used to find (a) the growth rate associated with a series of cash flows and (b) the interest rate associated with an equal-payment loan?

4–18 How can you determine the unknown number of periods when you know the present and future values—single amount or annuity—and the applicable rate of interest?

Summary

Focus on Value

Time value of money is an important tool that financial managers and other market participants use to assess the effects of proposed actions. Because firms have long lives and some decisions affect their long-term cash flows, the effective application of time-value-of-money techniques is extremely important. These techniques enable financial managers to evaluate cash flows occurring at different times so as to combine, compare, and evaluate them and link them to the firm's **overall goal of share price maximization.** It will become clear in

Chapters 6 and 7 that the application of time value techniques is a key part of the value determination process needed to make intelligent value-creating decisions.

Review of Learning Goals

Key definitions, formulas, and equations for this chapter are summarized in Table 4.9 (see page 180).

LG 1 **Discuss the role of time value in finance, the use of computational tools, and the basic patterns of cash flow.** Financial managers and investors use time-value-of-money techniques when assessing the value of expected cash flow streams. Alternatives can be assessed by either compounding to find future value or discounting to find present value. Financial managers rely primarily on present value techniques. Financial calculators, electronic spreadsheets, and financial tables can streamline the application of time value techniques. The cash flow of a firm can be described by its pattern—single amount, annuity, or mixed stream.

LG 2 **Understand the concepts of future value and present value, their calculation for single amounts, and the relationship between them.** Future value (FV) relies on compound interest to measure future amounts: The initial principal or deposit in one period, along with the interest earned on it, becomes the beginning principal of the following period.

The present value (PV) of a future amount is the amount of money today that is equivalent to the given future amount, considering the return that can be earned. Present value is the inverse of future value.

LG 3 **Find the future value and the present value of an ordinary annuity, and find the present value of a perpetuity.** An annuity is a pattern of equal periodic cash flows. For an ordinary annuity, the cash flows occur at the end of the period. For an annuity due, cash flows occur at the beginning of the period.

The future value of an ordinary annuity can be found by using the future value interest factor for an annuity. The present value of an ordinary annuity can be found by using the present value interest factor for an annuity. The present value of a perpetuity—an infinite-lived annuity—is found using 1 divided by the discount rate to represent the present value interest factor.

LG 4 **Calculate both the future value and the present value of a mixed stream of cash flows.** A mixed stream of cash flows is a stream of unequal periodic cash flows that reflect no particular pattern. The future value of a mixed stream of cash flows is the sum of the future values of each individual cash flow. Similarly, the present value of a mixed stream of cash flows is the sum of the present values of the individual cash flows.

LG 5 **Understand the effect that compounding interest more frequently than annually has on future value and on the effective annual rate of interest.** Interest can be compounded at intervals ranging from annually to daily, and even continuously. The more often interest is compounded, the larger the future amount that will be accumulated, and the higher the effective, or true, annual rate (EAR).

TABLE 4.9   Summary of Key Definitions, Formulas, and Equations for Time Value of Money

Definitions of variables

e = exponential function = 2.7183
EAR = effective annual rate
FV_n = future value or amount at the end of period n
FVA_n = future value of an n-year annuity
i = annual rate of interest
m = number of times per year interest is compounded
n = number of periods—typically years—over which money earns a return
PMT = amount deposited or received annually at the end of each year
PV = initial principal or present value
PVA_n = present value of an n-year annuity
t = period number index

Interest factor formulas

Future value of a single amount with annual compounding:

$$FVIF_{i,n} = (1 + i)^n$$ [Equation 4.5; factors in Table A–1]

Present value of a single amount:

$$PVIF_{i,n} = \frac{1}{(1 + i)^n}$$ [Equation 4.11; factors in Table A–2]

Future value of an ordinary annuity:

$$FVIFA_{i,n} = \sum_{t=1}^{n} (1 + i)^{t-1}$$ [Equation 4.13; factors in Table A–3]

Present value of an ordinary annuity:

$$PVIFA_{i,n} = \sum_{t=1}^{n} \frac{1}{(1 + i)^t}$$ [Equation 4.15; factors in Table A–4]

Present value of a perpetuity:

$$PVIFA_{i,\infty} = \frac{1}{i}$$ [Equation 4.17]

Future value with compounding more frequently than annually:

$$FVIF_{i,n} = \left(1 + \frac{i}{m}\right)^{m \times n}$$ [Equation 4.18]

For continuous compounding, $m = \infty$:

$$FVIF_{i,n} \text{ (continuous compounding)} = e^{i \times n}$$ [Equation 4.20]

To find the effective annual rate:

$$EAR = \left(1 + \frac{i}{m}\right)^m - 1$$ [Equation 4.22]

Basic equations

Future value (single amount):	$FV_n = PV \times (FVIF_{i,n})$	[Equation 4.6]
Present value (single amount):	$PV = FV_n \times (PVIF_{i,n})$	[Equation 4.12]
Future value (annuity):	$FVA_n = PMT \times (FVIFA_{i,n})$	[Equation 4.14]
Present value (annuity):	$PVA_n = PMT \times (PVIFA_{i,n})$	[Equation 4.16]

The annual percentage rate (APR)—a nominal annual rate—is quoted on credit cards and loans. The annual percentage yield (APY)—an effective annual rate—is quoted on savings products.

 6 **Describe the procedures involved in (1) determining deposits needed to accumulate a future sum, (2) loan amortization, (3) finding interest or growth rates, and (4) finding an unknown number of periods.** (1) The periodic deposit to accumulate a given future sum can be found by solving the equation for the future value of an annuity for the annual payment. (2) A loan can be amortized into equal periodic payments by solving the equation for the present value of an annuity for the periodic payment. (3) Interest or growth rates can be estimated by finding the unknown interest rate in the equation for the present value of a single amount or an annuity. (4) An unknown number of periods can be estimated by finding the unknown number of periods in the equation for the present value of a single amount or an annuity.

Self-Test Problems (Solutions in Appendix B)

 ST4–1 **Future values for various compounding frequencies**   Delia Martin has $10,000 that she can deposit in any of three savings accounts for a 3-year period. Bank A compounds interest on an annual basis, bank B compounds interest twice each year, and bank C compounds interest each quarter. All three banks have a stated annual interest rate of 4%.
a. What amount would Ms. Martin have at the end of the third year, leaving all interest paid on deposit, in each bank?
b. What *effective annual rate* (*EAR*) would she earn in each of the banks?
c. On the basis of your findings in parts **a** and **b**, which bank should Ms. Martin deal with? Why?
d. If a fourth bank (bank D), also with a 4% stated interest rate, compounds interest continuously, how much would Ms. Martin have at the end of the third year? Does this alternative change your recommendation in part **c**? Explain why or why not.

ST4–2 **Future values of annuities**   Ramesh Abdul wishes to choose the better of two equally costly cash flow streams: annuity X and annuity Y. Annuity X provides a cash inflow of $9,000 at the end of each of the next 6 years. Annuity Y provides a cash inflow of $10,000 at the end of each of the next 6 years. Assume that Ramesh can earn 11% on annuity X and 15% on annuity Y.
a. On a purely subjective basis, which annuity do you think is more attractive? Why?
b. Find the future value at the end of year 6, FVA_6, for both annuity X and annuity Y.
c. Use your finding in part **b** to indicate which annuity is more attractive. Compare your finding to your subjective response in part **a**.

ST4–3 **Present values of single amounts and streams**   You have a choice of accepting either of two 5-year cash flow streams or single amounts. One cash flow stream is an ordinary annuity, and the other is a mixed stream. You may accept alternative A or B—either as a cash flow stream or as a single amount. Given the cash flow stream and single amounts associated with each (see the following table), and assuming a

9% opportunity cost, which alternative (A or B) and in which form (cash flow stream or single amount) would you prefer?

	Cash flow stream	
End of year	Alternative A	Alternative B
1	$700	$1,100
2	700	900
3	700	700
4	700	500
5	700	300

	Single amount	
At time zero	$2,825	$2,800

 ST4–4 Deposits needed to accumulate a future sum   Judi Janson wishes to accumulate $8,000 by the end of 5 years by making equal, annual, end-of-year deposits over the next 5 years. If Judi can earn 7% on her investments, how much must she deposit at the *end of each year* to meet this goal?

Warm-Up Exercises

A blue box (■) indicates exercises available in .

 E4–1 Assume a firm makes a $2,500 deposit into its money market account. If this account is currently paying 0.7%, (yes, that's right, less than 1%!), what will the account balance be after 1 year?

  E4–2 If Bob and Judy combine their savings of $1,260 and $975, respectively, and deposit this amount into an account that pays 2% annual interest, compounded monthly, what will the account balance be after 4 years?

 E4–3 Gabrielle just won $2.5 million in the state lottery. She is given the option of receiving a total of $1.3 million now or she can elect to be paid $100,000 at the end of each of the next 25 years. If Gabrielle can earn 5% annually on her investments, from a strict economic point of view which option should she take?

 E4–4 Your firm has the option of making an investment in new software that will cost $130,000 today and is estimated to provide the savings shown in the following table over its 5-year life:

Year	Savings estimate
1	$35,000
2	50,000
3	45,000
4	25,000
5	15,000

Should the firm make this investment if it requires a minimum annual return of 9% on all investments?

E4–5 Joseph is a friend of yours. He has plenty of money but little financial sense. He received a gift of $12,000 for his recent graduation and is looking for a bank in which to deposit the funds. Partners' Savings Bank offers an account with an annual interest rate of 3% compounded semiannually, while Selwyn's offers an account with a 2.75% annual interest rate compounded continuously. Calculate the value of the two accounts at the end of one year and recommend to Joseph which account he should choose.

 E4–6 Jack and Jill have just had their first child. If college is expected to cost $150,000 per year in 18 years, how much should the couple begin depositing annually at the end of each year to accumulate enough funds to pay the first year's tuition at the beginning of the 19th year? Assume that they can earn a 6% annual rate of return on their investment.

 Go to the book's companion website at www.prenhall.com/gitman to find a series of Personal Finance Warm-Up Exercises.

Problems

A blue box (■) indicates problems available in myfinancelab.

 P4–1 **Using a time line**   The financial manager at Starbuck Industries is considering an investment that requires an initial outlay of $25,000 and is expected to result in cash inflows of $3,000 at the end of year 1, $6,000 at the end of years 2 and 3, $10,000 at the end of year 4, $8,000 at the end of year 5, and $7,000 at the end of year 6.
   a. Draw and label a time line depicting the cash flows associated with Starbuck Industries' proposed investment.
   b. Use arrows to demonstrate, on the time line in part **a,** how compounding to find future value can be used to measure all cash flows at the end of year 6.
   c. Use arrows to demonstrate, on the time line in part **b,** how discounting to find present value can be used to measure all cash flows at time zero.
   d. Which of the approaches—*future value* or *present value*—do financial managers rely on most often for decision making? Why?

 P4–2 **Future value calculation**   *Without referring to the preprogrammed function on your financial calculator or to tables,* use the basic formula for future value along with the given interest rate, i, and the number of periods, n, to calculate the future value interest factor in each of the cases shown in the following table. Compare the calculated value to the value in Appendix Table A–1.

Case	Interest rate, i	Number of periods, n
A	12%	2
B	6	3
C	9	2
D	3	4

P4-3 **Future value tables**   Use the future value interest factors in Appendix Table A–1 in each of the cases shown in the following table to estimate, to the nearest year, how long it would take an initial deposit, assuming no withdrawals,

a. To double.

b. To quadruple.

Case	Interest rate
A	7%
B	40
C	20
D	10

P4-4 **Future values**   For each of the cases shown in the following table, calculate the future value of the single cash flow deposited today that will be available at the end of the deposit period if the interest is compounded annually at the rate specified over the given period.

Case	Single cash flow	Interest rate	Deposit period (years)
A	$ 200	5%	20
B	4,500	8	7
C	10,000	9	10
D	25,000	10	12
E	37,000	11	5
F	40,000	12	9

PERSONAL FINANCE PROBLEM

P4-5 **Time value**   You have $1,500 to invest today at 7% interest compounded annually.

a. Find how much you will have accumulated in the account at the end of (1) 3 years, (2) 6 years, and (3) 9 years.

b. Use your findings in part **a** to calculate the amount of interest earned in (1) the first 3 years (years 1 to 3), (2) the second 3 years (years 4 to 6), and (3) the third 3 years (years 7 to 9).

c. Compare and contrast your findings in part **b**. Explain why the amount of interest earned increases in each succeeding 3-year period.

PERSONAL FINANCE PROBLEM

P4-6 **Time value**   As part of your financial planning, you wish to purchase a new car exactly 5 years from today. The car you wish to purchase costs $14,000 today, and your research indicates that its price will increase by 2% to 4% per year over the next 5 years.

a. Estimate the price of the car at the end of 5 years if inflation is (1) 2% per year and (2) 4% per year.

b. How much more expensive will the car be if the rate of inflation is 4% rather than 2%?

PERSONAL FINANCE PROBLEM

P4–7 **Time value**   You can deposit $10,000 into an account paying 9% annual interest either today or exactly 10 years from today. How much better off will you be at the end of 40 years if you decide to make the initial deposit today rather than 10 years from today?

PERSONAL FINANCE PROBLEM

P4–8 **Time value**   Misty needs to have $15,000 at the end of 5 years to fulfill her goal of purchasing a small sailboat. She is willing to invest the funds as a single amount today but wonders what sort of investment return she will need to earn. Use your calculator or the time value tables to figure out the approximate annually compounded rate of return needed in each of these cases:
a. Misty can invest $10,200 today.
b. Misty can invest $8,150 today.
c. Misty can invest $7,150 today.

PERSONAL FINANCE PROBLEM

P4–9 **Single-payment loan repayment**   A person borrows $200 to be repaid in 8 years with 14% annually compounded interest. The loan may be repaid at the end of any earlier year with no prepayment penalty.
a. What amount will be due if the loan is repaid at the end of year 1?
b. What is the repayment at the end of year 4?
c. What amount is due at the end of the eighth year?

P4–10 **Present value calculation**   *Without referring to the preprogrammed function on your financial calculator or to tables,* use the basic formula for present value, along with the given opportunity cost, i, and the number of periods, n, to calculate the present value interest factor in each of the cases shown in the following table. Compare the calculated value to the table value.

Case	Opportunity cost, i	Number of periods, n
A	2%	4
B	10	2
C	5	3
D	13	2

P4–11 **Present values**   For each of the cases shown in the following table, calculate the present value of the cash flow, discounting at the rate given and assuming that the cash flow is received at the end of the period noted.

Case	Single cash flow	Discount rate	End of period (years)
A	$ 7,000	12%	4
B	28,000	8	20
C	10,000	14	12
D	150,000	11	6
E	45,000	20	8

P4–12 **Present value concept**   Answer each of the following questions.
   a. What single investment made today, earning 12% annual interest, will be worth $6,000 at the end of 6 years?
   b. What is the present value of $6,000 to be received at the end of 6 years if the discount rate is 12%?
   c. What is the most you would pay today for a promise to repay you $6,000 at the end of 6 years if your opportunity cost is 12%?
   d. Compare, contrast, and discuss your findings in parts **a** through **c.**

PERSONAL FINANCE PROBLEM

 P4–13 **Time value**   Jim Nance has been offered a future payment of $500 three years from today. If his opportunity cost is 7% compounded annually, what value should he place on this opportunity today? What is the most he should pay to purchase this payment today?

 P4–14 **Time value**   An Iowa state savings bond can be converted to $100 at maturity 6 years from purchase. If the state bonds are to be competitive with U.S. savings bonds, which pay 8% annual interest (compounded annually), at what price must the state sell its bonds? Assume no cash payments on savings bonds prior to redemption.

PERSONAL FINANCE PROBLEM

 P4–15 **Time value and discount rates**   You just won a lottery that promises to pay you $1,000,000 exactly 10 years from today. Because the $1,000,000 payment is guaranteed by the state in which you live, opportunities exist to sell the claim today for an immediate single cash payment.
   a. What is the least you will sell your claim for if you can earn the following rates of return on similar-risk investments during the 10-year period?
       (1) 6%
       (2) 9%
       (3) 12%
   b. Rework part **a** under the assumption that the $1,000,000 payment will be received in 15 rather than 10 years.
   c. On the basis of your findings in parts **a** and **b,** discuss the effect of both the size of the rate of return and the time until receipt of payment on the present value of a future sum.

PERSONAL FINANCE PROBLEM

 P4–16 **Time value comparisons of single amounts**   In exchange for a $20,000 payment today, a well-known company will allow you to choose *one* of the alternatives shown in the following table. Your opportunity cost is 11%.

Alternative	Single amount
A	$28,500 at end of 3 years
B	$54,000 at end of 9 years
C	$160,000 at end of 20 years

   a. Find the value today of each alternative.
   b. Are all the alternatives acceptable—that is, worth $20,000 today?
   c. Which alternative, if any, will you take?

PERSONAL FINANCE PROBLEM

P4–17 **Cash flow investment decision**   Tom Alexander has an opportunity to purchase any of the investments shown in the following table. The purchase price, the amount of the single cash inflow, and its year of receipt are given for each investment. Which purchase recommendations would you make, assuming that Tom can earn 10% on his investments?

Investment	Price	Single cash inflow	Year of receipt
A	$18,000	$30,000	5
B	600	3,000	20
C	3,500	10,000	10
D	1,000	15,000	40

P4–18 **Future value of an annuity**   For each case in the accompanying table, calculate the future value of the annuity at the end of the deposit period, assuming that the annuity cash flows occur at the end of each year.

Case	Amount of annuity	Interest rate	Deposit period (years)
A	$ 2,500	8%	10
B	500	12	6
C	30,000	20	5
D	11,500	9	8
E	6,000	14	30

P4–19 **Present value of an annuity**   For each case in the following table, calculate the present value of the annuity, assuming that the annuity cash flows occur at the end of each year.

Case	Amount of annuity	Interest rate	Period (years)
A	$ 12,000	7%	3
B	55,000	12	15
C	700	20	9
D	140,000	5	7
E	22,500	10	5

PERSONAL FINANCE PROBLEM

P4–20 **Retirement planning**   Hal Thomas, a 25-year-old college graduate, wishes to retire at age 65. To supplement other sources of retirement income, he can deposit $2,000 each year into a tax-deferred individual retirement arrangement (IRA). The IRA will be invested to earn an annual return of 10%, which is assumed to be attainable over the next 40 years.
a. If Hal makes annual end-of-year $2,000 deposits into the IRA, how much will he have accumulated by the end of his sixty-fifth year?
b. If Hal decides to wait until age 35 to begin making annual end-of-year $2,000 deposits into the IRA, how much will he have accumulated by the end of his sixty-fifth year?

c. Using your findings in parts **a** and **b,** discuss the impact of delaying making deposits into the IRA for 10 years (age 25 to age 35) on the amount accumulated by the end of Hal's sixty-fifth year.

PERSONAL FINANCE PROBLEM

 P4–21 Value of a retirement annuity   An insurance agent is trying to sell you an immediate-retirement annuity, which for a single amount paid today will provide you with $12,000 at the end of each year for the next 25 years. You currently earn 9% on low-risk investments comparable to the retirement annuity. Ignoring taxes, what is the most you would pay for this annuity?

PERSONAL FINANCE PROBLEM

 P4–22 Funding your retirement   You plan to retire in exactly 20 years. Your goal is to create a fund that will allow you to receive $20,000 at the end of each year for the 30 years between retirement and death (a psychic told you would die exactly 30 years after you retire). You believe that you will be able to earn 11% per year during the 30-year retirement period.

a. How large a fund will you need *when you retire* in 20 years to provide the 30-year, $20,000 retirement annuity?
b. How much will you need *today* as a single amount to provide the fund calculated in part **a** if you earn only 9% per year during the 20 years preceding retirement?
c. What effect would an increase in the rate you can earn both during and prior to retirement have on the values found in parts **a** and **b**? Explain.

PERSONAL FINANCE PROBLEM

  Value of an annuity versus a single amount   Assume that you just won the state lottery. Your prize can be taken either in the form of $40,000 at the end of each of the next 25 years (i.e., $1,000,000 over 25 years) or as a single amount of $500,000 paid immediately.

a. If you expect to be able to earn 5% annually on your investments over the next 25 years, ignoring taxes and other considerations, which alternative should you take? Why?
b. Would your decision in part **a** change if you could earn 7% rather than 5% on your investments over the next 25 years? Why?
c. On a strictly economic basis, at approximately what earnings rate would you be indifferent between the two plans?

  Perpetuities   Consider the data in the following table.

Perpetuity	Annual amount	Discount rate
A	$ 20,000	8%
B	100,000	10
C	3,000	6
D	60,000	5

Determine, for each of the perpetuities:
a. The appropriate present value interest factor.
b. The present value.

P4–25 **Creating an endowment**   Upon completion of her introductory finance course, Marla Lee was so pleased with the amount of useful and interesting knowledge she gained that she convinced her parents, who were wealthy alumni of the university she was attending, to create an endowment. The endowment is to allow three needy students to take the introductory finance course each year in perpetuity. The guaranteed annual cost of tuition and books for the course is $600 per student. The endowment will be created by making a single payment to the university. The university expects to earn exactly 6% per year on these funds.

    a. How large an initial single payment must Marla's parents make to the university to fund the endowment?

    b. What amount would be needed to fund the endowment if the university could earn 9% rather than 6% per year on the funds?

P4–26 **Value of a mixed stream**   For each of the mixed streams of cash flows shown in the following table, determine the future value at the end of the final year if deposits are made at the *beginning of each year* into an account paying annual interest of 12%, assuming that no withdrawals are made during the period.

	Cash flow stream		
Year	A	B	C
1	$ 900	$30,000	$1,200
2	1,000	25,000	1,200
3	1,200	20,000	1,000
4		10,000	1,900
5		5,000	

P4–27 **Value of a single amount versus a mixed stream**   Gina Vitale has just contracted to sell a small parcel of land that she inherited a few years ago. The buyer is willing to pay $24,000 at the closing of the transaction or will pay the amounts shown in the following table at the *beginning* of each of the next 5 years. Because Gina doesn't really need the money today, she plans to let it accumulate in an account that earns 7% annual interest. Given her desire to buy a house at the end of 5 years after closing on the sale of the lot, she decides to choose the payment alternative— $24,000 single amount or the mixed stream of payments in the following table— that provides the higher future value at the end of 5 years.

Mixed stream	
Beginning of year	Cash flow
1	$ 2,000
2	4,000
3	6,000
4	8,000
5	10,000

a. What is the future value of the single amount at the end of year 5?
b. What is the future value of the mixed stream at the end of year 5?
c. On the basis of your findings in parts **a** and **b,** which alternative should Gina take?
d. If Gina could earn 10% rather than 7% on the funds, would your recommendation in part **c** change? Explain.

 P4–28 **Value of mixed streams**   Find the present value of the streams of cash flows shown in the following table. Assume that the firm's opportunity cost is 12%.

A		B		C	
Year	Cash flow	Year	Cash flow	Year	Cash flow
1	−$2,000	1	$10,000	1–5	$10,000/yr
2	3,000	2–5	5,000/yr	6–10	8,000/yr
3	4,000	6	7,000		
4	6,000				
5	8,000				

 P4–29 **Present value—Mixed streams**   Consider the mixed streams of cash flows shown in the following table.

	Cash flow stream	
Year	A	B
1	$ 50,000	$ 10,000
2	40,000	20,000
3	30,000	30,000
4	20,000	40,000
5	10,000	50,000
Totals	$150,000	$150,000

a. Find the present value of each stream using a 15% discount rate.
b. Compare the calculated present values and discuss them in light of the fact that the undiscounted cash flows total $150,000 in each case.

  P4–30 **Value of a mixed stream**   Harte Systems, Inc., a maker of electronic surveillance equipment, is considering selling to a well-known hardware chain the rights to market its home security system. The proposed deal calls for the hardware chain to pay Harte $30,000 and $25,000 at the end of years 1 and 2 and to make annual year-end payments of $15,000 in years 3 through 9. A final payment to Harte of $10,000 would be due at the end of year 10.
a. Lay out the cash flows involved in the offer on a time line.
b. If Harte applies a required rate of return of 12% to them, what is the present value of this series of payments?

c. A second company has offered Harte an immediate one-time payment of $100,000 for the rights to market the home security system. Which offer should Harte accept?

PERSONAL FINANCE PROBLEM

 P4–31 **Funding budget shortfalls**   As part of your personal budgeting process, you have determined that in each of the next 5 years you will have budget shortfalls. In other words, you will need the amounts shown in the following table at the end of the given year to balance your budget—that is, to make inflows equal outflows. You expect to be able to earn 8% on your investments during the next 5 years and wish to fund the budget shortfalls over the next 5 years with a single amount.

End of year	Budget shortfall
1	$ 5,000
2	4,000
3	6,000
4	10,000
5	3,000

a. How large must the single deposit today into an account paying 8% annual interest be to provide for full coverage of the anticipated budget shortfalls?
b. What effect would an increase in your earnings rate have on the amount calculated in part **a**? Explain.

 P4–32 **Relationship between future value and present value—Mixed stream**   Using *only* the information in the accompanying table, answer the questions that follow.

Year (*t*)	Cash flow	Future value interest factor at 5% ($FVIF_{5\%,n}$)
1	$ 800	1.050
2	900	1.102
3	1,000	1.158
4	1,500	1.216
5	2,000	1.276

a. Determine the *present value* of the mixed stream of cash flows using a 5% discount rate.
b. How much would you be willing to pay for an opportunity to buy this stream, assuming that you can at best earn 5% on your investments?
c. What effect, if any, would a 7% rather than a 5% opportunity cost have on your analysis? (Explain verbally.)

 P4–33 **Changing compounding frequency**   Using annual, semiannual, and quarterly compounding periods, for each of the following, (1) calculate the future value if $5,000 is deposited initially, and (2) determine the *effective annual rate (EAR)*.
a. At 12% annual interest for 5 years.
b. At 16% annual interest for 6 years.
c. At 20% annual interest for 10 years.

P4–34 **Compounding frequency, time value, and effective annual rates**   For each of the cases in the following table:
a. Calculate the future value at the end of the specified deposit period.
b. Determine the *effective annual rate, EAR*.
c. Compare the nominal annual rate, *i*, to the effective annual rate, EAR. What relationship exists between compounding frequency and the nominal and effective annual rates?

Case	Amount of initial deposit	Nominal annual rate, *i*	Compounding frequency, *m* (times/year)	Deposit period (years)
A	$ 2,500	6%	2	5
B	50,000	12	6	3
C	1,000	5	1	10
D	20,000	16	4	6

P4–35 **Continuous compounding**   For each of the cases in the following table, find the future value at the end of the deposit period, assuming that interest is compounded continuously at the given nominal annual rate.

Case	Amount of initial deposit	Nominal annual rate, *i*	Deposit period (years), *n*
A	$1,000	9%	2
B	600	10	10
C	4,000	8	7
D	2,500	12	4

PERSONAL FINANCE PROBLEM

P4–36 **Compounding frequency and time value**   You plan to invest $2,000 in an individual retirement arrangement (IRA) today at a *nominal annual rate* of 8%, which is expected to apply to all future years.
a. How much will you have in the account at the end of 10 years if interest is compounded (1) annually, (2) semiannually, (3) daily (assume a 365-day year), and (4) continuously?
b. What is the *effective annual rate, EAR*, for each compounding period in part **a**?
c. How much greater will your IRA balance be at the end of 10 years if interest is compounded continuously rather than annually?
d. How does the compounding frequency affect the future value and effective annual rate for a given deposit? Explain in terms of your findings in parts **a** through **c**.

PERSONAL FINANCE PROBLEM

P4–37 **Comparing compounding periods**   René Levin wishes to determine the future value at the end of 2 years of a $15,000 deposit made today into an account paying a nominal annual rate of 12%.

a. Find the future value of René's deposit, assuming that interest is compounded (1) annually, (2) quarterly, (3) monthly, and (4) continuously.

b. Compare your findings in part **a,** and use them to demonstrate the relationship between compounding frequency and future value.

c. What is the maximum future value obtainable given the $15,000 deposit, the 2-year time period, and the 12% nominal annual rate? Use your findings in part **a** to explain.

P4–38 Annuities and compounding   Janet Boyle intends to deposit $300 per year in a credit union for the next 10 years, and the credit union pays an annual interest rate of 8%.

a. Determine the future value that Janet will have at the end of 10 years, given that end-of-period deposits are made and no interest is withdrawn, if
   (1) $300 is deposited annually and the credit union pays interest annually.
   (2) $150 is deposited semiannually and the credit union pays interest semiannually.
   (3) $75 is deposited quarterly and the credit union pays interest quarterly.

b. Use your finding in part **a** to discuss the effect of more frequent deposits and compounding of interest on the future value of an annuity.

P4–39 Deposits to accumulate future sums   For each of the cases shown in the following table, determine the amount of the equal, annual, end-of-year deposits necessary to accumulate the given sum at the end of the specified period, assuming the stated annual interest rate.

Case	Sum to be accumulated	Accumulation period (years)	Interest rate
A	$ 5,000	3	12%
B	100,000	20	7
C	30,000	8	10
D	15,000	12	8

P4–40 Creating a retirement fund   To supplement your planned retirement in exactly 42 years, you estimate that you need to accumulate $220,000 by the end of 42 years from today. You plan to make equal, annual, end-of-year deposits into an account paying 8% annual interest.

a. How large must the annual deposits be to create the $220,000 fund by the end of 42 years?

b. If you can afford to deposit only $600 per year into the account, how much will you have accumulated by the end of the forty-second year?

P4–41 Accumulating a growing future sum   A retirement home at Deer Trail Estates now costs $185,000. Inflation is expected to cause this price to increase at 6% per year over the 20 years before C. L. Donovan retires. How large an equal, annual, end-of-year deposit must be made each year into an account paying an annual interest rate of 10% for Donovan to have the cash needed to purchase a home at retirement?

PERSONAL FINANCE PROBLEM

P4–42 **Deposits to create a perpetuity**   You have decided to endow your favorite university with a scholarship. It is expected to cost $6,000 per year to attend the university into perpetuity. You expect to give the university the endowment in 10 years and will accumulate it by making equal annual (end-of-year) deposits into an account. The rate of interest is expected to be 10% for all future time periods.
a. How large must the endowment be?
b. How much must you deposit at the end of each of the next 10 years to accumulate the required amount?

PERSONAL FINANCE PROBLEM

P4–43 **Inflation, time value, and annual deposits**   While vacationing in Florida, John Kelley saw the vacation home of his dreams. It was listed with a sale price of $200,000. The only catch is that John is 40 years old and plans to continue working until he is 65. Still, he believes that prices generally increase at the overall rate of inflation. John believes that he can earn 9% annually after taxes on his investments. He is willing to invest a fixed amount at the end of each of the next 25 years to fund the cash purchase of such a house (one that can be purchased today for $200,000) when he retires.
a. Inflation is expected to average 5% per year for the next 25 years. What will John's dream house cost when he retires?
b. How much must John invest at the *end* of each of the next 25 years to have the cash purchase price of the house when he retires?

P4–44 **Loan payment**   Determine the equal, annual, end-of-year payment required each year over the life of the loans shown in the following table to repay them fully during the stated term of the loan.

Loan	Principal	Interest rate	Term of loan (years)
A	$12,000	8%	3
B	60,000	12	10
C	75,000	10	30
D	4,000	15	5

PERSONAL FINANCE PROBLEM

P4–45 **Loan amortization schedule**   Joan Messineo borrowed $15,000 at a 14% annual rate of interest to be repaid over 3 years. The loan is amortized into three equal, annual, end-of-year payments.
a. Calculate the annual, end-of-year loan payment.
b. Prepare a loan amortization schedule showing the interest and principal breakdown of each of the three loan payments.
c. Explain why the interest portion of each payment declines with the passage of time.

P4–46 **Loan interest deductions**   Liz Rogers just closed a $10,000 business loan that is to be repaid in three equal, annual, end-of-year payments. The interest rate on the loan is 13%. As part of her firm's detailed financial planning, Liz wishes to determine the annual interest deduction attributable to the loan. (Because it is a business loan, the interest portion of each loan payment is tax-deductible to the business.)

a. Determine the firm's annual loan payment.

b. Prepare an amortization schedule for the loan.

c. How much interest expense will Liz's firm have in *each* of the next 3 years as a result of this loan?

PERSONAL FINANCE PROBLEM

P4–47 **Monthly loan payments**   Tim Smith is shopping for a used car. He has found one priced at $4,500. The dealer has told Tim that if he can come up with a down payment of $500, the dealer will finance the balance of the price at a 12% annual rate over 2 years (24 months).

a. Assuming that Tim accepts the dealer's offer, what will his *monthly* (end-of-month) payment amount be?

b. Use a financial calculator or Equation 4.15a (found in footnote 8) to help you figure out what Tim's *monthly* payment would be if the dealer were willing to finance the balance of the car price at a 9% annual rate.

P4–48 **Growth rates**   You are given the series of cash flows shown in the following table.

	Cash flows		
Year	A	B	C
1	$500	$1,500	$2,500
2	560	1,550	2,600
3	640	1,610	2,650
4	720	1,680	2,650
5	800	1,760	2,800
6		1,850	2,850
7		1,950	2,900
8		2,060	
9		2,170	
10		2,280	

a. Calculate the compound annual growth rate associated with each cash flow stream.

b. If year-1 values represent initial deposits in a savings account paying annual interest, what is the annual rate of interest earned on each account?

c. Compare and discuss the growth rate and interest rate found in parts **a** and **b**, respectively.

PERSONAL FINANCE PROBLEM

P4–49 **Rate of return**   Rishi Singh has $1,500 to invest. His investment counselor suggests an investment that pays no stated interest but will return $2,000 at the end of 3 years.

a. What annual rate of return will Rishi earn with this investment?

b. Rishi is considering another investment, of equal risk, that earns an annual return of 8%. Which investment should he make, and why?

P4–50 **Rate of return and investment choice**   Clare Jaccard has $5,000 to invest. Because she is only 25 years old, she is not concerned about the length of the investment's life. What she is sensitive to is the rate of return she will earn on the investment. With the help of her financial advisor, Clare has isolated four equally risky investments, each providing a single amount at the end of its life, as shown in the following table. All of the investments require an initial $5,000 payment.

Investment	Single amount	Investment life (years)
A	$ 8,400	6
B	15,900	15
C	7,600	4
D	13,000	10

a. Calculate, to the nearest 1%, the rate of return on each of the four investments available to Clare.
b. Which investment would you recommend to Clare, given her goal of maximizing the rate of return?

 Rate of return—Annuity   What is the rate of return on an investment of $10,606 if the company will receive $2,000 each year for the next 10 years?

P4–52 **Choosing the best annuity**   Raina Herzig wishes to choose the best of four immediate-retirement annuities available to her. In each case, in exchange for paying a single premium today, she will receive equal, annual, end-of-year cash benefits for a specified number of years. She considers the annuities to be equally risky and is not concerned about their differing lives. Her decision will be based solely on the rate of return she will earn on each annuity. The key terms of the four annuities are shown in the following table.

Annuity	Premium paid today	Annual benefit	Life (years)
A	$30,000	$3,100	20
B	25,000	3,900	10
C	40,000	4,200	15
D	35,000	4,000	12

a. Calculate to the nearest 1% the rate of return on each of the four annuities Raina is considering.
b. Given Raina's stated decision criterion, which annuity would you recommend?

P4–53 **Interest rate for an annuity**   Anna Waldheim was seriously injured in an industrial accident. She sued the responsible parties and was awarded a judgment of $2,000,000. Today, she and her attorney are attending a settlement conference with the defendants. The defendants have made an initial offer of $156,000 per year for

25 years. Anna plans to counteroffer at $255,000 per year for 25 years. Both the offer and the counteroffer have a present value of $2,000,000, the amount of the judgment. Both assume payments at the end of each year.

a. What interest rate assumption have the defendants used in their offer (rounded to the nearest whole percent)?
b. What interest rate assumption have Anna and her lawyer used in their counteroffer (rounded to the nearest whole percent)?
c. Anna is willing to settle for an annuity that carries an interest rate assumption of 9%. What annual payment would be acceptable to her?

PERSONAL FINANCE PROBLEM

 P4–54 **Loan rates of interest**   John Flemming has been shopping for a loan to finance the purchase of a used car. He has found three possibilities that seem attractive and wishes to select the one with the lowest interest rate. The information available with respect to each of the three $5,000 loans is shown in the following table.

Loan	Principal	Annual payment	Term (years)
A	$5,000	$1,352.81	5
B	5,000	1,543.21	4
C	5,000	2,010.45	3

a. Determine the interest rate associated with each of the loans.
b. Which loan should John take?

 P4–55 **Number of years to equal future amount**   For each of the following cases, determine the number of years it will take for the initial deposit to grow to equal the future amount at the given interest rate.

Case	Initial deposit	Future amount	Interest rate
A	$ 300	$ 1,000	7%
B	12,000	15,000	5
C	9,000	20,000	10
D	100	500	9
E	7,500	30,000	15

PERSONAL FINANCE PROBLEM

 P4–56 **Time to accumulate a given sum**   Manuel Rios wishes to determine how long it will take an initial deposit of $10,000 to double.
a. If Manuel earns 10% annual interest on the deposit, how long will it take for him to double his money?
b. How long will it take if he earns only 7% annual interest?
c. How long will it take if he can earn 12% annual interest?
d. Reviewing your findings in parts a, b, and c, indicate what relationship exists between the interest rate and the amount of time it will take Manuel to double his money.

P4–57 **Number of years to provide a given return**   In each of the following cases, determine the number of years that the given annual *end-of-year* cash flow must continue to provide the given rate of return on the given initial amount.

Case	Initial amount	Annual cash flow	Rate of return
A	$ 1,000	$ 250	11%
B	150,000	30,000	15
C	80,000	10,000	10
D	600	275	9
E	17,000	3,500	6

PERSONAL FINANCE PROBLEM

P4–58 **Time to repay installment loan**   Mia Salto wishes to determine how long it will take to repay a loan with initial proceeds of $14,000 where annual *end-of-year* installment payments of $2,450 are required.

   a. If Mia can borrow at a 12% annual rate of interest, how long will it take for her to repay the loan fully?

   b. How long will it take if she can borrow at a 9% annual rate?

   c. How long will it take if she has to pay 15% annual interest?

   d. Reviewing your answers in parts **a, b,** and **c,** describe the general relationship between the interest rate and the amount of time it will take Mia to repay the loan fully.

P4–59 **ETHICS PROBLEM**   A manager at a "check into cash" business defends his business practice of charging high percentage fees for cashing checks as simply "charging what the market will bear." "After all," says the manager, "we don't force people to come in the door." How would you respond to this ethical defense of the payday-advance business?

Chapter 4 Case

Funding Jill Moran's Retirement Annuity

Sunrise Industries wishes to accumulate funds to provide a retirement annuity for its vice president of research, Jill Moran. Ms. Moran, by contract, will retire at the end of exactly 12 years. Upon retirement, she is entitled to receive an annual end-of-year payment of $42,000 for exactly 20 years. If she dies prior to the end of the 20-year period, the annual payments will pass to her heirs. During the 12-year "accumulation period," Sunrise wishes to fund the annuity by making equal, annual, end-of-year deposits into an account earning 9% interest. Once the 20-year "distribution period" begins, Sunrise plans to move the accumulated monies into an account earning a guaranteed 12% per year. At the end of the distribution period, the account balance will equal zero. Note that the first deposit will be made at the end of year 1 and that the first distribution payment will be received at the end of year 13.

To Do

a. Draw a time line depicting all of the cash flows associated with Sunrise's view of the retirement annuity.

b. How large a sum must Sunrise accumulate by the end of year 12 to provide the 20-year, $42,000 annuity?

c. How large must Sunrise's equal, annual, end-of-year deposits into the account be over the 12-year accumulation period to fund fully Ms. Moran's retirement annuity?

d. How much would Sunrise have to deposit annually during the accumulation period if it could earn 10% rather than 9% during the accumulation period?

e. How much would Sunrise have to deposit annually during the accumulation period if Ms. Moran's retirement annuity were a perpetuity and all other terms were the same as initially described?

Spreadsheet Exercise

At the end of 2009, Uma Corporation was considering undertaking a major long-term project in an effort to remain competitive in its industry. The production and sales departments determined the potential annual cash flow savings that could accrue to the firm if it acts soon. Specifically, they estimate that a mixed stream of future cash flow savings will occur at the end of the years 2010 through 2015. The years 2016 through 2020 will see consecutive and equal cash flow savings at the end of each year. The firm estimates that its discount rate over the first 6 years will be 7%. The expected discount rate over the years 2016 through 2020 will be 11%.

The project managers will find the project acceptable if it results in present cash flow savings of at least $860,000. The following cash flow savings data are supplied to the finance department for analysis:

End of Year	Cash Flow Savings
2010	$110,000
2011	120,000
2012	130,000
2013	150,000
2014	160,000
2015	150,000
2016	90,000
2017	90,000
2018	90,000
2019	90,000
2020	90,000

To Do

Create spreadsheets similar to Tables 4.2 and 4.4 (which can be viewed at www .prenhall.com/gitman), and then answer the following questions:

a. Determine the value (at the beginning of 2010) of the future cash flow savings expected to be generated by this project.
b. Based solely on the one criterion set by management, should the firm undertake this specific project? Explain.
c. What is the "interest rate risk," and how might it influence the recommendation made in part **b**? Explain.

Web Exercise

Go to the book's companion website at www.prenhall.com/gitman to find the Web Exercise for this chapter.

Remember to check the book's website at www.prenhall.com/gitman to find additional resources, including Web Exercises and a Web Case.

5 | Risk and Return

WHY THIS CHAPTER MATTERS TO YOU

In Your Professional Life

Accounting: You need to understand the relationship between risk and return because of the effect that riskier projects will have on the firm's annual net income and on your efforts to stabilize reported net income.

Information systems: You need to understand how to do scenario and correlation analyses to build decision packages that help management analyze the risk and return of various business opportunities.

Management: You need to understand the relationship between risk and return, and how to measure that relationship to evaluate data that come from finance personnel and translate those data into decisions that increase the value of the firm.

Marketing: You need to understand that although higher-risk projects may produce higher returns, they may not be the best choice for the firm if they produce an erratic earnings pattern and fail to optimize the value of the firm.

Operations: You need to understand why investments in plant, equipment, and systems need to be evaluated in light of their impact on the firm's risk and return, which together will affect the firm's value.

In Your Personal Life

The tradeoff between risk and return enters into numerous personal financial decisions. You will use risk and return concepts when you select savings vehicles, buy real estate, finance major purchases, purchase insurance, invest in securities, and implement retirement plans. Although risk and return are difficult to measure precisely, you can get a feel for them and make decisions based upon the tradeoffs between risk and return in light of your personal disposition toward risk.

LEARNING GOALS

LG 1 Understand the meaning and fundamentals of risk, return, and risk preferences.

LG 2 Describe procedures for assessing and measuring the risk of a single asset.

LG 3 Discuss risk measurement for a single asset using the standard deviation and coefficient of variation.

LG 4 Understand the risk and return characteristics of a portfolio in terms of correlation and diversification, and the impact of international assets on a portfolio.

LG 5 Review the two types of risk and the derivation and role of beta in measuring the relevant risk of both a security and a portfolio.

LG 6 Explain the capital asset pricing model (CAPM), its relationship to the security market line (SML).

The concept that return should increase if risk increases is fundamental to modern management and finance. This relationship is regularly observed in the financial markets, and important clarification of it has led to Nobel prizes. In this chapter we discuss these two key factors in finance—risk and return—and introduce some quantitative tools and techniques used to measure risk and return for individual assets and for groups of assets.

5.1 | Risk and Return Fundamentals

To maximize share price, the financial manager must learn to assess two key determinants: risk and return. Each financial decision presents certain risk and return characteristics, and the unique combination of these characteristics has an impact on share price. Risk can be viewed as it is related either to a single asset or to a **portfolio**—a collection, or group, of assets. We will look at both, beginning with the risk of a single asset. First, though, it is important to introduce some fundamental ideas about risk, return, and risk preferences.

portfolio
A collection, or group, of assets.

Risk Defined

risk
The chance of financial loss or, more formally, the *variability of returns associated with a given asset.*

In the most basic sense, **risk** is the chance of financial loss. Assets having greater chances of loss are viewed as more risky than those with lesser chances of loss. More formally, the term *risk* is used interchangeably with *uncertainty* to refer to the *variability of returns associated with a given asset.* A $1,000 government bond that guarantees its holder $5 interest after 30 days has no risk, because there is no variability associated with the return. A $1,000 investment in a firm's common stock, which over the same 30 days may earn anywhere from $0 to $10, is very risky because of the high variability of its return. The more nearly certain the return from an asset, the less variability and therefore the less risk.

Some risks directly affect both financial managers and shareholders. Table 5.1 briefly describes the common sources of risk that affect both firms and their shareholders. As you can see, business risk and financial risk are more firm-specific and therefore are of greatest interest to financial managers. Interest rate, liquidity, and market risks are more shareholder-specific and therefore are of greatest interest to stockholders. Event, exchange rate, purchasing-power, and tax risk directly affect both firms and shareholders. The *Focus on Ethics* box on page 204 addresses another risk that affects both firms and shareholders—moral risk. A number of these risks are discussed in more detail later in this text. Clearly, both financial managers and shareholders must assess these and other risks as they make investment decisions.

Return Defined

return
The total gain or loss experienced on an investment over a given period of time; calculated by dividing the asset's cash distributions during the period, plus change in value, by its beginning-of-period investment value.

Obviously, if we are going to assess risk on the basis of variability of return, we need to be certain we know what *return* is and how to measure it. The **return** is the total gain or loss experienced on an investment over a given period of time. It is commonly measured as cash distributions during the period plus the change in

| TABLE 5.1 | Popular Sources of Risk Affecting Financial Managers and Shareholders |

Source of risk	Description
Firm-Specific Risks	
Business risk	The chance that the firm will be unable to cover its operating costs. Level is driven by the firm's revenue stability and the structure of its operating costs (fixed versus variable).
Financial risk	The chance that the firm will be unable to cover its financial obligations. Level is driven by the predictability of the firm's operating cash flows and its fixed-cost financial obligations.
Shareholder-Specific Risks	
Interest rate risk	The chance that changes in interest rates will adversely affect the value of an investment. Most investments lose value when the interest rate rises and increase in value when it falls.
Liquidity risk	The chance that an investment cannot be easily liquidated at a reasonable price. Liquidity is significantly affected by the size and depth of the market in which an investment is customarily traded.
Market risk	The chance that the value of an investment will decline because of market factors that are independent of the investment (such as economic, political, and social events). In general, the more a given investment's value responds to the market, the greater its risk; the less it responds, the smaller its risk.
Firm and Shareholder Risks	
Event risk	The chance that a totally unexpected event will have a significant effect on the value of the firm or a specific investment. These infrequent events, such as government-mandated withdrawal of a popular prescription drug, typically affect only a small group of firms or investments.
Exchange rate risk	The exposure of future expected cash flows to fluctuations in the currency exchange rate. The greater the chance of undesirable exchange rate fluctuations, the greater the risk of the cash flows and therefore the lower the value of the firm or investment.
Purchasing-power risk	The chance that changing price levels caused by inflation or deflation in the economy will adversely affect the firm's or investment's cash flows and value. Typically, firms or investments with cash flows that move with general price levels have a low purchasing-power risk, and those with cash flows that do not move with general price levels have a high purchasing-power risk.
Tax risk	The chance that unfavorable changes in tax laws will occur. Firms and investments with values that are sensitive to tax law changes are more risky.

value, expressed as a percentage of the beginning-of-period investment value. The expression for calculating the rate of return earned on any asset over period t, r_t, is commonly defined as

$$r_t = \frac{C_t + P_t - P_{t-1}}{P_{t-1}} \tag{5.1}$$

where

r_t = actual, expected, or required rate of return during period t

C_t = cash (flow) received from the asset investment in the time period $t-1$ to t

P_t = price (value) of asset at time t

P_{t-1} = price (value) of asset at time $t-1$

Focus on Ethics — What about Moral Risk?

The poster boy for "moral risk," exemplifying the devastating effects of unethical behavior for a company's investors, has to be Nick Leeson. As a futures trader, Leeson violated his bank's investing rules while secretly placing huge bets on the direction of the Japanese stock market. When those bets proved wrong, the $1.24 billion losses resulted in the 1995 demise of the centuries-old Barings Bank. More than any other single episode in world financial history, Leeson's misdeeds proved the importance of character in the financial industry.

Problems with ethics can be found throughout the business world. In a survey conducted by *CFO* magazine, 41 percent of surveyed chief financial officers admitted ethical problems in their organizations, and 48 percent of surveyed employees admitted engaging in unethical practices such as cheating on expense accounts or forging signatures. In the 2004 survey, 47 percent of CFOs said that they felt pressure from CEOs to use aggressive accounting to "make the numbers work." One

of the main reasons cited for accounting fraud uncovered in recent years was the pressure to "hit the numbers" expected by some Wall Street security analysts. The good news was that the same survey found CFOs standing up to CEO pressure and improving ethical standards in their departments, thanks to the 2002 Sarbanes-Oxley Act.

What can be done to minimize moral risk? A first step is to build awareness through a code of ethics. Almost all *Fortune* 500 companies and about half of all companies have an ethics code that spells out general principles of right and wrong conduct. Because ethical codes are often faulted for being vague and abstract, companies such as **Texas Instruments** have written detailed standards of conduct. Organizations also reveal their ethical commitment in other ways. Some administer honesty tests prior to hiring new workers; others require ethics training of mid-level managers. Additional methods of strengthening corporate ethics include providing whistle-blower protection for employees with ethics-related

concerns, establishing an *ethics director,* and evaluating managers' ethics in performance reviews.

The trend may be toward higher ethical standards, according to a study conducted by five Baylor University professors. They surveyed 10,000 U.S. business professionals three times over a 20-year period, asking the respondents to judge acceptable responses to 16 common business situations with questionable ethical dimensions. The responses, compiled into a single "ethics index" for each survey year, show an upward trend, according to the study published in 2006. Debate continues, however, over whether there is a gap between attitudes and actual actions. People who otherwise might do the right thing can be pressured to do something wrong.

■ *Is "hitting the numbers" an appropriate goal, given the Chapter 1 contrast of profit and shareholder wealth maximization? If not, why do executives emphasize it?*

The return, r_t, reflects the combined effect of cash flow, C_t, and changes in value, $P_t - P_{t-1}$, over period t.

Equation 5.1 is used to determine the rate of return over a time period as short as 1 day or as long as 10 years or more. However, in most cases, t is 1 year, and r therefore represents an annual rate of return.

Example

Robin's Gameroom, a high-traffic video arcade, wishes to determine the return on two of its video machines, Conqueror and Demolition. Conqueror was purchased 1 year ago for $20,000 and currently has a market value of $21,500. During the year, it generated $800 of after-tax cash receipts. Demolition was purchased

4 years ago; its value in the year just completed declined from $12,000 to $11,800. During the year, it generated $1,700 of after-tax cash receipts. Substituting into Equation 5.1, we can calculate the annual rate of return, r, for each video machine.

Conqueror (C):

$$r_C = \frac{\$800 + \$21,500 - \$20,000}{\$20,000} = \frac{\$2,300}{\$20,000} = \underline{\underline{11.5\%}}$$

Demolition (D):

$$r_D = \frac{\$1,700 + \$11,800 - \$12,000}{\$12,000} = \frac{\$1,500}{\$12,000} = \underline{\underline{12.5\%}}$$

Although the market value of Demolition declined during the year, its cash flow caused it to earn a higher rate of return than Conqueror earned during the same period. Clearly, the combined impact of cash flow and changes in value, as measured by the rate of return, is important.

Historical Returns

Investment returns vary both over time and between different types of investments. By averaging historical returns over a long period of time, it becomes possible to eliminate the impact of market and other types of risk. This enables the financial decision maker to focus on the differences in return that are attributable primarily to the types of investment. Table 5.2 shows the average annual rates of return for a number of popular security investments (and inflation) over the 81-year period January 1, 1926, through December 31, 2006. Each rate represents the average annual rate of return an investor would have realized had he or she purchased the investment on January 1, 1926, and sold it on December 31, 2006. You can see that significant differences exist between the average annual rates of return realized on the various types of stocks, bonds, and bills shown. Later in this chapter, we will see how these differences in return can be linked to differences in the risk of each of these investments.

TABLE 5.2   Historical Returns for Selected Security Investments (1926–2006)

Investment	Average annual return
Large-company stocks	12.3%
Small-company stocks	17.4
Long-term corporate bonds	6.2
Long-term government bonds	5.8
U.S. Treasury bills	3.8
Inflation	3.1%

Source: Stocks, Bonds, Bills, and Inflation, 2007 Yearbook (Chicago: Ibbotson Associates, Inc., 2007).

Risk Aversion

risk-averse
The attitude toward risk in which an increased return would be required for an increase in risk.

Financial managers generally seek to avoid risk. Most managers are **risk-averse;** for a given increase in risk, they require an increase in return. This attitude is believed consistent with that of the owners for whom the firm is being managed. Managers generally tend to be conservative rather than aggressive when accepting risk for their firm. Accordingly, a *risk-averse financial manager requiring higher returns for greater risk is assumed throughout this text.*

Hint Remember that most *shareholders* are risk-averse. Like risk-averse managers, for a given increase in risk, they require an increase in return on their investment in that firm.

REVIEW QUESTIONS

5–1   What is *risk* in the context of financial decision making?
5–2   Define *return*, and describe how to find the rate of return on an investment.
5–3   Describe the attitude toward return of a risk-averse financial manager.

5.2 | Risk of a Single Asset

The concept of risk can be developed by first considering a single asset held in isolation. We can look at expected-return behaviors to assess risk, and use statistics to measure it.

Risk Assessment

scenario analysis
An approach for assessing risk that uses several possible alternative outcomes (scenarios) to obtain a sense of the variability among returns.

Scenario analysis and probability distributions can be used to assess the general level of risk embodied in a given asset.

Scenario Analysis

range
A measure of an asset's risk, which is found by subtracting the return associated with the pessimistic (worst) outcome from the return associated with the optimistic (best) outcome.

Scenario analysis uses several possible alternative outcomes (scenarios) to obtain a sense of the variability among returns. One common method involves considering pessimistic (worst), most likely (expected), and optimistic (best) outcomes and the returns associated with them for a given asset. In this case, the asset's risk can be measured by the **range** of returns. The **range** is found by subtracting the return associated with the pessimistic outcome from the return associated with the optimistic outcome. The greater the range, the more variability, or risk, the asset is said to have.

Example

Norman Company, a custom golf equipment manufacturer, wants to choose the better of two investments, A and B. Each requires an initial outlay of $10,000, and each has a *most likely* annual rate of return of 15%. Management has estimated returns associated with each investment's *pessimistic* and *optimistic* outcomes. The three estimates for each asset, along with its range, are given in Table 5.3. Asset A appears to be less risky than asset B; its range of 4% (17% − 13%) is less than the range of 16% (23% − 7%) for asset B. The risk-averse decision maker would prefer asset A over asset B, because A offers the same most likely return as B (15%) with lower risk (smaller range).

TABLE 5.3	Assets A and B	
	Asset A	Asset B
Initial investment	$10,000	$10,000
Annual rate of return		
Pessimistic	13%	7%
Most likely	15%	15%
Optimistic	17%	23%
Range	4%	16%

Although the use of scenario analysis and the range is rather crude, it does give the decision maker a feel for the behavior of returns, which can be used to estimate the risk involved.

Probability Distributions

probability
The *chance* that a given outcome will occur.

Probability distributions provide a more quantitative insight into an asset's risk. The **probability** of a given outcome is its *chance* of occurring. An outcome with an 80 percent probability of occurrence would be expected to occur 8 out of 10 times. An outcome with a probability of 100 percent is certain to occur. Outcomes with a probability of zero will never occur.

Example

probability distribution
A model that relates probabilities to the associated outcomes.

Norman Company's past estimates indicate that the probabilities of the pessimistic, most likely, and optimistic outcomes are 25%, 50%, and 25%, respectively. Note that the sum of these probabilities must equal 100%; that is, they must be based on all the alternatives considered.

bar chart
The simplest type of probability distribution; shows only a limited number of outcomes and associated probabilities for a given event.

A **probability distribution** is a model that relates probabilities to the associated outcomes. The simplest type of probability distribution is the **bar chart**, which shows only a limited number of outcome–probability coordinates. The bar charts for Norman Company's assets A and B are shown in Figure 5.1. Although both assets have the same most likely return, the range of return is much greater, or more dispersed, for asset B than for asset A—16 percent versus 4 percent.

FIGURE 5.1

Bar Charts
Bar charts for asset A's and asset B's returns

FIGURE 5.2

Continuous Probability Distributions
Continuous probability distributions for asset A's and asset B's returns

continuous probability distribution
A probability distribution showing all the possible outcomes and associated probabilities for a given event.

If we knew all the possible outcomes and associated probabilities, we could develop a **continuous probability distribution**. This type of distribution can be thought of as a bar chart for a very large number of outcomes. Figure 5.2 presents continuous probability distributions for assets A and B. Note that although assets A and B have the same most likely return (15 percent), the distribution of returns for asset B has much greater *dispersion* than the distribution for asset A. Clearly, asset B is more risky than asset A.

Risk Measurement

In addition to considering its *range,* the risk of an asset can be measured quantitatively by using statistics. Here we consider two statistics—the standard deviation and the coefficient of variation—that can be used to measure the variability of asset returns.

Standard Deviation

standard deviation (σ_r)
The most common statistical indicator of an asset's risk; it measures the dispersion around the *expected value.*

expected value of a return ($\bar{r}$)
The most likely return on a given asset.

The most common statistical indicator of an asset's risk is the **standard deviation, σ_r,** which measures the dispersion around the *expected value.* The **expected value of a return, $\bar{r}$,** is the most likely return on an asset. It is calculated as follows:[1]

$$\bar{r} = \sum_{j=1}^{n} r_j \times Pr_j \qquad (5.2)$$

where

r_j = return for the *j*th outcome
Pr_j = probability of occurrence of the *j*th outcome
n = number of outcomes considered

---

1. The formula for finding the expected value of return, $\bar{r}$, when all of the outcomes, r_j, are known *and* their related probabilities are assumed to be equal, is a simple arithmetic average:

$$\bar{r} = \frac{\sum_{j=1}^{n} r_j}{n} \qquad (5.2a)$$

where *n* is the number of observations. Equation 5.2 is emphasized in this chapter because returns and related probabilities are often available.

| TABLE 5.4 | Expected Values of Returns for Assets A and B |

Possible outcomes	Probability (1)	Returns (2)	Weighted value [(1) × (2)] (3)
		Asset A	
Pessimistic	.25	13%	3.25%
Most likely	.50	15	7.50
Optimistic	.25	17	4.25
Total	1.00	Expected return	15.00%
		Asset B	
Pessimistic	.25	7%	1.75%
Most likely	.50	15	7.50
Optimistic	.25	23	5.75
Total	1.00	Expected return	15.00%

Example The expected values of returns for Norman Company's assets A and B are presented in Table 5.4. Column 1 gives the Pr_j's and column 2 gives the r_j's. In each case n equals 3. The expected value for each asset's return is 15%.

The expression for the *standard deviation of returns*, σ_r, is[2]

$$\sigma_r = \sqrt{\sum_{j=1}^{n} (r_j - \bar{r})^2 \times Pr_j}$$ (5.3)

In general, the higher the standard deviation, the greater the risk.

Example Table 5.5 (see page 210) presents the standard deviations for Norman Company's assets A and B, based on the earlier data. The standard deviation for asset A is 1.41%, and the standard deviation for asset B is 5.66%. The higher risk of asset B is clearly reflected in its higher standard deviation.

Historical Returns and Risk   We can now use the standard deviation as a measure of risk to assess the historical (1926–2006) investment return data in Table 5.2. Table 5.6 (see page 210) repeats the historical returns in column 1 and shows the standard deviations associated with each of them in column 2. A close

---

2. The formula that is commonly used to find the standard deviation of returns, σ_r, in a situation in which *all* outcomes are known *and* their related probabilities are assumed equal, is

$$\sigma_r = \sqrt{\frac{\sum_{j=1}^{n} (r_j - \bar{r})^2}{n - 1}}$$ (5.3a)

where n is the number of observations. Equation 5.3 is emphasized in this chapter because returns and related probabilities are often available.

TABLE 5.5	The Calculation of the Standard Deviation of the Returns for Assets A and B[a]

j	r_j	$\bar{r}$	$r_j - \bar{r}$	$(r_j - \bar{r})^2$	Pr_j	$(r_j - \bar{r})^2 \times Pr_j$
			Asset A			
1	13%	15%	−2%	4%	.25	1%
2	15	15	0	0	.50	0
3	17	15	2	4	.25	<u>1</u>

$$\sum_{j=1}^{3} (r_j - \bar{r})^2 \times Pr_j = 2\%$$

$$\sigma_{r_A} = \sqrt{\sum_{j=1}^{3} (r_j - \bar{r})^2 \times Pr_j} = \sqrt{2\%} = \underline{\underline{1.41\%}}$$

j	r_j	$\bar{r}$	$r_j - \bar{r}$	$(r_j - \bar{r})^2$	Pr_j	$(r_j - \bar{r})^2 \times Pr_j$
			Asset B			
1	7%	15%	−8%	64%	.25	16%
2	15	15	0	0	.50	0
3	23	15	8	64	.25	<u>16</u>

$$\sum_{j=1}^{3} (r_j - \bar{r})^2 \times Pr_j = 32\%$$

$$\sigma_{r_B} = \sqrt{\sum_{j=1}^{3} (r_j - \bar{r})^2 \times Pr_j} = \sqrt{32\%} = \underline{\underline{5.66\%}}$$

[a]Calculations in this table are made in percentage form rather than decimal form—e.g., 13% rather than 0.13. As a result, some of the intermediate computations may appear to be inconsistent with those that would result from using decimal form. Regardless, the resulting standard deviations are correct and identical to those that would result from using decimal rather than percentage form.

TABLE 5.6	Historical Returns, Standard Deviations, and Coefficients of Variation for Selected Security Investments (1926–2006)

Investment	Average annual return (1)	Standard deviation (2)	Coefficient of variation[a] (3)
Large-company stocks	12.3%	20.1%	1.63
Small-company stocks	17.4	32.7	1.88
Long-term corporate bonds	6.2	8.5	1.37
Long-term government bonds	5.8	9.2	1.59
U.S. Treasury bills	3.8	3.1	0.82
Inflation	3.1%	4.3%	1.39

[a]Calculated by dividing the standard deviation in column 2 by the average annual return in column 1.

Source: Stocks, Bonds, Bills, and Inflation, 2007 Yearbook (Chicago: Ibbotson Associates, Inc., 2007).

relationship can be seen between the investment returns and the standard deviations: Investments with higher returns have higher standard deviations. Because higher standard deviations are associated with greater risk, the historical data confirm the existence of a positive relationship between risk and return. That relationship reflects *risk aversion* by market participants, who require higher returns as compensation for greater risk. The historical data in columns 1 and 2 of Table 5.6 clearly show that during the 1926–2006 period, investors were rewarded with higher returns on higher-risk investments.

Coefficient of Variation

coefficient of variation (CV)
A measure of relative dispersion that is useful in comparing the risks of assets with differing expected returns.

The **coefficient of variation, *CV*,** is a measure of relative dispersion that is useful in comparing the risks of assets with differing expected returns. Equation 5.4 gives the expression for the coefficient of variation:

$$CV = \frac{\sigma_r}{\bar{r}} \tag{5.4}$$

The higher the coefficient of variation, the greater the risk and therefore the higher the expected return. This relationship can be seen by comparing the coefficients of variation in column 3 of Table 5.6, which shows historical 1926–2006 investment data, with the average annual returns in column 1. As with the standard deviations in column 2, higher returns are associated with higher coefficients of variation.

Example

When the standard deviations (from Table 5.5) and the expected returns (from Table 5.4) for assets A and B are substituted into Equation 5.4, the coefficients of variation for A and B are 0.094 (1.41% ÷ 15%) and 0.377 (5.66% ÷ 15%), respectively. Asset B has the higher coefficient of variation and is therefore more risky than asset A—which we already know from the standard deviation. (Because both assets have the same expected return, the coefficient of variation has not provided any new information.)

The real utility of the coefficient of variation comes in comparing the risks of assets that have *different* expected returns.

Example

A firm wants to select the less risky of two alternative assets—C and D. The expected return, standard deviation, and coefficient of variation for each of these assets' returns are

Statistics	Asset C	Asset D
(1) Expected return	12%	20%
(2) Standard deviation	9%[a]	10%
(3) Coefficient of variation [(2) ÷ (1)]	0.75	0.50[a]

[a]Preferred asset using the given risk measure.

Judging solely on the basis of their standard deviations, the firm would prefer asset C, which has a lower standard deviation than asset D (9% versus 10%). However, management would be making a serious error in choosing asset C over asset D, because the dispersion—the risk—of the asset, as reflected in the coefficient of variation, is lower for D (0.50) than for C (0.75). Clearly, using the coefficient of variation to compare asset risk is effective because it also considers the relative size, or expected return, of the assets.

Personal Finance Example   Marilyn Ansbro is reviewing stocks for inclusion in her investment portfolio. The stock she wishes to analyze is Danhaus Industries, Inc. (DII), a diversified manufacturer of pet products. One of her key concerns is risk; as a rule she will invest only in stocks with a coefficient of variation of returns below 0.75. She has gathered price and dividend data shown below for DII over the past 3 years, 2007–2009, and assumes that each year's return is equally probable.

| | Stock Price | | |
Year	Beginning	End	Dividend paid
2007	$35.00	$36.50	$3.50
2008	36.50	34.50	3.50
2009	34.50	35.00	4.00

Substituting the price and dividend data for each year into Equation 5.1, we get:

Year	Returns
2007	[$3.50 + ($36.50 − $35.00)]/$35.00 = $5.00 / $35.00 = 14.3%
2008	[$3.50 + ($34.50 − $36.50)]/$36.50 = $1.50 / $36.50 = 4.1%
2009	[$4.00 + ($35.00 − $34.50)]/$34.50 = $4.50 / $34.50 = 13.0%

Substituting into Equation 5.2a, given that the returns are equally probable, we get the average return, $\bar{r}_{2007-2009}$:

$$\bar{r}_{2007-2009} = (14.3\% + 4.1\% + 13.0\%)/3 = \mathbf{10.5\%}$$

Substituting the average return and annual returns into Equation 5.3a, we get the standard deviation, $\sigma_{r2007-2009}$:

$$\sigma_{r2007-2009} = \sqrt{[(14.3\% - 10.5\%)^2 + (4.1\% - 10.5\%)^2 + (13.0\% - 10.5\%)^2]/(3-1)}$$

$$= \sqrt{(14.44\% + 40.96\% + 6.25\%)/2} = \sqrt{30.825\%} = 5.6\%$$

Finally, substituting the standard deviation of returns and the average return into Equation 5.4, we get the coefficient of variation, CV:

$$CV = 5.6\%/10.5\% = \mathbf{0.53}$$

Because the coefficient of variation of returns on the DII stock over the 2007–2009 period of 0.53 is well below Marilyn's maximum coefficient of variation of 0.75, she concludes that the DII stock would be an acceptable investment.

efficient portfolio
A portfolio that maximizes return for a given level of risk or minimizes risk for a given level of return.

correlation
A statistical measure of the relationship between any two series of numbers representing data of any kind.

REVIEW QUESTIONS

5–4   Explain how the *range* is used in scenario analysis.
5–5   What does a plot of the *probability distribution* of outcomes show a decision maker about an asset's risk?
5–6   What relationship exists between the size of the *standard deviation* and the degree of asset risk?
5–7   When is the *coefficient of variation* preferred over the standard deviation for comparing asset risk?

5.3 | Risk of a Portfolio

In real-world situations, the risk of any single investment would not be viewed independently of other assets. (We did so for teaching purposes.) New investments must be considered in light of their impact on the risk and return of the *portfolio* of assets. The financial manager's goal is to create an **efficient portfolio,** one that maximizes return for a given level of risk or minimizes risk for a given level of return. First, we will look at the statistical concept of *correlation*, which underlies the process of diversification that is used to develop an efficient portfolio.

positively correlated
Describes two series that move in the same direction.

negatively correlated
Describes two series that move in opposite directions.

correlation coefficient
A measure of the degree of correlation between two series.

perfectly positively correlated
Describes two *positively correlated* series that have a *correlation coefficient* of +1.

perfectly negatively correlated
Describes two *negatively correlated* series that have a *correlation coefficient* of −1.

Correlation

Correlation is a statistical measure of the relationship between any two series of numbers. The numbers may represent data of any kind, from returns to test scores. If two series move in the same direction, they are **positively correlated.** If the series move in opposite directions, they are **negatively correlated.**

The degree of correlation is measured by the **correlation coefficient,** which ranges from +1 for **perfectly positively correlated** series to −1 for **perfectly negatively correlated** series. These two extremes are depicted for series M and N in Figure 5.3. The perfectly positively correlated series move exactly together; the perfectly negatively correlated series move in exactly opposite directions.

FIGURE 5.3

Correlations
The correlation between series M and series N

FIGURE 5.4

Diversification
Combining negatively
correlated assets to reduce,
or diversify, risk

Diversification

The concept of correlation is essential to developing an efficient portfolio. To reduce overall risk, it is best to *diversify* by combining, or adding to the portfolio, assets that have a negative (or a low positive) correlation. Combining negatively correlated assets can reduce the overall variability of returns. Figure 5.4 shows that a portfolio containing the negatively correlated assets F and G, both of which have the same expected return, $\bar{r}$, also has that same return $\bar{r}$ but has less risk (variability) than either of the individual assets. Even if assets are not negatively correlated, the lower the positive correlation between them, the lower the resulting risk.

uncorrelated
Describes two series that lack
any interaction and therefore
have a *correlation coefficient*
close to zero.

Some assets are **uncorrelated**—that is, there is no interaction between their returns. Combining uncorrelated assets can reduce risk, not so effectively as combining negatively correlated assets, but more effectively than combining positively correlated assets. The *correlation coefficient for uncorrelated assets is close to zero* and acts as the midpoint between perfect positive and perfect negative correlation.

The creation of a portfolio that combines two assets with perfectly positively correlated returns results in overall portfolio risk that at minimum equals that of the least risky asset and at maximum equals that of the most risky asset. However, a portfolio combining two assets with less than perfectly positive correlation *can* reduce total risk to a level below that of either of the components, which in certain situations may be zero. For example, assume that you manufacture machine tools. The business is very *cyclical*, with high sales when the economy is expanding and low sales during a recession. If you acquired another machine-tool company, with sales positively correlated with those of your firm, the combined sales would still be cyclical and risk would remain the same. Alternatively, however, you could acquire a sewing machine manufacturer, whose sales are *countercyclical*. It typically has low sales during economic expansion and high sales during recession (when consumers are more likely to make their own clothes). Combination with the sewing machine manufacturer, which has negatively correlated sales, should reduce risk.

Example

Table 5.7 presents the forecasted returns from three different assets—X, Y, and Z—over the next 5 years, along with their expected values and standard deviations. Each of the assets has an expected value of return of 12% and a standard deviation of 3.16%. The assets therefore have equal return and equal risk.

| TABLE 5.7 | **Forecasted Returns, Expected Values, and Standard Deviations for Assets X, Y, and Z and Portfolios XY and XZ** | | | | |

| | Assets | | | Portfolios | |
| | | | | XY[a] | XZ[b] |
Year	X	Y	Z	(50% X + 50% Y)	(50% X + 50% Z)
2010	8%	16%	8%	12%	8%
2011	10	14	10	12	10
2012	12	12	12	12	12
2013	14	10	14	12	14
2014	16	8	16	12	16
Statistics:[c]					
Expected value	12%	12%	12%	12%	12%
Standard deviation[d]	3.16%	3.16%	3.16%	0%	3.16%

[a]Portfolio XY, which consists of 50% of asset X and 50% of asset Y, illustrates *perfect negative correlation* because these two return streams behave in completely opposite fashion over the 5-year period. Its return values are calculated as shown in the following table.

| | Forecasted return | | | Expected portfolio |
| | Asset X | Asset Y | Portfolio return calculation[a] | return, r_p |
Year	(1)	(2)	(3)	(4)
2010	8%	16%	$(.50 \times 8\%) + (.50 \times 16\%) =$	12%
2011	10	14	$(.50 \times 10\%) + (.50 \times 14\%) =$	12
2012	12	12	$(.50 \times 12\%) + (.50 \times 12\%) =$	12
2013	14	10	$(.50 \times 14\%) + (.50 \times 10\%) =$	12
2014	16	8	$(.50 \times 16\%) + (.50 \times 8\%) =$	12

[b]Portfolio XZ, which consists of 50% of asset X and 50% of asset Z, illustrates *perfect positive correlation* because these two return streams behave identically over the 5-year period. Its return values are calculated using the same method demonstrated in note *a* above for portfolio XY.

[c]Because the probabilities associated with the returns are not given, the general equation, Equation 5.2a in footnote 1, is used to calculate expected values as demonstrated below for portfolio XY.

$$\bar{r}_{xy} = \frac{12\% + 12\% + 12\% + 12\% + 12\%}{5} = \frac{60\%}{5} = \underline{\underline{12\%}}$$

The same formula is applied to find the expected value of return for assets X, Y, and Z, and portfolio XZ.

[d]The portfolio standard deviations can be directly calculated from the standard deviations of the component assets with the following formula:

$$\sigma_{r_p} = \sqrt{w_1^2 \sigma_1^2 + w_2^2 \sigma_2^2 + 2 w_1 w_2 c_{1,2} \sigma_1 \sigma_2}$$

where w_1 and w_2 are the proportions of component assets 1 and 2, σ_1 and σ_2 are the standard deviations of component assets 1 and 2, and $c_{1,2}$ is the correlation coefficient between the returns of component assets 1 and 2.

The return patterns of assets X and Y are perfectly negatively correlated. They move in exactly opposite directions over time. The returns of assets X and Z are perfectly positively correlated. They move in precisely the same direction. (*Note:* The returns for X and Z are identical.)[3]

Portfolio XY Portfolio XY (shown in Table 5.7) is created by combining equal portions of assets X and Y, the perfectly negatively correlated assets.[4] The risk in this portfolio, as reflected by its standard deviation, is reduced to 0%, whereas the expected return remains at 12%. Thus the combination results in the complete elimination of risk. Whenever assets are perfectly negatively correlated, an optimal combination (similar to the 50–50 mix in the case of assets X and Y) exists for which the resulting standard deviation will equal 0.

Portfolio XZ Portfolio XZ (shown in Table 5.7) is created by combining equal portions of assets X and Z, the perfectly positively correlated assets. The risk in this portfolio, as reflected by its standard deviation, is unaffected by this combination. Risk remains at 3.16%, and the expected return value remains at 12%. Because assets X and Z have the same standard deviation, the minimum and maximum standard deviations are the same (3.16%).

Correlation, Diversification, Risk, and Return

In general, the lower the correlation between asset returns, the greater the potential diversification of risk. (This should be clear from the behaviors illustrated in Table 5.7.) For each pair of assets, there is a combination that will result in the lowest risk (standard deviation) possible. The amount that risk can be reduced by this combination depends on the degree of correlation. Many potential combinations (assuming divisibility) could be made, but only one combination of the infinite number of possibilities will minimize risk.

Three possible correlations—perfect positive, uncorrelated, and perfect negative—illustrate the effect of correlation on the diversification of risk and return. Table 5.8 summarizes the impact of correlation on the range of return and risk for various two-asset portfolio combinations. The table shows that as we move from perfect positive correlation to uncorrelated assets to perfect negative correlation, the ability to reduce risk is improved. Note that in no case will a portfolio of assets be riskier than the riskiest asset included in the portfolio. Further discussion of these relationships can be found at the book's website.

International Diversification

The ultimate example of portfolio diversification involves including foreign assets in a portfolio. The inclusion of assets from countries with business cycles that are not highly correlated with the U.S. business cycle reduces the portfolio's responsiveness to market movements and to foreign currency fluctuations.

---

3. Identical return streams are used in this example to permit clear illustration of the concepts, but it is *not* necessary for return streams to be identical for them to be perfectly positively correlated. Any return streams that move (i.e., vary) exactly together—regardless of the relative magnitude of the returns—are perfectly positively correlated.

4. For illustrative purposes it has been assumed that each of the assets—X, Y, and Z—can be divided up and combined with other assets to create portfolios. This assumption is made only to permit clear illustration of the concepts. The assets are not actually divisible.

TABLE 5.8	**Correlation, Return, and Risk for Various Two-Asset Portfolio Combinations**	
Correlation coefficient	Ranges of return	Ranges of risk
+1 (perfect positive)	Between returns of two assets held in isolation	Between risk of two assets held in isolation
0 (uncorrelated)	Between returns of two assets held in isolation	Between risk of most risky asset and an amount less than risk of least risky asset but greater than 0
−1 (perfect negative)	Between returns of two assets held in isolation	Between risk of most risky asset and 0

Returns from International Diversification

Over long periods, returns from internationally diversified portfolios tend to be superior to those of purely domestic ones. This is particularly so if the U.S. economy is performing relatively poorly and the dollar is depreciating in value against most foreign currencies. At such times, the dollar returns to U.S. investors on a portfolio of foreign assets can be very attractive. However, over any single short or intermediate period, international diversification can yield subpar returns, particularly when the dollar is appreciating in value relative to other currencies. When the U.S. currency gains in value, the dollar value of a foreign-currency-denominated portfolio of assets declines. Even if this portfolio yields a satisfactory return in local currency, the return to U.S. investors will be reduced when translated into dollars. Subpar local currency portfolio returns, coupled with an appreciating dollar, can yield truly dismal dollar returns to U.S. investors.

Overall, though, the logic of international portfolio diversification assumes that these fluctuations in currency values and relative performance will average out over long periods. Compared to similar, purely domestic portfolios, an internationally diversified portfolio will tend to yield a comparable return at a lower level of risk.

Risks of International Diversification

political risk
Risk that arises from the possibility that a host government will take actions harmful to foreign investors or that political turmoil will endanger investments.

In addition to the risk induced by currency fluctuations, several other financial risks are unique to international investing. Most important is **political risk,** which arises from the possibility that a host government will take actions harmful to foreign investors or that political turmoil will endanger investments. Political risks are particularly acute in developing countries, where unstable or ideologically motivated governments may attempt to block return of profits by foreign investors or even seize (nationalize) their assets in the host country. For example, reflecting President Chavez's desire to broaden the country's socialist revolution, Venezuela issued a list of priority goods for import that excluded a large percentage of the necessary inputs to the automobile production process. As a result, Toyota halted auto production in Venezuela, and three other auto manufacturers temporarily closed or deeply cut their production there. Chavez also has forced most foreign energy firms to reduce their stakes and give up control of oil projects in Venezuela.

Even where governments do not impose exchange controls or seize assets, international investors may suffer if a shortage of hard currency prevents payment of dividends or interest to foreigners. When governments are forced to allocate scarce foreign exchange, they rarely give top priority to the interests of foreign investors. Instead, hard-currency reserves are typically used to pay for necessary imports such as food, medicine, and industrial materials and to pay interest on the government's debt. Because most of the debt of developing countries is held by banks rather than individuals, foreign investors are often badly harmed when a country experiences political or economic problems.

REVIEW QUESTIONS

5–8   Why must assets be evaluated in a portfolio context?

5–9   Why is the *correlation* between asset returns important? How does diversification allow risky assets to be combined so that the risk of the portfolio is less than the risk of the individual assets in it?

5–10 How does international diversification enhance risk reduction? When might international diversification result in subpar returns? What are *political risks*, and how do they affect international diversification?

5.4 | Risk and Return: The Capital Asset Pricing Model (CAPM)

capital asset pricing model (CAPM)
The basic theory that links risk and return for all assets.

The most important aspect of risk is the *overall risk* of the firm as viewed by investors in the marketplace. Overall risk significantly affects investment opportunities and—even more important—the owners' wealth. The basic theory that links risk and return for all assets is the **capital asset pricing model (CAPM)**.[5] We will use CAPM to understand the basic risk–return tradeoffs involved in all types of financial decisions.

Types of Risk

To understand the basic types of risk, consider what happens to the risk of a portfolio consisting of a single security (asset), to which we add securities randomly selected from, say, the population of all actively traded securities. Using the standard deviation of return, σ_{r_p}, to measure the total portfolio risk, Figure 5.5 depicts the behavior of the total portfolio risk (y axis) as more securities are added (x axis). With the addition of securities, the total portfolio risk declines, as a result of the effects of diversification, and tends to approach a lower limit. Research has shown that, on average, most of the risk-reduction benefits of diversification can be gained by forming portfolios containing 15 to 20 randomly selected securities.

---

5. The initial development of this theory is generally attributed to William F. Sharpe, "Capital Asset Prices: A Theory of Market Equilibrium Under Conditions of Risk," *Journal of Finance* 19 (September 1964), pp. 425–442, and John Lintner, "The Valuation of Risk Assets and the Selection of Risky Investments in Stock Portfolios and Capital Budgets," *Review of Economics and Statistics* 47 (February 1965), pp. 13–37. A number of authors subsequently advanced, refined, and tested this now widely accepted theory.

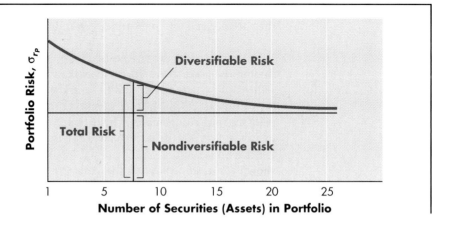

FIGURE 5.5

Risk Reduction
Portfolio risk and diversification

Diversifiable Risk

Portfolio Risk, σ_{r_P}

Total Risk

Nondiversifiable Risk

1   5   10   15   20   25

Number of Securities (Assets) in Portfolio

total risk
The combination of a security's *nondiversifiable risk* and *diversifiable risk.*

diversifiable risk
The portion of an asset's risk that is attributable to firm-specific, random causes; can be eliminated through diversification. Also called *unsystematic risk.*

nondiversifiable risk
The relevant portion of an asset's risk attributable to market factors that affect all firms; cannot be eliminated through diversification. Also called *systematic risk.*

The **total risk** of a security can be viewed as consisting of two parts:

$$\text{Total security risk} = \text{Nondiversifiable risk} + \text{Diversifiable risk} \qquad (5.5)$$

Diversifiable risk (sometimes called *unsystematic risk*) represents the portion of an asset's risk that is associated with random causes that can be eliminated through diversification. It is attributable to firm-specific events, such as strikes, lawsuits, regulatory actions, and loss of a key account. **Nondiversifiable risk** (also called *systematic risk*) is attributable to market factors that affect all firms; it cannot be eliminated through diversification. (It is the shareholder-specific *market risk* described in Table 5.1.) Factors such as war, inflation, international incidents, and political events account for nondiversifiable risk.

Because any investor can create a portfolio of assets that will eliminate virtually all diversifiable risk, *the only relevant risk is nondiversifiable risk.* Any investor or firm therefore must be concerned solely with nondiversifiable risk. The measurement of nondiversifiable risk is thus of primary importance in selecting assets with the most desired risk–return characteristics.

The Model: CAPM

The capital asset pricing model (CAPM) links nondiversifiable risk and return for all assets. We will discuss the model in four sections. The first deals with the beta coefficient, which is a measure of nondiversifiable risk. The second section presents an equation of the model itself, and the third graphically describes the relationship between risk and return. The final section offers some comments on the CAPM.

beta coefficient (*b*)
A relative measure of non-diversifiable risk. An *index* of the degree of movement of an asset's return in response to a change in the *market return.*

market return
The return on the market portfolio of all traded securities.

Beta Coefficient

The **beta coefficient, *b*,** is a relative measure of nondiversifiable risk. It is an *index* of the degree of movement of an asset's return in response to a change in the *market return.* An asset's historical returns are used in finding the asset's beta coefficient. The **market return** is the return on the market portfolio of all traded securities. The *Standard & Poor's 500 Stock Composite Index* or some similar stock index is commonly used as the market return. Betas for actively traded stocks can be obtained from a variety of sources, but you should understand how they are derived and interpreted and how they are applied to portfolios.

Deriving Beta from Return Data   An asset's historical returns are used in finding the asset's beta coefficient. Figure 5.6 plots the relationship between the returns of two assets—R and S—and the market return. Note that the horizontal (*x*) axis measures the historical market returns and that the vertical (*y*) axis measures the individual asset's historical returns. The first step in deriving beta involves plotting the coordinates for the market return and asset returns from various points in time. Such annual "market return–asset return" coordinates are shown *for asset S only* for the years 2002 through 2009. For example, in 2009, asset S's return was 20 percent when the market return was 10 percent. By use of statistical techniques, the "characteristic line" that best explains the relationship between the asset return and the market return coordinates is fit to the data points. The slope of this line is *beta*. The beta for asset R is about .80 and that for asset S is about 1.30. Asset S's higher beta (steeper characteristic line slope) indicates that its return is more responsive to changing market returns. *Therefore asset S is more risky than asset R.*

Interpreting Betas   The beta coefficient for the market is considered to be equal to 1.0. All other betas are viewed in relation to this value. Asset betas may be positive or negative, but positive betas are the norm. The majority of beta coefficients fall between .5 and 2.0. The return of a stock that is half as responsive as the market ($b = .5$) is expected to change by .5 percent for each 1 percent

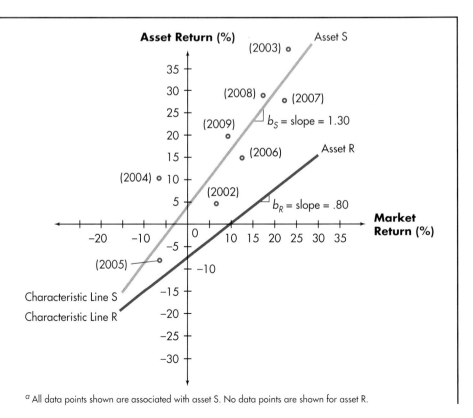

FIGURE 5.6

Beta Derivation[a]
Graphical derivation of beta for assets R and S

[a] All data points shown are associated with asset S. No data points are shown for asset R.

TABLE 5.9	Selected Beta Coefficients and Their Interpretations	
Beta	Comment	Interpretation
2.0	Move in same	Twice as responsive as the market
1.0	direction as	Same response as the market
.5	market	Only half as responsive as the market
0		Unaffected by market movement
−.5	Move in opposite	Only half as responsive as the market
−1.0	direction to	Same response as the market
−2.0	market	Twice as responsive as the market

Hint Remember that published betas are calculated using historical data. When investors use beta for decision making, they should recognize that past performance relative to the market average may not accurately predict future performance.

change in the return of the market portfolio. A stock that is twice as responsive as the market ($b = 2.0$) is expected to experience a 2 percent change in its return for each 1 percent change in the return of the market portfolio. Table 5.9 provides various beta values and their interpretations. Beta coefficients for actively traded stocks can be obtained from published sources such as *Value Line Investment Survey*, via the Internet, or through brokerage firms. Betas for some selected stocks are given in Table 5.10.

Portfolio Betas   The beta of a portfolio can be easily estimated by using the betas of the individual assets it includes. Letting w_j represent the proportion of the portfolio's total dollar value represented by asset j, and letting b_j equal the beta of asset j, we can use Equation 5.6 to find the portfolio beta, b_p:

$$b_p = (w_1 \times b_1) + (w_2 \times b_2) + \cdots + (w_n \times b_n) = \sum_{j=1}^{n} w_j \times b_j \qquad (5.6)$$

Of course, $\sum_{j=1}^{n} w_j = 1$, which means that 100 percent of the portfolio's assets must be included in this computation.

TABLE 5.10	Beta Coefficients for Selected Stocks (July 10, 2007)		
Stock	Beta	Stock	Beta
Amazon.com	1.20	JP Morgan Chase & Co.	1.40
Anheuser-Busch	.65	Merrill Lynch & Co.	1.35
DaimlerChrysler AG	1.30	Microsoft	.95
Disney	1.30	Nike, Inc.	.85
eBay	1.10	PepsiCo, Inc.	.75
ExxonMobil Corp.	.90	Qualcomm	1.00
Gap (The), Inc.	.95	Sempra Energy	1.05
General Electric	1.10	Wal-Mart Stores	.75
Intel	1.15	Xerox	1.40
Int'l Business Machines	1.05	Yahoo! Inc.	1.40

Source: Value Line Investment Survey (New York: Value Line Publishing, July 20, 2007).

Hint Mutual fund managers are key users of the portfolio beta and return concepts. They are continually evaluating what would happen to the fund's beta and return if the securities of a particular firm were added to or deleted from the fund's portfolio.

Portfolio betas are interpreted in the same way as the betas of individual assets. They indicate the degree of responsiveness of the *portfolio's* return to changes in the market return. For example, when the market return increases by 10 percent, a portfolio with a beta of .75 will experience a 7.5 percent increase in its return (.75 × 10%); a portfolio with a beta of 1.25 will experience a 12.5 percent increase in its return (1.25 × 10%). Clearly, a portfolio containing mostly low-beta assets will have a low beta, and one containing mostly high-beta assets will have a high beta.

Personal Finance Example   Mario Austino, an individual investor, wishes to assess the risk of two small portfolios he is considering—V and W. Both portfolios contain five assets, with the proportions and betas shown in Table 5.11. The betas for the two portfolios, b_V and b_W, can be calculated by substituting data from the table into Equation 5.7:

$$b_V = (.10 \times 1.65) + (.30 \times 1.00) + (.20 \times 1.30) + (.20 \times 1.10) + (.20 \times 1.25)$$
$$= .165 + .300 + .260 + .220 + .250 = 1.195 \approx \underline{1.20}$$

$$b_W = (.10 \times .80) + (.10 \times 1.00) + (.20 \times .65) + (.10 \times .75) + (.50 \times 1.05)$$
$$= .080 + .100 + .130 + .075 + .525 = \underline{.91}$$

Portfolio V's beta is about 1.20, and portfolio W's is .91. These values make sense, because portfolio V contains relatively high-beta assets, and portfolio W contains relatively low-beta assets. Mario's calculations show that portfolio V's returns are more responsive to changes in market returns and are therefore more risky than portfolio W's. He must now decide which, if either, portfolio he feels comfortable adding to his existing investments.

The Equation

Using the beta coefficient to measure nondiversifiable risk, the *capital asset pricing model (CAPM)* is given in Equation 5.7:

$$r_j = R_F + [b_j \times (r_m - R_F)] \tag{5.7}$$

TABLE 5.11   Mario Austino's Portfolios V and W

Asset	Portfolio V Proportion	Beta	Portfolio W Proportion	Beta
1	.10	1.65	.10	.80
2	.30	1.00	.10	1.00
3	.20	1.30	.20	.65
4	.20	1.10	.10	.75
5	.20	1.25	.50	1.05
Totals	1.00		1.00	

where

r_j = required return on asset j

R_F = risk-free rate of return, commonly measured by the return on a U.S. Treasury bill

b_j = beta coefficient or index of nondiversifiable risk for asset j

r_m = market return; return on the market portfolio of assets

risk-free rate of return, (R_F)
The required return on a *risk-free asset,* typically a 3-month U.S. Treasury bill.

U.S. Treasury bills (T-bills)
Short-term IOUs issued by the U.S. Treasury; considered the *risk-free asset.*

The CAPM can be divided into two parts: (1) the **risk-free rate of return, R_F,** which is the required return on a *risk-free asset,* typically a 3-month **U.S. Treasury bill (T-bill),** a short-term IOU issued by the U.S. Treasury, and (2) the *risk premium.* These are, respectively, the two elements on either side of the plus sign in Equation 5.7. The $(r_m - R_F)$ portion of the risk premium is called the *market risk premium,* because it represents the premium the investor must receive for taking the average amount of risk associated with holding the market portfolio of assets.[6]

Historical Risk Premiums   Using the historical return data for selected security investments for the 1926–2006 period shown in Table 5.2, we can calculate the risk premiums for each investment category. The calculation (consistent with Equation 5.7) involves merely subtracting the historical U.S. Treasury bill's average return from the historical average return for a given investment:

Investment	Risk premium[a]		
Large-company stocks	12.3%	− 3.8% =	8.5%
Small company stocks	17.4	− 3.8 =	13.6
Long-term corporate bonds	6.2	− 3.8 =	2.4
Long-term government bonds	5.8	− 3.8 =	2.0
U.S. Treasury bills	3.8	− 3.8 =	0.0

[a]Return values obtained from Table 5.2.

Reviewing the risk premiums calculated above, we can see that the risk premium is highest for small-company stocks, followed by large-company stocks, long-term corporate bonds, and long-term government bonds. This outcome makes sense intuitively because small-company stocks are riskier than large-company stocks, which are riskier than long-term corporate bonds (equity is riskier than debt investment). Long-term corporate bonds are riskier than long-term government bonds (because the government is less likely to renege on debt). And of course, U.S. Treasury bills, because of their lack of default risk and their very short maturity, are virtually risk-free, as indicated by their lack of any risk premium.

6. Although CAPM has been widely accepted, a broader theory, *arbitrage pricing theory (APT),* first described by Stephen A. Ross, "The Arbitrage Theory of Capital Asset Pricing," *Journal of Economic Theory* (December 1976), pp. 341–360, has received a great deal of attention in the financial literature. The theory suggests that the risk premium on securities may be better explained by a number of factors underlying and in place of the market return used in CAPM. The CAPM in effect can be viewed as being derived from APT. Although testing of APT confirms the importance of the market return, it has thus far failed to identify other risk factors clearly. As a result of this failure, as well as APT's lack of practical acceptance and usage, we concentrate our attention here on CAPM.

Example

Benjamin Corporation, a growing computer software developer, wishes to determine the required return on an asset Z, which has a beta of 1.5. The risk-free rate of return is 7%; the return on the market portfolio of assets is 11%. Substituting $b_Z = 1.5$, $R_F = 7\%$, and $r_m = 11\%$ into the capital asset pricing model given in Equation 5.8 yields a required return of

$$r_Z = 7\% + [1.5 \times (11\% - 7\%)] = 7\% + 6\% = \underline{\underline{13\%}}$$

The market risk premium of 4% (11% − 7%), when adjusted for the asset's index of risk (beta) of 1.5, results in a risk premium of 6% (1.5 × 4%). That risk premium, when added to the 7% risk-free rate, results in a 13% required return.

Other things being equal, *the higher the beta, the higher the required return, and the lower the beta, the lower the required return.*

The Graph: The Security Market Line (SML)

security market line (SML)
The depiction of the *capital asset pricing model* (*CAPM*) as a graph that reflects the required return in the marketplace for each level of nondiversifiable risk (beta).

When the capital asset pricing model (Equation 5.7) is depicted graphically, it is called the **security market line (SML)**. The SML will, in fact, be a straight line. It reflects the required return in the marketplace for each level of nondiversifiable risk (beta). In the graph, risk as measured by beta, b, is plotted on the x axis, and required returns, r, are plotted on the y axis. The risk–return tradeoff is clearly represented by the SML.

Example

In the preceding example for Benjamin Corporation, the risk-free rate, R_F, was 7%, and the market return, r_m, was 11%. The SML can be plotted by using the two sets of coordinates for the betas associated with R_F and r_m, b_{R_F} and b_m (that is, $b_{R_F} = 0$,[7] $R_F = 7\%$; and $b_m = 1.0$, $r_m = 11\%$). Figure 5.7 presents the resulting security market line. As traditionally shown, the security market line in Figure 5.7 presents the required return associated with all positive betas. The market risk premium of 4% (r_m of 11% − R_F of 7%) has been highlighted. For a beta for asset Z, b_Z, of 1.5, its corresponding required return, r_Z, is 13%. Also shown in the figure is asset Z's risk premium of 6% (r_Z of 13% − R_F of 7%). It should be clear that for assets with betas greater than 1, the risk premium is greater than that for the market; for assets with betas less than 1, the risk premium is less than that for the market.

Some Comments on CAPM

The capital asset pricing model generally relies on historical data. The betas may or may not actually reflect the *future* variability of returns. Therefore, the required returns specified by the model can be viewed only as rough approximations. Users of betas commonly make subjective adjustments to the historically determined betas to reflect their expectations of the future.

The CAPM was developed to explain the behavior of security prices and provide a mechanism whereby investors could assess the impact of a proposed security investment on their portfolio's overall risk and return. It is based on an

---

7. Because R_F is the rate of return on a risk-free asset, the beta associated with the risk-free asset, b_{R_F}, would equal 0. The zero beta on the risk-free asset reflects not only its absence of risk but also that the asset's return is unaffected by movements in the market return.

FIGURE 5.7

Security Market Line
Security market line (SML) with Benjamin Corporation's asset Z data shown

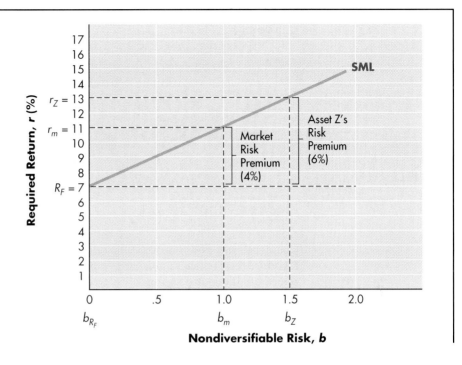

efficient market
A market with the following characteristics: many small investors, all having the same information and expectations with respect to securities; no restrictions on investment, no taxes, and no transaction costs; and rational investors, who view securities similarly and are risk-averse, preferring higher returns and lower risk.

assumed **efficient market** with the following characteristics: many small investors, all having the same information and expectations with respect to securities; no restrictions on investment, no taxes, and no transaction costs; and rational investors, who view securities similarly and are risk-averse, preferring higher returns and lower risk.

Although the perfect world of the efficient market appears to be unrealistic, studies have provided support for the existence of the expectational relationship described by CAPM in active markets such as the New York Stock Exchange.[8] In the case of real corporate assets, such as plant and equipment, research thus far has failed to prove the general applicability of CAPM because of indivisibility, relatively large size, limited number of transactions, and absence of an efficient market for such assets.

Despite the limitations of CAPM, it provides a useful conceptual framework for evaluating and linking risk and return. An awareness of this tradeoff and an attempt to consider risk as well as return in financial decision making should help financial managers achieve their goals.

REVIEW QUESTIONS

5–11 How are total risk, nondiversifiable risk, and diversifiable risk related? Why is nondiversifiable risk the *only relevant risk?*

---

8. A study by Eugene F. Fama and Kenneth R. French, "The Cross-Section of Expected Stock Returns," *Journal of Finance* 47 (June 1992), pp. 427–465, raised serious questions about the validity of CAPM. The study failed to find a significant relationship between the *historical* betas and *historical* returns on over 2,000 stocks during 1963–1990. In other words, it found that the magnitude of a stock's *historical* beta had no relationship to the level of its *historical* return. Although Fama and French's study continues to receive attention, CAPM has not been abandoned because its rejection as a *historical* model fails to discredit its validity as an *expectational* model. Therefore, in spite of this challenge, CAPM continues to be viewed as a logical and useful framework—both conceptually and operationally—for linking *expected* nondiversifiable risk and return.

5–12 What risk does *beta* measure? How can you find the beta of a portfolio?

5–13 Explain the meaning of each variable in the *capital asset pricing model (CAPM)* equation. What is the *security market line (SML)?*

5–14 Why do financial managers have some difficulty applying CAPM in financial decision making? Generally, what benefit does CAPM provide them?

Summary

Focus on Value

A firm's risk and expected return directly affect its share price. As we shall see in Chapter 7, risk and return are the two key determinants of the firm's value. It is therefore the financial manager's responsibility to assess carefully the risk and return of all major decisions so as to ensure that the expected returns justify the level of risk being introduced.

The financial manager can expect to achieve **the firm's goal of increasing its share price** (and thereby benefiting its owners) by taking only those actions that earn returns at least commensurate with their risk. Clearly, financial managers need to recognize, measure, and evaluate risk–return tradeoffs to ensure that their decisions contribute to the creation of value for owners.

Review of Learning Goals

Key definitions and formulas for this chapter are summarized in Table 5.12.

LG 1 **Understand the meaning and fundamentals of risk, return, and risk preferences.** Risk is the chance of loss or, more formally, the variability of returns. A number of sources of firm-specific and shareholder-specific risks exist. Return is any cash distributions plus the change in value over a given period of time expressed as a percentage of the initial value. Investment returns vary both over time and between different types of investments. Most financial decision makers are risk-averse. They require higher expected returns in exchange for greater risk.

LG 2 **Describe procedures for assessing and measuring the risk of a single asset.** The risk of a single asset is measured in much the same way as the risk of a portfolio of assets. Scenario analysis and probability distributions can be used to assess risk. The range, the standard deviation, and the coefficient of variation can be used to measure risk quantitatively.

LG 3 **Discuss risk measurement for a single asset using the standard deviation and coefficient of variation.** In addition to the range, which is the optimistic (best) outcome minus the pessimistic (worst) outcome, the standard deviation and the coefficient of variation can be used to measure risk quantitatively. The standard deviation measures the dispersion around an asset's expected value, and the coefficient of variation uses the standard deviation to measure dispersion on a relative basis.

TABLE 5.12   Summary of Key Definitions and Formulas for Risk and Return

Definitions of variables

b_j = beta coefficient or index of nondiversifiable risk for asset j

b_p = portfolio beta

C_t = cash received from the asset investment in the time period $t-1$ to t

CV = coefficient of variation

$\bar{r}$ = expected value of a return

r_j = return for the jth outcome; return on asset j; required return on asset j

r_m = market return; the return on the market portfolio of assets

r_p = portfolio return

r_t = actual, expected, or required rate of return during period t

n = number of outcomes considered

P_t = price (value) of asset at time t

P_{t-1} = price (value) of asset at time $t-1$

Pr_j = probability of occurrence of the jth outcome

R_F = risk-free rate of return

σ_r = standard deviation of returns

w_j = proportion of total portfolio dollar value represented by asset j

Risk and return formulas

Rate of return during period t:

$$r_t = \frac{C_t + P_t - P_{t-1}}{P_{t-1}}$$ [Equation 5.1]

Expected value of a return:

For probabilistic data:

$$\bar{r} = \sum_{j=1}^{n} r_j \times Pr_j$$ [Equation 5.2]

General formula:

$$\bar{r} = \frac{\sum_{j=1}^{n} r_j}{n}$$ [Equation 5.2a]

Standard deviation of return:

For probabilistic data:

$$\sigma_r = \sqrt{\sum_{j=1}^{n} (r_j - \bar{r})^2 \times Pr_j}$$ [Equation 5.3]

General formula:

$$\sigma_r = \sqrt{\frac{\sum_{j=1}^{n} (r_j - \bar{r})^2}{n-1}}$$ [Equation 5.3a]

Coefficient of variation:

$$CV = \frac{\sigma_r}{\bar{r}}$$ [Equation 5.4]

Total security risk = Nondiversifiable risk + Diversifiable risk [Equation 5.5]

Portfolio beta:

$$b_p = \sum_{j=1}^{n} w_j \times b_j$$ [Equation 5.6]

Capital asset pricing model (CAPM):

$$r_j = R_F + [b_j \times (r_m - R_F)]$$ [Equation 5.7]

Understand the risk and return characteristics of a portfolio in terms of correlation and diversification, and the impact of international assets on a portfolio. The financial manager's goal is to create an efficient portfolio that maximizes return for a given level of risk. The risk of a portfolio of assets may be reduced by diversification—combining assets with low correlation to reduce the risk of the portfolio. Correlation, the statistical relationship between asset returns, affects diversification. The more negative (or less positive) the correlation, the greater the risk-reducing benefits.

International diversification can further reduce a portfolio's risk. Foreign assets have the risk of currency fluctuation and political risks.

Review the two types of risk and the derivation and role of beta in measuring the relevant risk of both a security and a portfolio. The total risk of a security consists of nondiversifiable and diversifiable risk. Diversifiable risk can be eliminated through diversification. Nondiversifiable risk is the only relevant risk. Nondiversifiable risk is measured by the beta coefficient, which is a relative measure of the relationship between an asset's return and the market return. Beta is derived by finding the slope of the "characteristic line" that best explains the historical relationship between the asset's return and the market return. The beta of a portfolio is a weighted average of the betas of the individual assets that it includes.

Explain the capital asset pricing model (CAPM) and its relationship to the security market line (SML). The capital asset pricing model (CAPM) uses beta to relate an asset's risk relative to the market to the asset's required return. The graphical depiction of CAPM is the security market line (SML). Although it has some shortcomings, CAPM provides a useful conceptual framework for evaluating and linking risk and return.

Self-Test Problems (Solutions in Appendix B)

  ST5–1 Portfolio analysis You have been asked for your advice in selecting a portfolio of assets and have been given the following data:

| | Expected return | | |
Year	Asset A	Asset B	Asset C
2010	12%	16%	12%
2011	14	14	14
2012	16	12	16

No probabilities have been supplied. You have been told that you can create two portfolios—one consisting of assets A and B and the other consisting of assets A and C—by investing equal proportions (50%) in each of the two component assets.
a. What is the expected return for each asset over the 3-year period?
b. What is the standard deviation for each asset's return?
c. What is the expected return for each of the two portfolios?

d. How would you characterize the correlations of returns of the two assets making up each of the two portfolios identified in part **c**?

e. What is the standard deviation for each portfolio?

f. Which portfolio do you recommend? Why?

 ST5–2 Beta and CAPM   Currently under consideration is a project with a beta, *b*, of 1.50. At this time, the risk-free rate of return, R_F, is 7%, and the return on the market portfolio of assets, r_m, is 10%. The project is actually *expected* to earn an annual rate of return of 11%.

a. If the return on the market portfolio were to increase by 10%, what would you expect to happen to the project's *required return?* What if the market return were to decline by 10%?

b. Use the capital asset pricing model (CAPM) to find the *required return* on this investment.

c. On the basis of your calculation in part **b,** would you recommend this investment? Why or why not?

d. Assume that as a result of investors becoming less risk-averse, the market return drops by 1% to 9%. What impact would this change have on your responses in parts **b** and **c?**

Warm-Up Exercises   A blue box (■) indicates exercises available in 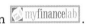.

E5–1   An analyst predicted last year that the stock of Logistics, Inc., would offer a total return of at least 10% in the coming year. At the beginning of the year, the firm had a stock market value of $10 million. At the end of the year, it had a market value of $12 million even though it experienced a loss, or negative net income, of $2.5 million. Did the analyst's prediction prove correct? Explain using the values for total annual return.

E5–2   Four analysts cover the stock of Fluorine Chemical. One forecasts a 5% return for the coming year. A second expects the return to be negative 5%. A third predicts a 10% return. A fourth expects a 3% return in the coming year. You are relatively confident that the return will be positive but not large, so you arbitrarily assign probabilities of being correct of 35%, 5%, 20%, and 40%, respectively, to the analysts' forecasts. Given these probabilities, what is Fluorine Chemical's *expected return* for the coming year?

E5–3   The expected annual returns are 15% for investment 1 and 12% for investment 2. The standard deviation of the first investment's return is 10%; the second investment's return has a standard deviation of 5%. Which investment is less risky based solely on *standard deviation?* Which investment is less risky based on *coefficient of variation?* Which is a better measure given that the expected returns of the two investments are not the same?

E5–4   Your portfolio has three asset classes. U.S. government T-bills account for 45% of the portfolio, large-company stocks constitute another 40%, and small-company stocks make up the remaining 15%. If the expected returns are 3.8% for the T-bills, 12.3% for the large-company stocks, and 17.4% for the small-company stocks, what is the expected return of the portfolio?

E5–5 You wish to calculate the risk level of your portfolio based on its beta. The five stocks in the portfolio with their respective weights and betas are shown below. Calculate the beta of your portfolio.

Stock	Portfolio weight	Beta
Alpha	20%	1.15
Centauri	10	.85
Zen	15	1.6
Wren	20	1.35
Yukos	35	1.85

E5–6
a. Calculate the required rate of return for an asset that has a beta of 1.8, given a risk-free rate of 5% and a market return of 10%.
b. If investors have become more risk-averse due to recent geopolitical events, and the market return rises to 13%, what is the required rate of return for the same asset?
c. Use your findings in part **a** to graph the initial *security market line (SML)*.

Problems

A blue box (■) indicates problems available in myfinancelab.

P5–1 **Rate of return** Douglas Keel, a financial analyst for Orange Industries, wishes to estimate the rate of return for two similar-risk investments, X and Y. Douglas's research indicates that the immediate past returns will serve as reasonable estimates of future returns. A year earlier, investment X had a market value of $20,000; investment Y had a market value of $55,000. During the year, investment X generated cash flow of $1,500 and investment Y generated cash flow of $6,800. The current market values of investments X and Y are $21,000 and $55,000, respectively.
a. Calculate the expected rate of return on investments X and Y using the most recent year's data.
b. Assuming that the two investments are equally risky, which one should Douglas recommend? Why?

P5–2 **Return calculations** For each of the investments shown in the following table, calculate the rate of return earned over the unspecified time period.

Investment	Cash flow during period	Beginning-of-period value	End-of-period value
A	− $ 100	$ 800	$ 1,100
B	15,000	120,000	118,000
C	7,000	45,000	48,000
D	80	600	500
E	1,500	12,500	12,400

P5–3 **Risk preferences** Sharon Smith, the financial manager for Barnett Corporation, wishes to evaluate three prospective investments: X, Y, and Z. Currently, the firm earns 12% on its investments, which have a risk index of 6%. The expected return and expected risk of the investments are shown below. If Sharon Smith is *risk-averse*, which investments would she select? Why?

Investment	Expected return	Expected risk index
X	14%	7%
Y	12	8
Z	10	9

P5–4 **Risk analysis** Solar Designs is considering an investment in an expanded product line. Two possible types of expansion are being considered. After investigating the possible outcomes, the company made the estimates shown in the following table:

	Expansion A	Expansion B
Initial investment	$12,000	$12,000
Annual rate of return		
Pessimistic	16%	10%
Most likely	20%	20%
Optimistic	24%	30%

a. Determine the *range* of the rates of return for each of the two projects.
b. Which project is less risky? Why?
c. If you were making the investment decision, which one would you choose? Why? What does this imply about your feelings toward risk?
d. Assume that expansion B's most likely outcome is 21% per year and that all other facts remain the same. Does this change your answer to part **c**? Why?

P5–5 **Risk and probability** Micro-Pub, Inc., is considering the purchase of one of two microfilm cameras, R and S. Both should provide benefits over a 10-year period, and each requires an initial investment of $4,000. Management has constructed the following table of estimates of rates of return and probabilities for pessimistic, most likely, and optimistic results.

	Camera R		Camera S	
	Amount	Probability	Amount	Probability
Initial investment	$4,000	1.00	$4,000	1.00
Annual rate of return				
Pessimistic	20%	.25	15%	.20
Most likely	25%	.50	25%	.55
Optimistic	30%	.25	35%	.25

a. Determine the *range* for the rate of return for each of the two cameras.
b. Determine the *expected value* of return for each camera.
c. Purchase of which camera is riskier? Why?

P5–6 Bar charts and risk   Swan's Sportswear is considering bringing out a line of designer jeans. Currently, it is negotiating with two different well-known designers. Because of the highly competitive nature of the industry, the two lines of jeans have been given code names. After market research, the firm has established the expectations shown in the following table about the annual rates of return:

Market acceptance	Probability	Annual rate of return Line J	Line K
Very poor	.05	.0075	.010
Poor	.15	.0125	.025
Average	.60	.0850	.080
Good	.15	.1475	.135
Excellent	.05	.1625	.150

Use the table to:
a. Construct a bar chart for each line's annual rate of return.
b. Calculate the *expected value* of return for each line.
c. Evaluate the relative riskiness for each jean line's rate of return using the bar charts.

P5–7 Coefficient of variation   Metal Manufacturing has isolated four alternatives for meeting its need for increased production capacity. The following table summarizes data gathered relative to each of these alternatives.

Alternative	Expected return	Standard deviation of return
A	20%	7.0%
B	22	9.5
C	19	6.0
D	16	5.5

a. Calculate the *coefficient of variation* for each alternative.
b. If the firm wishes to minimize risk, which alternative do you recommend? Why?

PERSONAL FINANCE PROBLEM

P5–8 Rate of return, standard deviation, coefficient of variation   Mike is searching for a stock to include in his current stock portfolio. He is interested in Apple Inc.; he has been impressed with the company's computer products and believes Apple is an innovative market player. However, Mike realizes that any time you consider a so-called high-tech stock, risk is a major concern. The rule he follows is to include only securities with a coefficient of variation of returns below 0.90.

Mike has obtained the following price information for the period 2006 through 2009. Apple stock, being growth-oriented, did not pay any dividends during these 4 years.

	Stock price	
Year	Beginning	End
2006	$14.36	$21.55
2007	21.55	64.78
2008	64.78	72.38
2009	72.38	91.80

a. Calculate the *rate of return* for each year, 2006 through 2009, for Apple stock.
b. Assume that each year's return is equally probable and calculate the *average return* over this time period.
c. Calculate the *standard deviation* of returns over the past 4 years. (*Hint:* Treat this data as a sample.)
d. Based on **b** and **c** determine the *coefficient of variation* of returns for the security.
e. Given the calculation in **d** what should be Mike's decision regarding the inclusion of Apple stock in his portfolio?

  P5–9 **Assessing return and risk**   Swift Manufacturing must choose between two asset purchases. The annual rate of return and the related probabilities given in the following table summarize the firm's analysis to this point.

Project 257		Project 432	
Rate of return	Probability	Rate of return	Probability
−10%	.01	10%	.05
10	.04	15	.10
20	.05	20	.10
30	.10	25	.15
40	.15	30	.20
45	.30	35	.15
50	.15	40	.10
60	.10	45	.10
70	.05	50	.05
80	.04		
100	.01		

a. For each project, compute:
   (1) The range of possible rates of return.
   (2) The expected value of return.
   (3) The standard deviation of the returns.
   (4) The coefficient of variation of the returns.
b. Construct a bar chart of each distribution of rates of return.
c. Which project would you consider less risky? Why?

P5–10 Integrative—Expected return, standard deviation, and coefficient of variation
Three assets—F, G, and H—are currently being considered by Perth Industries.
The probability distributions of expected returns for these assets are shown in the
following table.

	Asset F		Asset G		Asset H	
j	Pr_j	Return, r_j	Pr_j	Return, r_j	Pr_j	Return, r_j
1	.10	40%	.40	35%	.10	40%
2	.20	10	.30	10	.20	20
3	.40	0	.30	−20	.40	10
4	.20	− 5			.20	0
5	.10	−10			.10	−20

a. Calculate the expected value of return, $\bar{r}$, for each of the three assets.
Which provides the largest expected return?
b. Calculate the standard deviation, σ_r, for each of the three assets' returns.
Which appears to have the greatest risk?
c. Calculate the coefficient of variation, CV, for each of the three assets' returns.
Which appears to have the greatest *relative* risk?

PERSONAL FINANCE PROBLEM

P5–11 **Portfolio return and standard deviation**   Jamie Wong is considering building
an investment portfolio containing two stocks, L and M. Stock L will represent 40%
of the dollar value of the portfolio, and stock M will account for the other 60%.
The expected returns over the next 6 years, 2010–2015, for each of these stocks
are shown in the following table:

	Expected return	
Year	Stock L	Stock M
2010	14%	20%
2011	14	18
2012	16	16
2013	17	14
2014	17	12
2015	19	10

a. Calculate the expected portfolio return, r_p, for *each* of the 6 years.
b. Calculate the expected value of portfolio returns, $\bar{r}_p$, over the 6-year period.
c. Calculate the standard deviation of expected portfolio returns, σ_{r_p}, over the
6-year period.
d. How would you characterize the correlation of returns of the two stocks L
and M?
e. Discuss any benefits of diversification achieved by Jamie through creation of the
portfolio.

P5–12 **Portfolio analysis**   You have been given the expected return data shown in the first table on three assets—F, G, and H—over the period 2010–2013.

| | Expected return | | |
Year	Asset F	Asset G	Asset H
2010	16%	17%	14%
2011	17	16	15
2012	18	15	16
2013	19	14	17

Using these assets, you have isolated the three investment alternatives shown in the following table:

Alternative	Investment
1	100% of asset F
2	50% of asset F and 50% of asset G
3	50% of asset F and 50% of asset H

a. Calculate the expected return over the 4-year period for each of the three alternatives.
b. Calculate the standard deviation of returns over the 4-year period for each of the three alternatives.
c. Use your findings in parts **a** and **b** to calculate the coefficient of variation for each of the three alternatives.
d. On the basis of your findings, which of the three investment alternatives do you recommend? Why?

P5–13 **Correlation, risk, and return**   Matt Peters wishes to evaluate the risk and return behaviors associated with various combinations of assets V and W under three assumed degrees of correlation: perfect positive, uncorrelated, and perfect negative. The expected return and risk values calculated for each of the assets are shown in the following table.

Asset	Expected return, $\bar{r}$	Risk (standard deviation), σ_r
V	8%	5%
W	13	10

a. If the returns of assets V and W are *perfectly positively correlated* (correlation coefficient = +1), describe the *range* of (1) expected return and (2) risk associated with all possible portfolio combinations.
b. If the returns of assets V and W are *uncorrelated* (correlation coefficient = 0), describe the *approximate range* of (1) expected return and (2) risk associated with all possible portfolio combinations.

c. If the returns of assets V and W are *perfectly negatively correlated* (correlation coefficient $= -1$), describe the *range* of (1) expected return and (2) risk associated with all possible portfolio combinations.

PERSONAL FINANCE PROBLEM

  P5–14 **International investment returns** Joe Martinez, a U.S. citizen living in Brownsville, Texas, invested in the common stock of Telmex, a Mexican corporation. He purchased 1,000 shares at 20.50 pesos per share. Twelve months later, he sold them at 24.75 pesos per share. He received no dividends during that time.

a. What was Joe's investment return (in percentage terms) for the year, on the basis of the peso value of the shares?
b. The exchange rate for pesos was 9.21 pesos per US$1.00 at the time of the purchase. At the time of the sale, the exchange rate was 9.85 pesos per US$1.00. Translate the purchase and sale prices into US$.
c. Calculate Joe's investment return on the basis of the US$ value of the shares.
d. Explain why the two returns are different. Which one is more important to Joe? Why?

 P5–15 **Total, nondiversifiable, and diversifiable risk** David Talbot randomly selected securities from all those listed on the New York Stock Exchange for his portfolio. He began with a single security and added securities one by one until a total of 20 securities were held in the portfolio. After each security was added, David calculated the portfolio standard deviation, σ_{r_p}. The calculated values are shown in the following table.

Number of securities	Portfolio risk, σ_{r_p}	Number of securities	Portfolio risk, σ_{r_p}
1	14.50%	11	7.00%
2	13.30	12	6.80
3	12.20	13	6.70
4	11.20	14	6.65
5	10.30	15	6.60
6	9.50	16	6.56
7	8.80	17	6.52
8	8.20	18	6.50
9	7.70	19	6.48
10	7.30	20	6.47

a. On a set of "number of securities in portfolio (*x* axis)–portfolio risk (*y* axis)" axes, plot the portfolio risk data given in the preceding table.
b. Divide the total portfolio risk in the graph into its *nondiversifiable* and *diversifiable* risk components and label each of these on the graph.
c. Describe which of the two risk components is the *relevant risk*, and explain why it is relevant. How much of this risk exists in David Talbot's portfolio?

 P5–16 **Graphical derivation of beta** A firm wishes to estimate graphically the betas for two assets, A and B. It has gathered the return data shown in the following table for the market portfolio and for both assets over the last 10 years, 2000–2009.

	Actual return		
Year	Market portfolio	Asset A	Asset B
2000	6%	11%	16%
2001	2	8	11
2002	−13	− 4	−10
2003	− 4	3	3
2004	− 8	0	− 3
2005	16	19	30
2006	10	14	22
2007	15	18	29
2008	8	12	19
2009	13	17	26

a. On a set of "market return (x axis)–asset return (y axis)" axes, use the data given to draw the characteristic line for asset A and for asset B.
b. Use the characteristic lines from part **a** to estimate the betas for assets A and B.
c. Use the betas found in part **b** to comment on the relative risks of assets A and B.

P5–17 **Interpreting beta**   A firm wishes to assess the impact of changes in the market return on an asset that has a beta of 1.20.
a. If the market return increased by 15%, what impact would this change be expected to have on the asset's return?
b. If the market return decreased by 8%, what impact would this change be expected to have on the asset's return?
c. If the market return did not change, what impact, if any, would be expected on the asset's return?
d. Would this asset be considered more or less risky than the market? Explain.

P5–18 **Betas**   Answer the questions below for assets A to D shown in the following table.

Asset	Beta
A	.50
B	1.60
C	− .20
D	.90

a. What impact would a *10% increase* in the market return be expected to have on each asset's return?
b. What impact would a *10% decrease* in the market return be expected to have on each asset's return?
c. If you were certain that the market return would *increase* in the near future, which asset would you prefer? Why?
d. If you were certain that the market return would *decrease* in the near future, which asset would you prefer? Why?

PERSONAL FINANCE PROBLEM

P5–19 **Betas and risk rankings**   You are considering three stocks—A, B, and C—for possible inclusion in your investment portfolio. Stock A has a beta of .80, stock B has a beta of 1.40, and stock C has a beta of − .30.

a. Rank these stocks from the most risky to the least risky.
b. If the return on the market portfolio increased by 12%, what change would you expect in the return for each of the stocks?
c. If the return on the market portfolio decreased by 5%, what change would you expect in the return for each of the stocks?
d. If you felt that the stock market was getting ready to experience a significant decline, which stock would you probably add to your portfolio? Why?
e. If you anticipated a major stock market rally, which stock would you add to your portfolio? Why?

PERSONAL FINANCE PROBLEM

 P5–20 Portfolio betas   Rose Berry is attempting to evaluate two possible portfolios, which consist of the same five assets held in different proportions. She is particularly interested in using beta to compare the risks of the portfolios, so she has gathered the data shown in the following table.

		Portfolio weights	
Asset	Asset beta	Portfolio A	Portfolio B
1	1.30	10%	30%
2	.70	30	10
3	1.25	10	20
4	1.10	10	20
5	.90	40	20
Totals		100%	100%

a. Calculate the betas for portfolios A and B.
b. Compare the risks of these portfolios to the market as well as to each other. Which portfolio is more risky?

 P5–21 Capital asset pricing model (CAPM)   For each of the cases shown in the following table, use the capital asset pricing model to find the required return.

Case	Risk-free rate, R_F	Market return, r_m	Beta, b
A	5%	8%	1.30
B	8	13	.90
C	9	12	− .20
D	10	15	1.00
E	6	10	.60

PERSONAL FINANCE PROBLEM

  P5–22 Beta coefficients and the capital asset pricing model   Katherine Wilson is wondering how much risk she must undertake to generate an acceptable return on her portfolio. The risk-free return currently is 5%. The return on the average stock (market return) is 16%. Use the CAPM to calculate the beta coefficient associated with each of the following portfolio returns.

    a. 10%
    b. 15%
    c. 18%
    d. 20%
    e. Katherine is risk-averse. What is the highest return she can expect if she is unwilling to take more than an average risk?

 P5–23 Manipulating CAPM Use the basic equation for the capital asset pricing model (CAPM) to work each of the following problems.
    a. Find the *required return* for an asset with a beta of .90 when the risk-free rate and market return are 8% and 12%, respectively.
    b. Find the *risk-free rate* for a firm with a required return of 15% and a beta of 1.25 when the market return is 14%.
    c. Find the *market return* for an asset with a required return of 16% and a beta of 1.10 when the risk-free rate is 9%.
    d. Find the *beta* for an asset with a required return of 15% when the risk-free rate and market return are 10% and 12.5%, respectively.

PERSONAL FINANCE PROBLEM

     P5–24 Portfolio return and beta Jamie Peters invested $100,000 to set up the following portfolio one year ago:

Asset	Cost	Beta at purchase	Yearly income	Value today
A	$20,000	.80	$1,600	$20,000
B	35,000	.95	1,400	36,000
C	30,000	1.50	—	34,500
D	15,000	1.25	375	16,500

    a. Calculate the portfolio beta on the basis of the original cost figures.
    b. Calculate the percentage return of each asset in the portfolio for the year.
    c. Calculate the percentage return of the portfolio on the basis of original cost, using income and gains during the year.
    d. At the time Jamie made his investments, investors were estimating that the market return for the coming year would be 10%. The estimate of the risk-free rate of return averaged 4% for the coming year. Calculate an expected rate of return for each stock on the basis of its beta and the expectations of market and risk-free returns.
    e. On the basis of the actual results, explain how each stock in the portfolio performed relative to those CAPM-generated expectations of performance. What factors could explain these differences?

 P5–25 Security market line (SML) Assume that the risk-free rate, R_F, is currently 9% and that the market return, r_m, is currently 13%.
    a. Draw the security market line (SML) on a set of "nondiversifiable risk (x axis)–required return (y axis)" axes.
    b. Calculate and label the *market risk premium* on the axes in part **a.**
    c. Given the previous data, calculate the required return on asset A having a beta of .80 and asset B having a beta of 1.30.

d. Draw in the betas and required returns from part **c** for assets A and B on the axes in part **a**. Label the *risk premium* associated with each of these assets, and discuss them.

P5–26   Integrative—Risk, return, and CAPM   Wolff Enterprises must consider several investment projects, A through E, using the capital asset pricing model (CAPM) and its graphical representation, the security market line (SML). Relevant information is presented in the following table.

Item	Rate of return	Beta, *b*
Risk-free asset	9%	0
Market portfolio	14	1.00
Project A	—	1.50
Project B	—	.75
Project C	—	2.00
Project D	—	0
Project E	—	− .5

a. Calculate (1) the required rate of return and (2) the risk premium for each project, given its level of nondiversifiable risk.
b. Use your findings in part **a** to draw the security market line (required return relative to nondiversifiable risk).
c. Discuss the relative nondiversifiable risk of projects A through E.

P5–27   ETHICS PROBLEM   Integrity, especially honesty, is trait number one for being hired as a CFO in corporate America today. How might you assess a job candidate's honesty if you were interviewing a potential CFO candidate?

Chapter 5 Case

Analyzing Risk and Return on Chargers Products' Investments

Junior Sayou, a financial analyst for Chargers Products, a manufacturer of stadium benches, must evaluate the risk and return of two assets, X and Y. The firm is considering adding these assets to its diversified asset portfolio. To assess the return and risk of each asset, Junior gathered data on the annual cash flow and beginning- and end-of-year values of each asset over the immediately preceding 10 years, 2000–2009. These data are summarized in the following table. Junior's investigation suggests that both assets, on average, will tend to perform in the future just as they have during the past 10 years. He therefore believes that the expected annual return can be estimated by finding the average annual return for each asset over the past 10 years.

	Asset X	Value		Asset Y	Value	
Year	Cash flow	Beginning	Ending	Cash flow	Beginning	Ending
2000	$1,000	$20,000	$22,000	$1,500	$20,000	$20,000
2001	1,500	22,000	21,000	1,600	20,000	20,000
2002	1,400	21,000	24,000	1,700	20,000	21,000
2003	1,700	24,000	22,000	1,800	21,000	21,000
2004	1,900	22,000	23,000	1,900	21,000	22,000
2005	1,600	23,000	26,000	2,000	22,000	23,000
2006	1,700	26,000	25,000	2,100	23,000	23,000
2007	2,000	25,000	24,000	2,200	23,000	24,000
2008	2,100	24,000	27,000	2,300	24,000	25,000
2009	2,200	27,000	30,000	2,400	25,000	25,000

Title: Return Data for Assets X and Y, 2000–2009

Junior believes that each asset's risk can be assessed in two ways: in isolation and as part of the firm's diversified portfolio of assets. The risk of the assets in isolation can be found by using the standard deviation and coefficient of variation of returns over the past 10 years. The capital asset pricing model (CAPM) can be used to assess the asset's risk as part of the firm's portfolio of assets. Applying some sophisticated quantitative techniques, Junior estimated betas for assets X and Y of 1.60 and 1.10, respectively. In addition, he found that the risk-free rate is currently 7% and that the market return is 10%.

To Do

a. Calculate the annual rate of return for each asset in *each* of the 10 preceding years, and use those values to find the average annual return for each asset over the 10-year period.

b. Use the returns calculated in part **a** to find (1) the standard deviation and (2) the coefficient of variation of the returns for each asset over the 10-year period 2000–2009.

c. Use your findings in parts **a** and **b** to evaluate and discuss the return and risk associated with each asset. Which asset appears to be preferable? Explain.

d. Use the CAPM to find the required return for each asset. Compare this value with the average annual returns calculated in part **a**.

e. Compare and contrast your findings in parts **c** and **d**. What recommendations would you give Junior with regard to investing in either of the two assets? Explain to Junior why he is better off using beta rather than the standard deviation and coefficient of variation to assess the risk of each asset.

f. Rework parts **d** and **e** under each of the following circumstances:

(1) A rise of 1% in inflationary expectations causes the risk-free rate to rise to 8% and the market return to rise to 11%.

(2) As a result of favorable political events, investors suddenly become less risk-averse, causing the market return to drop by 1%, to 9%.

Spreadsheet Exercise

Jane is considering investing in three different stocks or creating three distinct two-stock portfolios. Jane considers herself to be a rather conservative investor. She is able to obtain forecasted returns for the three securities for the years 2010 through 2016. The data are as follows:

Year	Stock A	Stock B	Stock C
2010	10%	10%	12%
2011	13	11	14
2012	15	8	10
2013	14	12	11
2014	16	10	9
2015	14	15	9
2016	12	15	10

In any of the possible two-stock portfolios, the weight of each stock in the portfolio will be 50%. The three possible portfolio combinations are AB, AC, and BC.

To Do

Create a spreadsheet similar to Tables 5.7 and 5.8 (which can be viewed at www .prenhall.com/gitman) to answer the following:

a. Calculate the expected return for each individual stock.
b. Calculate the standard deviation for each individual stock.
c. Calculate the expected returns for portfolio AB, AC, and BC.
d. Calculate the standard deviations for portfolios AB, AC, and BC.
e. Would you recommend that Jane invest in the single stock A or the portfolio consisting of stocks A and B? Explain your answer from a risk–return viewpoint.
f. Would you recommend that Jane invest in the single stock B or the portfolio consisting of stocks B and C? Explain your answer from a risk–return viewpoint.

Web Exercise

Go to the book's companion website at www.prenhall.com/gitman to find the Web Exercise for this chapter.

Remember to check the book's website at www.prenhall.com/gitman to find additional resources, including Web Exercises and a Web Case.

6 Interest Rates and Bond Valuation

WHY THIS CHAPTER MATTERS TO YOU

In Your Professional Life

Accounting: You need to understand interest rates and the various types of bonds to be able to account properly for amortization of bond premiums and discounts and for bond purchases and retirements.

Information systems: You need to understand the data that you will need to track in bond amortization schedules and bond valuation.

Management: You need to understand the behavior of interest rates and how they will affect the types of funds the firm can raise and the timing and cost of bond issues and retirements.

Marketing: You need to understand how the interest rate level and the firm's ability to issue bonds may affect the availability of financing for marketing research projects and new-product development.

Operations: You need to understand how the interest rate level may affect the firm's ability to raise funds to maintain and grow the firm's production capacity.

In Your Personal Life

Interest rates have a direct impact on personal financial planning. Movements in interest rates occur frequently and affect the returns from and values of savings and investments. The rate of interest you are charged on credit cards and loans can have a profound effect on your personal finances. Understanding the basics of interest rates is important to your personal financial plans.

LEARNING GOALS

LG 1 Describe interest rate fundamentals, the term structure of interest rates, and risk premiums.

LG 2 Review the legal aspects of bond financing and bond cost.

LG 3 Discuss the general features, yields, prices, ratings, popular types, and international issues of corporate bonds.

LG 4 Understand the key inputs and basic model used in the valuation process.

LG 5 Apply the basic valuation model to bonds and describe the impact of required return and time to maturity on bond values.

LG 6 Explain yield to maturity (YTM), its calculation, and the procedure used to value bonds that pay interest semiannually.

The interactions of suppliers and demanders of funds in the financial markets affect interest rates. The interest rates (returns) required by suppliers of funds also depend on the perceived risk of an asset. In this chapter, we apply the concepts of risk and return in a process called valuation. This chapter discusses interest rates, describes the key aspects of corporate bonds, and demonstrates the valuation process for the easiest financial asset to value, bonds.

6.1 | Interest Rates and Required Returns

As noted in Chapter 1, financial institutions and markets create the mechanism through which funds flow between savers (funds suppliers) and investors (funds demanders). The level of funds flow between suppliers and demanders can significantly affect economic growth. The interest rate level acts as a regulating device that controls the flow of funds between suppliers and demanders. The *Board of Governors of the Federal Reserve System* regularly assesses economic conditions and, when necessary, initiates actions to raise or lower interest rates to control inflation and economic growth. Generally, the lower the interest rate, the greater the funds flow and therefore the greater the economic growth; the higher the interest rate, the lower the funds flow and economic growth.

interest rate
The compensation paid by the borrower of funds to the lender; from the borrower's point of view, the cost of borrowing funds.

required return
The cost of funds obtained by selling an ownership interest; it reflects the funds supplier's level of expected return.

liquidity preferences
General preferences of investors for shorter-term securities.

real rate of interest
The rate that creates an equilibrium between the supply of savings and the demand for investment funds in a perfect world, without inflation, where funds suppliers and demanders are indifferent to the term of loans or investments because they have no *liquidity preference,* and where all outcomes are certain.

Interest Rate Fundamentals

The *interest rate* or *required return* represents the cost of money. It is the compensation that a demander of funds must pay a supplier. When funds are lent, the cost of borrowing the funds is the **interest rate.** When funds are obtained by selling an ownership interest—as in the sale of stock—the cost to the issuer (demander) is commonly called the **required return,** which reflects the funds supplier's level of expected return. In both cases the supplier is compensated for providing funds. Ignoring risk factors, the cost of funds results from the *real rate of interest* adjusted for inflationary expectations and **liquidity preferences**—general preferences of investors for shorter-term securities.

The Real Rate of Interest

Assume a *perfect world* in which there is no inflation and in which funds suppliers and demanders are indifferent to the term of loans or investments because they have no *liquidity preference* and all outcomes are certain.[1] At any given point in time in that perfect world, there would be one cost of money—the **real rate of interest.** The real rate of interest creates an equilibrium between the supply of savings and the demand for investment funds. It represents the most basic cost of money. The real rate of interest in the United States is assumed to be stable and

---

1. These assumptions are made to describe the most basic interest rate, the *real rate of interest.* Subsequent discussions relax these assumptions to develop the broader concept of the interest rate and required return.

Supply–Demand Relationship
Supply of savings and demand for investment funds

equal to around 1 percent.[2] This supply–demand relationship is shown in Figure 6.1 by the supply function (labeled S_0) and the demand function (labeled D). An equilibrium between the supply of funds and the demand for funds ($S_0 = D$) occurs at a rate of interest r_0^*, the real rate of interest.

Clearly, the real rate of interest changes with changing economic conditions, tastes, and preferences. A trade surplus could result in an increased supply of funds, causing the supply function in Figure 6.1 to shift to, say, S_1. This could result in a lower real rate of interest, r_1^*, at equilibrium ($S_1 = D$). Likewise, a change in tax laws or other factors could affect the demand for funds, causing the real rate of interest to rise or fall to a new equilibrium level.

Inflation and the Cost of Money

Ignoring risk factors, the cost of funds—the interest rate or required return—is closely tied to inflationary expectations. This can be demonstrated by using the **risk-free rate of interest, R_F,** which was defined in Chapter 5 as the required return on the risk-free asset. The risk-free asset is typically considered to be a 3-month *U.S. Treasury bill (T-bill)*, which is a short-term IOU issued regularly by the U.S. Treasury.

Figure 6.2 (see page 246) illustrates the annual movement of the rate of inflation and the risk-free rate of return during the period 1978–2007. During this period the two rates tended to move in a similar fashion. Between 1978 and the early 1980s, inflation and interest rates were quite high, peaking at over 13 percent in 1980–1981. Since 1981 these rates have declined to levels generally below those in 1978. Note that between 2002 and 2005 the annual rate of inflation actually exceeded the average 3-month Treasury bill rate. The data in Figure 6.2 clearly illustrate the significant impact of inflation on the actual rate of interest charged by the supplier of funds and paid by the demander for the risk-free asset.

risk-free rate of interest, R_F
The required return on a risk-free asset, typically a 3-month *U.S. Treasury bill (T-bill)*.

---

2. Data in *Stocks, Bonds, Bills, and Inflation, 2007 Yearbook* (Chicago: Ibbotson Associates, Inc., 2007), show that over the period 1926–2006, U.S. Treasury bills provided an average annual real rate of return of about 0.70 percent. Because of certain major economic events that occurred during the 1926–2006 period, many economists believe that the real rate of interest during recent years has been about 1 percent.

1. Investors perceive less risk in short-term securities than in longer-term securities and are therefore willing to accept lower yields on them. The reason is that shorter-term securities are more liquid and less responsive to general interest rate movements.[3]
2. Borrowers are generally willing to pay a higher rate for long-term than for short-term financing. By locking in funds for a longer period of time, they can eliminate the potential adverse consequences of having to roll over short-term debt at unknown costs to obtain long-term financing.

Investors (lenders) tend to require a premium for tying up funds for longer periods, whereas borrowers are generally willing to pay a premium to obtain longer-term financing. These preferences of lenders and borrowers cause the yield curve to tend to be upward-sloping. Simply stated, longer maturities tend to have higher interest rates than shorter maturities.

market segmentation theory
Theory suggesting that the market for loans is segmented on the basis of maturity and that the supply of and demand for loans within each segment determine its prevailing interest rate; the slope of the yield curve is determined by the general relationship between the prevailing rates in each market segment.

Market Segmentation Theory   The **market segmentation theory** suggests that the market for loans is segmented on the basis of maturity and that the supply of and demand for loans within each segment determine its prevailing interest rate. In other words, the equilibrium between suppliers and demanders of short-term funds, such as seasonal business loans, would determine prevailing short-term interest rates, and the equilibrium between suppliers and demanders of long-term funds, such as real estate loans, would determine prevailing long-term interest rates. The slope of the yield curve would be determined by the general relationship between the prevailing rates in each market segment. Simply stated, low rates in the short-term segment and high rates in the long-term segment cause the yield curve to be upward-sloping. The opposite occurs for high short-term rates and low long-term rates.

Hint An upward-sloping yield curve will result if the supply outstrips the demand for short-term loans, thereby resulting in relatively low short-term rates at a time when long-term rates are high because the demand for long-term loans is far above their supply.

All three theories of term structure have merit. From them we can conclude that at any time, the slope of the yield curve is affected by (1) inflationary expectations, (2) liquidity preferences, and (3) the comparative equilibrium of supply and demand in the short- and long-term market segments. Upward-sloping yield curves result from higher future inflation expectations, lender preferences for shorter-maturity loans, and greater supply of short-term loans than of long-term loans relative to demand. The opposite behaviors would result in a downward-sloping yield curve. At any time, the interaction of these three forces determines the prevailing slope of the yield curve.

risk premium
The amount by which the interest rate or required return on a security exceeds the risk-free rate of interest R_F; it varies with specific issuer and issue characteristics.

Risk Premiums: Issuer and Issue Characteristics

So far we have considered only risk-free U.S. Treasury securities. We now add the element of risk, in order to assess what effect it has on the cost of funds. The amount by which the interest rate or required return exceeds the risk-free rate of interest, R_F, is a security's **risk premium**. The risk premium varies with specific

---

3. Later in this chapter we demonstrate that debt instruments with longer maturities are more sensitive to changing market interest rates. For a given change in market rates, the price or value of longer-term debts will be more significantly changed (up or down) than the price or value of debts with shorter maturities.

| TABLE 6.1 | Debt-Specific Issuer- and Issue-Related Risk Premium Components |

Component	Description
Default risk	The possibility that the issuer of debt will not pay the contractual interest or principal as scheduled. The greater the uncertainty as to the borrower's ability to meet these payments, the greater the risk premium. High bond ratings reflect low default risk, and low bond ratings reflect high default risk.
Maturity risk	The fact that the longer the maturity, the more the value of a security will change in response to a given change in interest rates. If interest rates on otherwise similar-risk securities suddenly rise as a result of a change in the money supply, the prices of long-term bonds will decline by more than the prices of short-term bonds, and vice versa.[a]
Contractual provision risk	Conditions that are often included in a debt agreement or a stock issue. Some of these reduce risk, whereas others may increase risk. For example, a provision allowing a bond issuer to retire its bonds prior to their maturity under favorable terms increases the bond's risk.

[a]A detailed discussion of the effects of interest rates on the price or value of bonds and other fixed-income securities is presented later in this chapter.

issuer and issue characteristics; it causes similar-maturity securities to have differing rates of interest.

The risk premium consists of a number of issuer- and issue-related components, including business risk, financial risk, interest rate risk, liquidity risk, and tax risk, which were defined in Table 5.1 on page 203, and the purely debt-specific risks—default risk, maturity risk, and contractual provision risk, briefly defined in Table 6.1. In general, the highest risk premiums and therefore the highest returns result from securities issued by firms with a high risk of default and from long-term maturities that have unfavorable contractual provisions.

REVIEW QUESTIONS

6–1   What is the *real rate of interest?* Differentiate it from the *risk-free rate of interest* for a 3-month U.S. Treasury bill.

6–2   What is the *term structure of interest rates,* and how is it related to the *yield curve?*

6–3   For a given class of similar-risk securities, what does each of the following yield curves reflect about interest rates: (a) downward-sloping; (b) upward-sloping; and (c) flat? Which form has been historically dominant?

6–4   Briefly describe the following theories of the general shape of the yield curve: (a) expectations theory; (b) liquidity preference theory; and (c) market segmentation theory.

6–5   List and briefly describe the potential issuer- and issue-related risk components that are embodied in the risk premium. Which are the purely debt-specific risks?

6.2 | Corporate Bonds

corporate bond
A long-term debt instrument indicating that a corporation has borrowed a certain amount of money and promises to repay it in the future under clearly defined terms.

coupon interest rate
The percentage of a bond's par value that will be paid annually, typically in two equal semiannual payments, as interest.

A **corporate bond** is a long-term debt instrument indicating that a corporation has borrowed a certain amount of money and promises to repay it in the future under clearly defined terms. Most bonds are issued with maturities of 10 to 30 years and with a par value, or face value, of $1,000. The **coupon interest rate** on a bond represents the percentage of the bond's par value that will be paid annually, typically in two equal semiannual payments, as interest. The bondholders, who are the lenders, are promised the semiannual interest payments and, at maturity, repayment of the principal amount.

Legal Aspects of Corporate Bonds

Certain legal arrangements are required to protect purchasers of bonds. Bondholders are protected primarily through the indenture and the trustee.

Bond Indenture

bond indenture
A legal document that specifies both the rights of the bondholders and the duties of the issuing corporation.

A **bond indenture** is a legal document that specifies both the rights of the bondholders and the duties of the issuing corporation. Included in the indenture are descriptions of the amount and timing of all interest and principal payments, various standard and restrictive provisions, and, frequently, sinking-fund requirements and security interest provisions.

standard debt provisions
Provisions in a *bond indenture* specifying certain record-keeping and general business practices that the bond issuer must follow; normally, they do not place a burden on a financially sound business.

Standard Provisions   The **standard debt provisions** in the bond indenture specify certain record-keeping and general business practices that the bond issuer must follow. Standard debt provisions do not normally place a burden on a financially sound business.

The borrower commonly must (1) *maintain satisfactory accounting records* in accordance with generally accepted accounting principles (GAAP); (2) periodically *supply audited financial statements*; (3) *pay taxes and other liabilities when due*; and (4) *maintain all facilities in good working order.*

restrictive covenants
Provisions in a *bond indenture* that place operating and financial constraints on the borrower.

Restrictive Provisions   Bond indentures also normally include certain **restrictive covenants,** which place operating and financial constraints on the borrower. These provisions help protect the bondholder against increases in borrower risk. Without them, the borrower could increase the firm's risk but not have to pay increased interest to compensate for the increased risk.

The most common restrictive covenants do the following:

1. Require a *minimum level of liquidity,* to ensure against loan default.
2. *Prohibit the sale of accounts receivable* to generate cash. Selling receivables could cause a long-run cash shortage if proceeds were used to meet current obligations.
3. Impose *fixed-asset restrictions*. The borrower must maintain a specified level of fixed assets to guarantee its ability to repay the bonds.
4. *Constrain subsequent borrowing.* Additional long-term debt may be prohibited, or additional borrowing may be *subordinated* to the original loan. **Subordination** means that subsequent creditors agree to wait until all claims of the *senior debt* are satisfied.

subordination
In a bond indenture, the stipulation that subsequent creditors agree to wait until all claims of the *senior debt* are satisfied.

5. *Limit the firm's annual cash dividend payments* to a specified percentage or amount.

Other restrictive covenants are sometimes included in bond indentures.

The violation of any standard or restrictive provision by the borrower gives the bondholders the right to demand immediate repayment of the debt. Generally, bondholders evaluate any violation to determine whether it jeopardizes the loan. They may then decide to demand immediate repayment, continue the loan, or alter the terms of the bond indenture.

Sinking-Fund Requirements   Another common restrictive provision is a **sinking-fund requirement.** Its objective is to provide for the systematic retirement of bonds prior to their maturity. To carry out this requirement, the corporation makes semiannual or annual payments that are used to retire bonds by purchasing them in the marketplace.

Security Interest   The bond indenture identifies any collateral pledged against the bond and specifies how it is to be maintained. The protection of bond collateral is crucial to guarantee the safety of a bond issue.

sinking-fund requirement
A restrictive provision often included in a bond indenture, providing for the systematic retirement of bonds prior to their maturity.

Trustee

A **trustee** is a third party to a *bond indenture*. The trustee can be an individual, a corporation, or (most often) a commercial bank trust department. The trustee is paid to act as a "watchdog" on behalf of the bondholders and can take specified actions on behalf of the bondholders if the terms of the indenture are violated.

trustee
A paid individual, corporation, or commercial bank trust department that acts as the third party to a *bond indenture* and can take specified actions on behalf of the bondholders if the terms of the indenture are violated.

Cost of Bonds to the Issuer

The cost of bond financing is generally greater than the issuer would have to pay for short-term borrowing. The major factors that affect the cost, which is the rate of interest paid by the bond issuer, are the bond's maturity, the size of the offering, the issuer's risk, and the basic cost of money.

Impact of Bond Maturity

Generally, as we noted earlier, long-term debt pays higher interest rates than short-term debt. In a practical sense, the longer the maturity of a bond, the less accuracy there is in predicting future interest rates, and therefore the greater the bondholders' risk of giving up an opportunity to lend money at a higher rate. In addition, the longer the term, the greater the chance that the issuer might default.

Impact of Offering Size

The size of the bond offering also affects the interest cost of borrowing, but in an inverse manner: Bond flotation and administration costs per dollar borrowed are likely to decrease with increasing offering size. On the other hand, the risk to the bondholders may increase, because larger offerings result in greater risk of default.

Impact of Issuer's Risk

The greater the issuer's *default risk*, the higher the interest rate. Some of this risk can be reduced through inclusion of appropriate restrictive provisions in the bond indenture. Clearly, bondholders must be compensated with higher returns for taking greater risk. Frequently, bond buyers rely on bond ratings (discussed later) to determine the issuer's overall risk.

Impact of the Cost of Money

The cost of money in the capital market is the basis for determining a bond's coupon interest rate. Generally, the rate on U.S. Treasury securities of equal maturity is used as the lowest-risk cost of money. To that basic rate is added a *risk premium* (as described earlier in this chapter) that reflects the factors mentioned above (maturity, offering size, and issuer's risk).

General Features of a Bond Issue

Three features sometimes included in a corporate bond issue are a conversion feature, a call feature, and stock purchase warrants. These features provide the issuer or the purchaser with certain opportunities for replacing or retiring the bond or supplementing it with some type of equity issue.

Convertible bonds offer a **conversion feature** that allows bondholders to change each bond into a stated number of shares of common stock. Bondholders convert their bonds into stock only when the market price of the stock is such that conversion will provide a profit for the bondholder. Inclusion of the conversion feature by the issuer lowers the interest cost and provides for automatic conversion of the bonds to stock if future stock prices appreciate noticeably.

The **call feature** is included in nearly all corporate bond issues. It gives the issuer the opportunity to repurchase bonds prior to maturity. The **call price** is the stated price at which bonds may be repurchased prior to maturity. Sometimes the call feature can be exercised only during a certain period. As a rule, the call price exceeds the par value of a bond by an amount equal to 1 year's interest. For example, a $1,000 bond with a 10 percent coupon interest rate would be callable for around $1,100 [$1,000 + (10% × $1,000)]. The amount by which the call price exceeds the bond's par value is commonly referred to as the **call premium**. This premium compensates bondholders for having the bond called away from them; to the issuer, it is the cost of calling the bonds.

The call feature enables an issuer to call an outstanding bond when interest rates fall and issue a new bond at a lower interest rate. When interest rates rise, the call privilege will not be exercised, except possibly to meet *sinking-fund requirements*. Of course, to sell a callable bond in the first place, the issuer must pay a higher interest rate than on noncallable bonds of equal risk, to compensate bondholders for the risk of having the bonds called away from them.

Bonds occasionally have stock purchase warrants attached as "sweeteners" to make them more attractive to prospective buyers. **Stock purchase warrants** are instruments that give their holders the right to purchase a certain number of shares of the issuer's common stock at a specified price over a certain period of time. Their inclusion typically enables the issuer to pay a slightly lower coupon interest rate than would otherwise be required.

---

conversion feature
A feature of *convertible bonds* that allows bondholders to change each bond into a stated number of shares of common stock.

call feature
A feature included in nearly all corporate bond issues that gives the issuer the opportunity to repurchase bonds at a stated *call price* prior to maturity.

call price
The stated price at which a bond may be repurchased, by use of a *call feature,* prior to maturity.

call premium
The amount by which a bond's *call price* exceeds its par value.

stock purchase warrants
Instruments that give their holders the right to purchase a certain number of shares of the issuer's common stock at a specified price over a certain period of time. Occasionally attached to bonds as "sweeteners."

Bond Yields

The *yield*, or rate of return, on a bond is frequently used to assess a bond's performance over a given period of time, typically 1 year. Because there are a number of ways to measure a bond's yield, it is important to understand popular yield measures. The three most widely cited bond yields are (1) *current yield*, (2) *yield to maturity (YTM)*, and (3) *yield to call (YTC)*. Each of these yields provides a unique measure of the return on a bond.

current yield
A measure of a bond's cash return for the year; calculated by dividing the bond's annual interest payment by its current price.

The simplest yield measure is the **current yield,** the annual interest payment divided by the current price. For example, a $1,000 par value bond with an 8% coupon interest rate that currently sells for $970 would have a current yield of 8.25% [(0.08 × $1,000)/$970]. This measure indicates the cash return for the year from the bond. However, because current yield ignores any change in bond value, it does not measure the total return. As we'll see later in this chapter, both the yield to maturity and the yield to call measure the total return.

Bond Prices

Because most corporate bonds are purchased and held by institutional investors, such as banks, insurance companies, and mutual funds, rather than individual investors, bond trading and price data are not readily available to individuals. Table 6.2 includes some assumed current data on the bonds of five companies, noted A through E. Looking at the data for Company C's bond, which is highlighted in the table, we see that the bond has a coupon interest rate of 7.200% and a maturity date of January 15, 2014. These data identify a specific bond issued by Company C. (The company could have more than a single bond issue outstanding.) The price represents the final price at which the bond traded on the current day.

Although most corporate bonds are issued with a *par*, or *face*, *value* of $1,000, *all bonds are quoted as a percentage of par*. A $1,000-par-value bond quoted at 94.007 is priced at $940.07 (94.007% × $1,000). Corporate bonds are quoted in dollars and cents. Thus, Company C's price of 103.143 for the day was $1,031.43—that is, 103.143% × $1,000.

The final column of Table 6.2 represents the bond's *yield to maturity (YTM)*, which is the compound annual rate of return that would be earned on the bond if it were purchased on the given day and held to maturity. (YTM is discussed in detail later in this chapter.)

TABLE 6.2	Data on Selected Bonds			
Company	Coupon	Maturity	Price	Yield (YTM)
Company A	6.125%	Nov. 15, 2011	105.336	4.788%
Company B	6.000	Oct. 31, 2036	94.007	6.454
Company C	7.200	Jan. 15, 2014	103.143	6.606
Company D	5.150	Jan. 15, 2017	95.140	5.814
Company E	5.850	Jan. 14, 2012	100.876	5.631

Focus on Ethics   Can We Trust the Bond Raters?

Assessing default risk requires an evaluation of creditworthiness. Most investors have neither the time nor the expertise to do their own credit appraisals for potential bond investments, so they rely on credit-rating agencies for this service. But how reliable are their ratings?

"The dominant rating agencies failed millions of investors by neglecting to lower their ratings on Enron, WorldCom, and other companies heading for bankruptcy," said Alabama Senator Richard Shelby, past-chair of the Senate Banking Committee and sponsor of legislation to hold rating agencies more accountable. "The absence of timely downgrades in these cases was a product of an industry that was beset with conflicts of interest and a lack of competition. Ultimately, this compromised the integrity of the market and investors paid the price," he concluded.

On September 29, 2006, President Bush signed the *Credit Rating Agency Reform Act of 2006*, which abolished the SEC's authority to designate credit-rating agencies as "nationally recognized rating agencies (NRSROs)." Instead, a credit-rating company with 3 years of experience that meets certain standards would be allowed to register with the SEC as a "statistical ratings organization."

The new law is designed to curb alleged abusive practices cited by members of Congress and corporate trade groups, including the practice of sending a company unsolicited ratings with a bill; *notching*, which occurs when a firm lowers ratings on asset-backed securities unless the firm rates a substantial portion of the underlying assets; and tying ratings to the purchase of additional services.

"Importantly, the new law gives the SEC the tools necessary to hold recognized rating agencies accountable if they fail to produce credible and reliable ratings," declared Jim Kaitz, president of the Association for Financial Professionals (AFP), in a statement. AFP represents 15,000 members working in corporate treasury and financial management functions.

One credit-rating agency, S&P, voiced its objection to the original House bill, saying that ratings agencies are members of the financial press and that the proposed legislation represented an unconstitutional infringement of the company's free speech. Despite their objection, the legislation is now law.

Performing risk–return analysis in the bond markets depends on having accurate and timely information. The increased scrutiny from the SEC along with increased competition should add to the value of the ratings received by the investing public.

■ *What effect will the new legislation likely have on the market share of the largest rating agencies? How will the new legislation affect the process of finding ratings information for investors?*

Bond Ratings

Independent agencies such as Moody's and Standard & Poor's assess the riskiness of publicly traded bond issues. These agencies derive their ratings by using financial ratio and cash flow analyses to assess the likely payment of bond interest and principal. Table 6.3 summarizes these ratings. For discussion of ethical issues related to the bond-rating agencies, see the *Focus on Ethics* box above.

Normally an inverse relationship exists between the quality of a bond and the rate of return that it must provide bondholders: High-quality (high-rated) bonds provide lower returns than lower-quality (low-rated) bonds. This reflects the lender's risk–return tradeoff. When considering bond financing, the financial manager must be concerned with the expected ratings of the bond issue, because these ratings affect salability and cost.

Hint Note that Moody's has 9 major ratings; Standard & Poor's has 10.

TABLE 6.3   Moody's and Standard & Poor's Bond Ratings[a]

Moody's	Interpretation	Standard & Poor's	Interpretation
Aaa	Prime quality	AAA	Bank investment quality
Aa	High grade	AA	
A	Upper medium grade	A	
Baa	Medium grade	BBB	
Ba	Lower medium grade	BB	Speculative
	or speculative	B	
B	Speculative		
Caa	From very speculative	CCC	
Ca	to near or in default	CC	
C	Lowest grade	C	Income bond
		D	In default

[a]Some ratings may be modified to show relative standing within a major rating category; for example, Moody's uses numerical modifiers (1, 2, 3), whereas Standard & Poor's uses plus (+) and minus (−) signs.

Sources: Moody's Investors Service, Inc. and Standard & Poor's Corporation.

Popular Types of Bonds

debentures
subordinated debentures
income bonds
mortgage bonds
collateral trust bonds
equipment trust certificates
See Table 6.4.

zero- (or low-) coupon bonds
junk bonds
floating-rate bonds
extendible notes
putable bonds
See Table 6.5 on page 257.

Bonds can be classified in a variety of ways. Here we break them into traditional bonds (the basic types that have been around for years) and contemporary bonds (newer, more innovative types). The traditional types of bonds are summarized in terms of their key characteristics and priority of lender's claim in Table 6.4 (see page 256). Note that the first three types—**debentures, subordinated debentures, and income bonds**—are unsecured, whereas the last three—**mortgage bonds, collateral trust bonds,** and **equipment trust certificates**—are secured.

Table 6.5 (see page 257) describes the key characteristics of five contemporary types of bonds: **zero- (or low-) coupon bonds, junk bonds, floating-rate bonds, extendible notes,** and **putable bonds.** These bonds can be either unsecured or secured. Changing capital market conditions and investor preferences have spurred further innovations in bond financing in recent years and will probably continue to do so.

International Bond Issues

Eurobond
A bond issued by an international borrower and sold to investors in countries with currencies other than the currency in which the bond is denominated.

Companies and governments borrow internationally by issuing bonds in two principal financial markets: the Eurobond market and the foreign bond market. Both give borrowers the opportunity to obtain large amounts of long-term debt financing quickly, in the currency of their choice and with flexible repayment terms.

A **Eurobond** is issued by an international borrower and sold to investors in countries with currencies other than the currency in which the bond is denominated. An example is a dollar-denominated bond issued by a U.S. corporation

TABLE 6.4   Characteristics and Priority of Lender's Claim of Traditional Types of Bonds

Bond type	Characteristics	Priority of lender's claim
Unsecured Bonds		
Debentures	Unsecured bonds that only creditworthy firms can issue. Convertible bonds are normally debentures.	Claims are the same as those of any general creditor. May have other unsecured bonds subordinated to them.
Subordinated debentures	Claims are not satisfied until those of the creditors holding certain (senior) debts have been fully satisfied.	Claim is that of a general creditor but not as good as a senior debt claim.
Income bonds	Payment of interest is required only when earnings are available. Commonly issued in reorganization of a failing firm.	Claim is that of a general creditor. Are not in default when interest payments are missed, because they are contingent only on earnings being available.
Secured Bonds		
Mortgage bonds	Secured by real estate or buildings.	Claim is on proceeds from sale of mortgaged assets; if not fully satisfied, the lender becomes a general creditor. The *first-mortgage* claim must be fully satisfied before distribution of proceeds to *second-mortgage* holders, and so on. A number of mortgages can be issued against the same collateral.
Collateral trust bonds	Secured by stock and (or) bonds that are owned by the issuer. Collateral value is generally 25% to 35% greater than bond value.	Claim is on proceeds from stock and (or) bond collateral; if not fully satisfied, the lender becomes a general creditor.
Equipment trust certificates	Used to finance "rolling stock"—airplanes, trucks, boats, railroad cars. A trustee buys the asset with funds raised through the sale of trust certificates and then leases it to the firm; after making the final scheduled lease payment, the firm receives title to the asset. A type of leasing.	Claim is on proceeds from the sale of the asset; if proceeds do not satisfy outstanding debt, trust certificate lenders become general creditors.

and sold to Belgian investors. From the founding of the Eurobond market in the 1960s until the mid-1980s, "blue chip" U.S. corporations were the largest single class of Eurobond issuers. Some of these companies were able to borrow in this market at interest rates below those the U.S. government paid on Treasury bonds. As the market matured, issuers became able to choose the currency in which they borrowed, and European and Japanese borrowers rose to prominence. In more recent years, the Eurobond market has become much more balanced in terms of the mix of borrowers, total issue volume, and currency of denomination.

foreign bond
A bond issued in a host country's financial market, in the host country's currency, by a foreign borrower.

In contrast, a **foreign bond** is issued in a host country's financial market, in the host country's currency, by a foreign borrower. A Swiss-franc–denominated bond issued in Switzerland by a U.S. company is an example of a foreign bond. The three largest foreign-bond markets are Japan, Switzerland, and the United States.

REVIEW QUESTIONS

6–6 What are typical maturities, denominations, and interest payments of a corporate bond? What mechanisms protect bondholders?

TABLE 6.5	Characteristics of Contemporary Types of Bonds
Bond type	Characteristics[a]
Zero- (or low-) coupon bonds	Issued with no (zero) or a very low coupon (stated interest) rate and sold at a large discount from par. A significant portion (or all) of the investor's return comes from gain in value (i.e., par value minus purchase price). Generally callable at par value. Because the issuer can annually deduct the current year's interest accrual without having to pay the interest until the bond matures (or is called), its cash flow each year is increased by the amount of the tax shield provided by the interest deduction.
Junk bonds	Debt rated Ba or lower by Moody's or BB or lower by Standard & Poor's. Commonly used by rapidly growing firms to obtain growth capital, most often as a way to finance mergers and takeovers. High-risk bonds with high yields—often yielding 2% to 3% more than the best-quality corporate debt.
Floating-rate bonds	Stated interest rate is adjusted periodically within stated limits in response to changes in specified money market or capital market rates. Popular when future inflation and interest rates are uncertain. Tend to sell at close to par because of the automatic adjustment to changing market conditions. Some issues provide for annual redemption at par at the option of the bondholder.
Extendible notes	Short maturities, typically 1 to 5 years, that can be renewed for a similar period at the option of holders. Similar to a floating-rate bond. An issue might be a series of 3-year renewable notes over a period of 15 years; every 3 years, the notes could be extended for another 3 years, at a new rate competitive with market interest rates at the time of renewal.
Putable bonds	Bonds that can be redeemed at par (typically, $1,000) at the option of their holder either at specific dates after the date of issue and every 1 to 5 years thereafter or when and if the firm takes specified actions, such as being acquired, acquiring another company, or issuing a large amount of additional debt. In return for its conferring the right to "put the bond" at specified times or when the firm takes certain actions, the bond's yield is lower than that of a nonputable bond.

[a]The claims of lenders (i.e., bondholders) against issuers of each of these types of bonds vary, depending on the bonds' other features. Each of these bonds can be unsecured or secured.

6–7   Differentiate between *standard debt provisions* and *restrictive covenants* included in a bond indenture. What are the consequences of violation of them by the bond issuer?

6–8   How is the cost of bond financing typically related to the cost of short-term borrowing? In addition to a bond's maturity, what other major factors affect its cost to the issuer?

6–9   What is a *conversion feature*? A *call feature*? *Stock purchase warrants*?

6–10   What is the *current yield* for a bond? How are bond prices quoted? How are bonds rated, and why?

6–11   Compare the basic characteristics of *Eurobonds* and *foreign bonds*.

6.3 | Valuation Fundamentals

valuation

The process that links risk and return to determine the worth of an asset.

Valuation is the process that links risk and return to determine the worth of an asset. It is a relatively simple process that can be applied to *expected* streams of benefits from bonds, stocks, income properties, oil wells, and so on. To determine an asset's worth at a given point in time, a financial manager uses the time-value-of-money techniques presented in Chapter 4 and the concepts of risk and return developed in Chapter 5.

Time line for bond valuation (Mills Company's 10% coupon interest rate, 10-year maturity, $1,000 par, January 1, 2010, issue paying annual interest; required return = 10%)

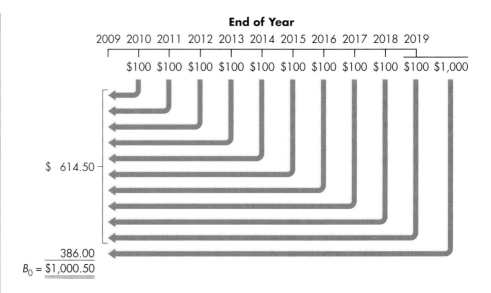

End of Year

2009 2010 2011 2012 2013 2014 2015 2016 2017 2018 2019

$100 $100 $100 $100 $100 $100 $100 $100 $100 $100 $1,000

$ 614.50

386.00

$B_0 = \$1,000.50$

Input	Function
10	N
10	I
100	PMT
1000	FV
	CPT
	PV

Solution

1,000

Calculator Use   Using the Mills Company's inputs shown at the left, you should find the bond value to be exactly $1,000. Note that *the calculated bond value is equal to its par value; this will always be the case when the required return is equal to the coupon interest rate.*

Spreadsheet Use   The value of the Mills Company bond also can be calculated as shown in the following Excel spreadsheet.

	A	B
1	BOND VALUE, ANNUAL INTEREST, REQUIRED RETURN = COUPON INTEREST RATE	
2	Annual interest payment	$100
3	Coupon interest rate	10%
4	Number of years to maturity	10
5	Par value	$1,000
6	Bond value	$1,000.00

Entry in Cell B6 is
(B2*(1-(1/(1+B3)^B4)))/B3 + (B6*(1/(1+B3)^B4))

The expression 1-(1/(1+B3)^B4))/B3 calculates the Present Value Interest Factor for an Annuity.
The expression 1/(1+B3)^B4 calculates the Present Value Interest Factor for a Single Amount.

Table Use   Substituting the appropriate values into Equation 6.7a yields

$$B_0 = \$100 \times (PVIFA_{10\%,10yrs}) + \$1,000 \times (PVIF_{10\%,10yrs})$$
$$= \$100 \times (6.145) + \$1,000 \times (0.386)$$
$$= \$614.50 + \$386.00 = \underline{\underline{\$1,000.50}}$$

The bond therefore has a value of approximately $1,000.[6]

---

6. Note that a slight rounding error ($0.50) results here from the use of the table factors, which are rounded to the nearest thousandth.

Bond Value Behavior

In practice, the value of a bond in the marketplace is rarely equal to its par value. In the bond data (see Table 6.2 on page 253), it can be seen that the prices of bonds often differ from their par values of 100 (100 percent of par). Some bonds are valued below par (current price below 100), and others are valued above par (current price above 100). A variety of forces in the economy, as well as the passage of time, tend to affect value. Although these external forces are in no way controlled by bond issuers or investors, it is useful to understand the impact that required return and time to maturity have on bond value.

Required Returns and Bond Values

Whenever the required return on a bond differs from the bond's coupon interest rate, the bond's value will differ from its par value. The required return is likely to differ from the coupon interest rate because either (1) economic conditions have changed, causing a shift in the basic cost of long-term funds, or (2) the firm's risk has changed. Increases in the basic cost of long-term funds or in risk will raise the required return; decreases in the cost of funds or in risk will lower the required return.

discount
The amount by which a bond sells at a value that is less than its par value.

premium
The amount by which a bond sells at a value that is greater than its par value.

Regardless of the exact cause, what is important is the relationship between the required return and the coupon interest rate: When the required return is greater than the coupon interest rate, the bond value, B_0, will be less than its par value, M. In this case, the bond is said to sell at a **discount**, which will equal $M - B_0$. When the required return falls below the coupon interest rate, the bond value will be greater than par. In this situation, the bond is said to sell at a **premium**, which will equal $B_0 - M$.

Example

Input	Function
10	N
12	I
100	PMT
1000	FV
	CPT
	PV

Solution
887.00

The preceding example showed that when the required return equaled the coupon interest rate, the bond's value equaled its $1,000 par value. If for the same bond the required return were to rise to 12% or fall to 8%, its value in each case would be found as follows (using Equation 6.3a):

Calculator Use   Using the inputs shown at the left and on the next page for the two different required returns, you will find the value of the bond to be below or above par. At a 12% required return, the bond would sell at a *discount* of $113.00 ($1,000 par value − $887.00 value). At the 8% required return, the bond would sell for a *premium* of about $134.00 ($1,134.00 value − $1,000 par value). The results of this and the following calculations for Mills Company's bond values are summarized in Table 6.7 and graphically depicted in Figure 6.4.

| TABLE 6.7 | Bond Values for Various Required Returns (Mills Company's 10% Coupon Interest Rate, 10-Year Maturity, $1,000 Par, January 1, 2010, Issue Paying Annual Interest) |

Required return, r_d	Bond value, B_0	Status
12%	$ 887.00	Discount
10	1,000.00	Par value
8	1,134.20	Premium

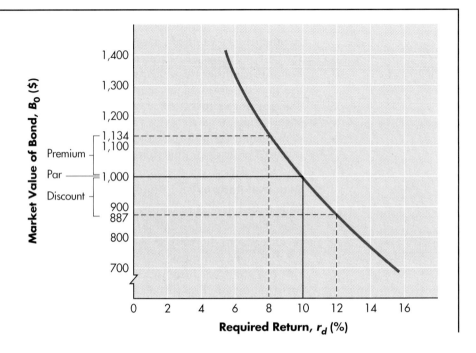

FIGURE 6.4

Bond Values and Required Returns
Bond values and required returns (Mills Company's 10% coupon interest rate, 10-year maturity, $1,000 par, January 1, 2010, issue paying annual interest)

Input	Function
10	N
8	I
100	PMT
1000	FV
	CPT
	PV

Solution
1,134.20

The inverse relationship between bond value and required return is clearly shown in the figure.

Spreadsheet Use   The values for the Mills Company bond at required returns of 12% and 8% also can be calculated as shown in the following Excel spreadsheet. (See the book's website, www.prenhall.com/gitman, Chapter 6, for another spreadsheet model that computes the values of the Mills Company bond at a discount and a premium.)

	A	B	C
1	BOND VALUE, ANNUAL INTEREST, REQUIRED RETURN NOT EQUAL TO COUPON INTEREST RATE		
2	Annual interest payment	$100	$100
3	Coupon interest rate	10%	10%
4	Required return	12%	8%
5	Number of years to maturity	10	10
6	Par value	$1,000	$1,000
7	Bond value	$887.00	$1,134.20

Entry in Cell B7, a **bond discount**, is
(B2*(1-(1/(1+B4)^B5))/B4) + (B6*(1/(1+B4)^B5))
The expression 1-(1/(1+B4)^B5))/B4) calculates the Present Value Interest Factor for an Annuity.
The expression 1/(1+B4)^B5 calculates the Present Value Interest Factor for a Single Amount.

Entry in Cell C7, a **bond premium**, is
(C2*(1-(1/(1+C4)^C5))/C4) + (C6*(1/(1+C4)^C5))
The expression 1-(1/(1+C4)^C5))/C4) calculates the Present Value Interest Factor for an Annuity.
The expression 1/(1+C4)^C5 calculates the Present Value Interest Factor for a Single Amount.

Table Use

Required Return = 12%	Required Return = 8%
$B_0 = \$100 \times (PVIFA_{12\%,10\text{yrs}}) + \$1,000$ $\times (PVIF_{12\%,10\text{yrs}})$	$B_0 = \$100 \times (PVIFA_{8\%,10\text{yrs}}) + \$1,000$ $\times (PVIF_{8\%,10\text{yrs}})$
$= \$887.00$	$= \$1,134.00$

Time to Maturity and Bond Values

Whenever the required return is different from the coupon interest rate, the amount of time to maturity affects bond value. An additional factor is whether required returns are constant or change over the life of the bond.

Constant Required Returns   When the required return is different from the coupon interest rate and is assumed to be *constant until maturity*, the value of the bond will approach its par value as the passage of time moves the bond's value closer to maturity. (Of course, when the required return *equals* the coupon interest rate, the bond's value will remain at par until it matures.)

Example

interest rate risk
The chance that interest rates will change and thereby change the required return and bond value. Rising rates, which result in decreasing bond values, are of greatest concern.

Figure 6.5 depicts the behavior of the bond values calculated earlier and presented in Table 6.7 for Mills Company's 10% coupon interest rate bond paying annual interest and having 10 years to maturity. Each of the three required returns—12%, 10%, and 8%—is assumed to remain constant over the 10 years to the bond's maturity. The bond's value at both 12% and 8% approaches and ultimately equals the bond's $1,000 par value at its maturity, as the discount (at 12%) or premium (at 8%) declines with the passage of time.

Changing Required Returns   The chance that interest rates will change and thereby change the required return and bond value is called **interest rate risk**. (This was described as a shareholder specific risk in Chapter 5, Table 5.1.)

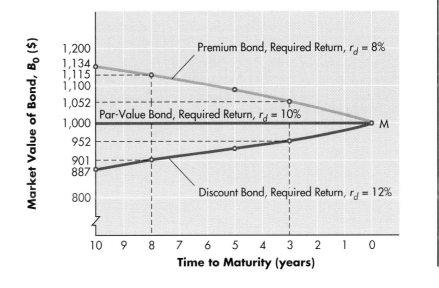

FIGURE 6.5

Time to Maturity and Bond Values
Relationship among time to maturity, required returns, and bond values (Mills Company's 10% coupon interest rate, 10-year maturity, $1,000 par, January 1, 2010, issue paying annual interest)

Bondholders are typically more concerned with rising interest rates because a rise in interest rates, and therefore in the required return, causes a decrease in bond value. The shorter the amount of time until a bond's maturity, the less responsive its market value to a given change in the required return. In other words, *short maturities have less interest rate risk than long maturities when all other features (coupon interest rate, par value, and interest payment frequency) are the same.* This is because of the mathematics of time value; the present values of short-term cash flows change far less than the present values of longer-term cash flows in response to a given change in the discount rate (required return).

> **Example**
>
> The effect of changing required returns on bonds with differing maturities can be illustrated by using Mills Company's bond and Figure 6.5. If the required return rises from 10% to 12% when the bond has 8 years to maturity (see the dashed line at 8 years), the bond's value decreases from $1,000 to $901—a 9.9% decrease. If the same change in required return had occurred with only 3 years to maturity (see the dashed line at 3 years), the bond's value would have dropped to just $952—only a 4.8% decrease. Similar types of responses can be seen for the change in bond value associated with decreases in required returns. The shorter the time to maturity, the less the impact on bond value caused by a given change in the required return.

Yield to Maturity (YTM)

yield to maturity (YTM)
The rate of return that investors earn if they buy a bond at a specific price and hold it until maturity. (Assumes that the issuer makes all scheduled interest and principal payments as promised.)

When investors evaluate bonds, they commonly consider **yield to maturity (YTM)**. This is the rate of return that investors earn if they buy the bond at a specific price and hold it until maturity. (The measure assumes, of course, that the issuer makes all scheduled interest and principal payments as promised.) The yield to maturity on a bond with a current price equal to its par value (that is, $B_0 = M$) will always equal the coupon interest rate. When the bond value differs from par, the yield to maturity will differ from the coupon interest rate.

Assuming that interest is paid annually, the yield to maturity on a bond can be found by solving Equation 6.3 for r_d. In other words, the current value, the annual interest, the par value, and the number of years to maturity are known, and the required return must be found. The required return is the bond's yield to maturity. The YTM can be found by using a financial calculator, by using an Excel spreadsheet, or by trial and error. The calculator provides accurate YTM values with minimum effort.

> **Personal Finance Example**
>
> Earl Washington wishes to find the YTM on the Mills Company bond. The bond currently sells for $1,080, has a 10% coupon interest rate and $1,000 par value, pays interest annually, and has 10 years to maturity. Because $B_0 = $1,080$, $I = 100 ($0.10 \times $1,000$), $M = $1,000$, and $n = 10$ years, substituting into Equation 6.3a yields
>
> $$\$1,080 = \$100 \times (PVIFA_{r_d,10yrs}) + \$1,000 \times (PVIF_{r_d,10yrs})$$
>
> Earl's objective is to solve the equation for r_d, the YTM.
>
> **Calculator Use** [*Note:* Most calculators require *either* the present value (B_0 in this case) or the future values (I and M in this case) to be input as negative num-

Input	Function
10	N
−1080	PV
100	PMT
1000	FV
	CPT
	I

Solution
8.766

bers to calculate yield to maturity. That approach is employed here.] Using the inputs shown at the left, you should find the YTM to be 8.766%.

Spreadsheet Use   The yield to maturity of the 10% coupon rate Mills Company bond also can be calculated as shown in the following Excel spreadsheet.

	A	B
1	YIELD TO MATURITY, ANNUAL INTEREST	
2	Annual interest payment	$100
3	Coupon interest rate	10%
4	Number of years to maturity	10
5	Par value	$1,000
6	Current bond price	$1,080
7	Yield to maturity	8.77%
8	**Trial and error method:**	
9	Choose various required rates and place them in Cell A14	
10	The spreadsheet will recalculate each time. Continue the process	
11	until the value ofthe bond equals the currentprice of the bond	
12	(in this example, it is $1,080).	
13		
14	8.77%	
15	**Payments** **PVIFA** **PVIF**	**PV**
16	$ 100 6.4831	$ 648.31
17	1,000 0.4314	431.40
18	Bond Value	≈ $1,080.00

Trial and Error   Because we know that a required return, r_d, of 10% (which equals the bond's 10% coupon interest rate) would result in a value of $1,000, the discount rate that would result in $1,080 must be less than 10%. (Remember that the lower the discount rate, the higher the present value, and the higher the discount rate, the lower the present value.) Trying 9%, we get

$$\$100 \times (PVIFA_{9\%,10yrs}) + \$1,000 \times (PVIF_{9\%,10yrs})$$
$$= \$100 \times (6.418) + \$1,000 \times (0.422)$$
$$= \$641.80 + \$422.00$$
$$= \$1,063.80$$

Because the 9% rate is not quite low enough to bring the value up to $1,080, we next try 8% and get

$$\$100 \times (PVIFA_{8\%,10yrs}) + \$1,000 \times (PVIF_{8\%,10yrs})$$
$$= \$100 \times (6.710) + \$1,000 \times (0.463)$$
$$= \$671.00 + \$463.00$$
$$= \$1,134.00$$

Because the value at the 8% rate is higher than $1,080 and the value at the 9% rate is lower than $1,080, the bond's yield to maturity must be between 8% and 9%. Because the $1,063.80 is closer to $1,080, the YTM to the nearest whole percent is 9%. (By using *interpolation*, we could eventually find the more precise YTM value to be 8.77%.)[7]

7. For information on how to interpolate to get a more precise answer, see the book's website at www.prenhall.com/gitman.

Semiannual Interest and Bond Values

The procedure used to value bonds paying interest semiannually is similar to that shown in Chapter 4 for compounding interest more frequently than annually, except that here we need to find present value instead of future value. It involves

1. Converting annual interest, I, to semiannual interest by dividing I by 2.
2. Converting the number of years to maturity, n, to the number of 6-month periods to maturity by multiplying n by 2.
3. Converting the required stated (rather than effective) annual return for similar-risk bonds that also pay semiannual interest from an annual rate, r_d, to a semiannual rate by dividing r_d by 2.

Substituting these three changes into Equation 6.3 yields

$$B_0 = \frac{I}{2} \times \left[\sum_{t=1}^{2n} \frac{1}{\left(1 + \frac{r_d}{2}\right)^t} \right] + M \times \left[\frac{1}{\left(1 + \frac{r_d}{2}\right)^{2n}} \right] \tag{6.4}$$

$$= \frac{I}{2} \times (PVIFA_{r_d/2,2n}) + M \times (PVIF_{r_d/2,2n}) \tag{6.4a}$$

Example

Assuming that the Mills Company bond pays interest semiannually and that the required stated annual return, r_d, is 12% for similar-risk bonds that also pay semiannual interest, substituting these values into Equation 6.4a yields

$$B_0 = \frac{\$100}{2} \times (PVIFA_{12\%/2,2 \times 10yrs}) + \$1,000 \times (PVIF_{12\%/2,2 \times 10yrs})$$

Input	Function
20	N
6	I
50	PMT
1000	FV
	CPT
	PV

Solution
885.30

Calculator Use   In using a calculator to find bond value when interest is paid semiannually, we must double the number of periods and divide both the required stated annual return and the annual interest by 2. For the Mills Company bond, we would use 20 periods (2×10 years), a required return of 6% ($12\% \div 2$), and an interest payment of $50 ($\$100 \div 2$). Using these inputs, you should find the bond value with semiannual interest to be $885.30, as shown at the left.

Spreadsheet Use   The value of the Mills Company bond paying semiannual interest at a required return of 12% also can be calculated as shown in the following Excel spreadsheet.

	A	B
1	BOND VALUE, SEMIANNUAL INTEREST	
2	Annual interest payment	$100
3	Stated annual return	12%
4	Number of years to maturity	10
5	Par value	$1,000
6	Bond value	$885.30

Entry in Cell B6 is
(B2/2*(1-(1/(1+B3/2)^(2*B4)))/(B3/2) + (B5*(1/(1+B3/2)^(2*B4)))
The expression 1-(1/(1+B3/2)^(2*B4)))/(B3/2) calculates the Present Value Interest Factor for an Annuity (semiannual interest).
The expression 1/(1+B3/2)^(2*B4) calculates the Present Value Interest Factor for a Single Amount (semiannual interest).

Table Use

$$B_0 = \$50 \times (PVIFA_{6\%,20\text{periods}}) + \$1,000 \times (PVIF_{6\%,20\text{periods}})$$
$$= \$50 \times (11.470) + \$1,000 \times (0.312) = \underline{\$885.50}$$

Note that this value is not as precise as that found using a financial calculator or spreadsheet.

Comparing this result with the $887.00 value found earlier for annual compounding (see Table 6.7 on page 263), we can see that the bond's value is lower when semiannual interest is paid. *This will always occur when the bond sells at a discount*. For bonds selling at a premium, the opposite will occur: The value with semiannual interest will be greater than with annual interest.

REVIEW QUESTIONS

6–16 What basic procedure is used to value a bond that pays annual interest? Semiannual interest?

6–17 What relationship between the required return and the coupon interest rate will cause a bond to sell at a *discount?* At a *premium?* At its *par value?*

6–18 If the required return on a bond differs from its coupon interest rate, describe the behavior of the bond value over time as the bond moves toward maturity.

6–19 As a risk-averse investor, would you prefer bonds with short or long periods until maturity? Why?

6–20 What is a bond's *yield to maturity (YTM)?* Briefly describe the use of a financial calculator, the use of an Excel spreadsheet, and the trial-and-error approach for finding YTM.

Summary

Focus on Value

Interest rates and required returns embody the real cost of money, inflationary expectations, and issuer and issue risk. They reflect the level of return required by market participants as compensation for the risk perceived in a specific security or asset investment. Because these returns are affected by economic expectations, they vary as a function of time, typically rising for longer-term maturities. The yield curve reflects such market expectations at any point in time.

The value of an asset can be found by calculating the present value of its expected cash flows, using the required return as the discount rate. Bonds are the easiest financial assets to value; both the amounts and the timing of their cash flows are contractual and therefore known with certainty. The financial manager needs to understand how to apply valuation techniques to bonds, stocks, and tangible assets (as we will demonstrate in the following chapters) to make decisions that are consistent with the firm's **share price maximization goal.**

Review of Learning Goals

Key definitions and formulas for this chapter are summarized in Table 6.8.

Describe interest rate fundamentals, the term structure of interest rates, and risk premiums. The flow of funds between savers and investors is regulated by the interest rate or required return. In a perfect, inflation-free, certain world there would be one cost of money—the real rate of interest.

For any class of similar-risk securities, the term structure of interest rates reflects the relationship between the interest rate or rate of return and the time to maturity. Yield curves can be downward-sloping (inverted), upward-sloping (normal), or flat. The expectations theory, liquidity preference theory, and market segmentation theory are cited to explain the shape of the yield curve. Risk premiums for non-Treasury debt issues result from business risk, financial risk, interest rate risk, liquidity risk, tax risk, default risk, maturity risk, and contractual provision risk.

Review the legal aspects of bond financing and bond cost. Corporate bonds are long-term debt instruments indicating that a corporation has borrowed an amount that it promises to repay in the future under clearly defined terms. Most bonds are issued with maturities of 10 to 30 years and a par value of $1,000. The bond indenture, enforced by a trustee, states all conditions of the bond issue. It contains both standard debt provisions and restrictive covenants, which may include a sinking-fund requirement and/or a security interest. The cost of a bond to an issuer depends on its maturity, offering size, and issuer risk and on the basic cost of money.

Discuss the general features, yields, prices, ratings, popular types, and international issues of corporate bonds. A bond issue may include a conversion feature, a call feature, or stock purchase warrants. The yield, or rate of return, on a bond can be measured by its current yield, yield to maturity (YTM), or yield to call (YTC). Bond prices are typically reported along with their coupon, maturity date, and yield to maturity (YTM). Bond ratings by independent agencies indicate the risk of a bond issue. Various types of traditional and contemporary bonds are available. Eurobonds and foreign bonds enable established creditworthy companies and governments to borrow large amounts internationally.

Understand the key inputs and basic model used in the valuation process. Key inputs to the valuation process include cash flows (returns), timing, and risk and the required return. The value of any asset is equal to the present value of all future cash flows it is *expected* to provide over the relevant time period.

Apply the basic valuation model to bonds and describe the impact of required return and time to maturity on bond values. The value of a bond is the present value of its interest payments plus the present value of its par

TABLE 6.8	Summary of Key Valuation Definitions and Formulas for Any Asset and for Bonds

Definitions of variables

B_0 = bond value

CF_t = cash flow *expected* at the end of year t

I = annual interest on a bond

r = appropriate required return (discount rate)

r_d = required return on a bond

M = par, or face, value of a bond

n = relevant time period, or number of years to maturity

V_0 = value of the asset at time zero

Valuation formulas

Value of any asset:

$$V_0 = \frac{CF_1}{(1+r)^1} + \frac{CF_2}{(1+r)^2} + \cdots + \frac{CF_n}{(1+r)^n} \qquad \text{[Equation 6.1]}$$

$$= [CF_1 \times (PVIF_{r,1})] + [CF_2 \times (PVIF_{r,2})] + \cdots + [CF_n \times (PVIF_{r,n})] \qquad \text{[Equation 6.2]}$$

Bond value:

$$B_0 = I \times \left[\sum_{t=1}^{n} \frac{1}{(1+r_d)^t} \right] + M \times \left[\frac{1}{(1+r_d)^n} \right] \qquad \text{[Equation 6.3]}$$

$$= I \times (PVIFA_{r_d,n}) + M \times (PVIF_{r_d,n}) \qquad \text{[Equation 6.3a]}$$

value. The discount rate used to determine bond value is the required return, which may differ from the bond's coupon interest rate. A bond can sell at a discount, at par, or at a premium, depending on whether the required return is greater than, equal to, or less than its coupon interest rate. The amount of time to maturity affects bond values. The value of a bond will approach its par value as the bond moves closer to maturity. The chance that interest rates will change and thereby change the required return and bond value is called interest rate risk. The shorter the amount of time until a bond's maturity, the less responsive is its market value to a given change in the required return.

LG 6 **Explain yield to maturity (YTM), its calculation, and the procedure used to value bonds that pay interest semiannually.** Yield to maturity is the rate of return investors earn if they buy a bond at a specific price and hold it until maturity. YTM can be calculated by using a financial calculator, by using an Excel spreadsheet, or by trial and error. Bonds that pay interest semiannually are valued by using the same procedure used to value bonds paying annual interest, except that the interest payments are one-half of the annual interest payments, the number of periods is twice the number of years to maturity, and the required return is one-half of the stated annual required return on similar-risk bonds.

Self-Test Problems (Solutions in Appendix B)

  ST6–1 **Bond valuation** Lahey Industries has outstanding a $1,000 par-value bond with an 8% coupon interest rate. The bond has 12 years remaining to its maturity date.
a. If interest is paid *annually*, find the value of the bond when the required return is (1) 7%, (2) 8%, and (3) 10%.
b. Indicate for each case in part **a** whether the bond is selling at a discount, at a premium, or at its par value.
c. Using the 10% required return, find the bond's value when interest is paid *semiannually*.

  ST6–2 **Bond yields** Elliot Enterprises' bonds currently sell for $1,150, have an 11% coupon interest rate and a $1,000 par value, pay interest *annually*, and have 18 years to maturity.
a. Calculate the bonds' *current yield*.
b. Calculate the bonds' *yield to maturity (YTM)*.
c. Compare the YTM calculated in part **b** to the bonds' coupon interest rate and current yield (calculated in part **a**). Use a comparison of the bonds' current price and par value to explain these differences.

Warm-Up Exercises

A blue box (■) indicates exercises available in .

 E6–1 The yields for Treasuries with differing maturities on a recent day were as shown in the following table:

Maturity	Yield
3 months	1.41%
6 months	1.71
2 years	2.68
3 years	3.01
5 years	3.70
10 years	4.51
30 years	5.25

Use the information above to construct a *yield curve* for this date.

  Recently, the annual inflation rate measured by the Consumer Price Index (CPI) was forecast to be 3.3%. How could a T-bill have had a negative real rate of return over the same period? How could it have had a zero real rate of return? What minimum rate of return must the T-bill have earned to meet your requirement of a 2% real rate of return?

E6–3 You have two assets and must calculate their values today based on their different payment streams and appropriate required returns. Asset 1 has a required return of 15% and will produce a stream of $500 at the end of each year indefinitely. Asset 2 has a required return of 10% and will produce an end-of-year cash flow of $1,200 in the first year, $1,500 in the second year, and $850 in its third and final year.

 E6–4 A bond with 5 years to maturity and a coupon rate of 6% has a par, or face, value of $20,000. Interest is paid annually. If you required a return of 8% on this bond, what is the value of this bond to you?

 E6–5 Assume a 5-year Treasury bond has a coupon rate of 4.5%.
a. Give examples of required rates of return that would make the bond sell at a discount, at a premium, and at par.
b. If this bond's par value is $10,000, calculate the differing values for this bond given the required rates you chose in part **a.**

Problems

A blue box (■) indicates problems available in myfinancelab.

 P6–1 **Yield curve**   A firm wishing to evaluate interest rate behavior has gathered yield data on five U.S. Treasury securities, each having a different maturity and all measured at the same point in time. The summarized data follow.

U.S. Treasury security	Time to maturity	Yield
A	1 year	12.6%
B	10 years	11.2
C	6 months	13.0
D	20 years	11.0
E	5 years	11.4

a. Draw the yield curve associated with these data.
b. Describe the resulting yield curve in part **a,** and explain the general expectations embodied in it.

 P6–2 **Term structure of interest rates**   The following yield data for a number of highest-quality corporate bonds existed at each of the three points in time noted.

| Time to maturity (years) | Yield | | |
	5 years ago	2 years ago	Today
1	9.1%	14.6%	9.3%
3	9.2	12.8	9.8
5	9.3	12.2	10.9
10	9.5	10.9	12.6
15	9.4	10.7	12.7
20	9.3	10.5	12.9
30	9.4	10.5	13.5

a. On the same set of axes, draw the yield curve at each of the three given times.

b. Label each curve in part **a** with its general shape (downward-sloping, upward-sloping, flat).

c. Describe the general inflationary and interest rate expectation existing at each of the three times.

 P6–3 **Risk-free rate and risk premiums**   The real rate of interest is currently 3%; the inflation expectation and risk premiums for a number of securities follow.

Security	Inflation expectation premium	Risk premium
A	6%	3%
B	9	2
C	8	2
D	5	4
E	11	1

a. Find the *risk-free rate of interest*, R_F, that is applicable to each security.

b. Although not noted, what factor must be the cause of the differing risk-free rates found in part **a**?

 P6–4 **Risk premiums**   Eleanor Burns is attempting to find the nominal rate of interest for each of two securities—A and B—issued by different firms at the same point in time. She has gathered the following data:

Characteristic	Security A	Security B
Time to maturity	3 years	15 years
Inflation expectation premium	9.0%	7.0%
Risk premium for:		
Liquidity risk	1.0%	1.0%
Default risk	1.0%	2.0%
Maturity risk	0.5%	1.5%
Other risk	0.5%	1.5%

a. If the real rate of interest is currently 2%, find the *risk-free rate of interest* applicable to each security.

b. Find the total risk premium attributable to each security's issuer and issue characteristics.

 P6–5 **Bond interest payments before and after taxes**   Charter Corp. has issued 2,500 debentures with a total principal value of $2,500,000. The bonds have a coupon interest rate of 7%.

a. What dollar amount of interest per bond can an investor expect to receive each year from Charter?

b. What is Charter's total interest expense per year associated with this bond issue?

c. Assuming that Charter is in a 35% corporate tax bracket, what is the company's net after-tax interest cost associated with this bond issue?

P6–6 **Bond prices and yields**   Assume that the Financial Management Corporation's $1,000-par-value bond had a 5.700% coupon, matured on May 15, 2017, had a current price quote of 97.708, and had a yield to maturity (YTM) of 6.034%. Given this information, answer the following questions.

a. What was the dollar price of the bond?
b. What is the bond's *current yield?*
c. Is the bond selling at par, at a discount, or at a premium? Why?
d. Compare the bond's current yield calculated in part **b** to its YTM and explain why they differ.

PERSONAL FINANCE PROBLEM

P6–7 **Valuation fundamentals**   Imagine that you are trying to evaluate the economics of purchasing an automobile. You expect the car to provide annual after-tax cash benefits of $1,200 at the end of each year, and assume that you can sell the car for after-tax proceeds of $5,000 at the end of the planned 5-year ownership period. All funds for purchasing the car will be drawn from your savings, which are currently earning 6% after taxes.

a. Identify the cash flows, their timing, and the required return applicable to valuing the car.
b. What is the maximum price you would be willing to pay to acquire the car? Explain.

P6–8 **Valuation of assets**   Using the information provided in the following table, find the value of each asset.

Asset	Cash flow		Appropriate required return
	End of year	Amount	
A	1	$ 5,000	18%
	2	5,000	
	3	5,000	
B	1 through ∞	$ 300	15%
C	1	$ 0	16%
	2	0	
	3	0	
	4	0	
	5	35,000	
D	1 through 5	$ 1,500	12%
	6	8,500	
E	1	$ 2,000	14%
	2	3,000	
	3	5,000	
	4	7,000	
	5	4,000	
	6	1,000	

f. If Annie buys the bond today at its $1,000 par value and holds it for exactly 3 years, at which time the required return is 7%, how much of a gain or loss will she experience in the value of the bond (ignoring interest already received and assuming annual interest)?

g. Rework part **f,** assuming that Annie holds the bond for 10 years and sells it when the required return is 7%. Compare your finding to that in part **f,** and comment on the bond's *maturity risk.*

h. Assume that Annie buys the bond at its current price of 98.380 and holds it until maturity. What will her *current yield* and *yield to maturity* (*YTM*) be, assuming annual interest?

i. After evaluating all of the issues raised above, what recommendation would you give Annie with regard to her proposed investment in the Atilier Industries bonds?

Spreadsheet Exercise

CSM Corporation has a bond issue outstanding at the end of 2009. The bond has 15 years remaining to maturity and carries a coupon interest rate of 6%. Interest on the bond is compounded on a semiannual basis. The par value of the CSM bond is $1,000 and it is currently selling for $874.42.

To Do

Create a spreadsheet similar to the spreadsheets for yield to maturity and semiannual interest that can be viewed at **www.prenhall.com/gitman**, to model the following:

a. Using the trial and error method, determine the *annual* required rate of return (r_d). Find one interest rate that results in a bond value greater than the current bond price, and then find another rate that results in a bond value lower than the current bond price.

b. What is the time to maturity (n)?

c. What is the semiannual coupon payment (pmt)?

d. What is the semiannual required rate of return ($r_d/2$)?

Web Exercise

Go to the book's companion website at **www.prenhall.com/gitman** to find the Web Exercise for this chapter.

Remember to check the book's website at **www.prenhall.com/gitman** to find additional resources, including Web Exercises and a Web Case.

7 | Stock Valuation

WHY THIS CHAPTER MATTERS TO YOU

LEARNING GOALS

LG 1 Differentiate between debt and equity capital.

LG 2 Discuss the rights, characteristics, and features of both common and preferred stock.

LG 3 Describe the process of issuing common stock, including venture capital, going public, and the investment banker, and interpreting stock quotations.

LG 4 Understand the concept of market efficiency and basic common stock valuation using zero-growth and constant-growth models.

LG 5 Discuss the free cash flow valuation model and the book value, liquidation value, and price/earnings (P/E) multiple approaches.

LG 6 Explain the relationships among financial decisions, return, risk, and the firm's value.

In recent years, many firms have issued two or more classes of common stock; they differ mainly in having unequal voting rights. A firm can use different classes of stock as a defense against a *hostile takeover* in which an outside group, without management support, tries to gain voting control of the firm by buying its shares in the marketplace. **Supervoting shares** of stock give each owner multiple votes. Supervoting shares allow "insiders" to maintain control against an outside group whose shares have only one vote each. At other times, a class of **nonvoting common stock** is issued when the firm wishes to raise capital through the sale of common stock but does not want to give up its voting control.

When different classes of common stock are issued on the basis of unequal voting rights, class A common is typically—but not universally—designated as nonvoting, and class B common has voting rights. Generally, higher classes of shares (class A, for example) are given preference in the distribution of earnings (dividends) and assets; lower-class shares, in exchange, receive voting rights. Treasury stock, which is held within the corporation, generally *does not* have voting rights, *does not* earn dividends, and *does not* have a claim on assets in liquidation.

Because most small stockholders do not attend the annual meeting to vote, they may sign a **proxy statement** transferring their votes to another party. The solicitation of proxies from shareholders is closely controlled by the Securities and Exchange Commission to ensure that proxies are not being solicited on the basis of false or misleading information. Existing management generally receives the stockholders' proxies, because it is able to solicit them at company expense.

Occasionally, when the firm is widely owned, outsiders may wage a **proxy battle** to unseat the existing management and gain control. To win a corporate election, votes from a majority of the shares voted are required. However, the odds of a nonmanagement group winning a proxy battle are generally slim.

Dividends

The payment of dividends to the firm's shareholders is at the discretion of the corporation's board of directors. Most corporations pay dividends quarterly. Dividends may be paid in cash, stock, or merchandise. Cash dividends are the most common, merchandise dividends the least.

Common stockholders are not promised a dividend, but they come to expect certain payments on the basis of the historical dividend pattern of the firm. Before dividends are paid to common stockholders, the claims of the government, all creditors, and preferred stockholders must be satisfied. Since passage of the *Jobs and Growth Tax Relief Reconciliation Act of 2003*, many firms now pay larger dividends to shareholders, who are subject to a maximum tax rate of 15 percent on dividends rather than the maximum tax rate of 39 percent in effect prior to passage of the act. Because of the importance of the dividend decision to the growth and valuation of the firm, dividends are discussed in greater detail in Chapter 12.

International Stock Issues

Although the international market for common stock is not as large as the international market for bonds, cross-border issuance and trading of common stock have increased dramatically in the past 30 years.

Some corporations *issue stock in foreign markets*. For example, the stock of General Electric trades in Frankfurt, London, Paris, and Tokyo; the stocks of Time Warner and Microsoft trade in Frankfurt and London; and the stock of McDonalds trades in Frankfurt, London, and Paris. The Frankfurt, London, and Tokyo markets are the most popular. Issuing stock internationally broadens the ownership base and helps a company to integrate itself into the local business scene. A listing on a foreign stock exchange both increases local business press coverage and serves as effective corporate advertising. Having locally traded stock can also facilitate corporate acquisitions, because shares can be used as an acceptable method of payment.

Foreign corporations have also discovered the benefits of trading their stock in the United States. The disclosure and reporting requirements mandated by the U.S. Securities and Exchange Commission have historically discouraged all but the largest foreign firms from directly listing their shares on the New York Stock Exchange or the American Stock Exchange. For example, in 1993, Daimler-Benz (now DaimlerChrysler) became the first large German company to be listed on the NYSE.

As an alternative, most foreign companies choose to tap the U.S. market through **American depositary receipts (ADRs)**. These are dollar-denominated receipts for the stocks of foreign companies that are held in the vaults of banks in the companies' home countries. They serve as backing for **American depositary shares (ADSs)**, which are securities that permit U.S. investors to hold shares of non-U.S. companies and trade them in U.S. markets. Because ADSs are issued, in dollars, to U.S. investors, they are subject to U.S. securities laws. At the same time, they give investors the opportunity to diversify their portfolios internationally.

Preferred Stock

Preferred stock gives its holders certain privileges that make them senior to common stockholders. Preferred stockholders are promised a fixed periodic dividend, which is stated either as a percentage or as a dollar amount. How the dividend is specified depends on whether the preferred stock has a *par value*. **Par-value preferred stock** has a stated face value, and its annual dividend is specified as a percentage of this value. **No-par preferred stock** has no stated face value, but its annual dividend is stated in dollars. Preferred stock is most often issued by public utilities, by acquiring firms in merger transactions, and by firms that are experiencing losses and need additional financing.

Basic Rights of Preferred Stockholders

The basic rights of preferred stockholders are somewhat more favorable than the rights of common stockholders. Preferred stock is often considered *quasi-debt* because, much like interest on debt, it specifies a fixed periodic payment (dividend). Of course, as ownership, preferred stock is unlike debt in that it has no maturity date. Because they have a fixed claim on the firm's income that takes precedence over the claim of common stockholders, preferred stockholders are exposed to less risk. They are consequently *not normally given a voting right*.

Preferred stockholders have *preference over common stockholders in the distribution of earnings*. If the stated preferred stock dividend is "passed" (not paid)

American depositary receipts (ADRs)
Dollar-denominated receipts for the stocks of foreign companies that are held in the vaults of banks in the companies' home countries.

American depositary shares (ADSs)
Securities, backed by *American depositary receipts (ADRs)*, that permit U.S. investors to hold shares of non-U.S. companies and trade them in U.S. markets.

par-value preferred stock
Preferred stock with a stated face value that is used with the specified dividend percentage to determine the annual dollar dividend.

no-par preferred stock
Preferred stock with no stated face value but with a stated annual dollar dividend.

by the board of directors, the payment of dividends to common stockholders is prohibited. It is this preference in dividend distribution that makes common stockholders the true risk takers.

Preferred stockholders are also usually given *preference over common stockholders in the liquidation of assets* in a legally bankrupt firm, although they must "stand in line" behind creditors. The amount of the claim of preferred stockholders in liquidation is normally equal to the par or stated value of the preferred stock.

Features of Preferred Stock

A preferred stock issue generally includes a number of features, which, along with the stock's par value, the amount of dividend payments, the dividend payment dates, and any restrictive covenants, are specified in an agreement similar to a *bond indenture*.

Restrictive Covenants   The restrictive covenants in a preferred stock issue focus on ensuring the firm's continued existence and regular payment of the dividend. These covenants include provisions about passing dividends, the sale of senior securities, mergers, sales of assets, minimum liquidity requirements, and repurchases of common stock. The violation of preferred stock covenants usually permits preferred stockholders either to obtain representation on the firm's board of directors or to force the retirement of their stock at or above its par or stated value.

cumulative (preferred stock)
Preferred stock for which all passed (unpaid) dividends in arrears, along with the current dividend, must be paid before dividends can be paid to common stockholders.

noncumulative (preferred stock)
Preferred stock for which passed (unpaid) dividends do not accumulate.

Cumulation   Most preferred stock is **cumulative** with respect to any dividends passed. That is, all dividends in arrears, along with the current dividend, must be paid before dividends can be paid to common stockholders. If preferred stock is **noncumulative,** passed (unpaid) dividends do not accumulate. In this case, only the current dividend must be paid before dividends can be paid to common stockholders. Because the common stockholders can receive dividends only after the dividend claims of preferred stockholders have been satisfied, it is in the firm's best interest to pay preferred dividends when they are due.[1]

Example   Utley Corporation, a manufacturer of specialty automobiles, currently has outstanding an issue of $6 preferred stock on which quarterly dividends of $1.50 are to be paid. Because of a cash shortage, the last two quarterly dividends were passed. The directors of the company have been receiving a large number of complaints from common stockholders, who have, of course, not received any dividends in the past two quarters either. If the preferred stock is *cumulative*, the company will have to pay its preferred stockholders $4.50 per share ($3.00 of dividends in arrears plus the current $1.50 dividend) prior to paying dividends to its common stockholders. If the preferred stock is *noncumulative*, the firm must pay only the current $1.50 dividend to its preferred stockholders prior to paying dividends to its common stockholders.

Other Features   Preferred stock is generally *callable*—the issuer can retire outstanding stock within a certain period of time at a specified price. The call

---

1. Most preferred stock is cumulative, because it is difficult to sell noncumulative stock. Common stockholders obviously prefer issuance of noncumulative preferred stock, because it does not place them in quite so risky a position. But it is often in the best interest of the firm to sell cumulative preferred stock because of its lower cost.

option generally cannot be exercised until after a specified date. The call price is normally set above the initial issuance price, but it may decrease as time passes. Making preferred stock callable provides the issuer with a way to bring the fixed-payment commitment of the preferred issue to an end if conditions in the financial markets make it desirable to do so.

Preferred stock quite often contains a **conversion feature** that allows *holders of convertible preferred stock* to change each share into a stated number of shares of common stock. Sometimes the number of shares of common stock that the preferred stock can be exchanged for changes according to a prespecified formula.

conversion feature (preferred stock)
A feature of *convertible preferred stock* that allows holders to change each share into a stated number of shares of common stock.

Issuing Common Stock

Because of the high risk associated with a business startup, a firm's initial financing typically comes from its founders in the form of a common stock investment. Until the founders have made an equity investment, it is highly unlikely that others will contribute either equity or debt capital. Early-stage investors in the firm's equity, as well as lenders who provide debt capital, want to be assured that they are taking no more risk than the founding owner(s). In addition, they want confirmation that the founders are confident enough in their vision for the firm that they are willing to risk their own money.

The initial nonfounder financing for business startups with attractive growth prospects comes from private equity investors. Then, as the firm establishes the viability of its product or service offering and begins to generate revenues, cash flow, and profits, it will often "go public" by issuing shares of common stock to a much broader group of investors.

Before we consider the initial *public* sales of equity, let's review some of the key aspects of early-stage equity financing in firms that have attractive growth prospects.

Venture Capital

venture capital
Privately raised external equity capital used to fund early-stage firms with attractive growth prospects.

venture capitalists (VCs)
Providers of venture capital; typically, formal businesses that maintain strong oversight over the firms they invest in and that have clearly defined exit strategies.

angel capitalists (angels)
Wealthy individual investors who do not operate as a business but invest in promising early-stage companies in exchange for a portion of the firm's equity.

The initial external equity financing privately raised by firms, typically early-stage firms with attractive growth prospects, is called **venture capital.** Those who provide venture capital are known as **venture capitalists (VCs).** They typically are formal business entities that maintain strong oversight over the firms they invest in and that have clearly defined exit strategies. Less visible early-stage investors called **angel capitalists** (or **angels**) tend to be investors who do not actually operate as a business; they are often wealthy individual investors who are willing to invest in promising early-stage companies in exchange for a portion of the firm's equity. Although angels play a major role in early-stage equity financing, we will focus on VCs because of their more formal structure and greater public visibility.

Organization and Investment Stages   Institutional venture capital investors tend to be organized in one of four basic ways, as described in Table 7.2 (see page 290). The *VC limited partnership* is by far the dominant structure. These funds have as their sole objective to earn high returns, rather than to obtain access to the companies in order to sell or buy other products or services.

VCs can invest in early-stage companies, later-stage companies, or buyouts and acquisitions. Generally, about 40 to 50 percent of VC investments are devoted to early-stage companies (for startup funding and expansion) and a similar percentage to later-stage companies (for marketing, production expansion, and

TABLE 7.2	Organization of Institutional Venture Capital Investors
Organization	Description
Small business investment companies (SBICs)	Corporations chartered by the federal government that can borrow at attractive rates from the U.S. Treasury and use the funds to make venture capital investments in private companies.
Financial VC funds	Subsidiaries of financial institutions, particularly banks, set up to help young firms grow and, it is hoped, become major customers of the institution.
Corporate VC funds	Firms, sometimes subsidiaries, established by nonfinancial firms, typically to gain access to new technologies that the corporation can access to further its own growth.
VC limited partnerships	Limited partnerships organized by professional VC firms, which serve as the general partner and organize, invest, and manage the partnership using the limited partners' funds; the professional VCs ultimately liquidate the partnership and distribute the proceeds to all partners.

preparation for public offering); the remaining 5 to 10 percent are devoted to the buyout or acquisition of other companies. Generally, VCs look for compound annual rates of return ranging from 20 to 50 percent or more, depending on both the development stage and the attributes of each company. Earlier-stage investments tend to demand higher returns than later-stage investments because of the higher risk associated with the earlier stages of a firm's growth.

Deal Structure and Pricing   Regardless of the development stage, venture capital investments are made under a legal contract that clearly allocates responsibilities and ownership interests between existing owners (founders) and the VC fund or limited partnership. The terms of the agreement will depend on numerous factors related to the founders; the business structure, stage of development, and outlook; and other market and timing issues. The specific financial terms will, of course, depend on the value of the enterprise, the amount of funding, and the perceived risk. To control the VC's risk, various covenants are included in the agreement, and the actual funding may be pegged to the achievement of *measurable milestones*. The VC will negotiate numerous other provisions into the contract, both to ensure the firm's success and to control its risk exposure. The contract will have an explicit exit strategy for the VC that may be tied both to measurable milestones and to time.

The amount of equity to which the VC is entitled will, of course, depend on the value of the firm, the terms of the contract, the exit terms, and the minimum compound annual rate of return required by the VC on its investment. Although each VC investment is unique and no standard contract exists, the transaction will be structured to provide the VC with a high rate of return that is consistent with the typically high risk of such transactions. The exit strategy of most VC investments is to take the firm public through an initial public offering.

Going Public

When a firm wishes to sell its stock in the primary market, it has three alternatives. It can make (1) a *public offering,* in which it offers its shares for sale to the general public; (2) a *rights offering*, in which new shares are sold to existing stockholders; or (3) a *private placement*, in which the firm sells new securities directly to an investor or group of investors. Here we focus on public offerings, particularly the **initial public offering (IPO)**, which is the first public sale of a firm's stock. IPOs are typically made by small, rapidly growing companies that either require additional capital to continue expanding or have met a milestone for going public that was established in a contract signed earlier in order to obtain VC funding.

initial public offering (IPO)
The first public sale of a firm's stock.

To go public, the firm must first obtain the approval of its current shareholders, the investors who own its privately issued stock. Next, the company's auditors and lawyers must certify that all documents for the company are legitimate. The company then finds an investment bank willing to *underwrite* the offering. This underwriter is responsible for promoting the stock and facilitating the sale of the company's IPO shares. The underwriter often brings in other investment banking firms as participants. We'll discuss the role of the investment banker in more detail in the next section.

The company files a registration statement with the SEC. One portion of the registration statement is called the **prospectus.** It describes the key aspects of the issue, the issuer, and its management and financial position. During the waiting period between the statement's filing and its approval, prospective investors can receive a preliminary prospectus. This preliminary version is called a **red herring,** because a notice printed in red on the front cover indicates the tentative nature of the offer. The cover of the preliminary prospectus describing the 2007 stock issue of Metro PCS Communications, Inc., is shown in Figure 7.1 (see page 292). Note the red herring printed vertically on its left edge.

prospectus
A portion of a security registration statement that describes the key aspects of the issue, the issuer, and its management and financial position.

red herring
A preliminary prospectus made available to prospective investors during the waiting period between the registration statement's filing with the SEC and its approval.

After the SEC approves the registration statement, the investment community can begin analyzing the company's prospects. However, from the time it files until at least one month after the IPO is complete, the company must observe a *quiet period*, during which there are restrictions on what company officials may say about the company. The purpose of the quiet period is to make sure that all potential investors have access to the same information about the company—the information presented in the preliminary prospectus—and not to any unpublished data that might give them an unfair advantage.

The investment bankers and company executives promote the company's stock offering through a *road show*, a series of presentations to potential investors around the country and sometimes overseas. In addition to providing investors with information about the new issue, road show sessions help the investment bankers gauge the demand for the offering and set an expected pricing range. After the underwriter sets terms and prices the issue, the SEC must approve the offering.

investment banker
Financial intermediary that specializes in selling new security issues and advising firms with regard to major financial transactions.

underwriting
The role of the *investment banker* in bearing the risk of reselling, at a profit, the securities purchased from an issuing corporation at an agreed-on price.

The Investment Banker's Role

Most public offerings are made with the assistance of an **investment banker.** The investment banker is a financial intermediary (such as Morgan Stanley or Goldman, Sachs) that specializes in selling new security issues and advising firms with regard to major financial transactions. The main activity of the investment banker is **underwriting.** This process involves purchasing the security issue from the issuing corporation at an agreed-on price and bearing the risk of reselling it to the public at a profit. The investment banker also provides the issuer with advice about pricing and other important aspects of the issue.

Cover of a Preliminary Prospectus for a Stock Issue
Some of the key factors related to the 2007 common stock issue by Metro PCS Communications, Inc., are summarized on the cover of the prospectus. The type printed vertically on the left edge is normally red, which explains its name "red herring." (*Source:* Metro PCS Communications, Inc., April 3, 2007, p. 1.)

The information in this prospectus is not complete and may be changed. We may not sell these securities until the registration statement filed with the Securities and Exchange Commission is effective. This prospectus is not an offer to sell these securities and it is not soliciting an offer to buy these securities in any jurisdiction where the offer or sale is not permitted.

SUBJECT TO COMPLETION, DATED APRIL 3, 2007

PROSPECTUS

50,000,000 Shares

MetroPCS Communications, Inc.
Common Stock

This is our initial public offering. We are offering 37,500,000 shares of our common stock and the selling stockholders identified in this prospectus are offering an additional 12,500,000 shares of our common stock. We will not receive any proceeds from the sale of our common stock by the selling stockholders. We currently expect the initial public offering price for our stock will be between $19.00 and $21.00 per share.

Unless otherwise indicated, all share numbers and per share prices in this prospectus give effect to a 3 for 1 stock split effected by means of a stock dividend of two shares of common stock for each share of common stock issued and outstanding at the close of business on March 14, 2007.

Prior to this offering, there has been no public market for our common stock. We have applied to list our common stock on the New York Stock Exchange under the symbol "PCS".

Investing in our common stock involves risks. See "Risk Factors" beginning on page 12.

	Per Share	Total
Public offering price	$	$
Underwriting discounts	$	$
Proceeds, before expenses, to us	$	$
Proceeds to the selling stockholders	$	$

Neither the Securities and Exchange Commission nor any state securities commission has approved or disapproved of these securities or passed upon the adequacy or accuracy of this prospectus. Any representation to the contrary is a criminal offense.

The underwriters expect to deliver the shares against payment in New York, New York on or about   , 2007.

The underwriters have a 30-day option to purchase up to 7,500,000 additional shares of common stock from the selling stockholders to cover over-allotments, if any. We will not receive any proceeds from the exercise of the over-allotment option.

Bear, Stearns & Co. Inc.
Banc of America Securities LLC
Merrill Lynch & Co.
Morgan Stanley

UBS Investment Bank
Thomas Weisel Partners LLC
Wachovia Securities
Raymond James

The date of this prospectus is   , 2007.

underwriting syndicate
A group of other bankers formed by an investment banker to share the financial risk associated with *underwriting* new securities.

selling group
A large number of brokerage firms that join the originating investment banker(s); each accepts responsibility for selling a certain portion of a new security issue on a commission basis.

In the case of very large security issues, the investment banker brings in other bankers as partners to form an **underwriting syndicate.** The syndicate shares the financial risk associated with buying the entire issue from the issuer and reselling the new securities to the public. The originating investment banker and the syndicate members put together a **selling group,** normally made up of themselves and a large number of brokerage firms. Each member of the selling group accepts the responsibility for selling a certain portion of the issue and is paid a commission on the securities it sells. The selling process for a large security issue is depicted in Figure 7.2.

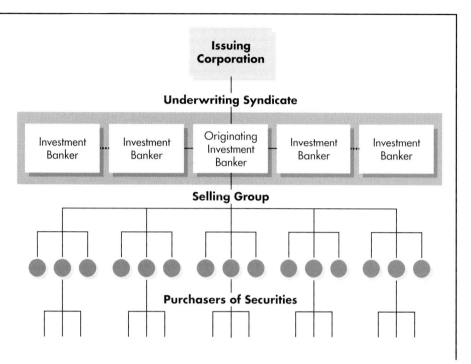

FIGURE 7.2

The Selling Process for a Large Security Issue
The investment banker hired by the issuing corporation may form an underwriting syndicate. The underwriting syndicate buys the entire security issue from the issuing corporation at an agreed-on price. The underwriters then have the opportunity (and bear the risk) of reselling the issue to the public at a profit. Both the originating investment banker and the other syndicate members put together a selling group to sell the issue on a commission basis to investors.

Compensation for underwriting and selling services typically comes in the form of a discount on the sale price of the securities. For example, an investment banker may pay the issuing firm $24 per share for stock that will be sold for $26 per share. The investment banker may then sell the shares to members of the selling group for $25.25 per share. In this case, the original investment banker earns $1.25 per share ($25.25 sale price − $24 purchase price). The members of the selling group earn 75 cents for each share they sell ($26 sale price − $25.25 purchase price). Although some primary security offerings are directly placed by the issuer, the majority of new issues are sold through public offering via the mechanism just described.

Interpreting Stock Quotations

The financial manager needs to stay abreast of the market values of the firm's outstanding stock, whether it is traded domestically or in international markets. Similarly, existing and prospective stockholders need to monitor the prices of the securities they own because these prices represent the current value of their investments. Price *quotations*, which include current price data along with statistics on recent price behavior, are readily available for actively traded stocks. The most up-to-date "quotes" can be obtained electronically, via a personal computer. Price information is available from stockbrokers and is widely published in news media. Popular sources of daily security price quotations include financial newspapers, such as the *Wall Street Journal* and *Investor's Business Daily,* and the business sections of daily general newspapers.

Figure 7.3 (see page 294) includes an excerpt from the NYSE quotations, reported in the *Wall Street Journal* on March 28, 2007, for transactions through

FIGURE 7.3

Stock Quotations
Selected stock quotations
for March 27, 2007

STOCK	SYM	CLOSE	NET CHG
Masco	MAS	27.80	–0.15
Masisa ADS	MYS	11.24	–0.03
MasseyEngy	MEE	24.20	–0.64
MasterCard	MA	107.25	–1.23
MatsuElec	MC	20.74	–0.22
Mattel	MAT	28.26	–0.47
McAfee	MFE	29.82	–0.07
ᵀ McClatchy A	MNI	37.61	–0.37
McCrmkCo	MKC	38.68	–0.43
McDermInt	MDR	49.82	–0.64
McDonalds	MCD	45.04	–0.08	← McDonald's
McGrawH	MHP	63.33	–0.26
McKesson	MCK	58.50	0.58
MeadWVaco	MWV	30.66	–0.03
Mechel OAO	MTL	31.75	–0.31
MedcoHlthSol	MHS	71.80	–0.57
♣ Medtronic	MDT	48.68	–1.15
MellonFnl	MEL	43.11	–0.47
MensWearhs	MW	48.26	–0.05

Source: Wall Street Journal,
March 28, 2007, p. C13.

Hint Preferred stock quotations typically are not listed in the financial press, but can be obtained online or through a stockbroker.

the close of trading on Tuesday, March 27, 2007. We'll look at the quotation for the common stock of McDonald's, highlighted in the figure. The quotations show that stock prices are quoted in dollars and cents. Listed to the right of the company's name is its *stock symbol;* McDonald's goes by "MCD." The next column, labeled "CLOSE," contains the closing (last) price at which the stock sold on the given day. The value for McDonald's was $45.04. The final column, "NET CHG," indicates the change in the closing price from that on the prior trading day. McDonald's closed down $0.08 from March 26, 2007, which means the closing price on that day was $45.12.

Similar quotations systems are used for stocks that trade in other markets such as the Nasdaq market. Also note that when a stock issue is not traded on a given day, it generally is not quoted in the financial and business press.

REVIEW QUESTIONS

7–2 What risks do common stockholders take that other suppliers of long-term capital do not?

7–3 How does a *rights offering* protect a firm's stockholders against the *dilution of ownership?*

7–4 Explain the relationships among authorized shares, outstanding shares, treasury stock, and issued shares.

7–5 What are the advantages to both U.S.-based and foreign corporations of issuing stock outside their home markets? What are *American depositary receipts (ADRs)?* What are *American depositary shares (ADSs)?*

7–6 What claims do preferred stockholders have with respect to distribution of earnings (dividends) and assets?

7–7 Explain the *cumulative feature* of preferred stock. What is the purpose of a *call feature* in a preferred stock issue?

7–8   What is the difference between a *venture capitalist* (VC) and an *angel capitalist* (*angel*)?

7–9   Into what bodies are institutional VCs most commonly organized? How are their deals structured and priced?

7–10   What general procedures must a private firm follow to go public via an *initial public offering* (IPO)?

7–11   What role does an *investment banker* play in a public offering? Explain the sequence of events in the issuing of stock.

7–12   What are the key sources of *stock quotations*? Describe the items of information included in a published stock quotation.

7.3 | Common Stock Valuation

Common stockholders expect to be rewarded through periodic cash dividends and an increasing—or at least nondeclining—share value. Like current owners, prospective owners and security analysts frequently estimate the firm's value. Investors purchase the stock when they believe that it is *undervalued*—when its true value is greater than its market price. They sell the stock when they feel that it is *overvalued*—when its market price is greater than its true value.

In this section, we will describe specific stock valuation techniques. First, though, we will look at the concept of an efficient market, which questions whether the prices of actively traded stocks can differ from their true values.

Market Efficiency

Economically rational buyers and sellers use their assessment of an asset's risk and return to determine its value. To a buyer, the asset's value represents the maximum price that he or she would pay to acquire it; a seller views the asset's value as a minimum sale price. In competitive markets with many active participants, such as the New York Stock Exchange, the interactions of many buyers and sellers result in an equilibrium price—the *market value*—for each security. This price reflects the collective actions that buyers and sellers take on the basis of all available information. Buyers and sellers are assumed to digest new information immediately as it becomes available and, through their purchase and sale activities, to create a new market equilibrium price quickly. This general concept is known as *market efficiency*.

efficient-market hypothesis (EMH)
Theory describing the behavior of an assumed "perfect" market in which (1) securities are typically in equilibrium, (2) security prices fully reflect all public information available and react swiftly to new information, and, (3) because stocks are fully and fairly priced, investors need not waste time looking for mispriced securities.

The Efficient-Market Hypothesis

As noted in Chapter 1, active broker and dealer markets, such as the New York Stock Exchange and the Nasdaq market, are *efficient*—they are made up of many rational investors who react quickly and objectively to new information. The **efficient-market hypothesis (EMH),** which is the basic theory describing the behavior of such a "perfect" market, specifically states that

1. Securities are typically in equilibrium, which means that they are fairly priced and that their expected returns equal their required returns.

2. At any point in time, security prices fully reflect all public information available about the firm and its securities,[2] and these prices react swiftly to new information.

3. Because stocks are fully and fairly priced, investors need not waste their time trying to find mispriced (undervalued or overvalued) securities.

Not all market participants are believers in the efficient-market hypothesis. Some feel that it is worthwhile to search for undervalued or overvalued securities and to trade them to profit from market inefficiencies. Others argue that it is mere luck that would allow market participants to anticipate new information correctly and as a result earn *excess returns*—that is, actual returns greater than required returns. They believe it is unlikely that market participants can *over the long run* earn excess returns. Contrary to this belief, some well-known investors such as Warren Buffett and Peter Lynch *have* over the long run consistently earned excess returns on their portfolios. It is unclear whether their success is the result of their superior ability to anticipate new information or of some form of market inefficiency.

The Behavioral Finance Challenge

Although considerable evidence supports the concept of market efficiency, a growing body of academic evidence has begun to cast doubt on the validity of this notion. The research documents various *anomalies*—deviations from accepted beliefs—in stock returns. A number of academics and practitioners have also recognized that emotions and other subjective factors play a role in investment decisions.

behavioral finance
A growing body of research that focuses on investor behavior and its impact on investment decisions and stock prices. Advocates are commonly referred to as "behaviorists."

This focus on investor behavior has resulted in a significant body of research, collectively referred to as **behavioral finance.** Advocates of behavioral finance are commonly referred to as "behaviorists." Daniel Kahneman was awarded the 2002 Nobel Prize in economics for his work in behavioral finance, specifically for integrating insights from psychology and economics. Ongoing research into the psychological factors that can affect investor behavior and the resulting effects on stock prices will likely result in growing acceptance of behavioral finance. For further discussion of some of the findings of behavioral finance, see the book's website.

Throughout this text we ignore both disbelievers and behaviorists and continue to assume market efficiency. This means that *the terms "expected return" and "required return" are used interchangeably,* because they should be equal in an efficient market. This also means that stock prices accurately reflect true value based on risk and return. In other words, we will operate under the assumption that a stock's market price at any point in time is the best estimate of its value. We're now ready to look closely at the mechanics of common stock valuation.

---

2. Those market participants who have nonpublic—*inside*—information may have an unfair advantage that enables them to earn an excess return. Since the mid-1980s disclosure of the insider-trading activities of a number of well-known financiers and investors, major national attention has been focused on the "problem" of insider trading and its resolution. Clearly, those who trade securities on the basis of inside information have an unfair and illegal advantage. Empirical research has confirmed that those with inside information do indeed have an opportunity to earn an excess return. Here we ignore this possibility, given its illegality and the fact that enhanced surveillance and enforcement by the securities industry and the government have in recent years (it appears) significantly reduced insider trading. We, in effect, assume that all relevant information is public and that therefore the market is efficient.

Basic Common Stock Valuation Equation

Like the value of a bond, which we discussed in Chapter 6, *the value of a share of common stock is equal to the present value of all future cash flows (dividends) that it is expected to provide over an infinite time horizon.* Although a stockholder can earn capital gains by selling stock at a price above that originally paid, what is really sold is the right to all future dividends. What about stocks that are not expected to pay dividends in the foreseeable future? Such stocks have a value attributable to a distant dividend expected to result from sale of the company or liquidation of its assets. Therefore, *from a valuation viewpoint, only dividends are relevant.*

By redefining terms, the basic valuation model in Equation 6.1 can be specified for common stock, as given in Equation 7.1:

$$P_0 = \frac{D_1}{(1+r_s)^1} + \frac{D_2}{(1+r_s)^2} + \cdots + \frac{D_\infty}{(1+r_s)^\infty} \tag{7.1}$$

where

P_0 = value of common stock

D_t = per-share dividend *expected* at the end of year t

r_s = required return on common stock

The equation can be simplified somewhat by redefining each year's dividend, D_t, in terms of anticipated growth. We will consider two models here: zero-growth and constant-growth. A third model—variable-growth—is defined below and discussed more fully at the book's website.

Zero-Growth Model

zero-growth model
An approach to dividend valuation that assumes a constant, nongrowing dividend stream.

The simplest approach to dividend valuation, the **zero-growth model**, assumes a constant, nongrowing dividend stream. In terms of the notation already introduced,

$$D_1 = D_2 = \cdots = D_\infty$$

When we let D_1 represent the amount of the annual dividend, Equation 7.1 under zero growth reduces to

$$P_0 = D_1 \times \sum_{t=1}^{\infty} \frac{1}{(1+r_s)^t} = D_1 \times (PVIFA_{r_s,\infty}) = D_1 \times \frac{1}{r_s} = \frac{D_1}{r_s} \tag{7.2}$$

The equation shows that with zero growth, the value of a share of stock would equal the present value of a perpetuity of D_1 dollars discounted at a rate r_s. (Perpetuities were introduced in Chapter 4; see Equation 4.17 and the related discussion.)

Personal Finance Example   Chuck Swimmer estimates that the dividend of Denham Company, an established textile producer, is expected to remain constant at $3 per share indefinitely. If his required return on its stock is 15%, the stock's value is $20 ($3 ÷ 0.15) per share.

Preferred Stock Valuation Because preferred stock typically provides its holders with a fixed annual dividend over its assumed infinite life, *Equation 7.2 can be used to find the value of preferred stock*. The value of preferred stock can be estimated by substituting the stated dividend on the preferred stock for D_1 and the required return for r_s in Equation 7.2. For example, a preferred stock paying a $5 stated annual dividend and having a required return of 13 percent would have a value of $38.46 ($5 ÷ 0.13) per share.

Constant-Growth Model

constant-growth model
A widely cited dividend valuation approach that assumes that dividends will grow at a constant rate, but a rate that is less than the required return.

The most widely cited dividend valuation approach, the **constant-growth model**, assumes that dividends will grow at a constant rate, but a rate that is less than the required return. (The assumption that the constant rate of growth, g, is less than the required return, r_s, is a necessary mathematical condition for deriving this model.) By letting D_0 represent the most recent dividend, we can rewrite Equation 7.1 as follows:

$$P_0 = \frac{D_0 \times (1 + g)^1}{(1 + r_s)^1} + \frac{D_0 \times (1 + g)^2}{(1 + r_s)^2} + \cdots + \frac{D_0 \times (1 + g)^\infty}{(1 + r_s)^\infty} \qquad (7.3)$$

If we simplify Equation 7.3, it can be rewritten as[3]

$$P_0 = \frac{D_1}{r_s - g} \qquad (7.4)$$

Gordon model
A common name for the *constant-growth model* that is widely cited in dividend valuation.

The constant-growth model in Equation 7.4 is commonly called the **Gordon model.** An example will show how it works.

Example

Lamar Company, a small cosmetics company, from 2004 through 2009 paid the following per-share dividends:

Year	Dividend per share
2009	$1.40
2008	1.29
2007	1.20
2006	1.12
2005	1.05
2004	1.00

---

3. For the interested reader, the calculations necessary to derive Equation 7.4 from Equation 7.3 follow. The first step is to multiply each side of Equation 7.3 by $(1 + r_s)/(1 + g)$ and subtract Equation 7.3 from the resulting expression. This yields

$$\frac{P_0 \times (1 + r_s)}{1 + g} - P_0 = D_0 - \frac{D_0 \times (1 + g)^\infty}{(1 + r_s)^\infty} \qquad (1)$$

Because r_s is assumed to be greater than g, the second term on the right side of Equation 1 should be zero. Thus

$$P_0 \times \left(\frac{1 + r_s}{1 + g} - 1\right) = D_0 \qquad (2)$$

Equation 2 is simplified as follows:

$$P_0 \times \left[\frac{(1 + r_s) - (1 + g)}{1 + g}\right] = D_0 \qquad (3)$$

$$P_0 \times (r_s - g) = D_0 \times (1 + g) \qquad (4)$$

$$P_0 = \frac{D_1}{r_s - g} \qquad (5)$$

Equation 5 equals Equation 7.4.

We assume that the historical compound annual growth rate of dividends is an accurate estimate of the future constant annual rate of dividend growth, g. Using a financial calculator, a spreadsheet, or Appendix Table A–2, we find that the historical compound annual growth rate of Lamar Company dividends equals 7%.[4] The company estimates that its dividend in 2010, D_1, will equal $1.50. The required return, r_s, is assumed to be 15%. By substituting these values into Equation 7.5, we find the value of the stock to be

$$P_0 = \frac{\$1.50}{0.15 - 0.07} = \frac{\$1.50}{0.08} = \underline{\underline{\$18.75}} \text{ per share}$$

Assuming that the values of D_1, r_s, and g are accurately estimated, Lamar Company's stock value is $18.75 per share.

Variable-Growth Model

variable-growth model
A dividend valuation approach that allows for a change in the dividend growth rate.

The zero- and constant-growth common stock models do not allow for any shift in expected growth rates. Because future growth rates might shift up or down because of changing expectations, it is useful to consider a **variable-growth model** that allows for a change in the dividend growth rate. For an explanation of how to use the variable-growth model to determine the value of a share of stock, see the book's website.

Free Cash Flow Valuation Model

free cash flow valuation model
A model that determines the value of an entire company as the present value of its expected *free cash flows* discounted at the firm's *weighted average cost of capital,* which is its expected average future cost of funds over the long run.

As an alternative to the dividend valuation models presented above, a firm's value can be estimated by using its projected *free cash flows* (FCFs). This approach is appealing when one is valuing firms that have no dividend history or are startups or when one is valuing an operating unit or division of a larger public company. Although dividend valuation models are widely used and accepted, in these situations it is preferable to use a more general free cash flow valuation model.

The **free cash flow valuation model** is based on the same basic premise as dividend valuation models: The value of a share of common stock is the present value of all future cash flows it is expected to provide over an infinite time horizon. However, in the free cash flow valuation model, instead of valuing the firm's expected dividends, we value the firm's expected *free cash flows*, defined in Equation 3.5 (on page 105). They represent the amount of cash flow available to

---

4. The technique involves solving the following equation for g:

$$D_{2009} = D_{2004} \times (1+g)^5$$

$$\frac{D_{2004}}{D_{2009}} = \frac{1}{(1+g)^5} = PVIF_{g,5}$$

To do so, we can use a financial calculator, a spreadsheet, or financial tables.

A financial calculator can be used. (*Note:* Most calculators require *either* the PV or FV value to be input as a negative number to calculate an unknown interest or growth rate. That approach is used here.) Using the inputs shown at the left, you should find the growth rate to be 6.96%, which we round to 7%.

An electronic spreadsheet could also be used to make this computation. Given space considerations, we have forgone that computational aid here.

We could also use a financial table. Two basic steps can be followed using the present value table. First, dividing the earliest dividend ($D_{2004} = \$1.00$) by the most recent dividend ($D_{2009} = \$1.40$) yields a factor for the present value of one dollar, *PVIF,* of 0.714 ($\$1.00 \div \$1.40$). Although six dividends are shown, *they reflect only 5 years of growth.* (The number of years of growth can also be found by subtracting the earliest year from the most recent year—that is, $2009 - 2004 = 5$ *years of growth.*) By looking across the Appendix Table A–2 at the *PVIF* for 5 years, we find that the factor closest to 0.714 occurs at 7% (0.713). Therefore, the growth rate of the dividends, rounded to the nearest whole percent, is 7%.

Input	Function
1.00	PV
−1.40	FV
5	N
	CPT
	I

Solution
6.96

investors—the providers of debt (creditors) and equity (owners)—after all other obligations have been met.

The free cash flow valuation model estimates the value of the entire company by finding the present value of its expected free cash flows discounted at its *weighted average cost of capital,* which is its expected average future cost of funds over the long run (see Chapter 10), as specified in Equation 7.5.

$$V_C = \frac{FCF_1}{(1 + r_a)^1} + \frac{FCF_2}{(1 + r_a)^2} + \cdots + \frac{FCF_\infty}{(1 + r_a)^\infty} \qquad (7.5)$$

where

V_C = value of the entire company

FCF_t = free cash flow *expected* at the end of year t

r_a = the firm's weighted average cost of capital

Note the similarity between Equations 7.5 and 7.1, the general stock valuation equation.

Because the value of the entire company, V_C, is the market value of the entire enterprise (that is, of all assets), to find common stock value, V_S, we must subtract the market value of all of the firm's debt, V_D, and the market value of preferred stock, V_P, from V_C.

$$V_S = V_C - V_D - V_P \qquad (7.6)$$

Because it is difficult to forecast a firm's free cash flow, specific annual cash flows are typically forecast for only about 5 years, beyond which a constant growth rate is assumed. Here we assume that the first 5 years of free cash flows are explicitly forecast and that a constant rate of free cash flow growth occurs beyond the end of year 5 to infinity. This model is methodologically similar to the variable-growth model presented earlier. Its application is best demonstrated with an example.

Example

Dewhurst, Inc., wishes to determine the value of its stock by using the free cash flow valuation model. To apply the model, the firm's CFO developed the data given in Table 7.3. Application of the model can be performed in four steps.

Step 1 Calculate the present value of the free cash flow occurring from the end of 2015 to infinity, measured at the beginning of 2015 (that is, at the end of 2014). Because a constant rate of growth in FCF is forecast beyond 2014, we can use the constant-growth dividend valuation model (Equation 7.4) to calculate the value of the free cash flows from the end of 2015 to infinity.

$$\text{Value of } FCF_{2015 \to \infty} = \frac{FCF_{2015}}{r_a - g_{FCF}}$$

$$= \frac{\$600,000 \times (1 + 0.03)}{0.09 - 0.03}$$

$$= \frac{\$618,000}{0.06} = \underline{\$10,300,000}$$

Note that to calculate the FCF in 2015, we had to increase the 2014 FCF value of $600,000 by the 3% FCF growth rate, g_{FCF}.

| TABLE 7.3 | Dewhurst, Inc.'s Data for the Free Cash Flow Valuation Model |

| Free cash flow | | |
Year (t)	$(FCF_t)^a$	Other data
2010	$400,000	Growth rate of FCF, beyond 2014 to infinity, $g_{FCF} = 3\%$
2011	450,000	Weighted average cost of capital, $r_a = 9\%$
2012	520,000	Market value of all debt, $V_D = \$3,100,000$
2013	560,000	Market value of preferred stock, $V_P = \$800,000$
2014	600,000	Number of shares of common stock outstanding = 300,000

^{a}Developed using Equations 3.4 and 3.5 (on pages 104 and 105).

Step 2   Add the present value of the FCF from 2015 to infinity, which is measured at the end of 2014, to the 2014 FCF value to get the total FCF in 2014.

$$\text{Total } FCF_{2014} = \$600,000 + \$10,300,000 = \$10,900,000$$

Step 3   Find the sum of the present values of the FCFs for 2010 through 2014 to determine the value of the entire company, V_C. This calculation is shown in Table 7.4, using present value interest factors, $PVIFs$, from Appendix Table A–2.

Step 4   Calculate the value of the common stock using Equation 7.6. Substituting into Equation 7.6 the value of the entire company, V_C, calculated in Step 3, and the market values of debt, V_D, and preferred stock, V_P, given in Table 7.3, yields the value of the common stock, V_S:

$$V_S = \$8,628,620 - \$3,100,000 - \$800,000 = \underline{\$4,728,620}$$

The value of Dewhurst's common stock is therefore estimated to be $4,728,620. By dividing this total by the 300,000 shares of common stock that the firm has outstanding, we get a common stock value of *$15.76 per share* ($4,728,620 ÷ 300,000).

| TABLE 7.4 | Calculation of the Value of the Entire Company for Dewhurst, Inc. |

| | | | Present value of FCF_t |
Year (t)	FCF_t (1)	$PVIF_{9\%,t}$ (2)	[(1) × (2)] (3)
2010	$ 400,000	0.917	$ 366,800
2011	450,000	0.842	378,900
2012	520,000	0.772	401,440
2013	560,000	0.708	396,480
2014	10,900,000^a	0.650	7,085,000
		Value of entire company, $V_C = \$8,628,620$	

^{a}This amount is the sum of the FCF_{2014} of $600,000 from Table 7.3 and the $10,300,000 value of the $FCF_{2015 \to \infty}$ calculated in Step 1.

It should now be clear that the free cash flow valuation model is consistent with the dividend valuation models presented earlier. The appeal of this approach is its focus on the free cash flow estimates rather than on forecast dividends, which are far more difficult to estimate, given that they are paid at the discretion of the firm's board. The more general nature of the free cash flow model is responsible for its growing popularity, particularly with CFOs and other financial managers.

Other Approaches to Common Stock Valuation

Many other approaches to common stock valuation exist. The more popular approaches include book value, liquidation value, and some type of price/earnings multiple.

book value per share
The amount per share of common stock that would be received if all of the firm's assets were *sold for their exact book (accounting) value* and the proceeds remaining after paying all liabilities (including preferred stock) were divided among the common stockholders.

Book Value

Book value per share is simply the amount per share of common stock that would be received if all of the firm's assets were *sold for their exact book (accounting) value* and the proceeds remaining after paying all liabilities (including preferred stock) were divided among the common stockholders. This method lacks sophistication and can be criticized on the basis of its reliance on historical balance sheet data. It ignores the firm's expected earnings potential and generally lacks any true relationship to the firm's value in the marketplace. Let us look at an example.

Example

At year-end 2009, Lamar Company's balance sheet shows total assets of $6 million, total liabilities (including preferred stock) of $4.5 million, and 100,000 shares of common stock outstanding. Its book value per share therefore would be

$$\frac{\$6,000,000 - \$4,500,000}{100,000 \text{ shares}} = \underline{\underline{\$15}} \text{ per share}$$

Because this value assumes that assets could be sold for their book value, it may not represent the minimum price at which shares are valued in the marketplace. As a matter of fact, although most stocks sell above book value, it is not unusual to find stocks selling below book value when investors believe either that assets are overvalued or that the firm's liabilities are understated.

liquidation value per share
The *actual amount* per share of common stock that would be received if all of the firm's assets were *sold for their market value*, liabilities (including preferred stock) were paid, and any remaining money were divided among the common stockholders.

Liquidation Value

Liquidation value per share is the *actual amount* per share of common stock that would be received if all of the firm's assets were *sold for their market value*, liabilities (including preferred stock) were paid, and any remaining money were divided among the common stockholders.[5] This measure is more realistic than book value—because it is based on the current market value of the firm's assets—but it still fails to consider the earning power of those assets. An example will illustrate.

---

5. In the event of liquidation, creditors' claims must be satisfied first, then those of the preferred stockholders. Anything left goes to common stockholders.

Example

Lamar Company found upon investigation that it could obtain only $5.25 million if it sold its assets today. The firm's liquidation value per share therefore would be

$$\frac{\$5,250,000 - \$4,500,000}{100,000 \text{ shares}} = \underline{\underline{\$7.50}} \text{ per share}$$

Ignoring liquidation expenses, this amount would be the firm's minimum value.

Price/Earnings (P/E) Multiples

price/earnings multiple approach
A popular technique used to estimate the firm's share value; calculated by multiplying the firm's expected earnings per share (EPS) by the average price/earnings (P/E) ratio for the industry.

The *price/earnings (P/E) ratio*, introduced in Chapter 2, reflects the amount investors are willing to pay for each dollar of earnings. The average P/E ratio in a particular industry can be used as the guide to a firm's value—if it is assumed that investors value the earnings of that firm in the same way they do the "average" firm in the industry. The **price/earnings multiple approach** is a popular technique used to estimate the firm's share value; it is calculated by multiplying the firm's expected earnings per share (EPS) by the average price/earnings (P/E) ratio for the industry. The average P/E ratio for the industry can be obtained from a source such as *Standard & Poor's Industrial Ratios*.

The P/E ratio valuation technique is a simple method of determining a stock's value and can be quickly calculated after firms make earnings announcements, which accounts for its popularity. Naturally, this has increased the demand for more frequent announcements or "guidance" regarding future earnings. Some firms feel that pre-earnings guidance creates additional costs and can lead to ethical issues, as discussed in the *Focus on Ethics* box on page 304.

The use of P/E multiples is especially helpful in valuing firms that are not publicly traded, whereas market price quotations can be used to value publicly traded firms. In any case, the price/earnings multiple approach is considered superior to the use of book or liquidation values because it considers *expected* earnings. An example will demonstrate the use of price/earnings multiples.

Personal Finance Example

Ann Perrier plans to use the price/earnings multiple approach to estimate the value of Lamar Company's stock, which she currently holds in her retirement account. She estimates that Lamar Company will earn $2.60 per share next year (2010). This expectation is based on an analysis of the firm's historical earnings trend and of expected economic and industry conditions. She finds the price/earnings (P/E) ratio for firms in the same industry to average 7. Multiplying Lamar's expected earnings per share (EPS) of $2.60 by this ratio gives her a value for the firm's shares of $18.20, assuming that investors will continue to value the average firm at 7 times its earnings.

So how much is Lamar Company's stock really worth? That's a trick question, because there's no one right answer. It is important to recognize that the answer depends on the assumptions made and the techniques used. Professional securities analysts typically use a variety of models and techniques to value stocks. For example, an analyst might use the constant-growth model, liquidation value, and a price/earnings (P/E) multiple to estimate the worth of a given stock. If the analyst feels comfortable with his or her estimates, the stock would be valued at no more than the largest estimate. Of course, should the firm's estimated liquidation value

IN PRACTICE

Focus on Ethics

Psst—Have You Heard Any Good Quarterly Earnings Forecasts Lately?

Corporate managers have long complained about the pressure to focus on the short term, and now business groups are coming to their defense. "The focus on the short term is a huge problem," says William Donaldson, former chairman of the Securities and Exchange Commission. "With all of the attention paid to quarterly performance, managers are taking their eyes off long-term strategic goals."

Donaldson, the U.S. Chamber of Commerce, and others believe that the best way to focus companies toward long-term goals is to do away with the practice of giving quarterly earnings guidance. In March 2007 the CFA Centre for Financial Market Integrity and the Business Roundtable Institute for Corporate Ethics proposed a template for quarterly earnings reports that would, in their view, obviate the need for earnings guidance.

Meanwhile, many companies are hesitant to give up issuing quarterly guidance. The practice of issuing earnings forecasts began in the early 1980s, a few years after the SEC's decision to allow companies to include forward-looking projections, provided they were accompanied by appropriate cautionary language. The result was what former SEC chairman Arthur Levitt once called a "game of winks and nods." Companies used earnings guidance to lower analysts' estimates; when the actual numbers came in higher, their stock prices jumped. The practice reached a fever pitch during the late 1990s when companies that missed the consensus earnings estimate, even by just a penny, saw their stock prices tumble.

One of the first companies to stop issuing earnings guidance was **Gillette**, in 2001. Others that abandoned quarterly guidance were **Coca-Cola, Intel,** and **McDonald's.** It became a trend. By 2005, just 61 percent of companies were offering quarterly projections to the public; according to the National Investor Relations Institute, the number declined to 52 percent in 2006.

Not everyone agrees with eliminating quarterly guidance. A survey conducted by New York University's Stern School of Business finance professor Baruch Lev, along with University of Florida professors Joel Houston and Jennifer Tucker, showed that companies that ended quarterly guidance reaped almost no benefit from doing so. Their study found no evidence that guidance-stoppers increased capital investments or research and development. So when should companies give up earnings guidance? According to Lev, they should do so only when they are not very good at predicting their earnings. "If you are not better than others at forecasting, then don't bother," he says.

■ *What are some of the real costs a company must face in preparing quarterly earnings guidance?*

Hint From an investor's perspective, the stock in this situation would be an attractive investment only if it could be purchased at a price below its liquidation value—which in an efficient market could never occur.

per share exceed its "going concern" value per share, estimated by using one of the valuation models (zero-, constant-, or variable-growth or free cash flow) or the P/E multiple approach, the firm would be viewed as being "worth more dead than alive." In such an event, the firm would lack sufficient earning power to justify its existence and should probably be liquidated.

REVIEW QUESTIONS

7–13 What does the *efficient-market hypothesis (EMH)* say about (**a**) securities prices, (**b**) their reaction to new information, and (**c**) investor opportunities to profit? What is the *behavioral finance* challenge to this hypothesis?

7–14 Describe, compare, and contrast the following common stock dividend valuation models: (**a**) zero-growth and (**b**) constant-growth.

7–15 Describe the *free cash flow valuation model* and explain how it differs from the dividend valuation models. What is the appeal of this model?

7–16 Explain each of the three other approaches to common stock valuation: **(a)** book value, **(b)** liquidation value, and **(c)** price/earnings (P/E) multiples. Which of these is considered the best?

7.4 | Decision Making and Common Stock Value

Valuation equations measure the stock value at a point in time based on expected return and risk. Any decisions of the financial manager that affect these variables can cause the value of the firm to change. Figure 7.4 depicts the relationship among financial decisions, return, risk, and stock value.

Changes in Expected Return

Assuming that economic conditions remain stable, any management action that would cause current and prospective stockholders to raise their dividend expectations should increase the firm's value. In Equation 7.4, we can see that P_0 will increase for any increase in D_1 or g. Any action of the financial manager that will increase the level of expected returns without changing risk (the required return) should be undertaken, because it will positively affect owners' wealth.

Example   Using the constant-growth model in an earlier example (on pages 298 and 299), we found Lamar Company to have a share value of $18.75. On the following day, the firm announced a major technological breakthrough that would revolutionize its industry. Current and prospective stockholders would not be expected to adjust their required return of 15%, but they would expect that future dividends will increase. Specifically, they expect that although the dividend next year, D_1, will remain at $1.50, the expected rate of growth thereafter will increase from 7% to 9%. If we substitute $D_1 = \$1.50$, $r_s = 0.15$, and $g = 0.09$ into Equation 7.4, the resulting share value is $25 [$1.50 ÷ (0.15 − 0.09)]. The increased value therefore resulted from the higher expected future dividends reflected in the increase in the growth rate.

FIGURE 7.4

Decision Making and Stock Value
Financial decisions, return, risk, and stock value

Decision Action by Financial Manager ┈┈▶ Effect on 1. Expected Return Measured by Expected Dividends, $D_1, D_2, ..., D_n$, and Expected Dividend Growth, g. 2. Risk Measured by the Required Return, r_s. ┈┈▶ Effect on Stock Value $P_0 = \dfrac{D_1}{r_s - g}$

Changes in Risk

Although r_s is defined as the required return, we know from Chapter 5 that it is directly related to the nondiversifiable risk, which can be measured by beta. The *capital asset pricing model (CAPM)* given in Equation 5.7 is restated here as Equation 7.7:

$$r_s = R_F + [b \times (r_m - R_F)] \tag{7.7}$$

With the risk-free rate, R_F, and the market return, r_m, held constant, the required return, r_s, depends directly on beta. Any action taken by the financial manager that increases risk (beta) will also increase the required return. In Equation 7.4, we can see that with everything else constant, an increase in the required return, r_s, will reduce share value, P_0. Likewise, a decrease in the required return will increase share value. Thus any action of the financial manager that increases risk contributes to a reduction in value, and any action that decreases risk contributes to an increase in value.

Example

Assume that Lamar Company's 15% required return resulted from a risk-free rate of 9%, a market return of 13%, and a beta of 1.50. Substituting into the capital asset pricing model, Equation 7.7, we get a required return, r_s, of 15%:

$$r_s = 9\% + [1.50 \times (13\% - 9\%)] = \underline{\underline{15\%}}$$

With this return, the firm's share value was calculated in an earlier example (on pages 298 and 299) to be $18.75.

Now imagine that the financial manager makes a decision that, without changing expected dividends, causes the firm's beta to increase to 1.75. Assuming that R_F and r_m remain at 9% and 13%, respectively, the required return will increase to 16% ($9\% + [1.75 \times (13\% - 9\%)]$) to compensate stockholders for the increased risk. Substituting $D_1 = \$1.50$, $r_s = 0.16$, and $g = 0.07$ into the valuation equation, Equation 7.4, results in a share value of $16.67 [$1.50 ÷ (0.16 − 0.07)]$. As expected, raising the required return, without any corresponding increase in expected return, causes the firm's stock value to decline. Clearly, the financial manager's action was not in the owners' best interest.

Combined Effect

A financial decision rarely affects return and risk independently; most decisions affect both factors. In terms of the measures presented, with an increase in risk (*b*), one would expect an increase in return (D_1 or *g*, or both), assuming that R_F and r_m remain unchanged. The net effect on value depends on the size of the changes in these variables.

Example

If we assume that the two changes illustrated for Lamar Company in the preceding examples occur simultaneously, key variable values would be $D_1 = \$1.50$, $r_s = 0.16$, and $g = 0.09$. Substituting into the valuation model, we obtain a share price of $21.43 [$1.50 ÷ (0.16 − 0.09)]$. The net result of the decision, which increased return (*g*, from 7% to 9%) as well as risk (*b*, from 1.50 to 1.75 and therefore r_s from 15% to 16%), is positive: The share price increased from $18.75 to $21.43. The decision appears to be in the best interest of the firm's owners, because it increases their wealth.

REVIEW QUESTIONS

7–17 Explain the linkages among financial decisions, return, risk, and stock value.

7–18 Assuming that all other variables remain unchanged, what impact would *each* of the following have on stock price? (**a**) The firm's beta increases. (**b**) The firm's required return decreases. (**c**) The dividend expected next year decreases. (**d**) The rate of growth in dividends is expected to increase.

Summary

Focus on Value

The price of each share of a firm's common stock is the value of each ownership interest. Although common stockholders typically have voting rights, which indirectly give them a say in management, their only significant right is their claim on the residual cash flows of the firm. This claim is subordinate to those of vendors, employees, customers, lenders, the government (for taxes), and preferred stockholders. The value of the common stockholders' claim is embodied in the cash flows they are entitled to receive from now to infinity. The present value of those expected cash flows is the firm's share value.

To determine this present value, forecast cash flows are discounted at a rate that reflects their risk. Riskier cash flows are discounted at higher rates, resulting in lower present values than less risky expected cash flows, which are discounted at lower rates. The value of the firm's common stock is therefore driven by its expected cash flows (returns) and risk (certainty of the expected cash flows).

In pursuing the firm's goal of **maximizing the stock price,** the financial manager must carefully consider the balance of return and risk associated with each proposal and must undertake only those actions that create value for owners. By focusing on value creation and by managing and monitoring the firm's cash flows and risk, the financial manager should be able to achieve the firm's goal of share price maximization.

Review of Learning Goals

Key definitions and formulas for this chapter are summarized in Table 7.5 (see page 308).

LG 1 **Differentiate between debt and equity capital.** Holders of equity capital (common and preferred stock) are owners of the firm. Typically, only common stockholders have a voice in management. Equity holders' claims on income and assets are secondary to creditors' claims, there is no maturity date, and dividends paid to stockholders are not tax-deductible.

TABLE 7.5	Summary of Key Valuation Definitions and Formulas for Common Stock

Definitions of variables

D_t = per-share dividend *expected* at the end of year t

FCF_t = free cash flow *expected* at the end of year t

g = constant rate of growth in dividends

g_1 = initial dividend growth rate (in variable-growth model)

g_2 = subsequent dividend growth rate (in variable-growth model)

r_a = weighted average cost of capital

r_s = required return on common stock

N = last year of initial growth period (in variable-growth model)

P_0 = value of common stock

V_C = value of the entire company

V_D = market value of all the firm's debt

V_P = market value of preferred stock

V_S = value of common stock

Valuation formulas

Basic stock value:

$$P_0 = \frac{D_1}{(1 + r_s)^1} + \frac{D_2}{(1 + r_s)^2} + \cdots + \frac{D_\infty}{(1 + r_s)^\infty} \qquad \text{[Equation 7.1]}$$

Common stock value:

  Zero-growth:

$$P_0 = \frac{D_1}{r_s} \text{ (also used to value preferred stock)} \qquad \text{[Equation 7.2]}$$

  Constant-growth:

$$P_0 = \frac{D_1}{r_s - g} \qquad \text{[Equation 7.4]}$$

Variable-growth: *See the book's website.*

FCF value of entire company:

$$V_C = \frac{FCF_1}{(1 + r_a)^1} + \frac{FCF_2}{(1 + r_a)^2} + \cdots + \frac{FCF_\infty}{(1 + r_a)^\infty} \qquad \text{[Equation 7.5]}$$

FCF common stock value:

$$V_S = V_C - V_D - V_P \qquad \text{[Equation 7.6]}$$

LG 2 **Discuss the rights, characteristics, and features of both common and preferred stock.** The common stock of a firm can be privately owned, closely owned, or publicly owned. It can be sold with or without a par value. Preemptive rights allow common stockholders to avoid dilution of ownership when new shares are issued. Not all shares authorized in the corporate charter are outstanding. If a firm has treasury stock, it will have issued more shares than are outstanding. Some firms have two or more classes of common stock that differ mainly in having unequal voting rights. Proxies transfer voting rights from one party to another. The decision to pay dividends to common stockholders is made by the firm's board of directors. Firms can issue stock in foreign markets. The stock of many foreign corporations is traded in U.S. markets in the form of American depositary shares (ADSs), which are backed by American depositary receipts (ADRs).

Preferred stockholders have preference over common stockholders with respect to the distribution of earnings and assets. They do not normally have voting privileges. Preferred stock issues may have certain restrictive covenants, cumulative dividends, a call feature, and a conversion feature.

LG 3 **Describe the process of issuing common stock, including venture capital, going public, and the investment banker, and interpreting stock quotations.** The initial nonfounder financing for business startups with attractive growth prospects typically comes from private equity investors. These investors can be either angel capitalists or venture capitalists (VCs). VCs usually invest in both early-stage and later-stage companies that they hope to take public so as to cash out their investments.

The first public issue of a firm's stock is called an initial public offering (IPO). The company selects an investment banker to advise it and to sell the securities. The lead investment banker may form a selling syndicate with other investment bankers. The IPO process includes getting SEC approval, promoting the offering to investors, and pricing the issue.

Stock quotations provide information on the closing (last) price at which the stock sold on the given day and the net price change from the prior trading day.

LG 4 **Understand the concept of market efficiency and basic common stock valuation using zero-growth and constant-growth models.** Market efficiency assumes that the quick reactions of rational investors to new information cause the market value of common stock to adjust quickly. The efficient-market hypothesis (EMH) suggests that securities are fairly priced, that they reflect fully all publicly available information, and that investors should therefore not waste time trying to find and capitalize on mispriced securities. Behavioral finance advocates challenge this hypothesis by arguing that emotion and other factors play a role in investment decisions.

The value of a share of common stock is the present value of all future dividends it is expected to provide over an infinite time horizon. Two dividend growth models—zero-growth and constant-growth—can be considered in common stock valuation. The most widely cited model is the constant-growth model. (A third model, the variable-growth model, allows for a change in the dividend growth rate.)

Discuss the free cash flow valuation model and the book value, liquidation value, and price/earnings (P/E) multiple approaches. The free cash flow valuation model values firms that have no dividend history, startups, or an operating unit or division of a larger public company. The model finds the value of the entire company by discounting the firm's expected free cash flow at its weighted average cost of capital. The common stock value is found by subtracting the market values of the firm's debt and preferred stock from the value of the entire company.

Book value per share is the amount per share of common stock that would be received if all of the firm's assets were *sold for their exact book (accounting) value* and the proceeds remaining after paying all liabilities (including preferred stock) were divided among the common stockholders. Liquidation value per share is the *actual amount* per share of common stock that would be received if all of the firm's assets were *sold for their market value*, liabilities (including preferred stock) were paid, and the remaining money were divided among the common stockholders. The price/earnings (P/E) multiple approach estimates stock value by multiplying the firm's expected earnings per share (EPS) by the average price/earnings (P/E) ratio for the industry.

Explain the relationships among financial decisions, return, risk, and the firm's value. In a stable economy, any action of the financial manager that increases the level of expected return without changing risk should increase share value; any action that reduces the level of expected return without changing risk should reduce share value. Similarly, any action that increases risk (required return) will reduce share value; any action that reduces risk will increase share value. An assessment of the combined effect of return and risk on stock value must be part of the financial decision-making process.

Self-Test Problems (Solutions in Appendix B)

 ST7–1 **Common stock valuation** Perry Motors' common stock currently pays an annual dividend of $1.80 per share. The required return on the common stock is 12%. Estimate the value of the common stock under each of the following assumptions about the dividend.
   a. Dividends are expected to grow at an annual rate of 0% to infinity.
   b. Dividends are expected to grow at a constant annual rate of 5% to infinity.

 ST7–2 **Free cash flow valuation** Erwin Footwear wishes to assess the value of its Active Shoe Division. This division has debt with a market value of $12,500,000 and no preferred stock. Its weighted average cost of capital is 10%. The Active Shoe Division's estimated free cash flow each year from 2010 through 2013 is given in the following table. Beyond 2013 to infinity, the firm expects its free cash flow to grow at 4% annually.

Year (*t*)	Free cash flow (*FCF_t*)
2010	$ 800,000
2011	1,200,000
2012	1,400,000
2013	1,500,000

a. Use the *free cash flow valuation model* to estimate the value of Erwin's entire Active Shoe Division.

b. Use your finding in part **a** along with the data provided above to find this division's common stock value.

c. If the Active Shoe Division as a public company will have 500,000 shares outstanding, use your finding in part **b** to calculate its value per share.

Warm-Up Exercises

A blue box (■) indicates exercises available in .

E7–1   A balance sheet balances assets with their sources of debt and equity financing. If a corporation has assets equal to $5.2 million and a debt ratio of 75.0%, how much debt does the corporation have on its books?

E7–2   Angina, Inc., has 5 million shares outstanding. The firm is considering issuing an additional 1 million shares. After selling these shares at their $20 per share offering price and netting 95% of the sale proceeds, the firm is obligated by an earlier agreement to sell an additional 250,000 shares at 90% of the offering price. In total, how much cash will the firm net from these stock sales?

E7–3   Figurate Industries has 750,000 shares of cumulative preferred stock outstanding. It has passed the last three quarterly dividends of $2.50 per share and now (at the end of the current quarter) wishes to distribute a total of $12 million to its shareholders. If Figurate has 3 million shares of common stock outstanding, how large a per-share common stock dividend will it be able to pay?

E7–4   Today the common stock of Gresham Technology closed at $24.60 per share, down $0.35 from yesterday. If the company has 4.6 million shares outstanding and annual earnings of $11.2 million, what is its P/E ratio today? What was its P/E ratio yesterday?

E7–5   Stacker Weight Loss currently pays an annual year-end dividend of $1.20 per share. It plans to increase this dividend by 5% next year and maintain it at the new level for the foreseeable future. If the required return on this firm's stock is 8%, what is the value of Stacker's stock?

E7–6   Brash Corporation initiated a new corporate strategy that fixes its annual dividend at $2.25 per share forever. Currently the risk-free rate is 4.5%, and Brash has a beta of 1.8. If the market return is 10.5%, what is the value of Brash's stock?

Problems

A blue box (■) indicates problems available in myfinancelab.

P7–1 Authorized and available shares   Aspin Corporation's charter authorizes issuance of 2,000,000 shares of common stock. Currently, 1,400,000 shares are outstanding and 100,000 shares are being held as treasury stock. The firm wishes to raise $48,000,000 for a plant expansion. Discussions with its investment bankers indicate that the sale of new common stock will net the firm $60 per share.

   a. What is the maximum number of new shares of common stock that the firm can sell without receiving further authorization from shareholders?

   b. Judging on the basis of the data given and your finding in part **a,** will the firm be able to raise the needed funds without receiving further authorization?

   c. What must the firm do to obtain authorization to issue more than the number of shares found in part **a?**

P7–2 Preferred dividends   Slater Lamp Manufacturing has an outstanding issue of preferred stock with an $80 par value and an 11% annual dividend.

   a. What is the annual dollar dividend? If it is paid quarterly, how much will be paid each quarter?

   b. If the preferred stock is *noncumulative* and the board of directors has passed the preferred dividend for the last 3 quarters, how much must be paid to preferred stockholders in the current quarter before dividends are paid to common stockholders?

   c. If the preferred stock is *cumulative* and the board of directors has passed the preferred dividend for the last 3 quarters, how much must be paid to preferred stockholders in the current quarter before dividends are paid to common stockholders?

P7–3 Preferred dividends   In each case in the following table, how many dollars of preferred dividends per share must be paid to preferred stockholders in the current period before common stock dividends are paid?

Case	Type	Par value	Dividend per share per period	Periods of dividends passed
A	Cumulative	$ 80	$ 5	2
B	Noncumulative	110	8%	3
C	Noncumulative	100	$11	1
D	Cumulative	60	8.5%	4
E	Cumulative	90	9%	0

P7–4 Convertible preferred stock   Valerian Corp. convertible preferred stock has a fixed conversion ratio of 5 common shares per 1 share of preferred stock. The preferred stock pays a dividend of $10.00 per share per year. The common stock currently sells for $20.00 per share and pays a dividend of $1.00 per share per year.

   a. Judging on the basis of the conversion ratio and the price of the common shares, what is the current conversion value of each preferred share?

b. If the preferred shares are selling at $96.00 each, should an investor convert the preferred shares to common shares?

c. What factors might cause an investor not to convert from preferred to common stock?

PERSONAL FINANCE PROBLEM

P7–5 **Stock quotation**   Assume that the following quote for the Advanced Business Machines stock (traded on the NYSE) was found in the Thursday, December 14, issue of the *Wall Street Journal*.

AdvBusMach   ABM   81.75   1.63

Given this information, answer the following questions:

a. On what day did the trading activity occur?

b. At what price did the stock sell at the end of the day on Wednesday, December 13?

c. What is the last price at which the stock traded on the day quoted?

d. How much, if any, of a change in stock price took place between the day quoted and the day before? At what price did the stock close on the day before?

P7–6 **Common stock valuation—Zero growth**   Scotto Manufacturing is a mature firm in the machine tool component industry. The firm's most recent common stock dividend was $2.40 per share. Because of its maturity as well as its stable sales and earnings, the firm's management feels that dividends will remain at the current level for the foreseeable future.

a. If the required return is 12%, what will be the value of Scotto's common stock?

b. If the firm's risk as perceived by market participants suddenly increases, causing the required return to rise to 20%, what will be the common stock value?

c. Judging on the basis of your findings in parts **a** and **b,** what impact does risk have on value? Explain.

PERSONAL FINANCE PROBLEM

P7–7 **Common stock value—Zero growth**   Kelsey Drums, Inc., is a well-established supplier of fine percussion instruments to orchestras all over the United States. The company's class A common stock has paid a dividend of $5.00 per share per year for the last 15 years. Management expects to continue to pay at that amount for the foreseeable future. Sally Talbot purchased 100 shares of Kelsey class A common 10 years ago at a time when the required rate of return for the stock was 16%. She wants to sell her shares today. The current required rate of return for the stock is 12%. How much capital gain or loss will Sally have on her shares?

P7–8 **Preferred stock valuation**   Jones Design wishes to estimate the value of its outstanding preferred stock. The preferred issue has an $80 par value and pays an annual dividend of $6.40 per share. Similar-risk preferred stocks are currently earning a 9.3% annual rate of return.

a. What is the market value of the outstanding preferred stock?

b. If an investor purchases the preferred stock at the value calculated in part **a,** how much does she gain or lose per share if she sells the stock when the required return on similar-risk preferreds has risen to 10.5%? Explain.

P7–9 **Common stock value—Constant growth**   Use the constant-growth model (Gordon model) to find the value of each firm shown in the following table.

Firm	Dividend expected next year	Dividend growth rate	Required return
A	$1.20	8%	13%
B	4.00	5	15
C	0.65	10	14
D	6.00	8	9
E	2.25	8	20

 P7–10 **Common stock value—Constant growth**   McCracken Roofing, Inc., common stock paid a dividend of $1.20 per share last year. The company expects earnings and dividends to grow at a rate of 5% per year for the foreseeable future.
   a. What required rate of return for this stock would result in a price per share of $28?
   b. If McCracken expects both earnings and dividends to grow at an annual rate of 10%, what required rate of return would result in a price per share of $28?

PERSONAL FINANCE PROBLEM
 P7–11 **Common stock value—Constant growth**   Elk County Telephone has paid the dividends shown in the following table over the past 6 years.

Year	Dividend per share
2009	$2.87
2008	2.76
2007	2.60
2006	2.46
2005	2.37
2004	2.25

The firm's dividend per share next year is expected to be $3.02.
   a. If you can earn 13% on similar-risk investments, what is the most you would be willing to pay per share?
   b. If you can earn only 10% on similar-risk investments, what is the most you would be willing to pay per share?
   c. Compare and contrast your findings in parts a and b, and discuss the impact of changing risk on share value.

PERSONAL FINANCE PROBLEM
 P7–12 **Common stock value—Both growth models**   You are evaluating the potential purchase of a small business currently generating $42,500 of after-tax cash flow $(D_0 = \$42,500)$. On the basis of a review of similar-risk investment opportunities, you must earn an 18% rate of return on the proposed purchase. Because you are relatively uncertain about future cash flows, you decide to estimate the firm's value using two possible assumptions about the growth rate of cash flows.
   a. What is the firm's value if cash flows are expected to grow at an annual rate of 0% from now to infinity?

b. What is the firm's value if cash flows are expected to grow at a constant annual rate of 7% from now to infinity?

P7–13 **Free cash flow valuation**   Nabor Industries is considering going public but is unsure of a fair offering price for the company. Before hiring an investment banker to assist in making the public offering, managers at Nabor have decided to make their own estimate of the firm's common stock value. The firm's CFO has gathered data for performing the valuation using the free cash flow valuation model.

The firm's weighted average cost of capital is 11%, and it has $1,500,000 of debt at market value and $400,000 of preferred stock at its assumed market value. The estimated free cash flows over the next 5 years, 2010 through 2014, are given below. Beyond 2014 to infinity, the firm expects its free cash flow to grow by 3% annually.

Year (t)	Free cash flow (FCF$_t$)
2010	$200,000
2011	250,000
2012	310,000
2013	350,000
2014	390,000

a. Estimate the value of Nabor Industries' entire company by using the *free cash flow valuation model.*
b. Use your finding in part **a,** along with the data provided above, to find Nabor Industries' common stock value.
c. If the firm plans to issue 200,000 shares of common sock, what is its estimated value per share?

PERSONAL FINANCE PROBLEM

P7–14 **Using the free cash flow valuation model to price an IPO**   Assume that you have an opportunity to buy the stock of CoolTech, Inc., an IPO being offered for $12.50 per share. Although you are very much interested in owning the company, you are concerned about whether it is fairly priced. To determine the value of the shares, you have decided to apply the free cash flow valuation model to the firm's financial data that you've developed from a variety of data sources. The key values you have compiled are summarized in the following table.

Year (t)	Free cash flow FCF$_t$	Other data
2010	$ 700,000	Growth rate of FCF, beyond 2013 to infinity = 2%
2011	800,000	Weighted average cost of capital = 8%
2012	950,000	Market value of all debt = $2,700,000
2013	1,100,000	Market value of preferred stock = $1,000,000
		Number of shares of common stock outstanding = 1,100,000

a. Use the *free cash flow valuation model* to estimate CoolTech's common stock value per share.

b. Judging on the basis of your finding in part **a** and the stock's offering price, should you buy the stock?

c. Upon further analysis, you find that the growth rate in FCF beyond 2013 will be 3% rather than 2%. What effect would this finding have on your responses in parts **a** and **b**?

P7–15 **Book and liquidation value**   The balance sheet for Gallinas Industries is as follows.

Gallinas Industries Balance Sheet December 31			
Assets		**Liabilities and Stockholders' Equity**	
Cash	$ 40,000	Accounts payable	$100,000
Marketable securities	60,000	Notes payable	30,000
Accounts receivable	120,000	Accrued wages	30,000
Inventories	160,000	Total current liabilities	$160,000
Total current assets	$380,000	Long-term debt	$180,000
Land and buildings (net)	$150,000	Preferred stock	$ 80,000
Machinery and equipment	250,000	Common stock (10,000 shares)	260,000
Total fixed assets (net)	$400,000	Retained earnings	100,000
Total assets	$780,000	Total liabilities and stockholders' equity	$780,000

Additional information with respect to the firm is available:
(1) Preferred stock can be liquidated at book value.
(2) Accounts receivable and inventories can be liquidated at 90% of book value.
(3) The firm has 10,000 shares of common stock outstanding.
(4) All interest and dividends are currently paid up.
(5) Land and buildings can be liquidated at 130% of book value.
(6) Machinery and equipment can be liquidated at 70% of book value.
(7) Cash and marketable securities can be liquidated at book value.

Given this information, answer the following:
a. What is Gallinas Industries' *book value per share?*
b. What is its *liquidation value per share?*
c. Compare, contrast, and discuss the values found in parts **a** and **b**.

P7–16 **Valuation with price/earnings multiples**   For each of the firms shown in the following table, use the data given to estimate its common stock value employing price/earnings (P/E) multiples.

Firm	Expected EPS	Price/earnings multiple
A	$3.00	6.2
B	4.50	10.0
C	1.80	12.6
D	2.40	8.9
E	5.10	15.0

P7–17 Management action and stock value   REH Corporation's most recent dividend was $3 per share, its expected annual rate of dividend growth is 5%, and the required return is now 15%. A variety of proposals are being considered by management to redirect the firm's activities. Determine the impact on share price for each of the following proposed actions, and indicate the best alternative.
a. Do nothing, which will leave the key financial variables unchanged.
b. Invest in a new machine that will increase the dividend growth rate to 6% and lower the required return to 14%.
c. Eliminate an unprofitable product line, which will increase the dividend growth rate to 7% and raise the required return to 17%.
d. Merge with another firm, which will reduce the growth rate to 4% and raise the required return to 16%.
e. Acquire a subsidiary operation from another manufacturer. The acquisition should increase the dividend growth rate to 8% and increase the required return to 17%.

  P7–18 Integrative—Valuation and CAPM formulas   Given the following information for the stock of Foster Company, calculate its beta.

Current price per share of common	$50.00
Expected dividend per share next year	$ 3.00
Constant annual dividend growth rate	9%
Risk-free rate of return	7%
Return on market portfolio	10%

  P7–19 Integrative—Risk and valuation   Giant Enterprises has a beta of 1.20, the risk-free rate of return is currently 10%, and the market return is 14%. The company, which plans to pay a dividend of $2.60 per share in the coming year, anticipates that its future dividends will increase at an annual rate consistent with that experienced over the 2003–2009 period, when the following dividends were paid:

Year	Dividend per share
2009	$2.45
2008	2.28
2007	2.10
2006	1.95
2005	1.82
2004	1.80
2003	1.73

a. Use the capital asset pricing model (CAPM) to determine the required return on Giant's stock.
b. Using the constant-growth model and your finding in part a, estimate the value of Giant's stock.
c. Explain what effect, if any, a decrease in beta would have on the value of Giant's stock.

  P7–20 Integrative—Valuation and CAPM   Hamlin Steel Company wishes to determine the value of Craft Foundry, a firm that it is considering acquiring for cash. Hamlin wishes to use the capital asset pricing model (CAPM) to determine the applicable

To Do

a. Given the data above, calculate the present value of this security. Use the constant-growth model (Equation 7.5) to find the stock value.

b. One year later, your broker offers to sell you additional shares of Azure at $73. The most recent dividend paid was $3.21, and the expected growth rate for earnings remains at 7%. To determine the required rate of return, you decide to use the capital asset pricing model (CAPM). The risk-free rate, R_F, is currently 5.25%; the market return, r_m, is 11.55%; and the stock's beta, b_{Azure}, is 1.07. Substitute the appropriate values into the CAPM (Equation 5.8) to determine the firm's current required return, r_{Azure}.

c. Applying Equation 7.5, determine the value of the stock using the new dividend and required return from part **b.**

d. Given your calculation in part **c,** would you buy the additional shares from your broker at $73 per share? Explain.

e. Given your calculation in part **c,** would you sell your old shares for $73? Explain.

Web Exercise

Go to the book's companion website at **www.prenhall.com/gitman** to find the Web Exercise for this chapter.

> Remember to check the book's website at **www.prenhall.com/gitman** to find additional resources, including Web Exercises and a Web Case.

Part Three
Long-Term Investment Decisions

Chapters in This Part

8

Capital Budgeting Cash Flows

Why This Chapter Matters to You

Learning Goals

LG 1 Understand the key motives for capital expenditure and the steps in the capital budgeting process.

LG 2 Define basic capital budgeting terminology.

LG 3 Discuss relevant cash flows, expansion versus replacement decisions, sunk costs and opportunity costs, and international capital budgeting.

LG 4 Calculate the initial investment associated with a proposed capital expenditure.

LG 5 Find the relevant operating cash inflows associated with a proposed capital expenditure.

LG 6 Determine the terminal cash flow associated with a proposed capital expenditure.

Before committing resources to expand, replace, or renew fixed assets or to undertake other types of long-term investments, firms carefully estimate and analyze the expected costs and benefits associated with these expenditures. This evaluation and selection process is called capital budgeting. We address this important topic in finance in two chapters. This chapter describes important aspects of the steps in the capital budgeting decision process and explains how the key cash flows that are inputs to it are developed.

8.1 | Capital Budgeting Decision Process

capital budgeting
The process of evaluating and selecting long-term investments that are consistent with the firm's goal of maximizing owner wealth.

Long-term investments represent sizable outlays of funds that commit a firm to some course of action. Consequently, the firm needs procedures to analyze and properly select its long-term investments. It must be able to measure cash flows and apply appropriate decision techniques. As time passes, fixed assets may become obsolete or may require an overhaul; at these points, too, financial decisions may be required. **Capital budgeting** is the process of evaluating and selecting long-term investments that are consistent with the firm's goal of maximizing owner wealth. Firms typically make a variety of long-term investments, but the most common for the manufacturing firm is in *fixed assets*, which include property (land), plant, and equipment. These assets, often referred to as *earning assets*, generally provide the basis for the firm's earning power and value.

Because firms treat capital budgeting (investment) and financing decisions *separately*, Chapters 8 and 9 concentrate on fixed-asset acquisition without regard to the specific method of financing used. We begin by discussing the motives for capital expenditure.

Motives for Capital Expenditure

capital expenditure
An outlay of funds by the firm that is expected to produce benefits over a period of time *greater than* 1 year.

operating expenditure
An outlay of funds by the firm resulting in benefits received *within* 1 year.

A **capital expenditure** is an outlay of funds by the firm that is expected to produce benefits over a period of time *greater than* 1 year. An **operating expenditure** is an outlay resulting in benefits received *within* 1 year. Fixed-asset outlays are capital expenditures, but not all capital expenditures are classified as fixed assets. A $60,000 outlay for a new machine with a usable life of 15 years is a capital expenditure that would appear as a fixed asset on the firm's balance sheet. A $60,000 outlay for an advertising campaign that is expected to produce benefits over a long period is also a capital expenditure, but would rarely be shown as a fixed asset.

Companies make capital expenditures for many reasons. The basic motives for capital expenditures are to expand operations, replace or renew fixed assets, or to obtain some other, less tangible benefit over a long period. Table 8.1 (see page 324) briefly describes the key motives for making capital expenditures.

Steps in the Process

capital budgeting process
Five distinct but interrelated steps: *proposal generation, review and analysis, decision making, implementation,* and *follow-up.*

The **capital budgeting process** consists of five distinct but interrelated steps.

1. *Proposal generation.* Proposals arc made at all levels within a business organization and are reviewed by finance personnel. Proposals that require large outlays are more carefully scrutinized than less costly ones.

TABLE 8.1	Key Motives for Making Capital Expenditures
Motive	Description
Expansion	The most common motive for a capital expenditure is to expand the level of operations—usually through acquisition of fixed assets. A growing firm often needs to acquire new fixed assets rapidly, as in the purchase of property and plant facilities.
Replacement or renewal	As a firm's growth slows and it reaches maturity, most capital expenditures will be made to increase efficiency by replacing or renewing obsolete or worn-out assets. Renewal may involve rebuilding, overhauling, or retrofitting an existing fixed asset. Each time a machine requires a major repair, the outlay for the repair should be compared to the outlay to replace the machine and the benefits of replacement.
Other purposes	Some capital expenditures do not result in the acquisition or transformation of tangible fixed assets. Instead, they involve a long-term commitment of funds in expectation of a future return. These expenditures include outlays for advertising campaigns, research and development, management consulting, and new products.

2. *Review and analysis.* Formal review and analysis is performed to assess the appropriateness of proposals and evaluate their economic viability. Once the analysis is complete, a summary report is submitted to decision makers.
3. *Decision making.* Firms typically delegate capital expenditure decision making on the basis of dollar limits. Generally, the board of directors must authorize expenditures beyond a certain amount. Often plant managers are given authority to make decisions necessary to keep the production line moving.
4. *Implementation.* Following approval, expenditures are made and projects implemented. Expenditures for a large project often occur in phases.
5. *Follow-up.* Results are monitored, and actual costs and benefits are compared with those that were expected. Action may be required if actual outcomes differ from projected ones.

Each step in the process is important. Review and analysis and decision making (Steps 2 and 3) consume the majority of time and effort, however. Follow-up (Step 5) is an important but often ignored step aimed at allowing the firm to improve the accuracy of its cash flow estimates continuously. Because of their fundamental importance, this and the following chapters give primary consideration to review and analysis and to decision making.

Personal Finance Example   Individuals can approach the acquisition of major assets much as do corporations. Using the five-step process:

1. A personal financial plan or a special situation initiates the proposed asset purchase. For example, your personal financial plan specifies a new car purchase in 2010.
2. Review and analyze the proposed asset purchase to isolate attractive alternatives in terms of features and costs. For the car purchase, you would shop for cars with the desired features and costs that are consistent with the budgeted amount.
3. Compare the features and costs of the alternative assets and choose the preferred alternative. That is, you would decide which car you are going to buy.
4. Make the purchase. This would involve arranging financing/payment for the car, possibly negotiating a trade-in price, closing the transaction, and taking delivery of the new car.

5. Compare the actual asset performance to its expected performance. You would assess how well the new car meets your expectations. If the actual performance fails to meet expectations, you might consider new alternatives (e.g., trade in the car).

Basic Terminology

Before we develop the concepts, techniques, and practices related to the capital budgeting process, we need to explain some basic terminology. In addition, we will present some key assumptions that are used to simplify the discussion in the remainder of this chapter and in Chapter 9.

Independent versus Mutually Exclusive Projects

independent projects
Projects whose cash flows are unrelated or independent of one another; the acceptance of one *does not eliminate* the others from further consideration.

mutually exclusive projects
Projects that compete with one another, so that the acceptance of one *eliminates* from further consideration all other projects that serve a similar function.

The two most common types of projects are (1) independent projects and (2) mutually exclusive projects. **Independent projects** are those whose cash flows are unrelated or independent of one another; the acceptance of one *does not eliminate* the others from further consideration. **Mutually exclusive projects** are those that have the same function and therefore compete with one another. The acceptance of one *eliminates* from further consideration all other projects that serve a similar function. For example, a firm in need of increased production capacity could obtain it by (1) expanding its plant, (2) acquiring another company, or (3) contracting with another company for production. Clearly, accepting any one option eliminates the need for either of the others.

Unlimited Funds versus Capital Rationing

unlimited funds
The financial situation in which a firm is able to accept all independent projects that provide an acceptable return.

capital rationing
The financial situation in which a firm has only a fixed number of dollars available for capital expenditures, and numerous projects compete for these dollars.

The availability of funds for capital expenditures affects the firm's decisions. If a firm has **unlimited funds** for investment, making capital budgeting decisions is quite simple: All independent projects that will provide an acceptable return can be accepted. Typically, though, firms operate under **capital rationing** instead. This means that they have only a fixed number of dollars available for capital expenditures and that numerous projects will compete for these dollars. Procedures for dealing with capital rationing are presented in Chapter 9. The discussions that follow here and in the following chapter assume unlimited funds.

Accept–Reject versus Ranking Approaches

accept–reject approach
The evaluation of capital expenditure proposals to determine whether they meet the firm's minimum acceptance criterion.

ranking approach
The ranking of capital expenditure projects on the basis of some predetermined measure, such as the rate of return.

Two basic approaches to capital budgeting decisions are available. The **accept–reject approach** involves evaluating capital expenditure proposals to determine whether they meet the firm's minimum acceptance criterion. This approach can be used when the firm has unlimited funds, as a preliminary step when evaluating mutually exclusive projects, or in a situation in which capital must be rationed. In these cases, only acceptable projects should be considered.

The second method, the **ranking approach**, involves ranking projects on the basis of some predetermined measure, such as the rate of return. The project with the highest return is ranked first, and the project with the lowest return is ranked last. Only acceptable projects should be ranked. Ranking is useful in selecting the "best" of a group of mutually exclusive projects and in evaluating projects with a view to capital rationing.

installed cost of new asset
The *cost of new asset* plus its *installation costs;* equals the asset's depreciable value.

after-tax proceeds from sale of old asset
The difference between the old asset's sale proceeds and any applicable taxes or tax refunds related to its sale.

proceeds from sale of old asset
The cash inflows, net of any *removal* or *cleanup costs*, resulting from the sale of an existing asset.

tax on sale of old asset
Tax that depends on the relationship between the old asset's sale price and *book value*, and on existing government tax rules.

book value
The strict accounting value of an asset, calculated by subtracting its accumulated depreciation from its installed cost.

any added costs that are necessary to place an asset into operation. The Internal Revenue Service (IRS) requires the firm to add installation costs to the purchase price of an asset to determine its depreciable value, which is expensed over a period of years. The **installed cost of new asset,** calculated by adding the *cost of new asset* to its *installation costs*, equals its depreciable value.

After-Tax Proceeds from Sale of Old Asset

Table 8.2 shows that the **after-tax proceeds from sale of old asset** decrease the firm's initial investment in the new asset. These proceeds are the difference between the old asset's sale proceeds and any applicable taxes or tax refunds related to its sale. The **proceeds from sale of old asset** are the net cash inflows it provides. This amount is net of any costs incurred in the process of removing the asset. Included in these *removal costs* are *cleanup costs*, such as those related to removal and disposal of chemical and nuclear wastes. These costs may not be trivial.

The proceeds from the sale of an old asset are normally subject to some type of tax.[2] This **tax on sale of old asset** depends on the relationship between its sale price and *book value*, and on existing government tax rules.

Book Value

The **book value** of an asset is its strict accounting value. It can be calculated by using the following equation:

$$\text{Book value} = \text{Installed cost of asset} - \text{Accumulated depreciation} \quad (8.1)$$

Example

Hudson Industries, a small electronics company, 2 years ago acquired a machine tool with an installed cost of $100,000. The asset was being depreciated under MACRS using a 5-year recovery period.[3] Table 3.2 (on page 98) shows that under MACRS for a 5-year recovery period, 20% and 32% of the installed cost would be depreciated in years 1 and 2, respectively. In other words, 52% (20% + 32%) of the $100,000 cost, or $52,000 (0.52 × $100,000), would represent the accumulated depreciation at the end of year 2. Substituting into Equation 8.1, we get

$$\text{Book value} = \$100,000 - \$52,000 = \underline{\underline{\$48,000}}$$

The book value of Hudson's asset at the end of year 2 is therefore $48,000.

Basic Tax Rules

Three potential tax situations can occur when a firm sells an asset. These situations depend on the relationship between the asset's sale price and its book value. The two key forms of taxable income and their associated tax treatments are

---

2. A brief discussion of the tax treatment of ordinary and capital gains income was presented in Chapter 1. Because corporate capital gains and ordinary income are taxed at the same rate, for convenience, we do not differ between them in the following discussions.

3. For a review of MACRS, see Chapter 3. Under current tax law, most manufacturing equipment has a 7-year recovery period, as noted in Table 3.1 (on page 97). Using this recovery period results in 8 years of depreciation, which unnecessarily complicates examples and problems. To simplify, *manufacturing equipment is treated as a 5-year asset in this and the following chapters.*

TABLE 8.3	**Tax Treatment on Sales of Assets**		
Form of taxable income	Definition	Tax treatment	Assumed tax rate
Gain on sale of asset	Portion of the sale price that is *greater than* book value.	All gains above book value are taxed as ordinary income.	40%
Loss on sale of asset	Amount by which sale price is *less than* book value.	If the asset is depreciable and used in business, loss is deducted from ordinary income.	40% of loss is a tax savings
		If the asset is *not* depreciable or is *not* used in business, loss is deductible only against capital gains.	40% of loss is a tax savings

defined and summarized in Table 8.3. The assumed tax rates used throughout this text are noted in the final column. There are three possible tax situations. The asset may be sold (1) for more than its book value, (2) for its book value, or (3) for less than its book value. An example will illustrate.

Example

The old asset purchased 2 years ago for $100,000 by Hudson Industries has a current book value of $48,000. What will happen if the firm now decides to sell the asset and replace it? The tax consequences depend on the sale price. Figure 8.5 (see page 334) depicts the taxable income resulting from four possible sale prices in light of the asset's initial purchase price of $100,000 and its current book value of $48,000. The taxable consequences of each of these sale prices are described below.

The sale of the asset for more than its book value   If Hudson sells the old asset for $110,000, it realizes a gain of $62,000 ($110,000 − $48,000). Technically this gain is made up of two parts—a capital gain and **recaptured depreciation,** which is the portion of the sale price that is above book value and below the initial purchase price. For Hudson, the capital gain is $10,000 ($110,000 sale price − $100,000 initial purchase price); recaptured depreciation is $52,000 (the $100,000 initial purchase price − $48,000 book value).[4]

recaptured depreciation
The portion of an asset's sale price that is above its book value and below its initial purchase price.

Both the $10,000 capital gain and the $52,000 recaptured depreciation are shown under the $110,000 sale price in Figure 8.5. The total gain above book value of $62,000 is taxed as ordinary income at the 40% rate, resulting in taxes of $24,800 (0.40 × $62,000). These taxes should be used in calculating the initial investment in the new asset, using the format in Table 8.2. In effect, the taxes raise the amount of the firm's initial investment in the new asset by reducing the proceeds from the sale of the old asset.

If Hudson instead sells the old asset for $70,000, it experiences a gain above book value (in the form of *recaptured depreciation*) of $22,000 ($70,000 − $48,000), as shown under the $70,000 sale price in Figure 8.5. This gain is taxed as ordinary income. Because the firm is assumed to be in the 40% tax bracket,

---

4. Although the current tax law requires corporate capital gains to be treated as ordinary income, the structure for corporate capital gains is retained under the law to facilitate a rate differential in the likely event of future tax revisions. For clarity and convenience, this distinction is *not* made throughout the text discussions.

FIGURE 8.5   **Taxable Income from Sale of Asset**

Taxable income from sale of asset at various sale prices for Hudson Industries

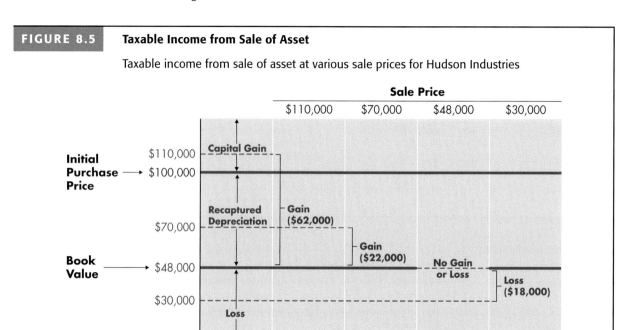

the taxes on the $22,000 gain are $8,800 (0.40 × $22,000). This amount in taxes should be used in calculating the initial investment in the new asset.

The sale of the asset for its book value   If the asset is sold for $48,000, its book value, the firm breaks even. There is no gain or loss, as shown under the $48,000 sale price in Figure 8.5. Because *no tax results from selling an asset for its book value*, there is no tax effect on the initial investment in the new asset.

The sale of the asset for less than its book value   If Hudson sells the asset for $30,000, it experiences a loss of $18,000 ($48,000 − $30,000), as shown under the $30,000 sale price in Figure 8.5. If this is a depreciable asset used in the business, the firm may use the loss to offset ordinary operating income. If the asset is *not* depreciable or is *not* used in the business, the firm can use the loss only to offset capital gains. In either case, the loss will save the firm $7,200 (0.40 × $18,000) in taxes. And, if current operating earnings or capital gains are not sufficient to offset the loss, the firm may be able to apply these losses to prior or future years' taxes.[5]

Change in Net Working Capital

net working capital
The amount by which a firm's current assets exceed its current liabilities.

Net working capital is the amount by which a firm's current assets exceed its current liabilities. This topic is treated in depth in Chapter 13; at this point it is important to note that changes in net working capital often accompany capital

---

5. The tax law provides detailed procedures for using *tax loss carrybacks/carryforwards*. Application of such procedures to capital budgeting is beyond the scope of this text, and they are therefore ignored in subsequent discussions.

expenditure decisions. If a firm acquires new machinery to expand its level of operations, it will experience an increase in levels of cash, accounts receivable, inventories, accounts payable, and accruals. These increases result from the need for more cash to support expanded operations, more accounts receivable and inventories to support increased sales, and more accounts payable and accruals to support increased outlays made to meet expanded product demand. As noted in Chapter 3, increases in cash, accounts receivable, and inventories are *outflows of cash*, whereas increases in accounts payable and accruals are *inflows of cash*.

change in net working capital
The difference between a change in current assets and a change in current liabilities.

The difference between the change in current assets and the change in current liabilities is the **change in net working capital.** Generally, current assets increase by more than current liabilities, resulting in an increased investment in net working capital. This increased investment is treated as an initial outflow. If the change in net working capital were negative, it would be shown as an initial inflow. The change in net working capital—regardless of whether it is an increase or a decrease—*is not taxable* because it merely involves a net buildup or net reduction of current accounts.

> *Example*

Danson Company, a metal products manufacturer, is contemplating expanding its operations. Financial analysts expect that the changes in current accounts summarized in Table 8.4 will occur and will be maintained over the life of the expansion. Current assets are expected to increase by $22,000, and current liabilities are expected to increase by $9,000, resulting in a $13,000 increase in net working capital. In this case, the change will represent an increased net working capital investment and will be treated as a cash outflow in calculating the initial investment.

Calculating the Initial Investment

A variety of tax and other considerations enter into the initial investment calculation. The following example illustrates calculation of the initial investment according to the format in Table 8.2.

TABLE 8.4	Calculation of Change in Net Working Capital for Danson Company	
Current account	Change in balance	
Cash	+ $ 4,000	
Accounts receivable	+ 10,000	
Inventories	+ 8,000	
(1) Current assets		+$22,000
Accounts payable	+$ 7,000	
Accruals	+ 2,000	
(2) Current liabilities		+ 9,000
Change in net working capital [(1) − (2)]		+$13,000

Example

Powell Corporation, a large, diversified manufacturer of aircraft components, is trying to determine the initial investment required to replace an old machine with a new, more sophisticated model. The proposed machine's purchase price is $380,000, and an additional $20,000 will be necessary to install it. It will be depreciated under MACRS using a 5-year recovery period. The present (old) machine was purchased 3 years ago at a cost of $240,000 and was being depreciated under MACRS using a 5-year recovery period. The firm has found a buyer willing to pay $280,000 for the present machine and to remove it at the buyer's expense. The firm expects that a $35,000 increase in current assets and an $18,000 increase in current liabilities will accompany the replacement; these changes will result in a $17,000 ($35,000 − $18,000) *increase* in net working capital. The firm pays taxes at a rate of 40%.

The only component of the initial investment calculation that is difficult to obtain is taxes. The book value of the present machine can be found by using the depreciation percentages from Table 3.2 (on page 98) of 20%, 32%, and 19% for years 1, 2, and 3, respectively. The resulting *book value is $69,600* ($240,000 − [(0.20 + 0.32 + 0.19) × $240,000]). A *gain* of $210,400 ($280,000 − $69,600) is realized on the sale. The total taxes on the gain are $84,160 (0.40 × $210,400). These taxes must be subtracted from the $280,000 sale price of the present machine to calculate the after-tax proceeds from its sale.

Substituting the relevant amounts into the format in Table 8.2 results in an initial investment of $221,160, which represents the net cash outflow required at time zero.

Installed cost of proposed machine		
Cost of proposed machine	$380,000	
+ Installation costs	20,000	
Total installed cost—proposed (depreciable value)		$400,000
− **After-tax proceeds from sale of present machine**		
Proceeds from sale of present machine	$280,000	
− Tax on sale of present machine	84,160	
Total after-tax proceeds—present		195,840
+ **Change in net working capital**		17,000
Initial investment		$221,160

REVIEW QUESTIONS

8–9 Explain how each of the following inputs is used to calculate the *initial investment:* (**a**) cost of new asset, (**b**) installation costs, (**c**) proceeds from sale of old asset, (**d**) tax on sale of old asset, and (**e**) change in net working capital.

8–10 How is the *book value* of an asset calculated? What are the two key forms of taxable income?

8–11 What three tax situations may result from the sale of an asset that is being replaced?

8–12 Referring to the basic format for calculating initial investment, explain how a firm would determine the *depreciable value* of the new asset.

8.4 | Finding the Operating Cash Inflows

The benefits expected from a capital expenditure or "project" are embodied in its *operating cash inflows*, which are *incremental after-tax cash inflows*. In this section we use the income statement format to develop clear definitions of the terms *after-tax*, *cash inflows*, and *incremental*.

Interpreting the Term After-Tax

Benefits expected to result from proposed capital expenditures must be measured on an *after-tax basis*, because the firm will not have the use of any benefits until it has satisfied the government's tax claims. These claims depend on the firm's taxable income, so deducting taxes *before* making comparisons between proposed investments is necessary for consistency when evaluating capital expenditure alternatives.

Interpreting the Term Cash Inflows

All benefits expected from a proposed project must be measured on a *cash flow basis*. Cash inflows represent dollars that can be spent, not merely "accounting profits." A simple accounting technique for converting after-tax net profits into operating cash inflows was given in Equation 3.1 on page 101. The basic calculation requires adding depreciation and any other *noncash charges* (amortization and depletion) deducted as expenses on the firm's income statement back to net profits after taxes. Because depreciation is commonly found on income statements, it is the only noncash charge we consider.

Example

Powell Corporation's estimates of its revenue and expenses (excluding depreciation and interest), with and without the proposed new machine described in the preceding example, are given in Table 8.5. Note that both the expected usable life of the proposed machine and the remaining usable life of the present machine are 5 years. The amount to be depreciated with the proposed machine is calculated by summing the purchase price of $380,000 and the installation costs of $20,000.

TABLE 8.5   Powell Corporation's Revenue and Expenses (Excluding Depreciation and Interest) for Proposed and Present Machines

	With proposed machine			With present machine	
Year	Revenue (1)	Expenses (excl. depr. and int.) (2)	Year	Revenue (1)	Expenses (excl. depr. and int.) (2)
1	$2,520,000	$2,300,000	1	$2,200,000	$1,990,000
2	2,520,000	2,300,000	2	2,300,000	2,110,000
3	2,520,000	2,300,000	3	2,400,000	2,230,000
4	2,520,000	2,300,000	4	2,400,000	2,250,000
5	2,520,000	2,300,000	5	2,250,000	2,120,000

TABLE 8.6	Depreciation Expense for Proposed and Present Machines for Powell Corporation

Year	Cost (1)	Applicable MACRS depreciation percentages (from Table 3.2) (2)	Depreciation [(1) × (2)] (3)
With proposed machine			
1	$400,000	20%	$ 80,000
2	400,000	32	128,000
3	400,000	19	76,000
4	400,000	12	48,000
5	400,000	12	48,000
6	400,000	5	20,000
Totals		100%	$400,000
With present machine			
1	$240,000	12% (year-4 depreciation)	$28,800
2	240,000	12 (year-5 depreciation)	28,800
3	240,000	5 (year-6 depreciation)	12,000
4		Because the present machine is at the end of the third year of its cost recovery at the time the analysis is performed, it has only the final 3 years of depreciation (as noted above) still applicable.	0
5			0
6			0
Total			$69,600[a]

[a]The total $69,600 represents the book value of the present machine at the end of the third year, as calculated in the preceding example.

The proposed machine is to be depreciated under MACRS using a 5-year recovery period.[6] The resulting depreciation on this machine for each of the 6 years, as well as the remaining 3 years of depreciation (years 4, 5, and 6) on the present machine, are calculated in Table 8.6.[7]

The *operating cash inflows* each year can be calculated by using the income statement format shown in Table 8.7. Note that we exclude interest because we are focusing purely on the "investment decision." The interest is relevant to the "financing decision," which is separately considered. Because we exclude interest expense, "earnings before interest and taxes (EBIT)" is equivalent to "net profits before taxes," and the calculation of "operating cash inflow" in Table 8.7 is equivalent to "operating cash flow (OCF)" (defined in Equation 3.4, on page 104). Simply stated, the income statement format calculates OCF.

Substituting the data from Tables 8.5 and 8.6 into this format and assuming a 40% tax rate, we get Table 8.8. It demonstrates the calculation of operating cash

---

6. As noted in Chapter 3, it takes $n + 1$ years to depreciate an n-year class asset under current tax law. Therefore, MACRS percentages are given for each of 6 years for use in depreciating an asset with a 5-year recovery period.

7. It is important to recognize that although both machines will provide 5 years of use, the proposed new machine will be depreciated over the 6-year period, whereas the present machine, as noted in the preceding example, has been depreciated over 3 years and therefore has remaining only its final 3 years (years 4, 5, and 6) of depreciation (12%, 12%, and 5%, respectively, under MACRS).

TABLE 8.7	Calculation of Operating Cash Inflows Using the Income Statement Format

Revenue
− Expenses (excluding depreciation and interest)
Earnings before depreciation, interest, and taxes (EBDIT)
− Depreciation
Earnings before interest and taxes (EBIT)
− Taxes (rate = T)
Net operating profit after taxes [NOPAT = EBIT $\times$ (1 − T)]
+ Depreciation
Operating cash inflows (same as OCF in Equation 3.4)

TABLE 8.8	Calculation of Operating Cash Inflows for Powell Corporation's Proposed and Present Machines

	Year 1	Year 2	Year 3	Year 4	Year 5	Year 6
With proposed machine						
Revenue[a]	$2,520,000	$2,520,000	$2,520,000	$2,520,000	$2,520,000	$ 0
− Expenses (excl. depr. and int.)[b]	2,300,000	2,300,000	2,300,000	2,300,000	2,300,000	0
Earnings before depr., int., and taxes	$ 220,000	$ 220,000	$ 220,000	$ 220,000	$ 220,000	$ 0
− Depreciation[c]	80,000	128,000	76,000	48,000	48,000	20,000
Earnings before interest and taxes	$ 140,000	$ 92,000	$ 144,000	$ 172,000	$ 172,000	−$20,000
− Taxes (rate, T = 40%)	56,000	36,800	57,600	68,800	68,800	− 8,000
Net operating profit after taxes	$ 84,000	$ 55,200	$ 86,400	$ 103,200	$ 103,200	−$12,000
+ Depreciation[c]	80,000	128,000	76,000	48,000	48,000	20,000
Operating cash inflows	$ 164,000	$ 183,200	$ 162,400	$ 151,200	$ 151,200	$ 8,000
With present machine						
Revenue[a]	$2,200,000	$2,300,000	$2,400,000	$2,400,000	$2,250,000	$ 0
− Expenses (excl. depr. and int.)[b]	1,990,000	2,110,000	2,230,000	2,250,000	2,120,000	0
Earnings before depr., int., and taxes	$ 210,000	$ 190,000	$ 170,000	$ 150,000	$ 130,000	$ 0
− Depreciation[c]	28,800	28,800	12,000	0	0	0
Earnings before interest and taxes	$ 181,200	$ 161,200	$ 158,000	$ 150,000	$ 130,000	$ 0
− Taxes (rate, T = 40%)	72,480	64,480	63,200	60,000	52,000	0
Net operating profit after taxes	$ 108,720	$ 96,720	$ 94,800	$ 90,000	$ 78,000	$ 0
+ Depreciation[c]	28,800	28,800	12,000	0	0	0
Operating cash inflows	$ 137,520	$ 125,520	$ 106,800	$ 90,000	$ 78,000	$ 0

[a]From column 1 of Table 8.5.
[b]From column 2 of Table 8.5.
[c]From column 3 of Table 8.6.

inflows for each year for both the proposed and the present machine. Because the proposed machine is depreciated over 6 years, the analysis must be performed over the 6-year period to capture fully the tax effect of its year-6 depreciation. The resulting operating cash inflows are shown in the final row of Table 8.8 for each machine. The $8,000 year-6 operating cash inflow for the proposed machine results solely from the tax benefit of its year-6 depreciation deduction.

Interpreting the Term Incremental

The final step in estimating the operating cash inflows for a proposed replacement project is to calculate the *incremental (relevant)* cash inflows. Incremental operating cash inflows are needed, because our concern is *only* with the change in operating cash inflows that result from the proposed project. Clearly, if this were an expansion project, the project's cash flows would be the incremental cash flows.

Example

Table 8.9 demonstrates the calculation of Powell Corporation's *incremental (relevant) operating cash inflows* for each year. The estimates of operating cash inflows developed in Table 8.8 appear in columns 1 and 2. Column 2 values represent the amount of operating cash inflows that Powell Corporation will receive if it does not replace the present machine. If the proposed machine replaces the present machine, the firm's operating cash inflows for each year will be those shown in column 1. Subtracting the present machine's operating cash inflows from the proposed machine's operating cash inflows, we get the incremental operating cash inflows for each year, shown in column 3. These cash flows represent the amounts by which each respective year's cash inflows will increase as a result of the replacement. For example, in year 1, Powell Corporation's cash inflows would increase by $26,480 if the proposed project were undertaken. Clearly, these are the relevant inflows to be considered when evaluating the benefits of making a capital expenditure for the proposed machine.

	Operating cash inflows		
			Incremental (relevant)
	Proposed machine[a]	Present machine[a]	[(1) − (2)]
Year	(1)	(2)	(3)
1	$164,000	$137,520	$26,480
2	183,200	125,520	57,680
3	162,400	106,800	55,600
4	151,200	90,000	61,200
5	151,200	78,000	73,200
6	8,000	0	8,000

TABLE 8.9   Incremental (Relevant) Operating Cash Inflows for Powell Corporation

[a]From final row for respective machine in Table 8.8.

REVIEW QUESTIONS

8–13 How does depreciation enter into the calculation of operating cash inflows? How does the income statement format in Table 8.7 relate to Equation 3.4 (on page 104) for finding operating cash flow (OCF)?

8–14 How are the *incremental (relevant) operating cash inflows* that are associated with a replacement decision calculated?

8.5 | Finding the Terminal Cash Flow

Terminal cash flow is the cash flow resulting from termination and liquidation of a project at the end of its economic life. It represents the after-tax cash flow, exclusive of operating cash inflows, that occurs in the final year of the project. When it applies, this flow can significantly affect the capital expenditure decision. Terminal cash flow can be calculated for replacement projects by using the basic format presented in Table 8.10.

Proceeds from Sale of Assets

The proceeds from sale of the new and the old asset, often called "salvage value," represent the amount *net of any removal or cleanup costs* expected upon termination of the project. For replacement projects, proceeds from both the new asset and the old asset must be considered. For expansion and renewal types of capital expenditures, the proceeds from the old asset are zero. Of course, it is not unusual for the value of an asset to be zero at the termination of a project.

Taxes on Sale of Assets

Earlier we calculated the tax on sale of old asset (as part of finding the initial investment). Similarly, taxes must be considered on the terminal sale of both the new and the old asset for replacement projects and on only the new asset in other

TABLE 8.10	**The Basic Format for Determining Terminal Cash Flow**

After-tax proceeds from sale of new asset =
  Proceeds from sale of new asset
  ∓ Tax on sale of new asset
− After-tax proceeds from sale of old asset =
  Proceeds from sale of old asset
  ∓ Tax on sale of old asset
± Change in net working capital
Terminal cash flow

cases. The tax calculations apply whenever an asset is sold for a value different from its book value. If the net proceeds from the sale are expected to exceed book value, a tax payment shown as an *outflow* (deduction from sale proceeds) will occur. When the net proceeds from the sale are less than book value, a tax rebate shown as a cash *inflow* (addition to sale proceeds) will result. For assets sold to net exactly book value, no taxes will be due.

Change in Net Working Capital

When we calculated the initial investment, we took into account any change in net working capital that is attributable to the new asset. Now, when we calculate the terminal cash flow, the change in net working capital represents the reversion of any initial net working capital investment. Most often, this will show up as a cash inflow due to the reduction in net working capital; with termination of the project, the need for the increased net working capital investment is assumed to end. Because the net working capital investment is in no way consumed, the amount recovered at termination will equal the amount shown in the calculation of the initial investment. Tax considerations are not involved.

Calculating the terminal cash flow involves the same procedures as those used to find the initial investment. In the following example, the terminal cash flow is calculated for a replacement decision.

Example

Continuing with the Powell Corporation example, assume that the firm expects to be able to liquidate the new machine at the end of its 5-year usable life to net $50,000 after paying removal and cleanup costs. The old machine can be liquidated at the end of the 5 years to net $10,000. The firm expects to recover its $17,000 net working capital investment upon termination of the project. The firm pays taxes at a rate of 40%.

From the analysis of the operating cash inflows presented earlier, we can see that the proposed (new) machine will have a book value of $20,000 (equal to the year-6 depreciation) at the end of 5 years. The present (old) machine will be fully depreciated and therefore have a book value of zero at the end of the 5 years. Because the sale price of $50,000 for the proposed (new) machine is below its initial installed cost of $400,000 but greater than its book value of $20,000, taxes will have to be paid only on the recaptured depreciation of $30,000 ($50,000 sale proceeds − $20,000 book value). Applying the ordinary tax rate of 40% to this $30,000 results in a tax of $12,000 (0.40 × $30,000) on the sale of the proposed machine. Its after-tax sale proceeds would therefore equal $38,000 ($50,000 sale proceeds − $12,000 taxes). Because the present machine would net $10,000 at termination, which is less than its original purchase price of $240,000 and above its book value of zero, it would experience a taxable gain of $10,000 ($10,000 sale price − $0 book value). Applying the 40% tax rate to the $10,000 gain, the firm will have to pay a tax of $4,000 (0.40 × $10,000) on the sale of the present machine at the end of year 5. Its after-tax sale proceeds from the present machine would therefore equal $6,000 ($10,000 sale price − $4,000 taxes). Substituting the appropriate values into the format in Table 8.10 results in the terminal cash inflow of $49,000.

After-tax proceeds from sale of proposed machine

Proceeds from sale of proposed machine	$50,000	
− Tax on sale of proposed machine	12,000	
Total after-tax proceeds—proposed		$38,000
− After-tax proceeds from sale of present machine		
Proceeds from sale of present machine	$10,000	
− Tax on sale of present machine	4,000	
Total after-tax proceeds—present		6,000
+ Change in net working capital		17,000
Terminal cash flow		**$49,000**

REVIEW QUESTION

8–15 Explain how the *terminal cash flow* is calculated for replacement projects.

8.6 | Summarizing the Relevant Cash Flows

Hint Capital expenditures are critical to a firm's success, and these funds are usually limited. Because of this, the process of determining cash flows should be finely tuned so that it is both objective and realistic.

The initial investment, operating cash inflows, and terminal cash flow together represent a project's *relevant cash flows*. These cash flows can be viewed as the incremental after-tax cash flows attributable to the proposed project. They represent, in a cash flow sense, how much better or worse off the firm will be if it chooses to implement the proposal.

Example

The relevant cash flows for Powell Corporation's proposed replacement expenditure can be shown graphically, on a time line. *Note that because the new asset is assumed to be sold at the end of its 5-year usable life, the year-6 incremental operating cash inflow calculated in Table 8.9 has no relevance; the terminal cash flow effectively replaces this value in the analysis.* As the following time line shows, the relevant cash flows follow a *conventional cash flow pattern*.

Time line for Powell Corporation's relevant cash flows with the proposed machine

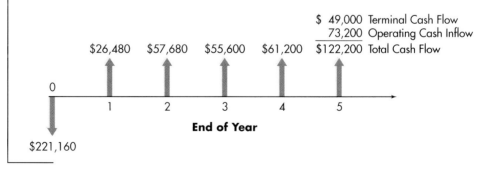

Techniques for analyzing conventional cash flow patterns to determine whether to undertake a proposed capital investment are discussed in Chapter 9.

the old asset. Expansion decisions are viewed as replacement decisions in which all cash flows from the old asset are zero. When estimating relevant cash flows, ignore sunk costs and include opportunity costs as cash outflows. In international capital budgeting, currency risks and political risks can be minimized through careful planning.

Calculate the initial investment associated with a proposed capital expenditure. The initial investment is the initial outflow required, taking into account the installed cost of the new asset, the after-tax proceeds from the sale of the old asset, and any change in net working capital. The initial investment is reduced by finding the after-tax proceeds from sale of the old asset. The book value of an asset is used to determine the taxes owed as a result of its sale. Either of two forms of taxable income—a gain or a loss—can result from sale of an asset, depending on whether the asset is sold for (1) more than book value, (2) book value, or (3) less than book value. The change in net working capital is the difference between the change in current assets and the change in current liabilities expected to accompany a given capital expenditure.

Find the relevant operating cash inflows associated with a proposed capital expenditure. The operating cash inflows are the incremental after-tax cash inflows expected to result from a project. The income statement format involves adding depreciation back to net operating profit after taxes and gives the operating cash inflows, which are the same as operating cash flows (OCF), associated with the proposed and present projects. The relevant (incremental) cash inflows for a replacement project are the difference between the operating cash inflows of the proposed project and those of the present project.

Determine the terminal cash flow associated with a proposed capital expenditure. The terminal cash flow represents the after-tax cash flow (exclusive of operating cash inflows) that is expected from liquidation of a project. It is calculated for replacement projects by finding the difference between the after-tax proceeds from sale of the new and the old asset at termination and then adjusting this difference for any change in net working capital. Sale price and depreciation data are used to find the taxes and the after-tax sale proceeds on the new and old assets. The change in net working capital typically represents the reversion of any initial net working capital investment.

Self-Test Problems (Solutions in Appendix B)

ST8–1 **Book value, taxes, and initial investment**   Irvin Enterprises is considering the purchase of a new piece of equipment to replace the current equipment. The new equipment costs $75,000 and requires $5,000 in installation costs. It will be depreciated under MACRS using a 5-year recovery period. The old piece of equipment was purchased 4 years ago for an installed cost of $50,000; it was being depreciated under MACRS using a 5-year recovery period. The old equipment can be sold today for $55,000 net of any removal or cleanup costs. As a result of the proposed replacement,

the firm's investment in net working capital is expected to increase by $15,000. The firm pays taxes at a rate of 40%. (Table 3.2 on page 98 contains the applicable MACRS depreciation percentages.)

a. Calculate the book value of the old piece of equipment.
b. Determine the taxes, if any, attributable to the sale of the old equipment.
c. Find the *initial investment* associated with the proposed equipment replacement.

ST8–2 Determining relevant cash flows   A machine currently in use was originally purchased 2 years ago for $40,000. The machine is being depreciated under MACRS using a 5-year recovery period; it has 3 years of usable life remaining. The current machine can be sold today to net $42,000 after removal and cleanup costs. A new machine, using a 3-year MACRS recovery period, can be purchased at a price of $140,000. It requires $10,000 to install and has a 3-year usable life. If the new machine is acquired, the investment in accounts receivable will be expected to rise by $10,000, the inventory investment will increase by $25,000, and accounts payable will increase by $15,000. *Earnings before depreciation, interest, and taxes* are expected to be $70,000 for each of the next 3 years with the old machine and to be $120,000 in the first year and $130,000 in the second and third years with the new machine. At the end of 3 years, the market value of the old machine will equal zero, but the new machine could be sold to net $35,000 before taxes. The firm is subject to a 40% tax rate. (Table 3.2 on page 98 contains the applicable MACRS depreciation percentages.)

a. Determine the *initial investment* associated with the proposed replacement decision.
b. Calculate the *incremental operating cash inflows* for years 1 to 4 associated with the proposed replacement. (*Note:* Only depreciation cash flows must be considered in year 4.)
c. Calculate the *terminal cash flow* associated with the proposed replacement decision. (*Note:* This is at the end of year 3.)
d. Depict on a time line the relevant cash flows found in parts **a, b,** and **c** that are associated with the proposed replacement decision, assuming that it is terminated at the end of year 3.

Warm-Up Exercises   A blue box (■) indicates exercises available in .

E8–1 If Halley Industries reimburses employees who earn master's degrees and who agree to remain with the firm for an additional 3 years, should the expense of the tuition reimbursement be categorized as a *capital expenditure* or an *operating expenditure?*

 E8–2 Canvas Reproductions, Inc., is considering two mutually exclusive investments. Project A requires an initial outlay of $20,000 and has expected cash inflows of $5,000 for each of the next 5 years. Project B requires an initial outlay of $25,000 and has expected cash inflows of $6,500 for each of the following 5 years. Use a simple rate of return measure to determine which project the company should choose.

Account	Change
Accruals	+ $ 40,000
Marketable securities	0
Inventories	– 10,000
Accounts payable	+ 90,000
Notes payable	0
Accounts receivable	+ 150,000
Cash	+ 15,000

a. Using the information given, calculate any *change in net working capital* that is expected to result from the proposed replacement action.
b. Explain why a change in these current accounts would be relevant in determining the *initial investment* for the proposed capital expenditure.
c. Would the change in net working capital enter into any of the other cash flow components that make up the relevant cash flows? Explain.

 P8–11 **Calculating initial investment** Vastine Medical, Inc., is considering replacing its existing computer system, which was purchased 2 years ago at a cost of $325,000. The system can be sold today for $200,000. It is being depreciated using MACRS and a 5-year recovery period (see Table 3.2, page 98). A new computer system will cost $500,000 to purchase and install. Replacement of the computer system would not involve any change in net working capital. Assume a 40% tax rate.
a. Calculate the *book value* of the existing computer system.
b. Calculate the after-tax proceeds of its sale for $200,000.
c. Calculate the *initial investment* associated with the replacement project.

 P8–12 **Initial investment—Basic calculation** Cushing Corporation is considering the purchase of a new grading machine to replace the existing one. The existing machine was purchased 3 years ago at an installed cost of $20,000; it was being depreciated under MACRS using a 5-year recovery period. (See Table 3.2 on page 98 for the applicable depreciation percentages.) The existing machine is expected to have a usable life of at least 5 more years. The new machine costs $35,000 and requires $5,000 in installation costs; it will be depreciated using a 5-year recovery period under MACRS. The existing machine can currently be sold for $25,000 without incurring any removal or cleanup costs. The firm is subject to a 40% tax rate. Calculate the *initial investment* associated with the proposed purchase of a new grading machine.

 P8–13 **Initial investment at various sale prices** Edwards Manufacturing Company (EMC) is considering replacing one machine with another. The old machine was purchased 3 years ago for an installed cost of $10,000. The firm is depreciating the machine under MACRS, using a 5-year recovery period. (See Table 3.2 on page 98 for the applicable depreciation percentages.) The new machine costs $24,000 and requires $2,000 in installation costs. The firm is subject to a 40% tax rate. In each of the following cases, calculate the *initial investment* for the replacement.
a. EMC sells the old machine for $11,000.
b. EMC sells the old machine for $7,000.
c. EMC sells the old machine for $2,900.
d. EMC sells the old machine for $1,500.

P8–14 **Depreciation**   A firm is evaluating the acquisition of an asset that costs $64,000 and requires $4,000 in installation costs. If the firm depreciates the asset under MACRS, using a 5-year recovery period (see Table 3.2 on page 98 for the applicable depreciation percentages), determine the depreciation charge for each year.

 P8–15 **Incremental operating cash inflows**   A firm is considering renewing its equipment to meet increased demand for its product. The cost of equipment modifications is $1.9 million plus $100,000 in installation costs. The firm will depreciate the equipment modifications under MACRS, using a 5-year recovery period. (See Table 3.2 on page 98 for the applicable depreciation percentages.) Additional sales revenue from the renewal should amount to $1.2 million per year, and additional operating expenses and other costs (excluding depreciation and interest) will amount to 40% of the additional sales. The firm is subject to a tax rate of 40%. (*Note:* Answer the following questions for each of the next *6 years.*)

a. What incremental earnings before depreciation, interest, and taxes will result from the renewal?

b. What incremental net operating profits after taxes will result from the renewal?

c. What *incremental operating cash inflows* will result from the renewal?

PERSONAL FINANCE PROBLEM

 P8–16 **Incremental operating cash flows**   Richard and Linda Thomson operate a local lawn maintenance service for commercial and residential property. They have been using a John Deere riding mower for the past several years and feel it is time to buy a new one. They would like to know the incremental (relevant) cash flows associated with the replacement of the old riding mower. The following data are available.

There are 5 years of remaining useful life on the old mower.

The old mower has a zero book value.

The new mower is expected to last 5 years.

The Thomsons will follow a 5-year MACRS recovery period for the new mower.

Depreciable value of the new law mower is $1,800.

They are subject to a 40% tax rate.

The new mower is expected to be more fuel-efficient, maneuverable, and durable than previous models and can result in reduced operating expenses of $500 per year.

The Thomsons will buy a maintenance contract that calls for annual payments of $120.

Create and *incremental operating cash flow* statement for the replacement of Richard and Linda's John Deere riding mower. Show the incremental operating cash flow for the next 6 years.

 P8–17 **Incremental operating cash inflows—Expense reduction**   Miller Corporation is considering replacing a machine. The replacement will reduce operating expenses (that is, increase earnings before depreciation, interest, and taxes) by $16,000 per year for each of the 5 years the new machine is expected to last. Although the old machine has zero book value, it can be used for 5 more years. The depreciable value of the new machine is $48,000. The firm will depreciate the machine under MACRS using a 5-year recovery period (see Table 3.2 on page 98 for the applicable depreciation percentages) and is subject to a 40% tax rate. Estimate the *incremental operating cash inflows* generated by the replacement. (*Note:* Be sure to consider the depreciation in year 6.)

P8–18 **Incremental operating cash inflows**   Strong Tool Company has been considering purchasing a new lathe to replace a fully depreciated lathe that will last 5 more years. The new lathe is expected to have a 5-year life and depreciation charges of $2,000 in year 1; $3,200 in year 2; $1,900 in year 3; $1,200 in both year 4 and year 5; and $500 in year 6. The firm estimates the revenues and expenses (excluding depreciation and interest) for the new and the old lathes to be as shown in the following table. The firm is subject to a 40% tax rate.

	New lathe		Old lathe	
Year	Revenue	Expenses (excl. depr. and int.)	Revenue	Expenses (excl. depr. and int.)
1	$40,000	$30,000	$35,000	$25,000
2	41,000	30,000	35,000	25,000
3	42,000	30,000	35,000	25,000
4	43,000	30,000	35,000	25,000
5	44,000	30,000	35,000	25,000

a. Calculate the *operating cash inflows* associated with each lathe. (*Note:* Be sure to consider the depreciation in year 6.)
b. Calculate the *incremental (relevant) operating cash inflows* resulting from the proposed lathe replacement.
c. Depict on a time line the incremental operating cash inflows calculated in part **b.**

P8–19 **Terminal cash flow—Various lives and sale prices**   Looner Industries is currently analyzing the purchase of a new machine that costs $160,000 and requires $20,000 in installation costs. Purchase of this machine is expected to result in an increase in net working capital of $30,000 to support the expanded level of operations. The firm plans to depreciate the machine under MACRS using a 5-year recovery period (see Table 3.2 on page 98 for the applicable depreciation percentages) and expects to sell the machine to net $10,000 before taxes at the end of its usable life. The firm is subject to a 40% tax rate.
a. Calculate the *terminal cash flow* for a usable life of (1) 3 years, (2) 5 years, and (3) 7 years.
b. Discuss the effect of usable life on terminal cash flows using your findings in part **a.**
c. Assuming a 5-year usable life, calculate the terminal cash flow if the machine were sold to net (1) $9,000 or (2) $170,000 (before taxes) at the end of 5 years.
d. Discuss the effect of sale price on terminal cash flow using your findings in part **c.**

P8–20 **Terminal cash flow—Replacement decision**   Russell Industries is considering replacing a fully depreciated machine that has a remaining useful life of 10 years with a newer, more sophisticated machine. The new machine will cost $200,000 and will require $30,000 in installation costs. It will be depreciated under MACRS using a 5-year recovery period (see Table 3.2 on page 98 for the applicable depreciation percentages). A $25,000 increase in net working capital will be required to support the new machine. The firm's managers plan to evaluate the potential replacement over a 4-year period. They estimate that the old machine could be sold at the end of 4 years to net $15,000 before taxes; the new machine at the end of 4 years will be worth $75,000 before taxes. Calculate the *terminal cash flow* at the end of year 4 that is relevant to the proposed purchase of the new machine. The firm is subject to a 40% tax rate.

   P8–21 Relevant cash flows for a marketing campaign Marcus Tube, a manufacturer of high-quality aluminum tubing, has maintained stable sales and profits over the past 10 years. Although the market for aluminum tubing has been expanding by 3% per year, Marcus has been unsuccessful in sharing this growth. To increase its sales, the firm is considering an aggressive marketing campaign that centers on regularly running ads in all relevant trade journals and exhibiting products at all major regional and national trade shows. The campaign is expected to require an *annual* tax-deductible expenditure of $150,000 over the next 5 years. Sales revenue, as shown in the income statement for 2009 below, totaled $20,000,000. If the proposed marketing campaign is not initiated, sales are expected to remain at this level in each of the next 5 years, 2010–2014. With the marketing campaign, sales are expected to rise to the levels shown in the accompanying table for each of the next 5 years; cost of goods sold is expected to remain at 80% of sales; general and administrative expense (exclusive of any marketing campaign outlays) is expected to remain at 10% of sales; and annual depreciation expense is expected to remain at $500,000. Assuming a 40% tax rate, find the *relevant cash flows* over the next 5 years associated with the proposed marketing campaign.

Marcus Tube Income Statement for the Year Ended December 31, 2009		
Sales revenue		$20,000,000
Less: Cost of goods sold (80%)		16,000,000
Gross profits		$ 4,000,000
Less: Operating expenses		
General and administrative expense (10%)	$2,000,000	
Depreciation expense	500,000	
Total operating expense		2,500,000
Earnings before interest and taxes		$ 1,500,000
Less: Taxes (rate = 40%)		600,000
Net operating profit after taxes		$ 900,000

Marcus Tube Sales Forecast	
Year	Sales revenue
2010	$20,500,000
2011	21,000,000
2012	21,500,000
2013	22,500,000
2014	23,500,000

  P8–22 Relevant cash flows—No terminal value Central Laundry and Cleaners is considering replacing an existing piece of machinery with a more sophisticated machine. The old machine was purchased 3 years ago at a cost of $50,000, and this amount was being depreciated under MACRS using a 5-year recovery period. The machine has 5 years of usable life remaining. The new machine that is being considered costs $76,000 and requires $4,000 in installation costs. The new machine would be depreciated under MACRS using a 5-year recovery period. The firm can currently sell the old machine for $55,000 without incurring any removal or cleanup costs. The firm is subject to a tax rate of 40%. The revenues and expenses (excluding depreciation and interest) associated with the new and the old machines for the next 5 years are given in the table below. (Table 3.2 on page 98 contains the applicable MACRS depreciation percentages.)

| | New machine | | Old machine | |
Year	Revenue	Expenses (excl. depr. and int.)	Revenue	Expenses (excl. depr. and int.)
1	$750,000	$720,000	$674,000	$660,000
2	750,000	720,000	676,000	660,000
3	750,000	720,000	680,000	660,000
4	750,000	720,000	678,000	660,000
5	750,000	720,000	674,000	660,000

a. Calculate the *initial investment* associated with replacement of the old machine by the new one.
b. Determine the *incremental operating cash inflows* associated with the proposed replacement. (*Note:* Be sure to consider the depreciation in year 6.)
c. Depict on a time line the *relevant cash flows* found in parts a and b associated with the proposed replacement decision.

 P8–23 Integrative—Determining relevant cash flows Lombard Company is contemplating the purchase of a new high-speed widget grinder to replace the existing grinder. The existing grinder was purchased 2 years ago at an installed cost of $60,000; it was being depreciated under MACRS using a 5-year recovery period. The existing grinder is expected to have a usable life of 5 more years. The new grinder costs $105,000 and requires $5,000 in installation costs; it has a 5-year usable life and would be depreciated under MACRS using a 5-year recovery period. Lombard can currently sell the existing grinder for $70,000 without incurring any removal or cleanup costs. To support the increased business resulting from purchase of the new grinder, accounts receivable would increase by $40,000, inventories by $30,000, and accounts payable by $58,000. At the end of 5 years, the existing grinder is expected to have a market value of zero; the new grinder would be sold to net $29,000 after removal and cleanup costs and before taxes. The firm is subject a 40% tax rate. The estimated *earnings before depreciation, interest, and taxes* over the 5 years for both the new and the existing grinder are shown in the following table. (Table 3.2 on page 98 contains the applicable MACRS depreciation percentages.)

| | Earnings before depreciation, interest, and taxes | |
Year	New grinder	Existing grinder
1	$43,000	$26,000
2	43,000	24,000
3	43,000	22,000
4	43,000	20,000
5	43,000	18,000

a. Calculate the *initial investment* associated with the replacement of the existing grinder by the new one.

b. Determine the *incremental operating cash inflows* associated with the proposed grinder replacement. (*Note:* Be sure to consider the depreciation in year 6.)

c. Determine the *terminal cash flow* expected at the end of year 5 from the proposed grinder replacement.

d. Depict on a time line the *relevant cash flows* associated with the proposed grinder replacement decision.

PERSONAL FINANCE PROBLEM

P8–24   Determining relevant cash flows for a new boat   Jan and Deana have been dreaming about owning a boat for some time and have decided that estimating its cash flows will help them in their decision process. They expect to have a disposable annual income of $24,000. Their cash flow estimates for the boat purchase are as follows:

Negotiated price of the new boat	$70,000
Sales tax rate (applicable to purchase price)	6.5%
Boat trade-in	0
Estimated value of new boat in 4 years	$40,000
Estimated monthly repair and maintenance	$800
Estimated monthly docking fee	$500

Using these cash flow estimates, calculate the following:

a. The initial investment

b. Operating cash flow

c. Terminal cash flow

d. Summary of annual cash flow

e. Based on their disposable annual income, what advice would you give Jan and Deana regarding the proposed boat purchase?

P8–25   ETHICS PROBLEM   According to academic research, capital budgeting cash flow projections are used rarely in practice by small firms, which often use accounting projections instead. What is the most likely explanation of this behavior?

Chapter 8 Case

Developing Relevant Cash Flows for Clark Upholstery Company's Machine Renewal or Replacement Decision

Bo Humphries, chief financial officer of Clark Upholstery Company, expects the firm's *net operating profit after taxes* for the next 5 years to be as shown in the following table.

Year	Net operating profit after taxes
1	$100,000
2	150,000
3	200,000
4	250,000
5	320,000

Bo is beginning to develop the relevant cash flows needed to analyze whether to renew or replace Clark's *only* depreciable asset, a machine that originally cost $30,000, has a current book value of zero, and can now be sold for $20,000. (*Note:* Because the firm's only depreciable asset is fully depreciated—its book value is zero—its expected operating cash inflows equal its net operating profit after taxes.) He estimates that at the end of 5 years, the existing machine can be sold to net $2,000 before taxes. Bo plans to use the following information to develop the relevant cash flows for each of the alternatives.

Alternative 1　Renew the existing machine at a total depreciable cost of $90,000. The renewed machine would have a 5-year usable life and would be depreciated under MACRS using a 5-year recovery period. Renewing the machine would result in the following projected revenues and expenses (excluding depreciation and interest):

Year	Revenue	Expenses (excl. depr. and int.)
1	$1,000,000	$801,500
2	1,175,000	884,200
3	1,300,000	918,100
4	1,425,000	943,100
5	1,550,000	968,100

The renewed machine would result in an increased investment in net working capital of $15,000. At the end of 5 years, the machine could be sold to net $8,000 before taxes.

Alternative 2　Replace the existing machine with a new machine that costs $100,000 and requires installation costs of $10,000. The new machine would have a 5-year usable life and would be depreciated under MACRS using a 5-year recovery period. The firm's projected revenues and expenses (excluding depreciation and interest), if it acquires the machine, would be as follows:

Year	Revenue	Expenses (excl. depr. and int.)
1	$1,000,000	$764,500
2	1,175,000	839,800
3	1,300,000	914,900
4	1,425,000	989,900
5	1,550,000	998,900

The new machine would result in an increased investment in net working capital of $22,000. At the end of 5 years, the new machine could be sold to net $25,000 before taxes.

The firm is subject to a 40% tax rate. As noted, the company uses MACRS depreciation. (See Table 3.2 on page 98 for the applicable depreciation percentages.)

To Do

a. Calculate the *initial investment* associated with each of Clark Upholstery's alternatives.
b. Calculate the *incremental operating cash inflows* associated with each of Clark's alternatives. (*Note:* Be sure to consider the depreciation in year 6.)
c. Calculate the *terminal cash flow* at the end of year 5 associated with each of Clark's alternatives.
d. Use your findings in parts **a, b,** and **c** to depict on a time line the *relevant cash flows* associated with each of Clark Upholstery's alternatives.
e. Solely on the basis of your comparison of their relevant cash flows, which alternative appears to be better? Why?

Spreadsheet Exercise

Damon Corporation, a sports equipment manufacturer, has a machine currently in use that was originally purchased 3 years ago for $120,000. The firm depreciates the machine under MACRS using a 5-year recovery period. Once removal and cleanup costs are taken into consideration, the expected net selling price for the present machine will be $70,000.

Damon can buy a new machine for a net price of $160,000 (including installation costs of $15,000). The proposed machine will be depreciated under MACRS using a 5-year recovery period. If the firm acquires the new machine, its working capital needs will change—accounts receivable will increase $15,000, inventory will increase $19,000, and accounts payable will increase $16,000.

Earnings before depreciation, interest, and taxes (EBDIT) for the present machine are expected to be $95,000 for each of the successive 5 years. For the proposed machine, the expected EBDIT for each of the next 5 years are $105,000, $110,000, $120,000, $120,000, and $120,000, respectively. The corporate tax rate (T) for the firm is 40%. (Table 3.2 on page 98 contains the applicable MACRS depreciation percentages.)

Damon expects to be able to liquidate the proposed machine at the end of its 5-year usable life for $24,000 (after paying removal and cleanup costs). The present machine is expected to net $8,000 upon liquidation at the end of the same period. Damon expects to recover its net working capital investment upon termination of the project. The firm is subject to a tax rate of 40%.

To Do

Create a spreadsheet similar to Tables 8.2, 8.6, 8.8, and 8.10 (or the spreadsheets that can be viewed at www.prenhall.com/gitman) to answer the following:

a. Create a spreadsheet to calculate the *initial investment*.
b. Create a spreadsheet to prepare a *depreciation schedule* for both the proposed and the present machine. Both machines are depreciated under MACRS using a 5-year recovery period. Remember, the present machine has only 3 years of depreciation remaining.
c. Create a spreadsheet to calculate the *operating cash inflows* for Damon Corporation for both the proposed and the present machine.
d. Create a spreadsheet to calculate the *terminal cash flow* associated with the project.

Web Exercise

Go to the book's companion website at **www.prenhall.com/gitman** to find the Web Exercise for this chapter.

> Remember to check the book's website at **www.prenhall.com/gitman** to find additional resources, including Web Exercises and a Web Case.

9

Capital Budgeting Techniques: Certainty and Risk

WHY THIS CHAPTER MATTERS TO YOU

In Your Professional Life

Accounting: You need to understand capital budgeting techniques to determine relevant cash flows associated with proposed capital expenditures and to appreciate how risk may affect the variability of cash flows.

Information systems: You need to understand capital budgeting techniques, including how to measure risk in those techniques, to design decision modules that help analyze proposed capital expenditures.

Management: You need to understand capital budgeting techniques, along with real options, capital rationing, and techniques for dealing with project risk, to analyze the relevant cash flows of proposed projects and decide whether to accept them.

Marketing: You need to understand capital budgeting techniques to grasp how proposals for new marketing programs, new products, and expansion of existing product lines will be evaluated by the firm's decision makers and how risk of proposed products is treated in capital budgeting.

Operations: You need to understand capital budgeting techniques to know how proposals for the acquisition of new equipment and plants will be evaluated by the firm's decision makers, especially when capital must be rationed.

In Your Personal Life

You can use capital budgeting techniques, such as the IRR technique, to measure both actual and forecast returns on investments in securities, real estate, the true cost of credit card debt, consumer loans, and leases. You also should consider risk when making personal-finance decisions.

LEARNING GOALS

LG 1 Calculate, interpret, and evaluate the payback period.

LG 2 Apply net present value (NPV) and internal rate of return (IRR) to relevant cash flows to choose acceptable capital expenditures.

LG 3 Use net present value profiles to compare the NPV and IRR techniques in light of conflicting rankings.

LG 4 Discuss two additional considerations in capital budgeting—recognizing real options and choosing projects under capital rationing.

LG 5 Recognize sensitivity analysis and scenario analysis, decision trees, and simulation as behavioral approaches for dealing with project risk, and the unique risks that multinational companies face.

LG 6 Understand the calculation and practical aspects of risk-adjusted discount rates (RADRs).

Firms use the relevant cash flows to make decisions about proposed capital expenditures. These decisions can be expressed in the form of project acceptance or rejection or of project rankings. A number of techniques are used in such decision making, some more sophisticated than others. These techniques are the topic of this chapter, wherein we describe the assumptions on which capital budgeting techniques are based, show how they are used in both certain and risky situations, and evaluate their strengths and weaknesses.

9.1 | Capital Budgeting Techniques

When firms have developed relevant cash flows, as demonstrated in Chapter 8, they analyze them to assess whether a project is acceptable or to rank projects. A number of techniques are available for performing such analyses. The preferred approaches integrate time value procedures, risk and return considerations, and valuation concepts to select capital expenditures that are consistent with the firm's goal of maximizing owners' wealth. This section and the next one focus on the use of these techniques in an environment of certainty. In subsequent sections, we will look at capital budgeting under uncertain circumstances.

Bennett Company's Relevant Cash Flows

We will use one basic problem to illustrate the capital budgeting techniques. The problem concerns Bennett Company, a medium-sized metal fabricator that is currently contemplating two projects: Project A requires an initial investment of $42,000; project B requires an initial investment of $45,000. The projected relevant cash flows for the two projects are presented in Table 9.1 and depicted on the time lines in Figure 9.1.[1] The projects exhibit *conventional cash flow pat-*

Hint Remember that the initial investment is an *outflow* occurring at time zero.

TABLE 9.1	**Capital Expenditure Data for Bennett Company**	
	Project A	Project B
Initial investment	$42,000	$45,000
Year	Operating cash inflows	
1	$14,000	$28,000
2	14,000	12,000
3	14,000	10,000
4	14,000	10,000
5	14,000	10,000

1. For simplification, these 5-year-lived projects with 5 years of cash inflows are used throughout this chapter. Projects with usable lives equal to the number of years of cash inflows are also included in the end-of-chapter problems. Recall from Chapter 8 that under current tax law, MACRS depreciation results in $n + 1$ years of depreciation for an n-year class asset. This means that projects will commonly have at least 1 year of cash flow beyond their recovery period. In actual practice, the usable lives of projects (and the associated cash inflows) may differ significantly from their depreciable lives. Generally, under MACRS, usable lives are longer than depreciable lives.

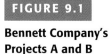

FIGURE 9.1

Bennett Company's Projects A and B
Time lines depicting the conventional cash flows of projects A and B

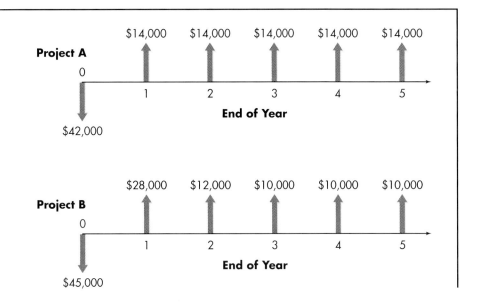

terns, which are assumed throughout the text. In addition, we initially assume that all projects' cash flows have the same level of risk, that projects being compared have equal usable lives, and that the firm has unlimited funds. Because very few are actually made under such conditions, later in the chapter we relax some of these simplifying instructions.

We begin with a look at the three most popular capital budgeting techniques: payback period, net present value, and internal rate of return.[2]

Payback Period

payback period
The amount of time required for a firm to recover its initial investment in a project, as calculated from *cash inflows.*

Payback periods are commonly used to evaluate proposed investments. The **payback period** is the amount of time required for the firm to recover its initial investment in a project, as calculated from *cash inflows.* In the case of an *annuity,* the payback period can be found by dividing the initial investment by the annual cash inflow. For a *mixed stream* of cash inflows, the yearly cash inflows must be accumulated until the initial investment is recovered. Although popular, the payback period is generally viewed as an *unsophisticated capital budgeting technique,* because it does not *explicitly* consider the time value of money.

---

2. Two other, closely related techniques that are sometimes used to evaluate capital budgeting projects are the *average (or accounting) rate of return (ARR)* and the *profitability index (PI).* The ARR is an unsophisticated technique that is calculated by dividing a project's average profits after taxes by its average investment. Because it fails to consider cash flows and the time value of money, it is ignored here. The PI, sometimes called the *benefit–cost ratio,* is calculated by dividing the present value of cash inflows by the initial investment. This technique, which does consider the time value of money, is sometimes used as a starting point in the selection of projects under *capital rationing*; the more popular NPV and IRR methods are discussed here.

Decision Criteria

When the payback period is used to make accept–reject decisions, the following decision criteria apply.

- If the payback period is *less than* the maximum acceptable payback period, *accept* the project.
- If the payback period is *greater than* the maximum acceptable payback period, *reject* the project.

The length of the maximum acceptable payback period is determined by management. This value is set *subjectively* on the basis of a number of factors, including the type of project (expansion, replacement or renewal, other), the perceived risk of the project, and the perceived relationship between the payback period and the share value. It is simply a value that management feels, on average, will result in value-creating investment decisions.

Example

We can calculate the payback period for Bennett Company's projects A and B using the data in Table 9.1. *For project A, which is an annuity, the payback period is 3.0 years ($42,000 initial investment ÷ $14,000 annual cash inflow).* Because project B generates a mixed stream of cash inflows, the calculation of its payback period is not as clear-cut. In year 1, the firm will recover $28,000 of its $45,000 initial investment. By the end of year 2, $40,000 ($28,000 from year 1 + $12,000 from year 2) will have been recovered. At the end of year 3, $50,000 will have been recovered. Only 50% of the year-3 cash inflow of $10,000 is needed to complete the payback of the initial $45,000. *The payback period for project B is therefore 2.5 years (2 years + 50% of year 3).*

If Bennett's maximum acceptable payback period were 2.75 years, project A would be rejected and project B would be accepted. If the maximum payback were 2.25 years, both projects would be rejected. If the projects were being ranked, B would be preferred over A, because it has a shorter payback period.

Pros and Cons of Payback Periods

Hint In *all three* of the decision methods presented in this text, the relevant data are *after-tax cash flows.* Accounting profit is used only to help determine the after-tax cash flow.

Hint The payback period indicates to firms taking on projects of high risk how quickly they can recover their investment. In addition, it tells firms with limited sources of capital how quickly the funds invested in a given project will become available for future projects.

Large firms usually use the payback period to evaluate small projects, and small firms use it to evaluate most projects. Its popularity results from its computational simplicity and intuitive appeal. It is also appealing in that it considers cash flows rather than accounting profits. By measuring how quickly the firm recovers its initial investment, the payback period also gives *implicit* consideration to the timing of cash flows and therefore to the time value of money. Because it can be viewed as a measure of *risk exposure*, many firms use the payback period as a decision criterion or as a supplement to other decision techniques. The longer the firm must wait to recover its invested funds, the greater the possibility of a calamity. Therefore, the shorter the payback period, the lower the firm's exposure to such risk.

The major weakness of the payback period is that the appropriate payback period is merely a subjectively determined number. It cannot be specified in light of the wealth maximization goal because it is not based on discounting cash flows to determine whether they add to the firm's value. Instead, the appropriate payback period is simply the maximum acceptable period of time over which management decides that a project's cash flows must break even (that is, just equal the initial investment).

Personal Finance Example   Seema Mehdi is considering investing $20,000 in a 5% interest in a rental property. Her good friend and real estate agent, Akbar Ahmed, put the deal together, and he conservatively estimates that Seema should receive between $4,000 and $6,000 per year in cash from her 5% interest in the property. The deal is structured in a way that forces all investors to maintain their investment in the property for at least 10 years. Seema expects to remain in the 25% income-tax bracket for quite a while. In order to be acceptable, Seema requires the investment to pay itself back in terms of after-tax cash flows in less than 7 years.

Seema's calculation of the payback period on this deal begins with calculation of the range of annual after-tax cash flow:

$$\text{After-tax cash flow} = (1 - \text{tax rate}) \times \text{Pre-tax cash flow}$$
$$= (1 - 0.25) \times \$4,000 = \$3,000$$
$$= (1 - 0.25) \times \$6,000 = \$4,500$$

The after-tax cash flow ranges from $3,000 to $4,500. Dividing the $20,000 initial investment by each of the estimated after-tax cash flows, we get the payback period:

$$\text{Payback period} = \text{Initial investment} \div \text{After-tax cash flow}$$
$$= \$20,000 \div \$3,000 = 6.67 \text{ years}$$
$$= \$20,000 \div \$4,500 = 4.44 \text{ years}$$

Because Seema's proposed rental property investment will pay itself back between 4.44 and 6.67 years, which is a range below her maximum payback of 7 years, the investment is acceptable.

A second weakness is that this approach fails to take *fully* into account the time factor in the value of money.[3] This weakness can be illustrated by an example.

Example   DeYarman Enterprises, a small medical appliance manufacturer, is considering two mutually exclusive projects, which it has named projects Gold and Silver. The firm uses only the payback period to choose projects. The relevant cash flows and payback period for each project are given in Table 9.2 (see page 366). Both projects have 3-year payback periods, which would suggest that they are equally desirable. But comparison of the pattern of cash inflows over the first 3 years shows that more of the $50,000 initial investment in project Silver is recovered sooner than is recovered for project Gold. For example, in year 1, $40,000 of the $50,000 invested in project Silver is recovered, whereas only $5,000 of the $50,000 investment in project Gold is recovered. Given the time value of money, project Silver would clearly be preferred over project Gold, in spite of the fact that both have identical 3-year payback periods. The payback approach does not fully account for the time value of money, which, if recognized, would cause project Silver to be preferred over project Gold.

─────────

3. To consider differences in timing explicitly in applying the payback method, the *discounted payback period* is sometimes used. It is found by first calculating the present value of the cash inflows at the appropriate discount rate and then finding the payback period by using the present value of the cash inflows.

TABLE 9.2	Relevant Cash Flows and Payback Periods for DeYarman Enterprises' Projects	
	Project Gold	Project Silver
Initial investment	$50,000	$50,000
Year	Operating cash inflows	
1	$ 5,000	$40,000
2	5,000	2,000
3	40,000	8,000
4	10,000	10,000
5	10,000	10,000
Payback period	3 years	3 years

A third weakness of payback is its failure to recognize cash flows that occur *after* the payback period.

Example   Rashid Company, a software developer, has two investment opportunities, X and Y. Data for X and Y are given in Table 9.3. The payback period for project X is 2 years; for project Y it is 3 years. Strict adherence to the payback approach suggests that project X is preferable to project Y. However, if we look beyond the payback period, we see that project X returns only an additional $1,200 ($1,000 in year 3 + $100 in year 4 + $100 in year 5), whereas project Y returns an additional $7,000 ($4,000 in year 4 + $3,000 in year 5). On the basis of this information, project Y appears preferable to X. The payback approach ignored the cash inflows occurring after the end of the payback period.[4]

TABLE 9.3	Calculation of the Payback Period for Rashid Company's Two Alternative Investment Projects	
	Project X	Project Y
Initial investment	$10,000	$10,000
Year	Operating cash inflows	
1	$5,000	$3,000
2	5,000	4,000
3	1,000	3,000
4	100	4,000
5	100	3,000
Payback period	2 years	3 years

4. To get around this weakness, some analysts add a desired dollar return to the initial investment and then calculate the payback period for the increased amount. For example, if the analyst wished to pay back the initial investment plus 20% for projects X and Y in Table 9.3, the amount to be recovered would be $12,000 [$10,000 + (0.20 × $10,000)]. For project X, the payback period would be infinite because the $12,000 would never be recovered; for project Y, the payback period would be 3.5 years [3 years + ($2,000 ÷ $4,000) years]. Clearly, project Y would be preferred.

Net Present Value (NPV)

Because *net present value (NPV)* gives explicit consideration to the time value of money, it is considered a *sophisticated capital budgeting technique*. All such techniques in one way or another discount the firm's cash flows at a specified rate. This rate—often called the *discount rate, required return, cost of capital,* or *opportunity cost*—is the minimum return that must be earned on a project to leave the firm's market value unchanged. In this chapter, we take this rate as a "given." In Chapter 11 we will explore how it is determined.

net present value (NPV)
A sophisticated capital budgeting technique; found by subtracting a project's initial investment from the present value of its cash inflows discounted at a rate equal to the firm's cost of capital.

The **net present value (NPV)** is found by subtracting a project's initial investment (CF_0) from the present value of its cash inflows (CF_t) discounted at a rate equal to the firm's cost of capital (r).

$$\text{NPV} = \text{Present value of cash inflows} - \text{Initial investment}$$

$$\text{NPV} = \sum_{t=1}^{n} \frac{CF_t}{(1+r)^t} - CF_0 \tag{9.1}$$

$$= \sum_{t=1}^{n} (CF_t \times PVIF_{r,t}) - CF_0 \tag{9.1a}$$

When NPV is used, both inflows and outflows are measured in terms of present dollars. Because we are dealing only with investments that have *conventional cash flow patterns*, the initial investment is automatically stated in terms of today's dollars. If it were not, the present value of a project would be found by subtracting the present value of outflows from the present value of inflows.

Decision Criteria

When NPV is used to make accept–reject decisions, the decision criteria are as follows:

- If the NPV is *greater than* $0, *accept* the project.
- If the NPV is *less than* $0, *reject* the project.

If the NPV is greater than $0, the firm will earn a return greater than its cost of capital. Such action should increase the market value of the firm, and therefore the wealth of its owners by an amount equal to the NPV.

Example

Project A

Input	Function
−42000	CF₀
14000	CF₁
5	N
10	I
	NPV

Solution
11,071.01

We can illustrate the net present value (NPV) approach by using the Bennett Company data presented in Table 9.1. If the firm has a 10% cost of capital, the net present values for projects A (an annuity) and B (a mixed stream) can be calculated as shown on the time lines in Figure 9.2 (see page 368). These calculations result in net present values for projects A and B of $11,071 and $10,924, respectively. Both projects are acceptable, because the net present value of each is greater than $0. If the projects were being ranked, however, project A would be considered superior to B, because it has a higher net present value than that of B ($11,071 versus $10,924).

Calculator Use   The preprogrammed NPV function in a financial calculator can be used to simplify the NPV calculation. The keystrokes for project A—the annuity—typically are as shown at left. Note that because project A is an annuity, only its first cash inflow, $CF_1 = 14000$, is input, followed by its frequency, $N = 5$.

FIGURE 9.2   Calculation of NPVs for Bennett Company's Capital Expenditure Alternatives

Time lines depicting the cash flows and NPV calculations for projects A and B

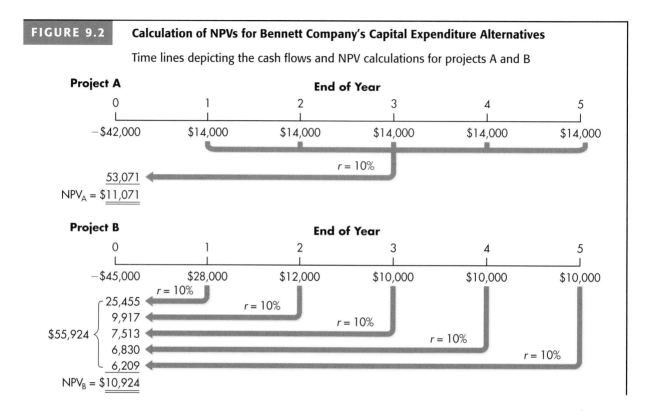

The keystrokes for project B—the mixed stream—are as shown at left. Because the last three cash inflows for project B are the same ($CF_3 = CF_4 = CF_5 = 10000$), after inputting the first of these cash inflows, CF_3, we merely input its frequency, $N = 3$.

The calculated NPVs for projects A and B of $11,071 and $10,924, respectively, agree with the NPVs cited above.

Spreadsheet Use   The NPVs can be calculated as shown on the following Excel spreadsheet.

	A	B	C
1	DETERMINING THE NET PRESENT VALUE		
2	Firm's cost of capital		10%
3		Year-End Cash Flow	
4	Year	Project A	Project B
5	0	$ (42,000)	$ (45,000)
6	1	$ 14,000	$ 28,000
7	2	$ 14,000	$ 12,000
8	3	$ 14,000	$ 10,000
9	4	$ 14,000	$ 10,000
10	5	$ 14,000	$ 10,000
11	NPV	$ 11,071	$ 10,924
12	Choice of project		Project A

Entry in Cell B11 is
=NPV(C2,B6:B10)+B5
Copy the entry in Cell B11 to Cell C11.
Entry in Cell C12 is =IF(B11>C11,B4,C4).

Internal Rate of Return (IRR)

internal rate of return (IRR)
A sophisticated capital budgeting technique; the discount rate that equates the NPV of an investment opportunity with $0 (because the present value of cash inflows equals the initial investment); it is the compound annual rate of return that the firm will earn if it invests in the project and receives the given cash inflows.

The *internal rate of return (IRR)* is probably the most widely used *sophisticated capital budgeting technique*. However, it is considerably more difficult than NPV to calculate by hand. The **internal rate of return (IRR)** is the discount rate that equates the NPV of an investment opportunity with $0 (because the present value of cash inflows equals the initial investment). It is the compound annual rate of return that the firm will earn if it invests in the project and receives the given cash inflows. Mathematically, the IRR is the value of *r* in Equation 9.1 that causes NPV to equal $0.

$$\$0 = \sum_{t=1}^{n} \frac{CF_t}{(1 + IRR)^t} - CF_0 \qquad \text{(9.2)}$$

$$\sum_{t=1}^{n} \frac{CF_t}{(1 + IRR)^t} = CF_0 \qquad \text{(9.2a)}$$

Decision Criteria

When IRR is used to make accept–reject decisions, the decision criteria are as follows:

- If the IRR is *greater than* the cost of capital, *accept* the project.
- If the IRR is *less than* the cost of capital, *reject* the project.

These criteria guarantee that the firm will earn at least its required return. Such an outcome should increase the market value of the firm and therefore the wealth of its owners.

Calculating the IRR

The actual calculation by hand of the IRR from Equation 9.2a is no easy chore. It involves a complex trial-and-error search technique that logically tries different discount rates until one is found that causes the project's present value of cash inflows to just equal its initial investment (or NPV to equal $0). Details of this technique are described and demonstrated on this text's website: www.prenhall .com/gitman. Fortunately, many financial calculators have a preprogrammed IRR function that can be used to simplify the IRR calculation. With these calculators, you merely punch in all cash flows just as if to calculate NPV and then depress IRR to find the internal rate of return. Computer software, including spreadsheets, is also available for simplifying these calculations. All NPV and IRR values presented in this and subsequent chapters are obtained by using these functions on a popular financial calculator.

Example We can demonstrate the internal rate of return (IRR) approach by using the Bennett Company data presented in Table 9.1. Figure 9.3 (see page 371) uses time lines to depict the framework for finding the IRRs for Bennett's projects A and B, both of which have conventional cash flow patterns. We can see in the figure that the IRR is the unknown discount rate that causes the NPV just to equal $0.

Calculator Use   To find the IRR using the preprogrammed function in a financial calculator, the keystrokes for each project are the same as those shown on pasge 000 and 000 for the NPV calculation, except that the last two NPV keystrokes (punching **I** and then **NPV**) are replaced by a single **IRR** keystroke.

Comparing the IRRs of projects A and B given in Figure 9.3 to Bennett Company's 10% cost of capital, we can see that both projects are acceptable because

$$IRR_A = 19.9\% > 10.0\% \text{ cost of capital}$$
$$IRR_B = 21.7\% > 10.0\% \text{ cost of capital}$$

Comparing the two projects' IRRs, we would prefer project B over project A because $IRR_B = 21.7\% > IRR_A = 19.9\%$. If these projects are mutually exclusive, the IRR decision technique would recommend project B.

Spreadsheet Use   The internal rate of return also can be calculated as shown on the following Excel spreadsheet.

	A	B	C
1	DETERMINING THE INTERNAL RATE OF RETURN		
2		Year-End Cash Flow	
3	Year	Project A	Project B
4	0	$ (42,000)	$ (45,000)
5	1	$ 14,000	$ 28,000
6	2	$ 14,000	$ 12,000
7	3	$ 14,000	$ 10,000
8	4	$ 14,000	$ 10,000
9	5	$ 14,000	$ 10,000
10	IRR	19.9%	21.7%
11	Choice of project		Project B

Entry in Cell B10 is =IRR(B4:B9).
Copy the entry in Cell B10 to Cell C10.
Entry in Cell C11 is =IF(B10>C10,B3,C3).

It is interesting to note in the preceding example that the IRR suggests that project B, which has an IRR of 21.7%, is preferable to project A, which has an IRR of 19.9%. This conflicts with the NPV rankings obtained in an earlier example. Such conflicts are not unusual. *There is no guarantee that NPV and IRR will rank projects in the same order. However, both methods should reach the same conclusion about the acceptability or nonacceptability of projects.*

Personal Finance Example   Tony DiLorenzo is evaluating an investment opportunity. He is comfortable with the investment's level of risk. Based on competing investment opportunities, he feels that this investment must earn a minimum compound annual after-tax return of 9% in order to be acceptable. Tony's initial investment would be $7,500, and he expects to receive annual after-tax cash flows of $500 per year in each of the first 4 years, followed by $700 per year at the end of years 5 through 8. He plans to sell the investment at the end of year 8 and net $9,000, after taxes.

To calculate the investment's IRR (compound annual return), Tony first summarizes the after-tax cash flows as shown in the following table:

Year	Cash flow (− or +)
0	−$7,500 (Initial investment)
1	+ 500
2	+ 500
3	+ 500
4	+ 500
5	+ 700
6	+ 700
7	+ 700
8	+ 9,700 ($700 + $9,000)

Substituting the after-tax cash flows for years 0 through 8 into a financial calculator or spreadsheet, he finds the investment's IRR of 9.54%. Given that the expected IRR of 9.54% exceeds Tony's required minimum IRR of 9%, the investment is acceptable.

REVIEW QUESTIONS

9–1 What is the *payback period?* How is it calculated? What weaknesses are commonly associated with the use of the payback period to evaluate a proposed investment?

FIGURE 9.3 **Calculation of IRRs for Bennett Company's Capital Expenditure Alternatives**

Time lines depicting the cash flows and IRR calculations for projects A and B

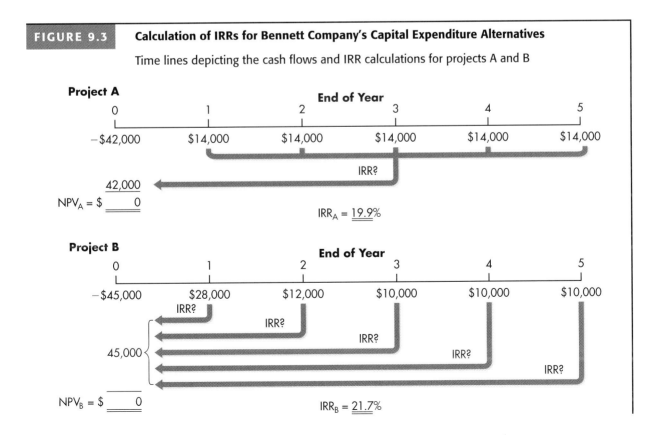

9–2   How is the *net present value (NPV)* calculated for a project with a *conventional cash flow pattern*? What are the acceptance criteria for NPV?

9–3   What is the *internal rate of return (IRR)* on an investment? How is it determined? What are the acceptance criteria for IRR?

9.2 | Comparing NPV and IRR Techniques

To understand the differences between the NPV and IRR techniques and decision makers' preferences in their use, we need to look at net present value profiles, conflicting rankings, and the question of which approach is better.

Net Present Value Profiles

net present value profile
Graph that depicts a project's NPVs for various discount rates.

Projects can be compared graphically by constructing **net present value profiles** that depict the project's NPVs for various discount rates. These profiles are useful in evaluating and comparing projects, especially when conflicting rankings exist. They are best demonstrated via an example.

Example   To prepare net present value profiles for Bennett Company's two projects, A and B, the first step is to develop a number of "discount rate–net present value" coordinates. Three coordinates can be easily obtained for each project; they are at discount rates of 0%, 10% (the cost of capital, r), and the IRR. The net present value at a 0% discount rate is found by merely adding all the cash inflows and subtracting the initial investment. Using the data in Table 9.1 and Figure 9.1, we get

For project A:

($14,000 + $14,000 + $14,000 + $14,000 + $14,000) − $42,000 = $28,000

For project B:

($28,000 + $12,000 + $10,000 + $10,000 + $10,000) − $45,000 = $25,000

The net present values for projects A and B at the 10% cost of capital are $11,071 and $10,924, respectively (from Figure 9.2). Because the IRR is the discount rate for which net present value equals zero, the IRRs (from Figure 9.3) of 19.9% for project A and 21.7% for project B result in $0 NPVs. The three sets of coordinates for each of the projects are summarized in Table 9.4.

TABLE 9.4	Discount Rate–NPV Coordinates for Projects A and B	
		Net present value
Discount rate	Project A	Project B
0 %	$28,000	$25,000
10	11,071	10,924
19.9	0	—
21.7	—	0

FIGURE 9.4

NPV Profiles
Net present value profiles for Bennett Company's projects A and B

Plotting the data from Table 9.4 results in the net present value profiles for projects A and B shown in Figure 9.4. The figure indicates that for any discount rate less than approximately 10.7%, the NPV for project A is greater than the NPV for project B. Beyond this point, the NPV for project B is greater. Because the net present value profiles for projects A and B cross at a positive NPV that occurs at a discount rate (10.7%), which is higher than the firm's cost of capital (10.0%), the IRRs for the projects result in conflicting rankings with their NPVs.

Conflicting Rankings

Ranking is an important consideration when projects are mutually exclusive or when capital rationing is necessary. When projects are mutually exclusive, ranking enables the firm to determine which project is best from a financial standpoint. When capital rationing is necessary, ranking projects will provide a logical starting point for determining which group of projects to accept. As we'll see, **conflicting rankings** using NPV and IRR result from *differences in the magnitude and timing of cash flows.*

conflicting rankings
Conflicts in the ranking given a project by NPV and IRR, resulting from *differences in the magnitude and timing of cash flows.*

intermediate cash inflows
Cash inflows received prior to the termination of a project.

The underlying cause of conflicting rankings is different implicit assumptions about the *reinvestment* of **intermediate cash inflows**—cash inflows received prior to the termination of a project. NPV assumes that intermediate cash inflows are reinvested at the cost of capital, whereas IRR assumes that intermediate cash inflows are reinvested at a rate equal to the project's IRR.[5]

In general, projects with similar-size investments and lower cash inflows in the early years tend to be preferred at lower discount rates. Projects that have

---

5. To eliminate the reinvestment rate assumption of the IRR, some practitioners calculate the *modified internal rate of return (MIRR)*. The MIRR is found by converting each operating cash inflow to its future value measured at the end of the project's life and then summing the future values of all inflows to get the project's *terminal value*. Each future value is found by using the cost of capital, thereby eliminating the reinvestment rate criticism of the traditional IRR. The MIRR represents the discount rate that causes the terminal value just to equal the initial investment. Because it uses the cost of capital as the reinvestment rate, the MIRR is generally viewed as a better measure of a project's true profitability than the IRR. Although this technique is frequently used in commercial real estate valuation and is a preprogrammed function on some financial calculators, its failure to resolve the issue of conflicting rankings and its theoretical inferiority to NPV have resulted in the MIRR receiving only limited attention and acceptance in the financial literature. For a thorough analysis of the arguments surrounding IRR and MIRR, see D. Anthony Plath and William F. Kennedy, "Teaching Return-Based Measures of Project Evaluation," *Financial Practice and Education* (Spring/Summer 1994), pp. 77–86.

TABLE 9.5	Preferences Associated with Extreme Discount Rates and Dissimilar Cash Inflow Patterns	
	Cash inflow pattern	
Discount rate	Lower early-year cash inflows	Higher early-year cash inflows
Low	Preferred, because higher late-year cash inflows are not greatly reduced and therefore dominate in terms of present value.	Not preferred
High	Not preferred	Preferred, because the higher early-year cash inflows are not greatly reduced and therefore dominate in terms of present value.

higher cash inflows in the early years tend to be preferred at higher discount rates. Why? Because at high discount rates, later-year cash inflows tend to be severely penalized in present value terms. For example, at a high discount rate, say 20 percent, the present value of $1 received at the end of 5 years is about 40 cents, whereas for $1 received at the end of 15 years it is less than 7 cents. Clearly, at high discount rates a project's early-year cash inflows count most in terms of its NPV. Table 9.5 summarizes the preferences associated with extreme discount rates and dissimilar cash inflow patterns.

Example ▶ Bennett Company's projects A and B were found to have conflicting rankings at the firm's 10% cost of capital (as depicted in Figure 9.4). If we review each project's cash inflow pattern as presented in Table 9.1 and Figure 9.1, we see that although the projects require similar initial investments, they have dissimilar cash inflow patterns. Table 9.5 indicates that project B, which has higher early-year cash inflows than project A, would be preferred over project A at higher discount rates. Figure 9.4 shows that this is in fact the case. At any discount rate in excess of 10.7%, project B's NPV surpasses that of project A. Clearly, the magnitude and timing of the projects' cash inflows do affect their rankings. ■

Which Approach Is Better?

Many companies use both the NPV and IRR techniques because current technology makes them easy to calculate. But it is difficult to choose one approach over the other, because the theoretical and practical strengths of the approaches differ. Clearly, it is wise to evaluate NPV and IRR techniques from both theoretical and practical points of view.

Theoretical View

On a purely theoretical basis, NPV is the better approach to capital budgeting as a result of several factors. Most important, the use of NPV implicitly assumes that any intermediate cash inflows generated by an investment are *reinvested at the firm's cost of capital.* The use of IRR assumes *reinvestment at the often high rate specified by the IRR.* Because the cost of capital tends to be a reasonable estimate of the rate at which the firm could *actually reinvest* intermediate cash inflows, the use of NPV, with its more conservative and realistic reinvestment rate, is in theory preferable.

In addition, certain mathematical properties may cause a project with a *nonconventional cash flow pattern* to have **multiple IRRs**—more than one IRR. Mathematically, the maximum number of *real* roots to an equation is equal to its number of sign changes. Take an equation like $x^2 - 5x + 6 = 0$, which has two sign changes in its coefficients—from positive $(+x^2)$ to negative $(-5x)$ and then from negative $(-5x)$ to positive $(+6)$. If we factor the equation (remember factoring from high school math?), we get $(x - 2) \times (x - 3)$, which means that x can equal either 2 or 3—there are two correct values for x. Substitute them back into the equation, and you'll see that both values work.

This same outcome can occur when finding the IRR for projects with nonconventional cash flows, because they have more than one sign change. Clearly, when multiple IRRs occur for nonconventional cash flows, the analyst faces the time-consuming need to interpret their meanings so as to evaluate the project. The fact that such a challenge does not exist when using NPV enhances its theoretical superiority.

multiple IRRs
More than one IRR resulting from a capital budgeting project with a *nonconventional cash flow pattern;* the maximum number of IRRs for a project is equal to the number of sign changes in its cash flows.

Practical View

Evidence suggests that in spite of the theoretical superiority of NPV, *financial managers prefer to use IRR.*[6] The preference for IRR is due to the general disposition of businesspeople toward *rates of return* rather than actual *dollar returns*. Because interest rates, profitability, and so on are most often expressed as annual rates of return, the use of IRR makes sense to financial decision makers. They tend to find NPV less intuitive because it does not measure benefits *relative to the amount invested*. Because a variety of techniques are available for avoiding the pitfalls of the IRR, its widespread use does not imply a lack of sophistication on the part of financial decision makers. Clearly, corporate financial analysts are responsible for identifying and resolving problems with the IRR before the decision makers use it as a decision technique.

REVIEW QUESTIONS

9–4   Do the net present value (NPV) and internal rate of return (IRR) always agree with respect to accept–reject decisions? With respect to ranking decisions? Explain.

9–5   How is a *net present value profile* used to compare projects? What causes conflicts in the ranking of projects via net present value and internal rate of return?

9–6   Does the assumption concerning the reinvestment of intermediate cash inflow tend to favor NPV or IRR? In practice, which technique is preferred and why?

---

6. For example, see John R. Graham and Campbell R. Harvey, "The Theory and Practice of Corporate Finance: Evidence from the Field," *Journal of Financial Economics* (May/June 2001,) pp. 187–243; Harold Bierman, Jr., "Capital Budgeting in 1992: A Survey," *Financial Management* (Autumn 1993), p. 24; and Lawrence J. Gitman and Charles E. Maxwell, "A Longitudinal Comparison of Capital Budgeting Techniques Used by Major U.S. Firms: 1986 versus 1976," *Journal of Applied Business Research* (Fall 1987), pp. 41–50, for discussions of evidence with respect to capital budgeting decision-making practices in major U.S. firms.

9.3 | Additional Considerations: Real Options and Capital Rationing

Two important issues that often confront the financial manager when making capital budgeting decisions are (1) the potential real options embedded in capital projects, and (2) the availability of only limited funding for acceptable projects. Here we briefly consider each of these situations.

Recognizing Real Options

The procedures described in Chapter 8 and thus far in this chapter suggest that to make capital budgeting decisions, we must (1) estimate relevant cash flows, (2) apply an appropriate decision technique such as NPV or IRR to those cash flows, and (3) recognize and adjust the decision technique for project risk. Although this traditional procedure is believed to yield good decisions, a more *strategic approach* to these decisions has emerged in recent years. This more modern view considers any **real options**—opportunities that are embedded in capital projects ("real," rather than financial, asset investments) that enable managers to alter their cash flows and risk in a way that affects project acceptability (NPV). Because these opportunities are more likely to exist in, and be more important to, large "strategic" capital budgeting projects, they are sometimes called *strategic options*.

Table 9.6 briefly describes some of the more common types of real options—abandonment, flexibility, growth, and timing. It should be clear from their

real options
Opportunities that are embedded in capital projects that enable managers to alter their cash flows and risk in a way that affects project acceptability (NPV). Also called *strategic options*.

TABLE 9.6	Major Types of Real Options
Option type	Description
Abandonment option	The option to abandon or terminate a project prior to the end of its planned life. This option allows management to avoid or minimize losses on projects that turn bad. Explicitly recognizing the abandonment option when evaluating a project often increases its NPV.
Flexibility option	The option to incorporate flexibility into the firm's operations, particularly production. It generally includes the opportunity to design the production process to accept multiple inputs, use flexible production technology to create a variety of outputs by reconfiguring the same plant and equipment, and purchase and retain excess capacity in capital-intensive industries subject to wide swings in output demand and long lead time in building new capacity from scratch. Recognition of this option embedded in a capital expenditure should increase the NPV of the project.
Growth option	The option to develop follow-on projects, expand markets, expand or retool plants, and so on, that would not be possible without implementation of the project that is being evaluated. If a project being considered has the measurable potential to open new doors if successful, then recognition of the cash flows from such opportunities should be included in the initial decision process. Growth opportunities embedded in a project often increase the NPV of the project in which they are embedded.
Timing option	The option to determine when various actions with respect to a given project are taken. This option recognizes the firm's opportunity to delay acceptance of a project for one or more periods, to accelerate or slow the process of implementing a project in response to new information, or to shut down a project temporarily in response to changing product market conditions or competition. As in the case of the other types of options, the explicit recognition of timing opportunities can improve the NPV of a project that fails to recognize this option in an investment decision.

descriptions that each of these types of options could be embedded in a capital budgeting decision and that explicit recognition of them would probably alter the cash flow and risk of a project and change its NPV.

By explicitly recognizing these options when making capital budgeting decisions, managers can make improved, more strategic decisions that consider in advance the economic impact of certain contingent actions on project cash flow and risk. The explicit recognition of real options embedded in capital budgeting projects will cause the project's *strategic NPV* to differ from its *traditional NPV* as indicated by Equation 9.3.

$$NPV_{strategic} = NPV_{traditional} + \text{Value of real options} \tag{9.3}$$

Application of this relationship is illustrated in the following example.

Example

Assume that a strategic analysis of Bennett Company's projects A and B finds no real options embedded in project A and two real options embedded in project B. The two real options in project B are as follows: (1) The project would have, during the first 2 years, some downtime that would result in unused production capacity that could be used to perform contract manufacturing for another firm, and (2) the project's computerized control system could, with some modification, control two other machines, thereby reducing labor cost, without affecting operation of the new project.

Bennett's management estimated the NPV of the contract manufacturing over the 2 years following implementation of project B to be $1,500 and the NPV of the computer control sharing to be $2,000. Management felt there was a 60% chance that the contract manufacturing option would be exercised and only a 30% chance that the computer control sharing option would be exercised. The combined value of these two real options would be the sum of their expected values.

Value of real options for project B = (0.60 × $1,500) + (0.30 × $2,000)
= $900 + $600 = $1,500

Substituting the $1,500 real options value along with the traditional NPV of $10,924 for project B (from Table 10.1) into Equation 10.7, we get the strategic NPV for project B.

$$NPV_{strategic} = \$10,924 + \$1,500 = \underline{\underline{\$12,424}}$$

Bennett Company's project B therefore has a strategic NPV of $12,424, which is above its traditional NPV and now exceeds project A's NPV of $11,071. Clearly, recognition of project B's real options improved its NPV (from $10,924 to $12,424) and causes it to be preferred over project A (NPV of $12,424 for B > NPV of $11,071 for A), which has no real options embedded in it.

It is important to realize that the recognition of attractive real options when determining NPV could cause an otherwise unacceptable project ($NPV_{traditional}$ < $0) to become acceptable ($NPV_{strategic}$ > $0). The failure to recognize the value of real options could therefore cause management to reject projects that are acceptable. Although doing so requires more strategic thinking and analysis, it is important for the financial manager to identify and incorporate real options in the NPV process. The procedures for doing this efficiently are emerging, and the use of the strategic NPV that incorporates real options is expected to become more commonplace in the future.

Choosing Projects under Capital Rationing

Firms commonly operate under *capital rationing*—they have more acceptable independent projects than they can fund. In theory, capital rationing should not exist. Firms should accept all projects that have positive NPVs (or IRRs > the cost of capital). However, in practice, most firms operate under capital rationing. Generally, firms attempt to isolate and select the best acceptable projects subject to a capital expenditure budget set by management. Research has found that management internally imposes capital expenditure constraints to avoid what it deems to be "excessive" levels of new financing, particularly debt. Although failing to fund all acceptable independent projects is theoretically inconsistent with the goal of maximizing owner wealth, here we will discuss capital rationing procedures because they are widely used in practice.

The objective of *capital rationing* is to select the group of projects that provides the *highest overall net present value* and does not require more dollars than are budgeted. As a prerequisite to capital rationing, the best of any mutually exclusive projects must be chosen and placed in the group of independent projects. Two basic approaches to project selection under capital rationing are discussed here.

internal rate of return approach
An approach to capital rationing that involves graphing project IRRs in descending order against the total dollar investment to determine the group of acceptable projects.

investment opportunities schedule (IOS)
The graph that plots project IRRs in descending order against the total dollar investment.

Internal Rate of Return Approach

The **internal rate of return approach** involves graphing project IRRs in descending order against the total dollar investment. This graph, which is discussed in more detail in Chapter 10, is called the **investment opportunities schedule (IOS)**. By drawing the cost-of-capital line and then imposing a budget constraint, the financial manager can determine the group of acceptable projects. The problem with this technique is that it does not guarantee the maximum dollar return to the firm. It merely provides a satisfactory solution to capital-rationing problems.

Example

Tate Company, a fast-growing plastics company, is confronted with six projects competing for its fixed budget of $250,000. The initial investment and IRR for each project are as follows:

Project	Initial investment	IRR
A	$ 80,000	12%
B	70,000	20
C	100,000	16
D	40,000	8
E	60,000	15
F	110,000	11

The firm has a cost of capital of 10%. Figure 9.5 presents the IOS that results from ranking the six projects in descending order on the basis of their IRRs.

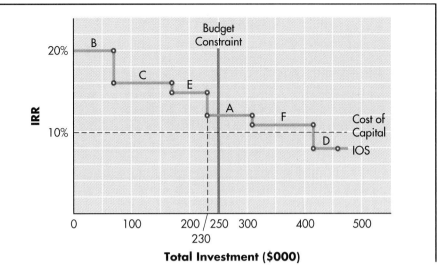

FIGURE 9.5

Investment Opportunities Schedule
Investment opportunities schedule (IOS) for Tate Company projects

According to the schedule, only projects B, C, and E should be accepted. Together they will absorb $230,000 of the $250,000 budget. Projects A and F are acceptable but cannot be chosen because of the budget constraint. Project D is not worthy of consideration; its IRR is less than the firm's 10% cost of capital.

The drawback of this approach is that there is no guarantee that the acceptance of projects B, C, and E will maximize *total dollar returns* and therefore owners' wealth.

Net Present Value Approach

net present value approach
An approach to capital rationing that is based on the use of present values to determine the group of projects that will maximize owners' wealth.

The **net present value approach** is based on the use of present values to determine the group of projects that will maximize owners' wealth. It is implemented by ranking projects on the basis of IRRs and then evaluating the present value of the benefits from each potential project to determine *the combination of projects with the highest overall present value.* This is the same as maximizing net present value, because the entire budget is viewed as the total initial investment. Any portion of the firm's budget that is not used does not increase the firm's value. At best, the unused money can be invested in marketable securities or returned to the owners in the form of cash dividends. In either case, the wealth of the owners is not likely to be enhanced.

Example

The projects described in the preceding example are ranked in Table 9.7 (see page 380) on the basis of IRRs. The present value of the cash inflows associated with the projects is also included in the table. Projects B, C, and E, which together require $230,000, yield a present value of $336,000. However, if projects B, C, and A were implemented, the total budget of $250,000 would be used, and the present value of the cash inflows would be $357,000. This is greater than the return expected from selecting the projects on the basis of the highest IRRs. Implementing B, C, and A is preferable, because they maximize the present value for the given budget. *The firm's objective is to use its budget to generate the highest present value of inflows.* Assuming that any unused portion of the budget does not gain or lose money, the total NPV for projects B, C, and E would be

TABLE 9.7	Rankings for Tate Company Projects		
Project	Initial investment	IRR	Present value of inflows at 10%
B	$ 70,000	20%	$112,000
C	100,000	16	145,000
E	60,000	15	79,000
A	80,000	12	100,000
F	110,000	11	126,500
D	40,000	8	36,000

Cutoff point (IRR < 10%) appears to the right of projects F and D.

$106,000 ($336,000 − $230,000), whereas the total NPV for projects B, C, and A would be $107,000 ($357,000 − $250,000). Selection of projects B, C, and A will therefore maximize NPV.

REVIEW QUESTIONS

9–7 What are *real options?* What are some major types of real options?

9–8 What is the difference between the *strategic NPV* and the *traditional NPV?* Do they always result in the same accept–reject decisions?

9–9 What is *capital rationing?* In theory, should capital rationing exist? Why does it frequently occur in practice?

9–10 Compare and contrast the *internal rate of return approach* and the *net present value approach* to capital rationing. Which is better? Why?

9.4 | Behavioral Approaches for Dealing with Risk

risk (in capital budgeting)
The chance that a project will prove unacceptable or, more formally, the degree of variability of cash flows.

In the context of capital budgeting, the term **risk** refers to the chance that a project will prove unacceptable—that is, NPV < $0 or IRR < cost of capital. More formally, risk in capital budgeting is the degree of variability of cash flows. Projects with a small chance of acceptability and a broad range of expected cash flows are more risky than projects that have a high chance of acceptability and a narrow range of expected cash flows.

In the conventional capital budgeting projects assumed here, risk stems almost entirely from *cash inflows,* because the initial investment is generally known with relative certainty. These inflows, of course, derive from a number of variables related to revenues, expenditures, and taxes. Examples include the level of sales, the cost of raw materials, labor rates, utility costs, and tax rates. We will concentrate on the risk in the cash inflows, but remember that this risk actually results from the interaction of these underlying variables.

Behavioral approaches can be used to get a "feel" for the level of project risk, whereas other approaches explicitly recognize project risk. Here we present a few behavioral approaches for dealing with risk in capital budgeting: risk and cash inflows, scenario analysis, and simulation. In a later section, we consider a popular approach that explicitly recognizes risk.

Scenario Analysis

Scenario analysis can be used to deal with project risk to capture the variability of cash inflows and NPVs. As noted in Chapter 5, *scenario analysis* is a behavioral approach that uses several possible alternative outcomes (scenarios), such as cash inflows, to obtain a sense of the variability among returns, measured here by NPV. This technique is often useful in getting a feel for the variability of return in response to changes in a key outcome. In capital budgeting, one of the most common scenario approaches is to estimate the NPVs associated with pessimistic (worst), most likely (expected), and optimistic (best) estimates of cash inflow. The *range* can be determined by subtracting the pessimistic-outcome NPV from the optimistic-outcome NPV.

Example

Treadwell Tire Company, a tire retailer with a 10% cost of capital, is considering investing in either of two mutually exclusive projects, A and B. Each requires a $10,000 initial investment, and both are expected to provide equal annual cash inflows over their 15-year lives. The firm's financial manager created three cash inflow outcome scenarios for each project: pessimistic, most likely, and optimistic. The cash inflow outcomes and resulting NPVs in each case are summarized in Table 9.8. Comparing the ranges of cash inflows ($1,000 for project A and $4,000 for B) and, more important, the ranges of NPVs ($7,606 for project A and $30,424 for B) makes it clear that project A is less risky than project B. Given that both projects have the same most likely NPV of $5,212, the assumed risk-averse decision maker will take project A because it has less risk (smaller NPV range) and no possibility of loss (all NPVs > $0).

TABLE 9.8	**Scenario Analysis of Treadwell's Projects A and B**	
	Project A	Project B
Initial investment	$10,000	$10,000
	Annual cash inflows	
Outcome		
Pessimistic	$1,500	$ 0
Most likely	2,000	2,000
Optimistic	2,500	4,000
Range	$1,000	$ 4,000
	Net present values[a]	
Outcome		
Pessimistic	$1,409	−$10,000
Most likely	5,212	5,212
Optimistic	9,015	20,424
Range	$7,606	$30,424

[a]These values were calculated by using the corresponding annual cash inflows. A 10% cost of capital and a 15-year life for the annual cash inflows were used.

The widespread availability of computers and spreadsheets has greatly enhanced the use of scenario analysis.

Decision Trees

decision trees
A behavioral approach that uses diagrams to map the various investment decision alternatives and payoffs, along with their probabilities of occurrence.

Decision trees are a behavioral approach that uses diagrams to map the various investment decision alternatives and payoffs, along with their probabilities of occurrence Their name derives from their resemblance to the branches of a tree (see Figure 9.6). Decision trees rely on estimates of the probabilities associated with the outcomes (payoffs) of competing courses of action. The payoffs of each course of action are weighted by the associated probability; the weighted payoffs are summed; and the expected value of each course of action is then determined. The alternative that provides the highest expected value is preferred.

Example

Convoy, Inc., a manufacturer of picture frames, wishes to choose between two equally risky projects, I and J. To make this decision, Convoy's management has gathered the necessary data, which are depicted in the decision tree in Figure 9.6. Project I requires an initial investment of $120,000; a resulting expected present value of cash inflows of $130,000 is shown in column 4. Project I's expected net present value, which is calculated below the decision tree, is therefore $10,000. The expected net present value of project J is determined in a similar fashion. Project J is preferred because it offers a higher NPV—$15,000.

FIGURE 9.6

Decision Tree for NPV
Decision Tree for Convoy, Inc.'s choice between projects I and J

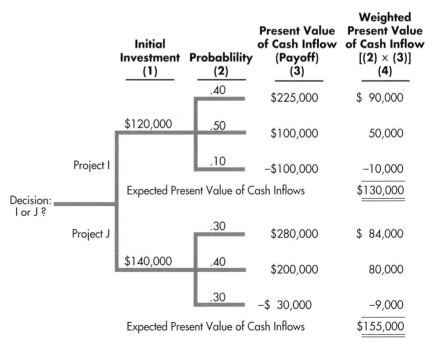

Expected NPV$_I$ = $130,000 − $120,000 = $10,000
Expected NPV$_J$ = $155,000 − $140,000 = $15,000
Because Expected NPV$_J$ > Expected NPV$_I$, Choose J.

Simulation

Simulation is a statistics-based behavioral approach that applies predetermined probability distributions and random numbers to estimate risky outcomes. By tying the various cash flow components together in a mathematical model and repeating the process numerous times, the financial manager can develop a probability distribution of project returns.

Figure 9.7 presents a flowchart of the simulation of the net present value of a project. The process of generating random numbers and using the probability distributions for cash inflows and cash outflows enables the financial manager to determine values for each of these variables. Substituting these values into the mathematical model results in an NPV. By repeating this process perhaps a thousand times, managers can create a probability distribution of net present values.

Although Figure 9.7 simulates only gross cash inflows and cash outflows, more sophisticated simulations using individual inflow and outflow components, such as sales volume, sale price, raw material cost, labor cost, or maintenance expense, are quite common. From the distribution of returns, the decision maker can determine not only the expected value of the return but also the probability of achieving or surpassing a given return. The use of computers has made the simulation approach feasible.

The output of simulation provides an excellent basis for decision making, because it enables the decision maker to view a continuum of risk–return trade-offs rather than a single-point estimate.

FIGURE 9.7

NPV Simulation
Flowchart of a net present value simulation

PART THREE

International Risk Considerations

Although the basic techniques of capital budgeting are the same for multinational companies (MNCs) as for purely domestic firms, firms that operate in several countries face risks that are unique to the international arena. Two types of risk are particularly important: exchange rate risk and political risk.

Exchange rate risk reflects the danger that an unexpected change in the exchange rate between the dollar and the currency in which a project's cash flows are denominated will reduce the market value of that project's cash flow. The dollar value of future cash inflows can be dramatically altered if the local currency depreciates against the dollar. In the short term, specific cash flows can be hedged by using financial instruments such as currency futures and options. Long-term exchange rate risk can best be minimized by financing the project, in whole or in part, in local currency.

Political risk is much harder to protect against. Once a foreign project is accepted, the foreign government can block the return of profits, seize the firm's assets, or otherwise interfere with a project's operation. The inability to manage political risk after the fact makes it even more important that managers account for political risks *before* making an investment. They can do so either by adjusting a project's expected cash inflows to account for the probability of political interference or by using *risk-adjusted discount rates* (discussed later in this chapter) in capital budgeting formulas. In general, it is much better to adjust individual project cash flows for political risk subjectively than to use a blanket adjustment for all projects.

In addition to unique risks that MNCs must face, several other special issues are relevant only for international capital budgeting. One of these special issues is *taxes*. Because only after-tax cash flows are relevant for capital budgeting, financial managers must carefully account for taxes paid to foreign governments on profits earned within their borders. They must also assess the impact of these tax payments on the parent company's U.S. tax liability.

Another special issue in international capital budgeting is *transfer pricing*. Much of the international trade involving MNCs is, in reality, simply the shipment of goods and services from one of a parent company's subsidiaries to another subsidiary located abroad. The parent company therefore has great discretion in setting **transfer prices,** the prices that subsidiaries charge each other for the goods and services traded between them. The widespread use of transfer pricing in international trade makes capital budgeting in MNCs very difficult unless the transfer prices that are used accurately reflect actual costs and incremental cash flows.

Finally, MNCs often must approach international capital projects from a *strategic point of view,* rather than from a strictly financial perspective. For example, an MNC may feel compelled to invest in a country to ensure continued access, even if the project itself may not have a positive net present value. This motivation was important for Japanese automakers that set up assembly plants in the United States in the early 1980s. For much the same reason, U.S. investment in Europe surged during the years before the market integration of the European Community in 1992. MNCs often invest in production facilities in the home country of major rivals to deny these competitors an uncontested home market. MNCs also may feel compelled to invest in certain industries or countries to achieve a broad corporate objective such as completing a product line or diversifying raw material sources, even when the project's cash flows may not be sufficiently profitable.

REVIEW QUESTIONS

9–11 Define *risk* in terms of the cash inflows from a capital budgeting project. How can determination of the *breakeven cash inflow* be used to gauge project risk? Briefly describe how each of the following behavioral approaches can be used to deal with project risk: (**a**) scenario analysis, (**b**) decision trees, and (**c**) simulation.

9–12 Briefly explain how the following items affect the capital budgeting decisions of multinational companies: (**a**) exchange rate risk; (**b**) political risk; (**c**) tax law differences; (**d**) transfer pricing; and (**e**) a strategic rather than a strict financial viewpoint.

9.5 | Risk-Adjusted Discount Rates

The approaches for dealing with risk that have been presented so far enable the financial manager to get a "feel" for project risk. Unfortunately, they do not explicitly recognize project risk. We will now illustrate the most popular risk-adjustment technique that employs the net present value (NPV) decision method.[7] The NPV decision rule of accepting only those projects with NPVs > \$0 will continue to hold. Close examination of the basic equation for NPV, Equation 9.1, should make it clear that because the initial investment (CF_0) is known with certainty, a project's risk is embodied in the present value of its cash inflows:

$$\sum_{t=1}^{n} \frac{CF_t}{(1 + r)^t}$$

Two opportunities to adjust the present value of cash inflows for risk exist: (1) The cash inflows (CF_t) can be adjusted, or (2) the discount rate (r) can be adjusted. Adjusting the cash inflows is highly subjective, so here we describe the more popular process of adjusting the discount rate. In addition, we consider the portfolio effects of project analysis as well as the practical aspects of the risk-adjusted discount rate.

Determining Risk-Adjusted Discount Rates (RADRs)

A popular approach for risk adjustment involves the use of risk-adjusted discount rates (RADRs). This approach uses Equation 9.1 but employs a risk-adjusted discount rate, as noted in the following expression:

risk-adjusted discount rate (RADR)
The rate of return that must be earned on a given project to compensate the firm's owners adequately—that is, to maintain or improve the firm's share price.

$$NPV = \sum_{t=1}^{n} \frac{CF_t}{(1 + RADR)^t} - CF_0 \qquad (9.4)$$

The **risk-adjusted discount rate (RADR)** is the rate of return that must be earned on a given project to compensate the firm's owners adequately—that is, to maintain or improve the firm's share price. The higher the risk of a project, the higher the RADR, and therefore the lower the net present value for a given stream of cash inflows.

---

7. The IRR could just as well have been used, but because NPV is theoretically preferable, it is used instead.

Personal Finance Example   Talor Namtig is considering investing $1,000 in either of two stocks—A or B. She plans to hold the stock for exactly 5 years and expects both stocks to pay $80 in annual end-of-year cash dividends. At the end of the year 5 she estimates that stock A can be sold to net $1,200 and stock B can be sold to net $1,500. Talor has carefully researched the two stocks and feels that although stock A has average risk, stock B is considerably riskier. Her research indicates that she should earn an annual return on an average risk stock of 11%. Because stock B is considerably riskier, she will require a 14% return from it. Talor makes the following calculations to find the risk-adjusted net present values (NPVs) for the two stocks:

$$NPV_A = [\$80 \times (PVIFA_{11\%,5yrs})] + [\$1,200 \times (PVIF_{11\%,5yrs})] - \$1,000$$

Using a financial calculator, she gets:
$$NPV_A = \$1,007.81 - \$1,000 = \underline{\underline{\$7.81}}$$

$$NPV_B = [\$80 \times (PVIFA_{14\%,5yrs})] + [\$1,500 \times (PVIF_{14\%,5yrs})] - \$1,000$$

Using a financial calculator, she gets:
$$NPV_B = \$1,053.70 - \$1,000 = \underline{\underline{\$53.70}}$$

Although Talor's calculations indicate that both stock investments are acceptable (NPVs > $0), on a risk-adjusted basis, she should invest in Stock B because it has a higher NPV.

The logic underlying the use of RADRs is closely linked to the capital asset pricing model (CAPM) developed in Chapter 5. For a brief review of the CAPM and further explanation of using the CAPM to find RADRs, see the book's website.

Applying RADRs

Because the CAPM is based on an assumed efficient market, which does *not* exist for real corporate (nonfinancial) assets such as plant and equipment, the CAPM is not directly applicable in making capital budgeting decisions. Financial managers therefore assess the *total risk* of a project and use it to determine the risk-adjusted discount rate (RADR), which can be used in Equation 9.4 to find the NPV.

To avoid damaging its market value, the firm must use the correct discount rate to evaluate a project. The *Focus on Ethics* box describes real examples of companies that failed to recognize (or that ignored) certain risks associated with their business operations. As a result, their firms experienced monetary sanctions. If a firm fails to incorporate all relevant risks in its decision-making process, it may discount a risky project's cash inflows at too low a rate and accept the project. The firm's market price may drop later as investors recognize that the firm itself has become more risky. Conversely, if the firm discounts a project's cash inflows at too high a rate, it will reject acceptable projects. Eventually the firm's market price may drop, because investors who believe that the firm is being overly conservative will sell their stock, putting downward pressure on the firm's market value.

Unfortunately, there is no formal mechanism for linking *total project risk* to the level of required return. As a result, most firms subjectively determine the RADR by adjusting their existing required return. They adjust it up or down

Focus on Ethics   Environmental Compliance: Honesty Is the Best Policy

IN PRACTICE

It doesn't matter whether you manufacture specialty chemicals or household cleansers, operate a paint shop, sell turf products, or dispose of complex products such as aircraft engines, regulators want you to account for the effect your operations have on the environment, consumer health, and employee safety.

Not only do today's firms need to find a way to track the product as well as the environmental and exposure specifications associated with environmental regulations, they also have to manage their manufacturing processes to ensure that their storage and distribution facilities, equipment, personnel, processes, and products conform. This goes well beyond finished-product quality testing against regulated specifications. Firms have to manage the level of emissions and waste created throughout the entire lifecycle of their products and facilities, from R&D through transportation to customers—and increasingly to disposal.

The Environmental Protection Agency (EPA) has the authority to levy significant fines on companies that violate environmental regulations. In May 2007, the EPA announced that a settlement had been reached with **Kerr-McGee** after the EPA discovered violations of the Clean Air Act at several of Kerr-McGee's natural gas compressor stations near Vernal, Utah. The agreement requires Kerr-McGee to pay a $200,000 penalty and spend $250,000 on environmental projects to benefit the area in which the violations occurred. In addition, Kerr-McGee announced that it would spend $18 million on pollution controls that will reduce harmful emissions and conserve natural gas at its production facilities. The EPA also announced a $2.9 million penalty assessed against **Total Petrochemical USA Inc.** for alleged violations of the Clean Air Act. According to Granta Nakayama, EPA's assistant administrator for Enforcement and Compliance Assurance, "With today's settlement,

86 refineries in 25 states across the nation have agreed to address environmental problems and invest more than $4.5 billion in new pollution control technologies."

Companies that self-disclose violations of federal environmental regulations are fined, but they face a smaller penalty than they otherwise would if the EPA discovered the violations first. On May 9, 2007, the EPA announced that **Kmart** would pay a $102,422 fine to settle self-disclosed violations of clean water, hazardous waste, and emergency planning and preparedness regulations. If the EPA had discovered Kmart's violations through an inspection, the company would have faced a fine of more than $1.6 million. Although still economically painful, when it comes to reporting environmental violations, honesty is the best policy.

■ *What are some factors to consider when prioritizing and budgeting environmental compliance initiatives?*

depending on whether the proposed project is more or less risky, respectively, than the average risk of the firm. This CAPM-type of approach provides a "rough estimate" of the project risk and required return because both the project risk measure and the linkage between risk and required return are estimates.

Example

Bennett Company wishes to use the risk-adjusted discount rate approach to determine, according to NPV, whether to implement project A or project B. In addition to the data presented earlier, Bennett's management after much analysis subjectively assigned "risk indexes" of 1.6 to project A and 1.0 to project B. The risk index is merely a numerical scale used to classify project risk: Higher index values are assigned to higher-risk projects, and vice versa. The CAPM-type relationship used by the firm to link risk (measured by the risk index) and the required return (RADR) is shown in the following table. Management developed this relationship after analyzing CAPM and the risk–return relationships of the projects that they considered and implemented during the past few years.

	Risk index	Required return (RADR)
	0.0	6% (risk-free rate, R_F)
	0.2	7
	0.4	8
	0.6	9
	0.8	10
Project B →	1.0	11
	1.2	12
	1.4	13
Project A →	1.6	14
	1.8	16
	2.0	18

Because project A is riskier than project B, its RADR of 14% is greater than project B's 11%. The net present value of each project, calculated using its RADR, is found as shown on the time lines in Figure 9.8. The results clearly show

---

FIGURE 9.8   **Calculation of NPVs for Bennett Company's Capital Expenditure Alternatives Using RADRs**

Time lines depicting the cash flows and NPV calculations using RADRs for projects A and B

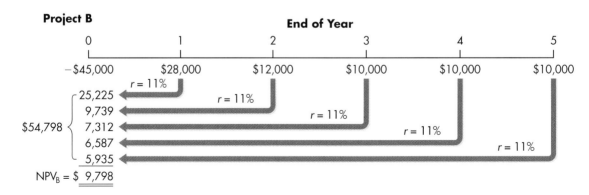

Note: When we use the risk indexes of 1.6 and 1.0 for projects A and B, respectively, along with the table above, a risk-adjusted discount rate (RADR) of 14% results for project A and a RADR of 11% results for project B.

Project A

Project B

that project B is preferable, because its risk-adjusted NPV of $9,798 is greater than the $6,063 risk-adjusted NPV for project A. As reflected by the NPVs in Figure 9.2, if the discount rates were not adjusted for risk, project A would be preferred to project B.

Calculator Use We can again use the preprogrammed NPV function in a financial calculator to simplify the NPV calculation. The keystrokes for project A—the annuity—typically are as shown at the left. The keystrokes for project B—the mixed stream—are also shown at the left. The calculated NPVs for projects A and B of $6,063 and $9,798, respectively, agree with those shown in Figure 9.8.

Spreadsheet Use Analysis of projects using risk-adjusted discount rates (RADRs) also can be performed as shown on the following Excel spreadsheet.

	A	B	C	D
1	ANALYSIS OF PROJECTS USING RISK-ADJUSTED DISCOUNT RATES			
2	Year	Cash Inflow	Present Value	Formulas for Calculated Values in Column C
3	Project A			
4	1-5	$ 14,000	$48,063	–PV(C7,5,B4,0)
5	Initial Investment		$42,000	
6	Net Present Value		$ 6,063	C4–C5
7	Required Return (RADAR)		14%	
8	Project B			
9	1	$ 28,000	$25,225	–PV(C17,A9,0,B9,0)
10	2	12,000	9,739	–PV(C17,A10,0,B10,0)
11	3	10,000	7,312	–PV(C17,A11,0,B11,0)
12	4	10,000	6,587	–PV(C17,A12,0,B12,0)
13	5	10,000	5,935	–PV(C17,A13,0,B13,0)
14	Present value		$54,798	SUM(C9:C13) or NPV(C17,B9:B13)
15	Initial Investment		$45,000	
16	Net Present Value		$ 9,798	C14–C15
17	Required Return (RADAR)		11%	
18	Choice of project	B		IF(C6>=C16,"A","B")

The minus signs appear before the entries in Cells D4 and D9:D13 to convert the results to positive values.

The usefulness of risk-adjusted discount rates should now be clear. The real difficulty lies in estimating project risk and linking it to the required return (RADR).

RADRs in Practice

In spite of the appeal of total risk, *RADRs are often used in practice.* Their popularity stems from two facts: (1) They are consistent with the general disposition of financial decision makers toward rates of return, and (2) they are easily estimated and applied. The first reason is clearly a matter of personal preference, but the second is based on the computational convenience and well-developed procedures involved in the use of RADRs.

In practice, firms often establish a number of *risk classes*, with an RADR assigned to each. Like the CAPM-type risk–return relationship described earlier, management develops the risk classes and RADRs based on both CAPM and the risk–return behaviors of past projects. Each new project is then subjectively placed in the appropriate risk class, and the corresponding RADR is used to evaluate it. This is sometimes done on a division-by-division basis, in which case each division has its own set of risk classes and associated RADRs, similar to those for Bennett Company in Table 9.9. The use of *divisional costs of capital* and associated risk classes enables a large multidivisional firm to incorporate differing levels of divisional risk into the capital budgeting process and still recognize differences in the levels of individual project risk.

Example

Assume that the management of Bennett Company decided to use risk classes to analyze projects and so placed each project in one of four risk classes according to its perceived risk. The classes ranged from I for the lowest-risk projects to IV for the highest-risk projects. Associated with each class was an RADR appropriate to the level of risk of projects in the class, as given in Table 9.9. Bennett classified as lower-risk those projects that tend to involve routine replacement or renewal activities; higher-risk projects involve expansion, often into new or unfamiliar activities.

The financial manager of Bennett has assigned project A to class III and project B to class II. The cash flows for project A would be evaluated using a 14% RADR, and project B's would be evaluated using a 10% RADR.[8] The NPV of project A at 14% was calculated in Figure 9.8 to be $6,063, and the NPV for project B at a 10% RADR was shown in Figure 9.2 to be $10,924. Clearly, with RADRs based on the use of risk classes, project B is preferred over project A. As noted earlier, this result is contrary to the preferences shown in Figure 9.2, where differing risks of projects A and B were not taken into account.

TABLE 9.9	**Bennett Company's Risk Classes and RADRs**	
Risk class	Description	Risk-adjusted discount rate, RADR
I	*Below-average risk:* Projects with low risk. Typically involve routine replacement without renewal of existing activities.	8%
II	*Average risk:* Projects similar to those currently implemented. Typically involve replacement or renewal of existing activities.	10%[a]
III	*Above-average risk:* Projects with higher than normal, but not excessive, risk. Typically involve expansion of existing or similar activities.	14%
IV	*Highest risk:* Projects with very high risk. Typically involve expansion into new or unfamiliar activities.	20%

[a]This RADR is actually the firm's cost of capital, which is discussed in detail in Chapter 10. It represents the firm's required return on its existing portfolio of projects, which is assumed to be unchanged with acceptance of the "average risk" project.

---

8. Note that the 10% RADR for project B using the risk classes in Table 9.9 differs from the 11% RADR used in the preceding example for project B. This difference is attributable to the less precise nature of the use of risk classes.

9–13 Describe the basic procedures involved in using *risk-adjusted discount rates (RADRs)*. How is this approach related to the *capital asset pricing model (CAPM)?*

9–14 How are *risk classes* often used to apply RADRs?

Summary

Focus on Value

After estimating the relevant cash flows, the financial manager must apply appropriate decision techniques to assess whether the project creates value. Net present value (NPV) and internal rate of return (IRR) are the generally preferred capital budgeting techniques. Both use the cost of capital as the required return. Both indicate whether a proposed investment creates or destroys shareholder value. NPV is the theoretically preferred approach, but IRR is preferred in practice because of its intuitive appeal.

Procedures for explicitly recognizing real options embedded in capital projects and procedures for selecting projects under capital rationing enable the financial manager to refine the capital budgeting process further. Not all capital budgeting projects have the same level of risk as the firm's existing portfolio of projects. The financial manager must adjust projects for differences in risk when evaluating their acceptability. Risk-adjusted discount rates (RADRs) provide a mechanism for adjusting the discount rate so that it is consistent with the risk–return preferences of market participants. These techniques should enable the financial manager to make capital budgeting decisions that are consistent with the firm's goal of **maximizing stock price.**

Review of Learning Goals

Key formulas and decision criteria for this chapter are summarized in Table 9.10 on page 392.

Calculate, interpret, and evaluate the payback period. The payback period is the amount of time required for the firm to recover its initial investment, as calculated from cash inflows. Shorter payback periods are preferred. The payback period is relatively easy to calculate, has simple intuitive appeal, considers cash flows, and measures risk exposure. Its weaknesses include lack of linkage to the wealth maximization goal, failure to consider time value explicitly, and the fact that it ignores cash flows that occur after the payback period.

Apply net present value (NPV) and internal rate of return (IRR) to relevant cash flows to choose acceptable capital expenditures. Sophisticated capital budgeting techniques use the cost of capital to consider the time factor in the value of money. NPV measures the amount of value created by a given project; only positive NPV projects are acceptable. IRR is the compound annual

TABLE 9.10	Summary of Key Formulas/Definitions and Decision Criteria for Capital Budgeting Techniques	
Technique	Formula/definition	Decision criteria
Payback period[a]	*For annuity:* $$\frac{\text{Initial investment}}{\text{Annual cash inflow}}$$ *For mixed stream:* Calculate cumulative cash inflows on year-to-year basis until the initial investment is recovered.	*Accept* if < maximum acceptable payback period. *Reject* if > maximum acceptable payback period.
Net present value (NPV)[b]	Present value of cash inflows − Initial investment.	*Accept* if > $0. *Reject* if < $0.
Internal rate of return (IRR)[b]	The discount rate that causes *NPV* = $0 (present value of cash inflows equals the initial investment).	*Accept* if > the cost of capital. *Reject* if < the cost of capital.

[a]Unsophisticated technique, because it does not give explicit consideration to the time value of money.

[b]Sophisticated technique, because it gives explicit consideration to the time value of money.

rate of return that the firm will earn by investing in a project and receiving the given cash inflows. Both NPV and IRR yield the same accept–reject decisions, but they often provide conflicting rankings.

LG 3 **Use net present value profiles to compare NPV and IRR techniques in the light of conflicting rankings.** A net present value profile graph projects' NPVs for various discount rates. NPV profiles are useful for comparing projets, especially when NPV and IRR rankings conflict. On a purely theoretical basis, NPV is preferred over IRR because NPV assumes the more conservative reinvestment rate and does not exhibit the mathematical problem of multiple IRRs that often occurs when IRRs are calculated for nonconventional cash flows. In practice, the IRR is more commonly used because it is consistent with the general preference of businesspeople for rates of return.

LG 4 **Discuss two additional considerations in capital budgeting—recognizing real options and choosing projects under capital rationing.** By explicitly recognizing real options—opportunities that are embedded in capital projects and that allow managers to alter their cash flow and risk in a way that affects project acceptability (NPV)—the financial manager can find a project's strategic NPV. Some of the more common types of real options are abandonment, flexibility, growth, and timing options. The strategic NPV improves the quality of the capital budgeting decision.

Capital rationing exists when firms have more acceptable independent projects than they can fund. Capital rationing commonly occurs in practice. Its objective is to select from all acceptable projects the group that provides the highest overall net present value and does not require more dollars than are budgeted. The two basic approaches for choosing projects under capital rationing are the internal rate of return approach and the net present value approach. The NPV approach better achieves the objective of using the budget to generate the highest present value of inflows.

LG 5 **Recognize sensitivity analysis and scenario analysis, decision trees, and simulation as behavioral approaches for dealing with project risk, and the unique risks that multinational companies face.** Risk in capital budgeting is concerned with either the chance that a project will prove unacceptable or, more formally, the degree of variability of cash flows. Sensitivity analysis and scenario analysis are two behavioral approaches for capturing the variability of cash inflows and NPVs. A decision tree is a behavioral approach for dealing with risk that relies on estimates of probabilities associated with the outcomes of competing courses of action to determine the expected values used to select a preferred action. Simulation is a statistics-based approach that results in a probability distribution of project returns.

Although the basic capital budgeting techniques are the same for multinational and purely domestic companies, firms that operate in several countries must also deal with exchange rate and political risks, tax law differences, transfer pricing, and strategic issues.

LG 6 **Understand the calculation and practical aspects of risk-adjusted discount rates (RADRs).** The risk-adjusted discount rate (RADR) uses a market-based adjustment of the discount rate to calculate NPV. The RADR is closely linked to CAPM, but because real corporate assets are generally not traded in an efficient market, the CAPM cannot be applied directly to capital budgeting. RADRs are commonly used in practice, because decision makers find rates of return easy to estimate and apply.

Self-Test Problems (Solutions in Appendix B)

 ST9–1 **All techniques with NPV profile—Mutually exclusive projects**   Fitch Industries is in the process of choosing the better of two equal-risk, mutually exclusive capital expenditure projects—M and N. The relevant cash flows for each project are shown in the following table. The firm's cost of capital is 14%.

	Project M	Project N
Initial investment (CF_0)	$28,500	$27,000
Year (t)	Cash inflows (CF_t)	
1	$10,000	$11,000
2	10,000	10,000
3	10,000	9,000
4	10,000	8,000

a. Calculate each project's *payback period*.
b. Calculate the *net present value (NPV)* for each project.

c. Calculate the *internal rate of return (IRR)* for each project.
d. Summarize the preferences dictated by each measure you calculated, and indicate which project you would recommend. Explain why.
e. Draw the *net present value profiles* for these projects on the same set of axes, and explain the circumstances under which a conflict in rankings might exist.

ST9–2 **Risk-adjusted discount rates**   CBA Company is considering two mutually exclusive projects, A and B. The following table shows the CAPM-type relationship between a risk index and the required return (RADR) applicable to CBA Company.

Risk index	Required return (RADR)
0.0	7.0% (risk-free rate, R_F)
0.2	8.0
0.4	9.0
0.6	10.0
0.8	11.0
1.0	12.0
1.2	13.0
1.4	14.0
1.6	15.0
1.8	16.0
2.0	17.0

Project data are shown as follows:

	Project A	Project B
Initial investment (CF_0)	$15,000	$20,000
Project life	3 years	3 years
Annual cash inflow (CF)	$7,000	$10,000
Risk index	0.4	1.8

a. Ignoring any differences in risk and assuming that the firm's cost of capital is 10%, calculate the *net present value (NPV)* of each project.
b. Use NPV to evaluate the projects, using *risk-adjusted discount rates (RADRs)* to account for risk.
c. Compare, contrast, and explain your findings in parts **a** and **b**.

Warm-Up Exercises   A blue box (■) indicates exercises available in .

E9–1 Elysian Fields, Inc., uses a maximum payback period of 6 years, and currently must choose between two mutually exclusive projects. Project Hydrogen requires an initial outlay of $25,000; project Helium requires an initial outlay of $35,000. Using the expected cash inflows given for each project in the following table, calculate each project's *payback period*. Which project meets Elysian's standards?

	Expected cash inflows	
Year	Hydrogen	Helium
1	$6,000	$7,000
2	6,000	7,000
3	8,000	8,000
4	4,000	5,000
5	3,500	5,000
6	2,000	4,000

 E9–2 Herky Foods is considering acquisition of a new wrapping machine. The initial investment is estimated at $1.25 million, and the machine will have a 5-year life with no salvage value. Using a 6% discount rate, determine the *net present value (NPV)* of the machine given its expected operating cash inflows shown in the following table. Based on the project's NPV, should Herky make this investment?

Year	Cash inflow
1	$400,000
2	375,000
3	300,000
4	350,000
5	200,000

E9–3 Billabong Tech uses the *internal rate of return (IRR)* to select projects. Calculate the IRR for each of the following projects and recommend the best project based on this measure. Project T-Shirt requires an initial investment of $15,000 and generates cash inflows of $8,000 per year for 4 years. Project Board Shorts requires an initial investment of $25,000 and produces cash inflows of $12,000 per year for 5 years.

  E9–4 Cooper Electronics uses *NPV profiles* to visually evaluate competing projects. Key data for the two projects under consideration is given in the following table. Using these data, graph, on the same set of axes, the NPV profiles for each project using discount rates of 0%, 8%, and the IRR.

	Terra	Firma
Initial investment	$30,000	$25,000
Year	Operating cash inflows	
1	$ 7,000	$ 6,000
2	10,000	9,000
3	12,000	9,000
4	10,000	8,000

Longchamps Electric is faced with a capital budget of $150,000 for the coming year. It is considering six investment projects and has a cost of capital of 7%. The six projects are listed in the follwing table, along with their initial investments and their IRRs. Using the data given, prepare an *investment opportunities schedule (IOS)*. Which projects does the IOS suggest should be funded? Does this group of projects maximize NPV? Explain.

Project	Initial investment	IRR
1	$75,000	8%
2	40,000	10
3	35,000	7
4	50,000	11
5	45,000	9
6	20,000	6

 E9–6 Like most firms in its industry, Yeastime Bakeries uses a subjective risk assessment tool of its own design. The tool is a simple index by which projects are ranked by level of perceived risk on a scale of 0–10. The scale is recreated below.

Risk	Required Return
0	4.0% (current risk-free rate)
1	4.5
2	5.0
3	5.5
4	6.0
5	6.5 (current IRR)
6	7.0
7	7.5
8	8.0
9	8.5
10	9.0

The firm is analyzing two projects based on their RADRs. Project Sourdough requires an initial investment of $12,500 and is assigned a risk index of 6. Project Greek Salad requires an initial investment of $7,500 and is assigned a risk index of 8. The two projects have 7-year lives. Sourdough is projected to generate cash inflows of $5,500 per year. Greek Salad is projected to generate cash inflows of $4,000 per year. Use each project's RADR to select the better project.

Problems   A blue box (■) indicates problems available in .

  Payback period   Jordan Enterprises is considering a capital expenditure that requires an initial investment of $42,000 and returns after-tax cash inflows of $7,000 per year for 10 years. The firm has a maximum acceptable payback period of 8 years.

a. Determine the *payback period* for this project.
b. Should the company accept the project? Why or why not?

 P9–2 **Payback comparisons**   Nova Products has a 5-year maximum acceptable payback period. The firm is considering the purchase of a new machine and must choose between two alternative ones. The first machine requires an initial investment of $14,000 and generates annual after-tax cash inflows of $3,000 for each of the next 7 years. The second machine requires an initial investment of $21,000 and provides an annual cash inflow after taxes of $4,000 for 20 years.
a. Determine the *payback period* for each machine.
b. Comment on the acceptability of the machines, assuming that they are independent projects.
c. Which machine should the firm accept? Why?
d. Do the machines in this problem illustrate any of the weaknesses of using payback? Discuss.

PERSONAL FINANCE PROBLEM

 P9–3 **Long-term investment decision, payback method**   Bill Williams has the opportunity to invest in project A that costs $9,000 today and promises to pay annual end-of-year payments of $2,200, $2,500, $2,500, $2,000, and $1,800 over the next 5 years. Or, Bill can invest $9,000 in project B that promises to pay annual end-of-year payments of $1,500, $1,500, $1,500, $3,500, and $4, 000 over the next 5 years.
a. How long will it take for Bill to recoup his initial investment in project A?
b. How long will it take for Bill to recoup his initial investment in project B?
c. Using the *payback period*, which project should Bill choose?
d. Do you see any problems with his choice?

 P9–4 **NPV**   Calculate the *net present value (NPV)* for the following 20-year projects. Comment on the acceptability of each. Assume that the firm has an opportunity cost of 14%.
a. Initial investment is $10,000; cash inflows are $2,000 per year.
b. Initial investment is $25,000; cash inflows are $3,000 per year.
c. Initial investment is $30,000; cash inflows are $5,000 per year.

P9–5 **NPV for varying costs of capital**   Dane Cosmetics is evaluating a new fragrance-mixing machine. The machine requires an initial investment of $24,000 and will generate after-tax cash inflows of $5,000 per year for 8 years. For each of the costs of capital listed, (1) calculate the *net present value (NPV)*, (2) indicate whether to accept or reject the machine, and (3) explain your decision.
a. The cost of capital is 10%.
b. The cost of capital is 12%.
c. The cost of capital is 14%.

 P9–6 **Net present value—Independent projects**   Using a 14% cost of capital, calculate the *net present value* for each of the independent projects shown in the table on page 398, and indicate whether each is acceptable.

	Project A	Project B	Project C	Project D	Project E
Initial investment (CF_0)	$26,000	$500,000	$170,000	$950,000	$80,000
Year (t)			Cash inflows (CF_t)		
1	$4,000	$100,000	$20,000	$230,000	$ 0
2	4,000	120,000	19,000	230,000	0
3	4,000	140,000	18,000	230,000	0
4	4,000	160,000	17,000	230,000	20,000
5	4,000	180,000	16,000	230,000	30,000
6	4,000	200,000	15,000	230,000	0
7	4,000		14,000	230,000	50,000
8	4,000		13,000	230,000	60,000
9	4,000		12,000		70,000
10	4,000		11,000		

P9–7 **NPV and maximum return**   A firm can purchase a fixed asset for a $13,000 initial investment. The asset generates an annual after-tax cash inflow of $4,000 for 4 years.
a. Determine the *net present value (NPV)* of the asset, assuming that the firm has a 10% cost of capital. Is the project acceptable?
b. Determine the maximum required rate of return (closest whole-percentage rate) that the firm can have and still accept the asset. Discuss this finding in light of your response in part **a**.

P9–8 **NPV—Mutually exclusive projects**   Hook Industries is considering the replacement of one of its old drill presses. Three alternative replacement presses are under consideration. The relevant cash flows associated with each are shown in the following table. The firm's cost of capital is 15%.

	Press A	Press B	Press C
Initial investment (CF_0)	$85,000	$60,000	$130,000
Year (t)		Cash inflows (CF_t)	
1	$18,000	$12,000	$50,000
2	18,000	14,000	30,000
3	18,000	16,000	20,000
4	18,000	18,000	20,000
5	18,000	20,000	20,000
6	18,000	25,000	30,000
7	18,000	—	40,000
8	18,000	—	50,000

a. Calculate the *net present value (NPV)* of each press.
b. Using NPV, evaluate the acceptability of each press.
c. Rank the presses from best to worst using NPV.

PERSONAL FINANCE PROBLEM

P9–9 **Long-term investment decision, NPV method**   Jenny Jenks has researched the financial pros and cons of entering into an elite MBA program at her state university. The tuition and needed books for a master's program will have an upfront cost of $100,000. On average, a person with an MBA degree earns an extra $20,000 per year over a business career of 40 years. Jenny feels that her opportunity cost of capital is 6%. Given her estimates, find the *net present value (NPV)* of entering this MBA program. Are the benefits of further education worth the associated costs?

P9–10 **Payback and NPV**   Neil Corporation has three projects under consideration. The cash flows for each project are shown in the following table. The firm has a 16% cost of capital.

	Project A	Project B	Project C
Initial investment (CF_0)	$40,000	$40,000	$40,000
Year (t)	Cash inflows (CF_t)		
1	$13,000	$ 7,000	$19,000
2	13,000	10,000	16,000
3	13,000	13,000	13,000
4	13,000	16,000	10,000
5	13,000	19,000	7,000

a. Calculate each project's *payback period.* Which project is preferred according to this method?
b. Calculate each project's *net present value (NPV).* Which project is preferred according to this method?
c. Comment on your findings in parts **a** and **b,** and recommend the best project. Explain your recommendation.

P9–11 **Internal rate of return**   For each of the projects shown in the following table, calculate the *internal rate of return (IRR).* Then indicate, for each project, the maximum cost of capital that the firm could have and still find the IRR acceptable.

	Project A	Project B	Project C	Project D
Initial investment (CF_0)	$90,000	$490,000	$20,000	$240,000
Year (t)	Cash inflows (CF_t)			
1	$20,000	$150,000	$7,500	$120,000
2	25,000	150,000	7,500	100,000
3	30,000	150,000	7,500	80,000
4	35,000	150,000	7,500	60,000
5	40,000	—	7,500	—

P9–12 **IRR—Mutually exclusive projects**   Bell Manufacturing is attempting to choose the better of two mutually exclusive projects for expanding the firm's warehouse capacity. The relevant cash flows for the projects are shown in the following table. The firm's cost of capital is 15%.

	Project X	Project Y
Initial investment (CF_0)	$500,000	$325,000
Year (t)	Cash inflows (CF_t)	
1	$100,000	$140,000
2	120,000	120,000
3	150,000	95,000
4	190,000	70,000
5	250,000	50,000

a. Calculate the *IRR* to the nearest whole percent for each of the projects.
b. Assess the acceptability of each project on the basis of the IRRs found in part **a**.
c. Which project, on this basis, is preferred?

PERSONAL FINANCE PROBLEM

P9–13 **Long-term investment decision, IRR method**   Billy and Mandy Jones have $25,000 to invest. On average, they do not make any investment that will not return at least 7.5% per year. They have been approached with an investment opportunity that requires $25,000 upfront and has a payout of $6,000 at the end of each of the next 5 years. Using the *internal rate of return (IRR)* method and their requirements, determine whether Billy and Mandy should undertake the investment.

P9–14 **IRR, investment life, and cash inflows**   Oak Enterprises accepts projects earning more than the firm's 15% cost of capital. Oak is currently considering a 10-year project that provides annual cash inflows of $10,000 and requires an initial investment of $61,450. (*Note:* All amounts are after taxes.)
a. Determine the *IRR* of this project. Is it acceptable?
b. Assuming that the cash inflows continue to be $10,000 per year, how many *additional years* would the flows have to continue to make the project acceptable (that is, to make it have an IRR of 15%)?
c. With the given life, initial investment, and cost of capital, what is the minimum annual cash inflow that the firm should accept?

P9–15 **NPV and IRR**   Benson Designs has prepared the following estimates for a long-term project it is considering. The initial investment is $18,250, and the project is expected to yield after-tax cash inflows of $4,000 per year for 7 years. The firm has a 10% cost of capital.
a. Determine the *net present value (NPV)* for the project.
b. Determine the *internal rate of return (IRR)* for the project.
c. Would you recommend that the firm accept or reject the project? Explain your answer.

P9–16 **Payback, NPV, and IRR**   Rieger International is attempting to evaluate the feasibility of investing $95,000 in a piece of equipment that has a 5-year life. The firm has estimated the *cash inflows* associated with the proposal as shown in the following table. The firm has a 12% cost of capital.

Year (t)	Cash inflows (CF_t)
1	$20,000
2	25,000
3	30,000
4	35,000
5	40,000

a. Calculate the *payback period* for the proposed investment.
b. Calculate the *net present value (NPV)* for the proposed investment.
c. Calculate the *internal rate of return (IRR)*, rounded to the nearest whole percent, for the proposed investment.
d. Evaluate the acceptability of the proposed investment using NPV and IRR. What recommendation would you make relative to implementation of the project? Why?

  P9–17 **NPV, IRR, and NPV profiles**   Thomas Company is considering two mutually exclusive projects. The firm, which has a 12% cost of capital, has estimated its cash flows as shown in the following table.

	Project A	Project B
Initial investment (CF_0)	$130,000	$85,000
Year (t)	**Cash inflows (CF_t)**	
1	$25,000	$40,000
2	35,000	35,000
3	45,000	30,000
4	50,000	10,000
5	55,000	5,000

a. Calculate the *NPV* of each project, and assess its acceptability.
b. Calculate the *IRR* for each project, and assess its acceptability.
c. Draw the *NPV profiles* for both projects on the same set of axes.
d. Evaluate and discuss the rankings of the two projects on the basis of your findings in parts **a**, **b**, and **c**.
e. Explain your findings in part **d** in light of the pattern of cash inflows associated with each project.

   P9–18 **All techniques—Decision among mutually exclusive investments**   Pound Industries is attempting to select the best of three mutually exclusive projects. The initial investment and after-tax cash inflows associated with these projects are shown in the table on page 402.

Cash flows	Project A	Project B	Project C
Initial investment (CF_0)	$60,000	$100,000	$110,000
Cash inflows (CF_t), $t = 1$ to 5	$20,000	$ 31,500	$ 32,500

a. Calculate the *payback period* for each project.
b. Calculate the *net present value (NPV)* of each project, assuming that the firm has a cost of capital equal to 13%.
c. Calculate the *internal rate of return (IRR)* for each project.
d. Draw the *net present value profiles* for both projects on the same set of axes, and discuss any conflict in ranking that may exist between NPV and IRR.
e. Summarize the preferences dictated by each measure, and indicate which project you would recommend. Explain why.

 P9–19 All techniques with NPV profile—Mutually exclusive projects Projects A and B, of equal risk, are alternatives for expanding Rosa Company's capacity. The firm's cost of capital is 13%. The cash flows for each project are shown in the following table.

	Project A	Project B
Initial investment (CF_0)	$80,000	$50,000
Year (t)	Cash inflows (CF_t)	
1	$15,000	$15,000
2	20,000	15,000
3	25,000	15,000
4	30,000	15,000
5	35,000	15,000

a. Calculate each project's *payback period*.
b. Calculate the *net present value (NPV)* for each project.
c. Calculate the *internal rate of return (IRR)* for each project.
d. Draw the *net present value profiles* for both projects on the same set of axes, and discuss any conflict in ranking that may exist between NPV and IRR.
e. Summarize the preferences dictated by each measure, and indicate which project you would recommend. Explain why.

 P9–20 Integrative—Complete investment decision Wells Printing is considering the purchase of a new printing press. The total installed cost of the press is $2.2 million. This outlay would be partially offset by the sale of an existing press. The old press has zero book value, cost $1 million 10 years ago, and can be sold currently for $1.2 million before taxes. As a result of acquisition of the new press, sales in each of the next 5 years are expected to be $1.6 million higher than with the existing press, but product costs (excluding depreciation) will represent 50% of sales. The new press will not affect the firm's net working capital requirements. The new press will be depreciated under MACRS using a 5-year recovery period (see Table 3.2 on page 98). The firm is subject to a 40% tax rate. Wells Printing's cost of capital is 11%. (*Note:* Assume that both the old and the new press will have terminal values of $0 at the end of year 6.)

a. Determine the *initial investment* required by the new press.
b. Determine the *operating cash inflows* attributable to the new press. (*Note:* Be sure to consider the depreciation in year 6.)
c. Determine the *payback period*.
d. Determine the *net present value (NPV)* and the *internal rate of return (IRR)* related to the proposed new press.
e. Make a recommendation to accept or reject the new press, and justify your answer.

P9–21 **Integrative—Investment decision**   Holliday Manufacturing is considering the replacement of an existing machine. The new machine costs $1.2 million and requires installation costs of $150,000. The existing machine can be sold currently for $185,000 before taxes. It is 2 years old, cost $800,000 new, and has a $384,000 book value and a remaining useful life of 5 years. It was being depreciated under MACRS using a 5-year recovery period (see Table 3.2 on page 98) and therefore has the final 4 years of depreciation remaining. If it is held for 5 more years, the machine's market value at the end of year 5 will be $0. Over its 5-year life, the new machine should reduce operating costs by $350,000 per year. The new machine will be depreciated under MACRS using a 5-year recovery period (see Table 3.2 on page 98). The new machine can be sold for $200,000 net of removal and cleanup costs at the end of 5 years. An increased investment in net working capital of $25,000 will be needed to support operations if the new machine is acquired. Assume that the firm has adequate operating income against which to deduct any loss experienced on the sale of the existing machine. The firm has a 9% cost of capital and is subject to a 40% tax rate.

a. Develop the *relevant cash flows* needed to analyze the proposed replacement.
b. Determine the *net present value (NPV)* of the proposal.
c. Determine the *internal rate of return (IRR)* of the proposal.
d. Make a recommendation to accept or reject the replacement proposal, and justify your answer.
e. What is the highest cost of capital that the firm could have and still accept the proposal? Explain.

P9–22 **Real options and the strategic NPV**   Jenny Rene, the CFO of Asor Products, Inc., has just completed an evaluation of a proposed capital expenditure for equipment that would expand the firm's manufacturing capacity. Using the traditional NPV methodology, she found the project unacceptable because

$$NPV_{traditional} = -\$1,700 < \$0$$

Before recommending rejection of the proposed project, she has decided to assess whether there might be real options embedded in the firm's cash flows. Her evaluation uncovered three options:

> *Option 1: Abandonment*—The project could be abandoned at the end of 3 years, resulting in an addition to NPV of $1,200.

> *Option 2: Growth*—If the projected outcomes occurred, an opportunity to expand the firm's product offerings further would become available at the end of 4 years. Exercise of this option is estimated to add $3,000 to the project's NPV.

> *Option 3: Timing*—Certain phases of the proposed project could be delayed if market and competitive conditions caused the firm's forecast revenues to develop more slowly than planned. Such a delay in implementation at that point has a NPV of $10,000.

Jenny estimated that there was a 25% chance that the abandonment option would need to be exercised, a 30% chance that the growth option would be exercised, and only a 10% chance that the implementation of certain phases of the project would affect timing.

a. Use the information provided to calculate the *strategic NPV*, $NPV_{strategic}$, for Asor Products' proposed equipment expenditure.

b. Judging on the basis of your findings in part **a**, what action should Jenny recommend to management with regard to the proposed equipment expenditure?

c. In general, how does this problem demonstrate the importance of considering real options when making capital budgeting decisions?

 P9–23 **Capital rationing—IRR and NPV approaches**   Valley Corporation is attempting to select the best of a group of independent projects competing for the firm's fixed capital budget of $4.5 million. The firm recognizes that any unused portion of this budget will earn less than its 15% cost of capital, thereby resulting in a present value of inflows that is less than the initial investment. The firm has summarized, in the following table, the key data to be used in selecting the best group of projects.

Project	Initial investment	IRR	Present value of inflows at 15%
A	$5,000,000	17%	$5,400,000
B	800,000	18	1,100,000
C	2,000,000	19	2,300,000
D	1,500,000	16	1,600,000
E	800,000	22	900,000
F	2,500,000	23	3,000,000
G	1,200,000	20	1,300,000

a. Use the *internal rate of return (IRR) approach* to select the best group of projects.
b. Use the *net present value (NPV) approach* to select the best group of projects.
c. Compare, contrast, and discuss your findings in parts **a** and **b**.
d. Which projects should the firm implement? Why?

  P9–24 **Capital rationing—NPV approach**   A firm with a 13% cost of capital must select the optimal group of projects from those shown in the following table, given its capital budget of $1 million.

Project	Initial investment	NPV at 13% cost of capital
A	$300,000	$ 84,000
B	200,000	10,000
C	100,000	25,000
D	900,000	90,000
E	500,000	70,000
F	100,000	50,000
G	800,000	160,000

a. Calculate the *present value of cash inflows* associated with each project.
b. Select the optimal group of projects, keeping in mind that unused funds are costly.

P9–25   **Basic scenario analysis**   Murdock Paints is in the process of evaluating two mutu-ally exclusive additions to its processing capacity. The firm's financial analysts have developed pessimistic, most likely, and optimistic estimates of the annual cash inflows associated with each project. These estimates are shown in the following table.

	Project A	Project B
Initial investment (CF_0)	$8,000	$8,000
Outcome	Annual cash inflows (CF)	
Pessimistic	$ 200	$ 900
Most likely	1,000	1,000
Optimistic	1,800	1,100

a. Determine the *range* of annual cash inflows for each of the two projects.
b. Assume that the firm's cost of capital is 10% and that both projects have 20-year lives. Construct a table similar to this for the NPVs for each project. Include the *range* of NPVs for each project.
c. Do parts **a** and **b** provide consistent views of the two projects? Explain.
d. Which project do you recommend? Why?

P9–26   **Scenario analysis**   James Secretarial Services is considering the purchase of one of two new personal computers, P and Q. The company expects both to provide benefits over a 10-year period, and each has a required investment of $3,000. The firm uses a 10% cost of capital. Management has constructed the following table of estimates of annual cash inflows for pessimistic, most likely, and optimistic results.

	Computer P	Computer Q
Initial investment (CF_0)	$3,000	$3,000
Outcome	Annual cash inflows (CF)	
Pessimistic	$ 500	$ 400
Most likely	750	750
Optimistic	1,000	1,200

a. Determine the *range* of annual cash inflows for each of the two computers.
b. Construct a table similar to this for the NPVs associated with each outcome for both computers.
c. Find the *range* of NPVs, and subjectively compare the risks associated with pur-chasing these computers.

P9–27   **Decision trees**   The Ouija Board-Games Company can bring out one of two new games this season. The *Signs Away* game has a higher initial cost but also a higher expected return. *Monopolistic Competition*, the alternative, has a slightly lower ini-tial cost but also a lower expected return. The present values and probabilities asso-ciated with each game are listed in the table on page 406.

Games	Initial investment	Present value of cash inflows	Probabilities
Signs Away	$140,000		1.00
		$320,000	.30
		220,000	.50
		− 80,000	.20
Monopolistic Competition	$120,000		1.00
		$260,000	.20
		$200,000	.45
		− 50,000	.35

a. Construct a *decision tree* to analyze the games.
b. Which game do you recommend (following a decision-tree analysis)?
c. Has your analysis captured the differences in the risks associated with these games? Explain.

P9–28 Simulation Ogden Corporation has compiled the following information on a capital expenditure proposal:
(1) The projected cash *inflows* are normally distributed with a mean of $36,000 and a standard deviation of $9,000.
(2) The projected cash *outflows* are normally distributed with a mean of $30,000 and a standard deviation of $6,000.
(3) The firm has an 11% cost of capital.
(4) The probability distributions of cash inflows and cash outflows are not expected to change over the project's 10-year life.
a. Describe how the foregoing data can be used to develop a simulation model for finding the net present value of the project.
b. Discuss the advantages of using a simulation to evaluate the proposed project.

P9–29 Risk-adjusted discount rates—Basic Country Wallpapers is considering investing in one of three mutually exclusive projects, E, F, and G. The firm's cost of capital, r, is 15%, and the risk-free rate, R_F, is 10%. The firm has gathered the following basic cash flow and risk index data for each project.

	Project (*j*)		
	E	F	G
Initial investment (CF_0)	$15,000	$11,000	$19,000
Year (*t*)	Cash inflows (CF_t)		
1	$ 6,000	$ 6,000	$ 4,000
2	6,000	4,000	6,000
3	6,000	5,000	8,000
4	6,000	2,000	12,000
Risk index (RI_j)	1.80	1.00	0.60

a. Find the *net present value (NPV)* of each project using the firm's cost of capital. Which project is preferred in this situation?
b. The firm uses the following equation to determine the risk-adjusted discount rate, RADR$_j$, for each project *j*:

$$\text{RADR}_j = R_F + [RI_j \times (r - R_F)]$$

where

R_F = risk-free rate of return
RI_j = risk index for project *j*
r = cost of capital

Substitute each project's risk index into this equation to determine its RADR.
c. Use the RADR for each project to determine its *risk-adjusted NPV*. Which project is preferable in this situation?
d. Compare and discuss your findings in parts **a** and **c**. Which project do you recommend that the firm accept?

P9–30 **Risk-adjusted discount rates—Tabular**   After a careful evaluation of investment alternatives and opportunities, Masters School Supplies has developed a CAPM-type relationship linking a risk index to the required return (RADR), as shown in the following table.

Risk index	Required return (RADR)
0.0	7.0% (risk-free rate, R_F)
0.2	8.0
0.4	9.0
0.6	10.0
0.8	11.0
1.0	12.0
1.2	13.0
1.4	14.0
1.6	15.0
1.8	16.0
2.0	17.0

The firm is considering two mutually exclusive projects, A and B. Following are the data the firm has been able to gather about the projects.

	Project A	Project B
Initial investment (CF_0)	$20,000	$30,000
Project life	5 years	5 years
Annual cash inflow (CF)	$7,000	$10,000
Risk index	0.2	1.4

All the firm's cash inflows have already been adjusted for taxes.
a. Evaluate the projects using *risk-adjusted discount rates*.
b. Discuss your findings in part **a**, and recommend the preferred project.

PERSONAL FINANCE PROBLEM

P9–31 **Mutually exclusive investments and risk**   Lara Fredericks is interested in two mutually exclusive investments. Both investments cover the same time horizon of 6 years.
The cost of the first investment is $10,000, and Lara expects equal and consecutive
year-end payments of $3,000. The second investment promises equal and consecu-
tive payments of $3,800 with an initial outlay of $12,000 required. The current
required return on the first investment is 8.5%, and the second carries a required
return of 10.5%.

a. What is the *net present value* of the first investment?
b. What is the *net present value* of the second investment?
c. Being mutually exclusive, which investment should Lara choose? Explain.
d. Which investment was relatively more risky? Explain.

P9–32 **Risk classes and RADR**   Moses Manufacturing is attempting to select the best of
three mutually exclusive projects, X, Y, and Z. Although all the projects have 5-year
lives, they possess differing degrees of risk. Project X is in class V, the highest-risk
class; project Y is in class II, the below-average-risk class; and project Z is in class
III, the average-risk class. The basic cash flow data for each project and the risk
classes and risk-adjusted discount rates (RADRs) used by the firm are shown in the
following tables.

	Project X	Project Y	Project Z
Initial investment (CF_0)	$180,000	$235,000	$310,000
Year (t)	Cash inflows (CF_t)		
1	$80,000	$50,000	$90,000
2	70,000	60,000	90,000
3	60,000	70,000	90,000
4	60,000	80,000	90,000
5	60,000	90,000	90,000

Risk Classes and RADRs		
Risk Class	Description	Risk-adjusted discount rate (RADR)
I	Lowest risk	10%
II	Below-average risk	13
III	Average risk	15
IV	Above-average risk	19
V	Highest risk	22

a. Find the *risk-adjusted NPV* for each project.
b. Which project, if any, would you recommend that the firm undertake?

P9–33 **ETHICS PROBLEM**   One way to avoid the EPA penalties (see *Focus on Ethics* on
page 387) for excessive air pollution is to use carbon credits. Carbon credits are a
tradable permit scheme that allows businesses that cannot meet their greenhouse-gas-

emissions limits to purchase carbon credits from businesses that are below their quota. By allowing credits to be bought and sold, a business for which reducing its emissions would be expensive or prohibitive can pay another business to make the reduction for it. Do you agree with this arrangement? How would you feel as an investor in a company that utilizes carbon credits to legally exceed its pollution limits?

Chapter 9 Case

Making Norwich Tool's Lathe Investment Decision

Norwich Tool, a large machine shop, is considering replacing one of its lathes with either of two new lathes—lathe A or lathe B. Lathe A is a highly automated, computer-controlled lathe; lathe B is a less expensive lathe that uses standard technology. To analyze these alternatives, Mario Jackson, a financial analyst, prepared estimates of the initial investment and incremental (relevant) cash inflows associated with each lathe. These are shown in the following table.

	Lathe A	Lathe B
Initial investment (CF_0)	$660,000	$360,000
Year (*t*)	\multicolumn{2}{c}{Cash inflows (CF_t)}

Year (*t*)	Cash inflows (CF_t)	
1	$128,000	$ 88,000
2	182,000	120,000
3	166,000	96,000
4	168,000	86,000
5	450,000	207,000

Note that Mario plans to analyze both lathes over a 5-year period. At the end of that time, the lathes would be sold, thus accounting for the large fifth-year cash inflows.

Mario believes that the two lathes are equally risky and that the acceptance of either of them will not change the firm's overall risk. He therefore decides to apply the firm's 13% cost of capital when analyzing the lathes. Norwich Tool requires all projects to have a maximum payback period of 4.0 years.

To Do

a. Use the *payback period* to assess the acceptability and relative ranking of each lathe.
b. Assuming equal risk, use the following sophisticated capital budgeting techniques to assess the acceptability and relative ranking of each lathe:
   (1) *Net present value (NPV)*.
   (2) *Internal rate of return (IRR)*.
c. Summarize the preferences indicated by the techniques used in parts **a** and **b**, and indicate which lathe you recommend, if either, (1) if the firm has unlimited funds and (2) if the firm has capital rationing.

  d. Repeat part **b** assuming that Mario decides that because of its greater risk, lathe A's cash inflows should be evaluated by using a 15% cost of capital.
  e. What effect, if any, does recognition of lathe A's greater risk in part **d** have on your recommendation in part **c**?

Spreadsheet Exercise

The Drillago Company is involved in searching for locations in which to drill for oil. The firm's current project requires an initial investment of $15 million and has an estimated life of 10 years. The expected future cash inflows for the project are as follows:

Year	Cash inflows
1	$ 600,000
2	1,000,000
3	1,000,000
4	2,000,000
5	3,000,000
6	3,500,000
7	4,000,000
8	6,000,000
9	8,000,000
10	12,000,000

The firm's current cost of capital is 13%.

To Do

Create a spreadsheet to answer the following:

  a. Calculate the project's *net present value (NPV)*. Is the project acceptable under the NPV technique? Explain.
  b. Calculate the project's *internal rate of return (IRR)*. Is the project acceptable under the IRR technique? Explain.
  c. In this case, did the two methods produce the same results? Generally, is there a preference between the NPV and IRR techniques? Explain.
  d. Calculate the *payback period* for the project. If the firm usually accepts projects that have payback periods between 1 and 7 years, is this project acceptable?

Web Exercise

Go to the book's companion website at **www.prenhall.com/gitman** to find the Web Exercise for this chapter.

Remember to check the book's website at **www.prenhall.com/gitman** to find additional resources, including Web Exercises and a Web Case.

Part Four
Long-Term Financial Decisions

Chapters in This Part

411

10 | The Cost of Capital

WHY THIS CHAPTER MATTERS TO YOU

In Your Professional Life

Accounting: You need to understand the various sources of capital and how their costs are calculated to provide the data necessary to determine the firm's overall cost of capital.

Information systems: You need to understand the various sources of capital and how their costs are calculated to develop systems that will estimate the costs of those sources of capital, as well as the overall cost of capital.

Management: You need to understand the cost of capital to select long-term investments after assessing their acceptability and relative rankings.

Marketing: You need to understand the firm's cost of capital because proposed projects must earn returns in excess of it to be acceptable.

Operations: You need to understand the firm's cost of capital to assess the economic viability of investments in plant and equipment needed to improve or grow the firm's capacity.

In Your Personal Life

You need to know, on average, how much you are paying for financing. You do not sell equity in your personal financial life, but you do borrow money and can therefore realize financial benefits by understanding cost of capital concepts. By knowing your *personal cost of capital,* you can make better long-term investment decisions and maximize the worth from each dollar of long-term investment.

LEARNING GOALS

LG 1 Understand the key assumptions, the basic concept, and the specific sources of capital associated with the cost of capital.

LG 2 Determine the cost of long-term debt and the cost of preferred stock.

LG 3 Calculate the cost of common stock equity and convert it into the cost of retained earnings and the cost of new issues of common stock.

LG 4 Calculate the weighted average cost of capital (WACC) and discuss alternative weighting schemes.

LG 5 Describe the procedures used to determine break points and the weighted marginal cost of capital (WMCC).

LG 6 Explain the weighted marginal cost of capital (WMCC) and its use with the investment opportunities schedule (IOS) to make financing/investment decisions.

he cost of capital is used to select capital investments that increase shareholder value. In applying the net present value and internal rate of return techniques in Chapter 9, we simply assumed a reasonable cost of capital. Now we will demonstrate how the cost of capital is calculated. This chapter considers the costs of long-term debt, preferred stock, common stock, and retained earnings and shows how to combine them to determine the cost of capital and related measures that the firm will use in making long-term financing/investment decisions.

10.1 | Overview of the Cost of Capital

cost of capital
The rate of return that a firm must earn on the projects in which it invests to maintain its market value and attract funds.

The **cost of capital** is the rate of return that a firm must earn on the projects in which it invests to maintain the market value of its stock. It can also be thought of as the rate of return required by the market suppliers of capital to attract their funds to the firm. If risk is held constant, projects with a rate of return above the cost of capital will increase the value of the firm, and projects with a rate of return below the cost of capital will decrease the value of the firm.

The cost of capital is an extremely important financial concept. It acts as a major link between the firm's long-term investment decisions (discussed in Part Three) and the wealth of the owners as determined by investors in the marketplace. It is, in effect, the "magic number" that is used to decide whether a proposed corporate investment will increase or decrease the firm's stock price. Clearly, only those investments that are expected to increase stock price (NPV > $0, or IRR > cost of capital) would be recommended. Because of its key role in financial decision making, the importance of the cost of capital cannot be overemphasized.

Some Key Assumptions

business risk
The risk to the firm of being unable to cover operating costs.

financial risk
The risk to the firm of being unable to cover required financial obligations (interest, lease payments, preferred stock dividends).

The cost of capital is a dynamic concept affected by a variety of economic and firm-specific factors. To isolate the basic structure of the cost of capital, we make some key assumptions relative to risk and taxes:

1. **Business risk**—the risk to the firm of being unable to cover operating costs—*is assumed to be unchanged.* This assumption means that the firm's acceptance of a given project does not affect its ability to meet operating costs.
2. **Financial risk**—the risk to the firm of being unable to cover required financial obligations (interest, lease payments, preferred stock dividends)—*is assumed to be unchanged.* This assumption means that projects are financed in such a way that the firm's ability to meet required financing costs is unchanged.
3. After-tax costs are considered relevant. In other words, *the cost of capital is measured on an after-tax basis.* This assumption is consistent with the after-tax framework used to make capital budgeting decisions.

Hint Because of the positive relationship between risk and return, a firm's financing cost (cost of capital) will change if the acceptance of a project changes the firm's business or financial risk. The cost of capital can therefore be more easily measured by assuming that new projects do not change these risks.

The Basic Concept

The cost of capital is estimated at a given point in time. It reflects the *expected average future cost of funds over the long run.* Although firms typically raise money in lumps, the cost of capital should reflect the interrelatedness of financing activities. For example, if a firm raises funds with debt (borrowing) today, it is likely that some form of equity, such as common stock, will have to be used the next time it needs funds. Most firms attempt to maintain a desired optimal mix of debt and equity financing. In practice, this mix is commonly a range, such as 40 percent to 50 percent debt, rather than a point, such as 55 percent debt. It is called a **target capital structure**—a topic that will be addressed in Chapter 11. Here, it is sufficient to say that although firms raise money in lumps, they tend toward some desired *mix of financing*.

To capture the interrelatedness of financing assuming the presence of a target capital structure, we need to look at the *overall cost of capital* rather than the cost of the specific source of funds used to finance a given expenditure.

Example

A firm is *currently* faced with an investment opportunity. Assume the following:

Best project available today

$$\text{Cost} = \$100,000$$
$$\text{Life} = 20 \text{ years}$$
$$\text{IRR} = 7\%$$

Cost of least-cost financing source available

$$\text{Debt} = 6\%$$

Because it can earn 7% on the investment of funds costing only 6%, the firm undertakes the opportunity. Imagine that *1 week later* a new investment opportunity is available:

Best project available 1 week later

$$\text{Cost} = \$100,000$$
$$\text{Life} = 20 \text{ years}$$
$$\text{IRR} = 12\%$$

Cost of least-cost financing source available

$$\text{Equity} = 14\%$$

In this instance, the firm rejects the opportunity, because the 14% financing cost is greater than the 12% expected return.

Were the firm's actions in the best interests of its owners? No; it accepted a project yielding a 7% return and rejected one with a 12% return. Clearly, there should be a better way, and there is: The firm can use a *combined* cost, which over the long run will yield better decisions. By weighting the cost of each source of financing by its *target proportion* in the firm's capital structure, the firm can obtain a *weighted average cost* that reflects the interrelationship of financing decisions. Assuming that a 50–50 mix of debt and equity is targeted, the weighted average cost here would be 10% [(0.50 × 6% debt) + (0.50 × 14% equity)]. With this cost, the first opportunity would have been rejected (7% IRR < 10% weighted average cost), and the second would have been accepted (12% IRR > 10% weighted average cost). Such an outcome would clearly be more desirable.

Specific Sources of Capital

This chapter focuses on finding the costs of specific sources of capital and combining them to determine the weighted average cost of capital. Our concern is only with the *long-term* sources of funds available to a business firm, because these sources supply the permanent financing. Long-term financing supports the firm's fixed-asset investments.[1] We assume throughout the chapter that such investments are selected by using appropriate capital budgeting techniques.

There are four basic sources of long-term funds for the business firm: long-term debt, preferred stock, common stock, and retained earnings. All entries on the right-hand side of the balance sheet, other than current liabilities, represent these sources:

Although not every firm will use all of these methods of financing, each firm is expected to have funds from some of these sources in its capital structure.

The *specific cost* of each source of financing is the *after-tax* cost of obtaining the financing *today,* not the historically based cost reflected by the existing financing on the firm's books. Techniques for determining the specific cost of each source of long-term funds are presented on the following pages. Although these techniques tend to develop precisely calculated values, the resulting values are at best *rough approximations* because of the numerous assumptions and forecasts that underlie them. Although we round calculated costs to the nearest 0.1 percent throughout this chapter, it is not unusual for practicing financial managers to use costs rounded to the nearest 1 percent because these values are merely estimates.

REVIEW QUESTIONS

10–1 What is the *cost of capital?* What role does it play in long-term investment decisions?

10–2 Why do we assume that *business risk* and *financial risk* are unchanged when evaluating the cost of capital? Discuss the implications of these assumptions on the acceptance and financing of new projects.

---

1. The role of both long-term and short-term financing in supporting both fixed- and current-asset investments is addressed in Chapter 13. Suffice it to say that long-term funds are at minimum used to finance fixed assets.

10–3 Why is the cost of capital measured on an *after-tax basis?* Why is use of a weighted average cost of capital rather than the cost of the specific source of funds recommended?

10–4 You have just been told, "Because we are going to finance this project with debt, its required rate of return must exceed the cost of debt." Do you agree or disagree? Explain.

10.2 | Cost of Long-Term Debt

cost of long-term debt, r_i
The after-tax cost today of raising long-term funds through borrowing.

The **cost of long-term debt,** r_i, is the after-tax cost today of raising long-term funds through borrowing. For convenience, we typically assume that the funds are raised through the sale of bonds. In addition, as we did in Chapter 6, we assume that the bonds pay *annual* (rather than *semiannual*) interest.

Net Proceeds

net proceeds
Funds actually received from the sale of a security.

flotation costs
The total costs of issuing and selling a security.

Most corporate long-term debts are incurred through the sale of bonds. The **net proceeds** from the sale of a bond, or any security, are the funds that are actually received from the sale. **Flotation costs**—the total costs of issuing and selling a security—reduce the net proceeds from the sale. These costs apply to all public offerings of securities—debt, preferred stock, and common stock. They include two components: (1) *underwriting costs*—compensation earned by investment bankers for selling the security, and (2) *administrative costs*—issuer expenses such as legal, accounting, printing, and other expenses.

Example | Duchess Corporation, a major hardware manufacturer, is contemplating selling $10 million worth of 20-year, 9% coupon (stated *annual* interest rate) bonds, each with a par value of $1,000. Because similar-risk bonds earn returns greater than 9%, the firm must sell the bonds for $980 to compensate for the lower coupon interest rate. The flotation costs are 2% of the par value of the bond ($0.02 \times \$1,000$), or $20. The *net proceeds* to the firm from the sale of each bond are therefore $960 ($980 − $20).

Before-Tax Cost of Debt

The before-tax cost of debt, r_d, for a bond can be obtained in any of three ways: quotation, calculation, or approximation.

Hint From the issuer's perspective, the IRR on a bond's cash flows is its *cost to maturity;* from the investor's perspective, the IRR on a bond's cash flows is its *yield to maturity (YTM),* as explained in Chapter 6. These two measures are conceptually similar, although their point of view is different.

Using Cost Quotations

When the net proceeds from sale of a bond equal its par value, the before-tax cost just equals the coupon interest rate. For example, a bond with a 10 percent coupon interest rate that nets proceeds equal to the bond's $1,000 par value would have a before-tax cost, r_d, of 10 percent.

A second quotation that is sometimes used is the *yield to maturity* (*YTM*) on a similar-risk bond[2] (see Chapter 6). For example, if a similar-risk bond has a YTM of 9.7 percent, this value can be used as the before-tax cost of debt, r_d.

Calculating the Cost

This approach finds the before-tax cost of debt by calculating the *internal rate of return* (*IRR*) on the bond cash flows. From the issuer's point of view, this value is the *cost to maturity* of the cash flows associated with the debt. The cost to maturity can be calculated by using a financial calculator, an electronic spreadsheet, or a trial-and-error technique.[3] It represents the annual before-tax percentage cost of the debt.

Example

In the preceding example, the net proceeds of a $1,000, 9% coupon interest rate, 20-year bond were found to be $960. The calculation of the annual cost is quite simple. The cash flow pattern is exactly the opposite of a conventional pattern; it consists of an initial inflow (the net proceeds) followed by a series of annual outlays (the interest payments). In the final year, when the debt is retired, an outlay representing the repayment of the principal also occurs. The cash flows associated with Duchess Corporation's bond issue are as follows:

End of year(s)	Cash flow
0	$ 960
1–20	−$ 90
20	−$1,000

The initial $960 inflow is followed by annual interest outflows of $90 (9% coupon interest rate × $1,000 par value) over the 20-year life of the bond. In year 20, an outflow of $1,000 (the repayment of the principal) occurs. We can determine the cost of debt by finding the IRR, which is the discount rate that equates the present value of the outflows to the initial inflow.

Calculator Use   [*Note:* Most calculators require either the present (net proceeds) or the future (annual interest payments and repayment of principal) values to be input as negative numbers when we calculate cost to maturity. That approach is used here.] Using the calculator and the inputs shown at the left, you should find the before-tax cost (cost to maturity) to be 9.452%.

Spreadsheet Use   The before-tax cost of debt on the Duchess Corporation bond also can be calculated as shown in the Excel spreadsheet on page 418.

---

2. Generally, the yield to maturity of bonds with a similar "rating" is used. Bond ratings, which are published by independent agencies, were discussed in Chapter 6.

3. The trial-and-error technique is presented at the book's website www.prenhall.com/gitman.

	A	B	C	D	E	F
1	FINDING THE IRR ON A 20-YEAR BOND					
2	Net proceeds from sale of bond	$ 960				
3	Coupon payment	$ 90				
4	Years to maturity	20				
5	Par value (principal)	$ 1,000				
6						
7	Use the Trial and Error Method to determine the before-tax cost of debt.					
8	The model:	Value of the bond = Coupon payment(PVIFA) + Par(PVIF)				
9	There is a before-tax rate that will discount the future cash flows back to the $960 value.					
10						
11		Before-tax cost of debt = 9.452%				
12						
13		Payment	PVIFA	Par	PVIF	= Value
14		$ 90	8.8420	$1,000	0.1643	960.03
15						

Approximating the Cost

The before-tax cost of debt, r_d, for a bond with a $1,000 par value can be approximated by using the following equation:

$$r_d = \frac{I + \frac{\$1,000 - N_d}{n}}{\frac{N_d + \$1,000}{2}} \qquad (10.1)$$

where

I = annual interest in dollars

N_d = net proceeds from the sale of debt (bond)

n = number of years to the bond's maturity

Example

Substituting the appropriate values from the Duchess Corporation example into the approximation formula given in Equation 10.1, we get

$$r_d = \frac{\$90 + \frac{\$1,000 - \$960}{20}}{\frac{\$960 + \$1,000}{2}} = \frac{\$90 + \$2}{\$980}$$

$$= \frac{\$92}{\$980} = \underline{9.4\%}$$

This approximate before-tax cost of debt is close to the 9.452% value calculated precisely in the preceding example.

After-Tax Cost of Debt

As indicated earlier, the *specific cost* of financing must be stated on an after-tax basis. Because interest on debt is tax deductible, it reduces the firm's taxable income. The after-tax cost of debt, r_i, can be found by multiplying the before-tax cost, r_d, by 1 minus the tax rate, T, as stated in the following equation:

$$r_i = r_d \times (1 - T) \tag{10.2}$$

Example Duchess Corporation has a 40% tax rate. Using the 9.4% before-tax debt cost calculated above, and applying Equation 10.2, we find an after-tax cost of debt of 5.6% [9.4% × (1 − 0.40)]. Typically, the cost of long-term debt is less than a given firm's cost of any of the alternative forms of long-term financing, primarily because of the tax deductibility of interest.

Personal Finance Example Kait and Kasim Sullivan, a married couple in the 28% federal income-tax bracket, wish to borrow $60,000 to fully pay for the purchase of a new luxury car. To finance the purchase, they can either borrow the $60,000 through the auto dealer at an annual interest rate of 6.0%, or they can take a $60,000 second mortgage on their home. The best annual rate they can get on the second mortgage is 7.2%. They already have qualified for both of the loans being considered.

If they borrow from the auto dealer, the interest on this "consumer loan" will not be deductible for federal tax purposes. Because their home, which is worth $400,000 today, currently has a mortgage balance of $240,000, the second mortgage of $60,000 would result in total mortgages against the property of $300,000. This amount is well below the $1.1 million maximum mortgage against which a homeowner can deduct interest for federal tax purposes. Therefore, the interest on the second mortgage would be tax-deductible.

To choose the least-cost financing, the Sullivans calculated the after-tax cost of both sources of long-term debt. Because interest on the auto loan is *not* tax-deductible, its after-tax cost equals its stated cost of 6.0%. Because the interest on the second mortgage *is* tax-deductible, its after-tax cost can be found using Equation 10.2:

After-tax cost of debt = Before-tax cost of debt × (1 − Tax rate)

7.2% × (1 − 0.28) = 7.2% × 0.72 = <u>5.2%</u>

Because the 5.2% after-tax cost of the second mortgage is less than the 6.0% cost of the auto loan, the Sullivans should use the second mortgage to finance the auto purchase.

REVIEW QUESTIONS

10–5 What are the *net proceeds* from the sale of a bond? What are *flotation costs* and how do they affect a bond's net proceeds?

10–6 What three methods can be used to find the before-tax cost of debt?

10–7 How is the before-tax cost of debt converted into the after-tax cost?

10.3 | Cost of Preferred Stock

Preferred stock represents a special type of ownership interest in the firm. It gives preferred stockholders the right to receive their *stated* dividends before the firm can distribute any earnings to common stockholders. Because preferred stock is a form of ownership, the proceeds from its sale are expected to be held for an infinite period of time. The key characteristics of preferred stock were described in Chapter 7. However, the one aspect of preferred stock that requires review is dividends.

Preferred Stock Dividends

Most preferred stock dividends are stated as a *dollar amount:* "*x* dollars per year." When dividends are stated this way, the stock is often referred to as "*x*-dollar preferred stock." Thus a "$4 preferred stock" is expected to pay preferred stockholders $4 in dividends each year on each share of preferred stock owned.

Sometimes preferred stock dividends are stated as an *annual percentage rate.* This rate represents the percentage of the stock's par, or face, value that equals the annual dividend. For instance, an 8 percent preferred stock with a $50 par value would be expected to pay an annual dividend of $4 per share ($0.08 \times \$50$ par = $4). Before the cost of preferred stock is calculated, any dividends stated as percentages should be converted to annual dollar dividends.

Calculating the Cost of Preferred Stock

cost of preferred stock, r_p
The ratio of the preferred stock dividend to the firm's net proceeds from the sale of preferred stock; calculated by dividing the annual dividend, D_p, by the net proceeds from the sale of the preferred stock, N_p.

The **cost of preferred stock,** r_p, is the ratio of the preferred stock dividend to the firm's net proceeds from the sale of the preferred stock. The net proceeds represents the amount of money to be received minus any flotation costs. Equation 10.3 gives the cost of preferred stock, r_p, in terms of the annual dollar dividend, D_p, and the net proceeds from the sale of the stock, N_p:

$$r_p = \frac{D_p}{N_p} \tag{10.3}$$

Because preferred stock dividends are paid out of the firm's *after-tax* cash flows, a tax adjustment is not required.

Example

Duchess Corporation is contemplating issuance of a 10% preferred stock that is expected to sell for its $87-per-share par value. The cost of issuing and selling the stock is expected to be $5 per share. The first step in finding the cost of the stock is to calculate the dollar amount of the annual preferred dividend, which is $8.70 ($0.10 \times \$87$). The net proceeds per share from the proposed sale of stock equals the sale price minus the flotation costs ($87 - \$5 = \$82$). Substituting the annual dividend, D_p, of $8.70 and the net proceeds, N_p, of $82 into Equation 10.3 gives the cost of preferred stock, 10.6% ($8.70 \div \$82$).

The cost of Duchess's preferred stock (10.6%) is much greater than the cost of its long-term debt (5.6%). This difference exists both because the cost of long-term debt (the interest) is tax deductible and because preferred stock is riskier than long-term debt.

10–8 How would you calculate the cost of preferred stock?

10.4 | Cost of Common Stock

The *cost of common stock* is the return required on the stock by investors in the marketplace. There are two forms of common stock financing: (1) retained earnings and (2) new issues of common stock. As a first step in finding each of these costs, we must estimate the cost of common stock equity.

Finding the Cost of Common Stock Equity

cost of common stock equity, r_s
The rate at which investors discount the expected dividends of the firm to determine its share value.

The **cost of common stock equity**, r_s, is the rate at which investors discount the expected dividends of the firm to determine its share value. Two techniques are used to measure the cost of common stock equity.[4] One relies on the constant-growth valuation model, the other on the capital asset pricing model (CAPM).

Using the Constant-Growth Valuation (Gordon) Model

constant-growth valuation (Gordon) model
Assumes that the value of a share of stock equals the present value of all future dividends (assumed to grow at a constant rate) that it is expected to provide over an infinite time horizon.

In Chapter 7 we found the value of a share of stock to be equal to the present value of all future dividends, which in one model were assumed to grow at a constant annual rate over an infinite time horizon. This is the **constant-growth valuation model,** also known as the **Gordon model.** The key expression derived for this model was presented as Equation 7.4 and is restated here:

$$P_0 = \frac{D_1}{r_s - g} \qquad (10.4)$$

where

P_0 = value of common stock

D_1 = per-share dividend *expected* at the end of year 1

r_s = required return on common stock

g = constant rate of growth in dividends

Solving Equation 10.4 for r_s results in the following expression for the *cost of common stock equity:*

$$r_s = \frac{D_1}{P_0} + g \qquad (10.5)$$

Equation 10.5 indicates that the cost of common stock equity can be found by dividing the dividend expected at the end of year 1 by the current price of the

---

4. Other, more subjective techniques are available for estimating the cost of common stock equity. One popular technique is the *bond yield plus a premium*; it estimates the cost of common stock equity by adding a premium, typically between 3% and 5%, to the firm's current cost of long-term debt. Another, even more subjective technique uses the firm's *expected return on equity (ROE)* as a measure of its cost of common stock equity. Here we focus only on the more theoretically based techniques.

stock (the "dividend yield") and adding the expected growth rate (the "capital gains yield"). Because common stock dividends are paid from *after-tax* income, no tax adjustment is required.

Example

Duchess Corporation wishes to determine its cost of common stock equity, r_s. The market price, P_0, of its common stock is $50 per share. The firm expects to pay a dividend, D_1, of $4 at the end of the coming year, 2010. The dividends paid on the outstanding stock over the past 6 years (2004–2009) were as follows:

Year	Dividend
2009	$3.80
2008	3.62
2007	3.47
2006	3.33
2005	3.12
2004	2.97

Using a financial calculator, electronic spreadsheet, or the table for the present value interest factors, *PVIF* (Table A–2), in conjunction with the technique described for finding growth rates in Chapter 4, we can calculate the annual growth rate of dividends, *g*. It turns out to be approximately 5% (more precisely, it is 5.05%). Substituting $D_1 = \$4$, $P_0 = \$50$, and $g = 5\%$ into Equation 10.5 yields the cost of common stock equity:

$$r_s = \frac{\$4}{\$50} + 0.05 = 0.08 + 0.05 = 0.130, \text{ or } \underline{13.0\%}$$

The 13.0% cost of common stock equity represents the return required by *existing* shareholders on their investment. If the actual return is less than that, shareholders are likely to begin selling their stock.

Using the Capital Asset Pricing Model (CAPM)

capital asset pricing model (CAPM)
Describes the relationship between the required return, r_s, and the nondiversifiable risk of the firm as measured by the beta coefficient, *b*.

Recall from Chapter 5 that the **capital asset pricing model (CAPM)** describes the relationship between the required return, r_s, and the nondiversifiable risk of the firm as measured by the beta coefficient, *b*. The basic CAPM is

$$r_s = R_F + [b \times (r_m - R_F)] \tag{10.6}$$

where

R_F = risk-free rate of return

r_m = market return; return on the market portfolio of assets

Using CAPM indicates that the cost of common stock equity is the return required by investors as compensation for the firm's nondiversifiable risk, measured by beta.

Example

Duchess Corporation now wishes to calculate its cost of common stock equity, r_s, by using the capital asset pricing model. The firm's investment advisors and its own analyses indicate that the risk-free rate, R_F, equals 7%; the firm's beta,

b, equals 1.5; and the market return, r_m, equals 11%. Substituting these values into Equation 10.6, the company estimates the cost of common stock equity, r_s, to be

$$r_s = 7.0\% + [1.5 \times (11.0\% - 7.0\%)] = 7.0\% + 6.0\% = \underline{13.0\%}$$

The 13.0% cost of common stock equity represents the required return of investors in Duchess Corporation common stock. It is the same as that found by using the constant-growth valuation model.

Cost of Retained Earnings

cost of retained earnings, r_r
The same as the cost of an *equivalent fully subscribed issue of additional common stock,* which is equal to the cost of common stock equity, r_s.

As you know, dividends are paid out of a firm's earnings. Their payment, made in cash to common stockholders, reduces the firm's retained earnings. Suppose a firm needs common stock equity financing of a certain amount. It has two choices relative to retained earnings: It can issue additional common stock in that amount and still pay dividends to stockholders out of retained earnings, or it can increase common stock equity by retaining the earnings (not paying the cash dividends) in the needed amount. In a strict accounting sense, the retention of earnings increases common stock equity in the same way that the sale of additional shares of common stock does. Thus the **cost of retained earnings, r_r,** to the firm is the same as the cost of an *equivalent fully subscribed issue of additional common stock.* Stockholders find the firm's retention of earnings acceptable only if they expect that it will earn at least their required return on the reinvested funds.

Hint Using retained earnings as a major source of financing for capital expenditures does not give away control of the firm and does not dilute present earnings per share, as would occur if new common stock were issued. However, the firm must effectively manage retained earnings to produce profits that increase future retained earnings.

Viewing retained earnings as a fully subscribed issue of additional common stock, we can set the firm's cost of retained earnings, r_r, equal to the cost of common stock equity as given by Equations 10.5 and 10.6.[5]

$$r_r = r_s \tag{10.7}$$

It is not necessary to adjust the cost of retained earnings for flotation costs, because by retaining earnings, the firm "raises" equity capital without incurring these costs.

Example

The cost of retained earnings for Duchess Corporation was actually calculated in the preceding examples: It is equal to the cost of common stock equity. Thus r_r equals 13.0%. As we will show in the next section, the cost of retained earnings is always lower than the cost of a new issue of common stock, because it entails no flotation costs.

Cost of New Issues of Common Stock

cost of a new issue of common stock, r_n
The cost of common stock, net of underpricing and associated flotation costs.

Our purpose in finding the firm's overall cost of capital is to determine the after-tax cost of *new* funds required for financing projects. The **cost of a new issue of common stock, r_n,** is determined by calculating the cost of common stock, net of

5. Technically, if a stockholder received dividends and wished to invest them in additional shares of the firm's stock, he or she would first have to pay personal taxes at capital gains rates on the dividends and then pay brokerage fees before acquiring additional shares. By using pt as the average stockholder's capital gains tax rate and bf as the average brokerage fees stated as a percentage, we can specify the cost of retained earnings, r_r, as $r_r = r_s \times (1 - pt) \times (1 - bf)$. Because of the difficulty in estimating pt and bf, only the simpler definition of r_r given in Equation 10.7 is used here.

underpriced
Stock sold at a price below its current market price, P_0.

underpricing and associated flotation costs. Normally, for a new issue to sell, it has to be **underpriced**—sold at a price below its current market price, P_0.

Firms underprice new issues for a variety of reasons. First, when the market is in equilibrium (that is, the demand for shares equals the supply of shares), additional demand for shares can be achieved only at a lower price. Second, when additional shares are issued, each share's percentage of ownership in the firm is diluted, thereby justifying a lower share value. Finally, many investors view the issuance of additional shares as a signal that management is using common stock equity financing because it believes that the shares are currently overpriced. Recognizing this information, they will buy shares only at a price below the current market price. Clearly, these and other factors necessitate underpricing of new offerings of common stock. Flotation costs paid for issuing and selling the new issue will further reduce proceeds.

We can use the constant-growth valuation model expression for the cost of existing common stock, r_s, as a starting point. If we let N_n represent the net proceeds from the sale of new common stock after subtracting underpricing and flotation costs, the cost of the new issue, r_n, can be expressed as follows:

$$r_n = \frac{D_1}{N_n} + g \tag{10.8}$$

The net proceeds from sale of new common stock, N_n, will be less than the current market price, P_0. Therefore, the cost of new issues, r_n, will always be greater than the cost of existing issues, r_s, which is equal to the cost of retained earnings, r_r. *The cost of new common stock is normally greater than any other long-term financing cost.* Because common stock dividends are paid from after-tax cash flows, no tax adjustment is required.

Example   In the constant-growth valuation example, we found Duchess Corporation's cost of common stock equity, r_s, to be 13%, using the following values: an expected dividend, D_1, of $4; a current market price, P_0, of $50; and an expected growth rate of dividends, g, of 5%.

To determine its cost of *new* common stock, r_n, Duchess Corporation has estimated that on the average, new shares can be sold for $47. The $3-per-share underpricing is due to the competitive nature of the market. A second cost associated with a new issue is flotation costs of $2.50 per share that would be paid to issue and sell the new shares. The total underpricing and flotation costs per share are therefore expected to be $5.50.

Subtracting the $5.50-per-share underpricing and flotation cost from the current $50 share price results in expected net proceeds of $44.50 per share ($50.00 − $5.50). Substituting $D_1 = \$4$, $N_n = \$44.50$, and $g = 5\%$ into Equation 10.8 results in a cost of new common stock, r_n, as follows:

$$r_n = \frac{\$4.00}{\$44.50} + 0.05 = 0.09 + 0.05 = 0.140, \text{ or } \underline{14.0\%}$$

Duchess Corporation's cost of new common stock is therefore 14.0%. This is the value to be used in subsequent calculations of the firm's overall cost of capital.

REVIEW QUESTIONS

10–9   What premise about share value underlies the constant-growth valuation (Gordon) model that is used to measure the cost of common stock equity, r_s?

10–10 Why is the cost of financing a project with retained earnings less than the cost of financing it with a new issue of common stock?

10.5 | Weighted Average Cost of Capital

weighted average cost of capital (WACC), r_a
Reflects the expected average future cost of funds over the long run; found by weighting the cost of each specific type of capital by its proportion in the firm's capital structure.

Now that we have calculated the cost of specific sources of financing, we can determine the overall cost of capital. As noted earlier, the **weighted average cost of capital (WACC)**, r_a, reflects the expected average future cost of funds over the long run. It is found by weighting the cost of each specific type of capital by its proportion in the firm's capital structure.

Calculating Weighted Average Cost of Capital (WACC)

Calculating the weighted average cost of capital (WACC) is straightforward: Multiply the specific cost of each form of financing by its proportion in the firm's capital structure and sum the weighted values. As an equation, the weighted average cost of capital, r_a, can be specified as follows:

$$r_a = (w_i \times r_i) + (w_p \times r_p) + (w_s \times r_{r \text{ or } n}) \tag{10.9}$$

where

w_i = proportion of long-term debt in capital structure
w_p = proportion of preferred stock in capital structure
w_s = proportion of common stock equity in capital structure
$w_i + w_p + w_s = 1.0$

Three important points should be noted in Equation 10.9:

1. For computational convenience, it is best to convert the weights into decimal form and leave the specific costs in percentage terms.
2. *The sum of the weights must equal 1.0.* Simply stated, all capital structure components must be accounted for.
3. The firm's common stock equity weight, w_s, is multiplied by either the cost of retained earnings, r_r, or the cost of new common stock, r_n. Which cost is used depends on whether the firm's common stock equity will be financed using retained earnings, r_r, or new common stock, r_n.

Example ▸

In earlier examples, we found the costs of the various types of capital for Duchess Corporation to be as follows:

Cost of debt, $r_i = $ 5.6%

Cost of preferred stock, $r_p = 10.6\%$

Cost of retained earnings, $r_r = 13.0\%$

Cost of new common stock, $r_n = 14.0\%$

The company uses the following weights in calculating its weighted average cost of capital:

Source of capital	Weight
Long-term debt	40%
Preferred stock	10
Common stock equity	50
Total	100%

   Because the firm expects to have a sizable amount of retained earnings available ($300,000), it plans to use its cost of retained earnings, r_r, as the cost of common stock equity. Duchess Corporation's weighted average cost of capital is calculated in Table 10.1. The resulting weighted average cost of capital for Duchess is 9.8%. Assuming an unchanged risk level, the firm should accept all projects that will earn a return greater than 9.8%.

Weighting Schemes

Firms can calculate weights on the basis of either *book value* or *market value* and using either *historical* or *target* proportions.

Book Value versus Market Value

book value weights
Weights that use accounting values to measure the proportion of each type of capital in the firm's financial structure.

market value weights
Weights that use market values to measure the proportion of each type of capital in the firm's financial structure.

Book value weights use accounting values to measure the proportion of each type of capital in the firm's financial structure. **Market value weights** measure the proportion of each type of capital at its market value. Market value weights are appealing, because the market values of securities closely approximate the actual dollars to be received from their sale. Moreover, because firms calculate the costs of the various types of capital by using prevailing market prices, it seems reasonable to use market value weights. In addition, the long-term investment cash

Hint For computational convenience, the financing proportion weights are listed in decimal form in column 1 and the specific costs are shown in percentage terms in column 2.

TABLE 10.1	Calculation of the Weighted Average Cost of Capital for Duchess Corporation		
Source of capital	Weight (1)	Cost (2)	Weighted cost [(1) × (2)] (3)
Long-term debt	0.40	5.6%	2.2%
Preferred stock	0.10	10.6	1.1
Common stock equity	0.50	13.0	6.5
Totals	1.00		9.8%

Weighted average cost of capital = 9.8%

flows to which the cost of capital is applied are estimated in terms of current as well as future market values. *Market value weights are clearly preferred over book value weights.*

Historical versus Target

historical weights
Either book or market value weights based on *actual* capital structure proportions.

Historical weights can be either book or market value weights based on *actual* capital structure proportions. For example, past or current book value proportions would constitute a form of historical weighting, as would past or current market value proportions. Such a weighting scheme would therefore be based on real—rather than desired—proportions.

target weights
Either book or market value weights based on *desired* capital structure proportions.

  Target weights, which can also be based on either book or market values, reflect the firm's *desired* capital structure proportions. Firms using target weights establish such proportions on the basis of the "optimal" capital structure they wish to achieve. (The development of these proportions and the optimal structure are discussed in detail in Chapter 11.)

  When one considers the somewhat approximate nature of the calculation of weighted average cost of capital, the choice of weights may not be critical. However, from a strictly theoretical point of view, the *preferred weighting scheme is target market value proportions,* and we assume these throughout this chapter.

Personal Finance Example   Chuck Solis currently has three loans outstanding, all of which mature in exactly 6 years and can be repaid without penalty any time prior to maturity. The outstanding balances and annual interest rates on these loans are noted below.

Loan	Outstanding Balance	Annual Interest Rate
1	$26,000	9.6%
2	9,000	10.6
3	45,000	7.4

After a thorough search, Chuck found a lender who would loan him $80,000 for 6 years at an annual interest rate 9.2% on the condition that the loan proceeds be used to fully repay the three outstanding loans, which combined have an outstanding balance of $80,000 ($26,000 + $9,000 + $45,000).

  Chuck wishes to choose the less costly alternative: (1) do nothing or (2) borrow the $80,000 and pay off all three loans. He calculates the weighted average cost of his current debt by weighting each debt's annual interest cost by the proportion of the $80,000 total it represents and then summing the three weighted values as follows:

$$\text{Weighted average cost of current debt} = [(\$26,000/\$80,000) \times 9.6\%] + [(\$9,000/\$80,000) \times 10.6\%]$$
$$+ [(\$45,000/\$80,000) \times 7.4\%]$$
$$= (.3250 \times 9.6\%) + (.1125 \times 10.6\%) + (.5625 \times 7.4\%)$$
$$= 3.12\% + 1.19\% + 4.16\% = 8.47\% \approx \underline{\underline{8.5\%}}$$

Given that the weighted average cost of the $80,000 of current debt of 8.5% is below the 9.2% cost of the new $80,000 loan, Chuck should do nothing, and just continue to pay off the three loans as originally scheduled.

REVIEW QUESTIONS

10–11 What is the *weighted average cost of capital (WACC)*, and how is it calculated?

10–12 Describe the logic underlying the use of *target weights* to calculate the WACC, and compare and contrast this approach with the use of *historical weights*. What is the preferred weighting scheme?

10.6 | Marginal Cost and Investment Decisions

The firm's weighted average cost of capital is a key input to the investment decision-making process. As demonstrated earlier in the chapter, the firm should make only those investments for which the expected return is greater than the weighted average cost of capital. A somewhat static approach to this decision is **economic value added (EVA®)**, which is a popular measure that firms can use to determine whether an investment—proposed or existing—contributes positively to the owners' wealth. The application of EVA® requires the use of the weighted average cost of capital (WACC). Despite the operational simplicity of EVA®-type models, here we continue to focus on the theoretically more sound NPV approach introduced in Chapter 9. The *Focus on Practice* box on page 429 further discusses value creation as measured by EVA®.

economic value added (EVA®)
A popular, but static, approach to investment decisions used by many firms to determine whether an investment contributes positively to the owners' wealth.

The use of NPV provides a more dynamic approach to investment decisions. It recognizes that at any given time, the firm's financing costs and investment returns will be affected by the volume of financing and investment undertaken. The *weighted marginal cost of capital* and the *investment opportunities schedule* are mechanisms whereby financing and investment decisions can be made simultaneously.

Weighted Marginal Cost of Capital (WMCC)

The weighted average cost of capital may vary over time, depending on the volume of financing that the firm plans to raise. *As the volume of financing increases, the costs of the various types of financing will increase, raising the firm's weighted average cost of capital.* Therefore, it is useful to calculate the **weighted marginal cost of capital (WMCC)**, which is simply the firm's weighted average cost of capital (WACC) associated with its *next dollar* of total new financing. This marginal cost is relevant to current decisions.

weighted marginal cost of capital (WMCC)
The firm's weighted average cost of capital (WACC) associated with its *next dollar* of total new financing.

The costs of the financing components (debt, preferred stock, and common stock) rise as larger amounts are raised. Suppliers of funds require greater returns in the form of interest, dividends, or growth as compensation for the increased risk introduced by larger volumes of *new* financing. The WMCC is therefore an increasing function of the level of total new financing.

Focus on Practice   EVAlue Creation

Answering the question, "Does the company use investors' money wisely?" is one of the financial manager's chief responsibilities and greatest challenges. At many firms—from Fortune 500 companies and investment firms to community hospitals—economic value added (EVA®) is the measurement tool of choice for making investment decisions, measuring overall financial performance, and motivating management.

Developed in 1983 by financial consultants **Stern Stewart & Co.** and protected by trademark, EVA is the difference between an investment's net operating profits after taxes and the cost of funds used to finance the investment (the amount of capital times the company's cost of capital). The EVA calculation is similar to calculating internal rate of return (IRR), except that the result is stated *in dollars* rather than percentages. It can be applied to the company as a whole as well as to specific

long-term investments such as new facilities and acquisitions.

According to its proponents, EVA represents "real" profits and provides a more accurate measure than accounting profits. Over time, it also has better correlation with stock prices than does earnings per share. Income calculations include only the cost of debt (interest expense), whereas EVA uses the total cost of capital, both debt and equity (an expensive form of capital). In addition, EVA treats research and development outlays as investments in future products or processes and capitalizes rather than expenses them. A growing EVA can signal future increases in stock prices.

Companies that use EVA believe doing so leads to better overall performance. Managers who apply it focus on allocating assets, not just accounting profits. They will accelerate the development of a hot new product even if it reduces earnings in the near

term. Companies write off R&D each year in line with generally accepted accounting practices, so speeding up new product development will reduce earnings in the near-term. Although earnings *may* drop for a few quarters, so will taxes—and cash flow eventually increases. One benefit of the EVA (non-GAAP) treatment of R&D expenses as a capitalized expense is that managers are less tempted to reduce valuable R&D expenditures just to improve current earnings because only a fraction of the reduction in R&D would impact current earnings.

EVA is not a panacea, however. Its critics say it may not be the right measure for many companies. They claim that because it favors big projects in big companies, EVA doesn't always do a good job on capital allocation.

■ *Why might a company use EVA as a measure of its performance in addition to the standard accounting measures?*

Another factor that causes the weighted average cost of capital to increase is the use of common stock equity financing. New financing provided by common stock equity will be provided by retaining earnings until this supply is exhausted, and then it will be obtained through new common stock financing. Because retained earnings are a less expensive form of common stock equity financing than the sale of new common stock, the weighted average cost of capital will rise with the addition of new common stock.

Finding Break Points

break point
The level of *total* new financing at which the cost of one of the financing components rises, thereby causing an upward shift in the *weighted marginal cost of capital (WMCC)*.

To calculate the WMCC, we must calculate **break points,** which reflect the level of *total* new financing at which the cost of one of the financing components rises. The following general equation can be used to find break points:

$$BP_j = \frac{AF_j}{w_j}$$

(10.10)

where

BP_j = break point for financing source j

AF_j = amount of funds available from financing source j at a given cost

w_j = capital structure weight (stated in decimal form) for financing source j

Example

When Duchess Corporation exhausts its $300,000 of available retained earnings (at $r_r = 13.0\%$), it must use the more expensive new common stock financing (at $r_n = 14.0\%$) to meet its common stock equity needs. In addition, the firm expects that it can borrow only $400,000 of debt at the 5.6% cost; additional debt will have an after-tax cost (r_i) of 8.4%. Two break points therefore exist: (1) when the $300,000 of retained earnings costing 13.0% is exhausted, and (2) when the $400,000 of long-term debt costing 5.6% is exhausted.

The break points can be found by substituting these values and the corresponding capital structure weights given earlier into Equation 10.10. We get the dollar amounts of *total* new financing at which the costs of the given financing sources rise:

$$BP_{\text{common equity}} = \frac{\$300,000}{0.50} = \$600,000$$

$$BP_{\text{long-term debt}} = \frac{\$400,000}{0.40} = \$1,000,000$$

Calculating the WMCC

Once we have determined the break points, the next step is to calculate the weighted average cost of capital over each range of total new financing between break points. First, we find the WACC for a level of total new financing between zero and the first break point. Next, we find the WACC for a level of total new financing between the first and second break points, and so on. By definition, for each of the ranges of total new financing between break points, certain component capital costs (such as common equity or debt) will increase. This will cause the weighted average cost of capital to increase to a higher level than that over the preceding range.

weighted marginal cost of capital (WMCC) schedule
Graph that relates the firm's weighted average cost of capital to the level of total new financing.

Together, these data can be used to prepare a **weighted marginal cost of capital (WMCC) schedule.** This graph relates the firm's weighted average cost of capital to the level of total new financing.

Example

Table 10.2 summarizes the calculation of the WACC for Duchess Corporation over the three ranges of total new financing created by the two break points—$600,000 and $1,000,000. Comparing the costs in column 3 of the table for each of the three ranges, we can see that the costs in the first range ($0 to $600,000) are those calculated in earlier examples and used in Table 10.1. The second range ($600,000 to $1,000,000) reflects the increase in the common stock equity cost to 14.0%. In the final range, the increase in the long-term debt cost to 8.4% is introduced.

The weighted average costs of capital (WACC) for the three ranges are summarized in the table shown at the bottom of Figure 10.1. These data describe the weighted marginal cost of capital (WMCC), which increases as levels of total new financing increase. Figure 10.1 presents the WMCC schedule. Again, it is clear that the WMCC is an increasing function of the amount of total new financing raised.

TABLE 10.2   Weighted Average Cost of Capital for Ranges of Total New Financing for Duchess Corporation

Range of total new financing	Source of capital (1)	Weight (2)	Cost (3)	Weighted cost [(2) × (3)] (4)
$0 to $600,000	Debt	.40	5.6%	2.2%
	Preferred	.10	10.6	1.1
	Common	.50	13.0	6.5
			Weighted average cost of capital	9.8%
$600,000 to $1,000,000	Debt	.40	5.6%	2.2%
	Preferred	.10	10.6	1.1
	Common	.50	14.0	7.0
			Weighted average cost of capital	10.3%
$1,000,000 and above	Debt	.40	8.4%	3.4%
	Preferred	.10	10.6	1.1
	Common	.50	14.0	7.0
			Weighted average cost of capital	11.5%

WMCC Schedule
Weighted marginal cost of capital (WMCC) schedule for Duchess Corporation

Range of total new financing	WACC
$0 to $600,000	9.8%
$600,000 to $1,000,000	10.3
$1,000,000 and above	11.5

Investment Opportunities Schedule (IOS)

investment opportunities schedule (IOS)
A ranking of investment possibilities from best (highest return) to worst (lowest return).

At any given time, a firm has certain investment opportunities available to it. These opportunities differ with respect to the size of investment, risk, and return.[6] The firm's **investment opportunities schedule (IOS)** is a ranking of investment possibilities from best (highest return) to worst (lowest return). Generally, the first project selected will have the highest return, the next project the second highest, and so on. The return on investments will *decrease* as the firm accepts additional projects.

Example | Column 1 of Table 10.3 shows Duchess Corporation's current investment opportunities schedule (IOS) listing the investment possibilities from best (highest return) to worst (lowest return). Column 2 of the table shows the initial investment required by each project. Column 3 shows the cumulative total invested funds necessary to finance all projects better than and including the corresponding investment opportunity. Plotting the project returns against the cumulative investment (column 1 against column 3) results in the firm's investment opportunities schedule (IOS). Figure 10.2 shows a graph of the IOS for Duchess Corporation.

Using the WMCC and IOS to Make Financing/Investment Decisions

As long as a project's internal rate of return is greater than the weighted marginal cost of new financing, the firm should accept the project.[7] The return will decrease with the acceptance of more projects, and the weighted marginal cost of

TABLE 10.3   Investment Opportunities Schedule (IOS) for Duchess Corporation

Investment opportunity	Internal rate of return (IRR) (1)	Initial investment (2)	Cumulative investment[a] (3)
A	15.0%	$100,000	$ 100,000
B	14.5	200,000	300,000
C	14.0	400,000	700,000
D	13.0	100,000	800,000
E	12.0	300,000	1,100,000
F	11.0	200,000	1,300,000
G	10.0	100,000	1,400,000

[a]The cumulative investment represents the total amount invested in projects with higher returns plus the investment required for the corresponding investment opportunity.

6. Because the calculated weighted average cost of capital does not apply to risk-changing investments, we assume that all opportunities have equal risk similar to the firm's risk.

7. Although net present value could be used to make these decisions, the internal rate of return is used here because of the ease of comparison it offers.

FIGURE 10.2

IOS and WMCC Schedules
Using the IOS and WMCC to select projects for Duchess Corporation

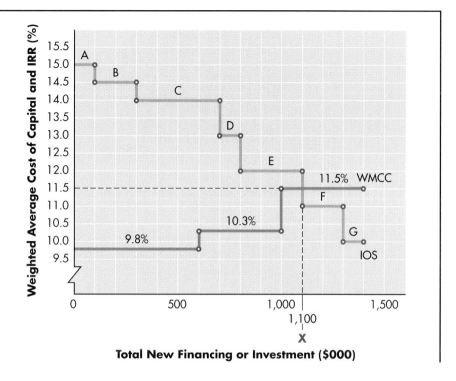

capital will increase because greater amounts of financing will be required. The decision rule therefore would be: *Accept projects up to the point at which the marginal return on an investment equals its weighted marginal cost of capital.* Beyond that point, its investment return will be less than its capital cost.

This approach is consistent with the maximization of net present value (NPV) for conventional projects for two reasons: (1) The NPV is positive as long as the IRR exceeds the weighted average cost of capital, r_a. (2) The larger the difference between the IRR and r_a, the larger the resulting NPV. Therefore, the acceptance of projects beginning with those that have the greatest positive difference between IRR and r_a, down to the point at which IRR just equals r_a, should result in the maximum total NPV for all independent projects accepted. Such an outcome is completely consistent with the firm's goal of maximizing owner wealth.

Example

Figure 10.2 shows Duchess Corporation's WMCC schedule and IOS on the same set of axes. By raising $1,100,000 of new financing and investing these funds in projects A, B, C, D, and E, the firm should maximize the wealth of its owners, because these projects result in the maximum total net present value. Note that the 12.0% return on the last dollar invested (in project E) *exceeds* its 11.5% weighted average cost. Investment in project F is not feasible, because its 11.0% return is *less than* the 11.5% cost of funds available for investment.

The firm's optimal capital budget of $1,100,000 is marked with an X in Figure 10.2. At that point, the IRR equals the weighted average cost of capital, and the firm's size as well as its shareholder value will be optimized. In a sense, the size of the firm is determined by the market—the availability of and returns on investment opportunities, and the availability and cost of financing.

In practice, most firms operate under *capital rationing*. That is, management imposes constraints that keep the capital expenditure budget below optimal (where IRR = r_a). Because of this, a gap frequently exists between the theoretically optimal capital budget and the firm's actual level of financing/investment.

REVIEW QUESTIONS

10–13 What is the *weighted marginal cost of capital (WMCC)?* What does the WMCC *schedule* represent? Why does this schedule increase?

10–14 What is the *investment opportunities schedule (IOS)?* Is it typically depicted as an increasing or a decreasing function? Why?

10–15 How can a firm use the WMCC schedule and the IOS to find the level of financing/investment that maximizes owner wealth? Why do many firms finance/invest at a level below this optimum?

Summary

Focus on Value

The cost of capital is an extremely important rate of return, particularly in capital budgeting decisions. It is the expected average future cost to the firm of funds over the long run. Because the cost of capital is the pivotal rate of return used in the investment decision process, its accuracy can significantly affect the quality of these decisions.

Even with good estimates of project cash flows, the application of NPV and IRR decision techniques, and adequate consideration of project risk, a poorly estimated cost of capital can result in the destruction of shareholder value. Underestimation of the cost of capital can result in the mistaken acceptance of poor projects; overestimation can cause good projects to be rejected. By applying the techniques presented in this chapter to estimate the firm's cost of capital, the financial manager will improve the likelihood that the firm's long-term decisions will be consistent with the firm's overall goal of **maximizing stock price (owner wealth)**.

Review of Learning Goals

Key definitions and formulas for this chapter are summarized in Table 10.4.

LG 1 **Understand the key assumptions, the basic concept, and the specific sources of capital associated with the cost of capital.** The cost of capital is the rate of return that a firm must earn on its investments to maintain its market value and attract needed funds. It is affected by business and financial risks, and is measured on an after-tax basis. A weighted average cost of capital should be used to find the expected average future cost of funds over the long run. The specific costs of the basic sources of capital (long-term debt, preferred stock, retained earnings, and common stock) can be calculated individually.

TABLE 10.4	**Summary of Key Definitions and Formulas for Cost of Capital**

Definitions of variables

AF_j = amount of funds available from financing source j at a given cost

b = beta coefficient or measure of nondiversifiable risk

BP_j = break point for financing source j

D_1 = per-share dividend *expected* at the end of year 1

D_p = annual preferred stock dividend (in dollars)

g = constant rate of growth in dividends

I = annual interest in dollars

r_a = weighted average cost of capital

r_d = before-tax cost of debt

r_i = after-tax cost of debt

r_m = required return on the market portfolio

r_n = cost of a new issue of common stock

r_p = cost of preferred stock

r_r = cost of retained earnings

r_s = required return on common stock

n = number of years to the bond's maturity

N_d = net proceeds from the sale of debt (bond)

N_n = net proceeds from the sale of new common stock

N_p = net proceeds from the sale of preferred stock

P_0 = value of common stock

R_F = risk-free rate of return

T = firm's tax rate

w_i = proportion of long-term debt in capital structure

w_j = capital structure proportion (historical or target, stated in decimal form) for financing source j

w_p = proportion of preferred stock in capital structure

w_s = proportion of common stock equity in capital structure

Cost of capital formulas

Before-tax cost of debt (approximation):

$$r_d = \frac{I + \frac{\$1,000 - N_d}{n}}{\frac{N_d + \$1,000}{2}}$$ [Equation 10.1]

After-tax cost of debt: $r_i = r_d \times (1 - T)$ [Equation 10.2]

Cost of preferred stock: $r_p = \frac{D_p}{N_p}$ [Equation 10.3]

Cost of common stock equity:

Using constant-growth valuation model: $r_s = \frac{D_1}{P_0} + g$ [Equation 10.5]

Using CAPM: $r_s = R_F + [b \times (r_m - R_F)]$ [Equation 10.6]

Cost of retained earnings: $r_r = r_s$ [Equation 10.7]

Cost of new issues of common stock: $r_n = \frac{D_1}{N_n} + g$ [Equation 10.8]

Weighted average cost of capital (WACC): $r_a = (w_i \times r_i) + (w_p \times r_p) + (w_s \times r_{r\ or\ n})$ [Equation 10.9]

Break point: $BP_j = \frac{AF_j}{w_j}$ [Equation 10.10]

LG 2 Determine the cost of long-term debt and the cost of preferred stock. The cost of long-term debt is the after-tax cost today of raising long-term funds through borrowing. Cost quotations, calculation, or an approximation can be used to find the before-tax cost of debt, which must then be tax-adjusted. The cost of preferred stock is the ratio of the preferred stock dividend to the firm's net proceeds from the sale of preferred stock.

LG 3 Calculate the cost of common stock equity and convert it into the cost of retained earnings and the cost of new issues of common stock. The cost of common stock equity can be calculated by using the constant-growth valuation (Gordon) model or the CAPM. The cost of retained earnings is equal to the cost of common stock equity. An adjustment in the cost of common stock equity to reflect underpricing and flotation costs is necessary to find the cost of new issues of common stock.

LG 4 Calculate the weighted average cost of capital (WACC) and discuss alternative weighting schemes. The firm's WACC reflects the expected average future cost of funds over the long run. It combines the costs of specific types of capital after weighting each of them by its proportion. The theoretically preferred approach uses target weights based on market values.

LG 5 Describe the procedures used to determine break points and the weighted marginal cost of capital (WMCC). As total new financing increases, the costs of the various types of financing will increase, raising the firm's WACC. The WMCC is the firm's WACC associated with its next dollar of total new financing. Break points represent the level of total new financing at which the cost of one of the financing components rises, causing an upward shift in the WMCC. The WMCC schedule relates the WACC to each level of total new financing.

LG 6 Explain the weighted marginal cost of capital (WMCC) and its use with the investment opportunities schedule (IOS) to make financing/investment decisions. The IOS ranks currently available investments from best to worst. It is used with the WMCC to find the level of financing/investment that maximizes owner wealth. The firm accepts projects up to the point at which the marginal return on its investment equals its weighted marginal cost of capital.

Self-Test Problem (Solution in Appendix B)

ST10–1 **Specific costs, WACC, WMCC, and IOS**   Humble Manufacturing is interested in measuring its overall cost of capital. The firm is in the 40% tax bracket. Current investigation has gathered the following data:

Debt   The firm can raise an unlimited amount of debt by selling $1,000-par-value, 10% coupon interest rate, 10-year bonds on which *annual interest* payments will be made. To sell the issue, an average discount of $30 per bond must be given. The firm must also pay flotation costs of $20 per bond.

Preferred stock   The firm can sell 11% (annual dividend) preferred stock at its $100-per-share par value. The cost of issuing and selling the preferred stock is expected to be $4 per share. An unlimited amount of preferred stock can be sold under these terms.

Common stock   The firm's common stock is currently selling for $80 per share. The firm expects to pay cash dividends of $6 per share next year. The firm's dividends have been growing at an annual rate of 6%, and this rate is expected to continue in the future. The stock will have to be underpriced by $4 per share, and flotation costs are expected to amount to $4 per share. The firm can sell an unlimited amount of new common stock under these terms.

Retained earnings   The firm expects to have $225,000 of retained earnings available in the coming year. Once these retained earnings are exhausted, the firm will use new common stock as the form of common stock equity financing.

a. Calculate the specific cost of each source of financing. (Round to the nearest 0.1%.)
b. The firm uses the weights shown in the following table, which are based on target capital structure proportions, to calculate its weighted average cost of capital. (Round to the nearest 0.1%.)

Source of capital	Weight
Long-term debt	40%
Preferred stock	15
Common stock equity	45
Total	100%

   (1) Calculate the single *break point* associated with the firm's financial situation. (*Hint:* This point results from the exhaustion of the firm's retained earnings.)
   (2) Calculate the weighted average cost of capital associated with total new financing *below* the break point calculated in part (1).
   (3) Calculate the weighted average cost of capital associated with total new financing *above* the break point calculated in part (1).
c. Using the results of part **b** along with the information shown in the following table on the available investment opportunities, draw the firm's weighted marginal cost of capital (WMCC) schedule and investment opportunities schedule (IOS) on the same set of axes (total new financing or investment on the *x* axis and weighted average cost of capital and IRR on the *y* axis).

Investment opportunity	Internal rate of return (IRR)	Initial investment
A	11.2%	$100,000
B	9.7	500,000
C	12.9	150,000
D	16.5	200,000
E	11.8	450,000
F	10.1	600,000
G	10.5	300,000

d. Which, if any, of the available investments do you recommend that the firm accept? Explain your answer. How much total new financing is required?

Warm-Up Exercises   A blue box (■) indicates exercises available in .

E10–1 Weekend Warriors, Inc., has 35% debt and 65% equity in its capital structure. The firm's estimated after-tax cost of debt is 8% and its estimated cost of equity is 13%. Determine the firm's *weighted average cost of capital (WACC)*.

E10–2 A firm raises capital by selling $20,000 worth of debt with flotation costs equal to 2% of its par value. If the debt matures in 10 years and has a coupon interest rate of 8%, what is the bond's *IRR*?

E10–3 Your firm, People's Consulting Group, has been asked to consult on a potential preferred stock offering by Brave New World. This 15% preferred stock issue would be sold at its par value of $35 per share. Flotation costs would total $3 per share. Calculate the *cost of this preferred stock*.

E10–4 Duke Energy has been paying dividends steadily for 20 years. During that time, dividends have grown at a compound annual rate of 7%. If Duke Energy's current stock price is $78 and the firm plans to pay a dividend of $6.50 next year, what is Duke's *cost of common stock equity*?

E10–5 Oxy Corporation uses debt, preferred stock, and common stock to raise capital. The firm's capital structure targets the following proportions: debt, 55%; preferred stock, 10%; and common stock, 35%. If the cost of debt is 6.7%, preferred stock costs 9.2%, and common stock costs 10.6%, what is Oxy's *weighted average cost of capital (WACC)*?

Problems   A blue box (■) indicates problems available in .

P10–1 **Concept of cost of capital** Wren Manufacturing is in the process of analyzing its investment decision-making procedures. The two projects evaluated by the firm during the past month were projects 263 and 264. The basic variables surrounding each project analysis, using the IRR decision technique, and the resulting decision actions are summarized in the following table.

Basic variables	Project 263	Project 264
Cost	$64,000	$58,000
Life	15 years	15 years
IRR	8%	15%
Least-cost financing		
Source	Debt	Equity
Cost (after-tax)	7%	16%
Decision		
Action	Accept	Reject
Reason	8% IRR > 7% cost	15% IRR < 16% cost

a. Evaluate the firm's decision-making procedures, and explain why the acceptance of project 263 and rejection of project 264 may not be in the owners' best interest.
b. If the firm maintains a capital structure containing 40% debt and 60% equity, find its *weighted average cost* using the data in the table.
c. If the firm had used the weighted average cost calculated in part **b,** what actions would have been indicated relative to projects 263 and 264?
d. Compare and contrast the firm's actions with your findings in part **c.** Which decision method seems more appropriate? Explain why.

P10–2 Cost of debt using both methods   Currently, Warren Industries can sell 15-year, $1,000-par-value bonds paying *annual interest* at a 12% coupon rate. As a result of current interest rates, the bonds can be sold for $1,010 each; flotation costs of $30 per bond will be incurred in this process. The firm is in the 40% tax bracket.
a. Find the net proceeds from sale of the bond, N_d.
b. Show the cash flows from the firm's point of view over the maturity of the bond.
c. Use the *IRR approach* to calculate the before-tax and after-tax costs of debt.
d. Use the *approximation formula* to estimate the before-tax and after-tax costs of debt.
e. Compare and contrast the costs of debt calculated in parts **c** and **d.** Which approach do you prefer? Why?

PERSONAL FINANCE PROBLEM

P10–3 Before-tax cost of debt and after-tax cost of debt   David Abbot is interested in purchasing a bond issued by Sony. He has obtained the following information on the security:

Sony Bond				
Par value	$1,000	Coupon interest rate	6%	Tax bracket 20%
Cost	$ 930	Years to maturity	10	

Answer the following questions.
a. Calculate the *before-tax cost* of the Sony bond using the IRR method.
b. Calculate the *after-tax cost* of the Sony bond given David's tax bracket.

P10–4 Cost of debt using the approximation formula   For each of the following $1,000-par-value bonds, assuming *annual interest* payment and a 40% tax rate, calculate the *after-tax* cost to maturity using the *approximation formula.*

Bond	Life	Underwriting fee	Discount (−) or premium (+)	Coupon interest rate
A	20 years	$25	−$20	9%
B	16	40	+ 10	10
C	15	30	− 15	12
D	25	15	Par	9
E	22	20	− 60	11

P10–5 **After-tax cost of debt**   Rick and Stacy Stark, a married couple, are interested in purchasing their first boat. They have decided to borrow the boat's purchase price of $100,000. The family is in the 28% federal income tax bracket. There are two choices for the Stark family: They can borrow the money from the boat dealer at an annual interest rate of 8%, or they could take out a $100,000 second mortgage on their home. Currently, home equity loans are at rates of 9.2%. There is no problem securing either of these two alternative financing choices.

Rick and Stacy learn that if they borrow from the boat dealership, the interest will not be tax-deductible. However, the interest on the second mortgage will qualify as being tax-deductible on their federal income tax return.

a. Calculate the *after-tax cost* of borrowing from the boat dealership.
b. Calculate the *after-tax cost* of borrowing through a second mortgage on their home.
c. Which source of borrowing is less costly for the Stark family?

P10–6 **Cost of preferred stock**   Taylor Systems has just issued preferred stock. The stock has a 12% annual dividend and a $100 par value and was sold at $97.50 per share. In addition, flotation costs of $2.50 per share must be paid.

a. Calculate the *cost of the preferred stock*.
b. If the firm sells the preferred stock with a 10% annual dividend and nets $90.00 after flotation costs, what is its cost?

P10–7 **Cost of preferred stock**   Determine the cost for each of the following preferred stocks.

Preferred stock	Par value	Sale price	Flotation cost	Annual dividend
A	$100	$101	$9.00	11%
B	40	38	$3.50	8%
C	35	37	$4.00	$5.00
D	30	26	5% of par	$3.00
E	20	20	$2.50	9%

P10–8 **Cost of common stock equity—CAPM**   J&M Corporation common stock has a beta, b, of 1.2. The risk-free rate is 6%, and the market return is 11%.

a. Determine the risk premium on J&M common stock.
b. Determine the required return that J&M common stock should provide.
c. Determine J&M's *cost of common stock equity* using the CAPM.

P10–9 **Cost of common stock equity**   Ross Textiles wishes to measure its cost of common stock equity. The firm's stock is currently selling for $57.50. The firm expects to pay a $3.40 dividend at the end of the year (2010). The dividends for the past 5 years are shown in the following table.

Year	Dividend
2009	$3.10
2008	2.92
2007	2.60
2006	2.30
2005	2.12

After underpricing and flotation costs, the firm expects to net $52 per share on a new issue.

a. Determine the growth rate of dividends.

b. Determine the net proceeds, N_n, that the firm will actually receive.

c. Using the constant-growth valuation model, determine the *cost of retained earnings*, r_r.

d. Using the constant-growth valuation model, determine the *cost of new common stock*, r_n.

 P10–10 **Retained earnings versus new common stock**   Using the data for each firm shown in the following table, calculate the *cost of retained earnings* and the *cost of new common stock* using the constant-growth valuation model.

Firm	Current market price per share	Dividend growth rate	Projected dividend per share next year	Underpricing per share	Flotation cost per share
A	$50.00	8%	$2.25	$2.00	$1.00
B	20.00	4	1.00	0.50	1.50
C	42.50	6	2.00	1.00	2.00
D	19.00	2	2.10	1.30	1.70

 P10–11 **WACC—Book weights**   Ridge Tool has on its books the amounts and specific (after-tax) costs shown in the following table for each source of capital.

Source of capital	Book value	Specific cost
Long-term debt	$700,000	5.3%
Preferred stock	50,000	12.0
Common stock equity	650,000	16.0

a. Calculate the firm's *weighted average cost of capital using book value weights.*

b. Explain how the firm can use this cost in the investment decision-making process.

 P10–12 **WACC—Book weights and market weights**   Webster Company has compiled the information shown in the following table.

Source of capital	Book value	Market value	After-tax cost
Long-term debt	$4,000,000	$3,840,000	6.0%
Preferred stock	40,000	60,000	13.0
Common stock equity	1,060,000	3,000,000	17.0
Totals	$5,100,000	$6,900,000	

a. Calculate the weighted average cost of capital using *book value weights.*

b. Calculate the weighted average cost of capital using *market value weights.*

c. Compare the answers obtained in parts **a** and **b**. Explain the differences.

P10–13 **WACC and target weights**   After careful analysis, Dexter Brothers has determined that its optimal capital structure is composed of the sources and target market value weights shown in the following table.

Source of capital	Target market value weight
Long-term debt	30%
Preferred stock	15
Common stock equity	55
Total	100%

The cost of debt is estimated to be 7.2%; the cost of preferred stock is estimated to be 13.5%; the cost of retained earnings is estimated to be 16.0%; and the cost of new common stock is estimated to be 18.0%. All of these are after-tax rates. The company's debt represents 25%, the preferred stock represents 10%, and the common stock equity represents 65% of total capital on the basis of the market values of the three components. The company expects to have a significant amount of retained earnings available and does not expect to sell any new common stock.

a. Calculate the weighted average cost of capital on the basis of *historical market value weights*.

b. Calculate the weighted average cost of capital on the basis of *target market value weights*.

c. Compare the answers obtained in parts **a** and **b**. Explain the differences.

    P10–14 **Calculation of specific costs, WACC, and WMCC**   Dillon Labs has asked its financial manager to measure the cost of each specific type of capital as well as the weighted average cost of capital. The weighted average cost is to be measured by using the following weights: 40% long-term debt, 10% preferred stock, and 50% common stock equity (retained earnings, new common stock, or both). The firm's tax rate is 40%.

Debt   The firm can sell for $980 a 10-year, $1,000-par-value bond paying *annual interest* at a 10% coupon rate. A flotation cost of 3% of the par value is required in addition to the discount of $20 per bond.

Preferred stock   Eight percent (annual dividend) preferred stock having a par value of $100 can be sold for $65. An additional fee of $2 per share must be paid to the underwriters.

Common stock   The firm's common stock is currently selling for $50 per share. The dividend expected to be paid at the end of the coming year (2010) is $4. Its dividend payments, which have been approximately 60% of earnings per share in each of the past 5 years, were as shown in the following table.

Year	Dividend
2009	$3.75
2008	3.50
2007	3.30
2006	3.15
2005	2.85

It is expected that to attract buyers, new common stock must be underpriced $5 per share, and the firm must also pay $3 per share in flotation costs. Dividend payments are expected to continue at 60% of earnings.

a. Calculate the specific cost of each source of financing. (Assume that $r_r = r_s$.)
b. If earnings available to common shareholders are expected to be $7 million, what is the *break point* associated with the exhaustion of retained earnings?
c. Determine the *weighted average cost of capital* between zero and the break point calculated in part **b.**
d. Determine the *weighted average cost of capital* just beyond the break point calculated in part **b.**

PERSONAL FINANCE PROBLEM

 Weighted average cost of capital   John Dough has just been awarded his degree in business. He has three education loans outstanding. They all mature in 5 years and can be repaid without penalty any time before maturity. The amounts owed on each loan and the annual interest rate associated with each loan are given in the following table.

Loan	Balance due	Annual interest rate
1	$20,000	6%
2	12,000	9
3	32,000	5

John can also combine the total of his three debts (i.e., $64,000) and create a consolidated loan from his bank. His bank will charge a 7.2% annual interest rate for a period of 5 years.

Should John do nothing (leave the three individual loans as is) or create a consolidated loan (the $64,000 question)?

   Calculation of specific costs, WACC, and WMCC   Lang Enterprises is interested in measuring its overall cost of capital. Current investigation has gathered the following data. The firm is in the 40% tax bracket.

Debt   The firm can raise an unlimited amount of debt by selling $1,000-par-value, 8% coupon interest rate, 20-year bonds on which *annual interest* payments will be made. To sell the issue, an average discount of $30 per bond would have to be given. The firm also must pay flotation costs of $30 per bond.

Preferred stock   The firm can sell 8% preferred stock at its $95-per-share par value. The cost of issuing and selling the preferred stock is expected to be $5 per share. An unlimited amount of preferred stock can be sold under these terms.

Common stock   The firm's common stock is currently selling for $90 per share. The firm expects to pay cash dividends of $7 per share next year. The firm's dividends have been growing at an annual rate of 6%, and this growth is expected to continue into the future. The stock must be underpriced by $7 per share, and flotation costs are expected to amount to $5 per share. The firm can sell an unlimited amount of new common stock under these terms.

Retained earnings   When measuring this cost, the firm does not concern itself with the tax bracket or brokerage fees of owners. It expects to have available $100,000 of retained earnings in the coming year; once these retained earnings are exhausted, the firm will use new common stock as the form of common stock equity financing.

a. Calculate the specific cost of each source of financing. (Round answers to the nearest 0.1%.)

b. The firm's capital structure weights used in calculating its weighted average cost of capital are shown in the following table. (Round answer to the nearest 0.1%.)

Source of capital	Weight
Long-term debt	30%
Preferred stock	20
Common stock equity	50
Total	100%

(1) Calculate the single *break point* associated with the firm's financial situation. (*Hint:* This point results from exhaustion of the firm's retained earnings.)

(2) Calculate the *weighted average cost of capital* associated with total new financing below the break point calculated in part (1).

(3) Calculate the *weighted average cost of capital* associated with total new financing above the break point calculated in part (1).

P10–17 Integrative—WACC, WMCC, and IOS   Cartwell Products has compiled the data shown in the following table for the current costs of its three basic sources of capital—long-term debt, preferred stock, and common stock equity—for various ranges of new financing.

Source of capital	Range of new financing	After-tax cost
Long-term debt	$0 to $320,000	6%
	$320,000 and above	8
Preferred stock	$0 and above	17%
Common stock equity	$0 to $200,000	20%
	$200,000 and above	24

The company's capital structure weights used in calculating its weighted average cost of capital are shown in the following table.

Source of capital	Weight
Long-term debt	40%
Preferred stock	20
Common stock equity	40
Total	100%

a. Determine the *break points* and ranges of *total* new financing associated with each source of capital.

b. Using the data developed in part **a,** determine the break points (levels of *total* new financing) at which the firm's weighted average cost of capital will change.

c. Calculate the *weighted average cost of capital* for each range of total new financing found in part **b.** (*Hint:* There are three ranges.)

    d. Using the results of part **c,** along with the following information on the available investment opportunities, draw the firm's *weighted marginal cost of capital (WMCC) schedule* and *investment opportunities schedule (IOS)* on the same set of axes (total new financing or investment on the *x* axis and weighted average cost of capital and IRR on the *y* axis).

Investment opportunity	Internal rate of return (IRR)	Initial investment
A	19%	$200,000
B	15	300,000
C	22	100,000
D	14	600,000
E	23	200,000
F	13	100,000
G	21	300,000
H	17	100,000
I	16	400,000

    e. Which, if any, of the available investments do you recommend that the firm accept? Explain your answer.

P10–18   **ETHICS PROBLEM**   Because the latency period for asbestos-related illnesses can be as long as 40 years, some claimants are filing for damages based on their previous work around the dangerous material even though they currently have no symptoms or impairments from their exposure to asbestos. If you were a company faced with such a claim, how would you refute the claim? If you were the claimant, how would you support your claim?

Chapter 10 Case

Making Star Products' Financing/Investment Decision

Star Products Company is a growing manufacturer of automobile accessories whose stock is actively traded on the over-the-counter (OTC) market. During 2009, the Dallas-based company experienced sharp increases in both sales and earnings. Because of this recent growth, Melissa Jen, the company's treasurer, wants to make sure that available funds are being used to their fullest. Management policy is to maintain the current capital structure proportions of 30% long-term debt, 10% preferred stock, and 60% common stock equity for at least the next 3 years. The firm is in the 40% tax bracket.

    Star's division and product managers have presented several competing investment opportunities to Jen. However, because funds are limited, choices of which projects to accept must be made. The investment opportunities schedule (IOS) is shown in the table on page 446.

Investment Opportunities Schedule (IOS) for Star Products Company		
Investment opportunity	Internal rate of return (IRR)	Initial investment
A	15%	$400,000
B	22	200,000
C	25	700,000
D	23	400,000
E	17	500,000
F	19	600,000
G	14	500,000

To estimate the firm's weighted average cost of capital (WACC), Jen contacted a leading investment banking firm, which provided the financing cost data shown in the following table.

Financing Cost Data Star Products Company
Long-term debt: The firm can raise $450,000 of additional debt by selling 15-year, $1,000-par-value, 9% coupon interest rate bonds that pay *annual interest*. It expects to net $960 per bond after flotation costs. Any debt in excess of $450,000 will have a before-tax cost, r_d, of 13%.
Preferred stock: Preferred stock, regardless of the amount sold, can be issued with a $70 par value and a 14% annual dividend rate and will net $65 per share after flotation costs.
Common stock equity: The firm expects dividends and earnings per share to be $0.96 and $3.20, respectively, in 2010 and to continue to grow at a constant rate of 11% per year. The firm's stock currently sells for $12 per share. Star expects to have $1,500,000 of retained earnings available in the coming year. Once the retained earnings have been exhausted, the firm can raise additional funds by selling new common stock, netting $9 per share after underpricing and flotation costs.

To Do

a. Calculate the cost of each source of financing, as specified:
   (1) Long-term debt, first $450,000.
   (2) Long-term debt, greater than $450,000.
   (3) Preferred stock, all amounts.
   (4) Common stock equity, first $1,500,000.
   (5) Common stock equity, greater than $1,500,000.
b. Find the *break points* associated with each source of capital, and use them to specify each of the ranges of total new financing over which the firm's weighted average cost of capital (WACC) remains constant.
c. Calculate the *weighted average cost of capital (WACC)* over each of the ranges of total new financing specified in part b.

d. Using your findings in part **c** along with the investment opportunities schedule (IOS), draw the firm's *weighted marginal cost of capital (WMCC)* and IOS on the same set of axes (total new financing or investment on the x axis and weighted average cost of capital and IRR on the y axis).

e. Which, if any, of the available investments would you recommend that the firm accept? Explain your answer.

Spreadsheet Exercise

Nova Corporation is interested in measuring the cost of each specific type of capital as well as the weighted average cost of capital. Historically, the firm has raised capital in the following manner:

Source of capital	Weight
Long-term debt	35%
Preferred stock	12
Common stock equity	53

The tax rate of the firm is currently 40%. The needed financial information and data are as follows:

Debt   Nova can raise an unlimited amount of debt by selling $1,000-par-value, 6.5% coupon interest rate, 10-year bonds on which *annual interest payments* will be made. To sell the issue, an average discount of $20 per bond needs to be given. There is an associated flotation cost of 2% of par value.

Preferred stock   An unlimited amount of preferred stock can be sold under the following terms: The security has a par value of $100 per share, the annual dividend rate is 6% of the par value, and the flotation cost is expected to be $4 per share. The preferred stock is expected to sell for $102 before cost considerations.

Common stock   The current price of Nova's common stock is $35 per share. The cash dividend is expected to be $3.25 per share next year. The firm's dividends have grown at an annual rate of 5%, and it is expected that the dividend will continue at this rate for the foreseeable future. The flotation costs are expected to be approximately $2 per share. Nova can sell an unlimited amount of new common stock under these terms.

Retained earnings   The firm expects to have available $100,000 of retained earnings in the coming year. Once these retained earnings are exhausted, the firm will use new common stock as the form of common stock equity financing. (*Note:* When measuring this cost, the firm does not concern itself with the tax bracket or brokerage fees of owners.)

To Do

Create a spreadsheet to answer the following questions:

a. Calculate the specific cost of *each source of financing*. (Round answers to the nearest 0.1%.)
b. Calculate the single *break point* associated with the firm's financial situation. This point results from exhaustion of the firm's retained earnings.
c. Calculate the *weighted average cost of capital (WACC)* associated with total financing *below* the break point calculated in part **b.**
d. Calculate the *weighted average cost of capital (WACC)* associated with total financing *above* the break point calculated in part **b.**

Web Exercise

Go to the book's companion website at www.prenhall.com/gitman to find the Web Exercise for this chapter.

Remember to check the book's website at www.prenhall.com/gitman to find additional resources, including Web Exercises and a Web Case.

11 Leverage and Capital Structure

WHY THIS CHAPTER MATTERS TO YOU

In Your Professional Life

Accounting: You need to understand how to calculate and analyze operating and financial leverage and to be familiar with the tax and earnings effects of various capital structures.

Information systems: You need to understand the types of capital and what capital structure is, because you will provide much of the information needed in management's determination of the best capital structure for the firm.

Management: You need to understand leverage so that you can control risk and magnify returns for the firm's owners and to understand capital structure theory so that you can make decisions about the firm's optimal capital structure.

Marketing: You need to understand breakeven analysis, which you will use in pricing and product feasibility decisions.

Operations: You need to understand the impact of fixed and variable operating costs on the firm's breakeven point and its operating leverage, because these costs will have a major impact on the firm's risk and return.

In Your Personal Life

Like corporations, you routinely incur debt, using both credit cards for short-term needs and negotiated long-term loans. When you borrow long-term, you experience the benefits and consequences of leverage. Also, the level of your outstanding debt relative to net worth is conceptually the same as a firm's capital structure. It reflects your financial risk and affects the availability and cost of borrowing.

LEARNING GOALS

LG 1 Discuss leverage, capital structure, breakeven analysis, the operating breakeven point, and the effect of changing costs on it.

LG 2 Understand operating, financial, and total leverage and the relationships among them.

LG 3 Describe the types of capital, external assessment of capital structure, the capital structure of non-U.S. firms, and capital structure theory.

LG 4 Explain the optimal capital structure using a graphical view of the firm's cost-of-capital functions and a zero-growth valuation model.

LG 5 Discuss the EBIT–EPS approach to capital structure.

LG 6 Review the return and risk of alternative capital structures, their linkage to market value, and other important considerations related to capital structure.

L everage involves the use of fixed costs to magnify returns. Its use in the capital structure of the firm has the potential to increase its return and risk. Leverage and capital structure are closely related concepts that are linked to capital budgeting decisions through the cost of capital. These concepts can be used to minimize the firm's cost of capital and maximize its owners' wealth. This chapter discusses leverage and capital-structure concepts and techniques and how the firm can use them to create the best capital structure.

  ## 11.1 | Leverage

leverage
Results from the use of fixed-cost assets or funds to magnify returns to the firm's owners.

capital structure
The mix of long-term debt and equity maintained by the firm.

Leverage results from the use of fixed-cost assets or funds to magnify returns to the firm's owners. Generally, increases in leverage result in increased return and risk, whereas decreases in leverage result in decreased return and risk. The amount of leverage in the firm's **capital structure**—the mix of long-term debt and equity maintained by the firm—can significantly affect its value by affecting return and risk. Unlike some causes of risk, management has almost complete control over the risk introduced through the use of leverage. Because of its effect on value, the financial manager must understand how to measure and evaluate leverage, particularly when making capital structure decisions.

The three basic types of leverage can best be defined with reference to the firm's income statement, as shown in the general income statement format in Table 11.1.

- *Operating leverage* is concerned with the relationship between the firm's sales revenue and its earnings before interest and taxes, or EBIT. (EBIT is a descriptive label for *operating profits*.)

- *Financial leverage* is concerned with the relationship between the firm's EBIT and its common stock earnings per share (EPS).

TABLE 11.1   General Income Statement Format and Types of Leverage

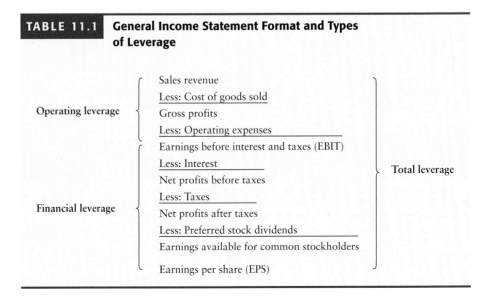

- *Total leverage* is concerned with the relationship between the firm's sales revenue and EPS.

We will examine the three types of leverage concepts in detail. First, though, we will look at breakeven analysis, which lays the foundation for leverage concepts by demonstrating the effects of fixed costs on the firm's operations.

Breakeven Analysis

breakeven analysis
Used to indicate the level of operations necessary to cover all costs and to evaluate the profitability associated with various levels of sales; also called *cost-volume-profit analysis*.

operating breakeven point
The level of sales necessary to cover all *operating costs*; the point at which EBIT = $0.

Firms use **breakeven analysis,** also called *cost-volume-profit analysis,* (1) to determine the level of operations necessary to cover all costs and (2) to evaluate the profitability associated with various levels of sales. The firm's **operating breakeven point** is the level of sales necessary to cover all *operating costs.* At that point, earnings before interest and taxes (EBIT) equals $0.[1]

The first step in finding the operating breakeven point is to divide the cost of goods sold and operating expenses into fixed and variable operating costs. *Fixed costs* are a function of time (dollars per period), not sales volume, and are typically contractual; rent, for example, is a fixed cost. *Variable costs* vary directly with sales and are a function of volume (dollars per unit), not time; shipping costs, for example, are a variable cost.[2]

Algebraic Approach

Using the following variables, we can recast the operating portion of the firm's income statement given in Table 11.1 into the algebraic representation shown in Table 11.2.

P = sale price per unit

Q = sales quantity in units

FC = fixed *operating* cost per period

VC = variable *operating* cost per unit

TABLE 11.2	**Operating Leverage, Costs, and Breakeven Analysis**	
	Item	Algebraic representation
Operating leverage	Sales revenue	$(P \times Q)$
	Less: Fixed operating costs	$- \quad FC$
	Less: Variable operating costs	$-(VC \times Q)$
	Earnings before interest and taxes	EBIT

---

1. Quite often, the breakeven point is calculated so that it represents the point at which *all costs—both operating and financial*—are covered. Our concern in this chapter is not with this overall breakeven point.

2. Some costs, commonly called *semifixed* or *semivariable,* are partly fixed and partly variable. An example is sales commissions that are fixed for a certain volume of sales and then increase to higher levels for higher volumes. For convenience and clarity, we assume that all costs can be classified as either fixed or variable.

Rewriting the algebraic calculations in Table 11.2 as a formula for earnings before interest and taxes yields Equation 11.1:

$$EBIT = (P \times Q) - FC - (VC \times Q) \tag{11.1}$$

Simplifying Equation 11.1 yields

$$EBIT = Q \times (P - VC) - FC \tag{11.2}$$

As noted above, the operating breakeven point is the level of sales at which all fixed and variable *operating costs* are covered—the level at which EBIT equals $0. Setting EBIT equal to $0 and solving Equation 12.2 for Q yield

$$Q = \frac{FC}{P - VC} \tag{11.3}$$

Q is the firm's operating breakeven point.

Example   Assume that Cheryl's Posters, a small poster retailer, has fixed operating costs of $2,500, its sale price per unit (poster) is $10, and its variable operating cost per unit is $5. Applying Equation 11.3 to these data yields

$$Q = \frac{\$2,500}{\$10 - \$5} = \frac{\$2,500}{\$5} = 500 \text{ units}$$

At sales of 500 units, the firm's EBIT should just equal $0. The firm will have positive EBIT for sales greater than 500 units and negative EBIT, or a loss, for sales less than 500 units. We can confirm this by substituting values above and below 500 units, along with the other values given, into Equation 11.1.

Graphical Approach

Figure 11.1 presents in graphical form the breakeven analysis of the data in the preceding example. The firm's operating breakeven point is the point at which its *total operating cost*—the sum of its fixed and variable operating costs—equals sales revenue. At this point, EBIT equals $0. The figure shows that for sales *below* 500 units, total operating cost exceeds sales revenue, and EBIT is less than $0 (a loss). For sales *above* the breakeven point of 500 units, sales revenue exceeds total operating cost, and EBIT is greater than $0.

Changing Costs and the Operating Breakeven Point

A firm's operating breakeven point is sensitive to a number of variables: fixed operating cost (FC), the sale price per unit (P), and the variable operating cost per unit (VC). The effects of increases or decreases in these variables can be readily seen by referring to Equation 11.3. The sensitivity of the breakeven sales volume (Q) to an *increase* in each of these variables is summarized in Table 11.3. As might be expected, an increase in cost (FC or VC) tends to increase the operating breakeven point, whereas an increase in the sale price per unit (P) decreases the operating breakeven point.

Example   Assume that Cheryl's Posters wishes to evaluate the impact of several options: (1) increasing fixed operating costs to $3,000, (2) increasing the sale price per unit to $12.50, (3) increasing the variable operating cost per unit to $7.50, and

FIGURE 11.1

Breakeven Analysis
Graphical operating
breakeven analysis

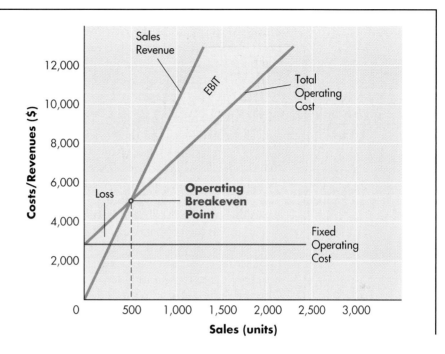

(4) simultaneously implementing all three of these changes. Substituting the appropriate data into Equation 11.3 yields the following results:

(1) Operating breakeven point $= \dfrac{\$3,000}{\$10 - \$5} = 600$ units

(2) Operating breakeven point $= \dfrac{\$2,500}{\$12.50 - \$5} = 333\frac{1}{3}$ units

(3) Operating breakeven point $= \dfrac{\$2,500}{\$10 - \$7.50} = 1,000$ units

(4) Operating breakeven point $= \dfrac{\$3,000}{\$12.50 - \$7.50} = 600$ units

TABLE 11.3   Sensitivity of Operating Breakeven Point to Increases in Key Breakeven Variables

Increase in variable	Effect on operating breakeven point
Fixed operating cost *(FC)*	Increase
Sale price per unit *(P)*	Decrease
Variable operating cost per unit *(VC)*	Increase

Note: Decreases in each of the variables shown would have the opposite effect on the operating breakeven point.

Comparing the resulting operating breakeven points to the initial value of 500 units, we can see that the cost increases (actions 1 and 3) raise the breakeven point, whereas the revenue increase (action 2) lowers the breakeven point. The combined effect of increasing all three variables (action 4) also results in an increased operating breakeven point.

Personal Finance Example   Rick Polo is considering having a new fuel-saving device installed in his car. The installed cost of the device is $240 paid up-front, plus a monthly fee of $15. He can terminate use of the device any time without penalty. Rick estimates that the device will reduce his average monthly gas consumption by 20%, which, assuming no change in his monthly mileage, translates into a savings of about $28 per month. He is planning to keep the car for 2 more years and wishes to determine whether he should have the device installed in his car.

To assess the financial feasibility of purchasing the device, Rick calculates the number of months it will take for him to break even on it. Letting the installed cost of $240 represent the fixed cost (FC), the monthly savings of $28 represent the benefit (P), and the monthly fee of $15 represent the variable cost (VC), and substituting these values into the breakeven point equation, Equation 11.3, we get:

$$\text{Breakeven point (in months)} = \$240/(\$28 - \$15) = \$240/\$13 = \underline{\underline{18.5 \text{ months}}}$$

Because the fuel-saving device pays itself back in 18.5 months, which is less than the 24 months that Rick is planning to continue owning the car, he should have the fuel-saving device installed in his car.

We now turn our attention to the three types of leverage. It is important to recognize that the demonstrations of leverage that follow are conceptual in nature and that the measures presented are *not* routinely used by financial managers for decision-making purposes.

Operating Leverage

operating leverage
The potential use of *fixed operating costs* to magnify the effects of changes in sales on the firm's earnings before interest and taxes.

Operating leverage results from the existence of *fixed operating costs* in the firm's income stream. Using the structure presented in Table 11.2, we can define **operating leverage** as the potential use of *fixed operating costs* to magnify the effects of changes in sales on the firm's earnings before interest and taxes.

Example   Using the data for Cheryl's Posters (sale price, $P = \$10$ per unit; variable operating cost, $VC = \$5$ per unit; fixed operating cost, $FC = \$2,500$), Figure 11.2 presents the operating breakeven graph originally shown in Figure 11.1. The additional notations on the graph indicate that as the firm's sales increase from 1,000 to 1,500 units (Q_1 to Q_2), its EBIT increases from $2,500 to $5,000 ($EBIT_1$ to $EBIT_2$). In other words, a 50% increase in sales (1,000 to 1,500 units) results in a 100% increase in EBIT ($2,500 to $5,000). Table 11.4 includes the data for Figure 11.2 as well as relevant data for a 500-unit sales level. We can illustrate two cases using the 1,000-unit sales level as a reference point.

Case 1   A 50% *increase* in sales (from 1,000 to 1,500 units) results in a 100% *increase* in earnings before interest and taxes (from $2,500 to $5,000).

FIGURE 11.2

Operating Leverage
Breakeven analysis and operating leverage

TABLE 11.4   **The EBIT for Various Sales Levels**

	Case 2		Case 1
	−50%		+50%
Sales (in units)	500	1,000	1,500
Sales revenue[a]	$5,000	$10,000	$15,000
Less: Variable operating costs[b]	2,500	5,000	7,500
Less: Fixed operating costs	2,500	2,500	2,500
Earnings before interest and taxes (EBIT)	$ 0	$ 2,500	$ 5,000
	−100%		+100%

[a]Sales revenue = $10/unit × sales in units.
[b]Variable operating costs = $5/unit × sales in units.

Case 2   A 50% *decrease* in sales (from 1,000 to 500 units) results in a 100% *decrease* in earnings before interest and taxes (from $2,500 to $0).

From the preceding example, we see that operating leverage works in *both directions*. When a firm has fixed operating costs, operating leverage is present. An increase in sales results in a more-than-proportional increase in EBIT; a decrease in sales results in a more-than-proportional decrease in EBIT.

Measuring the Degree of Operating Leverage (DOL)

degree of operating
leverage (DOL)
The numerical measure of
the firm's operating leverage.

The **degree of operating leverage** (DOL) is the numerical measure of the firm's operating leverage. It can be derived using the following equation:[3]

$$DOL = \frac{\text{Percentage change in EBIT}}{\text{Percentage change in sales}} \tag{11.4}$$

Whenever the percentage change in EBIT resulting from a given percentage change in sales is greater than the percentage change in sales, operating leverage exists. This means that as long as DOL is greater than 1, there is operating leverage.

Example

Applying Equation 11.4 to cases 1 and 2 in Table 11.4 yields the following results:[4]

Case 1: $\dfrac{+100\%}{+50\%} = 2.0$

Case 2: $\dfrac{-100\%}{-50\%} = 2.0$

Because the result is greater than 1, operating leverage exists. For a given base level of sales, the higher the value resulting from applying Equation 11.4, the greater the degree of operating leverage.

A more direct formula for calculating the degree of operating leverage at a base sales level, Q, is shown in Equation 11.5.

$$DOL \text{ at base sales level } Q = \frac{Q \times (P - VC)}{Q \times (P - VC) - FC} \tag{11.5}$$

Example

Substituting $Q = 1,000$, $P = \$10$, $VC = \$5$, and $FC = \$2,500$ into Equation 11.5 yields the following result:

$$DOL \text{ at } 1,000 \text{ units} = \frac{1,000 \times (\$10 - \$5)}{1,000 \times (\$10 - \$5) - \$2,500} = \frac{\$5,000}{\$2,500} = 2.0$$

The use of the formula results in the same value for DOL (2.0) as that found by using Table 11.4 and Equation 11.4.[5]

---

3. The degree of operating leverage also depends on the base level of sales used as a point of reference. The closer the base sales level used is to the operating breakeven point, the greater the operating leverage. *Comparison of the degree of operating leverage of two firms is valid only when the same base level of sales is used for both firms.*

4. Because the concept of leverage is *linear*, positive and negative changes of equal magnitude will always result in equal degrees of leverage when the same base sales level is used as a point of reference. This relationship holds for all types of leverage discussed in this chapter.

5. When total revenue in dollars from sales—instead of unit sales—is available, the following equation, in which TR = total revenue in dollars at a base level of sales and TVC = total variable operating costs in dollars, can be used:

$$DOL \text{ at base dollar sales } TR = \frac{TR - TVC}{TR - TVC - FC}$$

This formula is especially useful for finding the DOL for multiproduct firms. It should be clear that because in the case of a single-product firm, $TR = Q \times P$ and $TVC = Q \times VC$, substitution of these values into Equation 11.5 results in the equation given here.

Focus on Practice   Adobe's Leverage

Adobe Systems, the second largest PC software company in the United States, dominates the graphic design, imaging, dynamic media, and authoring-tool software markets. Website designers favor its Photoshop and Illustrator software applications, and Adobe's Acrobat software has become a standard for sharing documents online.

Adobe's ability to manage discretionary expenses helps keep its bottom line strong. Adobe has an additional advantage: *operating leverage,* the use of fixed operating costs to magnify the effect of changes in sales on earnings before interest and taxes (EBIT). Adobe and its peers in the software industry incur the bulk of their costs early in a product's life cycle, in the research and development and initial marketing stages. The up-front development costs are fixed, and subsequent production costs are practically zero. The economies of scale are

huge: Once a company sells enough copies to cover its fixed costs, incremental dollars go primarily to profit. Because the company has no long-term debt in its capital structure, its total leverage is derived only from fixed operating costs.

As demonstrated in the table below, operating leverage magnified Adobe's *decrease* in EBIT in 2002 while magnifying the increase in EBIT from 2003 to 2005. A 5.3 percent drop in 2002 sales resulted in an EBIT reduction of 24.6 percent. In 2003, a modest increase in sales—just over 11 percent— became a 33 percent increase

in EBIT. In 2006, Adobe, for the first time in 5 years, appeared to have lost its operating leverage. This can be attributed to its acquisition of Macromedia for approximately $3.5 billion in December 2005 and related restructuring charges during fiscal 2006. Once it has digested this purchase, Adobe should see its operating leverage rebound.

The table below demonstrates the impact of operating leverage on Adobe Systems in fiscal years (FYs) 2002–2006.

■ *What might cause the gradual decrease in operating leverage for Adobe?*

Item	FY2002	FY2003	FY2004	FY2005	FY2006
Sales revenue (millions)	$1,165	$1,295	$1,666	$1,966	$2,575
EBIT (millions)	$285	$380	$608	$766	$678
(1) Percent change in sales	−5.3%	11.2%	28.6%	18.0%	31.0%
(2) Percent change in EBIT	−24.6%	33.3%	60.0%	26.0%	−11.5%
DOL [(2) ÷ (1)]	4.6	3.0	2.1	1.4	−0.4

See the above *Focus on Practice* box for discussion of operating leverage at software maker Adobe.

Fixed Costs and Operating Leverage

Changes in fixed operating costs affect operating leverage significantly. Firms sometimes can incur fixed operating costs rather than variable operating costs and at other times may be able to substitute one type of cost for the other. For example, a firm could make fixed-dollar lease payments rather than payments equal to a specified percentage of sales. Or it could compensate sales representatives with a fixed salary and bonus rather than on a pure percent-of-sales commission basis. The effects of changes in fixed operating costs on operating leverage can best be illustrated by continuing our example.

Example

Assume that Cheryl's Posters exchanges a portion of its variable operating costs for fixed operating costs by eliminating sales commissions and increasing sales salaries. This exchange results in a reduction in the variable operating cost per

TABLE 11.5	Operating Leverage and Increased Fixed Costs		
		Case 2	Case 1
		−50%	+50%
Sales (in units)	500	1,000	1,500
Sales revenue[a]	$5,000	$10,000	$15,000
Less: Variable operating costs[b]	2,250	4,500	6,750
Less: Fixed operating costs	3,000	3,000	3,000
Earnings before interest and taxes (EBIT)	−$ 250	$ 2,500	$ 5,250
		−110%	+110%

[a]Sales revenue was calculated as indicated in Table 11.4.

[b]Variable operating costs = $4.50/unit × sales in units.

unit from $5 to $4.50 and an increase in the fixed operating costs from $2,500 to $3,000. Table 11.5 presents an analysis like that in Table 11.4, but using the new costs. Although the EBIT of $2,500 at the 1,000-unit sales level is the same as before the shift in operating cost structure, Table 11.5 shows that the firm has increased its operating leverage by shifting to greater fixed operating costs.

With the substitution of the appropriate values into Equation 11.5, the degree of operating leverage at the 1,000-unit base level of sales becomes

$$\text{DOL at 1,000 units} = \frac{1,000 \times (\$10 - \$4.50)}{1,000 \times (\$10 - \$4.50) - \$3,000} = \frac{\$5,500}{\$2,500} = 2.2$$

Comparing this value to the DOL of 2.0 before the shift to more fixed costs makes it clear that the higher the firm's fixed operating costs relative to variable operating costs, the greater the degree of operating leverage.

Financial Leverage

financial leverage

The potential use of *fixed financial costs* to magnify the effects of changes in earnings before interest and taxes on the firm's earnings per share.

Financial leverage results from the presence of *fixed financial costs* in the firm's income stream. Using the framework in Table 11.1, we can define **financial leverage** as the potential use of *fixed financial costs* to magnify the effects of changes in earnings before interest and taxes on the firm's earnings per share. The two fixed financial costs that may be found on the firm's income statement are (1) interest on debt and (2) preferred stock dividends. These charges must be paid regardless of the amount of EBIT available to pay them.[6]

6. As noted in Chapter 7, although preferred stock dividends can be "passed" (not paid) at the option of the firm's directors, it is generally believed that payment of such dividends is necessary. *This text treats the preferred stock dividend as a contractual obligation, not only to be paid as a fixed amount, but also to be paid as scheduled.* Although failure to pay preferred dividends cannot force the firm into bankruptcy, it increases the common stockholders' risk because they cannot be paid dividends until the claims of preferred stockholders are satisfied.

TABLE 11.6	**The EPS for Various EBIT Levels**[a]		
		Case 2	Case 1
		−40%	+40%
EBIT	$6,000	$10,000	$14,000
Less: Interest (I)	2,000	2,000	2,000
Net profits before taxes	$4,000	$ 8,000	$12,000
Less: Taxes ($T = 0.40$)	1,600	3,200	4,800
Net profits after taxes	$2,400	$ 4,800	$ 7,200
Less: Preferred stock dividends (PD)	2,400	2,400	2,400
Earnings available for common (EAC)	$ 0	$ 2,400	$ 4,800
Earnings per share (EPS)	$\dfrac{\$0}{1{,}000} = \$0$	$\dfrac{\$2{,}400}{1{,}000} = \$2.40$	$\dfrac{\$4{,}800}{1{,}000} = \$4.80$
		−100%	+100%

[a]As noted in Chapter 1, for accounting and tax purposes, interest is a *tax-deductible expense*, whereas dividends must be paid from after-tax cash flows.

Example

Chen Foods, a small Asian food company, expects EBIT of $10,000 in the current year. It has a $20,000 bond with a 10% (annual) coupon rate of interest and an issue of 600 shares of $4 (annual dividend per share) preferred stock outstanding. It also has 1,000 shares of common stock outstanding. The annual interest on the bond issue is $2,000 ($0.10 \times $20,000$). The annual dividends on the preferred stock are $2,400 ($4.00/share \times 600$ shares). Table 11.6 presents the EPS corresponding to levels of EBIT of $6,000, $10,000, and $14,000, assuming that the firm is in the 40% tax bracket. Two situations are shown:

Case 1   A 40% *increase* in EBIT (from $10,000 to $14,000) results in a 100% *increase* in earnings per share (from $2.40 to $4.80).

Case 2   A 40% *decrease* in EBIT (from $10,000 to $6,000) results in a 100% *decrease* in earnings per share (from $2.40 to $0).

The effect of financial leverage is such that an increase in the firm's EBIT results in a more-than-proportional increase in the firm's earnings per share, whereas a decrease in the firm's EBIT results in a more-than-proportional decrease in EPS.

Measuring the Degree of Financial Leverage (DFL)

degree of financial leverage (DFL)
The numerical measure of the firm's financial leverage.

The **degree of financial leverage (DFL)** is the numerical measure of the firm's financial leverage. Computing it is much like computing the degree of operating leverage. The following equation presents one approach for obtaining the DFL.[7]

---

7. This approach is valid only when the same base level of EBIT is used to calculate and compare these values. In other words, *the base level of EBIT must be held constant to compare the financial leverage associated with different levels of fixed financial costs.*

$$\text{DFL} = \frac{\text{Percentage change in EPS}}{\text{Percentage change in EBIT}} \tag{11.6}$$

Whenever the percentage change in EPS resulting from a given percentage change in EBIT is greater than the percentage change in EBIT, financial leverage exists. This means that whenever DFL is greater than 1, there is financial leverage.

Example

Applying Equation 11.6 to cases 1 and 2 in Table 11.6 yields

Case 1: $\dfrac{+100\%}{+40\%} = 2.5$

Case 2: $\dfrac{-100\%}{-40\%} = 2.5$

In both cases, the quotient is greater than 1, so financial leverage exists. The higher this value, the greater the degree of financial leverage.

Personal Finance Example   Shanta and Ravi Shandra, a married couple with no children, wish to assess the impact of additional long-term borrowing on their degree of financial leverage (DFL). The Shandras currently have $4,200 available after meeting all of their monthly living (operating) expenses, *before* making monthly loan payments. They currently have monthly loan payment obligations of $1,700 and are considering the purchase of a new car, which would result in a $500 per month increase (to $2,200) in their total monthly loan payments. Because a large portion of Ravi's monthly income represents commissions, the Shandras feel that the $4,200 per month currently available for making loan payments could vary by 20% above or below that amount.

In order to assess the potential impact of the additional borrowing on their financial leverage, the Shandras calculate their DFL for both their current ($1,700) and proposed ($2,200) loan payments as follows, using the currently available $4,200 as a base and a 20% change.

	Current DFL			Proposed DFL		
Available for making loan payments	$4,200	(+20%)	$5,040	$4,200	(+20%)	$5,040
Less: Loan payments	1,700		1,700	2,200		2,200
Available after loan payments	$2,500	(+33.6%)	$3,340	$2,000	(+42%)	$2,840
	DFL = +33.6%/+20% = 1.68			DFL = +42%/+20% = 2.10		

Based on their calculations, the amount the Shandras will have available after loan payments with their current debt changes by 1.68% for every 1% change in the amount they will have available for making the loan payments. This is considerably less responsive—and therefore less risky—than the 2.10% change in the amount available after loan payments for each 1% change in the amount available for making loan payments with the proposed additional $500 in monthly debt payments. Although it appears that the Shandras can afford the additional loan payments, they must decide if, given the variability of Ravi's income, they feel comfortable with the increased financial leverage and risk.

A more direct formula for calculating the degree of financial leverage at a base level of EBIT is given by Equation 11.7, where the notation from Table 11.6 is used. Note that in the denominator, the term $1/(1 - T)$ converts the after-tax preferred stock dividend to a before-tax amount for consistency with the other terms in the equation.

$$\text{DFL at base level EBIT} = \frac{\text{EBIT}}{\text{EBIT} - I - \left(PD \times \dfrac{1}{1 - T} \right)} \tag{11.7}$$

Example

Substituting EBIT = \$10,000, I = \$2,000, PD = \$2,400, and the tax rate (T = 0.40) into Equation 11.7 yields the following result:

$$\text{DFL at \$10,000 EBIT} = \frac{\$10,000}{\$10,000 - \$2,000 - \left(\$2,400 \times \dfrac{1}{1 - 0.40} \right)}$$

$$= \frac{\$10,000}{\$4,000} = 2.5$$

Note that the formula given in Equation 11.7 provides a more direct method for calculating the degree of financial leverage than the approach illustrated using Table 11.6 and Equation 11.6.

Total Leverage

total leverage
The potential use of *fixed costs, both operating and financial,* to magnify the effects of changes in sales on the firm's earnings per share.

We also can assess the combined effect of operating and financial leverage on the firm's risk by using a framework similar to that used to develop the individual concepts of leverage. This combined effect, or **total leverage,** can be defined as the potential use of *fixed costs, both operating and financial,* to magnify the effects of changes in sales on the firm's earnings per share. Total leverage can therefore be viewed as the *total impact of the fixed costs* in the firm's operating and financial structure.

Example

Cables Inc., a computer cable manufacturer, expects sales of 20,000 units at \$5 per unit in the coming year and must meet the following obligations: variable operating costs of \$2 per unit, fixed operating costs of \$10,000, interest of \$20,000, and preferred stock dividends of \$12,000. The firm is in the 40% tax bracket and has 5,000 shares of common stock outstanding. Table 11.7 on page 462 presents the levels of earnings per share associated with the expected sales of 20,000 units and with sales of 30,000 units.

The table illustrates that as a result of a 50% increase in sales (from 20,000 to 30,000 units), the firm would experience a 300% increase in earnings per share (from \$1.20 to \$4.80). Although it is not shown in the table, a 50% decrease in sales would, conversely, result in a 300% decrease in earnings per

TABLE 11.7   The Total Leverage Effect

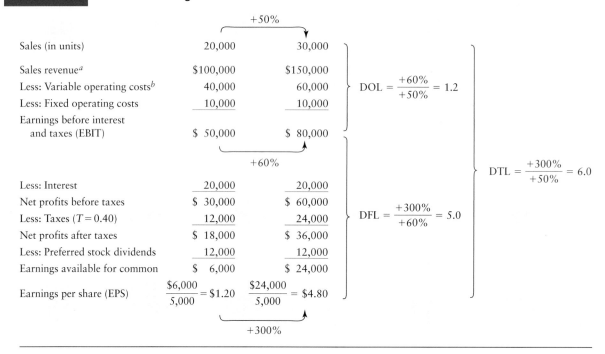

^{a}Sales revenue = $5/unit × sales in units.

^{b}Variable operating costs = $2/unit × sales in units.

share. The linear nature of the leverage relationship accounts for the fact that sales changes of equal magnitude in opposite directions result in EPS changes of equal magnitude in the corresponding direction. At this point, it should be clear that whenever a firm has fixed costs—operating or financial—in its structure, total leverage will exist.

Measuring the Degree of Total Leverage (DTL)

degree of total leverage (DTL)
The numerical measure of the firm's total leverage.

The **degree of total leverage (DTL)** is the numerical measure of the firm's total leverage. It can be computed much as operating and financial leverage are computed. The following equation presents one approach for measuring DTL:[8]

$$DTL = \frac{\text{Percentage change in EPS}}{\text{Percentage change in sales}} \tag{11.8}$$

Whenever the percentage change in EPS resulting from a given percentage change in sales is greater than the percentage change in sales, total leverage exists. This means that as long as the DTL is greater than 1, there is total leverage.

---

8. This approach is valid only when the same base level of sales is used to calculate and compare these values. In other words, *the base level of sales must be held constant if we are to compare the total leverage associated with different levels of fixed costs.*

Example

Applying Equation 11.8 to the data in Table 11.7 yields

$$\text{DTL} = \frac{+300\%}{+50\%} = 6.0$$

Because this result is greater than 1, total leverage exists. The higher the value, the greater the degree of total leverage.

A more direct formula for calculating the degree of total leverage at a given base level of sales, Q, is given by Equation 11.9, which uses the same notation that was presented earlier:

$$\text{DTL at base sales level } Q = \frac{Q \times (P - VC)}{Q \times (P - VC) - FC - I - \left(PD \times \frac{1}{1 - T}\right)} \quad (11.9)$$

Example

Substituting $Q = 20{,}000$, $P = \$5$, $VC = \$2$, $FC = \$10{,}000$, $I = \$20{,}000$, $PD = \$12{,}000$, and the tax rate ($T = 0.40$) into Equation 11.9 yields

DTL at 20,000 units

$$= \frac{20{,}000 \times (\$5 - \$2)}{20{,}000 \times (\$5 - \$2) - \$10{,}000 - \$20{,}000 - \left(\$12{,}000 \times \frac{1}{1 - 0.40}\right)}$$

$$= \frac{\$60{,}000}{\$10{,}000} = 6.0$$

Clearly, the formula used in Equation 11.9 provides a more direct method for calculating the degree of total leverage than the approach illustrated using Table 11.7 and Equation 11.8.

Relationship of Operating, Financial, and Total Leverage

Total leverage reflects the *combined impact* of operating and financial leverage on the firm. High operating leverage and high financial leverage will cause total leverage to be high. The opposite will also be true. The relationship between operating leverage and financial leverage is *multiplicative* rather than *additive*. The relationship between the degree of total leverage (DTL) and the degrees of operating leverage (DOL) and financial leverage (DFL) is given by Equation 11.10.

$$\text{DTL} = \text{DOL} \times \text{DFL} \quad (11.10)$$

Example

Substituting the values calculated for DOL and DFL, shown on the right-hand side of Table 11.7, into Equation 11.10 yields

$$\text{DTL} = 1.2 \times 5.0 = 6.0$$

The resulting degree of total leverage is the same value that we calculated directly in the preceding examples.

REVIEW QUESTIONS

11–1 What is meant by the term *leverage?* How are operating leverage, financial leverage, and total leverage related to the income statement?

11–2 What is the *operating breakeven point?* How do changes in fixed operating costs, the sale price per unit, and the variable operating cost per unit affect it?

11–3 What is *operating leverage?* What causes it? How is the *degree of operating leverage (DOL)* measured?

11–4 What is *financial leverage?* What causes it? How is the *degree of financial leverage (DFL)* measured?

11–5 What is the general relationship among operating leverage, financial leverage, and the total leverage of the firm? Do these types of leverage complement one another? Why or why not?

11.2 | The Firm's Capital Structure

Capital structure is one of the most complex areas of financial decision making because of its interrelationship with other financial decision variables.[9] Poor capital structure decisions can result in a high cost of capital, thereby lowering the NPVs of projects and making more of them unacceptable. Effective capital structure decisions can lower the cost of capital, resulting in higher NPVs and more acceptable projects—and thereby increasing the value of the firm. This section links together many of the concepts presented in Chapters 4, 5, 6, 7, and 10 and the discussion of leverage in this chapter.

Types of Capital

All of the items on the right-hand side of the firm's balance sheet, excluding current liabilities, are sources of capital. The following simplified balance sheet illustrates the basic breakdown of total capital into its two components, *debt capital* and *equity capital.*

---

9. Of course, although capital structure is financially important, it—like many business decisions—is generally not so important as the firm's products or services. In a practical sense, a firm can probably more readily increase its value by improving quality and reducing costs than by fine-tuning its capital structure.

Hint The various types and characterisitcs of *corporate bonds,* a major source of *debt capital,* were discussed in detail in Chapter 6.

The cost of debt is lower than the cost of other forms of financing. Lenders demand relatively lower returns because they take the least risk of any long-term contributors of capital: (1) They have a higher priority of claim against any earnings or assets available for payment. (2) They can exert far greater legal pressure against the company to make payment than can owners of preferred or common stock. (3) The tax deductibility of interest payments lowers the debt cost to the firm substantially.

Unlike debt capital, which must be repaid at some future date, *equity capital* is expected to remain in the firm for an indefinite period of time. The two basic sources of equity capital are (1) preferred stock and (2) common stock equity, which includes common stock and retained earnings. Common stock is typically the most expensive form of equity, followed by retained earnings and then preferred stock. Our concern here is the relationship between debt and equity capital. Because of equity's secondary position relative to debt, suppliers of equity capital take greater risk than suppliers of debt capital and therefore must be compensated with higher expected returns.

Hint Key differences between these two types of capital, relative to voice in management, claims on income and assets, maturity, and tax treatment, were summarized in Chapter 7, Table 7.1.

External Assessment of Capital Structure

We saw earlier that *financial leverage* results from the use of fixed-cost financing, such as debt and preferred stock, to magnify return and risk. The amount of leverage in the firm's capital structure can affect its value by affecting return and risk. Those outside the firm can make a rough assessment of capital structure by using measures found in the firm's financial statements. Some of these important debt ratios were presented in Chapter 2. For example, a direct measure of the degree of indebtedness is the *debt ratio.* The higher this ratio, the greater the relative amount of debt (or financial leverage) in the firm's capital structure. Measures of the firm's ability to meet contractual payments associated with debt include the *times interest earned ratio* and the *fixed-payment coverage ratio.* These ratios provide indirect information on financial leverage. Generally, the smaller these ratios, the greater the firm's financial leverage and the less able it is to meet payments as they come due.

The level of debt (financial leverage) that is acceptable for one industry or line of business can be highly risky in another, because different industries and lines of business have different operating characteristics. Table 11.8 (see page 466) presents the debt and times interest earned ratios for selected industries and lines of business. Significant industry differences can be seen in these data. Differences in debt positions are also likely to exist *within* an industry or line of business.

Personal Finance Example   Those who lend to individuals, like lenders to corporations, typically use ratios to assess the applicant's ability to meet the contractual payments associated with the requested debt. The lender, after obtaining information from a loan application and other sources, calculates ratios and compares them to predetermined allowable values. Typically, if the applicant's ratio values are within the acceptable range, the lender will make the requested loan.

The best example of this process is a real estate mortgage loan application. The mortgage lender usually invokes the following two requirements:

1. Monthly mortgage payments < 25% to 30% of monthly gross (before-tax) income

TABLE 11.8	Debt Ratios for Selected Industries and Lines of Business (Fiscal Years Ended 4/1/05 through 3/31/06)					
Industry or line of business	Debt ratio	Times interest earned ratio		Industry or line of business	Debt ratio	Times interest earned ratio
Manufacturing industries				**Retailing industries**		
Books printing	70.4%	2.9		Department stores	65.0%	3.0
Dairy products	70.3	3.1		New car dealers	82.2	1.8
Electronic computers	71.1	4.7		Supermarkets and grocery stores	72.9	3.4
Iron and steel forgings	59.9	4.9		**Service industries**		
Machine tools, metal cutting types	64.1	4.3		Advertising agencies	81.2	8.8
Wines and distilled alcoholic beverages	66.9	5.0		General automotive repair	85.3	2.8
Women's and girls' dresses	64.1	2.7		Insurance agencies and brokerages	80.4	7.3
Wholesaling industries				Offices of Certified Public Accountants	71.3	10.2
Furniture	69.3	4.0				
General groceries	70.5	3.0				
Men's and boys' clothing	66.9	3.7				

Source: RMA Annual Statement Studies, 2006–2007 (fiscal years ended 4/1/05 through 3/31/06) (Philadelphia: Risk Management Association, 2006). Copyright © 2006 by Risk Management Association.

Note: The Risk Management Association recommends that these ratios be regarded only as general guidelines and not as absolute industry norms. No claim is made as to the representativeness of these figures.

2. Total monthly installment payments (including the mortgage payment) < 33% to 38% of monthly gross (before-tax) income

Assume that the Loo family is applying for a mortgage loan. The family's monthly gross (before-tax) income is $5,380, and they currently have monthly installment loan obligations that total $560. The $200,000 mortgage loan they are applying for will require monthly payments of $1,400. The lender requires (1) the monthly mortgage payment to be less than 28% of monthly gross income and (2) total monthly installment payments (including the mortgage payment) to be less than 37% of monthly gross income. The lender calculates and evaluates these ratios for the Loos, as shown below.

1. Mort. pay./Gross income = $1,400/$5,380 = 26% < 28% maximum, therefore **OK**
2. Tot. instal. pay./Gross income = ($560 + $1,400)/$5,380 = $1,960/$5,380 = 36.4% < 37% maximum, therefore **OK**

Because the Loos' ratios meet the lender's standards, assuming they have adequate funds for the down payment and meet other lender requirements, the Loos will be granted the loan.

 ## Capital Structure of Non-U.S. Firms

In general, non-U.S. companies have much higher degrees of indebtedness than their U.S. counterparts. Most of the reasons relate to the fact that U.S. capital markets are more developed than those elsewhere and have played a greater role in corporate financing than has been the case in other countries. In most European countries and especially in Japan and other Pacific Rim nations, large commercial banks are more actively involved in the financing of corporate activity than has been true in the United States. Furthermore, in many of these countries, banks are allowed to make large equity investments in nonfinancial corporations—a practice prohibited for U.S. banks. Finally, share ownership tends to be more tightly controlled among founding-family, institutional, and even public investors in Europe and Asia than it is for most large U.S. corporations. Tight ownership enables owners to understand the firm's financial condition better, resulting in their willingness to tolerate a higher degree of indebtedness.

On the other hand, similarities do exist between U.S. corporations and corporations in other countries. First, the same industry patterns of capital structure tend to be found all around the world. For example, in nearly all countries, pharmaceutical and other high-growth industrial firms tend to have lower debt ratios than do steel companies, airlines, and electric utility companies. Second, the capital structures of the largest U.S.-based multinational companies, which have access to capital markets around the world, typically resemble the capital structures of multinational companies from other countries more than they resemble those of smaller U.S. companies. Finally, the worldwide trend is away from reliance on banks for financing and toward greater reliance on security issuance. Over time, the differences in the capital structures of U.S. and non-U.S. firms will probably lessen.

Capital Structure Theory

Research suggests that there is an optimal capital structure range. *It is not yet possible to provide financial managers with a specified methodology for use in determining a firm's optimal capital structure.* Nevertheless, financial theory does offer help in understanding how a firm's chosen financing mix affects the firm's value.

In 1958, Franco Modigliani and Merton H. Miller[10] (commonly known as "M and M") demonstrated algebraically that, assuming perfect markets,[11] the capital structure that a firm chooses does not affect its value. Many researchers, including M and M, have examined the effects of less restrictive assumptions on the relationship between capital structure and the firm's value. The result is a theoretical *optimal* capital structure based on balancing the benefits and costs of debt financing. The major benefit of debt financing is the *tax shield,* which allows interest payments to be deducted in calculating taxable income. The cost of debt financing results from (1) the increased probability of bankruptcy caused by debt obligations, (2) the *agency costs* of the lender's constraining the firm's actions, and (3) the costs associated with managers having more information about the firm's prospects than do investors.

Tax Benefits

Allowing firms to deduct interest payments on debt when calculating taxable income reduces the amount of the firm's earnings paid in taxes, thereby making

10. Franco Modigliani and Merton H. Miller, "The Cost of Capital, Corporation Finance, and the Theory of Investment," *American Economic Review* (June 1958), pp. 261–297.

11. Perfect-market assumptions include (1) no taxes, (2) no brokerage or flotation costs for securities, (3) symmetrical information—investors and managers have the same information about the firm's investment prospects, and (4) investor ability to borrow at the same rate as corporations.

more earnings available for bondholders and stockholders. The deductibility of interest means the cost of debt, r_i, to the firm is subsidized by the government. Letting r_d equal the before-tax cost of debt and letting T equal the tax rate, from Chapter 10 (Equation 10.2), we have $r_i = r_d \times (1 - T)$.

Probability of Bankruptcy

The chance that a firm will become bankrupt because of an inability to meet its obligations as they come due depends largely on its level of both business risk and financial risk.

Business Risk   In Chapter 10, we defined *business risk* as the risk to the firm of being unable to cover its operating costs. In general, the greater the firm's *operating leverage*—the use of fixed operating costs—the higher its business risk. Although operating leverage is an important factor affecting business risk, two other factors—revenue stability and cost stability—also affect it. *Revenue stability* reflects the relative variability of the firm's sales revenues. Firms with reasonably stable levels of demand and with products that have stable prices have stable revenues. The result is low levels of business risk. Firms with highly volatile product demand and prices have unstable revenues that result in high levels of business risk. *Cost stability* reflects the relative predictability of input prices such as those for labor and materials. The more predictable and stable these input prices are, the lower the business risk; the less predictable and stable they are, the higher the business risk.

Business risk varies among firms, regardless of their lines of business, and is not affected by capital structure decisions. The level of business risk must be taken as a "given." The higher a firm's business risk, the more cautious the firm must be in establishing its capital structure. Firms with high business risk therefore tend toward less highly leveraged capital structures, and firms with low business risk tend toward more highly leveraged capital structures. We will hold business risk constant throughout the discussions that follow.

Financial Risk   The firm's capital structure directly affects its *financial risk*, which is the risk to the firm of being unable to cover required financial obligations. The penalty for not meeting financial obligations is bankruptcy. The more fixed-cost financing—debt (including financial leases) and preferred stock—a firm has in its capital structure, the greater its financial leverage and risk. Financial risk depends on the capital structure decision made by the management, and that decision is affected by the business risk the firm faces.

> **Hint** The cash flows to investors from bonds are less risky than the dividends from preferred stock, which are less risky than dividends from common stock. Only with bonds is the issuer contractually obligated to pay the scheduled interest, and the amounts due to bondholders and preferred stockholders are usually fixed. Therefore, the required return for bonds is generally lower than that for preferred stock, which is lower than that for common stock.

Agency Costs Imposed by Lenders

As noted in Chapter 1, the managers of firms typically act as *agents* of the owners (stockholders). The owners give the managers the authority to manage the firm for the owners' benefit. The *agency problem* created by this relationship extends not only to the relationship between owners and managers but also to the relationship between owners and lenders.

When a lender provides funds to a firm, the interest rate charged is based on the lender's assessment of the firm's risk. The lender–borrower relationship, therefore, depends on the lender's expectations for the firm's subsequent behavior. The borrowing rates are, in effect, locked in when the loans are negotiated. After obtaining a loan at a certain rate, the firm could increase its risk by investing in risky projects or by incurring additional debt. Such action could weaken the lender's position in terms of its claim on the cash flow of the firm. From another point of view, if these risky investment strategies paid off, the stockholders would benefit. Because payment obligations to the lender remain unchanged, the excess cash flows generated by a positive outcome from the riskier action would enhance the value of the firm to its owners. In other words, if the risky investments pay off, the owners receive all the benefits; if the risky investments do not pay off, the lenders share in the costs.

Clearly, an incentive exists for the managers acting on behalf of the stockholders to "take advantage" of lenders. To avoid this situation, lenders impose certain monitoring techniques on borrowers, who as a result incur *agency costs*. The most obvious strategy is to deny subsequent loan requests or to increase the cost of future loans to the firm. But this strategy is an after-the-fact approach. Therefore, lenders typically protect themselves by including in the loan agreement provisions that limit the firm's ability to alter significantly its business and financial risk. These loan provisions tend to center on issues such as the minimum level of liquidity, asset acquisitions, executive salaries, and dividend payments.

By including appropriate provisions in the loan agreement, the lender can control the firm's risk and thus protect itself against the adverse consequences of this agency problem. Of course, in exchange for incurring agency costs by agreeing to the operating and financial constraints placed on it by the loan provisions, the firm should benefit by obtaining funds at a lower cost.

Hint Typical loan provisions included in corporate bonds are discussed in Chapter 6.

Asymmetric Information

Two surveys examined capital structure decisions.[12] Financial executives were asked which of two major criteria determined their financing decisions: (1) maintaining a *target capital structure* or (2) following a hierarchy of financing. This hierarchy, called a **pecking order,** begins with retained earnings, which is followed by debt financing and finally external equity financing. Respondents from 31 percent of *Fortune* 500 firms and from 11 percent of the (smaller) 500 largest over-the-counter firms answered target capital structure. Respondents from 69 percent of the *Fortune* 500 firms and 89 percent of the 500 largest OTC firms chose the pecking order.

At first glance, on the basis of financial theory, this choice appears to be inconsistent with wealth maximization goals, but Stewart Myers has explained how "asymmetric information" could account for the pecking order financing preferences of financial managers.[13] **Asymmetric information** results when managers of a firm have more information about operations and future prospects than do investors. Assuming that managers make decisions with the goal of maximizing the wealth of existing stockholders, then asymmetric information can affect the capital structure decisions that managers make.

pecking order
A hierarchy of financing that begins with retained earnings, which is followed by debt financing and finally external equity financing.

asymmetric information
The situation in which managers of a firm have more information about operations and future prospects than do investors.

---

12. The results of the survey of *Fortune* 500 firms are reported in J. Michael Pinegar and Lisa Wilbricht, "What Managers Think of Capital Structure Theory: A Survey," *Financial Management* (Winter 1989), pp. 82–91, and the results of a similar survey of the 500 largest OTC firms are reported in Linda C. Hittle, Kamal Haddad, and Lawrence J. Gitman, "Over-the-Counter Firms, Asymmetric Information, and Financing Preferences," *Review of Financial Economics* (Fall 1992), pp. 81–92.

13. Stewart C. Myers, "The Capital Structure Puzzle," *Journal of Finance* (July 1984), pp. 575–592.

Suppose, for example, that management has found a valuable investment that will require additional financing. Management believes that the prospects for the firm's future are very good and that the market, as indicated by the firm's current stock price, does not fully appreciate the firm's value. In this case, it would be advantageous to current stockholders if management raised the required funds using debt rather than issuing new stock. Using debt to raise funds is frequently viewed as a **signal** that reflects management's view of the firm's stock value. Debt financing is a *positive signal* suggesting that management believes that the stock is "undervalued" and therefore a bargain. When the firm's positive future outlook becomes known to the market, the increased value will be fully captured by existing owners, rather than having to be shared with new stockholders.

If, however, the outlook for the firm is poor, management may believe that the firm's stock is "overvalued." In that case, it would be in the best interest of existing stockholders for the firm to issue new stock. Therefore, investors often interpret the announcement of a stock issue as a *negative signal*—bad news concerning the firm's prospects—and the stock price declines. This decrease in stock value, along with high underwriting costs for stock issues (compared to debt issues), make new stock financing very expensive. When the negative future outlook becomes known to the market, the decreased value is shared with new stockholders, rather than being fully captured by existing owners.

Because conditions of asymmetric information exist from time to time, firms should maintain some reserve borrowing capacity by keeping debt levels low. This reserve allows the firm to take advantage of good investment opportunities without having to sell stock at a low value and thus send signals that unduly influence the stock price.

Optimal Capital Structure

What, then, *is* the optimal capital structure, even if it exists (so far) only in theory? To provide some insight into an answer, we will examine some basic financial relationships. It is generally believed that *the value of the firm is maximized when the cost of capital is minimized.* By using a modification of the simple zero-growth valuation model (see Equation 7.3 in Chapter 7), we can define the value of the firm, *V*, by Equation 11.11.

$$V = \frac{\text{EBIT} \times (1 - T)}{r_a} = \frac{\text{NOPAT}}{r_a} \qquad (11.11)$$

where

$\quad$ EBIT = earnings before interest and taxes

$\qquad T$ = tax rate

$\quad$ NOPAT = net operating profits after taxes, which (as noted in Chapters 3 and 8) is the after-tax operating earnings available to the debt and equity holders, EBIT $\times (1 - T)$

$\qquad r_a$ = weighted average cost of capital

Clearly, if we assume that NOPAT (and therefore EBIT) is constant, the value of the firm, *V*, is maximized by minimizing the weighted average cost of capital, r_a.

Cost Functions and Value
Capital costs and the
optimal capital structure

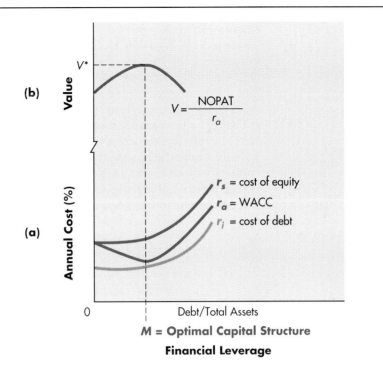

Cost Functions

Figure 11.3(*a*) plots three cost functions—the cost of debt, the cost of equity, and the weighted average cost of capital (WACC)—as a function of financial leverage measured by the debt ratio (debt to total assets). The *cost of debt*, r_i, remains low because of the tax shield, but it slowly increases as leverage increases, to compensate lenders for increasing risk. The *cost of equity*, r_s, is above the cost of debt. It increases as financial leverage increases, but it generally increases more rapidly than the cost of debt. The cost of equity rises because the stockholders require a higher return as leverage increases, to compensate for the higher degree of financial risk.

The *weighted average cost of capital*, r_a (WACC) results from a weighted average of the firm's debt and equity capital costs. At a debt ratio of zero, the firm is 100 percent equity-financed. As debt is substituted for equity and as the debt ratio increases, the WACC declines because the debt cost is less than the equity cost ($r_i < r_s$). As the debt ratio continues to increase, the increased debt and equity costs eventually cause the WACC to rise (after point *M* in Figure 11.3(*a*)). This behavior results in a U-shaped, or saucer-shaped, weighted average cost-of-capital function, r_a.

Graphical View of Optimal Structure

optimal capital structure
The capital structure at which the weighted average cost of capital is minimized, thereby maximizing the firm's value.

Because the maximization of value, *V*, is achieved when the overall cost of capital, r_a, is at a minimum (see Equation 11.11), the **optimal capital structure** is that at which the weighted average cost of capital, r_a, is minimized. In Figure 11.3(*a*), point *M* represents the *minimum weighted average cost of capital*—the point of optimal financial leverage and hence of optimal capital structure for the firm.

Figure 11.3(*b*) plots the value of the firm that results from substitution of r_a in Figure 11.3(*a*) for various levels of financial leverage into the zero-growth valuation model in Equation 11.11. As shown in Figure 11.3(*b*), at the optimal capital structure, point *M*, the value of the firm is maximized at V^*.

Generally, the lower the firm's weighted average cost of capital, the greater the difference between the return on a project and the WACC, and therefore the greater the owners' return. Simply stated, minimizing the weighted average cost of capital allows management to undertake a larger number of profitable projects, thereby further increasing the value of the firm.

As a practical matter, there is no way to calculate the optimal capital structure implied by Figure 11.3. Because it is impossible either to know or to remain at the precise optimal capital structure, firms generally try to operate in a *range* that places them near what they believe to be the optimal capital structure.

REVIEW QUESTIONS

11–6 What is a firm's *capital structure?* What ratios assess the degree of financial leverage in a firm's capital structure?

11–7 In what ways are the capital structures of U.S. and non-U.S. firms different? How are they similar?

11–8 What is the major benefit of debt financing? How does it affect the firm's cost of debt?

11–9 What are *business risk* and *financial risk?* How does each of them influence the firm's capital structure decisions?

11–10 Briefly describe the *agency problem* that exists between owners and lenders. How do lenders cause firms to incur *agency costs* to resolve this problem?

11–11 How does *asymmetric information* affect the firm's capital structure decisions? How do the firm's financing actions give investors *signals* that reflect management's view of stock value?

11–12 How do the cost of debt, the cost of equity, and the weighted average cost of capital (WACC) behave as the firm's financial leverage increases from zero? Where is the *optimal capital structure?* What is its relationship to the firm's value at that point?

11.3 | EBIT–EPS Approach to Capital Structure

EBIT–EPS approach
An approach for selecting the capital structure that maximizes earnings per share (EPS) over the expected range of earnings before interest and taxes (EBIT).

It should be clear from earlier chapters that the goal of the financial manager is to maximize owner wealth—that is, the firm's stock price. One of the widely followed variables affecting the firm's stock price is its earnings, which represents the returns earned on behalf of owners. In spite of the fact that focusing on earnings ignores risk (the other key variable affecting the firm's stock price), earnings per share (EPS) can be conveniently used to analyze alternative capital structures. The **EBIT–EPS approach** to capital structure involves selecting the capital structure that maximizes EPS over the expected range of earnings before interest and taxes (EBIT).

Presenting a Financing Plan Graphically

To analyze the effects of a firm's capital structure on the owners' returns, we consider the relationship between earnings before interest and taxes (EBIT) and earnings per share (EPS). A constant level of EBIT—constant *business risk*—is assumed, to isolate the effect on returns of the financing costs associated with alternative capital structures. EPS is used to measure the owners' returns, which are expected to be closely related to share price.

Data Required

To graph a financing plan, we need to know at least two EBIT–EPS coordinates. The following example illustrates the approach for obtaining coordinates.

Example

The current capital structure of JSG Company, a soft-drink manufacturer, is as shown in the following table. Note that JSG's capital structure currently contains only common stock equity; the firm has no debt or preferred stock. If (for convenience) we assume the firm has no current liabilities, its debt ratio (total liabilities ÷ total assets) is currently 0% ($0 ÷ $500,000); it therefore has *zero* financial leverage. Assume the firm is in the 40% tax bracket.

Current capital structure	
Long-term debt	$ 0
Common stock equity ($25,000 shares @ $20)	500,000
Total capital (assets)	$500,000

EBIT–EPS coordinates for JSG's current capital structure can be found by assuming two EBIT values and calculating the EPS associated with them.[14] Because the EBIT–EPS graph is a straight line, any two EBIT values can be used to find coordinates. Here we arbitrarily use values of $100,000 and $200,000.

	$100,000	$200,000
EBIT (assumed)	$100,000	$200,000
− Interest (rate × $0 debt)	0	0
Net profits before taxes	$100,000	$200,000
− Taxes ($T = 0.40$)	40,000	80,000
Net profits after taxes	$ 60,000	$120,000
EPS	$\dfrac{\$60,000}{25,000 \text{ sh.}} = \$2.40$	$\dfrac{\$120,000}{25,000 \text{ sh.}} = \$4.80$

The two EBIT–EPS coordinates resulting from these calculations are (1) $100,000 EBIT and $2.40 EPS and (2) $200,000 EBIT and $4.80 EPS.

---

14. A convenient method for finding one EBIT–EPS coordinate is to calculate the *financial breakeven point*, the level of EBIT for which the firm's EPS just equals $0. It is the level of EBIT needed just to cover all fixed financial costs—annual interest (I) and preferred stock dividends (PD). The equation for the financial breakeven point is

$$\text{Financial breakeven point} = I + \frac{PD}{1 - T}$$

where T is the tax rate. It can be seen that when $PD = \$0$, the financial breakeven point is equal to I, the annual interest payment.

Plotting the Data

financial breakeven point
The level of EBIT necessary
to just cover all *fixed financial
costs;* the level of EBIT for
which EPS = $0.

The JSG Company data can be plotted on a set of EBIT–EPS axes, as shown in Figure 11.4. The figure shows the level of EPS expected for each level of EBIT. For levels of EBIT below the *x*-axis intercept, a loss (negative EPS) results. Each of the *x*-axis intercepts is a **financial breakeven point**, the level of EBIT necessary to just cover all *fixed financial costs* (EPS = $0).

Comparing Alternative Capital Structures

We can compare alternative capital structures by graphing financing plans as shown in Figure 11.4.

> *Example*
>
> JSG Company, whose current zero-leverage capital structure was described above, is contemplating shifting its capital structure to either of two leveraged positions. To maintain its $500,000 of total capital, JSG's capital structure will be shifted to greater leverage by issuing debt and using the proceeds to retire an equivalent amount of common stock. The two alternative capital structures result in debt ratios of 30% and 60%, respectively. The basic information on the current and two alternative capital structures is summarized in Table 11.9.
>
> Using the data in Table 11.9, we can calculate the coordinates needed to plot the 30% and 60% debt capital structures. For convenience, using the $100,000 and $200,000 EBIT values used earlier to plot the current capital structure, we get the information in the following table.

	Capital structure			
	30% Debt ratio		60% Debt ratio	
EBIT (assumed)	$100,000	$200,000	$100,000	$200,000
− Interest (Table 11.9)	15,000	15,000	49,500	49,500
Net profits before taxes	$ 85,000	$185,000	$ 50,500	$150,500
− Taxes (T = 0.40)	34,000	74,000	20,200	60,200
Net profits after taxes	$ 51,000	$111,000	$ 30,300	$ 90,300
EPS	$\frac{\$51,000}{17,500 \text{ sh.}} = \$2.91$	$\frac{\$111,000}{17,500 \text{ sh.}} = \$6.34$	$\frac{\$30,300}{10,000 \text{ sh.}} = \$3.03$	$\frac{\$90,300}{10,000 \text{ sh.}} = \$9.03$

> The two sets of EBIT–EPS coordinates developed in the preceding table, along with those developed for the current zero-leverage capital structure, are summarized and plotted on the EBIT–EPS axes in Figure 11.5 (see page 476). This figure shows that each capital structure is superior to the others in terms of maximizing EPS over certain ranges of EBIT. The zero-leverage capital structure (debt ratio = 0%) is superior to either of the other capital structures for levels of EBIT between $0 and $50,000. Between $50,000 and $95,500 of EBIT, the capital structure associated with a debt ratio of 30% is preferred. And at a level of EBIT above $95,500, the 60% debt ratio capital structure provides the highest earnings per share.[15]

---

15. An algebraic technique can be used to find the *indifference points* between the capital structure alternatives. Due to its relative complexity, this technique is not presented. Instead, emphasis is given here to the visual estimation of these points from the graph.

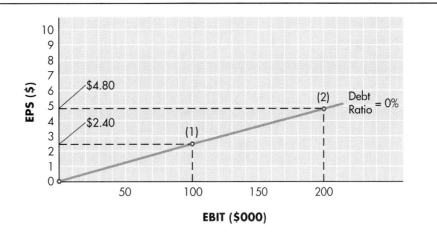

FIGURE 11.4

Graphic Presentation of a Financing Plan
JSG Company's zero-leverage financing plan

TABLE 11.9   **Basic Information on JSG Company's Current and Alternative Capital Structures**

Capital structure debt ratio (1)	Total assets[a] (2)	Debt [(1) × (2)] (3)	Equity [(2) − (3)] (4)	Interest rate on debt[b] (5)	Annual interest [(3) × (5)] (6)	Shares of common stock outstanding [(4) ÷ $20][c] (7)
0% (current)	$500,000	$ 0	$500,000	0 %	$ 0	25,000
30	500,000	150,000	350,000	10	15,000	17,500
60	500,000	300,000	200,000	16.5	49,500	10,000

[a]Because for convenience the firm is assumed to have no current liabilities, total assets equals total capital of $500,000.

[b]The interest rate on all debt increases with increases in the debt ratio due to the greater leverage and risk associated with higher debt ratios.

[c]The $20 value represents the book value of common stock equity.

Considering Risk in EBIT–EPS Analysis

When interpreting EBIT–EPS analysis, it is important to consider the risk of each capital structure alternative. Graphically, the risk of each capital structure can be viewed in light of two measures: (1) the *financial breakeven point* (EBIT-axis intercept) and (2) the *degree of financial leverage* reflected in the slope of the capital structure line: *The higher the financial breakeven point and the steeper the slope of the capital structure line, the greater the financial risk.*

Further assessment of risk can be performed by using ratios. As financial leverage (measured by the debt ratio) increases, we expect a corresponding decline in the firm's ability to make scheduled interest payments (measured by the times interest earned ratio).

FIGURE 11.5

EBIT–EPS Approach
A comparison of selected
capital structures for JSG
Company

Capital structure debt ratio	EBIT	
	$100,000	**$200,000**
	Earnings per share (EPS)	
0%	$2.40	$4.80
30	2.91	6.34
60	3.03	9.03

Example

Reviewing the three capital structures plotted for JSG Company in Figure 11.5, we can see that as the debt ratio increases, so does the financial risk of each alternative. Both the financial breakeven point and the slope of the capital structure lines increase with increasing debt ratios. If we use the $100,000 EBIT value, for example, the times interest earned ratio (EBIT ÷ interest) for the zero-leverage capital structure is infinity ($100,000 ÷ $0); for the 30% debt case, it is 6.67 ($100,000 ÷ $15,000); and for the 60% debt case, it is 2.02 ($100,000 ÷ $49,500). Because lower times interest earned ratios reflect higher risk, these ratios support the conclusion that the risk of the capital structures increases with increasing financial leverage. The capital structure for a debt ratio of 60% is riskier than that for a debt ratio of 30%, which in turn is riskier than the capital structure for a debt ratio of 0%.

Basic Shortcoming of EBIT–EPS Analysis

The most important point to recognize when using EBIT–EPS analysis is that this technique tends to concentrate on *maximizing earnings* rather than maximizing owner wealth as reflected in the firm's stock price. The use of an EPS-maximizing approach generally ignores risk. If investors did not require risk premiums (additional returns) as the firm increased the proportion of debt in its capital structure, a strategy involving maximizing EPS would also maximize stock price. But because risk premiums increase with increases in financial leverage, the maximization of EPS *does not* ensure owner wealth maximization. To select the best capital structure, firms must integrate both return (EPS) and risk (via the required return, r_s) into a valuation framework consistent with the capital structure theory presented earlier.

REVIEW QUESTION

11–13 Explain the *EBIT–EPS approach* to capital structure. Include in your explanation a graph indicating the *financial breakeven point*; label the axes. Is this approach consistent with maximization of the owners' wealth?

11.4 | Choosing the Optimal Capital Structure

A wealth maximization framework for use in making capital structure decisions should include the two key factors of return and risk. This section describes the procedures for linking to market value the return and risk associated with alternative capital structures.

Linkage

To determine the firm's value under alternative capital structures, the firm must find the level of return that it must earn to compensate owners for the risk being incurred. This approach is consistent with the overall valuation framework developed in Chapters 6 and 7 and applied to capital budgeting decisions in Chapter 9.

The required return associated with a given level of financial risk can be estimated in a number of ways. Theoretically, the preferred approach would be first to estimate the beta associated with each alternative capital structure and then to use the CAPM framework presented in Equation 5.7 to calculate the required return, r_s. A more operational approach involves linking the financial risk associated with each capital structure alternative directly to the required return. Such an approach is similar to the CAPM-type approach demonstrated in Chapter 9 for linking project risk and required return (RADR). Here it involves estimating the required return associated with each level of financial risk, as measured by a statistic such as the coefficient of variation of EPS. Regardless of the approach used, one would expect the required return to increase as the financial risk increases.

Example   Expanding the JSG Company example presented earlier, we assume that the firm is attempting to choose the best of seven alternative capital structures—debt ratios of 0%, 10%, 20%, 30%, 40%, 50%, and 60%. For each of these structures the

TABLE 11.10   **Calculation of Share Value Estimates Associated with Alternative Capital Structures for JSG Company**

Capital structure debt ratio	Expected EPS (1)	Estimated coefficient of variation of EPS (2)	Estimated required return, r_s (3)	Estimated share value [(1) ÷ (3)] (4)
0%	$2.40	0.71	.115	$20.87
10	2.55	0.74	.117	21.79
20	2.72	0.78	.121	22.48
30	2.91	0.83	.125	23.28
40	3.12	0.91	.140	22.29
50	3.18	1.07	.165	19.27
60	3.03	1.40	.190	15.95

firm estimated the (1) EPS, (2) coefficient of variation of EPS, and (3) required return, r_s. These values are shown in columns 1 through 3 of Table 11.10. Note that EPS (in column 1) is maximized at a 50% debt ratio though the risk of EPS measured by its coefficient of variation (in column 2) is constantly increasing. As expected, the estimated required return of owners, r_s (in column 3), increases with increasing risk, as measured by the coefficient of variation of EPS (in column 2). Simply stated, for higher degrees of financial leverage—debt ratios—owners require higher rates of return.

Estimating Value

The value of the firm associated with alternative capital structures can be estimated by using one of the standard valuation models. If, for simplicity, we assume that all earnings are paid out as dividends, we can use a zero-growth valuation model such as that developed in Chapter 7. The model, originally stated in Equation 7.2, is restated here with EPS substituted for dividends (because in each year the dividends would equal EPS):

$$P_0 = \frac{EPS}{r_s} \qquad (11.12)$$

By substituting the expected level of EPS and the associated required return, r_s, into Equation 11.12, we can estimate the per-share value of the firm, P_0.

Example   We can now estimate the value of JSG Company's stock under each of the alternative capital structures. Substituting the expected EPS (column 1 of Table 11.10) and the required returns, r_s (column 3 of Table 11.10 in decimal form), into Equation 11.12 for each of the capital structures, we obtain the share values given in column 4 of the table. Plotting the resulting share values against the associated debt ratios, as shown in Figure 11.6, clearly illustrates that the maximum share value occurs at the capital structure associated with a debt ratio of 30%.

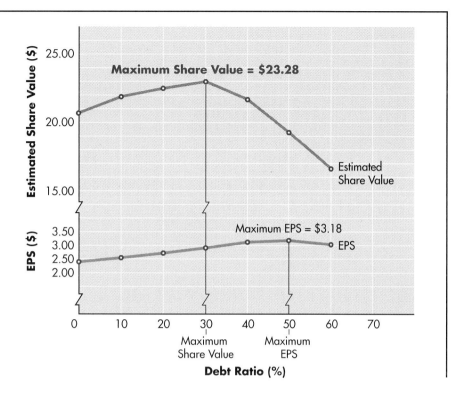

FIGURE 11.6

Estimating Value
Estimated share value and EPS for alternative capital structures for JSG Company

Maximizing Value versus Maximizing EPS

Throughout this text, we have specified the goal of the financial manager as maximizing owner wealth, not profit. Although some relationship exists between expected profit and value, there is no reason to believe that profit-maximizing strategies necessarily result in wealth maximization. It is therefore the wealth of the owners as reflected in the estimated share value that should serve as the criterion for selecting the best capital structure. A final look at JSG Company will highlight this point.

Example

Further analysis of Figure 11.6 clearly shows that although the firm's profits (EPS) are maximized at a debt ratio of 50%, share value is maximized at a 30% debt ratio. Therefore, the preferred capital structure would be the 30% debt ratio. The two approaches provide different conclusions because EPS maximization does not consider risk.

Some Other Important Considerations

Because there is really no practical way to calculate the optimal capital structure, any quantitative analysis of capital structure must be tempered with other important considerations. Table 11.11 on page 480 summarizes some of the more important additional factors involved in capital structure decisions.

TABLE 11.11	**Important Factors to Consider in Making Capital Structure Decisions**

Concern	Factor	Description
Business risk	Revenue stability	Firms that have stable and predictable revenues can more safely undertake highly leveraged capital structures than can firms with volatile patterns of sales revenue. Firms with growing sales tend to benefit from added debt; they can reap the positive benefits of financial leverage, which magnifies the effect of these increases.
	Cash flow	When considering a new capital structure, the firm must focus on its ability to generate the cash flows necessary to meet obligations. Cash forecasts reflecting an ability to service debts (and preferred stock) must support any shift in capital structure.
Agency costs	Contractual obligations	A firm may be contractually constrained with respect to the type of funds that it can raise. For example, a firm might be prohibited from selling additional debt except when the claims of holders of such debt are made subordinate to the existing debt. Contractual constraints on the sale of additional stock, as well as on the ability to distribute dividends on stock, might also exist.
	Management preferences	Occasionally, a firm will impose an internal constraint on the use of debt to limit its risk exposure to a level deemed acceptable to management. In other words, because of risk aversion, the firm's management constrains the firm's capital structure at a level that may or may not be the true optimum.
	Control	A management group concerned about control may prefer to issue debt rather than (voting) common stock. Under favorable market conditions, a firm that wanted to sell equity could make a *preemptive offering* or issue *nonvoting shares*, allowing each shareholder to maintain proportionate ownership. Generally, only in closely held firms or firms threatened by takeover does control become a major concern in the capital structure decision.
Asymmetric information	External risk assessment	The firm's ability to raise funds quickly and at favorable rates depends on the external risk assessments of lenders and bond raters. The firm must consider the impact of capital structure decisions both on share value and on published financial statements from which lenders and raters assess the firm's risk.
	Timing	At times when interest rates are low, debt financing might be more attractive; when interest rates are high, the sale of stock may be more appealing. Sometimes both debt and equity capital become unavailable at reasonable terms. General economic conditions—especially those of the capital market—can thus significantly affect capital structure decisions.

REVIEW QUESTIONS

11–14 Why do *maximizing EPS* and *maximizing value* not necessarily lead to the same conclusion about the optimal capital structure?

11–15 What important factors in addition to quantitative factors should a firm consider when it is making a capital structure decision?

Summary

Focus on Value

The amount of leverage (fixed-cost assets or funds) employed by a firm directly affects its risk, return, and share value. Generally, higher leverage raises risk and return, and lower leverage reduces risk and return. Operating leverage concerns the level of fixed operating costs; financial leverage focuses on fixed financial costs, particularly interest on debt and any preferred stock dividends. The firm's capital structure determines its financial leverage. Because of its fixed interest payments, the more debt a firm employs relative to its equity, the greater its financial leverage.

The value of the firm is clearly affected by its degree of operating leverage and by the composition of its capital structure. The financial manager must therefore carefully consider the types of operating and financial costs it incurs, recognizing that with greater fixed costs comes higher risk. Major decisions with regard to both operating cost structure and capital structure must therefore focus on their impact on the firm's value. The firm should implement only those leverage and capital structure decisions that are consistent with its goal of **maximizing its stock price.**

Review of Learning Goals

LG 1 **Discuss leverage, capital structure, breakeven analysis, the operating breakeven point, and the effect of changing costs on it.** Leverage results from the use of fixed costs to magnify returns to a firm's owners. Capital structure, the firm's mix of long-term debt and equity, affects leverage and therefore the firm's value. Breakeven analysis measures the level of sales necessary to cover total operating costs. The operating breakeven point may be calculated algebraically, by dividing fixed operating costs by the difference between the sale price per unit and variable operating cost per unit, or it may be determined graphically. The operating breakeven point increases with increased fixed and variable operating costs and decreases with an increase in sale price, and vice versa.

LG 2 **Understand operating, financial, and total leverage and the relationships among them.** Operating leverage is the use of fixed operating costs by the firm to magnify the effects of changes in sales on EBIT. The higher the fixed operating costs, the greater the operating leverage. Financial leverage is the use of fixed financial costs by the firm to magnify the effects of changes in EBIT on EPS. The higher the fixed financial costs, the greater the financial leverage. The total leverage of the firm is the use of fixed costs—both operating and financial—to magnify the effects of changes in sales on EPS.

LG 3 **Describe the types of capital, external assessment of capital structure, the capital structure of non-U.S. firms, and capital structure theory.** Debt capital and equity capital make up a firm's capital structure. Capital structure can be externally assessed by using financial ratios—debt ratio, times interest earned ratio, and fixed-payment coverage ratio. Non-U.S. companies tend to have much higher degrees of indebtedness than do their U.S. counterparts, primarily because U.S. capital markets are more developed.

Research suggests that there is an optimal capital structure that balances the firm's benefits and costs of debt financing. The major benefit of debt financing is the tax shield. The costs of debt financing include the probability of bankruptcy; agency costs imposed by lenders; and asymmetric information, which typically causes firms to raise funds in a pecking order so as to send positive signals to the market and thereby enhance shareholder wealth.

LG 4 **Explain the optimal capital structure using a graphical view of the firm's cost-of-capital functions and a zero-growth valuation model.** The zero-growth valuation model defines the firm's value as its net operating profits after taxes (NOPAT), or after-tax EBIT, divided by its weighted average cost of capital. Assuming that NOPAT is constant, the value of the firm is maximized by minimizing its weighted average cost of capital (WACC). The optimal capital structure minimizes the WACC. Graphically, the firm's WACC exhibits a U-shape, whose minimum value defines the optimal capital structure that maximizes owner wealth.

LG 5 **Discuss the EBIT–EPS approach to capital structure.** The EBIT–EPS approach evaluates capital structures in light of the returns they provide the firm's owners and their degree of financial risk. Under the EBIT–EPS approach, the preferred capital structure is the one that is expected to provide maximum EPS over the firm's expected range of EBIT. Graphically, this approach reflects risk in terms of the financial breakeven point and the slope of the capital structure line. The major shortcoming of EBIT–EPS analysis is that it concentrates on maximizing earnings (returns) rather than owners' wealth, which considers risk as well as return.

LG 6 **Review the return and risk of alternative capital structures, their linkage to market value, and other important considerations related to capital structure.** The best capital structure can be selected by using a valuation model to link return and risk factors. The preferred capital structure is the one that results in the highest estimated share value, not the highest EPS. Other important nonquantitative factors must also be considered when making capital structure decisions.

Self-Test Problems (Solutions in Appendix B)

  ST11–1 **Breakeven point and all forms of leverage**   TOR most recently sold 100,000 units at $7.50 each; its variable operating costs are $3.00 per unit, and its fixed operating costs are $250,000. Annual interest charges total $80,000, and the firm has 8,000

shares of $5 (annual dividend) preferred stock outstanding. It currently has 20,000 shares of common stock outstanding. Assume that the firm is subject to a 40% tax rate.

a. At what level of sales (in units) would the firm break even on operations (that is, EBIT = $0)?

b. Calculate the firm's *earnings per share (EPS)* in tabular form at (1) the current level of sales and (2) a 120,000-unit sales level.

c. Using the current $750,000 *level of sales as a base*, calculate the firm's degree of operating leverage (DOL).

d. Using the EBIT *associated with the $750,000 level of sales as a base*, calculate the firm's degree of financial leverage (DFL).

e. Use the degree of total leverage (DTL) concept to determine the effect (in percentage terms) of a 50% increase in TOR's sales *from the $750,000 base level* on its earnings per share.

 ST11–2 EBIT–EPS analysis Newlin Electronics is considering additional financing of $10,000. It currently has $50,000 of 12% (annual interest) bonds and 10,000 shares of common stock outstanding. The firm can obtain the financing through a 12% (annual interest) bond issue or through the sale of 1,000 shares of common stock. The firm has a 40% tax rate.

a. Calculate two EBIT–EPS coordinates for each plan by selecting any two EBIT values and finding their associated EPS values.

b. Plot the two financing plans on a set of EBIT–EPS axes.

c. On the basis of your graph in part **b,** at what level of EBIT does the bond plan become superior to the stock plan?

  ST11–3 Optimal capital structure Hawaiian Macadamia Nut Company has collected the following data with respect to its capital structure, expected earnings per share, and required return.

Capital structure debt ratio	Expected earnings per share	Required return, r_s
0%	$3.12	13%
10	3.90	15
20	4.80	16
30	5.44	17
40	5.51	19
50	5.00	20
60	4.40	22

a. Compute the *estimated share value* associated with each of the capital structures, using the simplified method described in this chapter (see Equation 11.12). (*Hint:* Be sure to convert required returns to decimal form.)

b. Determine the optimal capital structure on the basis of (1) maximization of expected earnings per share and (2) maximization of share value.

c. Which capital structure do you recommend? Why?

Warm-Up Exercises

A blue box (■) indicates exercises available in .

 E11–1 Canvas Reproductions has fixed operating costs of $12,500, variable operating costs of $10 per unit, and sells its paintings for $25 each. At what level of unit sales will the company breakeven in terms of EBIT?

 E11–2 The Great Fish Taco Corporation currently has fixed operating costs of $15,000, sells its pre-made tacos for $6 per box, and incurs variable operating costs of $2.50 per box. If the firm has a potential investment that would simultaneously raise its fixed costs to $16,500 and allow it to charge a per-box sale price of $6.50 due to better-textured tacos, what will the impact be on its operating breakeven point in boxes?

 E11–3 Chico's has sales of 15,000 units at a price of $20 per unit. The firm incurs fixed operating costs of $30,000 and variable operating costs of $12 per unit. What is Chico's *degree of operating leverage (DOL)* at a base level of sales of 15,000 units?

 E11–4 Parker Investments has EBIT of $20,000, interest expense of $3,000, and preferred dividends of $4,000. If it pays taxes at a rate of 38%, what is Parker's *degree of financial leverage (DFL)* at a base level of EBIT of $20,000?

 E11–5 Cobalt Industries had sales of 150,000 units at a price of $10 per unit. It faced fixed operating costs of $250,000 and variable operating costs of $5 per unit. The company is subject to a tax rate of 38% and has a weighted average cost of capital of 8.5%. Calculate Cobalt's *net operating profits after taxes (NOPAT)*, and use it to estimate the value of the firm.

Problems

A blue box (■) indicates problems available in .

 P11–1 **Breakeven point—Algebraic**   Kate Rowland wishes to estimate the number of flower arrangements she must sell at $24.95 to break even. She has estimated fixed operating costs of $12,350 per year and variable operating costs of $15.45 per arrangement. How many flower arrangements must Kate sell to break even on operating costs?

 P11–2 **Breakeven comparisons—Algebraic**   Given the price and cost data shown in the accompanying table for each of the three firms, F, G, and H, answer the following questions.

Firm	F	G	H
Sale price per unit	$ 18.00	$ 21.00	$ 30.00
Variable operating cost per unit	6.75	13.50	12.00
Fixed operating cost	45,000	30,000	90,000

a. What is the *operating breakeven point* in units for each firm?

b. How would you rank these firms in terms of their risk?

 P11–3 **Breakeven point—Algebraic and graphical** Fine Leather Enterprises sells its single product for $129.00 per unit. The firm's fixed operating costs are $473,000 annually, and its variable operating costs are $86.00 per unit.

a. Find the firm's *operating breakeven point* in units.

b. Label the *x* axis "Sales (units)" and the *y* axis "Costs/Revenues ($)," and then graph the firm's sales revenue, total operating cost, and fixed operating cost functions on these axes. In addition, label the operating breakeven point and the areas of loss and profit (EBIT).

 P11–4 **Breakeven analysis** Barry Carter is considering opening a music store. He wants to estimate the number of CDs he must sell to break even. The CDs will be sold for $13.98 each, variable operating costs are $10.48 per CD, and annual fixed operating costs are $73,500.

a. Find the *operating breakeven point* in number of CDs.

b. Calculate the total operating costs at the breakeven volume found in part **a**.

c. If Barry estimates that at a minimum he can sell 2,000 CDs *per month*, should he go into the music business?

d. How much EBIT will Barry realize if he sells the minimum 2,000 CDs per month noted in part **c**?

PERSONAL FINANCE PROBLEM

 P11–5 **Breakeven analysis** Paul Scott has a 2008 Cadillac that he wants to update with a geo-tracker device so he will have access to road maps and directions. After-market equipment can be fitted for a flat fee of $500, and the service provider requires monthly charges of $20. In his line of work as a traveling salesman, he estimates that this device can save him time and money—about $35 per month (as the price of gas keeps increasing).

In order to determine the financial feasibility of purchasing the geo-tracker, Paul wants to determine the number of months it will take to break even. He plans to keep the car for another 3 years.

a. Calculate the *breakeven point* for the device in months.

b. Based on **a,** should Paul have the tracker installed in his car?

 P11–6 **Breakeven point—Changing costs/revenues** JWG Company publishes *Creative Crosswords*. Last year the book of puzzles sold for $10 with variable operating cost per book of $8 and fixed operating costs of $40,000. How many books must JWG sell this year to achieve the *breakeven point* for the stated operating costs, given the following different circumstances?

a. All figures remain the same as for last year.

b. Fixed operating costs increase to $44,000; all other figures remain the same.

c. The selling price increases to $10.50; all costs remain the same as for last year.

d. Variable operating cost per book increases to $8.50; all other figures remain the same.

e. What conclusions about the operating breakeven point can be drawn from your answers?

P11–7   EBIT sensitivity   Stewart Industries sells its finished product for $9 per unit. Its fixed operating costs are $20,000, and the variable operating cost per unit is $5.
- a. Calculate the firm's earnings before interest and taxes (EBIT) for sales of 10,000 units.
- b. Calculate the firm's EBIT for sales of 8,000 and 12,000 units, respectively.
- c. Calculate the percentage changes in sales (from the 10,000-unit base level) and associated percentage changes in EBIT for the shifts in sales indicated in part **b.**
- d. On the basis of your findings in part **c,** comment on the sensitivity of changes in EBIT in response to changes in sales.

 P11–8   Degree of operating leverage   Grey Products has fixed operating costs of $380,000, variable operating costs of $16 per unit, and a selling price of $63.50 per unit.
- a. Calculate the *operating breakeven point* in units.
- b. Calculate the firm's EBIT at 9,000, 10,000, and 11,000 units, respectively.
- c. With 10,000 units as a base, what are the percentage changes in units sold and EBIT as sales move from the base to the other sales levels used in part **b?**
- d. Use the percentages computed in part **c** to determine the *degree of operating leverage (DOL).*
- e. Use the formula for degree of operating leverage to determine the DOL at 10,000 units.

 P11–9   Degree of operating leverage—Graphical   Levin Corporation has fixed operating costs of $72,000, variable operating costs of $6.75 per unit, and a selling price of $9.75 per unit.
- a. Calculate the *operating breakeven point* in units.
- b. Compute the *degree of operating leverage (DOL)* using the following unit sales levels as a base: 25,000, 30,000, 40,000. Use the formula given in the chapter.
- c. Graph the DOL figures that you computed in part **b** (on the *y* axis) against base sales levels (on the *x* axis).
- d. Compute the degree of operating leverage at 24,000 units; add this point to your graph.
- e. What principle do your graph and figures illustrate?

 P11–10   EPS calculations   Southland Industries has $60,000 of 16% (annual interest) bonds outstanding, 1,500 shares of preferred stock paying an annual dividend of $5 per share, and 4,000 shares of common stock outstanding. Assuming that the firm has a 40% tax rate, compute *earnings per share (EPS)* for the following levels of EBIT:
- a. $24,600
- b. $30,600
- c. $35,000

 P11–11   Degree of financial leverage   Northwestern Savings and Loan has a current capital structure consisting of $250,000 of 16% (annual interest) debt and 2,000 shares of common stock. The firm pays taxes at the rate of 40%.
- a. Using EBIT values of $80,000 and $120,000, determine the associated *earnings per share (EPS).*
- b. Using $80,000 of EBIT as a base, calculate the *degree of financial leverage (DFL).*

c. Rework parts **a** and **b** assuming that the firm has $100,000 of 16% (annual interest) debt and 3,000 shares of common stock.

PERSONAL FINANCE PROBLEM

 P11–12 **Financial leverage**   Max Small has outstanding school loans that require a monthly payment of $1,000. He needs to purchase a new car for work and estimates that this will add $350 per month to his existing monthly obligations. Max will have $3,000 available after meeting all of his monthly living (operating) expenses. This amount could vary by plus or minus 10%.

a. In order to assess the potential impact of the additional borrowing on his financial leverage, calculate the *DFL* in tabular form for both the current and proposed loan payments using Max's available $3,000 as a base and a 10% change.

b. Can Max afford the additional loan payment?

c. Should Max take on the additional loan payment?

  P11–13 **DFL and graphical display of financing plans**   Wells and Associates has EBIT of $67,500. Interest costs are $22,500, and the firm has 15,000 shares of common stock outstanding. Assume a 40% tax rate.

a. Use the degree of financial leverage (DFL) formula to calculate the *DFL* for the firm.

b. Using a set of EBIT–EPS axes, plot Wells and Associates' financing plan.

c. If the firm also has 1,000 shares of preferred stock paying a $6.00 annual dividend per share, what is the DFL?

d. Plot the financing plan, including the 1,000 shares of $6.00 preferred stock, on the axes used in part **b**.

e. Briefly discuss the graph of the two financing plans.

  P11–14 **Integrative—Multiple leverage measures**   Play-More Toys produces inflatable beach balls, selling 400,000 balls per year. Each ball produced has a variable operating cost of $0.84 and sells for $1.00. Fixed operating costs are $28,000. The firm has annual interest charges of $6,000, preferred dividends of $2,000, and a 40% tax rate.

a. Calculate the *operating breakeven point* in units.

b. Use the degree of operating leverage (DOL) formula to calculate *DOL*.

c. Use the degree of financial leverage (DFL) formula to calculate *DFL*.

d. Use the degree of total leverage (DTL) formula to calculate *DTL*. Compare this to the product of DOL and DFL calculated in parts **b** and **c**.

 P11–15 **Integrative—Leverage and risk**   Firm R has sales of 100,000 units at $2.00 per unit, variable operating costs of $1.70 per unit, and fixed operating costs of $6,000. Interest is $10,000 per year. Firm W has sales of 100,000 units at $2.50 per unit, variable operating costs of $1.00 per unit, and fixed operating costs of $62,500. Interest is $17,500 per year. Assume that both firms are in the 40% tax bracket.

a. Compute the degree of operating, financial, and total leverage for firm R.

b. Compute the degree of operating, financial, and total leverage for firm W.

c. Compare the relative risks of the two firms.

d. Discuss the principles of leverage that your answers illustrate.

P11–16 **Capital structure** Kirsten Neal is interested in purchasing a new house given that mortgage rates are at a historical low. Her bank has specific rules regarding an applicant's ability to meet the contractual payments associated with the requested debt. Kirsten must submit personal financial data for her income, expenses, and existing installment loan payments. The bank then calculates and compares certain ratios to predetermined allowable values to determine if it will make the requested loan. The requirements are as follows:

(1) Monthly mortgage payments < 28% of monthly gross (before-tax) income.
(2) Total monthly installment payments (including the mortgage payments) < 37% of monthly gross (before-tax) income.

Kirsten submits the following personal financial data:

Monthly gross (before-tax) income	$4,500
Monthly installment loan obligations	$375
Requested mortgage	$150,000
Monthly mortgage payments	$1,100

a. Calculate the ratio for requirement 1.
b. Calculate the ratio for requirement 2.
c. Assuming that Kirsten has adequate funds for the down payment and meets other lender requirements, will Kirsten be granted the loan?

P11–17 **Various capital structures** Charter Enterprises currently has $1 million in total assets and is totally equity-financed. It is contemplating a change in its capital structure. Compute the amount of debt and equity that would be outstanding if the firm were to shift to each of the following debt ratios: 10%, 20%, 30%, 40%, 50%, 60%, and 90%. (*Note:* The amount of total assets would not change.) Is there a limit to the debt ratio's value?

P11–18 **EBIT–EPS and capital structure** Data-Check is considering two capital structures. The key information is shown in the following table. Assume a 40% tax rate.

Source of capital	Structure A	Structure B
Long-term debt	$100,000 at 16% coupon rate	$200,000 at 17% coupon rate
Common stock	4,000 shares	2,000 shares

a. Calculate two *EBIT–EPS coordinates* for each of the structures by selecting any two EBIT values and finding their associated EPS values.
b. Plot the two capital structures on a set of EBIT–EPS axes.
c. Indicate over what EBIT range, if any, each structure is preferred.
d. Discuss the leverage and risk aspects of each structure.
e. If the firm is fairly certain that its EBIT will exceed $75,000, which structure would you recommend? Why?

P11–19 **EBIT–EPS and preferred stock** Litho-Print is considering two possible capital structures, A and B, shown in the table at the top of page 489. Assume a 40% tax rate.

Source of capital	Structure A	Structure B
Long-term debt	$75,000 at 16% coupon rate	$50,000 at 15% coupon rate
Preferred stock	$10,000 with an 18% annual dividend	$15,000 with an 18% annual dividend
Common stock	8,000 shares	10,000 shares

a. Calculate two *EBIT–EPS coordinates* for each of the structures by selecting any two EBIT values and finding their associated EPS values.
b. Graph the two capital structures on the same set of EBIT–EPS axes.
c. Discuss the leverage and risk associated with each of the structures.
d. Over what range of EBIT is each structure preferred?
e. Which structure do you recommend if the firm expects its EBIT to be $35,000? Explain.

    P11–20 **Integrative—Optimal capital structure**   Nelson Corporation has made the following forecast of sales, with the associated probabilities of occurrence noted.

Sales	Probability
$200,000	.20
300,000	.60
400,000	.20

The company has fixed operating costs of $100,000 per year, and variable operating costs represent 40% of sales. The existing capital structure consists of 25,000 shares of common stock that have a $10 per share book value. No other capital items are outstanding. The marketplace has assigned the following required returns to risky earnings per share.

Coefficient of variation of EPS	Estimated required return, r_s
0.43	15%
0.47	16
0.51	17
0.56	18
0.60	22
0.64	24

The company is contemplating *shifting its capital structure* by substituting debt in the capital structure for common stock. The three different debt ratios under consideration are shown in the following table, along with an estimate, for each ratio, of the corresponding required interest rate on *all* debt.

Debt ratio	Interest rate on *all* debt
20%	10%
40	12
60	14

The tax rate is 40%. The market value of the equity for a leveraged firm can be found by using the simplified method (see Equation 11.12).

a. Calculate the expected earnings per share (EPS), the standard deviation of EPS, and the coefficient of variation of EPS for the three proposed capital structures.

b. Determine the *optimal capital structure*, assuming (1) maximization of earnings per share and (2) maximization of share value.

c. Construct a graph (similar to Figure 11.6) showing the relationships in part **b.** (*Note:* You will probably have to sketch the lines, because you have only three data points.)

  P11–21 **Integrative—Optimal capital structure**   Triple D Corporation wishes to analyze five possible capital structures—0%, 15%, 30%, 45%, and 60% debt ratios. The firm's total assets of $1 million are assumed to be constant. Its common stock has a book value of $25 per share, and the firm is in the 40% tax bracket. The following additional data have been gathered for use in analyzing the five capital structures under consideration.

Capital structure debt ratio	Interest rate on debt, r_d	Expected EPS	Required return, r_s
0%	0.0%	$3.60	10.0%
15	8.0	4.03	10.5
30	10.0	4.50	11.6
45	13.0	4.95	14.0
60	17.0	5.18	20.0

a. Calculate the amount of debt, the amount of equity, and the number of shares of common stock outstanding for each of the capital structures being considered.

b. Calculate the annual interest on the debt under each of the capital structures being considered. (*Note:* The interest rate given is applicable to *all* debt associated with the corresponding debt ratio.)

c. Calculate the EPS associated with $150,000 and $250,000 of EBIT for each of the five capital structures being considered.

d. Using the EBIT–EPS data developed in part **c,** plot the capital structures on the same set of EBIT–EPS axes, and discuss the ranges over which each is preferred. What is the major problem with the use of this approach?

e. Using the valuation model given in Equation 11.12 and the appropriate data, estimate the share value for each of the capital structures being considered. (*Hint:* Be sure to convert required returns to decimal form.)

f. Construct a graph similar to Figure 11.6 showing the relationships between the debt ratio (*x* axis) and expected EPS (*y* axis) and share value (*y* axis).

g. Referring to the graph in part **f:** Which structure is preferred if the goal is to *maximize EPS?* Which structure is preferred if the goal is to *maximize share value?* Which capital structure do you recommend? Explain.

 P11–22 **ETHICS PROBLEM**   "Information asymmetry lies at the heart of the ethical dilemma that managers, stockholders, and bondholders confront when companies initiate management buyouts or swap debt for equity." Comment on this statement. What steps might a board of directors take to ensure that the company's actions are ethical to all parties?

Chapter 11 Case

Evaluating Tampa Manufacturing's Capital Structure

Tampa Manufacturing, an established producer of printing equipment, expects its sales to remain flat for the next 3 to 5 years because of both a weak economic outlook and an expectation of little new printing technology development over that period. On the basis of this scenario, the firm's board has instructed its management to institute programs that will allow it to operate more efficiently, earn higher profits, and, most important, maximize share value.

In this regard, the firm's chief financial officer (CFO), Jon Lawson, has been charged with evaluating the firm's capital structure. Lawson believes that the current capital structure, which contains 10% debt and 90% equity, may lack adequate financial leverage. To evaluate the firm's capital structure, Lawson has gathered the data summarized in the following table on the current capital structure (10% debt ratio) and two alternative capital structures—A (30% debt ratio) and B (50% debt ratio)—that he would like to consider.

	Capital structure[a]		
Source of capital	Current (10% debt)	A (30% debt)	B (50% debt)
Long-term debt	$1,000,000	$3,000,000	$5,000,000
Coupon interest rate[b]	9%	10%	12%
Common stock	100,000 shares	70,000 shares	40,000 shares
Required return on equity, r_s[c]	12%	13%	18%

[a]These structures are based on maintaining the firm's current level of $10,000,000 of total financing.
[b]Interest rate applicable to *all* debt.
[c]Market-based return for the given level of risk.

Lawson expects the firm's earnings before interest and taxes (EBIT) to remain at its current level of $1,200,000. The firm has a 40% tax rate.

To Do

a. Use the current level of EBIT to calculate the times interest earned ratio for each capital structure. Evaluate the current and two alternative capital structures using the times interest earned and debt ratios.

b. Prepare a single EBIT–EPS graph showing the current and two alternative capital structures.

c. On the basis of the graph in part **b,** which capital structure will maximize Tampa's earnings per share (EPS) at its expected level of EBIT of $1,200,000? Why might this *not* be the best capital structure?

d. Using the zero-growth valuation model given in Equation 11.12, find the market value of Tampa's equity under each of the three capital structures at the $1,200,000 level of expected EBIT.

e. On the basis of your findings in parts **c** and **d,** which capital structure would you recommend? Why?

Spreadsheet Exercise

Starstruck Company would like to determine its optimal capital structure. Several of its managers believe that the best method is to rely on the estimated earnings per share (EPS) of the firm, because they feel that profits and stock price are closely related. The financial managers have suggested another method that uses estimated required returns to estimate the share value of the firm. The following financial data are available.

Capital structure debt ratio	Estimated EPS	Estimated required return
0%	$1.75	11.40%
10	1.90	11.80
20	2.25	12.50
30	2.55	13.25
40	3.18	18.00
50	3.06	19.00
60	3.10	25.00

To Do

a. Based upon the given financial data, create a spreadsheet to calculate the estimated share values associated with the seven alternative capital structures. Refer to Table 11.10 in the text (or view it at www.prenhall.com/gitman).

b. Use Excel to graph the relationship between capital structure and the estimated EPS of the firm. What is the optimal debt ratio? Refer to Figure 11.6 in the text (or view it at www.prenhall.com/gitman).

c. Use Excel to graph the relationship between capital structure and the estimated share value of the firm. What is the optimal debt ratio? Refer to Figure 11.6 in the text (or view it at www.prenhall.com/gitman).

d. Do both methods lead to the same *optimal capital structure?* Which method do you favor? Explain.

e. What is the major difference between the EPS and share value methods?

Web Exercise

Go to the book's companion website at www.prenhall.com/gitman to find the Web Exercise for this chapter.

Remember to check the book's website at www.prenhall.com/gitman to find additional resources, including Web Exercises and a Web Case.

12 Dividend Policy

WHY THIS CHAPTER MATTERS TO YOU

In Your Professional Life

Accounting: You need to understand the types of dividends and payment procedures for them because you will need to record and report the declaration and payment of dividends; you also will provide the financial data that management must have to make dividend decisions.

Information systems: You need to understand types of dividends, payment procedures, and the financial data that the firm must have to make and implement dividend decisions.

Management: To make appropriate dividend decisions for the firm, you need to understand types of dividends, arguments about the relevance of dividends, the factors that affect dividend policy, and types of dividend policies.

Marketing: You need to understand factors affecting dividend policy because you may want to argue that the firm would be better off retaining funds for use in new marketing programs or products, rather than paying them out as dividends.

Operations: You need to understand factors affecting dividend policy because you may find that the firm's dividend policy imposes limitations on planned expansion, replacement, or renewal projects.

In Your Personal Life

Many individual investors buy common stock for the anticipated cash dividends. From a personal finance perspective, you should understand why and how firms pay dividends and the informational and financial implications of receiving them. Such understanding will help you select common stocks that have dividend-paying patterns consistent with your long-term financial goals.

LEARNING GOALS

LG 1 Understand cash dividend payment procedures, the tax treatment of dividends, and the role of dividend reinvestment plans.

LG 2 Describe the residual theory of dividends and the key arguments with regard to dividend irrelevance and relevance.

LG 3 Discuss the key factors involved in establishing a dividend policy.

LG 4 Review and evaluate the three basic types of dividend policies.

LG 5 Evaluate stock dividends from accounting, shareholder, and company points of view.

LG 6 Explain stock splits and stock repurchases and the firm's motivation for undertaking each of them.

Dividends represent a source of cash flow to stockholders and provide information about the firm's performance. Some stockholders expect to receive dividends. Others are content to see an increase in stock price and no dividends. The firm's dividend policy depends on various factors. This chapter considers whether dividends matter to stockholders and explains the key factors in dividend policy, basic types of dividend policies, and alternative forms of dividends.

12.1 | Dividend Fundamentals

Expected cash dividends are the key return variable from which owners and investors determine share value. They represent a source of cash flow to stockholders and provide information about the firm's current and future performance. Because **retained earnings,** earnings not distributed to owners as dividends, are a form of *internal* financing, the dividend decision can significantly affect the firm's *external* financing requirements. In other words, if the firm needs financing, the larger the cash dividend paid, the greater the amount of financing it must raise externally through borrowing or through the sale of common or preferred stock. (Remember that although dividends are charged to retained earnings, they are actually paid out of cash.) The first thing to know about cash dividends is the procedures for paying them.

retained earnings
Earnings not distributed to owners as dividends; a form of *internal* financing.

Cash Dividend Payment Procedures

At quarterly or semiannual meetings, a firm's board of directors decides whether and in what amount to pay cash dividends to corporate stockholders. The past period's financial performance and future outlook, as well as recent dividends paid, are key inputs to the dividend decision. The payment date of the cash dividend, if one is declared, must also be established.

Amount of Dividends

Whether dividends should be paid, and if so, in what amount, are important decisions that depend primarily on the firm's dividend policy. Most firms have a set policy with respect to the periodic dividend, but the firm's directors can change this amount, largely on the basis of significant increases or decreases in earnings.

Relevant Dates

If the directors of the firm declare a dividend, they also typically issue a statement indicating the dividend decision, the record date, and the payment date. This statement is generally quoted in the *Wall Street Journal* and other financial news media.

Record Date   All persons whose names are recorded as stockholders on the **date of record** set by the directors receive a declared dividend at a specified future time. These stockholders are often referred to as *holders of record*.

Because of the time needed to make bookkeeping entries when a stock is traded, the stock begins selling **ex dividend** 2 *business days* prior to the date of

date of record (dividends)
Set by the firm's directors, the date on which all persons whose names are recorded as stockholders receive a declared dividend at a specified future time.

ex dividend
Period, beginning 2 *business days* prior to the date of record, during which a stock is sold without the right to receive the current dividend.

record. Purchasers of a stock selling ex dividend do not receive the current dividend. A simple way to determine the first day on which the stock sells ex dividend is to subtract 2 days from the date of record; if a weekend intervenes, subtract 4 days. Ignoring general market fluctuations, the stock's price is expected to drop by the amount of the declared dividend on the ex dividend date.

payment date
Set by the firm's directors, the actual date on which the firm mails the dividend payment to the holders of record.

Payment Date   The **payment date,** also set by the directors, is the actual date on which the firm mails the dividend payment to the holders of record. It is generally a few weeks after the record date. An example will clarify the various dates and the accounting effects.

> **Example**
>
> At the quarterly dividend meeting of Rudolf Company, a distributor of office products, held on June 10, the directors declared an $0.80-per-share cash dividend for holders of record on Friday, July 2. The firm had 100,000 shares of common stock outstanding. The payment date for the dividend was Monday, August 2. Figure 12.1 shows a time line depicting the key dates relative to the Rudolf Company's dividend. Before the dividend was declared, the key accounts of the firm were as follows:
>
> | | | | |
> |---|---|---|---|
> | Cash | $200,000 | Dividends payable | $ 0 |
> | | | Retained earnings | 1,000,000 |
>
> When the dividend was announced by the directors, $80,000 of the retained earnings ($0.80 per share × 100,000 shares) was transferred to the dividends payable account. The key accounts thus became
>
> | | | | |
> |---|---|---|---|
> | Cash | $200,000 | Dividends payable | $ 80,000 |
> | | | Retained earnings | 920,000 |
>
> Rudolf Company's stock began selling ex dividend 2 *business days* prior to the date of record, which was Wednesday, June 30. This date was found by subtracting 2 days from the July 2 date of record. Purchasers of Rudolf's stock on Tuesday, June 29 or earlier received the rights to the dividends; those who purchased the stock on or after June 30 did not. Assuming a stable market, Rudolf's

FIGURE 12.1

Dividend Payment Time Line
Time line for the announcement and payment of a cash dividend for Rudolf Company

stock price was expected to drop by approximately $0.80 per share when it began selling ex dividend on June 30. On August 2 the firm mailed dividend checks to the holders of record as of July 2. This produced the following balances in the key accounts of the firm:

Cash	$120,000	Dividends payable	$ 0
		Retained earnings	920,000

The net effect of declaring and paying the dividend was to reduce the firm's total assets (and stockholders' equity) by $80,000.

Tax Treatment of Dividends

The *Jobs and Growth Tax Relief Reconciliation Act of 2003* significantly changed the tax treatment of corporate dividends for most taxpayers. Prior to passage of the 2003 law, dividends received by investors were taxed as ordinary income at rates as high as 35 percent. The 2003 act reduced the tax rate on corporate dividends for most taxpayers to the tax rate applicable to capital gains, which is a maximum rate of 5 percent to 15 percent, depending on the taxpayer's tax bracket. This change significantly diminishes the degree of "double taxation" of dividends, which results when the corporation is first taxed on its income and then when the investor who receives the dividend is also taxed on it. After-tax cash flow to dividend recipients is much greater at the lower applicable tax rate; the result is noticeably higher dividend payouts by corporations today than prior to passage of the 2003 legislation.

Personal Finance Example   The board of directors of Espinoza Industries, Inc., on October 4 of the current year, declared a quarterly dividend of $0.46 per share payable to all holders of record on Friday, October 30. They set a payment date of November 19. Rob and Kate Heckman, who purchased 500 shares of Espinoza's common stock on Thursday, October 15, wish to determine whether they will receive the recently declared dividend and, if so, when and how much they would net after taxes from the dividend given that the dividends would be subject to a 15% federal income tax.

Given the Friday, October 30, date of record, the stock would begin selling *ex dividend* 2 business days earlier on Wednesday, October 28. Purchasers of the stock on or before Tuesday, October 27, would receive the right to the dividend. Because the Heckmans purchased the stock on October 15, they would be eligible to receive the dividend of $0.46 per share. Thus, the Heckmans will receive $230 in dividends ($0.46 per share × 500 shares), which will be mailed to them on the November 19 payment date. Because they are subject to a 15% federal income tax on the dividends, the Heckmans will net $195.50 [(1 − 0.15) × $230] after taxes from the Espinoza Industries dividend.

dividend reinvestment plans (DRIPs)
Plans that enable stockholders to use dividends received on the firm's stock to acquire additional shares—even fractional shares—at little or no transaction cost.

Dividend Reinvestment Plans

Today many firms offer **dividend reinvestment plans (DRIPs)**, which enable stockholders to use dividends received on the firm's stock to acquire additional shares—even fractional shares—at little or no transaction cost. Some companies even allow investors to make their *initial purchases* of the firm's stock directly from the company without going through a broker. With DRIPs, plan participants typically can acquire shares at about 5 percent below the prevailing market price. From its point of view, the firm can issue new shares to participants more economically, avoiding the underpricing and flotation costs that would accompany the public sale of new shares. Clearly, the existence of a DRIP may enhance the market appeal of a firm's shares.

REVIEW QUESTIONS

12–1 Who are *holders of record*? When does a stock sell *ex dividend*?

12–2 What effect did the *Jobs and Growth Tax Relief Reconciliation Act of 2003* have on the taxation of corporate dividends? On corporate dividend payouts?

12–3 What benefit is available to participants in a *dividend reinvestment plan*? How might the firm benefit?

12.2 | Relevance of Dividend Policy

The financial literature has reported numerous theories and empirical findings concerning dividend policy. Although this research provides some interesting insights about dividend policy, capital budgeting and capital structure decisions are generally considered far more important than dividend decisions. In other words, firms should not sacrifice good investment and financing decisions for a dividend policy of questionable importance.

A number of key questions have yet to be resolved: Does dividend policy matter? What effect does dividend policy have on share price? Is there a model that can be used to evaluate alternative dividend policies in view of share value? Here we begin by describing the residual theory of dividends, which is used as a backdrop for discussion of the key arguments in support of dividend irrelevance and then those in support of dividend relevance.

Residual Theory of Dividends

residual theory of dividends
A school of thought that suggests that the dividend paid by a firm should be viewed as a *residual*—the amount left over after all acceptable investment opportunities have been undertaken.

The **residual theory of dividends** is a school of thought that suggests that the dividend paid by a firm should be viewed as a *residual*—the amount left over after all acceptable investment opportunities have been undertaken. Using this approach, the firm would treat the dividend decision in three steps, as follows:

Step 1 Determine its optimal level of capital expenditures, which would be the level generated by the point of intersection of the investment opportunities schedule (IOS) and weighted marginal cost of capital (WMCC) schedule (see Chapter 10).

Step 2 Using the optimal capital structure proportions (see Chapter 11), estimate the total amount of equity financing needed to support the expenditures generated in Step 1.

Step 3 Because the cost of retained earnings, r_r, is less than the cost of new common stock, r_n, use retained earnings to meet the equity requirement determined in Step 2. If retained earnings are inadequate to meet this need, sell new common stock. If the available retained earnings are in excess of this need, distribute the surplus amount—the residual—as dividends.

According to this approach, as long as the firm's equity need exceeds the amount of retained earnings, no cash dividend is paid. The argument for this approach is that it is sound management to be certain that the company has the money it needs to compete effectively. This view of dividends suggests that the required return of investors, r_s, is *not* influenced by the firm's dividend policy—a premise that in turn implies that dividend policy is irrelevant.

Example

Overbrook Industries, a manufacturer of canoes and other small watercraft, has available from the current period's operations $1.8 million that can be retained or paid out in dividends. The firm's optimal capital structure is at a debt ratio of 30%, which represents 30% debt and 70% equity. Figure 12.2 depicts the firm's weighted marginal cost of capital (WMCC) schedule along with three investment opportunities schedules. For each IOS, the level of total new financing or investment determined by the point of intersection of the IOS and the WMCC has been noted. For IOS_1, it is $1.5 million, for IOS_2 $2.4 million, and for IOS_3 $3.2 million. Although only one IOS will exist in practice, it is useful to look at the possible dividend decisions generated by applying the residual theory in each of the three cases. Table 12.1 summarizes this analysis.

Table 12.1 shows that if IOS_1 exists, the firm will pay out $750,000 in dividends, because only $1,050,000 of the $1,800,000 of available earnings is

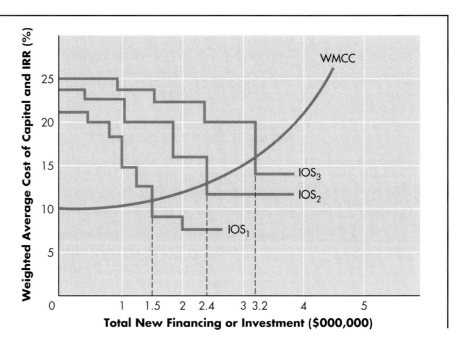

FIGURE 12.2

WMCC and IOSs
WMCC and IOSs for Overbrook Industries

TABLE 12.1	**Applying the Residual Theory of Dividends to Overbrook Industries for Each of Three IOSs (Shown in Figure 12.2)**		

| | Investment opportunities schedules | | |
Item	IOS_1	IOS_2	IOS_3
(1) New financing or investment (Fig. 12.2)	$1,500,000	$2,400,000	$3,200,000
(2) Retained earnings available (given)	$1,800,000	$1,800,000	$1,800,000
(3) Equity needed [70% × (1)]	1,050,000	1,680,000	2,240,000
(4) Dividends [(2) − (3)]	$ 750,000	$ 120,000	$ 0[a]
(5) Dividend payout ratio [(4) ÷ (2)]	41.7%	6.7%	0%

[a]In this case, additional new common stock in the amount of $440,000 ($2,240,000 needed − $1,800,000 available) would have to be sold; no dividends would be paid.

needed. A 41.7% payout ratio results. For IOS_2, dividends of $120,000 (a payout ratio of 6.7%) result. Should IOS_3 exist, the firm would pay no dividends (a 0% payout ratio), because its retained earnings of $1,800,000 would be less than the $2,240,000 of equity needed. In this case, the firm would have to obtain additional new common stock financing to meet the new requirements generated by the intersection of the IOS_3 and WMCC. Depending on which IOS exists, the firm's dividend would in effect be the residual, if any, remaining after all acceptable investments had been financed.

Arguments for Dividend Irrelevance

dividend irrelevance theory
Miller and Modigliani's theory that in a perfect world, the firm's value is determined solely by the earning power and risk of its assets (investments) and that the manner in which it splits its earnings stream between dividends and internally retained (and reinvested) funds does not affect this value.

informational content
The information provided by the dividends of a firm with respect to future earnings, which causes owners to bid up or down the price of the firm's stock.

The residual theory of dividends implies that if the firm cannot invest its earnings to earn a return (IRR) that is in excess of cost (WMCC), it should distribute the earnings by paying dividends to stockholders. This approach suggests that dividends represent an earnings residual rather than an active decision variable that affects the firm's value. Such a view is consistent with the **dividend irrelevance theory** put forth by Merton H. Miller and Franco Modigliani (M and M).[1] They argue that the firm's value is determined solely by the earning power and risk of its assets (investments) and that the manner in which it splits its earnings stream between dividends and internally retained (and reinvested) funds does not affect this value. M and M's theory suggests that in a perfect world (certainty, no taxes, no transactions costs, and no other market imperfections), the value of the firm is unaffected by the distribution of dividends.

However, studies have shown that large changes in dividends do affect share price. Increases in dividends result in increased share price, and decreases in dividends result in decreased share price. In response, M and M argue that these effects are attributable not to the dividend itself but rather to the **informational content** of dividends with respect to future earnings. In other words, say M and M, it is not the preference of shareholders for current dividends (rather than

1. Merton H. Miller and Franco Modigliani, "Dividend Policy, Growth and the Valuation of Shares," *Journal of Business* 34 (October 1961), pp. 411–433.

future capital gains) that is responsible for this behavior. Instead, investors view a change in dividends, up or down, as a *signal* that management expects future earnings to change in the same direction. Investors view an increase in dividends as a *positive signal,* and they bid up the share price. They view a decrease in dividends as a *negative signal* that causes a decrease in share price as investors sell their shares.

M and M further argue that a **clientele effect** exists: A firm attracts shareholders whose preferences for the payment and stability of dividends correspond to the firm's actual payment pattern and stability of dividends. Investors who desire stable dividends as a source of income hold the stock of firms that pay about the same dividend amount each period. Investors who prefer to earn capital gains are more attracted to growing firms that reinvest a large portion of their earnings, favoring growth over a stable pattern of dividends. Because the shareholders get what they expect, M and M argue, the value of their firm's stock is unaffected by dividend policy.

The views of M and M with respect to dividend irrelevance are consistent with the residual theory, which focuses on making the best investment decisions to maximize share value. The proponents of dividend irrelevance conclude that because dividends are irrelevant to a firm's value, the firm does not need to have a dividend policy. Although many research studies have been performed to validate or refute the dividend irrelevance theory, none has been successful in providing irrefutable evidence.

Arguments for Dividend Relevance

The key argument in support of **dividend relevance theory** is attributed to Myron J. Gordon and John Lintner,[2] who suggest that there is, in fact, a direct relationship between the firm's dividend policy and its market value. Fundamental to this proposition is their **bird-in-the-hand argument,** which suggests that investors see current dividends as less risky than future dividends or capital gains. "A bird in the hand is worth two in the bush." Gordon and Lintner argue that current dividend payments reduce investor uncertainty, causing investors to discount the firm's earnings at a lower rate and, all else being equal, to place a higher value on the firm's stock. Conversely, if dividends are reduced or are not paid, investor uncertainty will increase, raising the required return and lowering the stock's value.

Although many other arguments related to dividend relevance have been put forward, *empirical studies fail to provide conclusive evidence in support of the intuitively appealing dividend relevance argument.* In practice, however, the actions of both financial managers and stockholders tend to support the belief that dividend policy does affect stock value.[3] Because we focus on the day-to-day behavior of firms, the remainder of this chapter is consistent with the belief that *dividends are relevant*—that each firm must develop a dividend policy that fulfills the goals of its owners and maximizes their wealth as reflected in the firm's share price.

clientele effect
The argument that a firm attracts shareholders whose preferences for the payment and stability of dividends correspond to the firm's actual payment pattern and stability of dividends.

dividend relevance theory
The theory, advanced by Gordon and Lintner, that there is a direct relationship between a firm's dividend policy and its market value.

bird-in-the-hand argument
The belief, in support of *dividend relevance theory,* that investors see current dividends as less risky than future dividends or capital gains.

2. Myron J. Gordon, "Optimal Investment and Financing Policy," *Journal of Finance* 18 (May 1963), pp. 264–272, and John Lintner, "Dividends, Earnings, Leverage, Stock Prices, and the Supply of Capital to Corporations," *Review of Economics and Statistics* 44 (August 1962), pp. 243–269.

3. A common exception is small firms, because they frequently treat dividends as a residual remaining after all acceptable investments have been initiated. Small firms follow this course of action because they usually do not have ready access to capital markets. The use of retained earnings therefore is a key source of financing for growth, which is generally an important goal of a small firm.

REVIEW QUESTIONS

12–4 Does following the *residual theory of dividends* lead to a stable dividend? Is this approach consistent with dividend relevance?

12–5 Contrast the basic arguments about dividend policy advanced by Miller and Modigliani (M and M) and by Gordon and Lintner.

 ## 12.3 | Factors Affecting Dividend Policy

dividend policy
The firm's plan of action to be followed whenever it makes a dividend decision.

The firm's **dividend policy** represents a plan of action to be followed whenever it makes a dividend decision. Firms develop policies consistent with their goals. Before we review some of the popular types of dividend policies, we discuss six factors that firms consider in establishing a dividend policy. They are legal constraints, contractual constraints, internal constraints, the firm's growth prospects, owner considerations, and market considerations.

Legal Constraints

Most states prohibit corporations from paying out as cash dividends any portion of the firm's "legal capital," which is typically measured by the par value of common stock. Other states define legal capital to include not only the par value of the common stock, but also any paid-in capital in excess of par. These *capital impairment restrictions* are generally established to provide a sufficient equity base to protect creditors' claims. An example will clarify the differing definitions of capital.

> **Example**
>
> The stockholders' equity account of Miller Flour Company, a large grain processor, is presented in the following table.
>
> | Miller Flour Company Stockholders' Equity | |
> | --- | --- |
> | Common stock at par | $100,000 |
> | Paid-in capital in excess of par | 200,000 |
> | Retained earnings | 140,000 |
> | Total stockholders' equity | $440,000 |
>
> In states where the firm's legal capital is defined as the par value of its common stock, the firm could pay out $340,000 ($200,000 + $140,000) in cash dividends without impairing its capital. In states where the firm's legal capital includes all paid-in capital, the firm could pay out only $140,000 in cash dividends.

Firms sometimes impose an earnings requirement limiting the amount of dividends. With this restriction, the firm cannot pay more in cash dividends than the sum of its most recent and past retained earnings. However, *the firm is not prohibited from paying more in dividends than its current earnings.*[4]

---

4. A firm that has an operating loss in the current period can still pay cash dividends as long as sufficient retained earnings against which to charge the dividend are available and, of course, as long as it has the cash with which to make the payments.

Example

Assume that Miller Flour Company, from the preceding example, in the year just ended has $30,000 in earnings available for common stock dividends. As the preceding table indicates, the firm has past retained earnings of $140,000. Thus it can legally pay dividends of up to $170,000.

excess earnings accumulation tax
The tax the IRS levies on retained earnings above $250,000 for most businesses when it determines that the firm has accumulated an excess of earnings to allow owners to delay paying ordinary income taxes on dividends received.

If a firm has overdue liabilities or is legally insolvent or bankrupt, most states prohibit its payment of cash dividends. In addition, the Internal Revenue Service prohibits firms from accumulating earnings to reduce the owners' taxes. If the IRS can determine that a firm has accumulated an excess of earnings to allow owners to delay paying ordinary income taxes on dividends received, it may levy an **excess earnings accumulation tax** on any retained earnings above $250,000 for most businesses.

Contractual Constraints

Often the firm's ability to pay cash dividends is constrained by restrictive provisions in a loan agreement. Generally, these constraints prohibit the payment of cash dividends until the firm achieves a certain level of earnings, or they may limit dividends to a certain dollar amount or percentage of earnings. Constraints on dividends help to protect creditors from losses due to the firm's insolvency.

Internal Constraints

The firm's ability to pay cash dividends is generally constrained by the amount of liquid assets (cash and marketable securities) available. Although it is possible for a firm to borrow funds to pay dividends, lenders are generally reluctant to make such loans because they produce no tangible or operating benefits that will help the firm repay the loan.

Example

Miller Flour Company's stockholders' equity account, presented earlier, indicates that if the firm's legal capital is defined as all paid-in capital, the firm can pay $140,000 in dividends. If the firm has total liquid assets of $50,000 ($20,000 in cash plus marketable securities worth $30,000) and it needs $35,000 of this for operations, the maximum cash dividend the firm can pay is $15,000 ($50,000 − $35,000).

Growth Prospects

Hint Firms that grow very rapidly, such as high-tech firms, cannot afford to pay dividends. Their stockholders are influenced by the possibility of exceptionally higher share price and dividend levels in the future.

The firm's financial requirements are directly related to how much it expects to grow and what assets it will need to acquire. It must evaluate its profitability and risk to develop insight into its ability to raise capital externally. In addition, the firm must determine the cost and speed with which it can obtain financing. Generally, a large, mature firm has adequate access to new capital, whereas a rapidly growing firm may not have sufficient funds available to support its acceptable projects. A growth firm is likely to have to depend heavily on internal financing through retained earnings, so it is likely to pay out only a very small percentage of its earnings as dividends. A more established firm is in a better position to pay out a large proportion of its earnings, particularly if it has ready sources of financing.

Owner Considerations

The firm must establish a policy that has a favorable effect on the wealth of the *majority* of owners. One consideration is the *tax status of a firm's owners*. If a firm has a large percentage of wealthy stockholders who have sizable incomes, it may decide to pay out a *lower* percentage of its earnings to allow the owners to delay the payment of taxes until they sell the stock. Because cash dividends are taxed at the same rate as capital gains (as a result of the 2003 Tax Act), this strategy benefits owners through the tax deferral rather than as a result of a lower tax rate. Lower-income shareholders, however, who need dividend income, will prefer a *higher* payout of earnings.

A second consideration is the *owners' investment opportunities*. A firm should not retain funds for investment in projects yielding lower returns than the owners could obtain from external investments of equal risk. If it appears that the owners have better opportunities externally, the firm should pay out a higher percentage of its earnings. If the firm's investment opportunities are at least as good as similar-risk external investments, a lower payout is justifiable.

A final consideration is the *potential dilution of ownership*. If a firm pays out a high percentage of earnings, new equity capital will have to be raised with common stock. The result of a new stock issue may be dilution of both control and earnings for the existing owners. By paying out a low percentage of its earnings, the firm can minimize the possibility of such dilution.

Market Considerations

An awareness of the market's probable response to certain types of policies is also helpful in formulating dividend policy. Stockholders are believed to value a *fixed or increasing level of dividends* as opposed to a fluctuating pattern of dividends. This belief is supported by the research of John Lintner, who found that corporate managers are averse to changing the dollar amount of dividends in response to changes in earnings, particularly when earnings decline.[5] In addition, stockholders are believed to value a policy of *continuous dividend payment*. Because regularly paying a fixed or increasing dividend eliminates uncertainty about the frequency and magnitude of dividends, the returns of the firm are likely to be discounted at a lower rate. This should result in an increase in the market value of the stock and therefore an increase in the owners' wealth.

A final market consideration is *informational content*. As noted earlier, shareholders often view a dividend payment as a *signal* of the firm's future success. A stable and continuous dividend is a *positive signal,* conveying the firm's good financial health. Shareholders are likely to interpret a passed dividend payment due to a loss or to very low earnings as a *negative signal*. The nonpayment

Hint The risk–return concept also applies to the firm's dividend policy. A firm that lets its dividends fluctuate from period to period will be viewed as risky, and investors will require a higher rate of return, which will increase the firm's cost of capital.

---

5. John Lintner, "Distribution of Income of Corporations Among Dividends, Retained Earnings, and Taxes," *American Economic Review* 46 (May 1956), pp. 97–113.

of the dividend creates uncertainty about the future, which is likely to result in lower stock value. Owners and investors generally construe a dividend payment during a period of losses as an indication that the loss is merely temporary.

REVIEW QUESTION

12–6 What six factors do firms consider in establishing *dividend policy?* Briefly describe each of them.

12.4 | Types of Dividend Policies

The firm's dividend policy must be formulated with two basic objectives in mind: providing for sufficient financing and maximizing the wealth of the firm's owners. Three commonly used dividend policies are described in the following sections. A particular firm's cash dividend policy may incorporate elements of each.

Constant-Payout-Ratio Dividend Policy

dividend payout ratio
Indicates the percentage of each dollar earned that a firm distributes to the owners in the form of cash. It is calculated by dividing the firm's cash dividend per share by its earnings per share.

One type of dividend policy involves use of a constant payout ratio. The **dividend payout ratio** indicates the percentage of each dollar earned that the firm distributes to the owners in the form of cash. It is calculated by dividing the firm's cash dividend per share by its earnings per share. With a **constant-payout-ratio dividend policy,** the firm establishes that a certain percentage of earnings is paid to owners in each dividend period.

constant-payout-ratio dividend policy
A dividend policy based on the payment of a certain percentage of earnings to owners in each dividend period.

The problem with this policy is that if the firm's earnings drop or if a loss occurs in a given period, the dividends may be low or even nonexistent. Because dividends are often considered an indicator of the firm's future condition and status, the firm's stock price may be adversely affected.

Example

Peachtree Industries, a miner of potassium, has a policy of paying out 40% of earnings in cash dividends. In periods when a loss occurs, the firm's policy is to pay no cash dividends. Data on Peachtree's earnings, dividends, and average stock prices for the past 6 years follow.

Year	Earnings/share	Dividends/share	Average price/share
2009	−$0.50	$0.00	$42.00
2008	3.00	1.20	52.00
2007	1.75	0.70	48.00
2006	− 1.50	0.00	38.00
2005	2.00	0.80	46.00
2004	4.50	1.80	50.00

Dividends increased in 2007 and in 2008 but decreased in the other years. In years of decreasing dividends, the firm's stock price dropped; when dividends increased, the price of the stock increased. Peachtree's sporadic dividend payments appear to make its owners uncertain about the returns they can expect.

Although some firms use a constant-payout-ratio dividend policy, it is *not* recommended.

Regular Dividend Policy

The **regular dividend policy** is based on the payment of a fixed-dollar dividend in each period. This policy provides the owners with generally positive information, thereby minimizing their uncertainty. Often, firms that use this policy increase the regular dividend once a *proven* increase in earnings has occurred. Under this policy, dividends are almost never decreased.

Hint Regulated utilities in low-growth areas can use a constant-payout-ratio dividend policy. Their capital requirements are usually low and their earnings are more stable than those of most firms.

regular dividend policy
A dividend policy based on the payment of a fixed-dollar dividend in each period.

Example

The dividend policy of Woodward Laboratories, a producer of a popular artificial sweetener, is to pay annual dividends of $1.00 per share until per-share earnings have exceeded $4.00 for 3 consecutive years. At that point, the annual dividend is raised to $1.50 per share, and a new earnings plateau is established. The firm does not anticipate decreasing its dividend unless its liquidity is in jeopardy. Data for Woodward's earnings, dividends, and average stock prices for the past 12 years follow.

Year	Earnings/share	Dividends/share	Average price/share
2009	$4.50	$1.50	$47.50
2008	3.90	1.50	46.50
2007	4.60	1.50	45.00
2006	4.20	1.00	43.00
2005	5.00	1.00	42.00
2004	2.00	1.00	38.50
2003	6.00	1.00	38.00
2002	3.00	1.00	36.00
2001	0.75	1.00	33.00
2000	0.50	1.00	33.00
1999	2.70	1.00	33.50
1998	2.85	1.00	35.00

Whatever the level of earnings, Woodward Laboratories paid dividends of $1.00 per share through 2006. In 2007, the dividend increased to $1.50 per share because earnings in excess of $4.00 per share had been achieved for 3 years. In 2007, the firm also had to establish a new earnings plateau for further dividend increases. Woodward Laboratories' average price per share exhibited a stable, increasing behavior in spite of a somewhat volatile pattern of earnings.

target dividend-payout ratio
A dividend policy under which the firm attempts to pay out a certain *percentage* of earnings as a stated dollar dividend and adjusts that dividend toward a target payout as proven earnings increases occur.

Often a regular dividend policy is built around a **target dividend-payout ratio.** Under this policy, the firm attempts to pay out a certain *percentage* of earnings, but rather than let dividends fluctuate, it pays a stated dollar dividend and adjusts that dividend toward the target payout as proven earnings increases occur. For instance, Woodward Laboratories appears to have a target payout ratio of around 35 percent. The payout was about 35 percent ($1.00 ÷ $2.85) when the dividend policy was set in 1998, and when the dividend was raised to $1.50 in 2007, the payout ratio was about 33 percent ($1.50 ÷ $4.60).

Low-Regular-and-Extra Dividend Policy

Some firms establish a **low-regular-and-extra dividend policy,** paying a low regular dividend, supplemented by an additional ("extra") dividend when earnings are higher than normal in a given period. By calling the additional dividend an **extra dividend,** the firm avoids giving shareholders false hopes. This policy is especially common among companies that experience cyclical shifts in earnings.

By establishing a low regular dividend that is paid each period, the firm gives investors the stable income necessary to build confidence in the firm, and the extra dividend permits them to share in the earnings from an especially good period. Firms using this policy must raise the level of the regular dividend once proven increases in earnings have been achieved. The extra dividend should not be a regular event; otherwise, it becomes meaningless. The use of a target dividend-payout ratio in establishing the regular dividend level is advisable.

REVIEW QUESTION

12–7 Describe a constant-payout-ratio dividend policy, a regular dividend policy, and a low-regular-and-extra dividend policy. What are the effects of these policies?

12.5 | Other Forms of Dividends

Dividends can be paid in forms other than cash. Here we discuss two other methods of paying dividends—stock dividends and stock repurchases—as well as a closely related topic, stock splits.

Stock Dividends

A **stock dividend** is the payment, to existing owners, of a dividend in the form of stock. Often firms pay stock dividends as a replacement for or a supplement to cash dividends. Although stock dividends do not have a real value, stockholders may perceive them to represent something they did not have before.

Accounting Aspects

In an accounting sense, the payment of a stock dividend is a shifting of funds between stockholders' equity accounts rather than an outflow of funds. When a firm declares a stock dividend, the procedures for announcement and distribution are the same as those described earlier for a cash dividend. The accounting entries associated with the payment of a stock dividend vary depending on its size. A **small (ordinary) stock dividend** is a stock dividend that represents less than 20 percent to 25 percent of the common stock outstanding when the dividend is declared. Small stock dividends are most common.

Example

The current stockholders' equity on the balance sheet of Garrison Corporation, a distributor of prefabricated cabinets, is as shown in the following accounts.

Preferred stock	$ 300,000
Common stock (100,000 shares at $4 par)	400,000
Paid-in capital in excess of par	600,000
Retained earnings	700,000
Total stockholders' equity	$2,000,000

Garrison, which has 100,000 shares of common stock outstanding, declares a 10% stock dividend when the market price of its stock is $15 per share. Because 10,000 new shares (10% of 100,000) are issued at the prevailing market price of $15 per share, $150,000 ($15 per share × 10,000 shares) is shifted from retained earnings to the common stock and paid-in capital accounts. A total of $40,000 ($4 par × 10,000 shares) is added to common stock, and the remaining $110,000 [($15 − $4) × 10,000 shares] is added to the paid-in capital in excess of par. The resulting account balances are as follows:

Preferred stock	$ 300,000
Common stock (110,000 shares at $4 par)	440,000
Paid-in capital in excess of par	710,000
Retained earnings	550,000
Total stockholders' equity	$2,000,000

The firm's total stockholders' equity has not changed; funds have merely been *shifted* among stockholders' equity accounts.

Shareholder's Viewpoint

The shareholder receiving a stock dividend typically receives nothing of value. After the dividend is paid, the per-share value of the shareholder's stock decreases in proportion to the dividend in such a way that the market value of his or her total holdings in the firm remains unchanged. Therefore stock dividends are usually nontaxable. The shareholder's proportion of ownership in the firm also remains the same, and *as long as the firm's earnings remain unchanged*, so does his or her share of total earnings. (However, if the firm's earnings and cash dividends increase when the stock dividend is issued, an increase in share value is likely to result.)

Example

Ms. X owned 10,000 shares of Garrison Corporation's stock. The company's most recent earnings were $220,000, and earnings are not expected to change in the near future. Before the stock dividend, Ms. X owned 10% (10,000 shares ÷ 100,000 shares) of the firm's stock, which was selling for $15 per share. Earnings per share were $2.20 ($220,000 ÷ 100,000 shares). Because Ms. X owned 10,000 shares, her earnings were $22,000 ($2.20 per share × 10,000 shares). After receiving the 10% stock dividend, Ms. X has 11,000 shares, which again is 10% of the ownership (11,000 shares ÷ 110,000 shares). The market price of the stock can be expected to drop to $13.64 per share [$15 × (1.00 ÷ 1.10)], which means that the market value of Ms. X's holdings is $150,000 (11,000 shares × $13.64 per share). This is the same as the initial value of her holdings (10,000 shares $\times$ \$15 per share). The future earnings per share drops to \$2 (\$220,000 $\div$ 110,000 shares) because the same \$220,000 in earnings must now be divided among 110,000 shares. Because Ms. X still owns 10% of the stock, her share of total earnings is still \$22,000 (\$2 per share $\times$ 11,000 shares).

In summary, if the firm's earnings remain constant and total cash dividends do not increase, a stock dividend results in a lower per-share market value for the firm's stock.

The Company's Viewpoint

Stock dividends are more costly to issue than cash dividends, but certain advantages may outweigh these costs. Firms find the stock dividend to be a way to give owners something without having to use cash. Generally, when a firm needs to preserve cash to finance rapid growth, it uses a stock dividend. When the stockholders recognize that the firm is reinvesting the cash flow so as to maximize future earnings, the market value of the firm should at least remain unchanged. However, if the stock dividend is paid so as to retain cash to satisfy past-due bills, a decline in market value may result.

Stock Splits

stock split
A method commonly used to lower the market price of a firm's stock by increasing the number of shares belonging to each shareholder.

Although not a type of dividend, *stock splits* have an effect on a firm's share price similar to that of stock dividends. A **stock split** is a method commonly used to lower the market price of a firm's stock by increasing the number of shares belonging to each shareholder. In a 2-for-1 split, for example, two new shares are exchanged for each old share, with each new share being worth half the value of each old share. A stock split has no effect on the firm's capital structure and is usually nontaxable.

Quite often, a firm believes that its stock is priced too high and that lowering the market price will enhance trading activity. Stock splits are often made prior to issuing additional stock to enhance that stock's marketability and stimulate market activity. It is not unusual for a stock split to cause a slight increase in the market value of the stock, attributable to its informational content and to the fact that *total* dividends paid commonly increase slightly after a split.

Example

Delphi Company, a forest products concern, had 200,000 shares of \$2-par-value common stock and no preferred stock outstanding. Because the stock is selling at a high market price, the firm has declared a 2-for-1 stock split. The total before- and after-split stockholders' equity is shown in the following table.

Before split		After 2-for-1 split	
Common stock (200,000 shares at \$2 par)	\$ 400,000	Common stock (400,000 shares at \$1 part)	\$ 400,000
Paid-in capital in excess of par	4,000,000	Paid-in-capital in excess of part	4,000,000
Retained earnings	2,000,000	Retained earnings	2,000,000
Total stockholders' equity	\$6,400,000	Total stockholders' equity	\$6,400,000

The insignificant effect of the stock split on the firm's books is obvious.

reverse stock split
A method used to raise the market price of a firm's stock by exchanging a certain number of outstanding shares for one new share.

Stock can be split in any way desired. Sometimes a **reverse stock split** is made: The firm exchanges a certain number of outstanding shares for one new share. For example, in a 1-for-3 split, one new share is exchanged for three old shares. Reverse stock splits are initiated to raise the market price of a firm's stock when it is selling at too low a price to appear respectable.[6]

Personal Finance Example   Shakira Washington, a single investor in the 25% federal income tax bracket, owns 260 shares of Advanced Technology, Inc., common stock. She originally bought the stock 2 years ago at its initial public offering (IPO) price of $9 per share. The stock of this fast-growing technology company is currently trading for $60 per share, so the current value of her Advanced Technology stock is $15,600 (260 shares x $60 per share). Because the firm's board believes that the stock would trade more actively in the $20 to $30 price range, it just announced a 3-for-1 stock split. Shakira wishes to determine the impact of the stock split on her holdings and taxes.

Because the stock will split 3 for 1, after the split Shakira will own 780 shares (3×260 shares). She should expect the market price of the stock to drop to $20 ($1/3 \times \$60$) immediately after the split; the value of her after-split holding will be $15,600 (780 shares $\times$ $20 per share). Because the $15,600 value of her after-split holdings in Advanced Technology stock exactly equals the before-split value of $15,600, Shakira has experienced neither a gain nor a loss on the stock as a result of the 3-for-1 split. Even if there were a gain or loss attributable to the split, Shakira would not have any tax liability unless she actually sold the stock and realized that (or any other) gain or loss.

Stock Repurchases

stock repurchase
The repurchase by the firm of outstanding common stock in the marketplace; their popularity and importance is due to the fact that they either enhance shareholder value or help to discourage an unfriendly takeover.

In recent years, firms have increased their repurchasing of outstanding common stock in the marketplace. The practical motives for **stock repurchases** include obtaining shares to be used in acquisitions, having shares available for employee stock option plans, and retiring shares. The popularity and importance of stock repurchases is due to the fact that they either enhance shareholder value or help to discourage an unfriendly takeover. Stock repurchases enhance shareholder value by (1) reducing the number of shares outstanding and thereby raising earnings per share, (2) sending a *positive signal* to investors in the marketplace that management believes that the stock is undervalued, and (3) providing a temporary floor for the stock price, which may have been declining. The use of repurchases to discourage unfriendly takeovers is predicated on the belief that a corporate raider is less likely to gain control of the firm if there are fewer publicly traded shares available. Here we focus on retiring shares through repurchase, because this motive for repurchase is similar to the payment of cash dividends.

---

6. If a firm's stock is selling at a low price—possibly less than a few dollars—many investors are hesitant to purchase it because they believe it is "cheap." These somewhat unsophisticated investors correlate cheapness and quality, and they feel that a low-priced stock is a low-quality investment. A reverse stock split raises the stock price and increases per-share earnings.

Stock Repurchases Viewed as a Cash Dividend

When firms repurchase common stock for retirement, the underlying motive is to distribute excess cash to the owners. Generally, as long as earnings remain constant, the repurchase reduces the number of outstanding shares, raising the earnings per share and therefore the market price per share. In addition, an owner tax-deferral benefit may result. The repurchase of common stock results in a type of *reverse dilution*, because the EPS and the market price of stock are increased by reducing the number of shares outstanding. The net effect of the repurchase is similar to the payment of a cash dividend.

Example

Benton Company, a national sportswear chain, has released the following financial data:

Earnings available for common stockholders	$1,000,000
Number of shares of common stock outstanding	400,000
Earnings per share ($1,000,000 ÷ 400,000)	$2.50
Market price per share	$50
Price/earnings (P/E) ratio ($50 ÷ $2.50)	20

The firm wants to use $800,000 of its earnings either to pay cash dividends or to repurchase shares. If the firm paid cash dividends, the amount of the dividend would be $2 per share ($800,000 ÷ 400,000 shares). If the firm paid $52 per share to repurchase stock, it could repurchase approximately 15,385 shares ($800,000 ÷ $52 per share). As a result of this repurchase, 384,615 shares (400,000 shares − 15,385 shares) of common stock would remain outstanding. Earnings per share (EPS) would rise to $2.60 ($1,000,000 ÷ 384,615). If the stock still sold at 20 times earnings (P/E = 20), its market price could be estimated by multiplying the new EPS by this P/E ratio (the *price/earnings multiple approach* presented in Chapter 7). The price would therefore rise to $52 per share ($2.60 × 20). In both cases, the stockholders would receive $2 per share: a $2 cash dividend in the dividend case or a $2 increase in share price ($50 per share to $52 per share) in the repurchase case.

Besides the advantage of an increase in per-share earnings, an owner tax-deferral benefit results. Although the owners would have to pay capital gains taxes in either case (the $2 dividend or the $2 increase in market value), the dividend tax would be paid in the current year. In contrast, the tax on the gain from the repurchase would effectively be deferred until the stock is sold. Clearly, the repurchase provides the stockholder with the opportunity to defer taxes. The IRS is alleged to monitor firms that regularly repurchase stock and levies a penalty when it believes repurchases have been deliberately made to delay the payment of taxes by stockholders.

Accounting Entries

The accounting entries that result when firms repurchase common stock are a reduction in cash and the establishment of a contra capital account called "treasury stock," which is shown as a deduction from stockholders' equity. The label *treasury stock* is used on the balance sheet to indicate the presence of repurchased shares.

Repurchase Process

When a company intends to repurchase a block of outstanding shares, it should make shareholders aware of its intentions. Specifically, it should advise them of the purpose of the repurchase (acquisition, stock options, retirement) and the disposition (if any) planned for the repurchased shares (traded for shares of another firm, distribution to executives, or held in the treasury).

Three basic methods of repurchase are common. One is to purchase shares on the *open market*. This places upward pressure on the price of shares if the number of shares being repurchased is reasonably large in comparison with the total number outstanding. The second method is through tender offers. A **tender offer** is a formal offer to purchase a given number of shares of a firm's stock at a specified price. The price at which a tender offer is made is set above the current market price to attract sellers. If the number of shares desired cannot be repurchased through the tender offer, firms can obtain the additional shares on the open market. Tender offers are preferred when large numbers of shares are repurchased, because the company's intentions are clearly stated and each stockholder has an opportunity to sell shares at the tendered price. A third method involves

tender offer

A formal offer to purchase a given number of shares of a firm's stock at a specified price.

Focus on Ethics   Are Buybacks Really a Bargain?

IN PRACTICE

When **CBS** announced in March 2007 that it would buy back $1.4 billion worth of stock, its sagging share price saw the biggest spike since the media giant parted ways with **Viacom** in 2005. The 4.5 percent jump may be an omen of good fortune—at the very least it shows how much shareholders like buybacks.

Companies have been gobbling up their own shares faster than ever in a world of inexpensive capital and swollen balance sheets. Since 2003, the market for buybacks has boomed, with repurchases nearly on a par with capital expenditures. In 2006, $437 billion of stock was repurchased, according to Howard Silverblatt, an analyst at Standard & Poor's. Some, however, have questioned the moves and motives that lead to a big buyback.

In addition to simply returning cash to shareholders, companies also typically say they do so because they believe their stock is undervalued. Yet new research shows that companies often use creative financial reporting to push earnings downward before buybacks, making the stock seem undervalued and causing its price to bounce higher after the buyback. That pleases investors who then amplify the effect by pushing the price even higher.

"Managers who are acting opportunistically can use their reporting discretion to reduce the repurchase price by temporarily deflating earnings," argue Guojin Gong, Henock Louis, and Amy Sun at Penn State University's Smeal College of Business. Observing data from 1,720 companies, the authors say companies can easily create an apparent slump by speeding

up or slowing down expense recognition, changing inventory accounting, or revising estimates of bad debt—all classic methods of making the numbers look worse without actually breaking accounting rules.

The penalty for being caught deliberately managing earnings in advance of a buyback could be severe. With the backdating scandals that popped up regularly in the early 2000s, executives would no doubt be wary of deflating earnings just to get a boost from a buyback. Still, that's what Louis believes some are doing. "I don't think what they're doing is illegal," he says. "But it's misleading their investors."

■ *Do you agree that corporate managers would manipulate their stock's value prior to a buyback, or do you believe that corporations are more likely to initiate a buyback to enhance shareholder value?*

13 | Working Capital and Current Assets Management

WHY THIS CHAPTER MATTERS TO YOU

(In Your Professional Life)

Accounting: You need to understand the cash conversion cycle and the management of inventory, accounts receivable, and receipts and disbursements of cash.

Information systems: You need to understand the cash conversion cycle, inventory, accounts receivable, and receipts and disbursements of cash to design financial information systems that facilitate effective short-term financial management.

Management: You need to understand the management of working capital so that you can efficiently manage current assets and decide whether to finance the firm's funds requirements aggressively or conservatively.

Marketing: You need to understand credit selection and monitoring because sales will be affected by the availability of credit to purchasers; sales will also be affected by inventory management.

Operations: You need to understand the cash conversion cycle because you will be responsible for reducing the cycle through the efficient management of production, inventory, and costs.

(In Your Personal Life)

You often will be faced with short-term purchasing decisions, which tend to focus on consumable items. Many involve tradeoffs between quantity and price: Should you buy large quantities in order to pay a lower unit price, hold the items, and use them over time? Or should you buy smaller quantities more frequently and pay a slightly higher unit price? Analyzing these types of short-term purchasing decisions will help you make the most of your money.

LEARNING GOALS

LG 1 Understand short-term financial management, net working capital, and the related tradeoff between profitability and risk.

LG 2 Describe the cash conversion cycle, its funding requirements, and the key strategies for managing it.

LG 3 Discuss inventory management: differing views, common techniques, and international concerns.

LG 4 Explain the credit selection process and the quantitative procedure for evaluating changes in credit standards.

LG 5 Review the procedures for quantitatively considering cash discount changes, other aspects of credit terms, and credit monitoring.

LG 6 Understand the management of receipts and disbursements, including float, speeding up collections, slowing down payments, cash concentration, zero-balance accounts, and investing in marketable securities.

An important consideration for all firms is the ability to finance the transition from cash to inventories to receivables and back to cash. Various strategies exist for managing current assets in order to reduce the amount of financing needed to support this cycle. In addition to managing cash, firms also must manage the accounts that typically represent the firm's largest investment in current assets—inventories and accounts receivable. This chapter looks at the management of these various aspects of the firm's current assets.

13.1 | Net Working Capital Fundamentals

The firm's balance sheet provides information about the structure of the firm's investments on the one hand and the structure of its financing sources on the other hand. The structures chosen should consistently lead to the maximization of the value of the owners' investment in the firm.

Short-Term Financial Management

short-term financial management
Management of current assets and current liabilities.

Important components of the firm's financial structure include the level of investment in current assets and the extent of current liability financing. In U.S. manufacturing firms, current assets account for about 40 percent of total assets; current liabilities represent about 26 percent of total financing. Therefore, it should not be surprising to learn that **short-term financial management**—managing current assets and current liabilities—is one of the financial manager's most important and time-consuming activities. A study of *Fortune* 1000 firms found that more than one-third of financial management time is spent managing current assets and about one-fourth of financial management time is spent managing current liabilities.[1]

The goal of short-term financial management is to manage each of the firm's current assets (inventory, accounts receivable, cash, and marketable securities) and current liabilities (accounts payable, accruals, and notes payable) to achieve a balance between profitability and risk that contributes positively to the firm's value. This chapter does not discuss the optimal level of current assets and current liabilities that a firm should have. That issue is unresolved in the financial literature. Here, we first use *net working capital* to consider the basic relationship between current assets and current liabilities and then use the *cash conversion cycle* to consider the key aspects of current asset management. In the following chapter, we consider current liability management.

working capital
Current assets, which represent the portion of investment that circulates from one form to another in the ordinary conduct of business.

Net Working Capital

Current assets, commonly called **working capital,** represent the portion of investment that circulates from one form to another in the ordinary conduct of business. This idea embraces the recurring transition from cash to inventories to

---

1. Lawrence J. Gitman and Charles E. Maxwell, "Financial Activities of Major U.S. Firms: Survey and Analysis of Fortune's 1000," *Financial Management* (Winter 1985), pp. 57–65.

receivables and back to cash. As cash substitutes, *marketable securities* are considered part of working capital.

Current liabilities represent the firm's short-term financing, because they include all debts of the firm that come due (must be paid) in 1 year or less. These debts usually include amounts owed to suppliers (accounts payable), employees and governments (accruals), and banks (notes payable), among others.

As noted in Chapter 8, **net working capital** is commonly defined as the difference between the firm's current assets and its current liabilities. When the current assets exceed the current liabilities, the firm has *positive net working capital.* When current assets are less than current liabilities, the firm has *negative net working capital.*

The conversion of current assets from inventory to receivables to cash provides the cash used to pay the current liabilities. The cash outlays for current liabilities are relatively predictable. When an obligation is incurred, the firm generally knows when the corresponding payment will be due. What is difficult to predict are the cash inflows—the conversion of the current assets to more liquid forms. The more predictable its cash inflows, the less net working capital a firm needs. Because most firms are unable to match cash inflows to cash outflows with certainty, they usually need current assets that more than cover outflows for current liabilities. In general, the greater the margin by which a firm's current assets cover its current liabilities, the better able it will be to pay its bills as they come due.

net working capital
The difference between the firm's current assets and its current liabilities; can be *positive* or *negative.*

Hint Stated differently, some portion of current assets is usually held to provide liquidity in case it is unexpectedly needed.

Tradeoff between Profitability and Risk

A tradeoff exists between a firm's profitability and its risk. **Profitability,** in this context, is the relationship between revenues and costs generated by using the firm's assets—both current and fixed—in productive activities. A firm can increase its profits by (1) increasing revenues or (2) decreasing costs. **Risk,** in the context of short-term financial management, is the probability that a firm will be unable to pay its bills as they come due. A firm that cannot pay its bills as they come due is said to be **technically insolvent.** It is generally assumed that the greater the firm's net working capital, the lower its risk. In other words, the more net working capital, the more liquid the firm and therefore the lower its risk of becoming technically insolvent. Using these definitions of profitability and risk, we can demonstrate the tradeoff between them by considering changes in current assets and current liabilities separately.

profitability
The relationship between revenues and costs generated by using the firm's assets—both current and fixed—in productive activities.

risk (of technical insolvency)
The probability that a firm will be unable to pay its bills as they come due.

technically insolvent
Describes a firm that is unable to pay its bills as they come due.

Changes in Current Assets

We can demonstrate how changing the level of the firm's current assets affects its profitability–risk tradeoff by using the ratio of current assets to total assets. This ratio indicates the *percentage of total assets* that is current. For purposes of illustration, we will assume that the level of total assets remains unchanged.[2] The effects on both profitability and risk of an increase or decrease in this ratio are summarized in the upper portion of Table 13.1. When the ratio increases—that is, when current assets increase—profitability decreases. Why? Because current

---

2. To isolate the effect of changing asset and financing mixes on the firm's profitability and risk, we assume the level of total assets to be *constant* in this and the following discussion.

TABLE 13.1	Effects of Changing Ratios on Profits and Risk		
Ratio	Change in ratio	Effect on profit	Effect on risk
Current assets / Total assets	**Increase**	Decrease	Decrease
	Decrease	Increase	Increase
Current liabilities / Total assets	**Increase**	Increase	Increase
	Decrease	Decrease	Decrease

assets are less profitable than fixed assets. Fixed assets are more profitable because they add more value to the product than that provided by current assets. Without fixed assets, the firm could not produce the product.

The risk effect, however, decreases as the ratio of current assets to total assets increases. The increase in current assets increases net working capital, thereby reducing the risk of technical insolvency. In addition, as you go down the asset side of the balance sheet, the risk associated with the assets increases: Investment in cash and marketable securities is less risky than investment in accounts receivable, inventories, and fixed assets. Accounts receivable investment is less risky than investment in inventories and fixed assets. Investment in inventories is less risky than investment in fixed assets. The nearer an asset is to cash, the less risky it is. The opposite effects on profit and risk result from a decrease in the ratio of current assets to total assets.

Hint It is generally easier to turn receivables into the more liquid asset cash than it is to turn inventory into cash. As we will learn in Chapter 14, the firm can sell its receivables for cash. Often inventory is sold on credit and is therefore converted to a receivable before it becomes cash.

Changes in Current Liabilities

We also can demonstrate how changing the level of the firm's current liabilities affects its profitability–risk tradeoff by using the ratio of current liabilities to total assets. This ratio indicates the percentage of total assets that has been financed with current liabilities. Again, assuming that total assets remain unchanged, the effects on both profitability and risk of an increase or decrease in the ratio are summarized in the lower portion of Table 13.1. When the ratio increases, profitability increases. Why? Because the firm uses more of the less expensive current liabilities financing and less long-term financing. Current liabilities are less expensive because only notes payable, which represent about 20 percent of the typical manufacturer's current liabilities, have a cost. The other current liabilities are basically debts on which the firm pays no charge or interest. However, when the ratio of current liabilities to total assets increases, the risk of technical insolvency also increases, because the increase in current liabilities in turn decreases net working capital. The opposite effects on profit and risk result from a decrease in the ratio of current liabilities to total assets.

REVIEW QUESTIONS

13–1 Why is *short-term financial management* one of the most important and time-consuming activities of the financial manager? What is *net working capital?*

13–2 What is the relationship between the predictability of a firm's cash inflows and its required level of net working capital? How are net working capital, liquidity, and *risk of technical insolvency* related?

13–3 Why does an increase in the ratio of current assets to total assets decrease both profits and risk as measured by net working capital? How do changes in the ratio of current liabilities to total assets affect profitability and risk?

13.2 | Cash Conversion Cycle

Central to short-term financial management is an understanding of the firm's *cash conversion cycle*.[3] This cycle frames discussion of the management of the firm's current assets in this chapter and that of the management of current liabilities in Chapter 14. Here, we begin by demonstrating the calculation and application of the cash conversion cycle.

Calculating the Cash Conversion Cycle

operating cycle (OC)
The time from the beginning of the production process to collection of cash from the sale of the finished product.

A firm's **operating cycle** (OC) is the time from the beginning of the production process to collection of cash from the sale of the finished product. The operating cycle encompasses two major short-term asset categories: inventory and accounts receivable. It is measured in elapsed time by summing the *average age of inventory (AAI)* and the *average collection period (ACP)*.

$$OC = AAI + ACP \tag{13.1}$$

Hint A firm can lower its working capital if it can speed up its operating cycle. For example, if a firm accepts bank credit (like a Visa card), it will receive cash sooner after the sale is transacted than if it has to wait until the customer pays its accounts receivable.

However, the process of producing and selling a product also includes the purchase of production inputs (raw materials) on account, which results in accounts payable. Accounts payable reduce the number of days a firm's resources are tied up in the operating cycle. The time it takes to pay the accounts payable, measured in days, is the *average payment period (APP)*. The operating cycle less the average payment period is referred to as the **cash conversion cycle** (CCC). It represents the amount of time the firm's resources are tied up. The formula for the cash conversion cycle is

cash conversion cycle (CCC)
The amount of time a firm's resources are tied up; calculated by subtracting the average payment period from the *operating cycle*.

$$CCC = OC - APP \tag{13.2}$$

Substituting the relationship in Equation 13.1 into Equation 13.2, we can see that the cash conversion cycle has three main components, as shown in Equation 13.3: (1) average age of the inventory, (2) average collection period, and (3) average payment period.

$$CCC = AAI + ACP - APP \tag{13.3}$$

Clearly, if a firm changes any of these time periods, it changes the amount of resources tied up in the day-to-day operation of the firm.

---

3. The conceptual model that is used in this section to demonstrate basic short-term financial management strategies was developed by Lawrence J. Gitman in "Estimating Corporate Liquidity Requirements: A Simplified Approach," *The Financial Review* (1974), pp. 79–88, and refined and operationalized by Lawrence J. Gitman and Kanwal S. Sachdeva in "A Framework for Estimating and Analyzing the Required Working Capital Investment," *Review of Business and Economic Research* (Spring 1982), pp. 35–44.

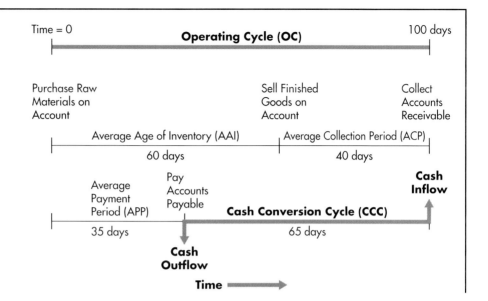

FIGURE 13.1

Time Line for MAX Company's Cash Conversion Cycle

MAX Company's operating cycle is 100 days, and its cash conversion cycle is 65 days.

Example

MAX Company, a producer of paper dinnerware, has annual sales of $10 million, a cost of goods sold of 75% of sales, and purchases that are 65% of cost of goods sold. MAX has an average age of inventory (AAI) of 60 days, an average collection period (ACP) of 40 days, and an average payment period (APP) of 35 days. Thus the cash conversion cycle for MAX is 65 days (60 + 40 − 35). Figure 13.1 presents MAX Company's cash conversion cycle as a time line.

The resources MAX has invested in this cash conversion cycle (assuming a 365-day year) are

Inventory	$= (\$10,000,000 \times 0.75) \times (60/365)$	$=$	$1,232,877
+ Accounts receivable	$= (\;10,000,000 \times 40/365)$	$=$	1,095,890
− Accounts payable	$= (\;10,000,000 \times 0.75 \times 0.65) \times (35/365) =$		467,466
	$=$ Resources invested	$=$	$1,861,301

Changes in any of the time periods will change the resources tied up in operations. For example, if MAX could reduce the average collection period on its accounts receivable by 5 days, it would shorten the cash conversion time line and thus reduce the amount of resources MAX has invested in operations. For MAX, a 5-day reduction in the average collection period would reduce the resources invested in the cash conversion cycle by $136,986 [$10,000,000 × (5/365)].

Funding Requirements of the Cash Conversion Cycle

We can use the cash conversion cycle as a basis for discussing how the firm funds its required investment in operating assets. We first differentiate between permanent and seasonal funding needs and then describe aggressive and conservative seasonal funding strategies.

permanent funding requirement
A constant investment in operating assets resulting from constant sales over time.

seasonal funding requirement
An investment in operating assets that varies over time as a result of cyclic sales.

Permanent versus Seasonal Funding Needs

If the firm's sales are constant, then its investment in operating assets should also be constant, and the firm will have only a **permanent funding requirement.** If the firm's sales are cyclic, then its investment in operating assets will vary over time with its sales cycles, and the firm will have **seasonal funding requirements** in addition to the permanent funding required for its minimum investment in operating assets.

Example

Nicholson Company holds, on average, $50,000 in cash and marketable securities, $1,250,000 in inventory, and $750,000 in accounts receivable. Nicholson's business is very stable over time, so its operating assets can be viewed as permanent. In addition, Nicholson's accounts payable of $425,000 are stable over time. Thus Nicholson has a permanent investment in operating assets of $1,625,000 ($50,000 + $1,250,0000 + $750,000 − $425,000). That amount would also equal its permanent funding requirement.

In contrast, Semper Pump Company, which produces bicycle pumps, has seasonal funding needs. Semper has seasonal sales, with its peak sales being driven by the summertime purchases of bicycle pumps. Semper holds, at minimum, $25,000 in cash and marketable securities, $100,000 in inventory, and $60,000 in accounts receivable. At peak times, Semper's inventory increases to $750,000, and its accounts receivable increase to $400,000. To capture production efficiencies, Semper produces pumps at a constant rate throughout the year. Thus accounts payable remain at $50,000 throughout the year. Accordingly, Semper has a permanent funding requirement for its minimum level of operating assets of $135,000 ($25,000 + $100,000 + $60,000 − $50,000) and peak seasonal funding requirements (in excess of its permanent need) of $990,000 [($25,000 + $750,000 + $400,000 − $50,000) − $135,000]. Semper's total funding requirements for operating assets vary from a minimum of $135,000 (permanent) to a seasonal peak of $1,125,000 ($135,000 + $990,000). Figure 13.2 depicts these needs over time.

---

aggressive funding strategy
A funding strategy under which the firm funds its seasonal requirements with short-term debt and its permanent requirements with long-term debt.

conservative funding strategy
A funding strategy under which the firm funds both its seasonal and its permanent requirements with long-term debt.

Aggressive versus Conservative Seasonal Funding Strategies

Short-term funds are typically less expensive than long-term funds. (The yield curve is typically upward-sloping.) However, long-term funds allow the firm to lock in its cost of funds over a period of time and thus avoid the risk of increases in short-term interest rates. Also, long-term funding ensures that the required funds are available to the firm when needed. Short-term funding exposes the firm to the risk that it may not be able to obtain the funds needed to cover its seasonal peaks. Under an **aggressive funding strategy,** the firm funds its seasonal requirements with short-term debt and its permanent requirements with long-term debt. Under a **conservative funding strategy,** the firm funds both its seasonal and its permanent requirements with long-term debt.

Example

Semper Pump Company has a permanent funding requirement of $135,000 in operating assets and seasonal funding requirements that vary between $0 and $990,000 and average $101,250 (calculated from data not shown). If Semper can borrow short-term funds at 6.25% and long-term funds at 8%, and if it can earn

FIGURE 13.2   Semper Pump Company's Total Funding Requirements

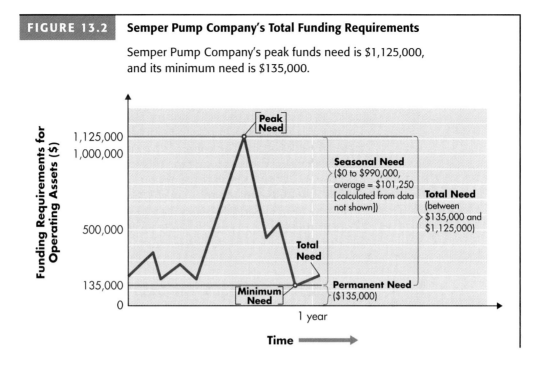

Semper Pump Company's peak funds need is $1,125,000, and its minimum need is $135,000.

5% on the investment of any surplus balances, then the annual cost of an aggressive strategy for seasonal funding will be

Cost of short-term financing = 0.0625 ×	$101,250 =	$ 6,328.13
+ Cost of long-term financing = 0.0800 ×	135,000 =	10,800.00
− Earnings on surplus balances[4] = 0.0500 ×	0 =	0
Total cost of aggressive strategy		$17,128.13

Alternatively, Semper can choose a conservative strategy, under which surplus cash balances are fully invested. (In Figure 13.2, this surplus will be the difference between the peak need of $1,125,000 and the total need, which varies between $135,000 and $1,125,000 during the year.) The cost of the conservative strategy will be

Cost of short-term financing = 0.0625 × $	0 = $	0
+ Cost of long-term financing = 0.0800 ×	1,125,000 =	90,000.00
− Earnings on surplus balances[5] = 0.0500 ×	888,750 =	44,437.50
Total cost of conservative strategy		$45,562.50

---

4. Because under this strategy the amount of financing exactly equals the estimated funding need, no surplus balances exist.

5. The average surplus balance would be calculated by subtracting the sum of the permanent need ($135,000) and the average seasonal need ($101,250) from the seasonal peak need ($1,125,000) to get $888,750 ($1,125,000 − $135,000 − $101,250). This represents the surplus amount of financing that on average could be invested in short-term vehicles that earn a 5% annual return.

It is clear from these calculations that for Semper, the aggressive strategy is far less expensive than the conservative strategy. However, it is equally clear that Semper has substantial peak-season operating-asset needs and that it must have adequate funding available to meet the peak needs and ensure ongoing operations.

Clearly, the aggressive strategy's heavy reliance on short-term financing makes it riskier than the conservative strategy because of interest rate swings and possible difficulties in obtaining needed short-term financing quickly when seasonal peaks occur. The conservative strategy avoids these risks through the locked-in interest rate and long-term financing, but it is more costly because of the negative spread between the earnings rate on surplus funds (5% in the example) and the cost of the long-term funds that create the surplus (8% in the example). Where the firm operates, between the extremes of the aggressive and conservative seasonal funding strategies, depends on management's disposition toward risk and the strength of its banking relationships.

Strategies for Managing the Cash Conversion Cycle

Some firms establish a *target* cash conversion cycle and then monitor and manage the *actual* cash conversion cycle toward the targeted value. A positive cash conversion cycle, as we saw for MAX Company in the earlier example, means the firm must use negotiated liabilities (such as bank loans) to support its operating assets. Negotiated liabilities carry an explicit cost, so the firm benefits by minimizing their use in supporting operating assets. Simply stated, the goal is to *minimize the length of the cash conversion cycle*, which minimizes negotiated liabilities. This goal can be realized through use of the following strategies:

1. *Turn over inventory as quickly as possible* without stockouts that result in lost sales.
2. *Collect accounts receivable as quickly as possible* without losing sales from high-pressure collection techniques.
3. *Manage mail, processing, and clearing time* to reduce them when collecting from customers and to increase them when paying suppliers.
4. *Pay accounts payable as slowly as possible* without damaging the firm's credit rating.

Techniques for implementing these four strategies are the focus of the remainder of this chapter and the following chapter.

REVIEW QUESTIONS

13–4 What is the difference between the firm's *operating cycle* and its *cash conversion cycle?*

13–5 Why is it helpful to divide the funding needs of a seasonal business into its permanent and seasonal funding requirements when developing a funding strategy?

13–6 What are the benefits, costs, and risks of an *aggressive funding strategy* and of a *conservative funding strategy?* Under which strategy is the borrowing often in excess of the actual need?

13–7 Why is it important for a firm to minimize the length of its cash conversion cycle?

13.3 | Inventory Management

The first component of the cash conversion cycle is the average age of inventory. The objective for managing inventory, as noted earlier, is to turn over inventory as quickly as possible without losing sales from stockouts. The financial manager tends to act as an advisor or "watchdog" in matters concerning inventory; he or she does not have direct control over inventory but does provide input to the inventory management process.

Differing Viewpoints about Inventory Level

Differing viewpoints about appropriate inventory levels commonly exist among a firm's finance, marketing, manufacturing, and purchasing managers. Each views inventory levels in light of his or her own objectives. The *financial manager's* general disposition toward inventory levels is to keep them low, to ensure that the firm's money is not being unwisely invested in excess resources. The *marketing manager,* on the other hand, would like to have large inventories of the firm's finished products. This would ensure that all orders could be filled quickly, eliminating the need for backorders due to stockouts.

The *manufacturing manager's* major responsibility is to implement the production plan so that it results in the desired amount of finished goods of acceptable quality available on time at a low cost. In fulfilling this role, the manufacturing manager would keep raw materials inventories high to avoid production delays. He or she also would favor large production runs for the sake of lower unit production costs, which would result in high finished goods inventories.

The *purchasing manager* is concerned solely with the raw materials inventories. He or she must have on hand, in the correct quantities at the desired times and at a favorable price, whatever raw materials are required by production. Without proper control, in an effort to get quantity discounts or in anticipation of rising prices or a shortage of certain materials, the purchasing manager may purchase larger quantities of resources than are actually needed at the time.

Common Techniques for Managing Inventory

Numerous techniques are available for effectively managing the firm's inventory. Here we briefly consider four commonly used techniques.

ABC System

ABC inventory system
Inventory management technique that divides inventory into three groups—A, B, and C, in descending order of importance and level of monitoring, on the basis of the dollar investment in each.

A firm using the **ABC inventory system** divides its inventory into three groups: A, B, and C. The A group includes those items with the largest dollar investment. Typically, this group consists of 20 percent of the firm's inventory items but 80 percent of its investment in inventory. The B group consists of items that account for the next largest investment in inventory. The C group consists of a large number of items that require a relatively small investment.

The inventory group of each item determines the item's level of monitoring. The A group items receive the most intense monitoring because of the high dollar investment. Typically, A group items are tracked on a perpetual inventory system that allows daily verification of each item's inventory level. B group items are frequently controlled through periodic, perhaps weekly, checking of their levels. C group items are monitored with unsophisticated techniques, such as the two-bin method. With the **two-bin method,** the item is stored in two bins. As an item is needed, inventory is removed from the first bin. When that bin is empty, an order is placed to refill the first bin while inventory is drawn from the second bin. The second bin is used until empty, and so on.

The large dollar investment in A and B group items suggests the need for a better method of inventory management than the ABC system. The EOQ model, discussed next, is an appropriate model for the management of A and B group items.

Economic Order Quantity (EOQ) Model

One of the most common techniques for determining the optimal order size for inventory items is the **economic order quantity (EOQ) model.** The EOQ model considers various costs of inventory and then determines what order size minimizes total inventory cost.

EOQ assumes that the relevant costs of inventory can be divided into *order costs* and *carrying costs*. (The model excludes the actual cost of the inventory item.) Each of them has certain key components and characteristics. **Order costs** include the fixed clerical costs of placing and receiving orders: the cost of writing a purchase order, of processing the resulting paperwork, and of receiving an order and checking it against the invoice. Order costs are stated in dollars per order. **Carrying costs** are the variable costs per unit of holding an item of inventory for a specific period of time. Carrying costs include storage costs, insurance costs, the costs of deterioration and obsolescence, and the opportunity or financial cost of having funds invested in inventory. These costs are stated in dollars per unit per period.

Order costs decrease as the size of the order increases. Carrying costs, however, increase with increases in the order size. The EOQ model analyzes the tradeoff between order costs and carrying costs to determine the *order quantity that minimizes the total inventory cost.*

Mathematical Development of EOQ   A formula can be developed for determining the firm's EOQ for a given inventory item, where

S = usage in units per period

O = order cost per order

C = carrying cost per unit per period

Q = order quantity in units

The first step is to derive the cost functions for order cost and carrying cost. The order cost can be expressed as the product of the cost per order and the number of orders. Because the number of orders equals the usage during the period divided by the order quantity (S/Q), the order cost can be expressed as follows:

$$\text{Order cost} = O \times S/Q \qquad \text{(13.4)}$$

The carrying cost is defined as the cost of carrying a unit of inventory per period multiplied by the firm's average inventory. The average inventory is the order

two-bin method
Unsophisticated inventory-monitoring technique that is typically applied to C group items and involves reordering inventory when one of two bins is empty.

economic order quantity (EOQ) model
Inventory management technique for determining an item's optimal order size, which is the size that minimizes the total of its *order costs* and *carrying costs*.

order costs
The fixed clerical costs of placing and receiving an inventory order.

carrying costs
The variable costs per unit of holding an item in inventory for a specific period of time.

quantity divided by 2 (Q/2), because inventory is assumed to be depleted at a constant rate. Thus carrying cost can be expressed as follows:

$$\text{Carrying cost} = C \times Q/2 \qquad (13.5)$$

total cost of inventory
The sum of order costs and carrying costs of inventory.

The firm's **total cost of inventory** is found by summing the order cost and the carrying cost. Thus the total cost function is

$$\text{Total cost} = (O \times S/Q) + (C \times Q/2) \qquad (13.6)$$

Hint The EOQ calculation helps management minimize the total cost of inventory. Lowering order costs will cause an increase in carrying costs and may increase total cost. Likewise, a decrease in total cost may result from reduced carrying costs. The goal, facilitated by using the EOQ calculation, is to lower total cost.

Because the EOQ is defined as the order quantity that minimizes the total cost function, we must solve the total cost function for the EOQ. The resulting equation is

$$EOQ = \sqrt{\frac{2 \times S \times O}{C}} \qquad (13.7)$$

Although the EOQ model has weaknesses, it is certainly better than subjective decision making. Despite the fact that the use of the EOQ model is outside the control of the financial manager, the financial manager must be aware of its utility and must provide certain inputs, specifically with respect to inventory carrying costs.

Personal Finance Example Individuals sometimes are confronted with personal finance decisions involving cost tradeoffs similar to the tradeoff between the fixed order costs and variable carrying costs of inventory that corporations face. Take the case of the von Dammes, who are trying to decide whether a conventional car (uses gas) or a hybrid car (uses gas and electric battery) would be more cost-effective.

The von Dammes plan to keep whichever car they choose for 3 years and expect to drive it 12,000 miles in each of those years. They will use the same dollar amount of financing repaid under the same terms for either car and they expect the cars to have identical repair costs over the 3-year ownership period. They also assume that the trade-in value of the two cars at the end of 3 years will be identical. Both cars use regular unleaded gas, which they estimate will cost, on average, $3.20 per gallon over the 3 years. The key data for each car follows:

	Conventional	Hybrid
Total cost	$24,500	$27,300
Average miles per gallon	27	42

We can begin by calculating the total fuel cost for each car over the 3-year ownership period:

Conventional: [(3 years × 12,000 miles per year)/27 miles per gallon] × $3.20 per gallon
= 1,333.33 gallons × $3.20 per gallon = $4,267

Hybrid: [(3 years × 12,000 miles per year)/42 miles per gallon] × $3.20 per gallon
= 857.14 gallons × $3.20 per gallon = $2,743

In order to buy the hybrid car, the von Dammes will have to pay $2,800 more ($27,300 − $24,500) than the cost of the conventional car, but they will save about $1,524 ($4,267 − $2,743) in fuel costs over the 3-year ownership period. Ignoring differences in timing, on a strict economic basis *they should buy the conventional car because the $2,800 marginal cost of the hybrid results in a marginal fuel cost savings of only $1,524.* Clearly, other factors such as environmental concerns and the reasonableness of the assumptions could affect their decision.

reorder point
The point at which to reorder inventory, expressed as days of lead time × daily usage.

Reorder Point   Once the firm has determined its economic order quantity, it must determine when to place an order. The **reorder point** reflects the number of days of lead time the firm needs to place and receive an order and the firm's daily usage of the inventory item. Assuming that inventory is used at a constant rate, the formula for the reorder point is

$$\text{Reorder point} = \text{Days of lead time} \times \text{Daily usage} \qquad (13.8)$$

For example, if a firm knows it takes 3 days to place and receive an order, and if it uses 15 units per day of the inventory item, then the reorder point is 45 units of inventory (3 days × 15 units/day). Thus, as soon as the item's inventory level falls to the reorder point (45 units, in this case) an order will be placed at the item's EOQ. If the estimates of lead time and usage are correct, then the order will arrive exactly as the inventory level reaches zero. However, lead times and usage rates are not precise, so most firms hold **safety stock** (extra inventory) to prevent stockouts of important items.

safety stock
Extra inventory that is held to prevent stockouts of important items.

Example

MAX Company has an A group inventory item that is vital to the production process. This item costs $1,500, and MAX uses 1,100 units of the item per year. MAX wants to determine its optimal order strategy for the item. To calculate the EOQ, we need the following inputs:

Order cost per order = $150
Carrying cost per unit per year = $200

Substituting into Equation 14.7, we get

$$EOQ = \sqrt{\frac{2 \times 1,100 \times \$150}{\$200}} \approx \underline{\underline{41}} \text{ units}$$

The reorder point for MAX depends on the number of days MAX operates per year. Assuming that MAX operates 250 days per year and uses 1,100 units of this item, its daily usage is 4.4 units (1,100 ÷ 250). If its lead time is 2 days and MAX wants to maintain a safety stock of 4 units, the reorder point for this item is 12.8 units [(2 × 4.4) + 4]. However, orders are made only in whole units, so the order is placed when the inventory falls to 13 units.

The firm's goal for inventory is to turn it over as quickly as possible without stockouts. Inventory turnover is best calculated by dividing cost of goods sold by average inventory. The EOQ model determines the optimal order size and, indirectly, through the assumption of constant usage, the average inventory. Thus the EOQ model determines the firm's optimal inventory turnover rate, given the firm's specific costs of inventory.

Just-in-Time (JIT) System

just-in-time (JIT) system
Inventory management technique that minimizes inventory investment by having materials arrive at exactly the time they are needed for production.

The **just-in-time (JIT) system** is used to minimize inventory investment. The philosophy is that materials should arrive at exactly the time they are needed for production. Ideally, the firm would have only work-in-process inventory. Because its objective is to minimize inventory investment, a JIT system uses no (or very little) safety stock. Extensive coordination among the firm's employees, its suppliers, and shipping companies must exist to ensure that material inputs arrive on time. Failure of materials to arrive on time results in a shutdown of the production line until the materials arrive. Likewise, a JIT system requires high-quality parts from suppliers. When quality problems arise, production must be stopped until the problems are resolved.

The goal of the JIT system is manufacturing efficiency. It uses inventory as a tool for attaining efficiency by emphasizing quality of the materials used and their timely delivery. When JIT is working properly, it forces process inefficiencies to surface. Knowing the level of inventory is, of course, an important part of any inventory management system.

Computerized Systems for Resource Control

materials requirement planning (MRP) system
Inventory management technique that applies EOQ concepts and a computer to compare production needs to available inventory balances and determine when orders should be placed for various items on a product's *bill of materials*.

manufacturing resource planning II (MRP II)
A sophisticated computerized system that integrates data from numerous areas such as finance, accounting, marketing, engineering, and manufacturing and generates production plans as well as numerous financial and management reports.

enterprise resource planning (ERP)
A computerized system that electronically integrates external information about the firm's suppliers and customers with the firm's departmental data so that information on all available resources—human and material—can be instantly obtained in a fashion that eliminates production delays and controls costs.

Today a number of systems are available for controlling inventory and other resources. One of the most basic is the **materials requirement planning (MRP) system.** It is used to determine what materials to order and when to order them. MRP applies EOQ concepts to determine how much to order. Using a computer, MRP simulates each product's bill of materials, inventory status, and manufacturing process. The *bill of materials* is simply a list of all parts and materials that go into making the finished product. For a given production plan, the computer simulates material requirements by comparing production needs to available inventory balances. On the basis of the time it takes for a product that is in process to move through the various production stages and the lead time to get materials, the MRP system determines when orders should be placed for various items on the bill of materials. The objective of this system is to lower the firm's inventory investment without impairing production. If the firm's opportunity cost of capital for investments of equal risk is 15 percent, every dollar of investment released from inventory will increase before-tax profits by $0.15.

A popular extension of MRP is **manufacturing resource planning II (MRP II)**, which integrates data from numerous areas such as finance, accounting, marketing, engineering, and manufacturing using a sophisticated computer system. This system generates production plans as well as numerous financial and management reports. In essence, it models the firm's processes so that the effects of changes in one area of operations on other areas can be assessed and monitored. For example, the MRP II system would allow the firm to assess the effect of an increase in labor costs on sales and profits.

Whereas MRP and MRP II tend to focus on internal operations, **enterprise resource planning (ERP)** systems expand the focus to the external environment by including information about suppliers and customers. ERP electronically integrates all of a firm's departments so that, for example, production can call up sales information and immediately know how much must be produced to fill customer orders. Because all available resources—human and material—are known, the system can eliminate production delays and control costs. ERP systems automatically note changes, such as a supplier's inability to meet a scheduled delivery date, so that necessary adjustments can be made.

International Inventory Management

International inventory management is typically much more complicated for exporters in general, and for multinational companies in particular, than for purely domestic firms. The production and manufacturing economies of scale that might be expected from selling products globally may prove elusive if products must be tailored for individual local markets, as frequently happens, or if actual production takes place in factories around the world. When raw materials, intermediate goods, or finished products must be transported over long distances—particularly by ocean shipping—there will be more delays, confusion, damage, and theft than occur in a one-country operation. The international inventory manager, therefore, puts a premium on flexibility. He or she is usually less concerned about ordering the economically optimal quantity of inventory than about making sure that sufficient quantities of inventory are delivered where they are needed, when they are needed, and in a condition to be used as planned.

REVIEW QUESTIONS

13–8   What are likely to be the viewpoints of each of the following managers about the levels of the various types of inventory: finance, marketing, manufacturing, and purchasing? Why is inventory an investment?

13–9   Briefly describe the following techniques for managing inventory: ABC system, economic order quantity (EOQ) model, just-in-time (JIT) system, and computerized systems for resource control—MRP, MRP II, and ERP.

13–10 What factors make managing inventory more difficult for exporters and multinational companies?

  ## 13.4 | Accounts Receivable Management

The second component of the cash conversion cycle is the average collection period. This period is the average length of time from a sale on credit until the payment becomes usable funds for the firm. The average collection period has two parts. The first part is the time from the sale until the customer mails the payment. The second part is the time from when the payment is mailed until the firm has the collected funds in its bank account. The first part of the average collection period involves managing the credit available to the firm's customers, and the second part involves collecting and processing payments. This section of the chapter discusses the firm's accounts receivable credit management.

The objective for managing accounts receivable is to collect accounts receivable as quickly as possible without losing sales from high-pressure collection techniques. Accomplishing this goal encompasses three topics: (1) credit selection and standards, (2) credit terms, and (3) credit monitoring.

> **Hint** Some small businesses resolve these problems by selling their accounts receivable to a third party at a discount. Though expensive, this strategy overcomes the problem of not having adequate personnel. It also creates a buffer between the small business and those customers who need a little prodding to stay current.

Credit Selection and Standards

Credit selection involves application of techniques for determining which customers should receive credit. This process involves evaluating the customer's creditworthiness and comparing it to the firm's **credit standards,** its minimum requirements for extending credit to a customer.

credit standards
The firm's minimum requirements for extending credit to a customer.

Five C's of Credit

five C's of credit
The five key dimensions—character, capacity, capital, collateral, and conditions—used by credit analysts to provide a framework for in-depth credit analysis.

One popular credit selection technique is the **five C's of credit,** which provides a framework for in-depth credit analysis. Because of the time and expense involved, this credit selection method is used for large-dollar credit requests. The five C's are

1. *Character:* The applicant's record of meeting past obligations.
2. *Capacity:* The applicant's ability to repay the requested credit, as judged in terms of financial statement analysis focused on cash flows available to repay debt obligations.
3. *Capital:* The applicant's debt relative to equity.
4. *Collateral:* The amount of assets the applicant has available for use in securing the credit. The larger the amount of available assets, the greater the chance that a firm will recover funds if the applicant defaults.
5. *Conditions:* Current general and industry-specific economic conditions, and any unique conditions surrounding a specific transaction.

Hint Computers are widely used to aid in the credit decision process. Data on each customer's payment patterns are maintained and can be called forth to evaluate requests for renewed or additional credit.

Analysis via the five C's of credit does not yield a specific accept/reject decision, so its use requires an analyst experienced in reviewing and granting credit requests. Application of this framework tends to ensure that the firm's credit customers will pay, without being pressured, within the stated credit terms.

Credit Scoring

credit scoring
A credit selection method commonly used with high-volume/small-dollar credit requests; relies on a credit score determined by applying statistically derived weights to a credit applicant's scores on key financial and credit characteristics.

Credit scoring is a method of credit selection that firms commonly use with high-volume/small-dollar credit requests. **Credit scoring** applies statistically derived weights to a credit applicant's scores on key financial and credit characteristics to predict whether he or she will pay the requested credit in a timely fashion. Simply stated, the procedure results in a score that measures the applicant's overall credit strength, and the score is used to make the accept/reject decision for granting the applicant credit. Credit scoring is most commonly used by large credit card operations, such as those of banks, oil companies, and department stores. The purpose of credit scoring is to make a relatively informed credit decision quickly and inexpensively, recognizing that the cost of a single bad scoring decision is small. However, if bad debts from scoring decisions increase, then the scoring system must be reevaluated. For a demonstration of credit scoring, including use of a spreadsheet for that purpose, see the book's website at www.prenhall.com/gitman.

Changing Credit Standards

Hint Relaxing the credit standards and/or credit terms will increase the risk of the firm, but it may also increase the return to the firm. The average collection period and bad debts will both increase with more lenient credit standards and/or credit terms, but the increased revenue may produce profits that exceed these costs.

The firm sometimes will contemplate changing its credit standards in an effort to improve its returns and create greater value for its owners. To demonstrate, consider the following changes and effects on profits expected to result from the *relaxation* of credit standards.

Effects of Relaxation of Credit Standards

Variable	Direction of change	Effect on profits
Sales volume	Increase	Positive
Investment in accounts receivable	Increase	Negative
Bad-debt expenses	Increase	Negative

If credit standards were tightened, the opposite effects would be expected.

Example

Dodd Tool, a manufacturer of lathe tools, is currently selling a product for $10 per unit. Sales (all on credit) for last year were 60,000 units. The variable cost per unit is $6. The firm's total fixed costs are $120,000.

The firm is currently contemplating a *relaxation of credit standards* that is expected to result in the following: a 5% increase in unit sales to 63,000 units; an increase in the average collection period from 30 days (the current level) to 45 days; an increase in bad-debt expenses from 1% of sales (the current level) to 2%. The firm's required return on equal-risk investments, which is the opportunity cost of tying up funds in accounts receivable, is 15%.

To determine whether to relax its credit standards, Dodd Tool must calculate its effect on the firm's additional profit contribution from sales, the cost of the marginal investment in accounts receivable, and the cost of marginal bad debts.

Additional Profit Contribution from Sales Because fixed costs are "sunk" and therefore are unaffected by a change in the sales level, the only cost relevant to a change in sales is variable costs. Sales are expected to increase by 5%, or 3,000 units. The profit contribution per unit will equal the difference between the sale price per unit ($10) and the variable cost per unit ($6). The profit contribution per unit therefore will be $4. The total additional profit contribution from sales will be $12,000 (3,000 units × $4 per unit).

Cost of the Marginal Investment in Accounts Receivable To determine the cost of the marginal investment in accounts receivable, Dodd must find the difference between the cost of carrying receivables under the two credit standards. Because its concern is only with the out-of-pocket costs, *the relevant cost is the variable cost*. The average investment in accounts receivable can be calculated by using the following formula:

$$\frac{\text{Average investment}}{\text{in accounts receivable}} = \frac{\text{Total variable cost of annual sales}}{\text{Turnover of accounts receivable}} \qquad (13.9)$$

where

$$\text{Turnover of accounts receivable} = \frac{365}{\text{Average collection period}}$$

The total variable cost of annual sales under the present and proposed plans can be found as follows, using the variable cost per unit of $6.

Total variable cost of annual sales

Under present plan: ($6 × 60,000 units) = $360,000
Under proposed plan: ($6 × 63,000 units) = $378,000

The turnover of accounts receivable is the number of times each year that the firm's accounts receivable are actually turned into cash. It is found by dividing the average collection period into 365 (the number of days assumed in a year).

Turnover of accounts receivable

Under present plan: $\frac{365}{30} = 12.2$

Under proposed plan: $\frac{365}{45} = 8.1$

By substituting the cost and turnover data just calculated into Equation 13.9 for each case, we get the following average investments in accounts receivable:

Average investment in accounts receivable

$$\text{Under present plan: } \frac{\$360,000}{12.2} = \$29,508$$

$$\text{Under proposed plan: } \frac{\$378,000}{8.1} = \$46,667$$

We calculate the marginal investment in accounts receivable and its cost as follows:

Cost of marginal investment in accounts receivable

Average investment under proposed plan	$46,667
− Average investment under present plan	29,508
Marginal investment in accounts receivable	$17,159
× Required return on investment	0.15
Cost of marginal investment in A/R	$ 2,574

The resulting value of $2,574 is considered a cost because it represents the maximum amount that could have been earned on the $17,159 had it been placed in the best equal-risk investment alternative available at the firm's required return on investment of 15%.

Cost of Marginal Bad Debts   We find the cost of marginal bad debts by taking the difference between the levels of bad debts before and after the proposed relaxation of credit standards.

Cost of marginal bad debts

Under proposed plan: $(0.02 \times \$10/\text{unit} \times 63,000 \text{ units})$	=	$12,600
Under present plan: $(0.01 \times \$10/\text{unit} \times 60,000 \text{ units})$	=	6,000
Cost of marginal bad debts		$ 6,600

Note that the bad-debt costs are calculated by using the sale price per unit ($10) to deduct not just the true loss of variable cost ($6) that results when a customer fails to pay its account, but also the profit contribution per unit (in this case $4) that is included in the "additional profit contribution from sales." Thus the resulting cost of marginal bad debts is $6,600.

Making the Credit Standard Decision   To decide whether to relax its credit standards, the firm must compare the additional profit contribution from sales to the added costs of the marginal investment in accounts receivable and marginal bad debts. If the additional profit contribution is greater than marginal costs, credit standards should be relaxed.

Example   The results and key calculations related to Dodd Tool's decision whether to relax its credit standards are summarized in Table 13.2 on page 542. The net addition to total profits resulting from such an action will be $2,826 per year. Therefore, the firm *should* relax its credit standards as proposed.

TABLE 13.2	Effects on Dodd Tool of a Relaxation of Credit Standards		
Additional profit contribution from sales			
[3,000 units × ($10 − $6)]			$12,000
Cost of marginal investment in A/R[a]			
Average investment under proposed plan:			
$\dfrac{\$6 \times 63,000}{8.1} = \dfrac{\$378,000}{8.1}$		$46,667	
Average investment under present plan:			
$\dfrac{\$6 \times 60,000}{12.2} = \dfrac{\$360,000}{12.2}$		29,508	
Marginal investment in A/R		$17,159	
Cost of marginal investment in A/R (0.15 × $17,159)			($ 2,574)
Cost of marginal bad debts			
Bad debts under proposed plan (0.02 × $10 × 63,000)	$12,600		
Bad debts under present plan (0.01 × $10 × 60,000)	6,000		
Cost of marginal bad debts			($ 6,600)
Net profit from implementation of proposed plan			$ 2,826

[a]The denominators 8.1 and 12.2 in the calculation of the average investment in accounts receivable under the proposed and present plans are the accounts receivable turnovers for each of these plans (365/45 = 8.1 and 365/30 = 12.2).

The procedure described here for evaluating a proposed change in credit standards is also commonly used to evaluate other changes in the management of accounts receivable. If Dodd Tool had been contemplating tightening its credit standards, for example, the cost would have been a reduction in the profit contribution from sales, and the return would have been from reductions in the cost of the investment in accounts receivable and in the cost of bad debts. Another application of this procedure is demonstrated later in the chapter.

 ### Managing International Credit

Credit management is difficult enough for managers of purely domestic companies, and these tasks become much more complex for companies that operate internationally. This is partly because (as we have seen before) international operations typically expose a firm to *exchange rate risk*. It is also due to the dangers and delays involved in shipping goods long distances and in having to cross at least two international borders.

Exports of finished goods are usually priced in the currency of the importer's local market; most commodities, on the other hand, are priced in dollars. Therefore, a U.S. company that sells a product in Japan, for example, would have to price that product in Japanese yen and extend credit to a Japanese wholesaler in the local currency (yen). If the yen *depreciates* against the dollar before the U.S. exporter collects on its account receivable, the U.S. company experiences an exchange rate loss; the yen collected are worth fewer dollars than expected at the time the sale was made. Of course, the dollar could just as easily depreciate against the yen, yielding an exchange rate gain to the U.S. exporter. Most companies fear the loss more than they welcome the gain.

For a major currency such as the Japanese yen, the exporter can *hedge* against this risk by using the currency futures, forward, or options markets, but it is costly to do so, particularly for relatively small amounts. If the exporter is selling to a customer in a developing country—where 40 percent of U.S. exports are now sold—there will probably be no effective instrument available for protecting against exchange rate risk at any price. This risk may be further magnified because credit standards may be much lower (and acceptable collection techniques much different) in developing countries than in the United States. Although it may seem tempting just "not to bother" with exporting, U.S. companies no longer can concede foreign markets to international rivals. These export sales, if carefully monitored and (where possible) effectively hedged against exchange rate risk, often prove to be very profitable.

Credit Terms

Credit terms are the terms of sale for customers who have been extended credit by the firm. Terms of *net 30* mean the customer has 30 days from the beginning of the credit period (typically *end of month* or *date of invoice)* to pay the full invoice amount. Some firms offer **cash discounts,** percentage deductions from the purchase price for paying within a specified time. For example, terms of *2/10 net 30* mean the customer can take a 2 percent discount from the invoice amount if the payment is made within 10 days of the beginning of the credit period or can pay the full amount of the invoice within 30 days.

A firm's business strongly influences its regular credit terms. For example, a firm selling perishable items will have very short credit terms, because its items have little long-term collateral value; a firm in a seasonal business may tailor its terms to fit the industry cycles. A firm wants its regular credit terms to conform to its industry's standards. If its terms are more restrictive than its competitors', it will lose business; if its terms are less restrictive than its competitors', it will attract poor-quality customers that probably could not pay under the standard industry terms. The bottom line is that a firm should compete on the basis of quality and price of its product and service offerings, not its credit terms. Accordingly, the firm's regular credit terms should match the industry standards, but individual customer terms should reflect the riskiness of the customer.

Cash Discount

Including a cash discount in the credit terms is a popular way to speed up collections without putting pressure on customers. The cash discount provides an incentive for customers to pay sooner. By speeding collections, the discount decreases the firm's investment in accounts receivable, but it also decreases the per-unit profit. Additionally, initiating a cash discount should reduce bad debts because customers will pay sooner, and it should increase sales volume because customers who take the discount pay a lower price for the product. Accordingly, firms that consider offering a cash discount must perform a benefit–cost analysis to determine whether extending a cash discount is profitable.

Example

MAX Company has an average collection period of 40 days (turnover = 365/40 = 9.1). In accordance with the firm's credit terms of net 30, this period is divided into 32 days until the customers place their payments in the mail (not everyone pays within 30 days) and 8 days to receive, process, and collect payments once they are mailed. MAX is considering initiating a cash discount by changing its credit terms from net 30 to 2/10 net 30. The firm expects this change to reduce the amount of time until the payments are placed in the mail, resulting in an average collection period of 25 days (turnover = 365/25 = 14.6).

As noted earlier in the EOQ example (on page 536), MAX has a raw material with current annual usage of 1,100 units. Each finished product produced requires 1 unit of this raw material at a variable cost of $1,500 per unit, incurs another $800 of variable cost in the production process, and sells for $3,000 on terms of net 30. Variable costs therefore total $2,300 ($1,500 + $800). MAX estimates that 80% of its customers will take the 2% discount and that offering the discount will increase sales of the finished product by 50 units (from 1,100 to 1,150 units) per year but will not alter its bad-debt percentage. MAX's opportunity cost of funds invested in accounts receivable is 14%. Should MAX offer the proposed cash discount? An analysis similar to that demonstrated earlier for the credit standard decision, presented in Table 13.3, shows a net loss from the cash discount of $6,640. Thus *MAX should not initiate the proposed cash discount.* However, other discounts may be advantageous.

Cash Discount Period

cash discount period
The number of days after the beginning of the credit period during which the cash discount is available.

The financial manager can change the **cash discount period,** the number of days after the beginning of the credit period during which the cash discount is available. The net effect of changes in this period is difficult to analyze because of the

TABLE 13.3   Analysis of Initiating a Cash Discount for MAX Company

Additional profit contribution from sales		
[50 units × ($3,000 − $2,300)]		$35,000
Cost of marginal investment in A/R[a]		
Average investment presently (without discount):		
$\frac{\$2,300 \times 1,100 \text{ units}}{9.1} = \frac{\$2,530,000}{9.1}$	$278,022	
Average investment with proposed cash discount:[b]		
$\frac{\$2,300 \times 1,150 \text{ units}}{14.6} = \frac{\$2,645,000}{14.6}$	181,164	
Reduction in accounts receivable investment	$96,858	
Cost savings from reduced investments in accounts receivable (0.14 × $96,858)[c]		$13,560
Cost of cash discount (0.02 × 0.80 × 1,150 × $3,000)		($55,200)
Net profit from initiation of proposed cash discount		($6,640)

[a]In analyzing the investment in accounts receivable, we use the variable cost of the product sold ($1,500 raw materials cost + $800 production cost = $2,300 per unit variable cost) instead of the sale price, because the variable cost is a better indicator of the firm's investment.

[b]The average investment in accounts receivable with the proposed cash discount is estimated to be tied up for an average of 25 days instead of the 40 days under the original terms.

[c]MAX's opportunity cost of funds is 14%.

nature of the forces involved. For example, if a firm were to increase its cash discount period by 10 days (for example, changing its credit terms from 2/10 net 30 to 2/20 net 30), the following changes would be expected to occur: (1) Sales would increase, positively affecting profit. (2) Bad-debt expenses would decrease, positively affecting profit. (3) The profit per unit would decrease as a result of more people taking the discount, negatively affecting profit.

The difficulty for the financial manager lies in assessing what impact an increase in the cash discount period would have on the firm's investment in accounts receivable. This investment will decrease because of non–discount takers now paying earlier. However, the investment in accounts receivable will increase for two reasons: (1) Discount takers will still get the discount but will pay later, and (2) new customers attracted by the new policy will result in new accounts receivable. If the firm were to decrease the cash discount period, the effects would be the opposite of those just described.

Credit Period

credit period
The number of days after the beginning of the credit period until full payment of the account is due.

Changes in the **credit period,** the number of days after the beginning of the credit period until full payment of the account is due, also affect a firm's profitability. For example, increasing a firm's credit period from net 30 days to net 45 days should increase sales, positively affecting profit. But both the investment in accounts receivable and bad-debt expenses would also increase, negatively affecting profit. The increased investment in accounts receivable would result from both more sales and generally slower pay, on average, as a result of the longer credit period. The increase in bad-debt expenses results from the fact that the longer the credit period, the more time available for a firm to fail, making it unable to pay its accounts payable. A decrease in the length of the credit period is likely to have the opposite effects. Note that the variables affected by an increase in the credit period behave in the same way they would have if the credit standards had been relaxed, as demonstrated earlier in Table 13.2.

Credit Monitoring

credit monitoring
The ongoing review of a firm's accounts receivable to determine whether customers are paying according to the stated credit terms.

The final issue a firm should consider in its accounts receivable management is credit monitoring. **Credit monitoring** is an ongoing review of the firm's accounts receivable to determine whether customers are paying according to the stated credit terms. If they are not paying in a timely manner, credit monitoring will alert the firm to the problem. Slow payments are costly to a firm because they lengthen the average collection period and thus increase the firm's investment in accounts receivable. Two frequently used techniques for credit monitoring are average collection period and aging of accounts receivable. In addition, a number of popular collection techniques are used by firms.

Average Collection Period

The *average collection period* is the second component of the cash conversion cycle. As noted in Chapter 2, it is the average number of days that credit sales are outstanding. The average collection period has two components: (1) the time from sale until the customer places the payment in the mail and (2) the time to receive, process, and collect the payment once it has been mailed by the customer. The formula for finding the average collection period is

$$\text{Average collection period} = \frac{\text{Accounts receivable}}{\text{Average sales per day}} \tag{13.10}$$

Assuming receipt, processing, and collection time is constant, the average collection period tells the firm, on average, when its customers pay their accounts.

Knowing its average collection period enables the firm to determine whether there is a general problem with accounts receivable. For example, a firm that has credit terms of net 30 would expect its average collection period (minus receipt, processing, and collection time) to equal about 30 days. If the actual collection period is significantly greater than 30 days, the firm has reason to review its credit operations. If the firm's average collection period is increasing over time, it has cause for concern about its accounts receivable management. A first step in analyzing an accounts receivable problem is to "age" the accounts receivable. By this process the firm can determine whether the problem exists in its accounts receivable in general or is attributable to a few specific accounts.

Aging of Accounts Receivable

aging schedule
A credit-monitoring technique that breaks down accounts receivable into groups on the basis of their time of origin; it indicates the percentages of the total accounts receivable balance that have been outstanding for specified periods of time.

An **aging schedule** breaks down accounts receivable into groups on the basis of their time of origin. The breakdown is typically made on a month-by-month basis, going back 3 or 4 months. The resulting schedule indicates the percentages of the total accounts receivable balance that have been outstanding for specified periods of time. The purpose of the aging schedule is to enable the firm to pinpoint problems. A simple example will illustrate the form and evaluation of an aging schedule.

Example

The accounts receivable balance on the books of Dodd Tool on December 31, 2009, was $200,000. The firm extends net 30-day credit terms to its customers. To gain insight into the firm's relatively lengthy—51.3-day—average collection period, Dodd prepared the following aging schedule.

Age of account	Balance outstanding	Percentage of total balance outstanding
0–30 days	$ 80,000	40%
31–60 days	36,000	18
61–90 days	52,000	26
91–120 days	26,000	13
Over 120 days	6,000	3
Totals at 12/31/09	$200,000	100%

Because Dodd extends 30-day credit terms to its customers, they have 30 days after the end of the month of sale to remit payment. Therefore, the 40% of the balance outstanding with an age of 0–30 days is *current*. The balances outstanding for 31–60 days, 61–90 days, 91–120 days, and over 120 days are *overdue*.

Reviewing the aging schedule, we see that 40% of the accounts are current (age < 30 days) and the remaining 60% are overdue (age > 30 days). Eighteen percent of the balance outstanding is 1–30 days overdue, 26% is 31–60 days overdue, 13% is 61–90 days overdue, and 3% is more than 90 days overdue. Although the collections seem generally slow, a noticeable irregularity in these data is the high percentage of the balance outstanding that is 31–60 days overdue (ages of 61–90 days). Clearly, a problem must have occurred 61–90 days ago. Investigation may find that the problem can be attributed to the hiring of a new credit manager, the acceptance of a new account that made a large credit purchase but has not yet paid for it, or ineffective collection policy. When these types of discrepancies are found in the aging schedule, the analyst should determine, evaluate, and remedy its cause.

Popular Collection Techniques

A number of collection techniques, ranging from letters to legal action, are employed. As an account becomes more and more overdue, the collection effort becomes more personal and more intense. In Table 13.4 the popular collection techniques are listed, and briefly described, in the order typically followed in the collection process.

REVIEW QUESTIONS

13–11 What is the role of the *five C's of credit* in the credit selection activity?

13–12 Explain why *credit scoring* is typically applied to consumer credit decisions rather than to mercantile credit decisions.

13–13 What are the basic tradeoffs in a *tightening* of credit standards?

TABLE 13.4	**Popular Collection Techniques**
Technique[a]	Brief description
Letters	After a certain number of days, the firm sends a polite letter reminding the customer of the overdue account. If the account is not paid within a certain period after this letter has been sent, a second, more demanding letter is sent.
Telephone calls	If letters prove unsuccessful, a telephone call may be made to the customer to request immediate payment. If the customer has a reasonable excuse, arrangements may be made to extend the payment period. A call from the seller's attorney may be used.
Personal visits	This technique is much more common at the consumer credit level, but it may also be effectively employed by industrial suppliers. Sending a local salesperson or a collection person to confront the customer can be very effective. Payment may be made on the spot.
Collection agencies	A firm can turn uncollectible accounts over to a collection agency or an attorney for collection. The fees for this service are typically quite high; the firm may receive less than 50 cents on the dollar from accounts collected in this way.
Legal action	Legal action is the most stringent step, an alternative to the use of a collection agency. Not only is direct legal action expensive, but it may force the debtor into bankruptcy without guaranteeing the ultimate receipt of the overdue amount.

[a]The techniques are listed in the order in which they are typically followed in the collection process.

13–14 Why are the risks involved in international credit management more complex than those associated with purely domestic credit sales?

13–15 Why do a firm's regular credit terms typically conform to those of its industry?

13–16 Why should a firm actively monitor the accounts receivable of its credit customers? How are the *average collection period* and an *aging schedule* used for credit monitoring?

13.5 | Management of Receipts and Disbursements

Hint The financial manager of a small business should maintain a strong relationship with a commercial banker. Because the small firm cannot afford to hire someone strictly as a manager of receipts and disbursements, the financial manager, who is probably a generalist, needs to rely on the expertise of the commercial banker for the firm's most cost-effective means of managing cash.

As discussed in the previous section, the average collection period (the second component of the cash conversion cycle) has two parts: (1) the time from sale until the customer mails the payment and (2) the receipt, processing, and collection time. The third component of the cash conversion cycle, the average payment period, also has two parts: (1) the time from purchase of goods on account until the firm mails its payment and (2) the receipt, processing, and collection time required by the firm's suppliers. The receipt, processing, and collection time for the firm, both from its customers and to its suppliers, is the focus of receipts and disbursements management.

Float

float
Funds that have been sent by the payer but are not yet usable funds to the payee.

mail float
The time delay between when payment is placed in the mail and when it is received.

processing float
The time between receipt of a payment and its deposit into the firm's account.

clearing float
The time between deposit of a payment and when spendable funds become available to the firm.

Float refers to funds that have been sent by the payer but are not yet usable funds to the payee. Float is important in the cash conversion cycle because its presence lengthens both the firm's average collection period and its average payment period. However, the goal of the firm should be to shorten its average collection period and lengthen its average payment period. Both can be accomplished by managing float.

Float has three component parts:

1. **Mail float** is the time delay between when payment is placed in the mail and when it is received.
2. **Processing float** is the time between receipt of the payment and its deposit into the firm's account.
3. **Clearing float** is the time between deposit of the payment and when spendable funds become available to the firm. This component of float is attributable to the time required for a check to clear the banking system.

Some popular techniques for managing the component parts of float to speed up collections and slow down payments are described here.

Hint One method of accelerating the collection of accounts receivable is to let someone else do the financing for you, such as by using bank credit cards or selling accounts receivable to a third party at a discount. Another method is to change the credit terms: Increase the cash discount and shorten the required payment period.

Speeding Up Collections

Speeding up collections reduces customer *collection float* time and thus reduces the firm's average collection period, which reduces the investment the firm must make in its cash conversion cycle. In our earlier examples, MAX Company had annual sales of $10 million and 8 days of total collection float (receipt, processing, and collection time). If MAX can reduce its float time by 3 days, it will reduce its investment in the cash conversion cycle by $82,192 [$10,000,000 × (3/365)].

A popular technique for speeding up collections is a lockbox system. A **lockbox system** works as follows: Instead of mailing payments to the company, customers mail payments to a post office box. The firm's bank empties the post office box regularly, processes each payment, and deposits the payments in the firm's account. Deposit slips, along with payment enclosures, are sent (or transmitted electronically) to the firm by the bank so that the firm can properly credit customers' accounts. Lockboxes are geographically dispersed to match the locations of the firm's customers. A lockbox system affects all three components of float. Lockboxes reduce mail time and often clearing time by being near the firm's customers. Lockboxes reduce processing time to nearly zero because the bank deposits payments before the firm processes them. Obviously a lockbox system reduces collection float time, but not without a cost; therefore, a firm must perform an economic analysis to determine whether to implement a lockbox system.

Lockbox systems are commonly used by large firms whose customers are geographically dispersed. However, a firm does not have to be large to benefit from a lockbox. Smaller firms can also benefit from a lockbox system. The benefit to small firms often comes primarily from transferring the processing of payments to the bank.

Slowing Down Payments

Float is also a component of the firm's average payment period. In this case, the float is in the favor of the firm. The firm may benefit by increasing all three of the components of its *payment float*. One popular technique for increasing payment float is **controlled disbursing**, which involves the strategic use of mailing points and bank accounts to lengthen mail float and clearing float, respectively. Firms must use this approach carefully, though, because longer payment periods may strain supplier relations.

The *Focus on Ethics* box on page 550 takes a closer look at the ethical issues involved in slowing down payments through controlled disbursing and other methods—a technique known collectively as *stretching accounts payable*. This is a topic we will come back to in Chapter 14.

In summary, a reasonable overall policy for float management is (1) to collect payments as quickly as possible, because once the payment is in the mail, the funds belong to the firm, and (2) to delay making payment to suppliers, because once the payment is mailed, the funds belong to the supplier.

Cash Concentration

Cash concentration is the process used by the firm to bring lockbox and other deposits together into one bank, often called the *concentration bank*. Cash concentration has three main advantages. First, it creates a large pool of funds for use in making short-term cash investments. Because there is a fixed-cost component in the transaction cost associated with such investments, investing a single pool of funds reduces the firm's transaction costs. The larger investment pool also

lockbox system A collection procedure in which customers mail payments to a post office box that is emptied regularly by the firm's bank, which processes the payments and deposits them in the firm's account. This system speeds up collection time by reducing processing time as well as mail and clearing time.

controlled disbursing The strategic use of mailing points and bank accounts to lengthen mail float and clearing float, respectively.

Hint Data on clearing times among banks located in various cities can be developed by the firm itself. They also can be obtained from a major bank's cash management service department or purchased from a firm that sells such information.

cash concentration The process used by the firm to bring lockbox and other deposits together into one bank, often called the *concentration bank.*

Focus on Ethics   Stretching Accounts Payable—Is It a Good Policy?

Stretching payables has often been considered good cash management. By delaying bill payments as long as possible without damaging the firm's credit, companies get interest-free loans from suppliers. Other businesses deliberately increase their accounts payable lag to cover temporary cash shortages.

There are two negative ramifications of stretching accounts payables (A/P). First, the stretching out of payables can be pushed too far, and a business can get tagged as a slow-payer. Vendors will eventually put increasing pressure on the company to make more timely payments.

Stretching accounts payables also raises ethical issues. First, it may cause the firm to violate the agreement it entered with its supplier when it purchased the merchandise. More important to investors, the firm may stretch A/P to artificially boost reported operating cash flow during a reporting period. In other words, firms can improve reported operating cash flows due solely to a decision to slow the payment

rate to vendors. Unfortunately for investors, the improvement in operating cash flows may be unsustainable if vendors force the company to improve its payment record; at a minimum, any year-over-year improvement in operating cash flow may be unsustainable.

The extension of payables can be identified by monitoring *days sales payables* (DSP), calculated as the end-of-period accounts payable balance divided by the cost of goods sold and multiplied by the number of days in the period. As DSP grows, operating cash flows are boosted.

A more complicated version of stretching payables is the financing of payables. This occurs when a company uses a third-party financial institution to pay the vendor in the current period and pays back the bank in a subsequent period. This approach reclassifies the amount from accounts payable to short-term loans. The reclassification results in a decrease to operating cash flow in that quarter and an increase in financing cash flow. Normally, cash expenditures for

accounts payable are included in operating activities. Because the timing and extent of vendor financing is at the discretion of company management, the temptation to manipulate operating cash flows may prove too great for some.

Setting aside the ethical ramifications of stretching accounts payable, there may be financial incentives for avoiding the practice. Companies that can move to an automated A/P system may be able to take advantage of beneficial early payment discounts that provide a far better risk-free rate of return than stretching out accounts payable. For example, a 2/10 net 30 discount equates to about a 36 percent annualized return. Viewed this way, an A/P balance may be the most expensive debt on the balance sheet.

■ *While vendor discounts for early payment are very rewarding, what are some of the difficulties that may arise to keep a firm from taking advantage of those discounts?*

allows the firm to choose from a greater variety of short-term investment vehicles. Second, concentrating the firm's cash in one account improves the tracking and internal control of the firm's cash. Third, having one concentration bank enables the firm to implement payment strategies that reduce idle cash balances.

There are a variety of mechanisms for transferring cash from the lockbox bank and other collecting banks to the concentration bank. One mechanism is a **depository transfer check (DTC)**, which is an unsigned check drawn on one of the firm's bank accounts and deposited in another. For cash concentration, a DTC is drawn on each lockbox or other collecting bank account and deposited in the concentration bank account. Once the DTC has cleared the bank on which it is drawn (which may take several days), the transfer of funds is completed. Most

depository transfer check (DTC)
An unsigned check drawn on one of a firm's bank accounts and deposited in another.

firms currently provide deposit information by telephone to the concentration bank, which then prepares and deposits into its account the DTC drawn on the lockbox or other collecting bank account.

A second mechanism is an **ACH (automated clearinghouse) transfer,** which is a preauthorized electronic withdrawal from the payer's account. A computerized clearing facility (called the *automated clearinghouse,* or *ACH*) makes a paperless transfer of funds between the payer and payee banks. An ACH settles accounts among participating banks. Individual accounts are settled by respective bank balance adjustments. ACH transfers clear in one day. For cash concentration, an ACH transfer is made from each lockbox bank or other collecting bank to the concentration bank. An ACH transfer can be thought of as an electronic DTC, but because the ACH transfer clears in one day, it provides benefits over a DTC; however, both banks in the ACH transfer must be members of the clearinghouse.

A third cash concentration mechanism is a **wire transfer.** A wire transfer is an electronic communication that, via bookkeeping entries, removes funds from the payer's bank and deposits them in the payee's bank. Wire transfers can eliminate mail and clearing float and may reduce processing float as well. For cash concentration, the firm moves funds using a wire transfer from each lockbox or other collecting account to its concentration account. Wire transfers are a substitute for DTC and ACH transfers, but they are more expensive.

It is clear that the firm must balance the costs and benefits of concentrating cash to determine the type and timing of transfers from its lockbox and other collecting accounts to its concentration account. The transfer mechanism selected should be the one that is most profitable. (The profit per period of any transfer mechanism equals earnings on the increased availability of funds minus the cost of the transfer system.)

Zero-Balance Accounts

Zero-balance accounts (ZBAs) are disbursement accounts that always have an end-of-day balance of zero. The purpose is to eliminate nonearning cash balances in corporate checking accounts. A ZBA works well as a disbursement account under a cash concentration system.

ZBAs work as follows: Once all of a given day's checks are presented for payment from the firm's ZBA, the bank notifies the firm of the total amount of checks, and the firm transfers funds into the account to cover the amount of that day's checks. This leaves an end-of-day balance of $0 (zero dollars). The ZBA enables the firm to keep all of its operating cash in an interest-earning account, thereby eliminating idle cash balances. Thus a firm that used a ZBA in conjunction with a cash concentration system would need two accounts. The firm would concentrate its cash from the lockboxes and other collecting banks into an interest-earning account and would write checks against its ZBA. The firm would cover the exact dollar amount of checks presented against the ZBA with transfers from the interest-earning account, leaving the end-of-day balance in the ZBA at $0.

A ZBA is a disbursement-management tool. As we discussed earlier, the firm would prefer to maximize its payment float. However, some cash managers feel that actively attempting to increase float time on payments is unethical. A ZBA enables the firm to maximize the use of float on each check without altering the

---

ACH (automated clearinghouse) transfer
Preauthorized electronic withdrawal from the payer's account and deposit into the payee's account via a settlement among banks by the *automated clearinghouse,* or *ACH.*

wire transfer
An electronic communication that, via bookkeeping entries, removes funds from the payer's bank and deposits them in the payee's bank.

zero-balance account (ZBA)
A disbursement account that always has an end-of-day balance of zero because the firm deposits money to cover checks drawn on the account only as they are presented for payment each day.

float time of payments to its suppliers. Keeping all the firm's cash in an interest-earning account enables the firm to maximize earnings on its cash balances by capturing the full float time on each check it writes.

Personal Finance Example   Megan Laurie, a 25-year-old nurse, works at a hospital that pays her every 2 weeks by direct deposit into her checking account, which pays no interest and has no minimum balance requirement. She takes home about $1,800 every 2 weeks—or about $3,600 per month. She maintains a checking account balance of around $1,500. Whenever it exceeds that amount she transfers the excess into her savings account, which currently pays 1.5% annual interest. She currently has a savings account balance of $17,000 and estimates that she transfers about $600 per month from her checking account into her savings account.

Megan pays her bills immediately when she receives them. Her monthly bills average about $1,900, and her monthly cash outlays for food and gas total about $900. An analysis of Megan's bill payments indicates that on average she pays her bills 8 days early. Most marketable securities are currently yielding about 4.2% annual interest. Megan is interested in learning how she might better manage her cash balances.

Megan talks with her sister, who has had a finance course, and they come up with three ways for Megan to better manage her cash balance:

1. **Invest current balances.** Megan can transfer her current savings account balances into a liquid marketable security, thereby increasing the rate of interest earned from 1.5% to about 4.2%. On her current $17,000 balance, she will immediately increase her annual interest earnings by about $460 [(0.042 − 0.015) × $17,000].
2. **Invest monthly surpluses.** Megan can transfer monthly the $600 from her checking account to the liquid marketable security, thereby increasing the annual earnings on each monthly transfer by about $16 [(0.042 − 0.015) × $600], which for the 12 transfers would generate additional annual earnings of about $192 (12 months × $16).
3. **Slow down payments.** Rather than paying her bills immediately upon receipt, Megan can pay her bills nearer their due date. By doing this she can gain 8 days of disbursement float each month, or 96 days per year (8 days per month × 12 months), on an average of $1,900 of bills. Assuming she can earn 4.2% annual interest on the $1,900, slowing down her payments would save about $21 annually [(96/365) × 0.042 × $1,900].

Based on these three recommendations, Megan would increase her annual earnings by a total of about $673 ($460 + $192 + $21). Clearly, Megan can grow her earnings by better managing her cash balances.

Investing in Marketable Securities

Marketable securities are short-term, interest-earning, money market instruments that can easily be converted into cash.[6] Marketable securities are classified as part of the firm's liquid assets. The firm uses them to earn a return on temporarily idle

---

6. As explained in Chapter 1, the *money market* results from a financial relationship between the suppliers and demanders of short-term funds, that is, marketable securities.

funds. To be truly marketable, a security must have (1) a ready market so as to minimize the amount of time required to convert it into cash, and (2) safety of principal, which means that it experiences little or no loss in value over time.

The securities that are most commonly held as part of the firm's marketable-securities portfolio are divided into two groups: (1) government issues, which have relatively low yields as a consequence of their low risk, and (2) nongovernment issues, which have slightly higher yields than government issues with similar maturities because of the slightly higher risk associated with them. Table 13.5 (see page 554) summarizes the key features and recent (July 23, 2007) yields for popular marketable securities.

REVIEW QUESTIONS

13–17 What is *float* and what are its three components?

13–18 What are the firm's objectives with regard to *collection float* and to *payment float?*

13–19 What are the three main advantages of *cash concentration?*

13–20 What are three mechanisms of cash concentration? What is the objective of using a *zero-balance account (ZBA)* in a cash concentration system?

13–21 What two characteristics make a security marketable? Why are the yields on nongovernment marketable securities generally higher than the yields on government issues with similar maturities?

Summary

Focus on Value

It is important for a firm to maintain a reasonable level of net working capital. To do so, it must balance the high profit and high risk associated with low levels of current assets and high levels of current liabilities against the low profit and low risk that result from high levels of current assets and low levels of current liabilities. A strategy that achieves a reasonable balance between profits and risk should positively contribute to the firm's value.

Similarly, the firm should manage its cash conversion cycle by turning inventory quickly; collecting accounts receivable quickly; managing mail, processing, and clearing time; and paying accounts payable slowly. These strategies should enable the firm to manage its current accounts efficiently and to minimize the amount of resources invested in operating assets.

The financial manager can manage inventory, accounts receivable, and cash receipts to minimize the firm's operating cycle investment, thereby reducing the amount of resources needed to support its business. Employing these strategies, and managing accounts payable and cash disbursements so as to shorten the cash conversion cycle, should minimize the negotiated liabilities needed to support the firm's resource requirements. Active management of the firm's net working capital and current assets should positively contribute to the firm's goal of **maximizing its stock price.**

TABLE 13.5   Features and Recent Yields on Popular Marketable Securities[a]

Security	Issuer	Description	Initial maturity	Risk and return	Yield on July 23, 2007[b]
Government Issues					
Treasury bills	U.S. Treasury	Issued weekly at auction; sold at a discount; strong secondary market	4, 13, and 26 weeks	Lowest, virtually risk-free	4.97%
Treasury notes	U.S. Treasury	Stated interest rate; interest paid semiannually; strong secondary market	1 to 10 years	Low, but slightly higher than U.S. Treasury bills	5.03%
Federal agency issues	Agencies of federal goverment	Not an obligation of U.S. Treasury; strong secondary market	9 months to 30 years	Slightly higher than U.S. Treasury issues	5.17%[c]
Nongovernment Issues					
Negotiable certificates of deposit (CDs)	Commercial banks	Represent specific cash deposits in commercial banks; amounts and maturities tailored to investor needs; large denominations; good secondary market	1 month to 3 years	Higher than U.S. Treasury issues and comparable to commercial paper	4.95%
Commercial paper	Corporation with a high credit standing	Unsecured note of issuer; large denominations	3 to 270 days	Higher than U.S. Treasury issues and comparable to negotiable CDs	5.23%
Banker's acceptances	Banks	Results from a bank guarantee of a business transaction; sold at discount from maturity value	30 to 180 days	About the same as negotiable CDs and commercial paper but higher than U.S. Treasury issues	5.31%
Eurodollar deposits	Foreign banks	Deposits of currency not native to the country in which the bank is located; large denominations; active secondary market	1 day to 3 years	High, due to less regulation of despository banks and some foreign exchange risk	5.36%
Money market mutual funds	Professional portfolio management companies	Professionally managed portfolios of marketable securities; provide instant liquidity	None—depends on wishes of investor	Vary, but generally higher than U.S. Treasury issues and comparable to negotiable CDs and commercial paper	4.98%[d]
Repurchase agreements	Bank or security dealer	Bank or security dealer sells specific securities to firm and agrees to repurchase them at a specific price and time	Customized to purchaser's needs	Generally slightly below that associated with the outright purchase of the security	5.13%

[a]The prime rate of interest at this time was 8.25%.

[b]Yields obtained for 3-month maturities of each security.

[c]Federal National Mortgage Association (Fannie Mae) issue with 3 months to maturity is used here.

[d]Fidelity Cash Reserves Fund with an average maturity of 51 days is used here in the absence of any average-yield data.

Source: Wall Street Journal, July 24, 2007, p. C6.

Review of Learning Goals

LG 1 **Understand short-term financial management, net working capital, and the related tradeoff between profitability and risk.** Short-term financial management focuses on managing each of the firm's current assets (inventory, accounts receivable, cash, and marketable securities) and current liabilities (accounts payable, accruals, and notes payable) in a manner that positively contributes to the firm's value. Net working capital is the difference between current assets and current liabilities. Risk, in the context of short-term financial decisions, is the probability that a firm will be unable to pay its bills as they come due. Assuming a constant level of total assets, the higher a firm's ratio of current assets to total assets, the less profitable the firm, and the less risky it is. The converse is also true. With constant total assets, the higher a firm's ratio of current liabilities to total assets, the more profitable and the more risky the firm is. The converse of this statement is also true.

LG 2 **Describe the cash conversion cycle, its funding requirements, and the key strategies for managing it.** The cash conversion cycle has three components: (1) average age of inventory, (2) average collection period, and (3) average payment period. The length of the cash conversion cycle determines the amount of time resources are tied up in the firm's day-to-day operations. The firm's investment in short-term assets often consists of both permanent and seasonal funding requirements. The seasonal requirements can be financed using either an aggressive (low-cost, high-risk) financing strategy or a conservative (high-cost, low-risk) financing strategy. The firm's funding decision for its cash conversion cycle ultimately depends on management's disposition toward risk and the strength of the firm's banking relationships. To minimize its reliance on negotiated liabilities, the financial manager seeks to (1) turn over inventory as quickly as possible, (2) collect accounts receivable as quickly as possible, (3) manage mail, processing, and clearing time, and (4) pay accounts payable as slowly as possible. Use of these strategies should minimize the length of the cash conversion cycle.

LG 3 **Discuss inventory management: differing views, common techniques, and international concerns.** The viewpoints of marketing, manufacturing, and purchasing managers about the appropriate levels of inventory tend to cause higher inventories than those deemed appropriate by the financial manager. Four commonly used techniques for effectively managing inventory to keep its level low are (1) the ABC system, (2) the economic order quantity (EOQ) model, (3) the just-in-time (JIT) system, and (4) computerized systems for resource control—MRP, MRP II, and ERP. International inventory managers place greater emphasis on making sure that sufficient quantities of inventory are delivered where and when needed, and in the right condition, than on ordering the economically optimal quantities.

LG 4 **Explain the credit selection process and the quantitative procedure for evaluating changes in credit standards.** Credit selection techniques determine which customers' creditworthiness is consistent with the firm's credit standards. Two popular credit selection techniques are the five C's of credit and credit scoring. Changes in credit standards can be evaluated mathematically by assessing the effects of a proposed change on profits from sales, the cost of accounts receivable investment, and bad-debt costs.

LG 5 **Review the procedures for quantitatively considering cash discount changes, other aspects of credit terms, and credit monitoring.** Changes in credit terms—the cash discount, the cash discount period, and the credit period—can be quantified similarly to changes in credit standards. Credit monitoring, the ongoing review of accounts receivable, frequently involves use of the average collection period and an aging schedule. Firms use a number of popular collection techniques.

LG 6 **Understand the management of receipts and disbursements, including float, speeding up collections, slowing down payments, cash concentration, zero-balance accounts, and investing in marketable securities.** Float refers to funds that have been sent by the payer but are not yet usable funds to the payee. The components of float are mail time, processing time, and clearing time. Float occurs in both the average collection period and the average payment period. One technique for speeding up collections is a lockbox system. A popular technique for slowing payments is controlled disbursing.

The goal for managing operating cash is to balance the opportunity cost of nonearning balances against the transaction cost of temporary investments. Firms commonly use depository transfer checks (DTCs), ACH transfers, and wire transfers to transfer lockbox receipts to their concentration banks quickly. Zero-balance accounts (ZBAs) can be used to eliminate nonearning cash balances in corporate checking accounts. Marketable securities are short-term, interest-earning, money market instruments used by the firm to earn a return on temporarily idle funds. They may be government or nongovernment issues.

Self-Test Problems (Solutions in Appendix B)

 ST13–1 **Cash conversion cycle** Hurkin Manufacturing Company pays accounts payable on the tenth day after purchase. The average collection period is 30 days, and the average age of inventory is 40 days. The firm currently has annual sales of about $18 million. The firm is considering a plan that would stretch its accounts payable by 20 days. If the firm pays 12% per year for its resource investment, what annual savings can it realize by this plan? Assume no difference in the investment per dollar of sales in inventory, receivables, and payables; no discount for early payment of accounts payable; and a 365-day year.

 ST13–2 **EOQ analysis** Thompson Paint Company uses 60,000 gallons of pigment per year. The cost of ordering pigment is $200 per order, and the cost of carrying the pigment in inventory is $1 per gallon per year. The firm uses pigment at a constant rate every day throughout the year.
a. Calculate the EOQ.
b. Assuming that it takes 20 days to receive an order once it has been placed, determine the reorder point in terms of gallons of pigment. *(Note:* Use a 365-day year.)

ST13–3 **Relaxing credit standards**   Regency Rug Repair Company is trying to decide whether it should relax its credit standards. The firm repairs 72,000 rugs per year at an average price of $32 each. Bad-debt expenses are 1% of sales, the average collection period is 40 days, and the variable cost per unit is $28. Regency expects that if it does relax its credit standards, the average collection period will increase to 48 days and that bad debts will increase to 1½% of sales. Sales will increase by 4,000 repairs per year. If the firm has a required rate of return on equal-risk investments of 14%, what recommendation would you give the firm? Use your analysis to justify your answer. (*Note:* Use a 365-day year.)

Warm-Up Exercises   A blue box (■) indicates exercises available in .

 E13–1   Sharam Industries has a 120-day *operating cycle*. If its average age of inventory is 50 days, how long is its average collection period? If its average payment period is 30 days, what is its *cash conversion cycle?* Place all of this information on a time line similar to Figure 13.1 on page 529.

 E13–2   Icy Treats, Inc., is a seasonal business that sells frozen desserts. At the peak of its summer selling season the firm has $35,000 in cash, $125,000 in inventory, $70,000 in accounts receivable, and $65,000 in accounts payable. During the slow winter period the firm holds $10,000 in cash, $55,000 in inventory, $40,000 in accounts receivable, and $35,000 in accounts payable. Calculate Icy Treats' minimum and peak funding requirements.

 E13–3   Mama Leone's Frozen Pizzas uses 50,000 units of cheese per year. Each unit costs $2.50. The ordering cost for the cheese is $250 per order, and its carrying cost is $0.50 per unit per year. Calculate the firm's *economic order quantity (EOQ)* for the cheese. Mama Leone's operates 250 days per year and maintains a minimum inventory level of 2 days' worth of cheese as a safety stock. If the lead time to receive orders of cheese is 3 days, calculate the *reorder point*.

 E13–4   Forrester Fashions has annual credit sales of 250,000 units with an average collection period of 70 days. The company has a per-unit variable cost of $20 and a per-unit sale price of $30. Bad debts currently are 5% of sales. The firm estimates that a proposed relaxation of credit standards would not affect its 70-day average collection period, but would increase bad debts to 7.5% of sales, which would increase to 300,000 units per year. Forrester requires a 12% return on investments. Show all necessary calculations required to evaluate Forrester's proposed relaxation of credit standards.

 E13–5   Klein's Tools is considering offering a cash discount to speed up the collection of accounts receivable. Currently the firm has an average collection period of 65 days, annual sales are 35,000 units, the per-unit price is $40, and the per-unit variable cost is $29. A 2% cash discount is being considered. Klein's Tools estimates that 80% of its customers will take the 2% discount. If sales are expected to rise to 37,000 units per year and the firm has a 15% required rate of return, what minimum average collection period is required to approve the cash discount plan?

Problems   A blue box (■) indicates problems available in myfinancelab .

P13–1 **Cash conversion cycle**   American Products is concerned about managing cash efficiently. On the average, inventories have an age of 90 days, and accounts receivable are collected in 60 days. Accounts payable are paid approximately 30 days after they arise. The firm has annual sales of about $30 million. Assume there is no difference in the investment per dollar of sales in inventory, receivables, and payables; and a 365-day year.
a. Calculate the firm's *operating cycle*.
b. Calculate the firm's *cash conversion cycle*.
c. Calculate the amount of resources needed to support the firm's cash conversion cycle.
d. Discuss how management might be able to reduce the cash conversion cycle.

P13–2 **Changing cash conversion cycle**   Camp Manufacturing turns over its inventory 8 times each year, has an average payment period of 35 days, and has an average collection period of 60 days. The firm's annual sales are $3.5 million. Assume there is no difference in the investment per dollar of sales in inventory, receivables, and payables; and a 365-day year.
a. Calculate the firm's *operating cycle* and *cash conversion cycle*.
b. Calculate the firm's daily cash operating expenditure. How much in resources must be invested to support its cash conversion cycle?
c. If the firm pays 14% for these resources, by how much would it increase its annual profits by *favorably* changing its current cash conversion cycle by 20 days?

P13–3 **Multiple changes in cash conversion cycle**   Garrett Industries turns over its inventory 6 times each year; it has an average collection period of 45 days and an average payment period of 30 days. The firm's annual sales are $3 million. Assume there is no difference in the investment per dollar of sales in inventory, receivables, and payables; and a 365-day year.
a. Calculate the firm's *cash conversion cycle*, its daily cash operating expenditure, and the amount of resources needed to support its cash conversion cycle.
b. Find the firm's cash conversion cycle and resource investment requirement if it makes the following changes simultaneously.
    (1) Shortens the average age of inventory by 5 days.
    (2) Speeds the collection of accounts receivable by an average of 10 days.
    (3) Extends the average payment period by 10 days.
c. If the firm pays 13% for its resource investment, by how much, if anything, could it increase its annual profit as a result of the changes in part **b**?
d. If the annual cost of achieving the profit in part **c** is $35,000, what action would you recommend to the firm? Why?

P13–4 **Aggressive versus conservative seasonal funding strategy**   Dynabase Tool has forecast its total funds requirements for the coming year as shown in the following table.

Month	Amount	Month	Amount
January	$2,000,000	July	$12,000,000
February	2,000,000	August	14,000,000
March	2,000,000	September	9,000,000
April	4,000,000	October	5,000,000
May	6,000,000	November	4,000,000
June	9,000,000	December	3,000,000

a. Divide the firm's monthly funds requirement into (1) a *permanent* component and (2) a *seasonal* component, and find the monthly average for each of these components.

b. Describe the amount of long-term and short-term financing used to meet the total funds requirement under (1) an *aggressive funding strategy* and (2) a *conservative funding strategy.* Assume that under the aggressive strategy, long-term funds finance permanent needs and short-term funds are used to finance seasonal needs.

c. Assuming that short-term funds cost 12% annually and that the cost of long-term funds is 17% annually, use the averages found in part **a** to calculate the total cost of each of the strategies described in part **b.**

d. Discuss the profitability–risk tradeoffs associated with the aggressive strategy and those associated with the conservative strategy.

LG 3 **P13–5** **EOQ analysis**   Tiger Corporation purchases 1,200,000 units per year of one component. The fixed cost per order is $25. The annual carrying cost of the item is 27% of its $2 cost.

a. Determine the EOQ under each of the following conditions: (1) no changes, (2) order cost of zero, and (3) carrying cost of zero.

b. What do your answers illustrate about the EOQ model? Explain.

LG 3 **P13–6** **EOQ, reorder point, and safety stock**   Alexis Company uses 800 units of a product per year on a continuous basis. The product has a fixed cost of $50 per order, and its carrying cost is $2 per unit per year. It takes 5 days to receive a shipment after an order is placed, and the firm wishes to hold 10 days' usage in inventory as a safety stock.

a. Calculate the EOQ.

b. Determine the average level of inventory. *(Note:* Use a 365-day year to calculate daily usage.)

c. Determine the *reorder point.*

d. Indicate which of the following variables change if the firm does not hold the safety stock: (1) order cost, (2) carrying cost, (3) total inventory cost, (4) reorder point, (5) economic order quantity. Explain.

PERSONAL FINANCE PROBLEM

LG 3 **P13–7** **Marginal costs**   Jimmy Johnson is interested in buying a new Jeep SUV. There are two options available, a V-6 model and a V-8 model. Whichever model he chooses, he plans to drive it for a period of 5 years and then sell it. Assume that the trade-in value of the two vehicles at the end of the 5-year ownership period will be identical.

There are definite differences between the two models and Jimmy needs to make a financial comparison. The manufacturer's suggested retail price (MSRP) of the V-6 and V-8 are $30,260 and $44,320, respectively. Jimmy believes the difference of $14,060 to be the marginal cost difference between the two vehicles. However, there is much more data available, and you suggest to Jimmy that his analysis may be too simple and will lead him to a poor financial decision. Assume that the prevailing discount rate for both vehicles is 5.5% annually. Other pertinent information on this purchase is shown in the following table:

	V-6	V-8
MSRP	$30,260	$44,320
Engine (liters)	3.7	5.7
Cylinders	6	8
Depreciation over 5 years	$17,337	$25,531
Finance charges* over entire 5-year period	$5,171	$7,573
Insurance over 5 years	$7,546	$8,081
Taxes and fees over 5 years	$2,179	$2,937
Maintenance/repairs over 5 years	$5,600	$5,600
Average miles per gallon	19	14
Ownership period in years	5	5
Miles driven per year over 5 years	15,000	15,000
Cost per gallon of gas over 5 year ownership	$3.15	$3.15

*The finance charges are the difference between the total principal and interest paid over the entire 5-year period less the actual cost of the SUV. Assuming an annual 5.5% discount rate over each of the 5 years and the respective present values of $30,260 for the V-6 and $44,320 for the V-8, the annual annuity payments are $7,086.20 and $10,379.70, respectively. [V-6: $(5 \times \$7,086.20) - \$30,260 = \$5,171$, and V-8: $(5 \times \$10,379.70) - \$44,320 = \$7,573$]

a. Calculate the total "true" cost for each vehicle over the 5-year ownership period.
b. Calculate the total fuel cost for each vehicle over the 5-year ownership period.
c. What is the marginal fuel cost from purchasing the larger V-8 SUV?
d. What is the marginal cost of purchasing the larger and more expensive V-8 SUV?
e. What is the total marginal cost associated with purchasing the V-8 SUV? How does this figure compare with the $14,060 that Jimmy calculated?

 P13–8 **Accounts receivable changes without bad debts**   Tara's Textiles currently has credit sales of $360 million per year and an average collection period of 60 days. Assume that the price of Tara's products is $60 per unit and that the variable costs are $55 per unit. The firm is considering an accounts receivable change that will result in a 20% increase in sales and a 20% increase in the average collection period. No change in bad debts is expected. The firm's equal-risk opportunity cost on its investment in accounts receivable is 14%. (*Note:* Use a 365-day year.)

a. Calculate the *additional profit contribution from sales* that the firm will realize if it makes the proposed change.
b. What *marginal investment in accounts receivable* will result?
c. Calculate the *cost of the marginal investment in accounts receivable*.
d. Should the firm implement the proposed change? What other information would be helpful in your analysis?

P13–9   **Accounts receivable changes with bad debts**   A firm is evaluating an accounts receivable change that would increase bad debts from 2% to 4% of sales. Sales are currently 50,000 units, the selling price is $20 per unit, and the variable cost per unit is $15. As a result of the proposed change, sales are forecast to increase to 60,000 units.

a. What are bad debts in dollars currently and under the proposed change?

b. Calculate the *cost of the marginal bad debts* to the firm.

c. Ignoring the additional profit contribution from increased sales, if the proposed change saves $3,500 and causes no change in the average investment in accounts receivable, would you recommend it? Explain.

d. Considering *all* changes in costs and benefits, would you recommend the proposed change? Explain.

e. Compare and discuss your answers in parts **c** and **d**.

P13–10   **Relaxation of credit standards**   Lewis Enterprises is considering relaxing its credit standards to increase its currently sagging sales. As a result of the proposed relaxation, sales are expected to increase by 10% from 10,000 to 11,000 units during the coming year; the average collection period is expected to increase from 45 to 60 days; and bad debts are expected to increase from 1% to 3% of sales. The sale price per unit is $40, and the variable cost per unit is $31. The firm's required return on equal-risk investments is 25%. Evaluate the proposed relaxation, and make a recommendation to the firm. (*Note:* Assume a 365-day year.)

P13–11   **Initiating a cash discount**   Gardner Company currently makes all sales on credit and offers no cash discount. The firm is considering offering a 2% cash discount for payment within 15 days. The firm's current average collection period is 60 days, sales are 40,000 units, selling price is $45 per unit, and variable cost per unit is $36. The firm expects that the change in credit terms will result in an increase in sales to 42,000 units, that 70% of the sales will take the discount, and that the average collection period will fall to 30 days. If the firm's required rate of return on equal-risk investments is 25%, should the proposed discount be offered? (*Note:* Assume a 365-day year.)

P13–12   **Shortening the credit period**   A firm is contemplating *shortening* its credit period from 40 to 30 days and believes that as a result of this change, its average collection period will decline from 45 to 36 days. Bad-debt expenses are expected to decrease from 1.5% to 1% of sales. The firm is currently selling 12,000 units but believes that as a result of the proposed change, sales will decline to 10,000 units. The sale price per unit is $56, and the variable cost per unit is $45. The firm has a required return on equal-risk investments of 25%. Evaluate this decision, and make a recommendation to the firm. (*Note:* Assume a 365-day year.)

P13–13   **Lengthening the credit period**   Parker Tool is considering lengthening its credit period from 30 to 60 days. All customers will continue to pay on the net date. The firm currently bills $450,000 for sales and has $345,000 in variable costs. The change in credit terms is expected to increase sales to $510,000. Bad-debt expenses will increase from 1% to 1.5% of sales. The firm has a required rate of return on equal-risk investments of 20%. (*Note:* Assume a 365-day year.)

a. What *additional profit contribution from sales* will be realized from the proposed change?

b. What is the *cost of the marginal investment in accounts receivable?*

c. What is the *cost of the marginal bad debts?*
d. Do you recommend this change in credit terms? Why or why not?

 P13–14 **Float**   Simon Corporation has daily cash receipts of $65,000. A recent analysis of its collections indicated that customers' payments were in the mail an average of 2.5 days. Once received, the payments are processed in 1.5 days. After payments are deposited, it takes an average of 3 days for these receipts to clear the banking system.
a. How much *collection float (in days)* does the firm currently have?
b. If the firm's opportunity cost is 11%, would it be economically advisable for the firm to pay an annual fee of $16,500 to reduce collection float by 3 days? Explain why or why not.

 P13–15 **Lockbox system**   Eagle Industries feels that a lockbox system can shorten its accounts receivable collection period by 3 days. Credit sales are $3,240,000 per year, billed on a continuous basis. The firm has other equally risky investments that earn a return of 15%. The cost of the lockbox system is $9,000 per year. (*Note:* Assume a 365-day year.)
a. What amount of cash will be made available for other uses under the lockbox system?
b. What net benefit (cost) will the firm realize if it adopts the lockbox system? Should it adopt the proposed lockbox system?

 P13–16 **Zero-balance account**   Union Company is considering establishment of a zero-balance account. The firm currently maintains an average balance of $420,000 in its disbursement account. As compensation to the bank for maintaining the zero-balance account, the firm will have to pay a monthly fee of $1,000 and maintain a $300,000 non–interest-earning deposit in the bank. The firm currently has no other deposits in the bank. Evaluate the proposed zero-balance account, and make a recommendation to the firm, assuming that it has a 12% opportunity cost.

PERSONAL FINANCE PROBLEM

 P13–17 **Management of cash balance**   Alexis Morris, an assistant manager at a local department store, gets paid every 2 weeks by direct deposit into her checking account. This account pays no interest and has no minimum balance requirement. Her monthly income is $4,200. Alexis has a "target" cash balance of around $1,200, and whenever it exceeds that amount she transfers the excess into her savings account, which currently pays 2.0% annual interest. Her current savings balance is $15,000, and Alexis estimates she transfers about $500 per month from her checking account into her savings account. Alexis doesn't waste any time in paying her bills, and her monthly bills average about $2,000. Her monthly cash outlay for food, gas, and other sundry items totals about $850. Reviewing her payment habits indicates that on average she pays her bills 9 days early. At this time, most marketable securities are yielding about 4.75% annual interest.

   Show how Alexis can better manage her cash balance:
a. What can Alexis do regarding the handling of her current balances?
b. What do you suggest that she do with her monthly surpluses?
c. What do you suggest Alexis do about the manner in which she pays her bills?
d. Can Alexis grow her earnings by better managing her cash balances? Show your work.

P13–18 **ETHICS PROBLEM**   A group of angry shareholders has placed a corporate resolution before all shareholders at a company's annual stockholders' meeting. The resolution demands that the company *stretch its accounts payable*, because these shareholders have determined that all of the company's competitors do so, and the firm operates in a highly competitive industry. How could management at the annual stockholders' meeting defend the firm's practice of paying suppliers on time?

Chapter 13 Case

Assessing Roche Publishing Company's Cash Management Efficiency

Lisa Pinto, vice president of finance at Roche Publishing Company, a rapidly growing publisher of college texts, is concerned about the firm's high level of short-term resource investment. She believes that the firm can improve the management of its cash and, as a result, reduce this investment. In this regard, she charged Arlene Bessenoff, the treasurer, with assessing the firm's cash management efficiency. Arlene decided to begin her investigation by studying the firm's operating and cash conversion cycles.

Arlene found that Roche's average payment period was 25 days. She consulted industry data, which showed that the average payment period for the industry was 40 days. Investigation of three similar publishing companies revealed that their average payment period was also 40 days. She estimated the annual cost of achieving a 40-day payment period to be $53,000.

Next, Arlene studied the production cycle and inventory policies. The average age of inventory was 120 days. She determined that the industry standard as reported in a survey done by *Publishing World*, the trade association journal, was 85 days. She estimated the annual cost of achieving an 85-day average age of inventory to be $150,000.

Further analysis showed Arlene that the firm's average collection period was 60 days. The industry average, derived from the trade association data and information on three similar publishing companies, was found to be 42 days—30% lower than Roche's. Arlene estimated that if Roche initiated a 2% cash discount for payment within 10 days of the beginning of the credit period, the firm's average collection period would drop from 60 days to the 42-day industry average. She also expected the following to occur as a result of the discount: Annual sales would increase from $13,750,000 to $15,000,000; bad debts would remain unchanged; and the 2% cash discount would be applied to 75% of the firm's sales. The firm's variable costs equal 80% of sales.

Roche Publishing Company is currently spending $12,000,000 per year on its operating-cycle investment, but it expects that initiating a cash discount will increase its operating-cycle investment to $13,100,000 per year. (*Note:* The operating-cycle investment per dollar of inventory, receivables, and payables is assumed to be the same.) Arlene's concern was whether the firm's cash management was as efficient as it could be. Arlene knew that the company paid 12% annual interest for its resource investment and therefore viewed this value as the firm's required return. For this reason, she was concerned about the resource investment cost resulting from any inefficiencies in the management of Roche's cash conversion cycle. (*Note:* Assume a 365-day year.)

To Do

a. Assuming a constant rate for purchases, production, and sales throughout the year, what are Roche's existing *operating cycle (OC), cash conversion cycle (CCC),* and *resource investment* need?

b. If Roche can optimize operations according to industry standards, what would its *operating cycle (OC), cash conversion cycle (CCC),* and *resource investment* need be under these more efficient conditions?

c. In terms of resource investment requirements, what is the annual cost of Roche's operational inefficiency?

d. Evaluate whether Roche's strategy for speeding its collection of accounts receivable would be acceptable. What annual net profit or loss would result from implementation of the cash discount?

e. Use your finding in part **d,** along with the payables and inventory costs given, to determine the total annual cost the firm would incur to achieve the industry level of operational efficiency.

f. Judging on the basis of your findings in parts **c** and **e,** should the firm incur the annual cost to achieve the industry level of operational efficiency? Explain why or why not.

Spreadsheet Exercise

The current balance in accounts receivable for Eboy Corporation is $443,000. This level was achieved with annual (365 days) credit sales of $3,544,000. The firm offers its customers credit terms of *net 30.* However, in an effort to help its cash flow position and to follow the actions of its rivals, the firm is considering changing its credit terms from net 30 to *2/10 net 30.* The objective is to speed up the receivable collections and thereby improve the firm's cash flows. Eboy would like to increase its accounts receivable turnover to 12.0.

The firm works with a raw material whose current annual usage is 1,450 units. Each finished product requires 1 unit of this raw material at a variable cost of $2,600 per unit and sells for $4,200 on terms of net 30. It is estimated that 70% of the firm's customers will take the 2% cash discount and that with the discount, sales of the finished product will increase by 50 units per year. The firm's opportunity cost of funds invested in accounts receivable is 12.5%

In analyzing the investment in accounts receivable, use the variable cost of the product sold instead of the sale price, because the variable cost is a better indicator of the firm's investment.

To Do

Create a spreadsheet similar to Table 13.3 to analyze whether the firm should initiate the proposed cash discount. What is your advice? Make sure you calculate the following:

a. Additional profit contribution from sales.
b. Average investment in accounts receivable at present (without cash discount).
c. Average investment in accounts receivable with the proposed cash discount.
d. Reduction in investment in accounts receivable.
e. Cost savings from reduced investment in accounts receivable.
f. Cost of the cash discount.
g. Net profit (loss) from initiation of proposed cash discount.

Web Exercise

Go to the book's companion website at www.prenhall.com/gitman to find the Web Exercise for this chapter.

Remember to check the book's website at www.prenhall.com/gitman to find additional resources, including Web Exercises and a Web Case.

14 | Current Liabilities Management

LEARNING GOALS

LG 1 Review accounts payable, the key components of credit terms, and the procedures for analyzing those terms.

LG 2 Understand the effects of stretching accounts payable on their cost, and the use of accruals.

LG 3 Describe interest rates and the basic types of unsecured bank sources of short-term loans.

LG 4 Discuss the basic features of commercial paper and the key aspects of international short-term loans.

LG 5 Explain the characteristics of secured short-term loans and the use of accounts receivable as short-term-loan collateral.

LG 6 Describe the various ways in which inventory can be used as short-term-loan collateral.

Accounts payable and accruals represent forms of spontaneous financing for the firm. The longer the firm can hold the cash intended for paying those accounts, the longer it can use those funds for its own purposes. Firms typically, though, must arrange for short-term loans to even out seasonal cash flows or to cover unexpected outlays. This chapter looks at various aspects of current liabilities management—spontaneous liabilities and how best to manage them, and both unsecured and secured sources of short-term loans.

14.1 | Spontaneous Liabilities

spontaneous liabilities
Financing that arises from the normal course of business; the two major short-term sources of such liabilities are accounts payable and accruals.

Spontaneous liabilities arise from the normal course of business. The two major spontaneous sources of short-term financing are accounts payable and accruals. As the firm's sales increase, accounts payable increase in response to the increased purchases necessary to produce at higher levels. Also in response to increasing sales, the firm's accruals increase as wages and taxes rise because of greater labor requirements and the increased taxes on the firm's increased earnings. There is normally no explicit cost attached to either of these current liabilities, although they do have certain implicit costs. In addition, both are forms of **unsecured short-term financing**—short-term financing obtained without pledging specific assets as collateral. The firm should take advantage of these "interest-free" sources of unsecured short-term financing whenever possible.

unsecured short-term financing
Short-term financing obtained without pledging specific assets as collateral.

Accounts Payable Management

Hint An account payable of a purchaser is an account receivable on the supplier's books. Chapter 13 highlighted the key strategies and considerations involved in extending credit to customers.

Accounts payable are the major source of unsecured short-term financing for business firms. They result from transactions in which merchandise is purchased but no formal note is signed to show the purchaser's liability to the seller. The purchaser in effect agrees to pay the supplier the amount required in accordance with credit terms normally stated on the supplier's invoice. The discussion of accounts payable here is presented from the viewpoint of the purchaser.

Role in the Cash Conversion Cycle

The average payment period is the final component of the *cash conversion cycle* introduced in Chapter 13. The average payment period has two parts: (1) the time from the purchase of raw materials until the firm mails the payment and (2) payment float time (the time it takes after the firm mails its payment until the supplier has withdrawn spendable funds from the firm's account). In the preceding chapter, we discussed issues related to payment float time. Here we discuss the firm's management of the time that elapses between its purchase of raw materials and its mailing payment to the supplier. This activity is **accounts payable management.**

accounts payable management
Management by the firm of the time that elapses between its purchase of raw materials and its mailing payment to the supplier.

The firm's goal is to pay as slowly as possible without damaging its credit rating. This means that accounts should be paid on the last day possible, given the supplier's stated credit terms. For example, if the terms are net 30, then the account should be paid 30 days from the *beginning of the credit period*, which is typically either the *date of invoice* or the *end of the month* (EOM) in which the purchase was made. This allows for the maximum use of an interest-free loan from the supplier and will not damage the firm's credit rating (because the account is paid within the stated credit terms).

| Example | In the demonstration of the cash conversion cycle in Chapter 13 (see pages 528–529), MAX Company had an average payment period of 35 days (consisting of 30 days until payment was mailed and 5 days of payment float), which resulted in average accounts payable of $467,466. Thus the daily accounts payable generated by MAX totaled $13,356 ($467,466/35). If MAX were to mail its payments in 35 days instead of 30 days, its accounts payable would increase by $66,780 (5 × $13,356). As a result, MAX's cash conversion cycle would decrease by 5 days, and the firm would reduce its investment in operations by $66,780. Clearly, if this action did not damage MAX's credit rating, it would be in the company's best interest. |

Analyzing Credit Terms

The credit terms that a firm is offered by its suppliers enable it to delay payments for its purchases. Because the supplier's cost of having its money tied up in merchandise after it is sold is probably reflected in the purchase price, the purchaser is already indirectly paying for this benefit. The purchaser should therefore carefully analyze credit terms to determine the best trade credit strategy. If a firm is extended credit terms that include a cash discount, it has two options—to take the cash discount or to give it up.

Taking the Cash Discount   If a firm intends to take a cash discount, it should pay on the last day of the discount period. There is no cost associated with taking a cash discount.

| Example | Lawrence Industries, operator of a small chain of video stores, purchased $1,000 worth of merchandise on February 27 from a supplier extending terms of 2/10 net 30 EOM. If the firm takes the cash discount, it must pay $980 [$1,000 − (0.02 × $1,000)] by March 10, thereby saving $20. |

cost of giving up a cash discount
The implied rate of interest paid to delay payment of an account payable for an additional number of days.

Giving Up the Cash Discount   If the firm chooses to give up the cash discount, it should pay on the final day of the credit period. There is an implicit cost associated with giving up a cash discount. The **cost of giving up a cash discount** is the implied rate of interest paid to delay payment of an account payable for an additional number of days. In other words, it is the interest being paid by the firm to keep its money for a number of days. This cost can be illustrated by a simple example. The example assumes that payment will be made on the last possible day (either the final day of the cash discount period or the final day of the credit period).

| Example | In the prior example, we saw that Lawrence Industries could take the cash discount on its February 27 purchase by paying $980 on March 10. If Lawrence gives up the cash discount, it can pay on March 30. To keep its money for an extra 20 days, the firm must give up an opportunity to pay $980 for its $1,000 purchase. In other words, it will cost the firm $20 to delay payment for 20 days. Figure 14.1 shows the payment options that are open to the company. |

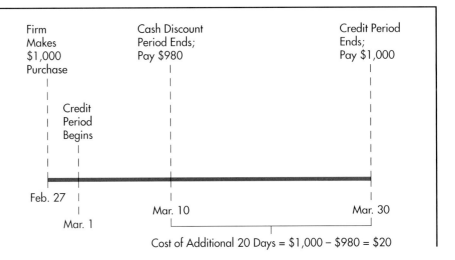

FIGURE 14.1

Payment Options
Payment options for
Lawrence Industries

To calculate the cost of giving up the cash discount, the *true purchase price* must be viewed as the *discounted cost of the merchandise,* which is $980 for Lawrence Industries. The annual percentage cost of giving up the cash discount can be calculated using Equation 14.1:

$$\text{Cost of giving up cash discount} = \frac{CD}{100\% - CD} \times \frac{365}{N} \qquad (14.1)$$

where

CD = stated cash discount in percentage terms

N = number of days that payment can be delayed by giving up the cash discount

Substituting the values for CD (2%) and N (20 days) into Equation 14.1 results in an annualized cost of giving up the cash discount of 37.24% [(2% ÷ 98%) × (365 ÷ 20)]. A 365-day year is assumed.

A simple way to *approximate* the cost of giving up a cash discount is to use the stated cash discount percentage, CD, in place of the first term of Equation 14.1:

$$\text{Approximate cost of giving up cash discount} = CD \times \frac{365}{N} \qquad (14.2)$$

The smaller the cash discount, the closer the approximation to the actual cost of giving it up. Using this approximation, the cost of giving up the cash discount for Lawrence Industries is 36.5% [2% × (365 ÷ 20)].

Using the Cost of Giving Up a Cash Discount in Decision Making The financial manager must determine whether it is advisable to take a cash discount. Financial managers must remember that taking cash discounts may represent an important source of additional profitability.

TABLE 14.1	Cash Discounts and Associated Costs for Mason Products	
Supplier	Credit terms	Approximate cost of giving up a cash discount
A	2/10 net 30 EOM	36.5%
B	1/10 net 55 EOM	8.1
C	3/20 net 70 EOM	21.9
D	4/10 net 60 EOM	29.2

Example

Mason Products, a large building-supply company, has four possible suppliers, each offering different credit terms. Otherwise, their products and services are identical. Table 14.1 presents the credit terms offered by suppliers A, B, C, and D and the cost of giving up the cash discounts in each transaction. The approximation method of calculating the cost of giving up a cash discount (Equation 14.2) has been used. The cost of giving up the cash discount from supplier A is 36.5%; from supplier B, 8.1%; from supplier C, 21.9%; and from supplier D, 29.2%.

If the firm needs short-term funds, which it can borrow from its bank at an interest rate of 13%, and if each of the suppliers is viewed *separately*, which (if any) of the suppliers' cash discounts will the firm give up? In dealing with supplier A, the firm takes the cash discount, because the cost of giving it up is 36.5%, and then borrows the funds it requires from its bank at 13% interest. With supplier B, the firm would do better to give up the cash discount, because the cost of this action is less than the cost of borrowing money from the bank (8.1% versus 13%). With either supplier C or supplier D, the firm should take the cash discount, because in both cases the cost of giving up the discount is greater than the 13% cost of borrowing from the bank.

The example shows that the cost of giving up a cash discount is relevant when one is evaluating a single supplier's credit terms in light of certain *bank borrowing costs*. However, other factors relative to payment strategies may also need to be considered. For example, some firms, particularly small firms and poorly managed firms, routinely give up *all* discounts because they either lack alternative sources of unsecured short-term financing or fail to recognize the implicit costs of their actions.

Effects of Stretching Accounts Payable

stretching accounts payable
Paying bills as late as possible without damaging the firm's credit rating.

A strategy that is often employed by a firm is **stretching accounts payable**—that is, paying bills as late as possible without damaging its credit rating. Such a strategy can reduce the cost of giving up a cash discount.

Example

Lawrence Industries was extended credit terms of 2/10 net 30 EOM. The cost of giving up the cash discount, assuming payment on the last day of the credit period, was approximately 36.5% [$2\% \times (365 \div 20)$]. If the firm were able to stretch its account payable to 70 days without damaging its credit rating, the cost of giving up the cash discount would be only 12.2% [$2\% \times (365 \div 60)$]. Stretching accounts payable reduces the implicit cost of giving up a cash discount.

Although stretching accounts payable may be financially attractive, it raises an important ethical issue: It may cause the firm to violate the agreement it entered into with its supplier when it purchased merchandise. Clearly, a supplier would not look kindly on a customer who regularly and purposely postponed paying for purchases.

Personal Finance Example   Jack and Mary Nobel, a young married couple, are in the process of purchasing a 42-inch HD TV at a cost of $1,900. The electronics dealer currently has a special financing plan that would allow them to either (1) put $200 down and finance the balance of $1,700 at 3% annual interest over 24 months, resulting in payments of $73 per month, or (2) receive an immediate $150 cash rebate, thereby paying only $1,750 cash. The Nobels, who have saved enough to pay cash for the TV, can currently earn 5% annual interest on their savings. They wish to determine whether to borrow or to pay cash to purchase the TV.

The upfront outlay for the financing alternative is the $200 down payment, whereas the Nobels will pay out $1,750 upfront under the cash purchase alternative. So the cash purchase will require an initial outlay that is $1,550 ($1,750 − $200) greater than under the financing alternative. Given that they can earn 5% on savings, the cash purchase will cause the Nobels to give up an opportunity to earn $155 (2 years × 0.05 × $1,550) over the 2 years.

If they choose the financing alternative, the $1,550 would grow to $1,705 ($1,550 + $155) at the end of 2 years. But under the financing alternative, the Nobels will pay out a total of $1,752 (24 months × $73 per month) over the 2-year loan term. Ignoring the time value of money, the cost of the financing alternative can be viewed as $1,752 and the cost of the cash payment (including forgone interest earnings) would be $1,705. Because it is less expensive, *the Nobels should pay cash for the TV.* The lower cost of the cash alternative is largely the result of the $150 cash rebate.

Accruals

accruals
Liabilities for services received for which payment has yet to be made.

The second spontaneous source of short-term business financing is accruals. **Accruals** are liabilities for services received for which payment has yet to be made. The most common items accrued by a firm are wages and taxes. Because taxes are payments to the government, their accrual cannot be manipulated by the firm. However, the accrual of wages can be manipulated to some extent. This is accomplished by delaying payment of wages, thereby receiving an interest-free loan from employees who are paid sometime after they have performed the work. The pay period for employees who earn an hourly rate is often governed by union regulations or by state or federal law. However, in other cases, the frequency of payment is at the discretion of the company's management.

Example   Tenney Company, a large janitorial service company, currently pays its employees at the end of each work week. The weekly payroll totals $400,000. If the firm were to extend the pay period so as to pay its employees 1 week later throughout an entire year, the employees would in effect be lending the firm $400,000 for a year. If the firm could earn 10% annually on invested funds, such a strategy would be worth $40,000 per year (0.10 × $400,000).

REVIEW QUESTIONS

14–1 What are the two major sources of spontaneous short-term financing for a firm? How do their balances behave relative to the firm's sales?

14–2 Is there a cost associated with *taking a cash discount?* Is there any cost associated with *giving up a cash discount?* How do short-term borrowing costs affect the cash discount decision?

14–3 What is "stretching accounts payable"? What effect does this action have on the cost of giving up a cash discount?

14.2 | Unsecured Sources of Short-Term Loans

Businesses obtain unsecured short-term loans from two major sources, banks and sales of commercial paper. Unlike the spontaneous sources of unsecured short-term financing, bank loans and commercial paper are negotiated and result from actions taken by the firm's financial manager. Bank loans are more popular, because they are available to firms of all sizes; commercial paper tends to be available only to large firms. In addition, firms can use international loans to finance international transactions.

Bank Loans

short-term, self-liquidating loan
An unsecured short-term loan in which the use to which the borrowed money is put provides the mechanism through which the loan is repaid.

Banks are a major source of unsecured short-term loans to businesses. The major type of loan made by banks to businesses is the **short-term, self-liquidating loan.** These loans are intended merely to carry the firm through seasonal peaks in financing needs that are due primarily to buildups of inventory and accounts receivable. As the firm converts inventories and receivables into cash, the funds needed to retire these loans are generated. In other words, the use to which the borrowed money is put provides the mechanism through which the loan is repaid—hence the term *self-liquidating.* Though most business borrowers take out loans honestly and repay them as agreed, a few do not. The *Focus on Ethics* box discusses the issue of loan fraud.

Banks lend unsecured, short-term funds in three basic ways: through single-payment notes, lines of credit, and revolving credit agreements. Before we look at these types of loans, we consider loan interest rates.

Loan Interest Rates

prime rate of interest (prime rate)
The lowest rate of interest charged by leading banks on business loans to their most important business borrowers.

The interest rate on a bank loan can be a fixed or a floating rate, typically based on the prime rate of interest. The **prime rate of interest (prime rate)** is the lowest rate of interest charged by leading banks on business loans to their most important business borrowers.[1] The prime rate fluctuates with changing supply-and-

---

1. A trend away from using the prime rate as a benchmark has begun in the United States in response to various borrower lawsuits against banks. Some banks now use the term *base rate* or *reference rate* rather than *prime rate* for pricing corporate and other loans. In fact, the use of the *London Interbank Offered Rate* (*LIBOR*) is gaining momentum as a base lending rate in the United States.

Focus on Ethics   Loan Fraud

IN PRACTICE

In June 2007, the creator of the Backstreet Boys and 'N Sync was indicted by a federal grand jury on charges that he defrauded a bank out of $20 million. He was accused of fraudulently securing millions in bank loans with documents from a fake accounting firm.

What constitutes *loan fraud?* A loan fraud is a scheme or artifice or making false statements orally or in writing in order to receive a loan. Loan frauds may sometimes be committed with the assistance of outside agents such as appraisers who inflate appraisals that support loans or, as in the case just cited, a fake or disreputable accounting firm.

Loan fraud is covered under a variety of federal statutes, and the perpetrator can be fined up to $1 million and imprisoned for up to 30 years. More extensive loan frauds, in which criminal enterprises commit a series of specified crimes against financial institutions, are covered by the "S&L Kingpin" statute. This law

provides for fines of up to $20 million for organizational defendants and up to $10 million and life imprisonment for individuals.

Common types of loan fraud include making false application, loans to nonexistent borrowers, nominee loans, double pledging of collateral, and misapplication of loan funds. *False applications* can include false information about persons, understated or missing debts, and/or overstated asset valuations. They also may include false income tax documents or false financial statements. *Loans to nonexistent borrowers* are loan frauds perpetrated by individuals or businesses who supply false names and addresses. *Nominee loans* are loans taken out by one party for the benefit of a second party whose identity is concealed from the financial institution. Some borrowers fraudulently secure two loans by *pledging the same collateral with different lenders* before the liens are recorded and without telling the lenders.

Misapplication of loan funds involves using the money for a purpose other than that stated in the loan.

How does a bank or lending institution protect itself from loan fraud? Deterioration in a borrower's finances can be a red flag. Lenders can calculate horizontal analyses by comparing financial ratios over several periods. Lenders can also perform vertical analysis in which they compare ratios to total assets or total sales and to benchmark ratios for similar companies.

Second, strong internal controls such as independent reviews, internal auditors, committee and officer lending limits, and sound underwriting can help prevent loan fraud. Physical inspections of collateral can also help detect a potential fraud.

■ *How might lenders use sales tax information to verify portions of the financial statements?*

---

fixed-rate loan
A loan with a rate of interest that is determined at a set increment above the prime rate and remains unvarying until maturity.

demand relationships for short-term funds.[2] Banks generally determine the rate to be charged to various borrowers by adding a premium to the prime rate to adjust it for the borrower's "riskiness." The premium may amount to 4 percent or more, although most unsecured short-term loans carry premiums of less than 2 percent.

Fixed- and Floating-Rate Loans   Loans can have either fixed or floating interest rates. On a **fixed-rate loan,** the rate of interest is determined at a set increment above the prime rate on the date of the loan and remains unvarying at that

---

2. During the past 25 years, the prime rate has varied from a record high of 21.5% (December 1980) to a low of 4.00% (July 2003 through June 2004). Since January 2001, it has fluctuated in the range from a high of 9.50% to a low of 4.00%.

floating-rate loan
A loan with a rate of interest initially set at an increment above the prime rate and allowed to "float," or vary, above prime *as the prime rate varies* until maturity.

fixed rate until maturity. On a **floating-rate loan,** the increment above the prime rate is initially established, and the rate of interest is allowed to "float," or vary, above prime *as the prime rate varies* until maturity. Generally, the increment above the prime rate will be *lower* on a floating-rate loan than on a fixed-rate loan of equivalent risk, because the lender bears less risk with a floating-rate loan. As a result of the volatile nature of the prime rate during recent years, today *most short-term business loans are floating-rate loans.*

Method of Computing Interest   Once the *nominal (or stated) annual rate* is established, the method of computing interest is determined. Interest can be paid either when a loan matures or in advance. If interest is paid *at maturity*, the *effective (or true) annual rate*—the actual rate of interest paid—for an assumed 1-year period[3] is equal to

$$\frac{\text{Interest}}{\text{Amount borrowed}} \tag{14.3}$$

Most bank loans to businesses require the interest payment at maturity.

discount loans
Loans on which interest is paid in advance by being deducted from the amount borrowed.

When interest is paid *in advance,* it is deducted from the loan so that the borrower actually receives less money than is requested. Loans on which interest is paid in advance are called **discount loans.** The *effective annual rate for a discount loan,* assuming a 1-year period, is calculated as

$$\frac{\text{Interest}}{\text{Amount borrowed} - \text{Interest}} \tag{14.4}$$

Paying interest in advance raises the effective annual rate above the stated annual rate.

Example   Wooster Company, a manufacturer of athletic apparel, wants to borrow $10,000 at a stated annual rate of 10% interest for 1 year. If the interest on the loan is paid at maturity, the firm will pay $1,000 (0.10 × $10,000) for the use of the $10,000 for the year. Substituting into Equation 14.3 reveals that the effective annual rate is therefore

$$\frac{\$1,000}{\$10,000} = 10.0\%$$

If the money is borrowed at the same *stated* annual rate for 1 year but interest is paid in advance, the firm still pays $1,000 in interest, but it receives only $9,000 ($10,000 − $1,000). The effective annual rate in this case is

$$\frac{\$1,000}{\$10,000 - \$1,000} = \frac{\$1,000}{\$9,000} = 11.1\%$$

Paying interest in advance thus makes the effective annual rate (11.1%) greater than the stated annual rate (10.0%).

---

3. Effective annual rates (EARs) for loans with maturities of less than 1 year can be found by using the technique presented in Chapter 4 for finding EARs when interest is compounded more frequently than annually. See Equation 4.24.

Single-Payment Notes

single-payment note
A short-term, one-time loan made to a borrower who needs funds for a specific purpose for a short period.

A **single-payment note** can be obtained from a commercial bank by a credit-worthy business borrower. This type of loan is usually a one-time loan made to a borrower who needs funds for a specific purpose for a short period. The resulting instrument is a *note*, signed by the borrower, that states the terms of the loan, including the length of the loan and the interest rate. This type of short-term note generally has a maturity of 30 days to 9 months or more. The interest charged is usually tied in some way to the prime rate of interest.

Example

Gordon Manufacturing, a producer of rotary mower blades, recently borrowed $100,000 from each of two banks—bank A and bank B. The loans were incurred on the same day, when the prime rate of interest was 6%. Each loan involved a 90-day note with interest to be paid at the end of 90 days. The interest rate was set at 1½% above the prime rate on bank A's *fixed-rate note*. Over the 90-day period, the rate of interest on this note will remain at 7½% (6% prime rate + 1½% increment) regardless of fluctuations in the prime rate. The total interest cost on this loan is $1,849 [$100,000 × (7½% × 90/365)]. The effective 90-day rate on this loan is 1.85% ($1,849/$100,000).

Assuming that the loan from bank A is rolled over each 90 days throughout the year under the same terms and circumstances, we can find its effective *annual* interest rate by using Equation 4.24. Because the loan costs 1.85% for 90 days, it is necessary to compound $(1 + 0.0185)$ for 4.06 periods in the year (that is, 365/90) and then subtract 1:

$$\text{Effective annual rate} = (1 + 0.0185)^{4.06} - 1$$
$$= 1.0773 - 1 = 0.0773 = \underline{7.73\%}$$

The effective annual rate of interest on the fixed-rate, 90-day note is 7.73%.

Bank B set the interest rate at 1% above the prime rate on its *floating-rate note*. The rate charged over the 90 days will vary directly with the prime rate. Initially, the rate will be 7% (6% + 1%), but when the prime rate changes, so will the rate of interest on the note. For instance, if after 30 days the prime rate rises to 6.5%, and after another 30 days it drops to 6.25%, the firm will be paying 0.575% for the first 30 days (7% × 30/365), 0.616% for the next 30 days (7.5% × 30/365), and 0.596% for the last 30 days (7.25% × 30/365). Its total interest cost will be $1,787 [$100,000 × (0.575% + 0.616% + 0.596%)], resulting in an effective 90-day rate of 1.79% ($1,787/$100,000).

Again, assuming the loan is rolled over each 90 days throughout the year under the same terms and circumstances, its effective *annual* rate is 7.46%:

$$\text{Effective annual rate} = (1 + 0.01787)^{4.06} - 1$$
$$= 1.0746 - 1 = 0.0746 = \underline{7.46\%}$$

Clearly, in this case the floating-rate loan would have been less expensive than the fixed-rate loan because of its generally lower effective annual rate.

Personal Finance Example   Megan Schwartz has been approved by Clinton National Bank for a 180-day loan of $30,000 that will allow her to make the down payment and close the loan on her new condo. She needs the funds to bridge the time until the sale of her current condo closes and she receives the $42,000 in proceeds from it.

Clinton National offered Megan the following two financing options for the $30,000 loan: (1) a *fixed-rate loan* at 2% above the prime rate, or (2) a *variable-rate loan* at 1% above the prime rate. Currently, the prime rate of interest is 8% and the consensus forecast of a group of mortgage economists for changes in the prime rate over the next 180 days are as follows:

60 days from today the prime rate will rise by 1%

90 days from today the prime rate will rise another ½%

150 days from today the prime rate will drop by 1%

Using the forecast prime rate changes, Megan wishes to determine the lowest interest-cost loan for the next 6 months.

Fixed-rate loan: Total interest cost over 180 days
$$= \$30{,}000 \times (0.08 + 0.02) \times (180/365)$$
$$= \$30{,}000 \times 0.04932 \approx \underline{\$1{,}480}$$

Variable-rate loan: The applicable interest rate would begin at 9% (8% + 1%) and remain there for 60 days. Then the applicable rate would rise to 10% (9% + 1%) for the next 30 days, and then to 10.50% (10% + 0.50%) for the next 60 days. Finally the applicable rate would drop to 9.50% (10.50% − 1%) for the final 30 days.

Total interest cost over 180 days
$$= \$30{,}000 \times [(0.09 \times 60/365) + (0.10 \times 30/365)$$
$$+ (0.105 \times 60/365) + (0.095 \times 30/365)]$$
$$= \$30{,}000 \times (0.01479 + 0.00822 + 0.01726 + 0.00781)$$
$$= \$30{,}000 \times 0.04808 \approx \underline{\$1{,}442}$$

Because the estimated total interest cost on the variable-rate loan of $1,442 is less than the total interest cost of $1,480 on the fixed-rate loan, *Megan should take the variable-rate loan.* By doing this she will save about $38 ($1,480 − $1,442) in interest cost over the 180 days.

Lines of Credit

line of credit
An agreement between a commercial bank and a business specifying the amount of unsecured short-term borrowing the bank will make available to the firm over a given period of time.

A **line of credit** is an agreement between a commercial bank and a business, specifying the amount of unsecured short-term borrowing the bank will make available to the firm over a given period of time. It is similar to the agreement under which issuers of bank credit cards, such as MasterCard, Visa, and Discover, extend preapproved credit to cardholders. A line-of-credit agreement is typically made for a period of 1 year and often places certain constraints on the borrower. It is *not a guaranteed loan* but indicates that if the bank has sufficient funds available, it will allow the borrower to owe it *up to* a certain amount of money. The amount of a line of credit is the *maximum amount the firm can owe the bank* at any point in time.

When applying for a line of credit, the borrower may be required to submit such documents as its cash budget, pro forma income statement, pro forma balance sheet, and recent financial statements. If the bank finds the customer acceptable, the line of credit will be extended. The major attraction of a line of credit from the bank's point of view is that it eliminates the need to examine the creditworthiness of a customer each time it borrows money within the year.

14–8   What is a *revolving credit agreement?* How does this arrangement differ from the line-of-credit agreement? What is a *commitment fee?*

14–9   How do firms use *commercial paper* to raise short-term funds? Who can issue commercial paper? Who buys commercial paper?

14–10 What is the important difference between international and domestic transactions? How is a *letter of credit* used in financing international trade transactions? How is "netting" used in transactions between subsidiaries?

14.3 | Secured Sources of Short-Term Loans

secured short-term financing
Short-term financing (loan) that has specific assets pledged as collateral.

security agreement
The agreement between the borrower and the lender that specifies the collateral held against a secured loan.

When a firm has exhausted its sources of unsecured short-term financing, it may be able to obtain additional short-term loans on a secured basis. **Secured short-term financing** has specific assets pledged as collateral. The *collateral* commonly takes the form of an asset, such as accounts receivable or inventory. The lender obtains a security interest in the collateral through the execution of a **security agreement** with the borrower that specifies the collateral held against the loan. In addition, the terms of the loan against which the security is held form part of the security agreement. A copy of the security agreement is filed in a public office within the state—typically, a county or state court. Filing provides subsequent lenders with information about which assets of a prospective borrower are unavailable for use as collateral. The filing requirement protects the lender by legally establishing the lender's security interest.

Characteristics of Secured Short-Term Loans

Although many people believe that holding collateral as security reduces the risk of a loan, lenders do not usually view loans in this way. Lenders recognize that holding collateral can reduce losses if the borrower defaults, but *the presence of collateral has no impact on the risk of default.* A lender requires collateral to ensure recovery of some portion of the loan in the event of default. What the lender wants above all, however, is to be repaid as scheduled. In general, lenders prefer to make less risky loans at lower rates of interest than to be in a position in which they must liquidate collateral.

Collateral and Terms

percentage advance
The percentage of the book value of the collateral that constitutes the principal of a secured loan.

Lenders of secured short-term funds prefer collateral that has a duration closely matched to the term of the loan. Current assets are the most desirable short-term-loan collateral, because they can normally be converted into cash much sooner than fixed assets. Thus, the short-term lender of secured funds generally accepts only liquid current assets as collateral.

Typically, the lender determines the desirable **percentage advance** to make against the collateral. This percentage advance constitutes the principal of the secured loan and is normally between 30 and 100 percent of the book value of the collateral. It varies according to the type and liquidity of collateral.

Hint Remember that firms typically borrow on a secured basis only after exhausting less costly, unsecured sources of short-term funds.

The interest rate that is charged on secured short-term loans is typically *higher* than the rate on unsecured short-term loans. Lenders do not normally consider secured loans less risky than unsecured loans. In addition, negotiating and administering secured loans is more troublesome for the lender than negotiating and administering unsecured loans. The lender therefore normally requires added compensation in the form of a service charge, a higher interest rate, or both.

Institutions Extending Secured Short-Term Loans

commercial finance companies
Lending institutions that make *only* secured loans—both short-term and long-term—to businesses.

The primary sources of secured short-term loans to businesses are commercial banks and commercial finance companies. Both institutions deal in short-term loans secured primarily by accounts receivable and inventory. We have already described the operations of commercial banks. **Commercial finance companies** are lending institutions that make *only* secured loans—both short-term and long-term—to businesses. Unlike banks, finance companies are not permitted to hold deposits.

Only when its unsecured and secured short-term borrowing power from the commercial bank is exhausted will a borrower turn to the commercial finance company for additional secured borrowing. Because the finance company generally ends up with higher-risk borrowers, its interest charges on secured short-term loans are usually higher than those of commercial banks. The leading U.S. commercial finance companies include The CIT Group and GE Corporate Financial Services.

Use of Accounts Receivable as Collateral

Two commonly used means of obtaining short-term financing with accounts receivable are *pledging accounts receivable* and *factoring accounts receivable*. Actually, only a pledge of accounts receivable creates a secured short-term loan; factoring really entails the *sale* of accounts receivable at a discount. Although factoring is not actually a form of secured short-term borrowing, it does involve the use of accounts receivable to obtain needed short-term funds.

Pledging Accounts Receivable

pledge of accounts receivable
The use of a firm's accounts receivable as security, or collateral, to obtain a short-term loan.

A **pledge of accounts receivable** is often used to secure a short-term loan. Because accounts receivable are normally quite liquid, they are an attractive form of short-term-loan collateral.

The Pledging Process   When a firm requests a loan against accounts receivable, the lender first evaluates the firm's accounts receivable to determine their desirability as collateral. The lender makes a list of the acceptable accounts, along with the billing dates and amounts. If the borrowing firm requests a loan for a fixed amount, the lender needs to select only enough accounts to secure the funds requested. If the borrower wants the maximum loan available, the lender evaluates all the accounts to select the maximum amount of acceptable collateral.

After selecting the acceptable accounts, the lender normally adjusts the dollar value of these accounts for expected returns on sales and other allowances. If a customer whose account has been pledged returns merchandise or receives some type of allowance, such as a cash discount for early payment, the amount of the collateral is automatically reduced. For protection from such occurrences, the lender normally reduces the value of the acceptable collateral by a fixed percentage.

Next, the percentage to be advanced against the collateral must be determined. The lender evaluates the quality of the acceptable receivables and the expected cost of their liquidation. This percentage represents the principal of the loan and typically ranges between 50 and 90 percent of the face value of acceptable accounts receivable. To protect its interest in the collateral, the lender files a **lien,** which is a publicly disclosed legal claim on the collateral. For an example of the complete pledging process, see the book's website at www.prenhall.com/gitman.

Notification   Pledges of accounts receivable are normally made on a **nonnotification basis,** meaning that a customer whose account has been pledged as collateral is not notified. Under the nonnotification arrangement, the borrower still collects the pledged account receivable, and the lender trusts the borrower to remit these payments as they are received. If a pledge of accounts receivable is made on a **notification basis,** the customer is notified to remit payment directly to the lender.

Pledging Cost   The stated cost of a pledge of accounts receivable is normally 2 to 5 percent above the prime rate. In addition to the stated interest rate, a service charge of up to 3 percent may be levied by the lender to cover its administrative costs. Clearly, pledges of accounts receivable are a high-cost source of short-term financing.

Factoring Accounts Receivable

Factoring accounts receivable involves selling them outright, at a discount, to a financial institution. A **factor** is a financial institution that specializes in purchasing accounts receivable from businesses. Although it is not the same as obtaining a short-term loan, factoring accounts receivable is similar to borrowing with accounts receivable as collateral.

Factoring Agreement   A factoring agreement normally states the exact conditions and procedures for the purchase of an account. The factor, like a lender against a pledge of accounts receivable, chooses accounts for purchase, selecting only those that appear to be acceptable credit risks. Where factoring is to be on a continuing basis, the factor will actually make the firm's credit decisions, because this will guarantee the acceptability of accounts.[4] Factoring is normally done on a *notification basis,* and the factor receives payment of the account directly from the customer. In addition, most sales of accounts receivable to a factor are made on a **nonrecourse basis,** meaning that the factor agrees to accept all credit risks. Thus, if a purchased account turns out to be uncollectible, the factor must absorb the loss.

---

lien
A publicly disclosed legal claim on loan collateral.

nonnotification basis
The basis on which a borrower, having pledged an account receivable, continues to collect the account payments without notifying the account customer.

notification basis
The basis on which an account customer whose account has been pledged (or factored) is notified to remit payment directly to the lender (or factor).

factoring accounts receivable
The outright sale of accounts receivable at a discount to a *factor* or other financial institution.

factor
A financial institution that specializes in purchasing accounts receivable from businesses.

nonrecourse basis
The basis on which accounts receivable are sold to a factor with the understanding that the factor accepts all credit risks on the purchased accounts.

---

4. The use of credit cards such as MasterCard, Visa, and Discover by consumers has some similarity to factoring, because the vendor that accepts the card is reimbursed at a discount for purchases made with the card. The difference between factoring and credit cards is that cards are nothing more than a line of credit extended by the issuer, which charges the vendors a fee for accepting the cards. In factoring, the factor does not analyze credit until after the sale has been made; in many cases (except when factoring is done on a continuing basis), the initial credit decision is the responsibility of the vendor, not the factor that purchases the account.

Typically, the factor is not required to pay the firm until the account is collected or until the last day of the credit period, whichever occurs first. The factor sets up an account similar to a bank deposit account for each customer. As payment is received or as due dates arrive, the factor deposits money into the seller's account, from which the seller is free to make withdrawals as needed.

In many cases, if the firm leaves the money in the account, a *surplus* will exist on which the factor will pay interest. In other instances, the factor may make *advances* to the firm against uncollected accounts that are not yet due. These advances represent a negative balance in the firm's account, on which interest is charged.

Factoring Cost   Factoring costs include commissions, interest levied on advances, and interest earned on surpluses. The factor deposits in the firm's account the book value of the collected or due accounts purchased by the factor, less the commissions. The commissions are typically stated as a 1 to 3 percent discount from the book value of factored accounts receivable. The *interest levied on advances* is generally 2 to 4 percent above the prime rate. It is levied on the actual amount advanced. The *interest paid on surpluses* is generally between 0.2 percent and 0.5 percent per month. An example of the factoring process is included on the book's website at **www.prenhall.com/gitman**.

Although its costs may seem high, factoring has certain advantages that make it attractive to many firms. One is the ability it gives the firm to *turn accounts receivable immediately into cash* without having to worry about repayment. Another advantage is that it ensures a *known pattern of cash flows*. In addition, if factoring is undertaken on a continuing basis, the firm *can eliminate its credit and collection departments*.

Use of Inventory as Collateral

Inventory is generally second to accounts receivable in desirability as short-term loan collateral. Inventory normally has a market value that is greater than its book value, which is used to establish its value as collateral. A lender whose loan is secured with inventory will probably be able to sell that inventory for at least book value if the borrower defaults on its obligations.

The most important characteristic of inventory being evaluated as loan collateral is *marketability*. A warehouse of *perishable* items, such as fresh peaches, may be quite marketable, but if the cost of storing and selling the peaches is high, they may not be desirable collateral. *Specialized items*, such as moon-roving vehicles, are not desirable collateral either, because finding a buyer for them could be difficult. When evaluating inventory as possible loan collateral, the lender looks for items with very stable market prices that have ready markets and that lack undesirable physical properties.

Floating Inventory Liens

floating inventory lien
A secured short-term loan against inventory under which the lender's claim is on the borrower's inventory in general.

A lender may be willing to secure a loan under a **floating inventory lien,** which is a claim on inventory in general. This arrangement is most attractive when the firm has a stable level of inventory that consists of a diversified group of relatively inexpensive merchandise. Inventories of items such as auto tires, screws and bolts, and shoes are candidates for floating-lien loans. Because it is difficult for a lender to verify the presence of the inventory, the lender generally advances less than 50 percent of the book value of the average inventory. The interest charge on a floating lien is 3 to 5 percent above the prime rate. Commercial banks often require floating liens as extra security on what would otherwise be an unsecured loan. Floating-lien inventory loans may also be available from commercial finance companies. An example of a floating inventory lien is included on the book's website at www.prenhall.com/gitman.

Trust Receipt Inventory Loans

trust receipt inventory loan
A secured short-term loan against inventory under which the lender advances 80 to 100 percent of the cost of the borrower's relatively expensive inventory items in exchange for the borrower's promise to repay the lender, with accrued interest, immediately after the sale of each item of collateral.

A **trust receipt inventory loan** often can be made against relatively expensive automotive, consumer durable, and industrial goods that can be identified by serial number. Under this agreement, the borrower keeps the inventory, and the lender may advance 80 to 100 percent of its cost. The lender files a *lien* on all the items financed. The borrower is free to sell the merchandise but is *trusted* to remit the amount lent, along with accrued interest, to the lender immediately after the sale. The lender then releases the lien on the item. The lender makes periodic checks of the borrower's inventory to make sure that the required collateral remains in the hands of the borrower. The interest charge to the borrower is normally 2 percent or more above the prime rate.

Trust receipt loans are often made by manufacturers' wholly owned financing subsidiaries, known as *captive finance companies,* to their customers. Captive finance companies are especially popular in industries that manufacture consumer durable goods, because they provide the manufacturer with a useful sales tool. For example, General Motors Acceptance Corporation (GMAC), the financing subsidiary of General Motors, grants these types of loans to its dealers. Trust receipt loans are also available through commercial banks and commercial finance companies.

Warehouse Receipt Loans

warehouse receipt loan
A secured short-term loan against inventory under which the lender receives control of the pledged inventory collateral, which is stored by a designated warehousing company on the lender's behalf.

A **warehouse receipt loan** is an arrangement whereby the lender, which may be a commercial bank or finance company, receives control of the pledged inventory collateral, which is stored by a designated agent on the lender's behalf. After selecting acceptable collateral, the lender hires a warehousing company to act as its agent and take possession of the inventory.

Two types of warehousing arrangements are possible. A *terminal warehouse* is a central warehouse that is used to store the merchandise of various customers. The lender normally uses such a warehouse when the inventory is easily transported and can be delivered to the warehouse relatively inexpensively. Under a *field warehouse* arrangement, the lender hires a field-warehousing company to set up a warehouse on the borrower's premises or to lease part of the borrower's warehouse to store the pledged collateral. Regardless of the type of warehouse, the warehousing company places a guard over the inventory. Only on written approval of the lender can any portion of the secured inventory be released by the warehousing company.

The actual lending agreement specifically states the requirements for the release of inventory. As in the case of other secured loans, the lender accepts only collateral that is believed to be readily marketable and advances only a portion—generally 75 to 90 percent—of the collateral's value. The specific costs of warehouse receipt loans are generally higher than those of any other secured lending arrangements because of the need to hire and pay a warehousing company to guard and supervise the collateral. The basic interest charged on warehouse receipt loans is higher than that charged on unsecured loans, generally ranging from 3 to 5 percent above the prime rate. In addition to the interest charge, the borrower must absorb the costs of warehousing by paying the warehouse fee, which is generally between 1 and 3 percent of the amount of the loan. The borrower is normally also required to pay the insurance costs on the warehoused merchandise. An example of the procedures and costs of a warehouse receipt loan is included on the book's website at www.prenhall.com/gitman.

REVIEW QUESTIONS

14–11 Are secured short-term loans viewed as more risky or less risky than unsecured short-term loans? Why?

14–12 In general, what interest rates and fees are levied on secured short-term loans? Why are these rates generally *higher* than the rates on unsecured short-term loans?

14–13 Describe and compare the basic features of the following methods of using *accounts receivable* to obtain short-term financing: (**a**) pledging accounts receivable, and (**b**) factoring accounts receivable. Be sure to mention the institutions that offer each of them.

14–14 For the following methods of using *inventory* as short-term loan collateral, describe the basic features of each, and compare their use: (**a**) floating lien, (**b**) trust receipt loan, and (**c**) warehouse receipt loan.

Summary

Focus on Value

Current liabilities represent an important and generally inexpensive source of financing for a firm. The level of short-term (current liabilities) financing employed by a firm affects its profitability and risk. Accounts payable and accruals are spontaneous liabilities that should be carefully managed because they represent free financing. Notes payable, which represent negotiated short-term financing, should be obtained at the lowest cost under the best possible terms. Large, well-known firms can obtain unsecured short-term financing through the sale of commercial paper. On a secured basis, the firm can obtain loans from banks or commercial finance companies, using either accounts receivable or inventory as collateral.

The financial manager must obtain the right quantity and form of current liabilities financing to provide the lowest-cost funds with the least risk. Such a strategy should positively contribute to the firm's goal of **maximizing the stock price.**

Review of Learning Goals

Key features of the common sources of short-term financing are summarized in Table 14.2 on pages 588–589.

LG 1 **Review accounts payable, the key components of credit terms, and the procedures for analyzing those terms.** The major spontaneous source of short-term financing is accounts payable. They are the primary source of short-term funds. Credit terms may differ with respect to the credit period, cash discount, cash discount period, and beginning of the credit period. Cash discounts should be given up only when a firm in need of short-term funds must pay an interest rate on borrowing that is greater than the cost of giving up the cash discount.

LG 2 **Understand the effects of stretching accounts payable on their cost, and the use of accruals.** Stretching accounts payable can lower the cost of giving up a cash discount. Accruals, which result primarily from wage and tax obligations, are virtually free.

LG 3 **Describe interest rates and the basic types of unsecured bank sources of short-term loans.** Banks are the major source of unsecured short-term loans to businesses. The interest rate on these loans is tied to the prime rate of interest by a risk premium and may be fixed or floating. It should be evaluated by using the effective annual rate. Whether interest is paid when the loan matures or in advance affects the rate. Bank loans may take the form of a single-payment note, a line of credit, or a revolving credit agreement.

LG 4 **Discuss the basic features of commercial paper and the key aspects of international short-term loans.** Commercial paper is an unsecured IOU issued by firms with a high credit standing. International sales and purchases expose firms to exchange rate risk. Such transactions are larger and of longer maturity than domestic transactions, and they can be financed by using a letter of credit, by borrowing in the local market, or through dollar-denominated loans from international banks. On transactions between subsidiaries, "netting" can be used to minimize foreign exchange fees and other transaction costs.

LG 5 **Explain the characteristics of secured short-term loans and the use of accounts receivable as short-term-loan collateral.** Secured short-term loans are those for which the lender requires collateral—typically, current assets such as accounts receivable or inventory. Only a percentage of the book value of acceptable collateral is advanced by the lender. These loans are more expensive than unsecured loans. Commercial banks and commercial finance companies make secured short-term loans. Both pledging and factoring involve the use of accounts receivable to obtain needed short-term funds.

LG 6 **Describe the various ways in which inventory can be used as short-term-loan collateral.** Inventory can be used as short-term-loan collateral under a floating lien, a trust receipt arrangement, or a warehouse receipt loan.

TABLE 14.2   Summary of Key Features of Common Sources of Short-Term Financing

Type of short-term financing	Source	Cost or conditions	Characteristics
I. Spontaneous liabilities			
Accounts payable	Suppliers of merchandise	No stated cost except when a cash discount is offered for early payment.	Credit extended on open account for a specified number of days. The largest source of short-term financing.
Accruals	Employees and government	Free.	Result because wages (employees) and taxes (government) are paid at discrete points in time after the service has been rendered. Hard to manipulate this source of financing.
II. Unsecured sources of short-term loans			
Bank sources			
(1) Single-payment notes	Commercial banks	Prime plus 0% to 4% risk premium—fixed or floating rate.	A single-payment loan used to meet a funds shortage expected to last only a short period of time.
(2) Lines of credit	Commercial banks	Prime plus 0% to 4% risk premium—fixed or floating rate. Often must maintain 10% to 20% compensating balance and clean up the line annually.	A prearranged borrowing limit under which funds, if available, will be lent to allow the borrower to meet seasonal needs.
(3) Revolving credit agreements	Commercial banks	Prime plus 0% to 4% risk premium—fixed or floating rate. Often must maintain 10% to 20% compensating balance and pay a commitment fee of approximately 0.5% of the average unused balance.	A line-of-credit agreement under which the availability of funds is guaranteed. Often for a period greater than 1 year.
Commercial paper	Business firms—both nonfinancial and financial	Generally 2% to 4% below the prime rate of interest.	A short-term, unsecured promissory note issued by the most financially sound firms.

(continued)

Type of short-term financing	Source	Cost or conditions	Characteristics
III. Secured sources of short-term loans			
Accounts receivable collateral			
(1) Pledging	Commercial banks and commercial finance companies	2% to 5% above prime plus up to 3% in fees. Advance 50% to 90% of collateral value.	Selected accounts receivable are used as collateral. The borrower is trusted to remit to the lender on collection of pledged accounts. Done on a nonnotification basis.
(2) Factoring	Factors, commercial banks, and commercial finance companies	1% to 3% discount from face value of factored accounts. Interest of 2% to 4% above prime levied on advances. Interest between 0.2% and 0.5% per month earned on surplus balances left with factor.	Selected accounts are sold—generally without recourse—at a discount. All credit risks go with the accounts. Factor will lend (make advances) against uncollected accounts that are not yet due. Factor will also pay interest on surplus balances. Typically done on a notification basis.
Inventory collateral			
(1) Floating liens	Commercial banks and commercial finance companies	3% to 5% above prime. Advance less than 50% of collateral value.	A loan against inventory in general. Made when firm has stable inventory of a variety of inexpensive items.
(2) Trust receipts	Manufacturers' captive financing subsidiaries, commercial banks, and commercial finance companies	2% or more above prime. Advance 80% to 100% of cost of collateral.	Loan against relatively expensive automotive, consumer durable, and industrial goods that can be identified by serial number. Collateral remains in possession of the borrower, who is trusted to remit proceeds to the lender upon its sale.
(3) Warehouse receipts	Commercial banks and commercial finance companies	3% to 5% above prime plus a 1% to 3% warehouse fee. Advance 75% to 90% of collateral value.	Inventory used as collateral is placed under control of the lender either through a terminal warehouse or through a field warehouse. A third party—a warehousing company—guards the inventory for the lender. Inventory is released only on written approval of the lender.

Self-Test Problem (Solution in Appendix B)

  ST14–1 Cash discount decisions   The credit terms for each of three suppliers are shown in the following table. (*Note:* Assume a 365-day year.)

Supplier	Credit terms
X	1/10 net 55 EOM
Y	2/10 net 30 EOM
Z	2/20 net 60 EOM

a. Determine the *approximate* cost of giving up the cash discount from each supplier.
b. Assuming that the firm needs short-term financing, indicate whether it would be better to give up the cash discount or take the discount and borrow from a bank at 15% annual interest. Evaluate each supplier *separately* using your findings in part **a**.
c. What impact, if any, would the fact that the firm could stretch its accounts payable (net period only) by 20 days from supplier Z have on your answer in part **b** relative to this supplier?

Warm-Up Exercises

A blue box (■) indicates exercises available in .

 E14–1 Lyman Nurseries purchased seeds costing $25,000 with terms of 3/15 net 30 EOM on January 12. How much will the firm pay if it takes the cash discount? What is the *approximate cost of giving up the cash discount,* using the simplified formula?

 E14–2 Cleaner's, Inc., is switching to paying employees every 2 weeks rather than weekly and will therefore "skip" 1 week's pay. The firm has 25 employees who work a 60-hour week and earn an average wage of $12.50 per hour. Using a 10% rate of interest, how much will this change save the firm annually?

 E14–3 Jasmine Scents has been given two competing offers for short-term financing. Both offers are for borrowing $15,000 for 1 year. The first offer is a *discount loan* at 8%; the second offer is for interest to be paid *at maturity* at a stated interest rate of 9%. Calculate the *effective annual rates* for each loan and indicate which loan offers the better terms.

 E14–4 Jackson Industries has borrowed $125,000 under a line-of-credit agreement. While the company normally maintains a checking account balance of $15,000 in the lending bank, this credit line requires a 20% compensating balance. The stated interest rate on the borrowed funds is 10%. What is the *effective annual rate of interest* on the line of credit?

 E14–5 Horizon Telecom sold $300,000 worth of 120-day commercial paper for $298,000. What is the dollar amount of interest paid on the commercial paper? What is the *effective 120-day rate* on the paper?

Problems

A blue box (■) indicates problems available in .

 P14–1 **Payment dates**   Determine when a firm must pay for purchases made and invoices dated on November 25 under each of the following credit terms.
a. net 30 date of invoice
b. net 30 EOM
c. net 45 date of invoice
d. net 60 EOM

 P14–2 **Cost of giving up cash discounts**   Determine the *cost of giving up cash discounts* under each of the following terms of sale. (*Note:* Assume a 365-day year.)
a. 2/10 net 30   e. 1/10 net 60
b. 1/10 net 30   f. 3/10 net 30
c. 2/10 net 45   g. 4/10 net 180
d. 3/10 net 45

 P14–3 **Credit terms**   Purchases made on credit are due in full by the end of the billing period. Many firms extend a discount for payment made in the first part of the billing period. The original invoice contains a type of "short-hand" notation that explains the credit terms that apply. (*Note:* Assume a 365-day year.)
a. Write the short-hand expression of credit terms for each of the following.

Cash discount	Cash discount period	Credit period	Beginning of credit period
1%	15 days	45 days	date of invoice
2	10	30	end of month
2	7	28	date of invoice
1	10	60	end of month

b. For each of the sets of credit terms in part **a**, calculate the number of days until full payment is due for invoices dated March 12.
c. For each of the sets of credit terms, calculate the *cost of giving up the cash discount*.
d. If the firm's cost of short-term financing is 8%, what would you recommend in regard to taking the discount or giving it up in each case?

  P14–4 **Cash discount versus loan**   Erica Stone works in an accounts payable department. She has attempted to convince her boss to take the discount on the 3/10 net 45 credit terms most suppliers offer, but her boss argues that giving up the 3% discount is less costly than a short-term loan at 14%. Prove to whoever is wrong that the other is correct. (*Note:* Assume a 365-day year.)

PERSONAL FINANCE PROBLEM

 P14–5 **Borrow or pay cash for an asset**   Bob and Carol Gibbs are set to move into their first apartment. They visited Furniture R'Us, looking for a dining room table and buffet. Dining room sets are typically one of the more expensive home furnishing items, and the store offers financing arrangements to customers. Bob and Carol have

ST5–2 a. When the market return increases by 10%, the project's required return would be expected to increase by 15% ($1.50 \times 10\%$). When the market return decreases by 10%, the project's required return would be expected to decrease by 15% [$1.50 \times (-10\%)$].

b. $r_j = R_F + [b_j \times (r_m - R_F)]$
$= 7\% + [1.50 \times (10\% - 7\%)]$
$= 7\% + 4.5\% = \underline{11.5\%}$

c. No, the project should be rejected, because its *expected* return of 11% is less than the 11.5% return *required* from the project.

d. $r_j = 7\% + [1.50 \times (9\% - 7\%)]$
$= 7\% + 3\% = \underline{10\%}$

The project would now be acceptable, because its *expected* return of 11% is now in excess of the *required* return, which has declined to 10% as a result of investors in the marketplace becoming less risk-averse.

Chapter 6

ST6–1 a. $B_0 = I \times (PVIFA_{r_d,n}) + M \times (PVIF_{r_d,n})$
$I = 0.08 \times \$1,000 = \$80$
$M = \$1,000$
$n = 12$ yrs
(1) $r_d = 7\%$
$B_0 = \$80 \times (PVIFA_{7\%,12yrs}) + \$1,000 \times (PVIF_{7\%,12yrs})$
$= (\$80 \times 7.943) + (\$1,000 \times 0.444)$
$= \$635.44 + \$444.00 = \underline{\$1,079.44}$
(Calculator solution = $1,079.43)
(2) $r_d = 8\%$
$B_0 = \$80 \times (PVIFA_{8\%,12yrs}) + \$1,000 \times (PVIF_{8\%,12yrs})$
$= (\$80 \times 7.536) + (\$1,000 \times 0.397)$
$= \$602.88 + \$397.00 = \underline{\$999.88}$
(Calculator solution = $1,000)
(3) $r_d = 10\%$
$B_0 = \$80 \times (PVIFA_{10\%,12yrs}) + \$1,000 \times (PVIF_{10\%,12yrs})$
$= (\$80 \times 6.814) + (\$1,000 \times 0.319)$
$= \$545.12 + \$319.00 = \underline{\$864.12}$
(Calculator solution = $863.73)

b. (1) $r_d = 7\%$, $B_0 = \$1,079.44$; sells at a *premium*

(2) $r_d = 8\%$, $B_0 = \$999.88 \approx \$1,000.00$; sells at its *par value*

(3) $r_d = 10\%$, $B_0 = \$864.12$; sells at a *discount*

c. $B_0 = \dfrac{I}{2} \times (PVIFA_{r_{d/2},2n}) + M \times (PVIF_{r_{d/2},2n})$

$= \dfrac{\$80}{2} \times (PVIFA_{10\%/2,2\times12\text{periods}}) + \$1,000 \times (PVIF_{10\%/2,2\times12\text{periods}})$

$= \$40 \times (PVIFA_{5\%,24\text{periods}}) + \$1,000 \times (PVIF_{5\%,24\text{periods}})$

$= (\$40 \times 13.799) + (\$1,000 \times 0.310)$

$= \$551.96 + \$310.00 = \underline{\underline{\$861.96}}$

(Calculator solution = \$862.01)

ST6–2 a. $B_0 = \$1,150$

$I = 0.11 \times \$1,000 = \$110$

$M = \$1,000$

$n = 18$ yrs

$\text{Current yield} = \dfrac{\text{annual interest}}{\text{current price}}$

$= \dfrac{\$110}{\$1,150} = 9.57\%$

b. $\$1,150 = \$110 \times (PVIFA_{r_d,18\text{yrs}}) + \$1,000 \times (PVIF_{r_d,18\text{yrs}})$

Because if $r_d = 11\%$, $B_0 = \$1,000 = M$, try $r_d = 10\%$.

$B_0 = \$110 \times (PVIFA_{10\%,18\text{yrs}}) + \$1,000 \times (PVIF_{10\%,18\text{yrs}})$

$= (\$110 \times 8.201) + (\$1,000 \times 0.180)$

$= \$902.11 + \$180.00 = \$1,082.11$

Because $\$1,082.11 < \$1,150$, try $r_d = 9\%$.

$B_0 = \$110 \times (PVIFA_{9\%,18\text{yrs}}) + \$1,000 \times (PVIF_{9\%,18\text{yrs}})$

$= (\$110 \times 8.756) + (\$1,000 \times 0.212)$

$= \$963.16 + \$212.00 = \$1,175.16$

Because the \$1,175.16 value at 9% is higher than \$1,150, and the \$1,082.11 value at 10% rate is lower than \$1,150, the bond's yield to maturity must be between 9% and 10%. Because the \$1,175.16 value is closer to \$1,150, rounding to the nearest whole percent, the YTM is 9%. (By using interpolation, the more precise YTM value is 9.27%.)

(Calculator solution = 9.26%)

c. The calculated YTM of 9.26% is below both the bond's 11% coupon interest rate and its current yield of 9.57% calculated in part **a**, because the bond's market value of \$1,150 is above its \$1,000 par value. Whenever a bond's market value is above its par value (it sells at a *premium*), its YTM and current yield will be below its coupon interest rate; when a bond sells at *par*, the YTM and current yield will equal its coupon interest rate; and when the bond sells for less than par (at a *discount*), its YTM and current yield will be greater than its coupon interest rate.

Chapter 7

ST7–1 $D_0 = \$1.80/\text{share}$

$r_s = 12\%$

a. *Zero growth:*

$$P_0 = \frac{D_1}{r_s} = \frac{D_1 = D_0 = \$1.80}{0.12} = \$15/\text{share}$$

b. *Constant growth, g = 5%:*

$$D_1 = D_0 \times (1 + g) = \$1.80 = (1 + 0.05) = \$1.89/\text{share}$$

$$P_0 = \frac{D_1}{r_s - g} = \frac{\$1.89}{0.12 - 0.05} = \frac{\$1.89}{0.07} = \$27/\text{share}$$

ST7–2 a. **Step 1:** Present value of free cash flow from end of 2011 to infinity measured at the end of 2010.

$$FCF_{2014} = \$1,500,000 \times (1 + 0.04) = \$1,560,000$$

$$\text{Value of } FCF_{2014\to\infty} = \frac{\$1,560,000}{0.10 - 0.04} = \frac{\$1,560,000}{0.06} = \$26,000,000$$

Step 2: Add the value found in Step 1 to the 2013 FCF.

Total $FCF_{2013} = \$1,500,000 + \$26,000,000 = \$27,500,000$

Step 3: Find the sum of the present values of the FCFs for 2010 through 2013 to determine company value, V_C.

Year (t)	FCF_t (1)	$PVIF_{10\%,t}$ (2)	Present value of FCF_t [(1) × (2)] (3)
2010	$ 800,000	0.909	$ 727,200
2011	1,200,000	0.826	991,200
2012	1,400,000	0.751	1,051,400
2013	27,500,000	0.683	18,782,500
		Value of entire company, V_C =	$21,552,300

(Calculator solution = $21,553,719)

b. Common Stock value, $V_S = V_C - V_D - V_P$

$V_C = \$21,552,300$ (calculated in part **a**)

$V_D = \$12,500,000$ (given)

$V_P = \$0$ (given)

$V_S = \$21,552,300 - \$12,500,000 - \$0 = \$9,052,300$

(Calculator solution = $9,053,719)

c. Price per share $= \dfrac{\$9,052,300}{500,000} = \$18.10/\text{share}$

(Calculator solution = $18.11/share)

Chapter 8

ST8–1 **a.** Book value = Installed cost − Accumulated depreciation
Installed cost = $50,000
Accumulated depreciation = $50,000 × (0.20 + 0.32 + 0.19 + 0.12)
$$= \$50,000 \times 0.83 = \$41,500$$
Book value = $50,000 − $41,500 = $8,500

b. Taxes on sale of old equipment:
Gain on sale = Sale price − Book value
$$= \$55,000 - \$8,500 = \$46,500$$
Taxes = 0.40 × $46,500 = $18,600

c. Initial investment:

Installed cost of new equipment		
Cost of new equipment	$75,000	
+ Installation costs	5,000	
Total installed cost—new		$80,000
− After-tax proceeds from sale of old equipment		
Proceeds from sale of old equipment	$55,000	
− Taxes on sale of old equipment	18,600	
Total after-tax proceeds—old		36,400
+ Change in net working capital		15,000
Initial investment		$58,600

ST8–2 **a.** Initial investment:

Installed cost of new machine		
Cost of new machine	$140,000	
+ Installation costs	10,000	
Total installed cost—new (depreciable value)		$150,000
− After-tax proceeds from sale of old machine		
Proceeds from sale of old machine	$ 42,000	
− Taxes on sale of old machine[1]	9,120	
Total after-tax proceeds—old		32,880
+ Change in net working capital[2]		20,000
Initial investment		$137,120

---

[1]Book value of old machine = $40,000 − [(0.20 + 0.32) × $40,000]
$$= \$40,000 - (0.52 \times \$40,000)$$
$$= \$40,000 - \$20,800 = \$19,200$$
Gain on sale = $42,000 − $19,200 = $22,800
Taxes = .40 × $22,800 = $9,120

[2]Change in net working capital = +$10,000 + $25,000 − $15,000
$$= \$35,000 - \$15,000 = \$20,000$$

b. Incremental operating cash inflows:

Calculation of Depreciation Expense

Year	Cost (1)	Applicable MACRS depreciation percentages (from Table 3.2) (2)	Depreciation [(1) × (2)] (3)
With new machine			
1	$150,000	33%	$ 49,500
2	150,000	45	67,500
3	150,000	15	22,500
4	150,000	7	10,500
		Totals 100%	$150,000
With old machine			
2	$ 40,000	19% (year-3 depreciation)	$ 7,600
2	40,000	12 (year-4 depreciation)	4,800
3	40,000	12 (year-5 depreciation)	4,800
4	40,000	5 (year-6 depreciation)	2,000
		Total	$19,200[a]

[a]The total of $19,200 represents the book value of the old machine at the end of the second year, which was calculated in part **a**.

Calculation of Operating Cash Inflows

	Year 1	Year 2	Year 3	Year 4
With new machine				
Earnings before depr., int., and taxes[a]	$120,000	$130,000	$130,000	$ 0
− Depreciation[b]	49,500	67,500	22,500	10,500
Earnings before int. and taxes	$ 70,500	$ 62,500	$107,500	−$10,500
− Taxes (rate, $T = 40\%$)	28,200	25,000	43,000	− 4,200
Net operating profit after taxes	$ 42,300	$ 37,500	$ 64,500	−$ 6,300
+ Depreciation[b]	49,500	67,500	22,500	10,500
Operating cash inflows	$ 91,800	$105,000	$ 87,000	$ 4,200
With old machine				
Earnings before depr., int., and taxes[a]	$ 70,000	$ 70,000	$ 70,000	$ 0
− Depreciation[c]	7,600	4,800	4,800	2,000
Earnings before int. and taxes	$ 62,400	$ 65,200	$ 65,200	−$ 2,000
− Taxes (rate, $T = 40\%$)	24,960	26,080	26,080	− 800
Net operating profit after taxes	$ 37,440	$ 39,120	$ 39,120	−$ 1,200
+ Depreciation	7,600	4,800	4,800	2,000
Operating cash inflows	$ 45,040	$ 43,920	$ 43,920	$ 800

[a]Given in the problem.

[b]From column 3 of the preceding table, top.

[c]From column 3 of the preceding table, bottom.

Calculation of Incremental Operating Cash Inflows

	Operating cash inflows		
Year	New machine[a] (1)	Old machine[a] (2)	Incremental (relevant) [(1) − (2)] (3)
1	$ 91,800	$45,040	$46,760
2	105,000	43,920	61,080
3	87,000	43,920	43,080
4	4,200	800	3,400

[a]From the final row for the respective machine in the preceding table.

c. Terminal cash flow (end of year 3):

After-tax proceeds from sale of new machine		
Proceeds from sale of new machine	$35,000	
Total after-tax proceeds—new[1]	9,800	
Total after-tax proceeds—new		$25,200
− After-tax proceeds from sale of old machine		
Proceeds from sale of old machine	$ 0	
− Tax on sale of old machine[2]	− 800	
Total after-tax proceeds—old		800
+ Change in net working capital		20,000
Terminal cash flow		$44,400

———————

[1]Book value of new machine at end of year 3
$$= \$150,000 - [(0.33 + 0.45 + 0.15) \times \$150,000] = \$150,000 - (0.93 \times \$150,000)$$
$$= \$15,000 - \$139,500 = \$10,500$$
Tax on sale $= 0.40 \times (\$35,000$ sale price $- \$10,500$ book value$)$
$$= 0.40 \times \$24,500 = \underline{\$9,800}$$

[2]Book value of old machine at end of year 3
$$= \$40,000 - [(0.20 + 0.32 + 0.19 + 0.12 + 0.12) \times \$40,000] = \$40,000 - (0.95 \times \$40,000)$$
$$= \$40,000 - \$38,000 = \$2,000$$
Tax on sale $= 0.40 \times (\$0$ sale price $- \$2,000$ book value$)$
$$= 0.40 \times (-\$2,500 = -\underline{\$800} \text{ (i.e., \$800 tax saving)}$$

d.

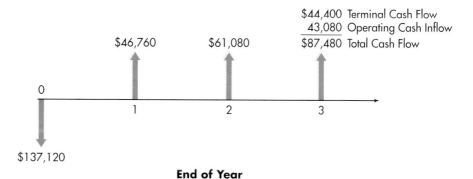

$44,400 Terminal Cash Flow
 43,080 Operating Cash Inflow
$87,480 Total Cash Flow

$46,760 $61,080

0

1   2   3

$137,120

End of Year

Note: The year-4 incremental operating cash inflow of $3,400 is not directly included; it is instead reflected in the book values used to calculate the taxes on sale of the machines at the end of year 3 and is therefore part of the terminal cash flow.

Chapter 9

ST9–1 **a.** Payback period:

Project M: $\dfrac{\$28,500}{\$10,000} = \underline{\underline{2.85}}$ years

Project N:

Year *(t)*	Cash inflows *(CF$_t$)*	Cumulative cash inflows
1	$11,000	$11,000
2	10,000	21,000 ←
3	9,000	30,000
4	8,000	38,000

$2 + \dfrac{\$27,000 - \$21,000}{\$9,000}$ years

$2 + \dfrac{\$6,000}{\$9,000}$ years $= \underline{\underline{2.67}}$ years

b. Net present value (NPV):

Project M: $\text{NPV} = (\$10,000 \times PVIFA_{14\%,4yrs}) - \$28,500$

$= (\$10,000 \times 2.914) - \$28,500$

$= \$29,140 - \$28,500 = \underline{\underline{\$640}}$

(Calculator solution $= \$637.12$)

Project N:

Year *(t)*	Cash inflows *(CF$_t$)* (1)	$PVIF_{14\%,t}$ (2)	Present value at 14% [(1) ÷ (2)] (3)
1	$11,000	0.877	$ 9,647
2	10,000	0.769	7,690
3	9,000	0.675	6,075
4	8,000	0.592	4,736
		Present value of cash inflows	$28,148
		− Initial investment	27,000
		Net present value (NPV)	$ 1,148

(Calculator solution $= \$1,155.18$)

c. Internal rate of return (IRR):

Project M: $\dfrac{\$28,500}{\$10,000} = 2.850$

$PVIFA_{IRR,4yrs} = 2.850$
From Table A–4:
$PVIFA_{15\%,4yrs} = 2.855$
$PVIFA_{16\%,4yrs} = 2.798$
IRR $= \underline{\underline{15}}\%$ (2.850 is closest to 2.855)
(Calculator solution $= 15.09\%$)
Project N:

Average annual cash inflow $= \dfrac{\$11,000 + \$10,000 + \$9,000 + \$8,000}{4}$

$$= \dfrac{\$38,000}{4} = \$9,500$$

$PVIFA_{r,4yrs} = \dfrac{\$27,000}{\$9,500} = 2.842$

$r \approx 15\%$

Try 16%, because there are more cash inflows in early years.

Year (t)	CF_t (1)	$PVIF_{16\%,t}$ (2)	Present value at 16% [(1) × (2)] (3)	$PVIF_{17\%,t}$ (4)	Present value at 17% [(1) × (4)] (5)
1	$11,000	0.862	$ 9,482	0.855	$ 9,405
2	10,000	0.743	7,430	0.731	7,310
3	9,000	0.641	5,769	0.624	5,616
4	8,000	0.552	4,416	0.534	4,272
	Present value of cash inflows		$27,097		$26,603
	− Initial investment		27,000		27,000
	NPV		$ 97		−$ 397

IRR $= \underline{\underline{16}}\%$ (rounding to nearest whole percent)
(Calculator solution $= 16.19\%$)

d.

	Project M	Project N
Payback period	2.85 years	2.67 years[a]
NPV	$640	$1,148[a]
IRR	15%	16%[a]

[a]Preferred project.

Project N is recommended, because it has the shorter payback period and the higher NPV, which is greater than zero, and the larger IRR, which is greater than the 14% cost of capital.

e. Net present value profiles:

	Data	
	NPV	
Discount rate	Project M	Project N
0%	$11,500[a]	$11,000[b]
14	640	1,148
15	0	—
16	—	0

[a]($10,000 + $10,000 + $10,000 + $10,000) − $28,500
= $40,000 − $28,500
= $11,500

[b]($11,000 + $10,000 + $9,000 + $8,000) − $27,000
= $38,000 − $27,000
= $11,000

From the NPV profile that follows, it can be seen that if the firm has a cost of capital below approximately 6% (exact value is 5.75%), conflicting rankings of the projects would exist using the NPV and IRR decision techniques. Because the firm's cost of capital is 14%, it can be seen in part **d** that no conflict exists.

ST9–2   a. $NPV_A = (\$7,000 \times PVIFA_{10\%,3yrs}) - \$15,000$

$= (\$7,000 \times 2.487) - \$15,000$

$= \$17,409 - \$15,000 = \underline{\underline{\$2,409}}$

(Calculator solution = $2,407.96)

$$\text{NPV}_B = (\$10,000 \times PVIFA_{10\%,3\text{yrs}}) - \$20,000$$
$$= (\$10,000 - 2.487) - \$20,000$$
$$= \$24,870 - \$20,000 = \underline{\underline{\$4,870}}^*$$

(Calculator solution = \$4,868.52)

*Preferred project, because higher NPV.

b. From the CAPM-type relationship, the risk-adjusted discount rate ($RADR$) for project A, which has a risk index of 0.4, is 9%; for project B, with a risk index of 1.8, the $RADR$ is 16%.

$$\text{NPV}_A = (\$7,000 \times PVIFA_{9\%,3\text{yrs}}) - \$15,000$$
$$= (\$7,000 \times 2.531) - \$15,000$$
$$= \$17,717 - \$15,000 = \underline{\underline{\$2,717}}^*$$

(Calculator solution = \$2,719.06)

$$\text{NPV}_B = (\$10,000 \times PVIFA_{16\%,3\text{yrs}}) - \$20,000$$
$$= (\$10,000 \times 2.246) - \$20,000$$
$$= \$22,460 - \$20,000 = \underline{\underline{\$2,460}}$$

(Calculator solution = \$2,458.90)

*Preferred project, because higher NPV.

c. When the differences in risk were ignored in part **a**, project B was preferred over project A; but when the higher risk of project B is incorporated into the analysis using risk-adjusted discount rates in part **b**, *project A is preferred over project B*. Clearly, project A should be implemented.

Chapter 10

ST10–1   a. Cost of debt, r_i (using approximation formula)

$$r_d = \frac{I + \dfrac{\$1,000 - N_d}{n}}{\dfrac{N_d + \$1,000}{2}}$$

$$I = 0.10 \times \$1,000 = \$100$$
$$N_d = \$1,000 - \$30 \text{ discount} - \$20 \text{ flotation cost} = \$950$$
$$n = 10 \text{ years}$$

$$r_d = \frac{\$100 + \dfrac{\$1,000 - \$950}{10}}{\dfrac{\$950 + \$1,000}{2}} = \frac{\$100 + \$5}{\$975} = 10.8\%$$

(Calculator solution = 10.8%)

$$r_i = r_d \times (1 - T)$$
$$T = 0.40$$
$$r_i = 10.8\% \times (1 - 0.40) = \underline{\underline{6.5\%}}$$

Cost of preferred stock, r_p

$$r_p = \frac{D_p}{N_p}$$

$D_p = 0.11 \times \$100 = \$11$

$N_p = \$100 - \$4 \text{ flotation cost} = \$96$

$$r_p = \frac{\$11}{\$96} = \underline{\underline{11.5\%}}$$

Cost of retained earnings, r_r

$$r_r = r_s = \frac{D_1}{P_0} + g$$

$$= \frac{\$6}{\$80} + 6.0\% = 7.5\% + 6.0\% = \underline{\underline{13.5\%}}$$

Cost of new common stock, r_n

$$r_n = \frac{D_1}{N_n} + g$$

$D_1 = \$6$

$N_n = \$80 - \$4 \text{ underpricing} - \$4 \text{ flotation cost} = \$72$

$g = 6.0\%$

$$r_n = \frac{\$6}{\$72} + 6.0\% = 8.3\% + 6.0\% = \underline{\underline{14.3\%}}$$

b. (1) Break point, BP

$$BP_{\text{common equity}} = \frac{AF_{\text{common equity}}}{w_{\text{common equity}}}$$

$AF_{\text{common equity}} = \$225,000$

$w_{\text{common equity}} = 45\%$

$$BP_{\text{common equity}} = \frac{\$225,000}{0.45} = \$500,000$$

(2) WACC for total new financing $< \$500,000$

Source of capital	Weight (1)	Cost (2)	Weighted cost [(1) × (2)] (3)
Long-term debt	.40	6.5%	2.6%
Preferred stock	.15	11.5	1.7
Common stock equity	.45	13.5	6.1
Totals	1.00		10.4%

Weighted average cost of capital = 10.4%

(3) WACC for total new financing > $500,000

Source of capital	Weight (1)	Cost (2)	Weighted cost [(1) × (2)] (3)
Long-term debt	.40	6.5%	2.6%
Preferred stock	.15	11.5	1.7
Common stock equity	.45	14.3	6.4
Totals	1.00		10.7%

Weighted average cost of capital = 10.7%

c. IOS data for graph

Investment opportunity	Internal rate of return (IRR)	Initial investment	Cumulative investment
D	16.5%	$200,000	$ 200,000
C	12.9	150,000	350,000
E	11.8	450,000	800,000
A	11.2	100,000	900,000
G	10.5	300,000	1,200,000
F	10.1	600,000	1,800,000
B	9.7	500,000	2,300,000

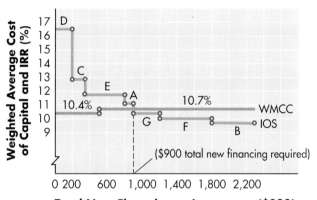

d. Projects D, C, E, and A should be accepted because their respective IRRs exceed the WMCC. They will require $900,000 of total new financing.

Chapter 11

ST11–1 a. $Q = \dfrac{FC}{P - VC}$

$$= \dfrac{\$250,000}{\$7.50 - \$3.00} = \dfrac{\$250,000}{\$4.50} = \underline{\underline{55,556}} \text{ units}$$

b.

	+20%	
Sales (in units)	100,000	120,000
Sales revenue (units × $7.50/unit)	$750,000	$900,000
Less: Variable operating costs (units × $3.00/unit)	300,000	360,000
Less: Fixed operating costs	250,000	250,000
Earnings before interest and taxes (EBIT)	$200,000	$290,000

+45%

Less: Interest	80,000	80,000
Net profits before taxes	$120,000	$210,000
Less: Taxes ($T = 0.40$)	48,000	84,000
Net profits after taxes	$ 72,000	$126,000
Less: Preferred dividends (8,000 shares × $5.00/share)	40,000	40,000
Earnings available for common	$132,000	$ 86,000
Earnings per share (EPS)	$32,000/20,000 = $1.60/share	$86,000/20,000 = $4.30/share

+169%

c. $\text{DOL} = \dfrac{\% \text{ change in EBIT}}{\% \text{ change in sales}} = \dfrac{+45\%}{+20\%} = \underline{\underline{2.25}}$

d. $\text{DFL} = \dfrac{\% \text{ change in EPS}}{\% \text{ change in EBIT}} = \dfrac{+169\%}{+45} = \underline{\underline{3.76}}$

e. $\text{DTL} = \text{DOL} \times \text{DFL}$

$= 2.25 \times 3.76 = \underline{\underline{8.46}}$

Using the other DTL formula:

$\text{DTL} = \dfrac{\% \text{ change in EPS}}{\% \text{ change in sales}}$

$8.46 = \dfrac{\% \text{ change in EPS}}{+50\%}$

% change in EPS $= 8.46 \times 0.50 = 4.23 = \underline{\underline{+423\%}}$

ST11–2

Data summary for alternative plans

Source of capital	Plan A (bond)	Plan B (stock)
Long-term debt	$60,000 at 12% annual interest	$50,000 at 12% annual interest
Annual interest =	0.12 = $60,000 = $7,200	0.12 × $50,000 = $6,000
Common stock	10,000 shares	11,000 shares

a.

	Plan A (bond)		Plan B (stock)	
EBIT[a]	$30,000	$40,000	$30,000	$40,000
Less: Interest	7,200	7,200	6,000	6,000
Net profits before taxes	$22,800	$32,800	$24,000	$34,000
Less: Taxes ($T = 0.40$)	9,120	13,120	9,600	13,600
Net profits after taxes	$13,680	$19,680	$14,400	$20,400
EPS (10,000 shares)	$1.37	$1.97		
(11,000 shares)			$1.31	$1.85

[a]Values were arbitrarily selected; other values could have been used.

Coordinates

	EBIT	
	$30,000	$40,000
Financing plan	Earnings per share (EPS)	
A (Bond)	$1.37	$1.97
B (Stock)	1.31	1.85

b.

c. The bond plan (Plan A) becomes superior to the stock plan (Plan B) at *around $20,000* of EBIT, as represented by the dashed vertical line in the figure in part **b.** (*Note:* The actual point is $19,200, which can be determined algebraically by using the technique described in more advanced texts.)

B-23   APPENDIX B

ST12–3   a.

Capital structure debt ratio	Expected EPS (1)	Required return, r_s (2)	Estimated share value [(1) ÷ (2)] (3)
0%	$3.12	.13	$24.00
10	3.90	.15	26.00
20	4.80	.16	30.00
30	5.44	.17	32.00
40	5.51	.19	29.00
50	5.00	.20	25.00
60	4.40	.22	20.00

    b. Using the table in part **a**:

       (1) Maximization of EPS: *40% debt ratio*, EPS = $5.51/share (see column 1).

       (2) Maximization of share value: *30% debt ratio*, share value = $32.00 (see column 3).

    c. Recommend *30% debt ratio*, because it results in the maximum share value and is therefore consistent with the firm's goal of owner wealth maximization.

Chapter 12

ST12–1   a. Earnings per share (EPS) = $\dfrac{\$2,000,000 \text{ earnings available}}{500,000 \text{ shares of common outstanding}}$

$= \underline{\$4.00/\text{share}}$

Price/earnings (P/E) ratio = $\dfrac{\$60 \text{ market price}}{\$4.00 \text{ EPS}} = \underline{15}$

    b. Proposed dividends = 500,000 shares × $2 per share = $1,000,000

Shares that can be repurchased = $\dfrac{\$1,000,000}{\$62} = \underline{16,129}$ shares

    c. *After proposed repurchase:*

Shares outstanding = 500,000 − 16,129 = 483,871

EPS = $\dfrac{\$2,000,000}{483,871} = \underline{\$4.13/\text{share}}$

    d. Market price = $4.13/share × 15 = $\underline{\$61.95/\text{share}}$

    e. The earnings per share (EPS) are higher after the repurchase, because there are fewer shares of stock outstanding (483,871 shares versus 500,000 shares) to divide up the firm's $2,000,000 of available earnings.

    f. In both cases, the stockholders would receive $2 per share—a $2 cash dividend in the dividend case or an approximately $2 increase in share price ($60.00 per share to $61.95 per share) in the repurchase case. [*Note:* The difference of $0.05 per share ($2.00 − $1.95) difference is due to rounding.]

Chapter 13

ST13–1

Basic data

Time component	Current	Proposed
Average payment period (APP)	10 days	30 days
Average collection period (ACP)	30 days	30 days
Average age of inventory (AAI)	40 days	40 days

$$\text{Cash conversion cycle (CCC)} = \text{AAI} + \text{ACP} - \text{APP}$$
$$\text{CCC}_{\text{current}} = 40 \text{ days} + 30 \text{ days} - 10 \text{ days} = 60 \text{ days}$$
$$\text{CCC}_{\text{proposed}} = 40 \text{ days} + 30 \text{ days} - 30 \text{ days} = \underline{40} \text{ days}$$
$$\text{Reduction in CCC} \quad \underline{\underline{20}} \text{ days}$$

Annual operating cycle investment = \$18,000,000
Daily expenditure = \$18,000,000 ÷ 365 = \$49,315
Reduction in resource investment = \$49,315 × 20 days = \$986,300
Annual profit increase = 0.12 × \$986,300 = $\underline{\underline{\$118,356}}$

ST13–2   **a.** *Data:*

S = 60,000 gallons
O = \$200 per order
C = \$1 per gallon per year

Calculation:

$$EOQ = \sqrt{\frac{2 \times S \times O}{C}}$$

$$= \sqrt{\frac{2 \times 60{,}000 \times \$200}{\$1}}$$

$$= \sqrt{24{,}000{,}000}$$

$$= \underline{\underline{4{,}899}} \text{ gallons}$$

b. *Data:*

Lead time = 20 days
Daily usage = 60,000 gallons/365 days
$\qquad\qquad$ = 164.38 gallons/day

Calculation:

Reorder point = lead time in days × daily usage
$\qquad\qquad$ = 20 days × 164.38 gallons/day
$\qquad\qquad$ = $\underline{\underline{3{,}287.6}}$ gallons

ST13–3   Tabular Calculation of the Effects of Relaxing Credit Standards on Regency Rug Repair Company:

Additional profit contribution from sales	
[4,000 rugs × ($32 avg. sale price − $28 var. cost)]	$16,000
Cost of marginal investment in accounts receivable	
Average investment under proposed plan:	

$$\frac{(\$28 \times 76{,}000 \text{ rugs})}{365/48} = \frac{\$2{,}128{,}000}{7.6} \qquad \$280{,}000$$

Average investment under present plan:

$$\frac{(\$28 \times 72{,}000 \text{ rugs})}{365/40} = \frac{\$2{,}016{,}000}{9.1} \qquad \underline{221{,}538}$$

Marginal investment in A/R	$ 58,462
Cost of marginal investment in	
A/R (0.14 × $58,462)	($ 8,185)
Cost of marginal bad debts	
Bad debts under proposed plan	
(0.015 × $32 × 76,000 rugs)	$ 36,480
Bad debts under present plan	
(0.010 × $32 × 72,000 rugs)	23,040
Cost of marginal bad debts	($13,440)
Net loss from implementation of proposed plan	($ 5,625)

Recommendation: Because a net loss of $5,625 is expected to result from relaxing credit standards, *the proposed plan should not be implemented.*

Chapter 14

ST14–1 a.

Supplier	Approximate cost of giving up cash discount
X	1% × [365/(55 − 10)] = 1% × 365/45 = 1% × 8 = 8.1%
Y	2% × [365/(30 − 10)] = 2% × 365/20 = 2% × 18 = 36.5%
Z	2% × [365/(60 − 20)] = 2% × 365/40 = 2% × 9 = 18.3%

b.

Supplier	Recommendation
X	8.1% cost of giving up discount < 15% interest cost from bank; therefore, *give up discount.*
Y	36.5% cost of giving up discount > 15% interest cost from bank; therefore, *take discount and borrow from bank.*
Z	18.3% cost of giving up discount > 15% interest cost from bank; therefore, *take discount and borrow from bank.*

c. Stretching accounts payable for supplier Z would change the cost of giving up the cash discount to

$$2\% \times [365/[(60 + 20) - 20]] = 2\% \times 365/60 = 2\% \times 6.1 = \underline{12.2\%}$$

In this case, in light of the 15% interest cost from the bank, the recommended strategy in part **b** would be to *give up the discount*, because the 12.2% cost of giving up the discount would be less than the 15% interest cost from the bank.

Appendix C

Answers to Selected End-of-Chapter Problems

The following list of answers to selected problems and portions of problems is included to provide "check figures" for use in preparing detailed solutions to end-of-chapter problems requiring calculations. For problems that are relatively straightforward, the key answer is given; for more complex problems, answers to a number of parts of the problem are included. Detailed calculations are not shown—only the final and, in some cases, intermediate answers, which should help to confirm whether the correct solution is being developed. Answers to problems involving present and future value were solved by using the appropriate tables; calculator solutions are not given. For problems containing a variety of cases for which similar calculations are required, the answers for only one or two cases have been included. The only verbal answers included are simple yes-or-no or "choice of best alternative" responses; answers to problems requiring detailed explanations or discussions are not given

The problems and portions of problems for which answers have been included were selected randomly; therefore, there is no discernible pattern to the choice of problem answers given. The answers given are based on what are believed to be the most obvious and reasonable assumptions related to the given problem; in some cases, other reasonable assumptions could result in equally correct answers.

1–1   a. Ms. Harper has unlimited liability: $60,000
      c. Ms. Harper has limited liability
1–2   a. $160,000
      b. $150,000
1–4   a. Cash inflows: $4,950
1–6   a. $19,700
      b. $72,800
      c. 21.3%
1–9   e. Total tax liability: $206,400
1–10 a. Earnings after tax: $18,000
1–11 b. Asset X: $100
          Asset Y: $2,000
2–3   a. Net profit after tax: $38,500
2–5   a. Earnings per share: $1.162
2–7   a. Total liquid assets: $5,700
          Total current liabilities: $2,400
2–9   Initial sales price: $9.50
2–10 b. Earnings per share: $2.36
      c. Cash dividend per share: $1.50
2–12 a.

Current ratio		2006: 1.88	2008: 1.79
Quick ratio		2006: 1.22	2008: 1.24

2–15 a. 45.62 days
2–16

	Creek	Industry
Debt ratio	0.73	0.51
Times interest earned	3.00	7.30

2–20 a.

	Actual 2009
Current ratio:	1.04
Average collection period:	57 days
Debt ratio:	61.3%
Net profit margin:	4.1%
Return on equity:	11.3%

2–21 a. 2006 Johnson ROE = 21.21%
                Industry ROE = 14.46%
3–5   b. $1,620
      c. $13,367
3–7

	April	May
		($000)
Cash 1 month delay	168	183
Cash 2 months delay	120	134.4
Total disbursements	465.3	413.1

3–9   c. Cumulative cash surplus at end
          of October 2010: $907
3–13 a. To retained earnings: $146,600
      b. To retained earnings: $157,400
3–14 a. Total assets: $1,383,000
          Total current liabilities: $510,000
          External funds required: $53,000
3–16 a. To retained earnings: $32,500
      c. $11,250
4–3   C: 3 years $< n <$ 4 years
4–4   A: $530.60
      D: $78.450
4–6   a. (1) $15,456

4–8   a. 8% $< i <$ 9%
4–11 B: $6,020
      D $80,250
4–22 b. $30,950.64
4–24 b. B: $1,000,000
          D: $1,200,000
4–26 a. A: $3,862.50
4–28 b. B: $26,039
4–31 a. $22,215
4–33 b. B: 12.6%
          D: 17.0%
4–33 a.

(1) Annual:		$8,810
Semiannual:		$8,955
Quarterly:		$9,030

4–39 B: $2,439.32
4–42 a. $60,000
      b. $3,764.82
4–44 A: $4,656.58
      B: $10,619.47
      C: $7,955.87
4–48 a. A: 12% $< i <$ 13%
          Calculator solution 12.47%
          C: 2% $< i <$ 3%
          Calculator solution 2.50%
4–50 a. B: 8% $< i <$ 9%
          Calculator solution 8.02%
          D: 10% $< i <$ 11%
          Calculator solution 10.03%
4–55 A: 17 $< n <$ 18
          Calculator solution 17.79
      D: 18 $< n <$ 19
          Calculator solution 18.68
5–1   a. X: 12.50%
          Y: 12.36%
5–2   A: 25%
5–4   a. A: 8%
          B: 20%
5–5   a. R: 10%
          S: 20%
      b. R: 25%
          S: 25.5%
5–8   a. 2008 return (hypothetical): 11.73%
5–9   a. (4) Project 257 CV: .368
              Project 432 CV: .354
5–10 a. F: 4%
      b. F: 13.38%
      c. F: 3.345
5–11 b. Portfolio return: 15.5%
      c. Standard deviation: 1.511%
5–14 a. 20.73%
      c. 12.89%
5–17 a. 18% increase
      b. 9.6% decrease
      c. No change

5–21	A: 8.9%	8–9	a. Total tax: $49,600
	D: 15%		d. Total tax: ($6,400)
5–23	b. 10%	8–12	Initial investment $22,680
6–3	a. A: 9%	8–13	a. Initial investment: $18,240
	B: 12%		c. Initial investment: $23,100
6–5	b. $175,000	8–15	c. Cash inflow, Year 3: $584,000
	c. $113,750	8–16	Incremental operating cash flow, Year 2: $458
6–7	b. $8,789.40	8–18	b. Incremental cash flow, Year 3: $1,960
6–8	C: $16,660.00	8–20	Terminal cash flow: $76,640
	D: $9,717.00	8–24	b. Operating cash flow, Year 1: ($15,600)
6–10	a. $1,156.88		
6–14	a. (1) $1,120.23	9–2	a. Machine 1: 4 years, 8 months
	(2) $1,000.00		Machine 2: 5 years, 3 months
	(3) $896.63	9–3	a. Project A payback: 3.9 years
6–17	a. A: approximate: 12.36%	9–4	a. $3,246 Accept
	Calculator solution: 12.71%		b. −$5,131 Reject
	C: approximate: 10.38%	9–5	a. $2,675 Accept
	Calculator solution: 10.22%		c. −$805 Reject
	E: approximate: 8.77%	9–10	a. Project A: 3.08 years
	Calculator solution: 8.95%		Project C: 2.38 years
6–19	A: $1,152.35		b. Project C: NPV $5,451
	C: $464.72	9–11	a. Project A: 17%
	E: $76.11		Project D: 21%
7–1	b. 800,000 shares	9–15	a. NPV = $1,222
7–3	A: $15.00		b. IRR = 12%
	C: $11.00		c. Accept
	D: $25.50	9–20	a. Initial Investment: $1,480,000
7–6	a. $20		b. Year Cash Flow
	b. $12		1 $656,000
7–8	a. $68.82		2 761,600
	b. $60.95		3 647,200
7–9	A: $24.00		4 585,600
	B: $40.00		5 585,600
	E: $18.75		6 44,000
7–10	a. $37.75		c. 2.1 years
	b. $60.40		d. NPV = $959,289
7–13	a. (1) $5,021,250		IRR = 35%
	(2) $5,411,250	9–22	a. Value of real options: $2,200
	(3) $4,049,331		NPV$_{strategic}$: $500
	b. $2,191,331	9–25	a. Range A: $1,600
	c. $10.96		Range B: $200
7–15	a. Book value: $36.00	9–26	b. Project A:
	b. Liquidation value: $30.20		Pessimistic: $73
8–1	a. Operating expenditure		Most likely: $1,609
	d. Operating expenditure		Optimistic: $3,145
	f. Capital expenditure	9–29	a. Project E: $2,130; Project F: $1,678
8–4	Year Relevant cash flow		c. Project E: $834; Project F: $1,678
	1 $4,000	9–31	b. $2,223
	2 $6,000	9–32	a. Project X: NPV = $14,960
	4 $10,000		Project Y: NPV = $2,650
8–7	A: $275,500	10–2	a. $980
	B: $26,800		d. 7.36% after tax
8–8	a. $23,200	10–3	a. $930
	b. @$100,000: $30,720	10–8	a. 6%
	@$56,000: $13,120		b. 12%

10–9	d.	16.54%
10–13	a.	13.55%
	b.	12.985%
11–1		1,300
11–4	a.	21,000 CDs
	b.	$293,580
	d.	$10,500
11–5	a.	36 months
11–8	a.	8,000 units
	b.	@ 10,000 units: $95,000
11–11	b.	2
	c.	1.25
11–12	a.	DFL, current: 1.50
11–19	a.	Structure A:
		EBIT $30,000: EPS $1.125
		Structure B:
		EBIT $50,000: EPS 2.28
12–4	a.	$4.75 per share
	b.	$0.40 per share

12–6 a.
Year	$ Dividend
2000	0.10
2004	0.96
2007	1.28
2009	1.60

c.
Year	$ Dividend
2000	0.50
2004	0.50
2007	0.66
2009	1.30

12–8	a.	Common stock: $21,000
		Paid in capital: $294,000
		Retained earnings: $85,000
12–10	a.	$2.00
	d.	$20.00 per share
12–12	a.	1,200,000 shares @ $1.50 par
	d.	3,600,000 shares @ $0.50 par

12–13	a.	1,600 shares
12–15	a.	19,047 shares
	b.	$2.10
13–1	a.	OC = 150 days
	b.	CCC = 120 days
	c.	$9,863,013.70
13–2	b.	CCC = 70 days
	c.	$26,849
13–4	a.	Average season requirement: $4,000,000
13–6	a.	200 units
	b.	121.92 units
	c.	32.88 units
13–7	d.	$4,441
13–10		Loss from implementation: $4,659
13–12		Loss from implementation: $11,972
13–14	a.	7 days
	b.	$21,450
14–2	a.	37.21%
	b.	18.43%
	c.	7.37%
14–5	b.	$119/month
	e.	$2,429
14–7		$1,300,000
14–8		$82,500
14–11		14.29%
14–12	a.	Effective rate: 12.94%
	b.	Effective rate: 11.73%
14–15	a.	Effective 90-day rate: 2.25%
	b.	Effective annual rate: 13.89%

14–19
	Amount remitted
A:	$196,000
C:	$107,800
F:	$176,400
G:	$ 88,200

Glossary

ABC inventory system   Inventory management technique that divides inventory into three groups—A, B, and C, in descending order of importance and level of monitoring, on the basis of the dollar investment in each. (Chapter 13)

ability to service debts   The ability of a firm to make the payments required on a scheduled basis over the life of a debt. (Chapter 2)

accept–reject approach   The evaluation of capital expenditure proposals to determine whether they meet the firm's minimum acceptance criterion. (Chapter 8)

accounts payable management   Management by the firm of the time that elapses between its purchase of raw materials and its mailing payment to the supplier. (Chapter 14)

accrual basis   In preparation of financial statements, recognizes revenue at the time of sale and recognizes expenses when they are incurred. (Chapter 1)

accruals   Liabilities for services received for which payment has yet to be made. (Chapter 14)

ACH (automated clearinghouse) transfer   Preauthorized electronic withdrawal from the payer's account and deposit into the payee's account via a settlement among banks by the *automated clearinghouse*, or *ACH*. (Chapter 13)

activity ratios   Measure the speed with which various accounts are converted into sales or cash—inflows or outflows. (Chapter 2)

after-tax proceeds from sale of old asset   The difference between the old asset's sale proceeds and any applicable taxes or tax refunds related to its sale. (Chapter 8)

agency costs   The costs borne by stockholders to maintain a *governance structure* that minimizes agency problems and contributes to the maximization of owner wealth. (Chapter 1)

agency problem   The likelihood that managers may place personal goals ahead of corporate goals. (Chapter 1)

aggressive funding strategy   A funding strategy under which the firm funds its seasonal requirements with short-term debt and its permanent requirements with long-term debt. (Chapter 13)

aging schedule   A credit-monitoring technique that breaks down accounts receivable into groups on the basis of their time of origin; it shows the percentages of the total accounts receivable balance that have been outstanding for specified periods of time. (Chapter 13)

American depositary receipts (ADRs)   Claims issued by U.S. banks representing ownership of shares of a foreign company's stock held on deposit by the U.S. bank in the foreign market and issued in dollars to U.S. investors. (Chapter 7)

American depositary shares (ADSs)   Securities backed by *American depositary receipts (ADRs)* that permit U.S. investors to hold shares of non-U.S. companies and trade them in U.S. markets. (Chapter 7)

angel capitalists (angels)   Wealthy individual investors who do not operate as a business but invest in promising early-stage companies in exchange for a portion of the firm's equity. (Chapter 7)

annual cleanup   The requirement that for a certain number of days during the year borrowers under a line of credit carry a zero loan balance (that is, owe the bank nothing). (Chapter 14)

annual percentage rate (APR)   The *nominal annual rate* of interest, found by multiplying the periodic rate by the number of periods in 1 year, that must be disclosed to consumers on credit cards and loans as a result of "truth-in-lending laws." (Chapter 4)

annual percentage yield (APY)   The *effective annual rate* of interest that must be disclosed to consumers by banks on their savings products as a result of "truth-in-savings laws." (Chapter 4)

annuity   A stream of equal periodic cash flows, over a specified time period. These cash flows can be *inflows* of returns earned on investments or *outflows* of funds invested to earn future returns. (Chapter 4)

annuity due   An annuity for which the cash flow occurs at the *beginning* of each period. (Chapter 4)

articles of partnership   The written contract used to formally establish a business partnership. (Chapter 1)

ask price   The lowest price at which a security is offered for sale. (Chapter 1)

asymmetric information   The situation in which managers of a firm have more information about operations and future prospects than do investors. (Chapter 11)

authorized shares   The number of shares of common stock that a firm's corporate charter allows it to issue. (Chapter 7)

average age of inventory   Average number of days' sales in inventory. (Chapter 2)

average collection period   The average amount of time needed to collect accounts receivable. (Chapter 2)

average payment period   The average amount of time needed to pay accounts payable. (Chapter 2)

average tax rate   A firm's taxes divided by its taxable income. (Chapter 1)

balance sheet   Summary statement of the firm's financial position at a given point in time. (Chapter 2)

bar chart   The simplest type of probability distribution; shows only a limited number of outcomes and associated probabilities for a given event. (Chapter 5)

behavioral finance   A growing body of research that focuses on investor behavior and its impact on investment decisions and stock prices. Advocates are commonly referred to as "behaviorists." (Chapter 7)

benchmarking   A type of *cross-sectional analysis* in which the firm's ratio values are compared to those of a key competitor or group of competitors that it wishes to emulate. (Chapter 2)

beta coefficient (*b*)   A relative measure of nondiversifiable risk. An *index* of the degree of movement of an asset's return in response to a change in the *market return*. (Chapter 5)

bid price   The highest price offered to purchase a security. (Chapter 1)

bird-in-the-hand argument   The belief, in support of *dividend relevance theory*, that investors see current dividends as less risky than future dividends or capital gains. (Chapter 12)

board of directors   Group elected by the firm's stockholders and typically responsible for developing strategic goals and plans, setting general policy, guiding corporate affairs, approving major expenditures, and hiring/firing, compensating, and monitoring key officers and executives. (Chapter 1)

bond   Long-term debt instrument used by business and government to raise large sums of money, generally from a diverse group of lenders. (Chapter 1)

bond indenture   A legal document that specifies both the rights of the bondholders and the duties of the issuing corporation. (Chapter 6)

book value   The strict accounting value of an asset, calculated by subtracting its accumulated depreciation from its installed cost. (Chapter 8)

book value per share   The amount per share of common stock that would be received if all of the firm's assets were *sold for their exact book (accounting) value* and the proceeds remaining after paying all liabilities (including preferred stock) were divided among the common stockholders. (Chapter 7)

book value weights   Weights that use accounting values to measure the proportion of each type of capital in the firm's financial structure. (Chapter 10)

breakeven analysis   Indicates the level of operations necessary to cover all operating costs and the profitability associated with various levels of sales. (Chapter 11)

break point   The level of *total* new financing at which the cost of one of the financing components rises, thereby causing an upward shift in the *weighted marginal cost of capital (WMCC)*. (Chapter 10)

broker market   The securities exchanges on which the two sides of a transaction, the buyer and seller, are brought together to trade securities. (Chapter 1)

business ethics   Standard of conduct or moral judgment that applies to persons engaged in commerce. (Chapter 1)

business risk   The risk to the firm of being unable to cover operating costs. (Chapter 10)

call feature   A feature included in nearly all corporate bond issues that gives the issuer the opportunity to repurchase bonds at a stated *call price* prior to maturity. (Chapter 6)

call premium   The amount by which a bond's *call price* exceeds its par value. (Chapter 6)

call price   The stated price at which a bond may be repurchased, by use of a *call feature*, prior to maturity. (Chapter 6)

capital   The long-term funds of a firm; all items on the right-hand side of the firm's balance sheet, *excluding current liabilities*. (Chapter 7)

capital asset pricing model (CAPM)   The basic theory that links risk and return for all assets; describes the relationship between the required return, r_s, and the nondiversifiable risk of the firm as measured by the beta coefficient, *b*. (Chapters 5 and 10)

capital budgeting   The process of evaluating and selecting long-term investments that are consistent with the firm's goal of maximizing owner wealth. (Chapter 8)

capital budgeting process   Five distinct but interrelated steps: *proposal generation, review and analysis, decision making, implementation*, and *follow-up*. (Chapter 8)

capital expenditure An outlay of funds by the firm that is expected to produce benefits over a period of time *greater than* 1 year. (Chapter 8)

capital gain The amount by which the sale price of an asset exceeds the asset's initial purchase price. (Chapter 1)

capital market A market that enables suppliers and demanders of *long-term funds* to make transactions. (Chapter 1)

capital rationing The financial situation in which a firm has only a fixed number of dollars available for capital expenditures, and numerous projects compete for these dollars. (Chapter 8)

capital structure The mix of long-term debt and equity maintained by the firm. (Chapter 11)

carrying costs The variable costs per unit of holding an item in inventory for a specific period of time. (Chapter 13)

cash basis Recognizes revenues and expenses only with respect to actual inflows and outflows of cash. (Chapter 1)

cash bonuses Cash paid to management for achieving certain performance goals. (Chapter 1)

cash budget (cash forecast) A statement of the firm's planned inflows and outflows of cash that is used to estimate its short-term cash requirements. (Chapter 3)

cash concentration The process used by the firm to bring lockbox and other deposits together into one bank, often called the *concentration bank*. (Chapter 13)

cash conversion cycle (CCC) The amount of time a firm's resources are tied up; calculated by subtracting the average payment period from the *operating cycle*. (Chapter 13)

cash disbursements All outlays of cash by the firm during a given financial period. (Chapter 3)

cash discount A percentage deduction from the purchase price; available to the credit customer who pays its account within a specified time. (Chapter 13)

cash discount period The number of days after the beginning of the credit period during which the cash discount is available. (Chapter 13)

cash receipts All of a firm's inflows of cash in a given financial period. (Chapter 3)

change in net working capital The difference between a change in current assets and a change in current liabilities. (Chapter 8)

clearing float The time between deposit of a payment and when spendable funds become available to the firm. (Chapter 13)

clientele effect The argument that a firm attracts shareholders whose preferences for the payment and stability of dividends correspond to the payment pattern and stability of the firm itself. (Chapter 12)

closely owned (stock) All common stock of a firm owned by a small group of investors (such as a family). (Chapter 7)

coefficient of variation (CV) A measure of relative dispersion that is useful in comparing the risks of assets with differing expected returns. (Chapter 5)

collateral trust bonds See Table 6.4. (Chapter 6)

commercial finance companies Lending institutions that make *only* secured loans—both short-term and long-term—to businesses. (Chapter 14)

commercial paper A form of financing consisting of short-term, unsecured promissory notes issued by firms with a high credit standing. (Chapter 14)

commitment fee The fee that is normally charged on a *revolving credit agreement*; it often applies to the average unused balance of the borrower's credit line. (Chapter 14)

common stock The purest and most basic form of corporate ownership. (Chapter 1)

common-size income statement An income statement in which each item is expressed as a percentage of sales. (Chapter 2)

compensating balance A required checking account balance equal to a certain percentage of the amount borrowed from a bank under a line-of-credit or revolving credit agreement. (Chapter 14)

compound interest Interest that is earned on a given deposit and has become part of the principal at the end of a specified period. (Chapter 4)

conflicting rankings Conflicts in the ranking given a project by NPV and IRR, resulting from *differences in the magnitude and timing of cash flows*. (Chapter 9)

conservative funding strategy A funding strategy under which the firm funds both its seasonal and its permanent requirements with long-term debt. (Chapter 13)

constant-growth model A widely cited dividend valuation approach that assumes that dividends will grow at a constant rate, but a rate that is less than the required return. (Chapter 7)

constant-growth valuation (Gordon) model Assumes that the value of a share of stock equals the present value of all future dividends (assumed to grow at a constant rate) that it is expected to provide over an infinite time horizon. (Chapter 10)

constant-payout-ratio dividend policy A dividend policy based on the payment of a certain percentage of earnings to owners in each dividend period. (Chapter 12)

continuous compounding   Compounding of interest an infinite number of times per year at intervals of microseconds. (Chapter 4)

continuous probability distribution   A probability distribution showing all the possible outcomes and associated probabilities for a given event. (Chapter 5)

controlled disbursing   The strategic use of mailing points and bank accounts to lengthen mail float and clearing float, respectively. (Chapter 13)

controller   The firm's chief accountant, who is responsible for the firm's accounting activities, such as corporate accounting, tax management, financial accounting, and cost accounting. (Chapter 1)

conventional cash flow pattern   An initial outflow followed only by a series of inflows. (Chapter 8)

conversion feature   An option that is included as part of a bond or a preferred stock issue and allows its holder to change the security into a stated number of shares of common stock. (Chapter 6)

conversion feature (preferred stock)   A feature of *convertible preferred stock* that allows holders to change each share into a stated number of shares of common stock. (Chapter 7)

corporate bond   A long-term debt instrument indicating that a corporation has borrowed a certain amount of money and promises to repay it in the future under clearly defined terms. (Chapter 6)

corporate governance   The system used to direct and control a corporation. Defines the rights and responsibilities of key corporate participants, decision-making procedures, and the way in which the firm will set, achieve, and monitor objectives. (Chapter 1)

corporation   An artificial being created by law (often called a "legal entity"). (Chapter 1)

correlation   A statistical measure of the relationship between any two series of numbers representing data of any kind. (Chapter 5)

correlation coefficient   A measure of the degree of correlation between two series. (Chapter 5)

cost of capital   The rate of return that a firm must earn on the projects in which it invests to maintain its market value and attract funds. (Chapter 10)

cost of common stock equity, r_s   The rate at which investors discount the expected dividends of the firm to determine its share value. (Chapter 10)

cost of giving up a cash discount   The implied rate of interest paid to delay payment of an account payable for an additional number of days. (Chapter 14)

cost of long-term debt, r_i   The after-tax cost today of raising long-term funds through borrowing. (Chapter 10)

cost of new asset   The net outflow necessary to acquire a new asset. (Chapter 8)

cost of a new issue of common stock, r_n   The cost of common stock, net of underpricing and associated flotation costs. (Chapter 10)

cost of preferred stock, r_p   The ratio of the preferred stock dividend to the firm's net proceeds from the sale of preferred stock; calculated by dividing the annual dividend, D_p, by the net proceeds from the sale of the preferred stock, N_p. (Chapter 10)

cost of retained earnings, r_r   The same as the cost of an *equivalent fully subscribed issue of additional common stock*, which is equal to the cost of common stock equity, r_s. (Chapter 10)

coupon interest rate   The percentage of a bond's par value that will be paid annually, typically in two equal semiannual payments, as interest. (Chapter 6)

coverage ratios   Ratios that measure the firm's ability to pay certain fixed charges. (Chapter 2)

credit monitoring   The ongoing review of a firm's accounts receivable to determine whether customers are paying according to the stated credit terms. (Chapter 13)

credit period   The number of days after the beginning of the credit period until full payment of the account is due. (Chapter 13)

credit scoring   A credit selection method commonly used with high-volume/small-dollar credit requests; relies on a credit score determined by applying statistically derived weights to a credit applicant's scores on key financial and credit characteristics. (Chapter 13)

credit standards   The firm's minimum requirements for extending credit to a customer. (Chapter 13)

credit terms   The terms of sale for customers who have been extended credit by the firm. (Chapter 13)

cross-sectional analysis   Comparison of different firms' financial ratios at the same point in time; involves comparing the firm's ratios to those of other firms in its industry or to industry averages. (Chapter 2)

cumulative preferred stock   Preferred stock for which all passed (unpaid) dividends in arrears, along with the current dividend, must be paid before dividends can be paid to common stockholders. (Chapter 7)

current assets   Short-term assets, expected to be converted into cash within 1 year or less. (Chapter 2)

current liabilities   Short-term liabilities, expected to be paid within 1 year or less. (Chapter 2)

current rate (translation) method   Technique used by U.S.-based companies to translate their foreign-currency-denominated assets and liabilities into dollars, for consolidation with the parent company's financial statements, using the exchange rate prevailing at the fiscal year ending date (the current rate). (Chapter 2)

current ratio   A measure of liquidity calculated by dividing the firm's current assets by its current liabilities. (Chapter 2)

current yield   A measure of a bond's cash return for the year; calculated by dividing the bond's annual interest payment by its current price. (Chapter 6)

date of record (dividends)   Set by the firm's directors, the date on which all persons whose names are recorded as stockholders receive a declared dividend at a specified future time. (Chapter 12)

dealer market   The market in which the buyer and seller are not brought together directly but instead have their orders executed by securities dealers that "make markets" in the given security. (Chapter 1)

debentures   See Table 6.4. (Chapter 6)

debt capital   All long-term borrowing incurred by a firm, including bonds. (Chapter 7)

debt ratio   Measures the proportion of total assets financed by the firm's creditors. (Chapter 2)

decision trees   A behavioral approach that uses diagrams to map the various investment decision alternatives and payoffs, along with their probabilities of occurrence. (Chapter 9)

degree of financial leverage (DFL)   The numerical measure of the firm's financial leverage. (Chapter 11)

degree of indebtedness   Measures the amount of debt relative to other significant balance sheet amounts. (Chapter 2)

degree of operating leverage (DOL)   The numerical measure of the firm's operating leverage. (Chapter 11)

degree of total leverage (DTL)   The numerical measure of the firm's total leverage. (Chapter 11)

depository transfer check (DTC)   An unsigned check drawn on one of a firm's bank accounts and deposited in another. (Chapter 13)

depreciable life   Time period over which an asset is depreciated. (Chapter 3)

depreciation   The systematic charging of a portion of the costs of fixed assets against annual revenues over time. (Chapter 3)

dilution of ownership   Occurs when a new stock issue results in each present shareholder having a claim on a *smaller* part of the firm's earnings than previously. (Chapter 7)

discount   The amount by which a bond sells at a value that is less than its par value. (Chapter 6)

discount loans   Loans on which interest is paid in advance by being deducted from the amount borrowed. (Chapter 14)

discounting cash flows   The process of finding present values; the inverse of compounding interest. (Chapter 4)

diversifiable risk   The portion of an asset's risk that is attributable to firm-specific, random causes; can be eliminated through diversification. Also called *unsystematic risk*. (Chapter 5)

dividend irrelevance theory   Miller and Modigliani's theory that in a perfect world, the firm's value is determined solely by the earning power and risk of its assets (investments) and that the manner in which it splits its earnings stream between dividends and internally retained (and reinvested) funds does not affect this value. (Chapter 12)

dividend payout ratio   Indicates the percentage of each dollar earned that is distributed to the owners in the form of cash. It is calculated by dividing the firm's cash dividend per share by its earnings per share. (Chapter 12)

dividend per share (DPS)   The dollar amount of cash distributed during the period on behalf of each outstanding share of common stock. (Chapter 2)

dividend policy   The firm's plan of action to be followed whenever a dividend decision is made. (Chapter 12)

dividend reinvestment plans (DRIPs)   Plans that enable stockholders to use dividends received on the firm's stock to acquire additional shares—even fractional shares—at little or no transaction cost. (Chapter 12)

dividend relevance theory   The theory, advanced by Gordon and Lintner, that there is a direct relationship between a firm's dividend policy and its market value. (Chapter 12)

dividends   Periodic distributions of earnings to the stockholders of a firm. (Chapter 1)

double taxation   Occurs when the already once-taxed earnings of a corporation are distributed as cash dividends to stockholders, who must pay taxes of up to a maximum rate of 15 percent on them. (Chapter 1)

DuPont formula   Multiplies the firm's *net profit margin* by its *total asset turnover* to calculate the firm's *return on total assets (ROA)*. (Chapter 2)

DuPont system of analysis   System used to dissect the firm's financial statements and to assess its financial condition. (Chapter 2)

earnings per share (EPS)   The amount earned during the period on behalf of each outstanding share of common stock, calculated by dividing the period's total earnings available for the firm's common stockholders by the number of shares of common stock outstanding. (Chapter 1)

EBIT–EPS approach   An approach for selecting the capital structure that maximizes earnings per share (EPS) over the expected range of earnings before interest and taxes (EBIT). (Chapter 11)

economic order quantity (EOQ) model   Inventory management technique for determining an item's optimal order size, which is the size that minimizes the total of its *order costs* and *carrying costs*. (Chapter 13)

economic value added (EVA®)   A popular measure used by many firms to determine whether an investment contributes positively to the owners' wealth; calculated as the difference between an investment's *net operating profit after taxes (NOPAT)* and the cost of funds used to finance the investment which is found by multiplying the dollar amount of funds used to finance the investment by the firm's weighted average cost of capital (WACC). (Chapter 10)

effective (true) annual rate (EAR)   The annual rate of interest actually paid or earned. (Chapter 4)

efficient market   A market that allocates funds to their most productive uses as a result of competition among wealth-maximizing investors that determines and publicizes prices that are believed to be close to their true value; a market with the following characteristics: many small investors, all having the same information and expectations with respect to securities; no restrictions on investment, no taxes, and no transaction costs; and rational investors, who view securities similarly and are risk-averse, preferring higher returns and lower risk. (Chapters 1 and 5)

efficient-market hypothesis   Theory describing the behavior of an assumed "perfect" market in which (1) securities are typically in equilibrium, (2) security prices fully reflect all public information available and react swiftly to new information, and, (3) because stocks are fully and fairly priced, investors need not waste time looking for mispriced securities. (Chapter 7)

efficient portfolio   A portfolio that maximizes return for a given level of risk or minimizes risk for a given level of return. (Chapter 5)

ending cash   The sum of the firm's beginning cash and its net cash flow for the period. (Chapter 3)

enterprise resource planning (ERP)   A computerized system that electronically integrates external information about the firm's suppliers and customers with the firm's departmental data so that information on all available resources—human and material—can be instantly obtained in a fashion that eliminates production delays and controls costs. (Chapter 13)

equipment trust certificates   See Table 6.4. (Chapter 6)

equity capital   The long-term funds provided by the firm's owners, the stockholders. (Chapter 7)

Eurobond   An *international bond* that is sold primarily in countries other than the country of the currency in which the issue is denominated. (Chapter 6)

Eurobond market   The market in which corporations and governments typically issue bonds denominated in dollars and sell them to investors located outside the United States. (Chapter 1)

Eurocurrency market   International equivalent of the domestic money market. (Chapter 1)

ex dividend   Period, beginning 2 *business days* prior to the date of record, during which a stock is sold without the right to receive the current dividend. (Chapter 12)

excess cash balance   The (excess) amount available for investment by the firm if the period's ending cash is greater than the desired minimum cash balance; assumed to be invested in marketable securities. (Chapter 3)

excess earnings accumulation tax   The tax the IRS levies on retained earnings above $250,000 when it determines that the firm has accumulated an excess of earnings to allow owners to delay paying ordinary income taxes on dividends received. (Chapter 12)

exchange rate risk   The danger that an unexpected change in the exchange rate between the dollar and the currency in which a project's cash flows are denominated will reduce the market value of that project's cash flow; the risk caused by varying exchange rates between two currencies. (Chapter 9)

expectations theory   The theory that the yield curve reflects investor expectations about future interest rates; an increasing inflation expectation results in an upward-sloping yield curve, and a decreasing inflation expectation results in a downward-sloping yield curve. (Chapter 6)

expected value of a return ($\bar{r}$)   The most likely return on a given asset. (Chapter 5)

extendible notes   See Table 6.5. (Chapter 6)

external financing required ("plug" figure)   Under the judgmental approach for developing a pro forma balance sheet, the amount of external financing needed to bring the statement into balance. It can be either a positive or a negative value. (Chapter 3)

external forecast   A sales forecast based on the relationships observed between the firm's sales and certain key external economic indicators. (Chapter 3)

extra dividend   An additional dividend optionally paid by the firm if earnings are higher than normal in a given period. (Chapter 12)

factor   A financial institution that specializes in purchasing accounts receivable from businesses. (Chapter 14)

factoring accounts receivable   The outright sale of accounts receivable at a discount to a *factor* or other financial institution. (Chapter 14)

finance   The art and science of managing money. (Chapter 1)

Financial Accounting Standards Board (FASB) Standard No. 52   Mandates that U.S.-based companies translate their foreign-currency-denominated assets and liabilities into dollars, for consolidation with the parent company's financial statements. This is done by using the *current rate (translation method)*. (Chapter 2)

Financial Accounting Standards Board (FASB)   The accounting profession's rule-setting body, which authorizes *generally accepted accounting principles (GAAP)*. (Chapter 2)

financial breakeven point   The level of EBIT necessary to just cover all *fixed financial costs*; the level of EBIT for which EPS = \$0. (Chapter 11)

financial institution   An intermediary that channels the savings of individuals, businesses, and governments into loans or investments. (Chapter 1)

financial leverage multiplier (FLM)   The ratio of the firm's total assets to its common stock equity. (Chapter 2)

financial leverage   The potential use of *fixed financial costs* to magnify the effects of changes in earnings before interest and taxes on the firm's earnings per share. (Chapters 2 and 11)

financial manager   Actively manages the financial affairs of any type of business, whether financial or nonfinancial, private or public, large or small, profit-seeking or not-for-profit. (Chapter 1)

financial markets   Forums in which suppliers of funds and demanders of funds can transact business directly. (Chapter 1)

financial planning process   Planning that begins with long-term, or *strategic*, financial plans that in turn guide the formulation of short-term, or *operating*, plans and budgets. (Chapter 3)

financial risk   The risk to the firm of being unable to cover required financial obligations (interest, lease payments, preferred stock dividends). (Chapter 10)

financial services   The part of finance concerned with the design and delivery of advice and financial products to individuals, business, and government. (Chapter 1)

financing flows   Cash flows that result from debt and equity financing transactions; includes incurrence and repayment of debt, cash inflow from the sale of stock, and cash outflows to pay cash dividends or repurchase stock. (Chapter 3)

five C's of credit   The five key dimensions—character, capacity, capital, collateral, and conditions—used by credit analysts to provide a framework for in-depth credit analysis. (Chapter 13)

fixed-payment coverage ratio   Measures the firm's ability to meet all fixed-payment obligations. (Chapter 2)

fixed-rate loan   A loan with a rate of interest that is determined at a set increment above the prime rate and at which it remains fixed until maturity. (Chapter 14)

flat yield curve   A yield curve that reflects relatively similar borrowing costs for both short- and longer-term loans. (Chapter 6)

float   Funds that have been sent by the payer but are not yet usable funds to the payee. (Chapter 13)

floating inventory lien   A secured short-term loan against inventory under which the lender's claim is on the borrower's inventory in general. (Chapter 14)

floating-rate bonds   See Table 6.5. (Chapter 6)

floating-rate loan   A loan with a rate of interest initially set at an increment above the prime rate and allowed to "float," or vary, above prime *as the prime rate varies* until maturity. (Chapter 14)

flotation costs   The total costs of issuing and selling a security. (Chapter 10)

foreign bond   Bond that is issued by a foreign corporation or government and is denominated in the investor's home currency and sold in the investor's home market. (Chapters 1 and 6)

foreign direct investment (FDI)   The transfer by a multinational firm of capital, managerial, and technical assets from its home country to a host country. (Chapter 8)

foreign exchange manager   The manager responsible for monitoring and managing the firm's exposure to loss from currency fluctuations. (Chapter 1)

free cash flow (FCF)   The amount of cash flow available to investors (creditors and owners) after the firm has met all operating needs and paid for investments in net fixed assets and net current assets. (Chapter 3)

free cash flow valuation model   A model that determines the value of an entire company as the present value of its expected free cash flows discounted at the firm's *weighted average cost of capital*, which is its expected average future cost of funds over the long run. (Chapter 7)

future value   The value at a given future date of a present amount placed on deposit today and earning interest at a specified rate. Found by applying *compound interest* over a specified period of time. (Chapter 4)

future value interest factor   The multiplier used to calculate, at a specified interest rate, the future value of a present amount as of a given time. (Chapter 4)

future value interest factor for an ordinary annuity   The multiplier used to calculate the future value of an *ordinary annuity* at a specified interest rate over a given period of time. (Chapter 4)

generally accepted accounting principles (GAAP)   The practice and procedure guidelines used to prepare and maintain financial records and reports; authorized by the *Financial Accounting Standards Board (FASB)*. (Chapter 2)

Gordon model   A common name for the *constant-growth model* that is widely cited in dividend valuation. (Chapter 7)

gross profit margin   Measures the percentage of each sales dollar remaining after the firm has paid for its goods. (Chapter 2)

historical weights   Either book or market value weights based on *actual* capital structure proportions. (Chapter 10)

incentive plans   Management compensation plans that tend to tie management compensation to share price; most popular incentive plan involves the grant of *stock options*. (Chapter 1)

income bonds   See Table 6.4. (Chapter 6)

income statement   Provides a financial summary of the firm's operating results during a specified period. (Chapter 2)

incremental cash flows   The *additional* cash flows—out-flows or inflows—expected to result from a proposed capital expenditure. (Chapter 8)

independent projects   Projects whose cash flows are unrelated or independent of one another; the acceptance of one *does not eliminate* the others from further consideration. (Chapter 8)

individual investors   Investors who buy relatively small quantities of shares in order to meet personal investment goals. (Chapter 1)

informational content   The information provided by the dividends of a firm with respect to future earnings, which causes owners to bid up or down the price of the firm's stock. (Chapter 12)

initial investment   The relevant cash outflow for a proposed project at time zero. (Chapter 8)

initial public offering (IPO)   The first public sale of a firm's stock. (Chapter 7)

installation costs   Any added costs that are necessary to place an asset into operation. (Chapter 8)

installed cost of new asset   The cost of *a new asset* plus its *installation costs*; equals the asset's depreciable value. (Chapter 8)

institutional investors   Investment professionals, such as insurance companies, mutual funds, and pension funds, that are paid to manage other people's money and that trade large quantities of securities. (Chapter 1)

interest rate   The compensation paid by the borrower of funds to the lender; from the borrower's point of view, the cost of borrowing funds. (Chapter 6)

interest rate risk   The chance that interest rates will change and thereby change the required return and bond value. Rising rates, which result in decreasing bond values, are of greatest concern. (Chapter 6)

intermediate cash inflows   Cash inflows received prior to the termination of a project. (Chapter 9)

internal forecast   A sales forecast based on a buildup, or consensus, of sales forecasts through the firm's own sales channels. (Chapter 3)

internal rate of return (IRR)   A sophisticated capital budgeting technique; the discount rate that equates the NPV of an investment opportunity with $0 (because the present value of cash inflows equals the initial investment); it is the compound annual rate of return that the firm will earn if it invests in the project and receives the given cash inflows. (Chapter 9)

internal rate of return approach   An approach to capital rationing that involves graphing project IRRs in descending order against the total dollar investment to determine the group of acceptable projects. (Chapter 9)

international equity market   A market that allows corporations to sell blocks of shares to investors in a number of different countries simultaneously. (Chapter 1)

inventory turnover   Measures the activity, or liquidity, of a firm's inventory. (Chapter 2)

inverted yield curve   A *downward-sloping* yield curve that indicates generally cheaper long-term borrowing costs than short-term borrowing costs. (Chapter 6)

investment bankers   Financial intermediaries who, in addition to their role in selling new security issues, can be hired by acquirers in mergers to find suitable target companies and assist in negotiations. (Chapter 7)

investment flows   Cash flows associated with purchase and sale of both fixed assets and equity investments in other firms. (Chapter 3)

investment opportunities schedule (IOS)   A ranking of investment possibilities from best (highest return) to worst (lowest return); the graph that plots project IRRs in descending order against the total dollar investment. (Chapters 9 and 10)

issued shares   The number of shares of common stock that have been put into circulation; the sum of outstanding shares and treasury stock. (Chapter 7)

judgmental approach   A simplified approach for preparing the pro forma balance sheet under which the values of certain balance sheet accounts are estimated, some as a percentage of sales and others by management assumption, and the firm's external financing is used as a balancing, or "plug," figure. (Chapter 3)

junk bonds   See Table 6.5. (Chapter 6)

just-in-time (JIT) system   Inventory management technique that minimizes inventory investment by having materials arrive at exactly the time they are needed for production. (Chapter 13)

letter of credit   A letter written by a company's bank to the company's foreign supplier, stating that the bank guarantees payment of an invoiced amount if all the underlying agreements are met. (Chapter 14)

letter to stockholders   Typically, the first element of the annual stockholders' report and the primary communication from management. (Chapter 2)

leverage   Results from the use of fixed-cost assets or funds to magnify returns to the firm's owners. (Chapter 11)

lien   A publicly disclosed legal claim on collateral. (Chapter 14)

limited liability corporation (LLC)   See Table 1.2. (Chapter 1)

limited liability partnership (LLP)   See Table 1.2. (Chapter 1)

limited partnership (LP)   See Table 1.2. (Chapter 1)

line of credit   An agreement between a commercial bank and a business specifying the amount of unsecured short-term borrowing the bank will make available to the firm over a given period of time. (Chapter 14)

liquidation value per share   The *actual amount* per share of common stock that would be received if all of the firm's assets were *sold for their market value*, liabilities (including preferred stock) were paid, and any remaining money were divided among the common stockholders. (Chapter 7)

liquidity   A firm's ability to satisfy its short-term obligations *as they come due.* (Chapter 2)

liquidity preferences   General preferences of investors for shorter-term securities. (Chapter 6)

liquidity preference theory   Theory suggesting that for any given issuer, long-term interest rates tend to be higher than short-term rates because (1) lower liquidity and higher responsiveness to general interest rate movements of longer-term securities exists and (2) borrower willingness to pay a higher rate for long-term financing causes the yield curve to be upward-sloping. (Chapter 6)

loan amortization   The determination of the equal periodic loan payments necessary to provide a lender with a specified interest return and to repay the loan principal over a specified period. (Chapter 4)

loan amortization schedule   A schedule of equal payments to repay a loan. It shows the allocation of each loan payment to interest and principal. (Chapter 4)

lockbox system   A collection procedure in which customers mail payments to a post office box that is emptied regularly by the firm's bank, who processes the payments and deposits them in the firm's account. This system speeds up collection time by reducing processing time as well as mail and clearing time. (Chapter 13)

long-term debt   Debts for which payment is not due in the current year. (Chapter 2)

long-term (strategic) financial plans   Lay out a company's planned financial actions and the anticipated impact of those actions over periods ranging from 2 to 10 years. (Chapter 3)

low-regular-and-extra dividend policy   A dividend policy based on paying a low regular dividend, supplemented by an additional dividend when earnings are higher than normal in a given period. (Chapter 12)

mail float   The time delay between when payment is placed in the mail and when it is received. (Chapter 13)

managerial finance   Concerns the duties of the financial manager in the business firm. (Chapter 1)

manufacturing resource planning II (MRP II)   A sophisticated computerized system that integrates data from numerous areas such as finance, accounting, marketing, engineering, and manufacturing and generates production plans as well as numerous financial and management reports. (Chapter 13)

marginal cost-benefit analysis   Economic principle that states that financial decisions should be made and actions taken only when the added benefits exceed the added costs. (Chapter 1)

marginal tax rate   The rate at which *additional income* is taxed. (Chapter 1)

market/book (M/B) ratio   Provides an assessment of how investors view the firm's performance. Firms expected to earn high returns relative to their risk typically sell at higher M/B multiples. (Chapter 2)

market makers   Securities dealers who "make markets" by offering to buy or sell certain securities at stated prices. (Chapter 1)

market ratios   Relate a firm's market value, as measured by its current share price, to certain accounting values. (Chapter 2)

market return   The return on the market portfolio of all traded securities. (Chapter 5)

market segmentation theory   Theory suggesting that the market for loans is segmented on the basis of maturity and that the supply of and demand for loans within each segment determine its prevailing interest rate; the slope of the yield curve is determined by the general relationship between the prevailing rates in each segment. (Chapter 6)

market value weights   Weights that use market values to measure the proportion of each type of capital in the firm's financial structure. (Chapter 10)

marketable securities   Short-term debt instruments, such as U.S. Treasury bills, commercial paper, and negotiable certificates of deposit issued by government, business, and financial institutions, respectively. (Chapter 1)

materials requirement planning (MRP) system   Applies EOQ concepts to determine what materials to order and when to order them; simulates each product's bill of materials, inventory status, and manufacturing process. (Chapter 13)

mixed stream   A stream of unequal periodic cash flows that reflect no particular pattern. (Chapter 4)

modified accelerated cost recovery system (MACRS)   System used to determine the depreciation of assets for tax purposes. (Chapter 3)

modified DuPont formula   Relates the firm's *return on total assets (ROA)* to its *return on common equity (ROE)* using the *financial leverage multiplier (FLM)*. (Chapter 2)

money market   A financial relationship created between suppliers and demanders of *short-term funds*. (Chapter 1)

mortgage bonds   See Table 6.4. (Chapter 6)

multiple IRRs   More than one IRR resulting from a capital budgeting project with a *nonconventional cash flow pattern*; the maximum number of IRRs for a project is equal to the number of sign changes in its cash flows. (Chapter 9)

mutually exclusive projects   Projects that compete with one another, so that the acceptance of one *eliminates* from further consideration all other projects that serve a similar function. (Chapter 8)

Nasdaq market   An all-electronic trading platform used to execute securities trades. (Chapter 1)

negatively correlated   Describes two series that move in opposite directions. (Chapter 5)

net cash flow   The mathematical difference between the firm's cash receipts and its cash disbursements in each period. (Chapter 3)

net operating profits after taxes (NOPAT)   A firm's earnings before interest and after taxes, EBIT $\times$ $(1 - T)$. (Chapter 3)

net present value (NPV)   A sophisticated capital budgeting technique; found by subtracting a project's initial investment from the present value of its cash inflows discounted at a rate equal to the firm's cost of capital. (Chapter 9)

net present value approach   An approach to capital rationing that is based on the use of present values to determine the group of projects that will maximize owners' wealth. (Chapter 9)

net present value profile   Graph that depicts a project's NPV for various discount rates. (Chapter 9)

net proceeds   Funds actually received from the sale of a security. (Chapter 10)

net profit margin   Measures the percentage of each sales dollar remaining after all costs and expenses, *including* interest, taxes, and preferred stock dividends, have been deducted. (Chapter 2)

net working capital   The amount by which a firm's current assets exceed its current liabilities; can be *positive* or *negative*. (Chapters 8 and 13)

nominal (stated) annual rate   Contractual annual rate of interest charged by a lender or promised by a borrower. (Chapter 4)

noncash charge   An expense that is deducted on the income statement but does not involve the actual outlay of cash during the period; includes depreciation, amortization, and depletion. (Chapter 3)

nonconventional cash flow pattern   An initial outflow followed by a series of inflows *and* outflows. (Chapter 8)

noncumulative preferred stock   Preferred stock for which passed (unpaid) dividends do not accumulate. (Chapter 7)

nondiversifiable risk   The relevant portion of an asset's risk attributable to market factors that affect all firms; cannot be eliminated through diversification. Also called *systematic risk*. (Chapter 5)

nonnotification basis   The basis on which a borrower, having pledged an account receivable, continues to collect the account payments without notifying the account customer. (Chapter 14)

nonrecourse basis   The basis on which accounts receivable are sold to a factor with the understanding that the factor accepts all credit risks on the purchased accounts. (Chapter 14)

nonvoting common stock   Common stock that carries no voting rights; issued when the firm wishes to raise capital through the sale of common stock but does not want to give up its voting control. (Chapter 7)

no-par preferred stock　Preferred stock with no stated face value but with a stated annual dollar dividend. (Chapter 7)

normal yield curve　An *upward-sloping* yield curve that indicates generally cheaper short-term borrowing costs than long-term borrowing costs. (Chapter 6)

notes to the financial statements　Footnotes detailing information on the accounting policies, procedures, calculations, and transactions underlying entries in the financial statements. (Chapter 2)

notification basis　The basis on which an account customer whose account has been pledged (or factored) is notified to remit payment directly to the lender (or factor). (Chapter 14)

operating breakeven point　The level of sales necessary to cover all *operating costs*; the point at which EBIT = $0. (Chapter 11)

operating cash flow (OCF)　The cash flow a firm generates from its normal operations; calculated as EBIT − taxes + depreciation. (Chapter 3)

operating cash inflows　The incremental after-tax cash inflows resulting from implementation of a project during its life. (Chapter 8)

operating cycle (OC)　The time from the beginning of the production process to the collection of cash from the sale of the finished product. (Chapter 13)

operating expenditure　An outlay of funds by the firm resulting in benefits received *within* 1 year. (Chapter 8)

operating flows　Cash flows directly related to sale and production of the firm's products and services. (Chapter 3)

operating leverage　The potential use of *fixed operating costs* to magnify the effects of changes in sales on the firm's earnings before interest and taxes. (Chapter 11)

operating profit margin　Measures the percentage of each sales dollar remaining after all costs and expenses *other than* interest, taxes, and preferred stock dividends are deducted; the "pure profits" earned on each sales dollar. (Chapter 2)

operating-change restrictions　Contractual restrictions that a bank may impose on a firm's financial condition or operations as part of a line-of-credit agreement. (Chapter 14)

opportunity costs　Cash flows that could be realized from the best alternative use of an owned asset. (Chapter 8)

optimal capital structure　The capital structure at which the weighted average cost of capital is minimized, thereby maximizing the firm's value. (Chapter 11)

order costs　The fixed clerical costs of placing and receiving an inventory order. (Chapter 13)

ordinary annuity　An annuity for which the cash flow occurs at the *end* of each period. (Chapter 4)

ordinary income　Income earned through the sale of a firm's goods or services. (Chapter 1)

outstanding shares　The number of shares of common stock held by the public. (Chapter 7)

over-the-counter (OTC) market　Market where smaller, unlisted securities are traded. (Chapter 1)

paid-in capital in excess of par　The amount of proceeds in excess of the par value received from the original sale of common stock. (Chapter 2)

partnership　A business owned by two or more people and operated for profit. (Chapter 1)

par value (stock)　A relatively useless value for a stock established for legal purposes in the firm's corporate charter. (Chapter 7)

par-value preferred stock　Preferred stock with a stated face value that is used with the specified dividend percentage to determine the annual dollar dividend. (Chapter 7)

payback period　The amount of time required for a firm to recover its initial investment in a project, as calculated from *cash inflows*. (Chapter 9)

payment date　Set by the firm's directors, the actual date on which the firm mails the dividend payment to the holders of record. (Chapter 12)

pecking order　A hierarchy of financing that begins with retained earnings, which is followed by debt financing and finally external equity financing. (Chapter 11)

percentage advance　The percent of the book value of the collateral that constitutes the principal of a secured loan. (Chapter 14)

percent-of-sales method　A simple method for developing the pro forma income statement; it forecasts sales and then expresses the various income statement items as percentages of projected sales. (Chapter 3)

perfectly negatively correlated　Describes two *negatively correlated* series that have a *correlation coefficient* of −1. (Chapter 5)

perfectly positively correlated　Describes two *positively correlated* series that have a *correlation coefficient* of +1. (Chapter 5)

performance plans　Plans that tie management compensation to measures such as EPS, growth in EPS, and other ratios of return. *Performance shares* and/or *cash bonuses* are used as compensation under these plans. (Chapter 1)

performance shares　Shares of stock given to management for meeting stated performance goals. (Chapter 1)

permanent funding requirement A constant investment in operating assets resulting from constant sales over time. (Chapter 13)

perpetuity An annuity with an infinite life, providing continual annual cash flow. (Chapter 4)

pledge of accounts receivable The use of a firm's accounts receivable as security, or collateral, to obtain a short-term loan. (Chapter 14)

political risk Risk that arises from the possibility that a host government will take actions harmful to foreign investors or that political turmoil in a country will endanger investments there. (Chapter 5)

portfolio A collection, or group, of assets. (Chapter 5)

positively correlated Describes two series that move in the same direction. (Chapter 5)

preemptive right Allows common stockholders to maintain their *proportionate* ownership in the corporation when new shares are issued. (Chapter 7)

preferred stock A special form of ownership having a fixed periodic dividend that must be paid prior to payment of any common stock dividends. (Chapter 1)

premium The amount by which a bond sells at a value that is greater than its par value. (Chapter 6)

present value The current dollar value of a future amount—the amount of money that would have to be invested today at a given interest rate over a specified period to equal the future amount. (Chapter 4)

present value interest factor The multiplier used to calculate, at a specified discount rate, the present value of an amount to be received in a future period. (Chapter 4)

present value interest factor for an ordinary annuity The multiplier used to calculate the present value of an *ordinary annuity* at a specified discount rate over a given period of time. (Chapter 4)

president or chief executive officer (CEO) Corporate official responsible for managing the firm's day-to-day operations and carrying out the policies established by the board of directors. (Chapter 1)

price/earnings multiple approach A popular technique used to estimate the firm's share value; calculated by multiplying the firm's expected earnings per share (EPS) by the average price/earnings (P/E) ratio for the industry. (Chapter 7)

price/earnings (P/E) ratio Measures the amount that investors are willing to pay for each dollar of a firm's earnings; the higher the P/E ratio, the greater is investor confidence. (Chapter 2)

primary market Financial market in which securities are initially issued; the only market in which the issuer is directly involved in the transaction. (Chapter 1)

prime rate of interest (prime rate) The lowest rate of interest charged by leading banks on business loans to their most important business borrowers. (Chapter 14)

principal The amount of money on which interest is paid. (Chapter 4)

private placement The sale of a new security issue, typically bonds or preferred stock, directly to an investor or group of investors. (Chapter 1)

privately owned (stock) All common stock of a firm owned by a single individual. (Chapter 7)

pro forma statements Projected, or forecast, income statements and balance sheets. (Chapter 3)

probability The *chance* that a given outcome will occur. (Chapter 5)

probability distribution A model that relates probabilities to the associated outcomes. (Chapter 5)

proceeds from sale of old asset The cash inflows, net of any *removal* or *cleanup costs*, resulting from the sale of an existing asset. (Chapter 8)

processing float The time between receipt of a payment and its deposit into the firm's account. (Chapter 13)

profitability The relationship between revenues and costs generated by using the firm's assets—both current and fixed—in productive activities. (Chapter 13)

prospectus A portion of a security registration statement that describes the key aspects of the issue, the issuer, and its management and financial position. (Chapter 7)

proxy battle The attempt by a nonmanagement group to gain control of the management of a firm by soliciting a sufficient number of proxy votes. (Chapter 7)

proxy statement A statement giving the votes of a stockholder to another party. (Chapter 7)

Public Company Accounting Oversight Board (PCAOB) A not-for-profit corporation established by the *Sarbanes-Oxley Act of 2002* to protect the interests of investors and further the public interest in the preparation of informative, fair, and independent audit reports. (Chapter 2)

public offering The nonexclusive sale of either bonds or stocks to the general public. (Chapter 1)

publicly owned (stock) Common stock of a firm owned by a broad group of unrelated individual or institutional investors. (Chapter 7)

putable bonds See Table 6.5. (Chapter 6)

quarterly compounding Compounding of interest over four periods within the year. (Chapter 4)

quick (acid-test) ratio A measure of liquidity calculated by dividing the firm's current assets minus inventory by its current liabilities. (Chapter 2)

range   A measure of an asset's risk, which is found by subtracting the pessimistic (worst) outcome from the optimistic (best) outcome. (Chapter 5)

ranking approach   The ranking of capital expenditure projects on the basis of some predetermined measure, such as the rate of return. (Chapter 8)

ratio analysis   Involves methods of calculating and interpreting financial ratios to analyze and monitor the firm's performance. (Chapter 2)

real options   Opportunities that are embedded in capital projects that enable managers to alter their cash flows and risk in a way that affects project acceptability (NPV). Also called *strategic options*. (Chapter 9)

real rate of interest   The rate that creates an equilibrium between the supply of savings and the demand for investment funds in a perfect world, without inflation, where funds suppliers and demanders are indifferent to the term of loans or investments and have no liquidity preference, and where all outcomes are certain. (Chapter 6)

recaptured depreciation   The portion of an asset's sale price that is above its book value and below its initial purchase price. (Chapter 8)

recovery period   The appropriate depreciable life of a particular asset as determined by MACRS. (Chapter 3)

red herring   A preliminary prospectus made available to prospective investors during the waiting period between the registration statement's filing with the SEC and its approval. (Chapter 7)

regular dividend policy   A dividend policy based on the payment of a fixed-dollar dividend in each period. (Chapter 12)

relevant cash flows   The *incremental cash outflow (investment) and resulting subsequent inflows* associated with a proposed capital expenditure. (Chapter 8)

reorder point   The point at which to reorder inventory, expressed as days of lead time × daily usage. (Chapter 13)

required return   The cost of funds obtained by selling an ownership interest; it reflects the funds supplier's level of expected return. (Chapter 6)

required total financing   Amount of funds needed by the firm if the ending cash for the period is less than the desired minimum cash balance; typically represented by notes payable. (Chapter 3)

residual theory of dividends   A school of thought that suggests that the dividend paid by a firm should be viewed as a *residual*—the amount left over after all acceptable investment opportunities have been undertaken. (Chapter 12)

restrictive covenants   Provisions in a *bond indenture* that place operating and financial constraints on the borrower. (Chapter 6)

retained earnings   The cumulative total of all earnings, net of dividends, that have been retained and reinvested in the firm since its inception; earnings not distributed to owners as dividends—a form of *internal* financing. (Chapters 2 and 12)

return   The total gain or loss experienced on an investment over a given period of time; calculated by dividing the asset's cash distributions during the period, plus change in value, by its beginning-of-period investment value. (Chapter 5)

return on common equity (ROE)   Measures the return earned on the common stockholders' investment in the firm. (Chapter 2)

return on total assets (ROA)   Measures the overall effectiveness of management in generating profits with its available assets; also called the *return on investment (ROI)*. (Chapter 2)

reverse stock split   A method used to raise the market price of a firm's stock by exchanging a certain number of outstanding shares for one new share. (Chapter 12)

revolving credit agreement   A line of credit *guaranteed* to a borrower by a commercial bank regardless of the scarcity of money. (Chapter 14)

rights   Financial instruments that permit stockholders to purchase additional shares at a price below the market price, in direct proportion to their number of owned shares. (Chapter 7)

risk   The chance of financial loss or, more formally, the *variability of returns associated with a given asset*. (Chapters 1 and 5)

risk (in capital budgeting)   The chance that a project will prove unacceptable or, more formally, the degree of variability of cash flows. (Chapter 9)

risk (of technical insolvency)   The probability that a firm will be unable to pay its bills as they come due. (Chapter 13)

risk premium   The amount by which the interest rate or required return on a security exceeds the risk-free rate of interest R_F; it varies with specific issuer and issue characteristics. (Chapter 6)

risk-adjusted discount rate (RADR)   The rate of return that must be earned on a given project to compensate the firm's owners adequately—that is, to maintain or improve the firm's share price. (Chapter 9)

risk-averse   The attitude toward risk in which an increased return would be required for an increase in risk. (Chapters 1 and 5)

risk-free rate of interest, R_F   The required return on a risk-free asset, typically a 3-month *U.S. Treasury bill (T-bill)*. (Chapter 6)

risk-free rate of return, R_F   The required return on a *risk-free asset*, typically a 3-month *U.S. Treasury bill*. (Chapter 5)

S corporation (S corp)   See Table 1.2. (Chapter 1)

safety stock   Extra inventory that is held to prevent stockouts of important items. (Chapter 13)

sales forecast   The prediction of the firm's sales over a given period, based on external and/or internal data; used as the key input to the short-term financial planning process. (Chapter 3)

Sarbanes-Oxley Act of 2002 (SOX)   An act aimed at eliminating corporate disclosure and conflict of interest. Contains provisions about corporate financial disclosures and the relationships among corporations, analysts, auditors, attorneys, directors, officers, and shareholders. (Chapter 1)

scenario analysis   A behavioral approach that evaluates the impact on the firm's return of simultaneous changes in a number of variables. (Chapter 5)

seasonal funding requirement   An investment in operating assets that varies over time as a result of cyclic sales. (Chapter 13)

secondary market   Financial market in which preowned securities (those that are not new issues) are traded. (Chapter 1)

secured short-term financing   Short-term financing (loan) that has specific assets pledged as collateral. (Chapter 14)

Securities and Exchange Commission (SEC)   The federal regulatory body that governs the sale and listing of securities. (Chapter 2)

securities exchanges   Organizations that provide the marketplace in which firms can raise funds through the sale of new securities and purchasers can resell securities. (Chapter 1)

security agreement   The agreement between the borrower and the lender that specifies the collateral held against a secured loan. (Chapter 14)

security market line (SML)   The depiction of the *capital asset pricing model* (*CAPM*) as a graph that reflects the required return in the marketplace for each level of nondiversifiable risk (beta). (Chapter 5)

selling group   A large number of brokerage firms that join the originating investment banker(s); each accepts responsibility for selling a certain portion of a new security issue on a commission basis. (Chapter 7)

semiannual compounding   Compounding of interest over two periods within the year. (Chapter 4)

short-term (operating) financial plans   Specify short-term financial actions and the anticipated impact of those actions. (Chapter 3)

short-term financial management   Management of current assets and current liabilities. (Chapter 13)

short-term, self-liquidating loan   An unsecured short-term loan in which the use to which the borrowed money is put provides the mechanism through which the loan is repaid. (Chapter 14)

signal   A financing action by management that is believed to reflect its view of the firm's stock value; generally, debt financing is viewed as a *positive signal* that management believes the stock is "undervalued," and a stock issue is viewed as a *negative signal* that management believes the stock is "overvalued." (Chapter 11)

simulation   A statistics-based behavioral approach that applies predetermined probability distributions and random numbers to estimate risky outcomes. (Chapter 9)

single-payment note   A short-term, one-time loan made to a borrower who needs funds for a specific purpose for a short period. (Chapter 14)

sinking-fund requirement   A restrictive provision often included in a bond indenture, providing for the systematic retirement of bonds prior to their maturity. (Chapter 6)

small (ordinary) stock dividend   A stock dividend representing less than 20 to 25 percent of the common stock outstanding when the dividend is declared. (Chapter 12)

sole proprietorship   A business owned by one person and operated for his or her own profit. (Chapter 1)

spontaneous liabilities   Financing that arises from the normal course of business; the two major short-term sources of such liabilities are accounts payable and accruals. (Chapter 14)

stakeholders   Groups such as employees, customers, suppliers, creditors, owners, and others who have a direct economic link to the firm. (Chapter 1)

standard debt provisions   Provisions in a *bond indenture* specifying certain record-keeping and general business practices that the bond issuer must follow; normally, they do not place a burden on a financially sound business. (Chapter 6)

standard deviation (σ_r)   The most common statistical indicator of an asset's risk; it measures the dispersion around the *expected value*. (Chapter 5)

statement of cash flows   Provides a summary of the firm's operating, investment, and financing cash flows and reconciles them with changes in its cash and marketable securities during the period. (Chapter 2)

statement of retained earnings   Reconciles the net income earned during a given year, and any cash dividends paid, with the change in retained earnings between the start and the end of that year. An abbreviated form of the *statement of stockholders' equity*. (Chapter 2)

statement of stockholders' equity   Shows all equity account transactions that occur during a given year. (Chapter 2)

stock dividend   The payment, to existing owners, of a dividend in the form of stock. (Chapter 12)

stock options   An incentive allowing managers to purchase stock at the market price set at the time of the grant. (Chapter 1)

stock purchase warrants   Instruments that give their holders the right to purchase a certain number of shares of the issuer's common stock at a specified price over a certain period of time. (Chapter 6)

stock repurchase   The repurchase by the firm of outstanding common stock in the marketplace; desired effects of stock repurchases are that they either enhance shareholder value or help to discourage an unfriendly takeover. (Chapter 12)

stock split   A method commonly used to lower the market price of a firm's stock by increasing the number of shares belonging to each shareholder. (Chapter 12)

stockholders   The owners of a corporation, whose ownership, or *equity*, is evidenced by either common stock or preferred stock. (Chapter 1)

stockholders' report   Annual report that publicly owned corporations must provide to stockholders; it summarizes and documents the firm's financial activities during the past year. (Chapter 2)

stretching accounts payable   Paying bills as late as possible without damaging the firm's credit rating. (Chapter 14)

subordinated debentures   See Table 6.4. (Chapter 6)

subordination   In a bond indenture, the stipulation that subsequent creditors agree to wait until all claims of the *senior debt* are satisfied. (Chapter 6)

sunk costs   Cash outlays that have already been made (past outlays) and therefore have no effect on the cash flows relevant to a current decision. (Chapter 8)

supervoting shares   Stock that carries with it multiple votes per share rather than the single vote per share typically given on regular shares of common stock. (Chapter 7)

target capital structure   The desired optimal mix of debt and equity financing that most firms attempt to maintain. (Chapter 10)

target dividend-payout ratio   A dividend policy under which the firm attempts to pay out a certain *percentage* of earnings as a stated dollar dividend and adjusts that dividend toward a target payout as proven earnings increases occur. (Chapter 12)

target weights   Either book or market value weights based on *desired* capital structure proportions. (Chapter 10)

tax on sale of old asset   Tax that depends on the relationship among the old asset's sale price, initial purchase price, and *book value*, and on existing government tax rules. (Chapter 8)

technically insolvent   Describes a firm that is unable to pay its bills as they come due. (Chapter 13)

tender offer   A formal offer to purchase a given number of shares of a firm's stock at a specified price. (Chapter 12)

term structure of interest rates   The relationship between the interest rate or rate of return and the time to maturity. (Chapter 6)

terminal cash flow   The after-tax nonoperating cash flow occurring in the final year of a project. It is usually attributable to liquidation of the project. (Chapter 8)

time line   A horizontal line on which time zero appears at the leftmost end and future periods are marked from left to right; can be used to depict investment cash flows. (Chapter 4)

times interest earned ratio   Measures the firm's ability to make contractual interest payments; sometimes called the *interest coverage ratio*. (Chapter 2)

time-series analysis   Evaluation of the firm's financial performance over time using financial ratio analysis. (Chapter 2)

total asset turnover   Indicates the efficiency with which the firm uses its assets to generate sales. (Chapter 2)

total cost of inventory   The sum of order costs and carrying costs of inventory. (Chapter 13)

total leverage   The potential use of *fixed costs, both operating and financial*, to magnify the effect of changes in sales on the firm's earnings per share. (Chapter 11)

total risk   The combination of a security's *nondiversifiable* and *diversifiable risk*. (Chapter 5)

transfer prices   Prices that subsidiaries charge each other for the goods and services traded between them. (Chapter 9)

treasurer   The firm's chief financial manager, who is responsible for the firm's financial activities, such as financial planning and fund raising, making capital expenditure decisions, and managing cash, credit, the pension fund, and foreign exchange. (Chapter 1)

treasury stock The number of shares of outstanding stock that have been repurchased by the firm. (Chapter 7)

trust receipt inventory loan A secured short-term loan against inventory under which the lender advances 80 to 100 percent of the cost of the borrower's relatively expensive inventory items in exchange for the borrower's promise to repay the lender, with accrued interest, immediately after the sale of each item of collateral. (Chapter 14)

trustee A paid individual, corporation, or commercial bank trust department that acts as the third party to a bond indenture and can take specified actions on behalf of the bondholders if the terms of the indenture are violated. (Chapter 6)

two-bin method Unsophisticated inventory-monitoring technique that is typically applied to C group items and involves reordering inventory when one of two bins is empty. (Chapter 13)

uncorrelated Describes two series that lack any interaction and therefore have a correlation coefficient close to zero. (Chapter 5)

U.S. Treasury bills (T-bills) Short-term IOUs issued by the U.S. Treasury; considered the *risk-free asset*. (Chapter 5)

underpriced Stock sold at a price below its current market price, P_0. (Chapter 10)

underwriting The role of the *investment banker* in bearing the risk of reselling, at a profit, the securities purchased from an issuing corporation at an agreed-on price. (Chapter 7)

underwriting syndicate A group formed by an investment banker to share the financial risk associated with *underwriting* new securities. (Chapter 7)

unlimited funds The financial situation in which a firm is able to accept all independent projects that provide an acceptable return. (Chapter 8)

unlimited liability The condition of a sole proprietorship (or general partnership) allowing the owner's total wealth to be taken to satisfy creditors. (Chapter 1)

unsecured short-term financing Short-term financing obtained without pledging specific assets as collateral. (Chapter 14)

valuation The process that links risk and return to determine the worth of an asset. (Chapter 6)

variable-growth model A dividend valuation approach that allows for a change in the dividend growth rate. (Chapter 7)

venture capital Privately raised external equity capital used to fund early-stage firms with attractive growth prospects. (Chapter 7)

venture capitalists (VCs) Providers of venture capital; typically, formal businesses that maintain strong oversight over the firms they invest in and that have clearly defined exit strategies. (Chapter 7)

warehouse receipt loan A secured short-term loan against inventory under which the lender receives control of the pledged inventory collateral, which is stored by a designated warehousing company on the lender's behalf. (Chapter 14)

weighted average cost of capital (WACC), r_a Reflects the expected average future cost of funds over the long run; found by weighting the cost of each specific type of capital by its proportion in the firm's capital structure. (Chapter 10)

weighted marginal cost of capital (WMCC) The firm's weighted average cost of capital (WACC) associated with its *next dollar* of total new financing. (Chapter 10)

weighted marginal cost of capital (WMCC) schedule Graph that relates the firm's weighted average cost of capital to the level of total new financing. (Chapter 10)

wire transfer An electronic communication that, via bookkeeping entries, removes funds from the payer's bank and deposits them in the payee's bank. (Chapter 13)

working capital Current assets, which represent the portion of investment that circulates from one form to another in the ordinary conduct of business. (Chapter 13)

yield curve A graph of the relationship between the debt's remaining time to maturity (*x* axis) and its yield to maturity (*y* axis); it shows the yield to maturity for debts of equal quality and different maturities. Graphically depicts the *term structure of interest rates*. (Chapter 6)

yield to maturity Compound annual rate of return earned on a debt security purchased on a given day and held to maturity. (Chapter 6)

zero- (or low-) coupon bonds See Table 6.5. (Chapter 6)

zero-balance account (ZBA) A disbursement account that always has an end-of-day balance of zero because the firm deposits money to cover checks drawn on the account only as they are presented for payment each day. (Chapter 13)

zero-growth model An approach to dividend valuation that assumes a constant, nongrowing dividend stream. (Chapter 7)

Index